IMAGES
of America

DOUGLAS

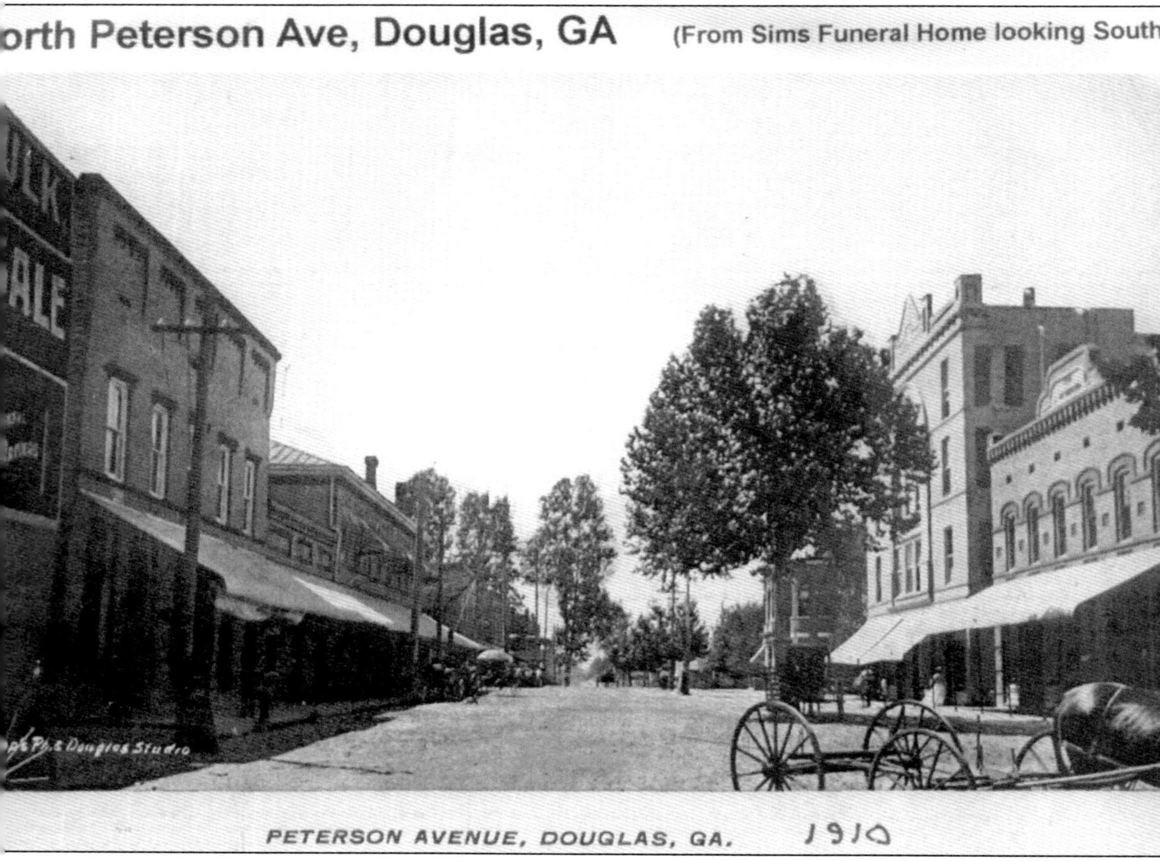

Peterson Avenue is seen here in 1910. The view looks south from the original location of the Sims Funeral Home on the 200 block of North Peterson Avenue. At the time, a city law prohibited cars on Peterson, as vehicles scared the horses. This was the first settled area of the city, where commerce, entertainment, and political power were concentrated. It was then—and thanks to urban renewal and Main Street programs, still is—the focus of business, shopping, and culture. (Courtesy of Joanne Hanna Lott.)

On the Cover: The family of Daniel (1851–1918) and Sophronia Fussell Newbern (1858–1931) are shown in a c. 1914 photograph in front of the family home on Newbern Road northeast of Broxton. The couple is surrounded by their five adult children, their children's spouses, and their grandchildren. Daniel was a successful farmer who served as the county's inferior court judge. His business interests included owning stock in the Union Bank and the Broxton Banking Company. The spinal meningitis epidemic of 1870 claimed the lives of his parents and four of his siblings. (Courtesy of Dr. James A. Cottingham.)

IMAGES
of America

DOUGLAS

Leann Elizabeth Griffiths

ARCADIA
PUBLISHING

ISBN 978-1-4671-1103-4

Published by Arcadia Publishing
Charleston, South Carolina

Printed in the United States of America

Library of Congress Control Number: 2013938998

For all general information, please contact Arcadia Publishing:
Telephone 843-853-2070
Fax 843-853-0044
E-mail sales@arcadiapublishing.com
For customer service and orders:
Toll-Free 1-888-313-2665

Visit us on the Internet at www.arcadiapublishing.com

This book is dedicated to my husband Charlie, my son Harley, and my parents. Thank you for your love and support.

Contents

Acknowledgments

This book would not have been possible without Charlie Griffiths for technical support, photographs, and research assistance. I am indebted to the World War II Flight Training Museum, Susan Harrington for photographs, Mr. Hugh T. Harrington for his tour of the museum, Tom Reilly for allowing me to see his work, Don Brooks for allowing me access to both the museum and Brooks Aviation, and Weezie Barendse for a tour and photographs.

In addition, I would like to thank South Georgia State College, Virginia Carson, Kayla Tillman, Walda Kight, Delectia Vickers, and Kellie Luke Moore and her environmental lab class: Ashleigh Hulett, Connor Gillis, Caroline McGhee, Keisha Fletcher, Jana Merritt, Brittany Allen, Katelyn Morgan, Grace Garrity, Tiffany Roberson, and Jeremy Walker.

Gratitude is also expressed to the Heritage Station Museum, Irene Murray for research assistance, Douglas City Hall, Roger Goddard, Dale Batten, Ivalene Clark, Judy Carter, Ken Hayes, the Douglas City-Coffee County Chamber of Commerce, JoAnne Ray Lewis for both photographs and research assistance, and the Satilla Regional Library Genealogy Department.

Private donors include Dr. James Cottingham (whose knowledge of history was just as valuable as his collection), Yolanda Crosby (photographs, research assistance, networking, and encouragement), Carol Morgan (research assistance), Frankie Snow, John Martin, Joanne Hanna Lott, Richard and Rose Ann Martin (photographs and research assistance), Martha Meeks (photographs), Wanell Hutchison (research assistance), Marceleno Moran (research assistance), Maria Baez (research assistance), Angela Elder Henderson (technical advice), Sue McDuffie, Cathy Harper, Danny Maley, Bill Anderson, John Braddy, Gwendolyn and Joe Reliford (photographs and research assistance), and Yvonne Lott.

INTRODUCTION

Douglas is located in Coffee County in the Magnolia Midlands of southeast Georgia. The area was inhabited early on by the Creek Indians. Settlers moved into the region after the development of the Columbus and Blackshear Roads. The county was created in 1854 and named after Gen. John Coffee, a hero of the War of 1812. The city itself was named for Stephen A. Douglas, the Southern candidate for president who ran against Lincoln. Douglas, the county seat of Coffee County, was incorporated in 1895.

The Twenty Mile Creek had been home to Methodist revivals and baptisms from as early as 1830. Camp meetings were popular with rural Georgians. Not only a time for spiritual renewal, they also served as gathering grounds where families and friends could reunite. Before the town was incorporated, revivals brought people to the area, and the *Douglas Breeze* (now the *Douglas Enterprise*) was reporting the news to isolated pioneer families.

The river does not run through Douglas, there are no major airports, and the closest interstate is nearly an hour away in any direction. For all intents and purposes, Douglas is the middle of nowhere. Nevertheless, trailblazing individuals from surrounding counties and businesses from as far away as Japan have been travelling here for over a century to forge a living.

Douglas is the product of rural industrialization. Driving through the woods to get here, one might think that farming was the chief industry of the area. But, after the Civil War, businessmen from the Carolinas came to the Wiregrass Region and developed turpentine camps in the piney woods around the county. Each camp had slaves, families, blacksmiths, a post office, schools, mills, stores, and a turpentine still. Douglas was a booming city that had tall buildings with turrets and horse races before the Civil War; however, after the war, the courthouse was little more than a stable for goats. In an effort to rebuild the community, local business owner and large landholder Benjah Peterson donated land and joined with others to build a new courthouse, new schools, and several new churches.

The pioneers brought art and architecture with them. In the historic district, one will find the architectural wonders of William J.J. Chase, Abreu & Robeson, and Haralson Bleckley on Gaskin Avenue. Farther up the road is the Ashley-Slater House, which aside from being an architectural wonder also holds a story of romance and scandal. It is said to be haunted by one of the six people who died there.

The Georgia & Florida Railway came to Douglas in 1907 and was a major employer for the community until the 1980s, when passenger rail service ceased in the area. In 1999, Georgia & Florida Railway employees and concerned citizens renovated the depot and reopened it as Heritage Station Museum.

During the Great Depression, most areas were hit hard. While many suffered, Douglas was fortunate because the tobacco industry came along just as the boll weevil was crippling the cotton industry. Douglas was the largest tobacco market in Georgia, and harvest day was like Christmas, with tobacco buyers offering prizes and presents at the market. Even those who did not win prizes had more money in their pockets after the crops were sold. Crowds of people came to market and gathered for the festivities.

South Georgia College, along with the Richard Aviation School, trained pilots for the war. The town raised money and grew Victory Gardens. While men were learning to fly, women were learning to build airplane engines and service planes. These skills came in handy after the war.

Douglas extended the flight school's runway so that businesses like TRW Aerospace Group could land their corporate jets. In 1977, TRW opened the first airplane-engine plant in Douglas. This was the first industry outside of agriculture for the local community. Its successor, PCC Airfoils, continues to be a leading employer.

Soldiers returning from World War II were too restless to just work. As in most areas, the population boomed in Douglas after the wars. Douglas even had its own minor-league baseball team, sponsored by the Cincinnati Reds, in the Georgia State League. Many young men came to the area to play baseball, and some stayed and later became successful local businessmen. Not to be left out of all the fun, the college had a football team, which many locals now miss and would like to see reinstated. Bobby Bowden, the winningest coach in all of college football history, got his start coaching in Douglas; however, after 1958 he left for Howard College and football ceased for Georgia's two-year colleges.

During the 1950s and 1960s, the town was home to several dance halls and theaters, and the schools offered local plays and music recitals. Douglas was one of the first small towns to implement an urban renewal plan to abolish slum housing. Public parks were revitalized, and General Coffee State Park was founded.

By the 1960s, poultry processing and manufactured housing were major industries in the city. Coffee County is part of the Georgia Small Business Development Center (SBDC) network, offering business-development services in partnership with the SBDC through its office on the campus of South Georgia State College. Coffee County products now ship to over 30 countries around the world. Industries today include poultry processing, distribution warehousing, manufactured housing, and the production of jet engine parts and small engines.

Almost as early as the town was founded, the 11th District A&M School—a two-year unit of the University System of Georgia and the state's first publicly supported junior college—was founded. It is the only junior college to have offered dormitory living and study-abroad opportunities, allowing students from the rural area to receive a global education. And, like the chamber of commerce, some assert that the college also has a resident ghost in Peterson Hall.

The college has grown and evolved to meet the needs of the community. South Georgia College consolidated with Waycross College and has recently become the state's newest four-year college, offering baccalaureate degrees in nursing and health sciences. In 2013, the institution changed its name to South Georgia State College.

The Douglas community has numerous recreational facilities, including 10 municipal parks, a walking trail, a swimming pool, General Coffee State Park, four golf courses, and the Douglas Recreation Department to facilitate programs for the community. Through the efforts of the Nature Conservancy, the Broxton Rocks preserves rare flora and wildlife species and hosts local community events. Douglas Motorsports Speedway draws racing fans from all over to the area. For several years, Douglas has been host to national hunting and barbeque events. There is a little something for nearly everyone in Douglas.

One

THE FOUNDING YEARS

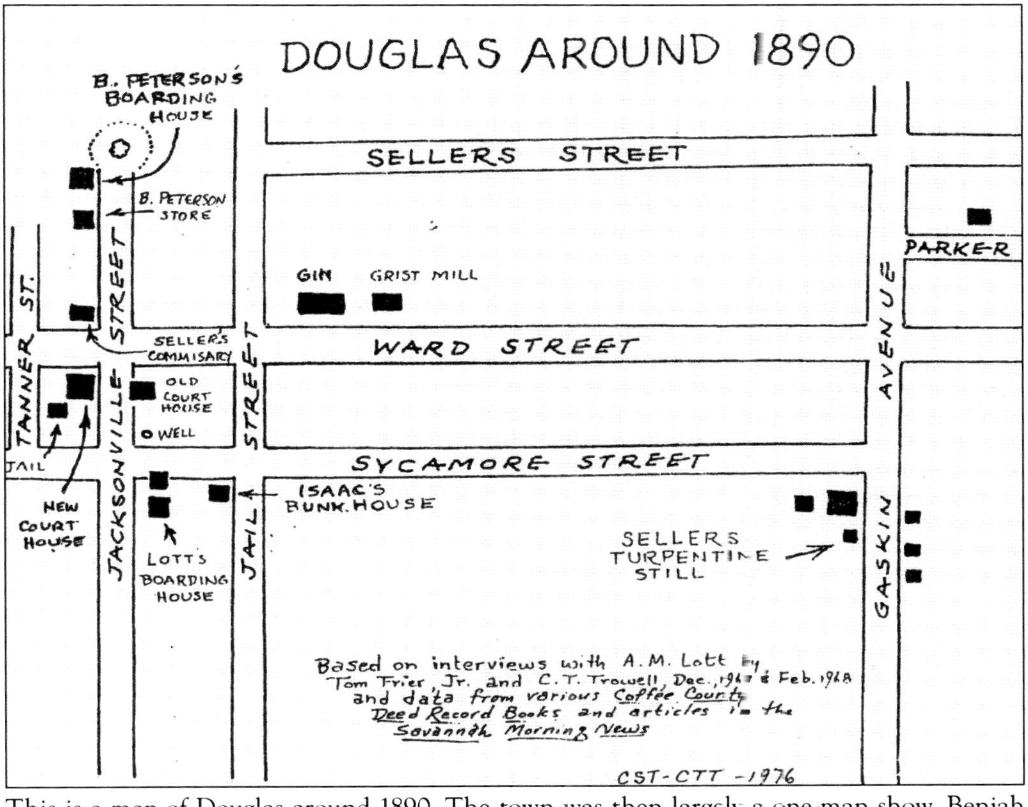

This is a map of Douglas around 1890. The town was then largely a one-man show. Benjah Peterson, who had acquired large amounts of land in 1884, played the role of hotel owner, post office operator, merchant, and sheepherder, and he literally fed the judge and jury; however, he did not actually name Peterson Avenue after himself. Naming of the north-south roads Peterson and Madison came later. Jacksonville and Jail Streets marked the center of town at this time. (Courtesy of C.T. Trowell.)

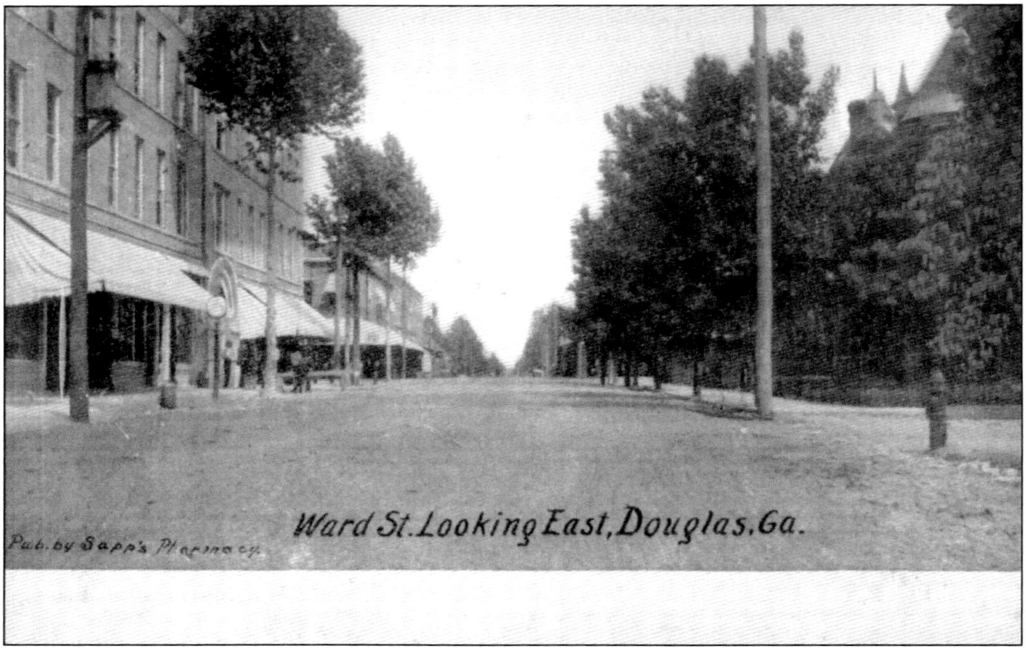

When the neighboring town of Pearson wanted the county seat moved there, Peterson donated and sold land to the City of Douglas. He worked with other businessmen and sold additional property in an effort to develop the community. This is Ward Street looking east. (Courtesy of Joanne Hanna Lott.)

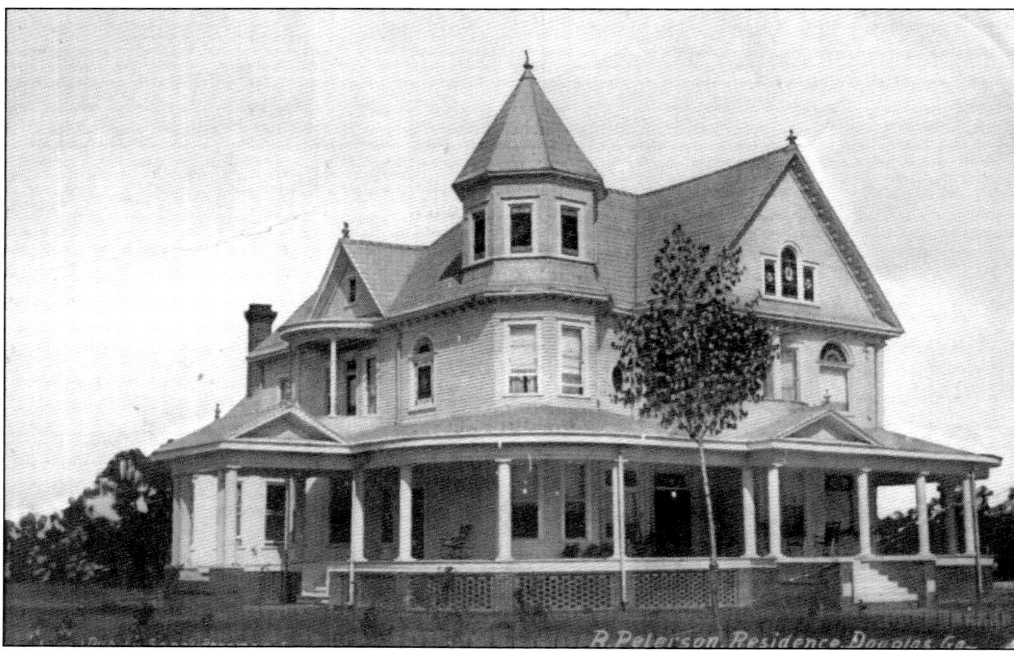

Built by Coffee County pioneer Benjah Peterson and later known as Stapleton's Boarding House, this Victorian landmark became the location of Sims Funeral Home in 1945. (Courtesy of Joanne Hanna Lott.)

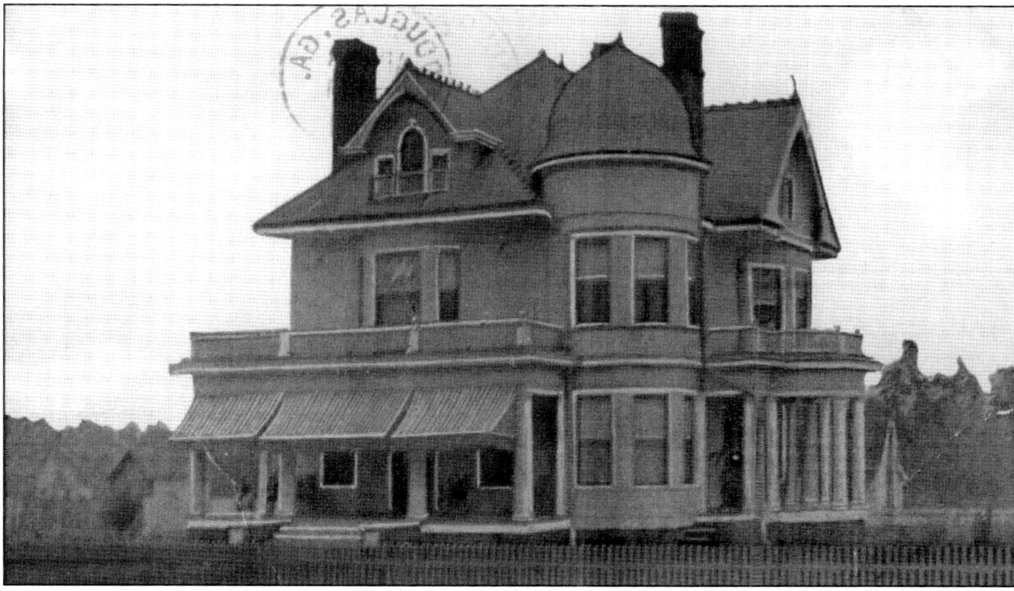

Pictured around 1910, this is O. Peterson's residence, better known as the Lonnie Pope House (not to be confused with the Benjah Peterson House). The home was designed by the architectural firm Barber & Klutz. It was relocated to Jackson Street and is now just off the Douglas Trail. Lonnie Pope was mayor of Douglas from 1933 to 1938 and donated the land for the hospital to be rebuilt in its current location. (Courtesy of Joanne Hanna Lott.)

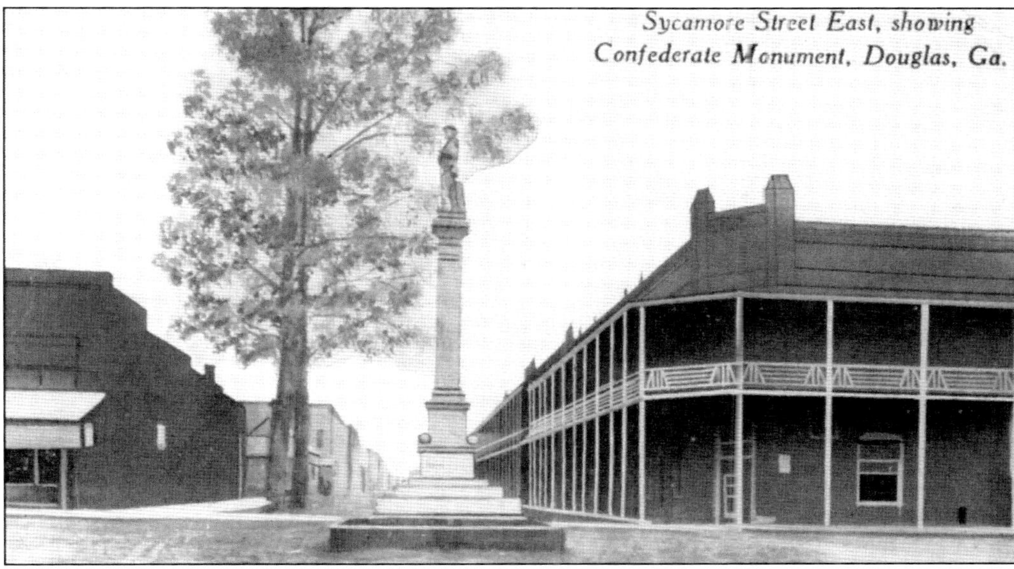

The Confederate monument in front of the courthouse was dedicated by a group of people that included "Little Miss Margaret Shelton." The monument had been erected for some time, but the United Daughters of the Confederacy were waiting for an appropriate date to unveil it. The event started with a parade and featured a presentation to the veterans, and the Willacoochee Band played while everybody in attendance sang "Dixie." A rifle salute was provided by the cadets of the agriculture school. As seen here, the monument was originally located on Sycamore Street but was later moved to the corner of Peterson Avenue and Ward Street. (Courtesy of Dr. James A. Cottingham.)

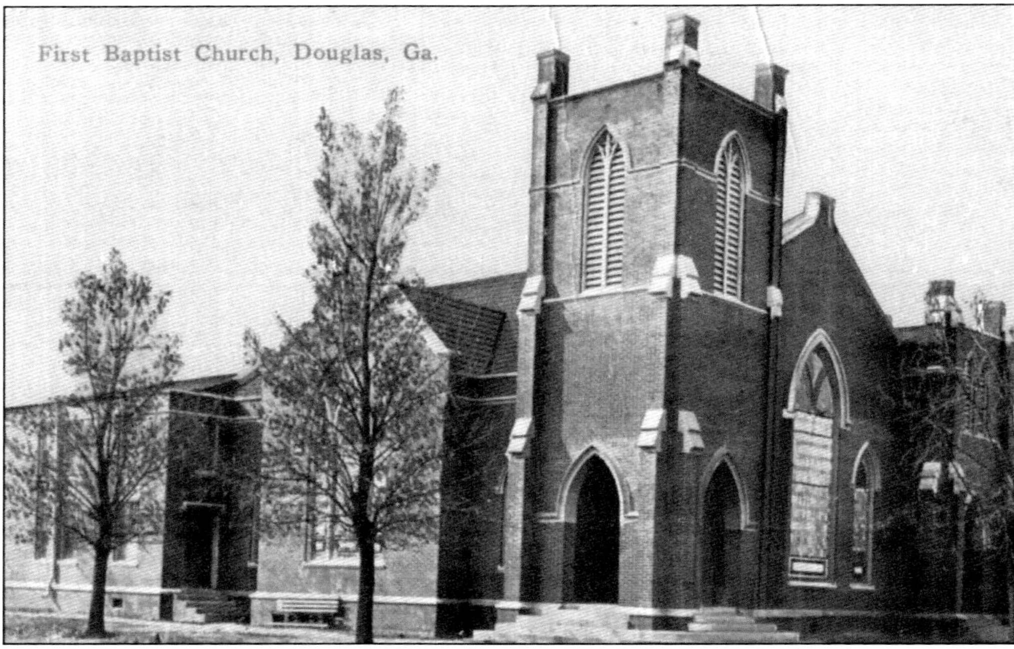

The First Baptist Church of Douglas was established in 1893. The original building site for the church was on the corner of Ward Street and Coffee Avenue, where the Cottingham home is today. The base of original baptismal font is still intact under the residence. The structure shown here was on the southwest corner of Ward Street and Gaskin Avenue. (Courtesy of Dr. James A. Cottingham.)

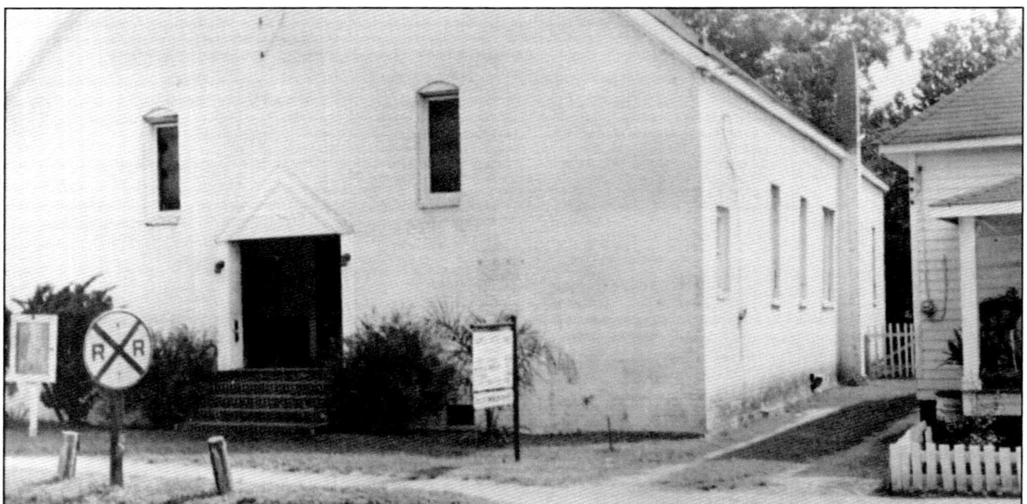

Gaines Chapel African Methodist Episcopal Church was established in the 1890s on Pearl Avenue by the railroad tracks. This was one of the buildings created from Benjah Peterson's donation and business ventures; the others included four additional churches, 12 stores, a gristmill, a ginnery, two livery stables, three hotels, a Masonic hall, and an Odd Fellows lodge. During the urban renewal project in the 1960s, this building was relocated to Coffee Avenue. The church building was expanded in size and is now a brick structure. (Courtesy of City of Douglas.)

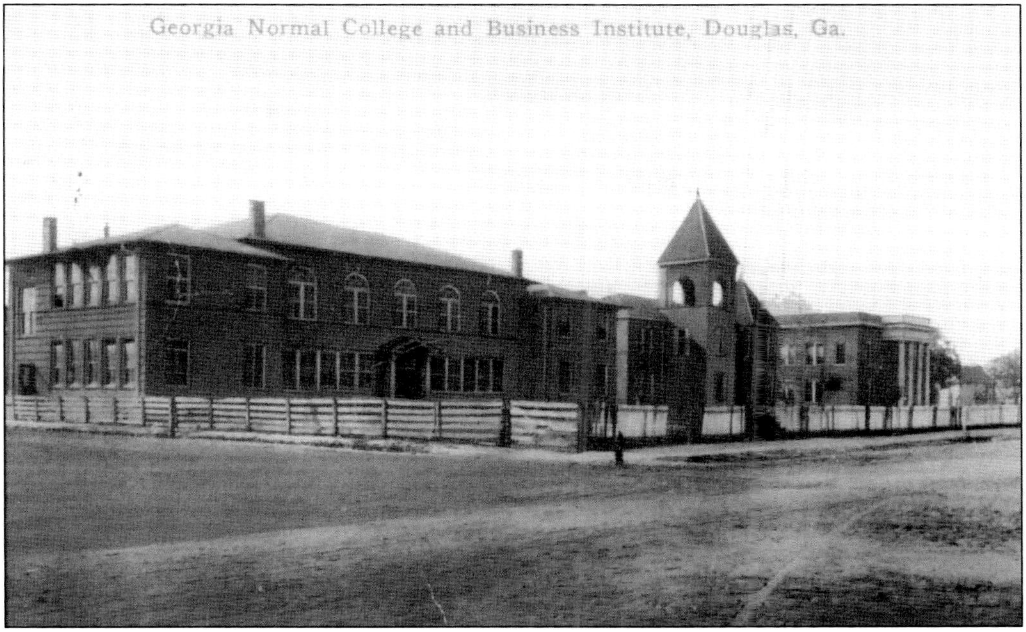

Georgia Normal College and Business Institute was originally opened in Abbeville in 1897, but Professors Little and Kuhl were persuaded to bring the school to Douglas in 1908. By the end of that year, 5,500 students had graduated from the institute. (Courtesy of Dr. James A. Cottingham.)

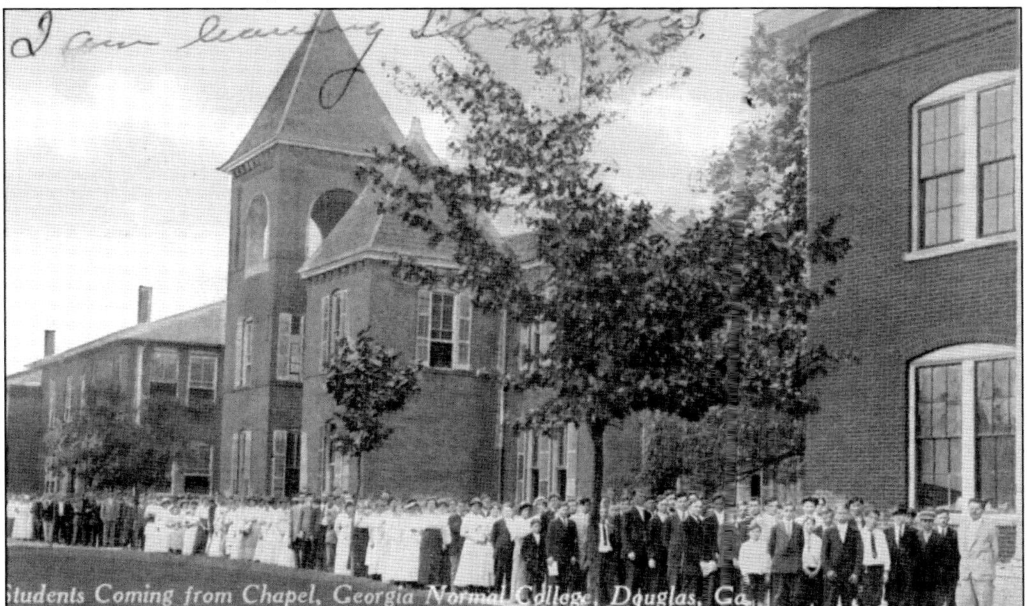

In the early 1900s, church service was a central part of public education. Colleges often required that pastors be employed as a part of the regular staff, and many presidents or vice presidents of colleges were pastors who served double duty. The students of Georgia Normal College and Business Institute can be seen here leaving the chapel. The gentleman on the far right is Prof. A.A. Kuhl. (Courtesy of Joanne Hanna Lott.)

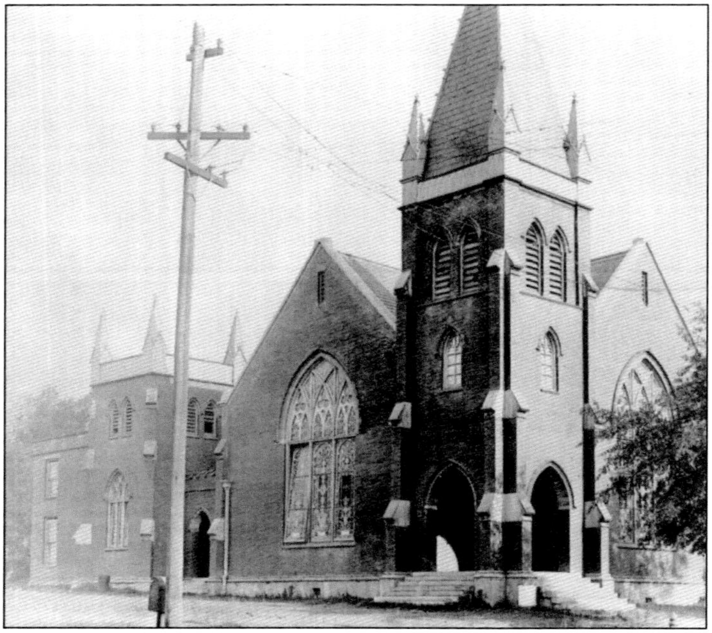

Methodist ministers traveled across the United States to spread the denomination in the 1800s. They went on horseback to rural areas like Coffee County, thereby becoming known as circuit riders. The First United Methodist Church in Douglas, Georgia, was established in August 1888. A year later, a new courthouse was built, and the Methodists bought the old courthouse building and moved it to Jackson Street to serve as a place of worship. (Courtesy of Dr. James A. Cottingham.)

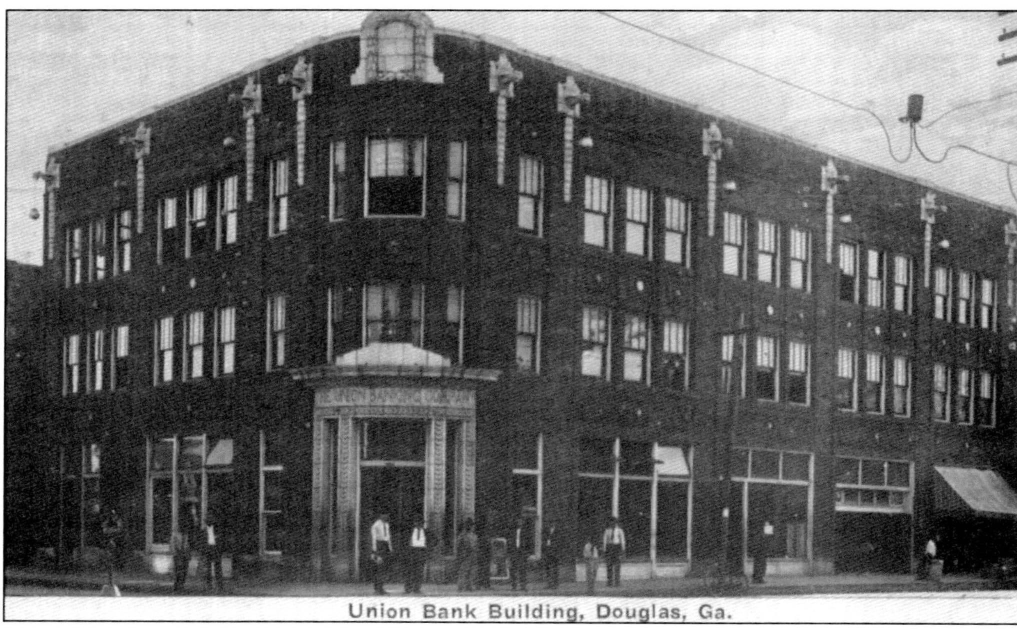

Pictured here in 1910 when it opened, the Union Company Banking Building (later the Coffee County Bank Building) was the first bank established in Douglas. The structure was designed by Valdosta resident R.N. McEachren. (Courtesy of Joanne Hanna Lott.)

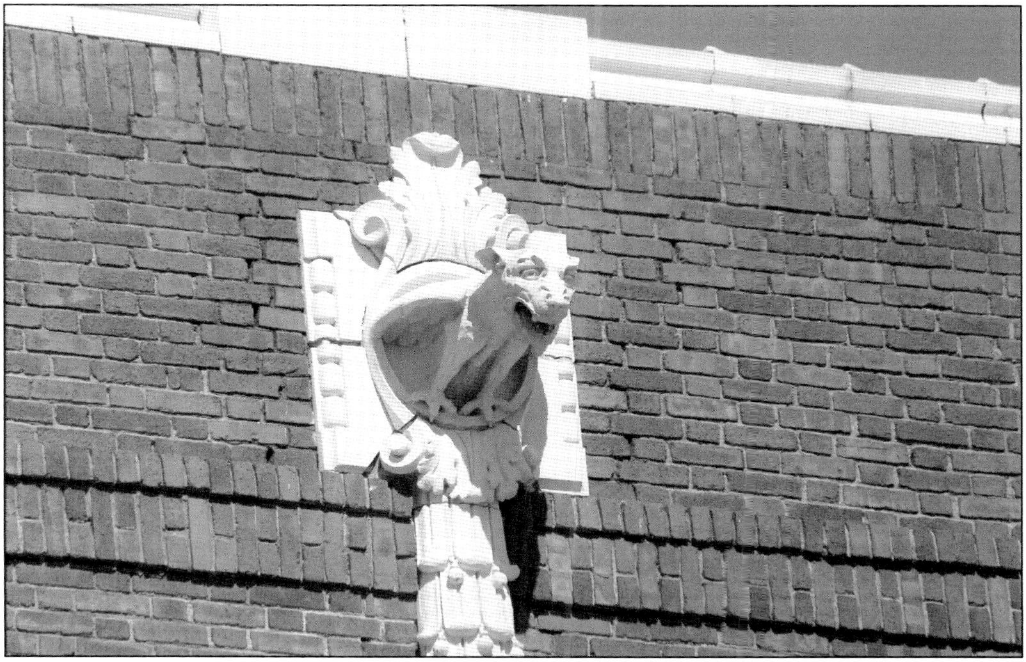

Trespassers beware, as gargoyles guard over the bank. Structurally, the gargoyles are just rainspouts, but their frightening appearance makes this building the most notable one in town. (Courtesy of Charles E. Griffiths II.)

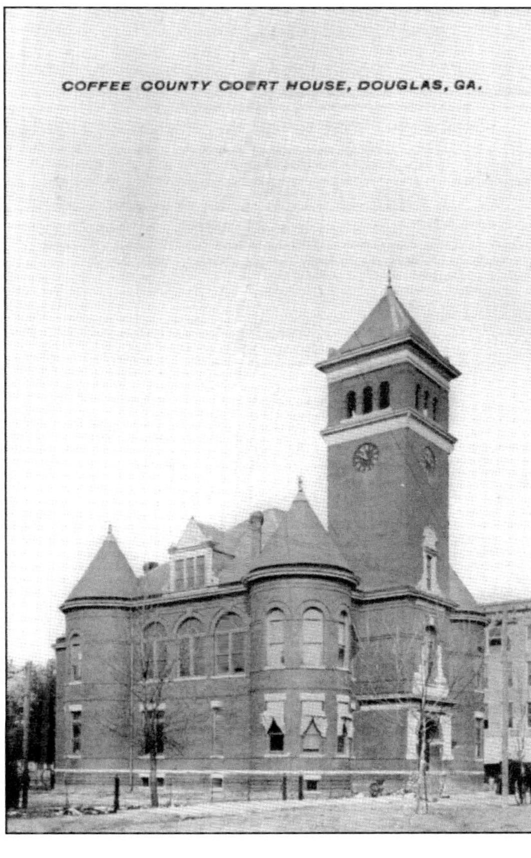

The earlier courthouse was once impressive, but it had become little more than a barn and schoolhouse during the Civil War. This courthouse was built in 1902 but burned in 1930. (Courtesy of Dr. James A. Cottingham.)

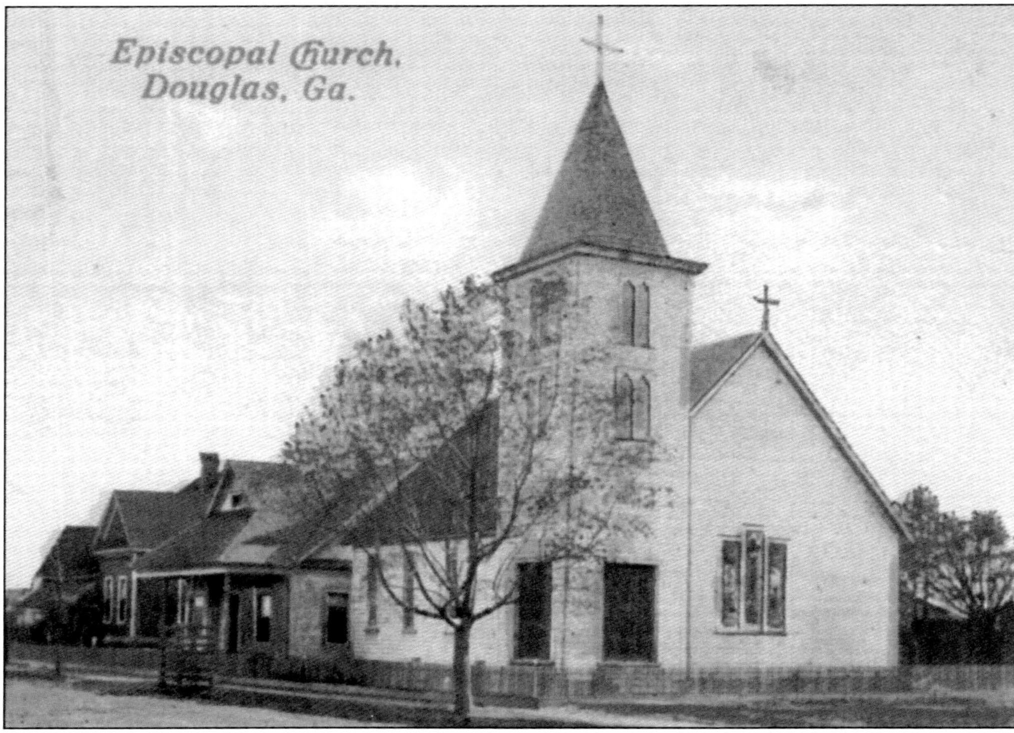

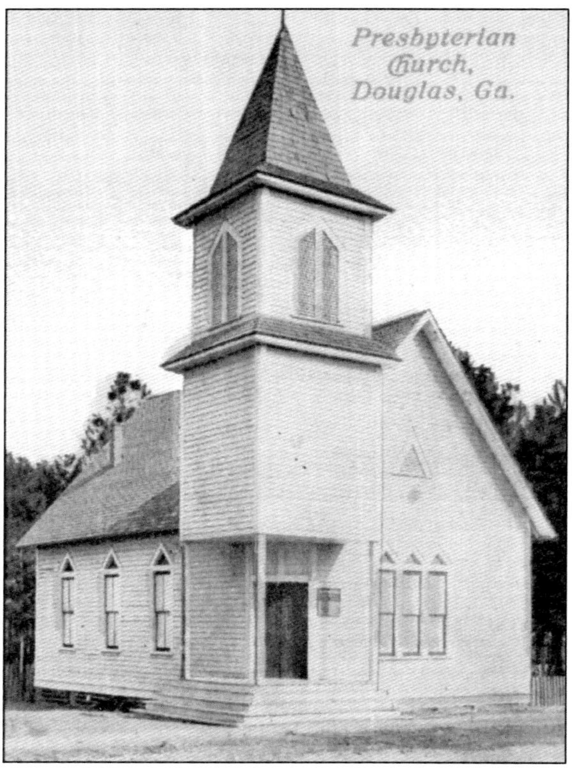

In 1899, a small group of people held a meeting to organize the Episcopal church. For almost two years, the new congregation met in neighboring church buildings. The first meeting held in this building took place in September 1901. By 1903, the church had nine stained-glass windows, and the remaining windows were covered in cloth to keep out the cold. The Baptist and Methodist churches gave a gift of one stained-glass window each to the congregation. In 1993, the building burned, but the stained-glass windows were saved for the new building. (Courtesy of Joanne Hanna Lott.)

For a few years, the Methodist and Baptist churches shared their buildings so that the Presbyterian congregation in the community could have occasional services. Presbyterian trustees raised $40 to purchase land for their own building in 1902, and the Presbyterian church was built in 1903. (Courtesy of Joanne Hanna Lott.)

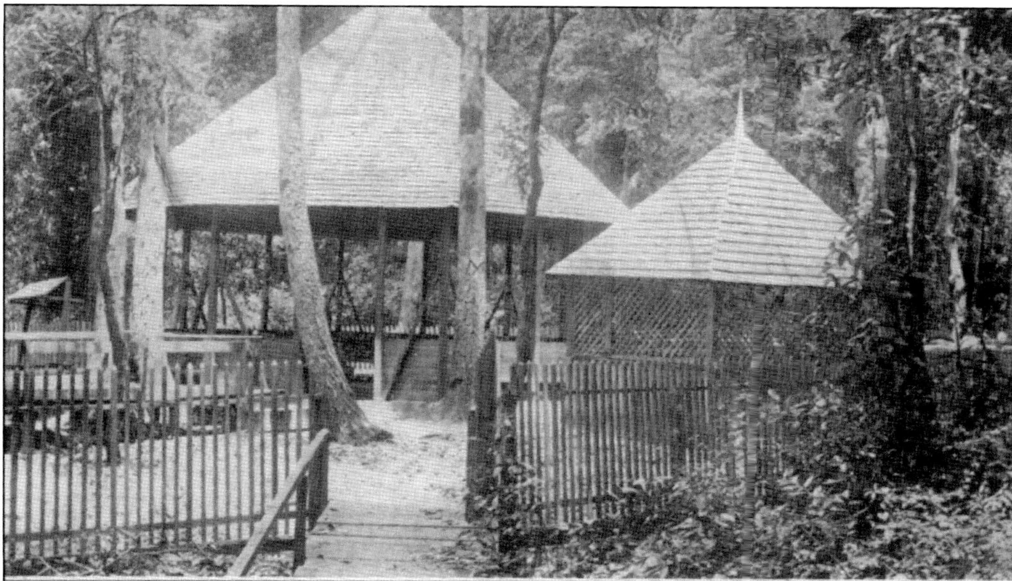
Gaskin's Springs, Douglas Ga.

This is the well at Gaskin's Springs Church Camp. Gaskin's Springs Camp meetings were started around 1895 by founder Joel Gaskin and sponsored by the First Methodist Church of Douglas, Georgia. The presiding elder was in charge of the grounds and the selection of the preachers. During some revival meetings, tents were pitched in addition to the permanent cottages. In 1946, Rev. M.J. Wood of Fort Valley, Georgia, held a revival meeting at Lone Hill Methodist Church and later at the old camp property. This meeting inspired Reverend Wood to build a new tabernacle, which was completed in 1950 with the help of E.A. Weathers, of Lone Hill Methodist Church, and the people of Douglas. Due to inclement weather, the meetings were not held for a few years. Some claimed the property had been abandoned, though after some deliberation and a number of years, Gaskin's Springs reopened. The original circular springhouse is gone, but the last two decades have witnessed a renewed interest in the historic retreat. (Courtesy of Dr. James A. Cottingham.)

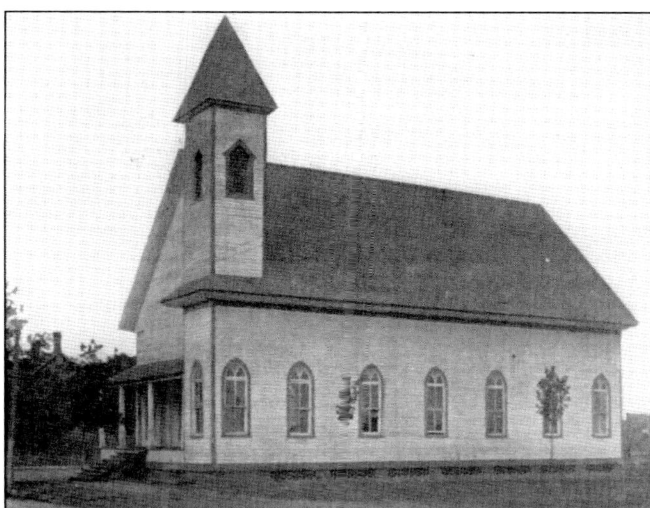

After the Civil War, the Baptist churches in Georgia underwent reformation. Prior to the war, African Americans had been forced to have membership in white churches. Some churches resisted any change in doctrine, and the Primitive Baptist congregations emerged. Still, further objections created Free Will, Holiness, and Independent Baptists. The Broxton Baptist Church is a living example of these times and was finally chartered in 1920. (Courtesy of Joanne Hanna Lott.)

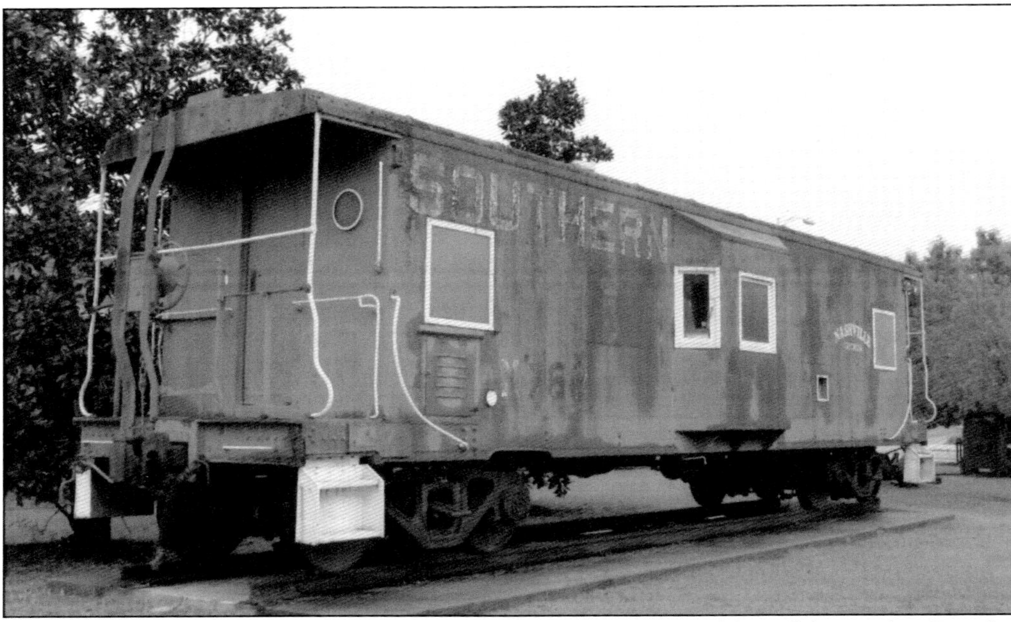

In 1895, Douglas welcomed its first train, which connected McDonald's Mill (Axson) to Douglas. Three years later, in 1898, the train line extended to the surrounding towns of Nicholls and Waycross, Georgia. Shortly thereafter, another line connected Douglas to Broxton and Fitzgerald, Georgia. The Atlanta, Birmingham & Coast Railroad and the Georgia & Florida Railway were the key operators in Douglas's early rail history. (Courtesy of Charles E. Griffiths II.)

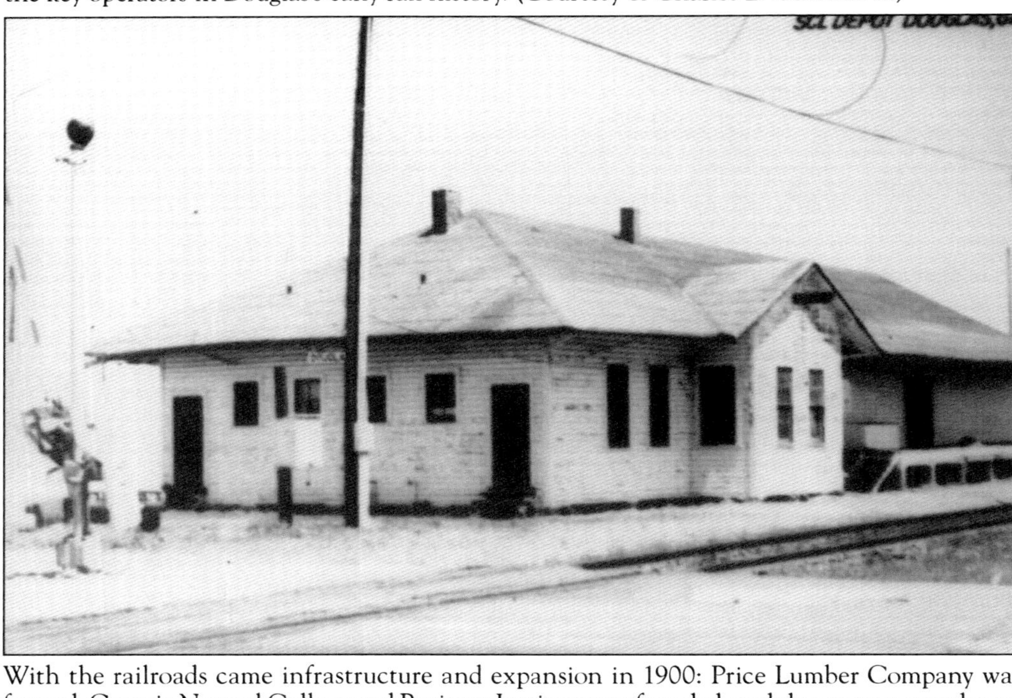

With the railroads came infrastructure and expansion in 1900: Price Lumber Company was formed, Georgia Normal College and Business Institute was founded, and the current courthouse was built with bricks the trains brought in. (Courtesy of Joanne Hanna Lott.)

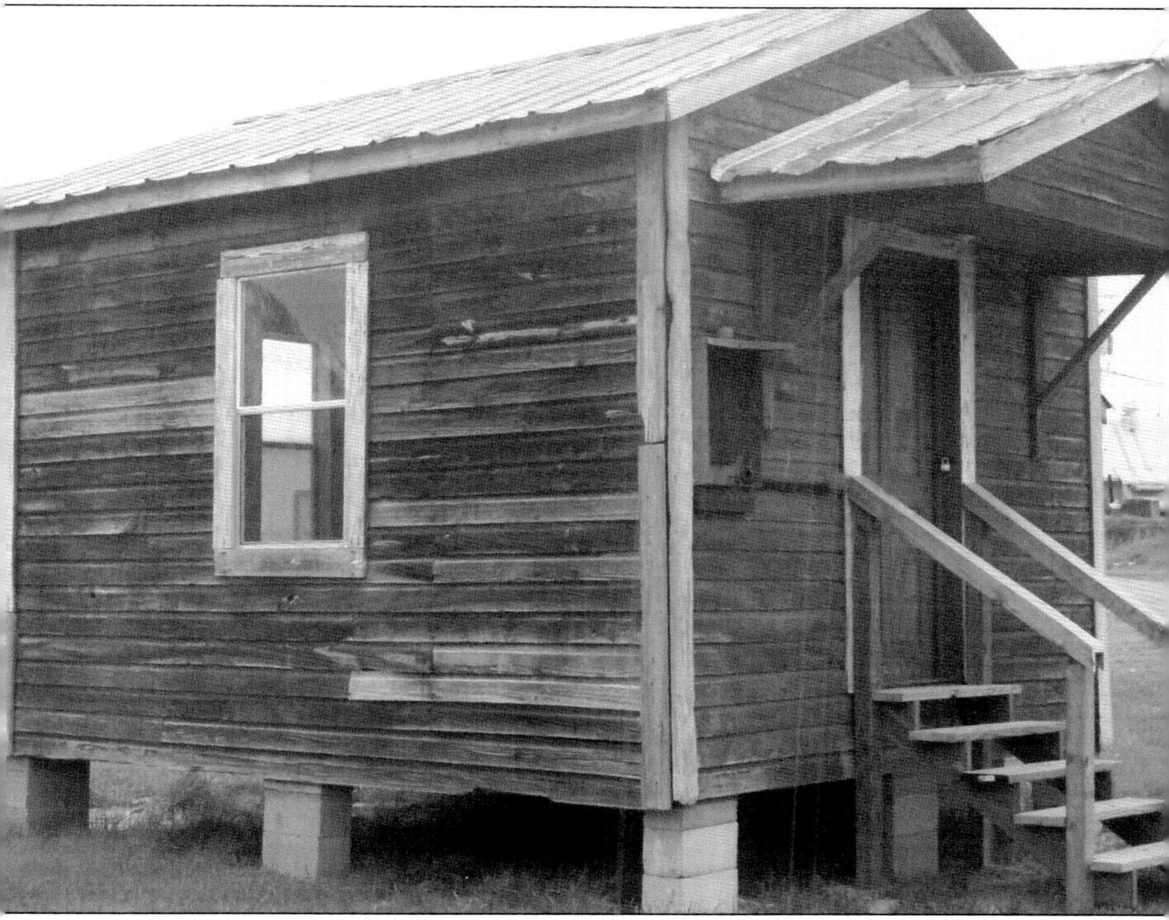

The railroad was a major industry in the community for 60 years. Trains still come through today, but passenger transportation stopped in the 1980s. This depot, built by the Vernon Company for passenger service, was dormant for many years. Concerned citizens and the Georgia & Florida Railway restored the building, and it is now home to the Heritage Station Museum, which features history of the railroad industry in the area, as well as history of local businesses. (Courtesy of Charles E. Griffiths II.)

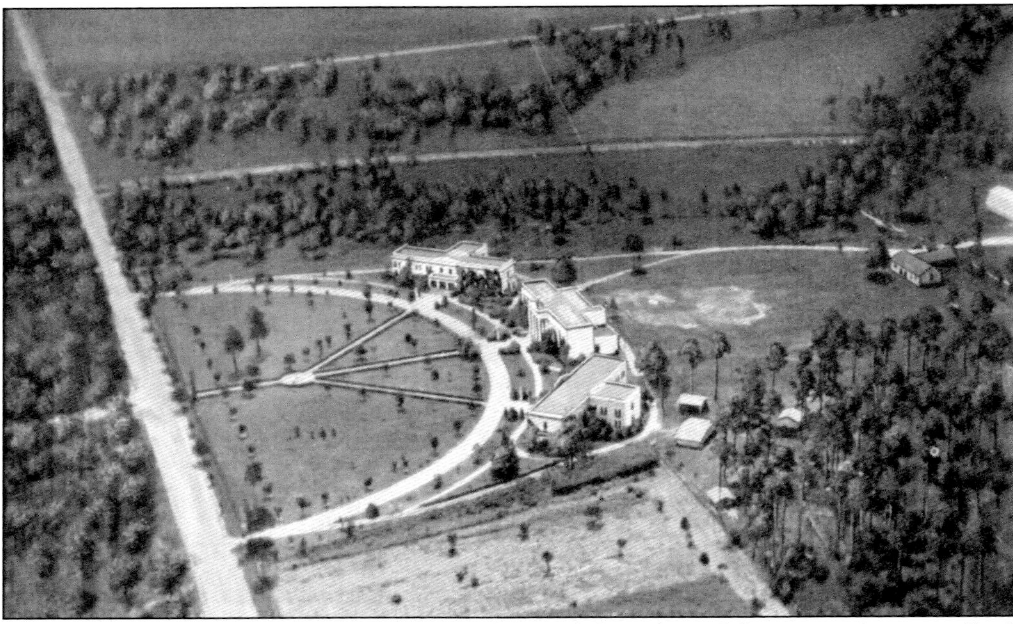

In 1906, few Georgians attended school beyond the eighth grade, and there was a shortage of high schools in the state. Georgia decided to open 12 district agricultural and mechanical (A&M) schools throughout the state to fulfill this educational need. Concerned Douglas citizens decided to offer the state a deal they could not refuse. Prominent landowner Benjah Peterson provided 300 acres of land for a school and free water for 10 years in return for the state agreeing to place one of those 12 schools in Douglas. Without this tempting offer, a rural town with fewer than 1,000 citizens would have been overlooked by the state. Seen here are the three original buildings of the 11th district A&M school; this is now South Georgia State College. (Courtesy of Dr. James A. Cottingham.)

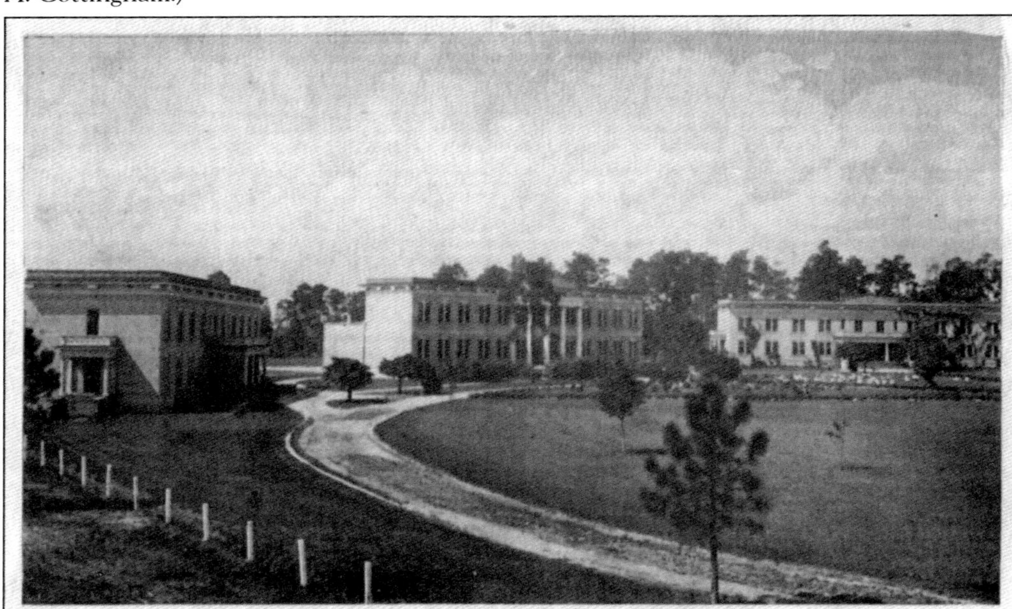

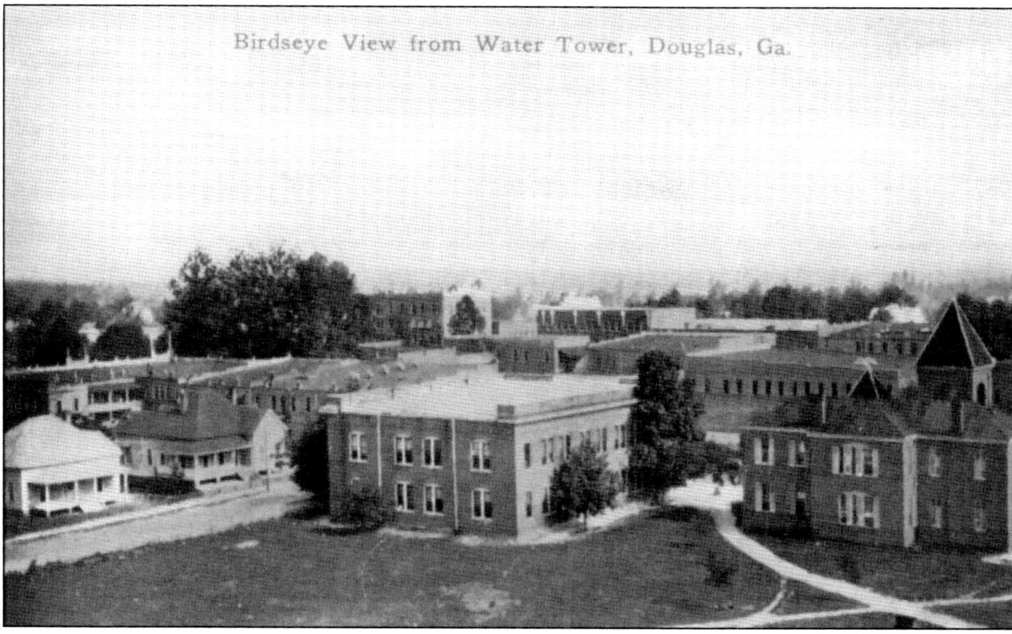

One of the most important steps for pioneers to make Douglas grow was to create a waterworks. Shallow wells ran dry and were polluted, and they were not reliable for fire protection. In 1897, a deep well, windmill, and elevated water tank were created. This is a view of Douglas from that water tower. (Courtesy of Joanne Hanna Lott.)

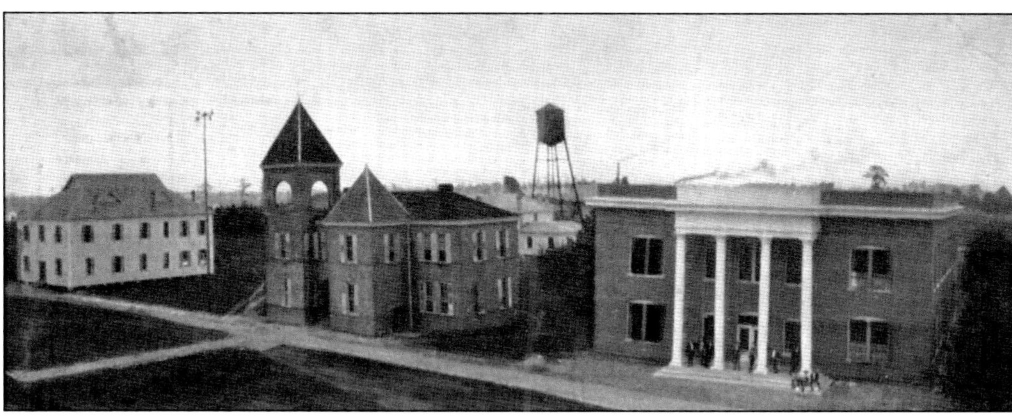

The water tower seen here behind the Georgia Normal College and Business Institute is near the site of one of the city's current towers, just east of city hall. (Courtesy of Dr. James A. Cottingham.)

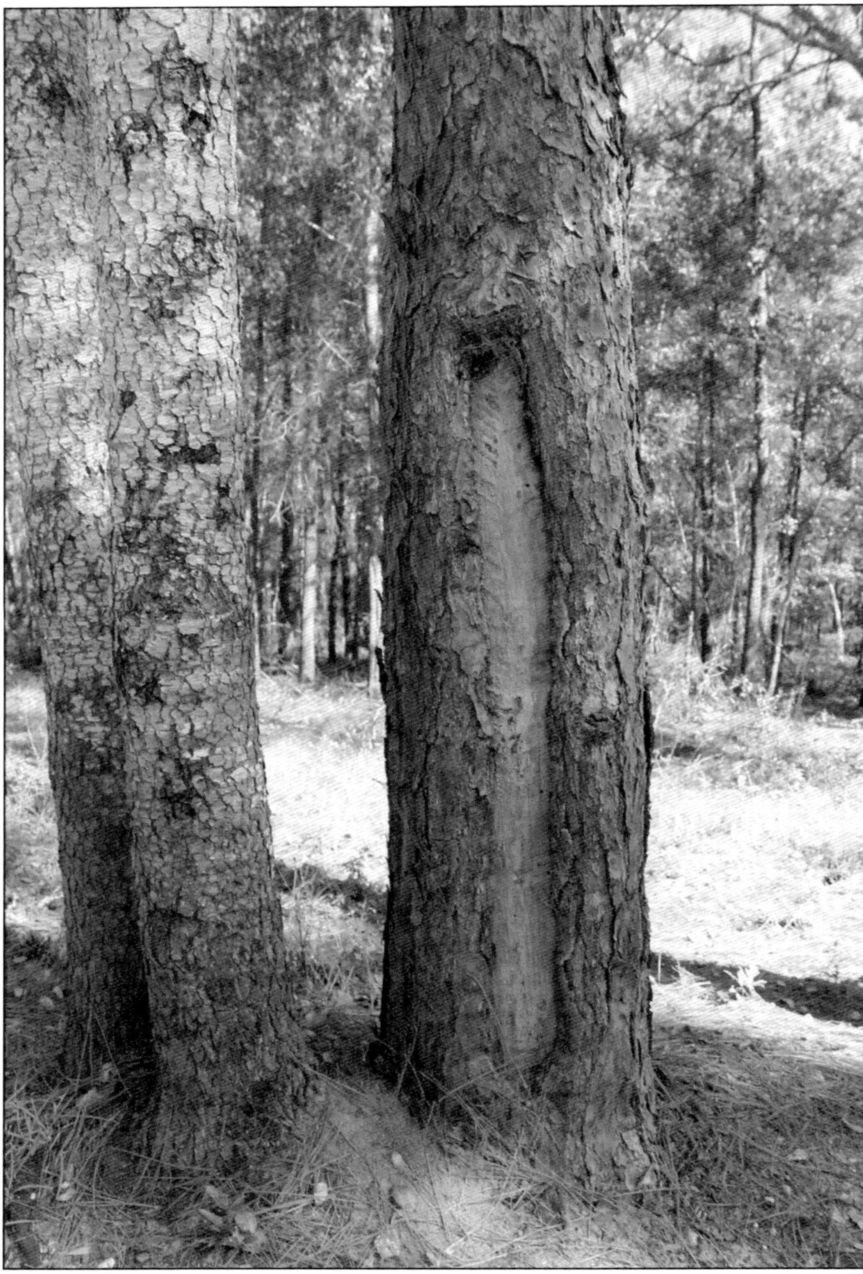

Douglas gained its first industry founders with turpentine stills. Business leaders such as McNiel & McNiel, Lewis & Ashley, Merrit & Powell, Lott & McLean, E.A Buck, and Miles Wilson Howell funded the newfound turpentine industry through housing, churches, hotels, and manpower. Turpentine harvested from pine trees was used in many products, including medications, waxes, cleaners, insecticides, explosives, and paints. Sapping the pine trees of turpentine exposed the them to pathogens, and a tree would form a scar where it was cut to protect itself. Pictured is one of the "catfaces" that mark hundreds of acres of trees across southern Georgia. (Courtesy of Charles E. Griffiths II.)

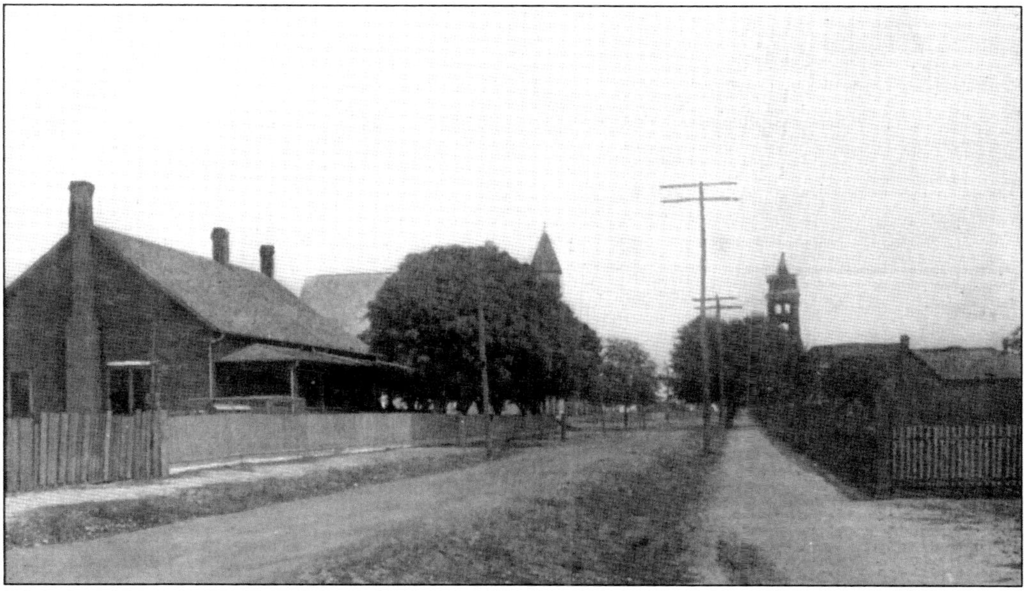

This is a photograph of a street in that area. There was no town here at this time, and like many of the temporary turpentine communities, the buildings and street pictured began as a working community. In 1908, the Dorminy Price Lumber Company drilled a 400-foot-deep well to be used for lumber boiler supply and domestic drinking. Like today, many people commuted to and from Douglas and surrounding areas to work. (Courtesy of Joanne Hanna Lott.)

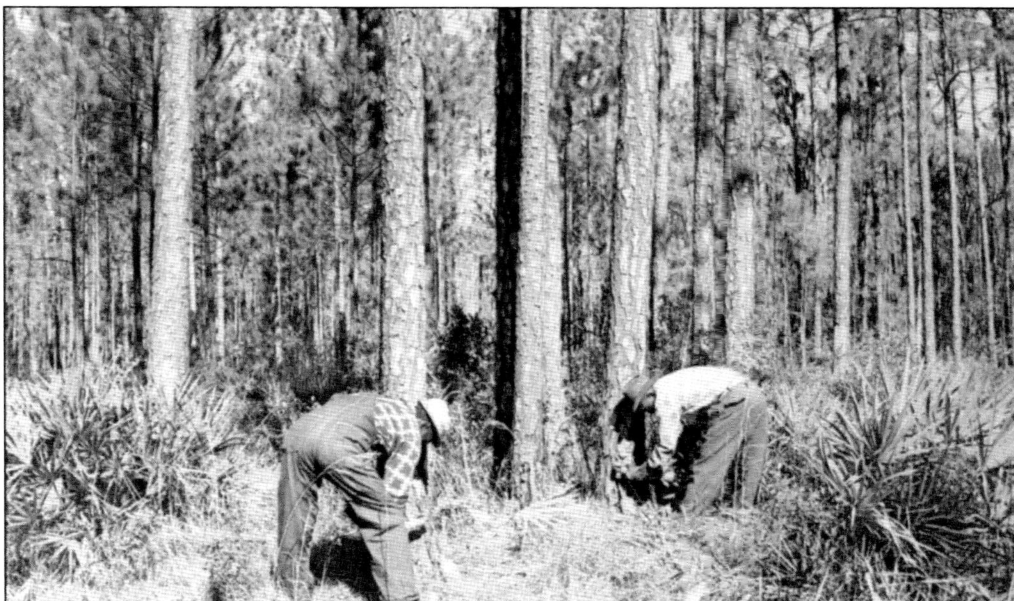

These turpentine workers labored in the northern part of the county near the area that is now Broxton. In 1904, the Dorminy Price Lumber Company purchased an extensive tract of timberland from the Ocmulgee River Company, including several thousand acres in Coffee County. It turpentined first and then milled trees, putting out two locomotives full of lumber daily. (Courtesy of Joanne Hanna Lott.)

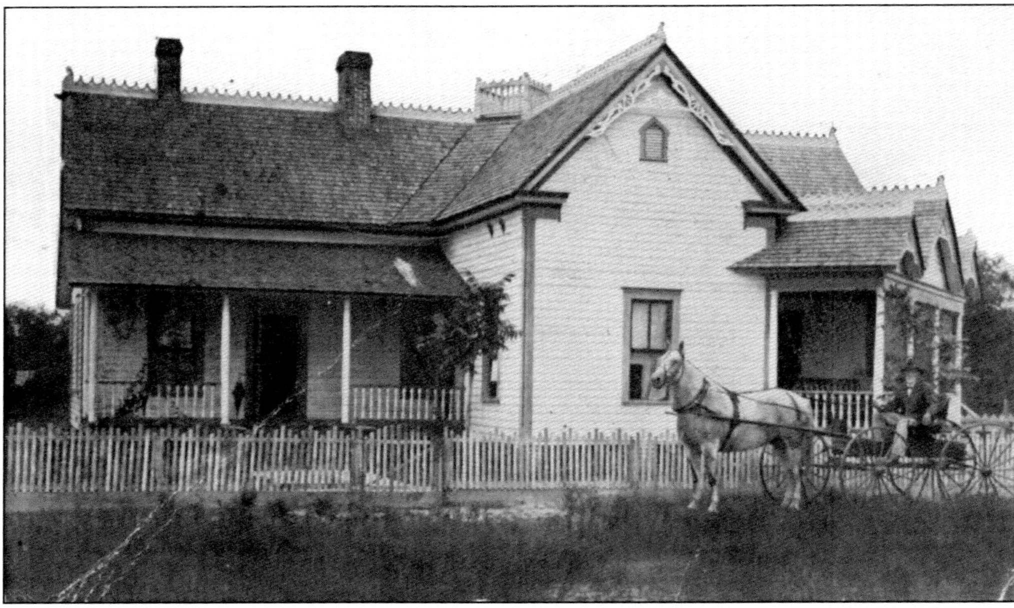

Picture is J.W. Price at his home in Broxton. Note the bird-spike trim and small picket fence on top of the roof. At this time, homes of wealthier families had trim that was not only decorative but also prevented birds from perching and making a mess. Metal or wood fencing trimmed with copper cable was placed on the roof to serve as a lightning rod, and rooster or weather-vane rods were generally placed on the barn. (Courtesy of Joanne Hanna Lott.)

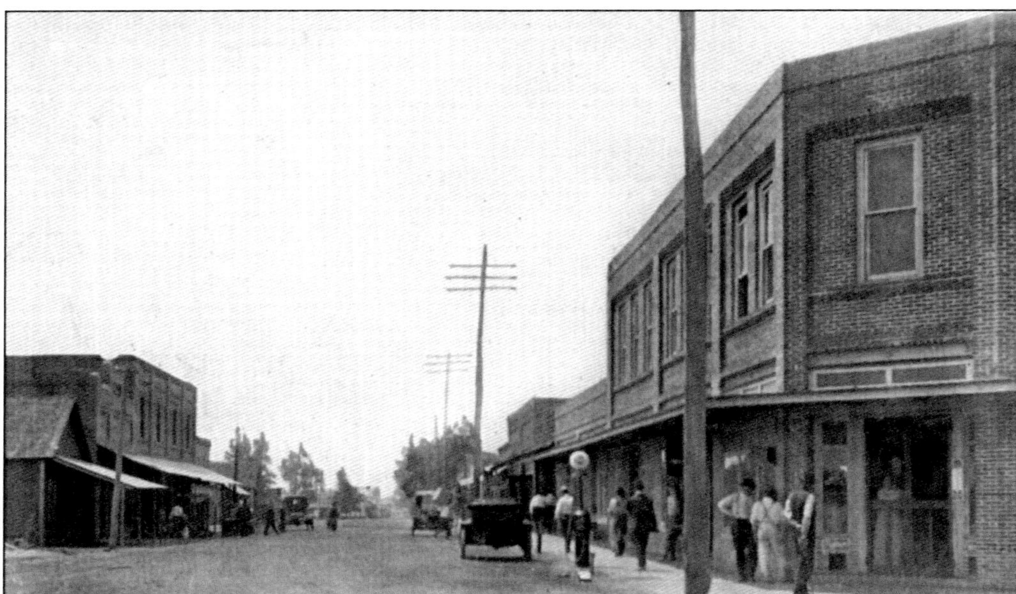

This is Ocmulgee Street in Broxton around 1910. Broxton was not established until 1932, but many people had been travelling down this road from Douglas for work and to picnic at the Broxton Rocks for a half century before incorporation. (Courtesy of Joanne Hanna Lott.)

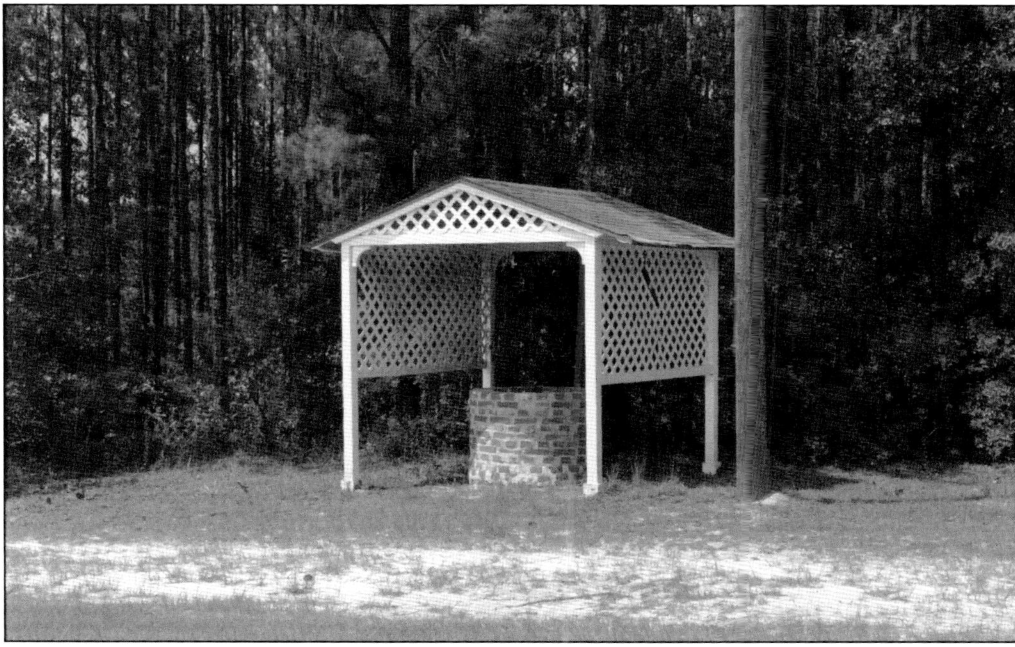

Sand Hill Church, located about seven miles east of Douglas, is one of the oldest churches in the area. In its early years, it held a historic, large association meeting on the grounds in a log building situated where the old well still stands. Preachers and congregations gathered from all over the country. It became the birthplace of the Smyrna Baptist Association, which currently comprises 39 churches. (Courtesy of Charles E. Griffiths II.)

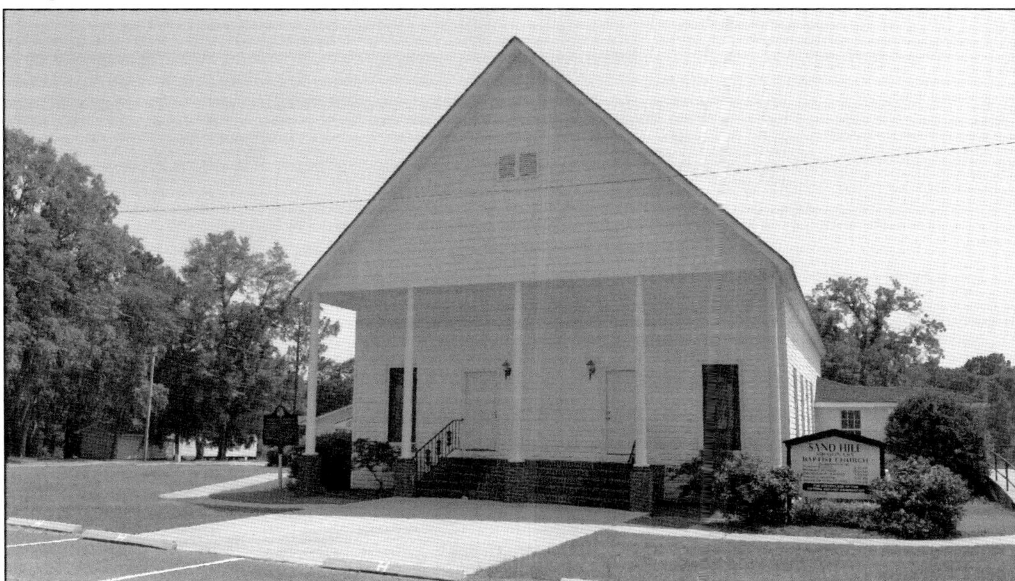

G.W. Newbern, Johnie Taylor, Gilford Lastinger, Thomas P. O'Neal, Elder Barber, and W.R. Frier Sr. (father of the editor of the *Douglas Enterprise*) attended the historic meeting and James Vining, S.P. Gaskins, and others preached. The existing sanctuary was built around 1905. (Courtesy of Charles E. Griffiths II.)

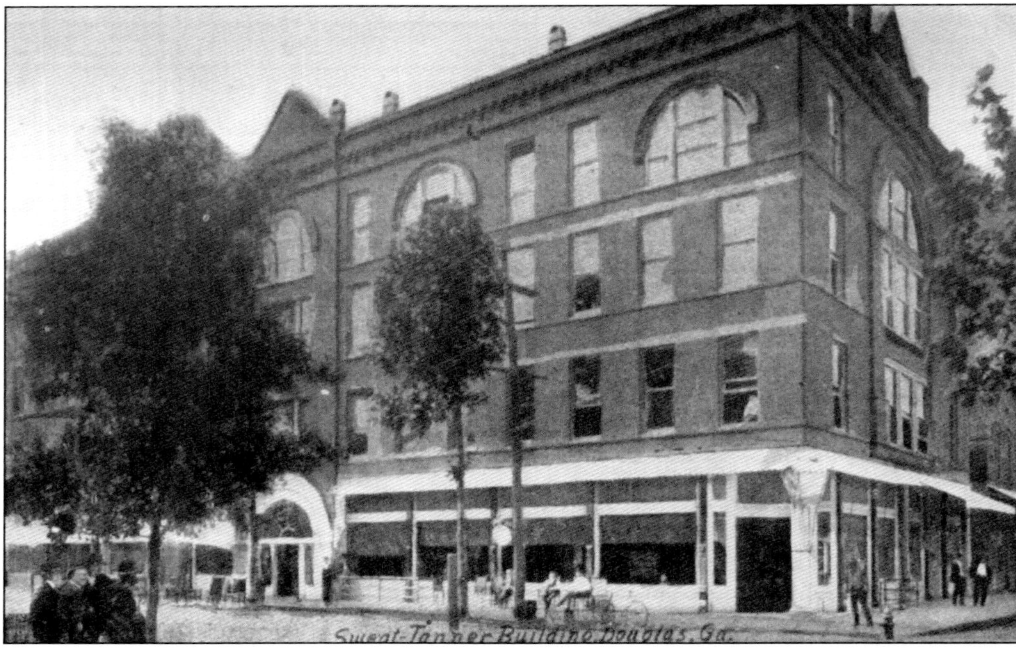

Pictured here in 1910, the Sweat Tanner Building was constructed in 1907 for business. One of the first tenants was Dr. Whipple, whose dentist practice occupied four suites. The building was constructed by B.H. Tanner in partnership with Frank L. Sweat. In the late 1800s and early 1900s, they built the edifices that currently encompass, among others, the Bordeaux Suites, Solid Waste, Drew House, the Sweat-Dent Building, and Norris Shoe. (Courtesy of Joanne Hanna Lott.)

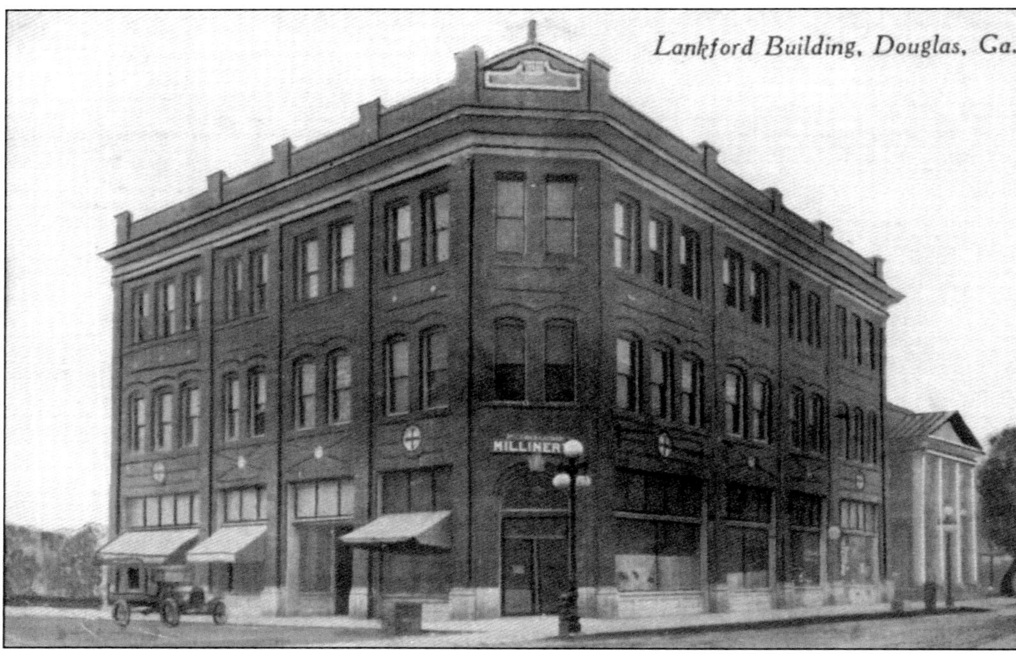

Around 1910, the W.C. Lankford Building was home to The Misses Douglas. All the fashionable young ladies of the time would get their spring millinery here. (Courtesy of Joanne Hanna Lott.)

Two

The Pioneers

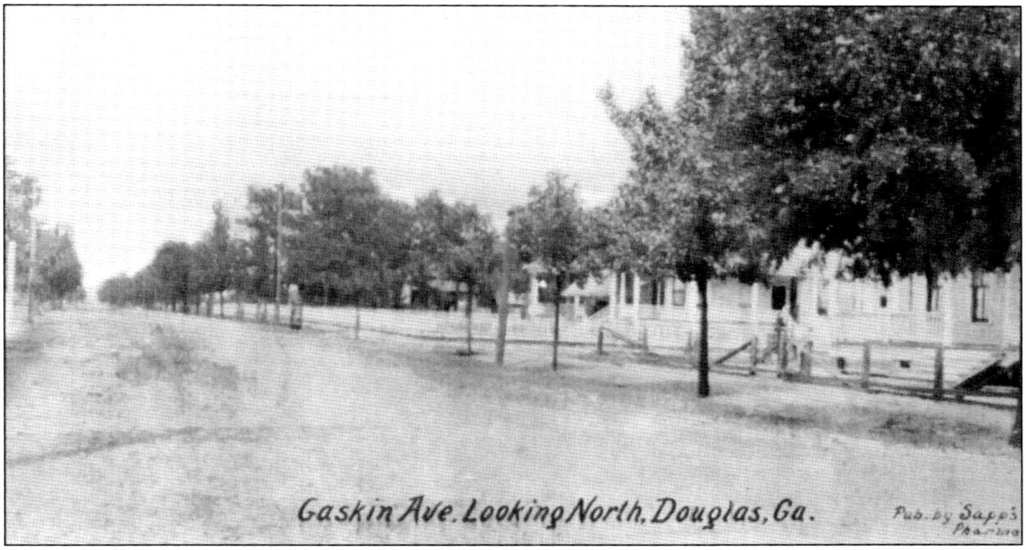

Coffee County was created in 1854, and in less than a century it sent its men to battle against the Seminole Indians and to fight in the Civil War, the Spanish-American War, and World Wars I and II. Douglas also faced a meningitis epidemic and influenza pandemics. Many pioneers perished before they found success. The Douglas City Cemetery is located on North Gaskin Avenue, which understandably became known as "Graveyard Road." Despite this, historic Gaskin Avenue was where the finest homes were located at this time, and the majority of the houses on this road and nearby are registered in the National Historic Registry. (Courtesy of Joanne Hanna Lott.)

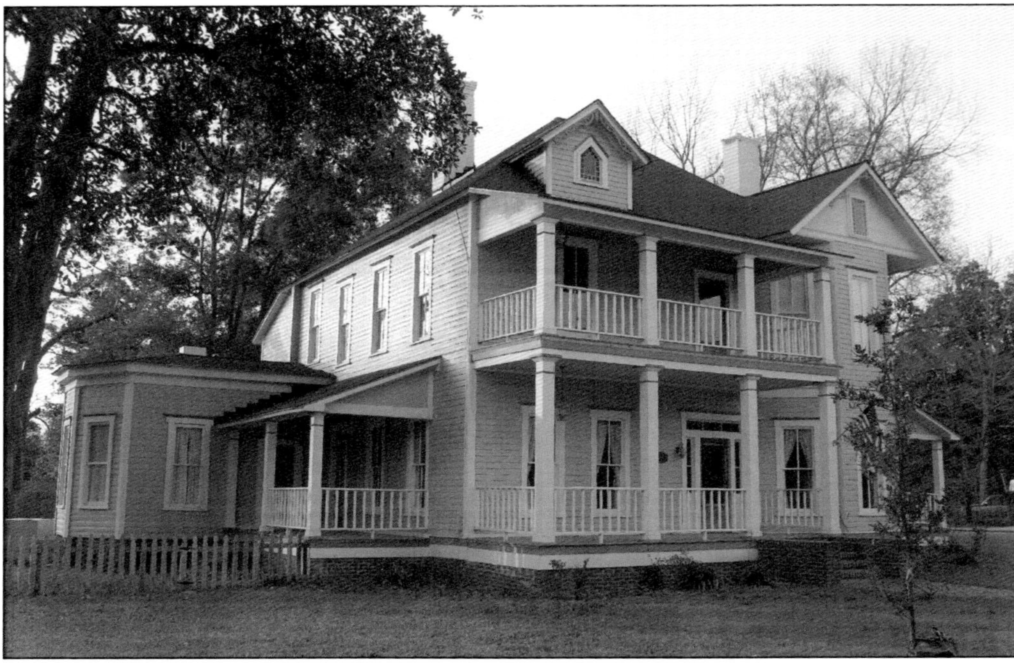

This Victorian home was built in 1901 by John and Anne Latimer McLean at 415 North Gaskin Avenue. The McLean family owned the house for a number of years, and it later served as an apartment building and a boarding school. (Courtesy of Charles E. Griffiths II.)

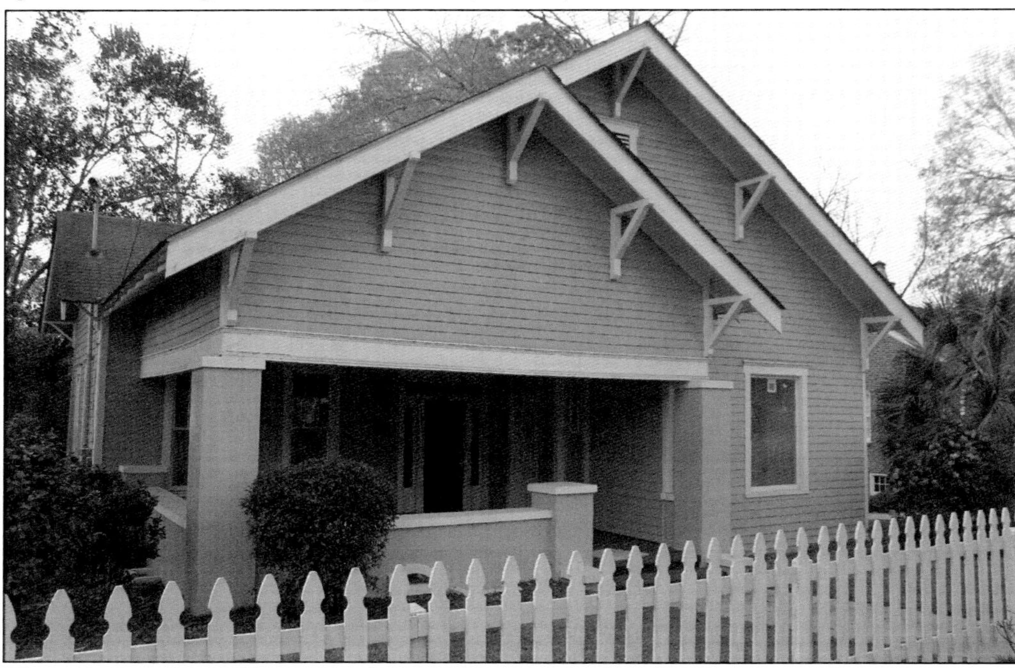

This one-story bungalow was built in 1901. It was the home of J. Walter Hendrick, a classics teacher and the principal of the Southern Normal Institute. It was later the home of the W.H. Bone family. (Courtesy of Charles E. Griffiths II.)

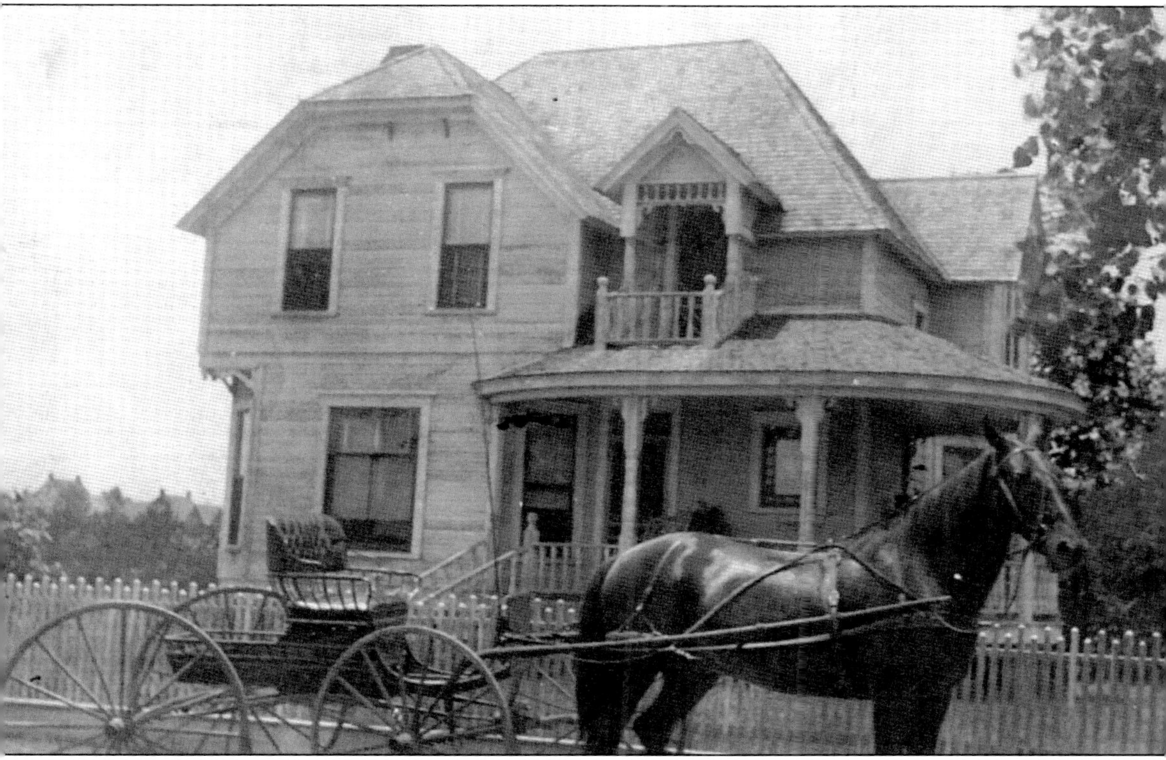

John Land Shelton, an employee of the Union Banking Company, was an animal lover and was especially fond of horses. He could frequently be seen driving a horse-drawn carriage around Douglas. One of his favorite thoroughbreds is seen here pulling a carriage in front of the Shelton home on North Gaskin Avenue. (Courtesy of Mary Clyde Scott.)

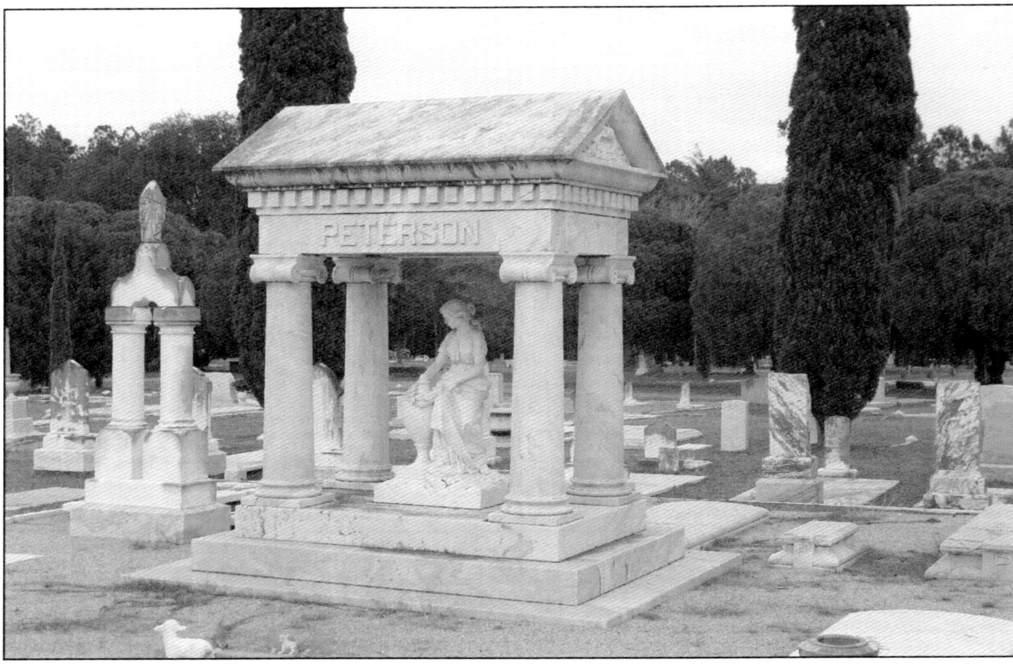

Currently 40 acres in size, it is believed the Douglas City Cemetery began with a donation of land from the Peterson family in the early 1860s. Pictured is the Peterson family plot. (Courtesy of Charles E. Griffiths II.)

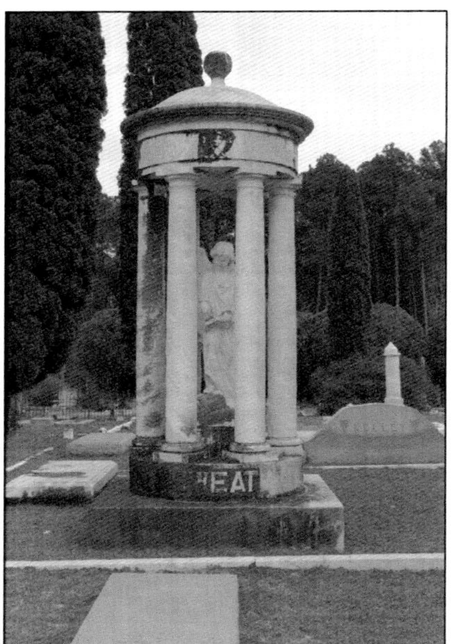

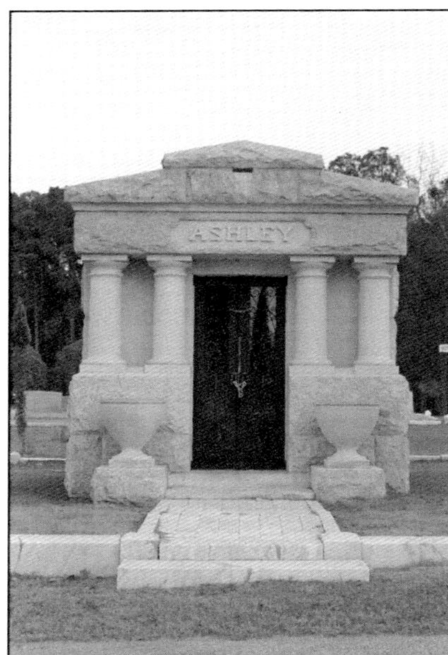

Today, it is customary to be quiet and solemn in graveyards, but this cemetery was expected to be visited and enjoyed. Seen here are headstones for pioneers Ashley and Sweat, who are buried in the older section of the cemetery. Take note of the trees; the city cemetery was designed to be a park. Tall Italian Cypress trees reaching more than 50 feet can be found in the older section of the graveyard. (Courtesy of Charles E. Griffiths II.)

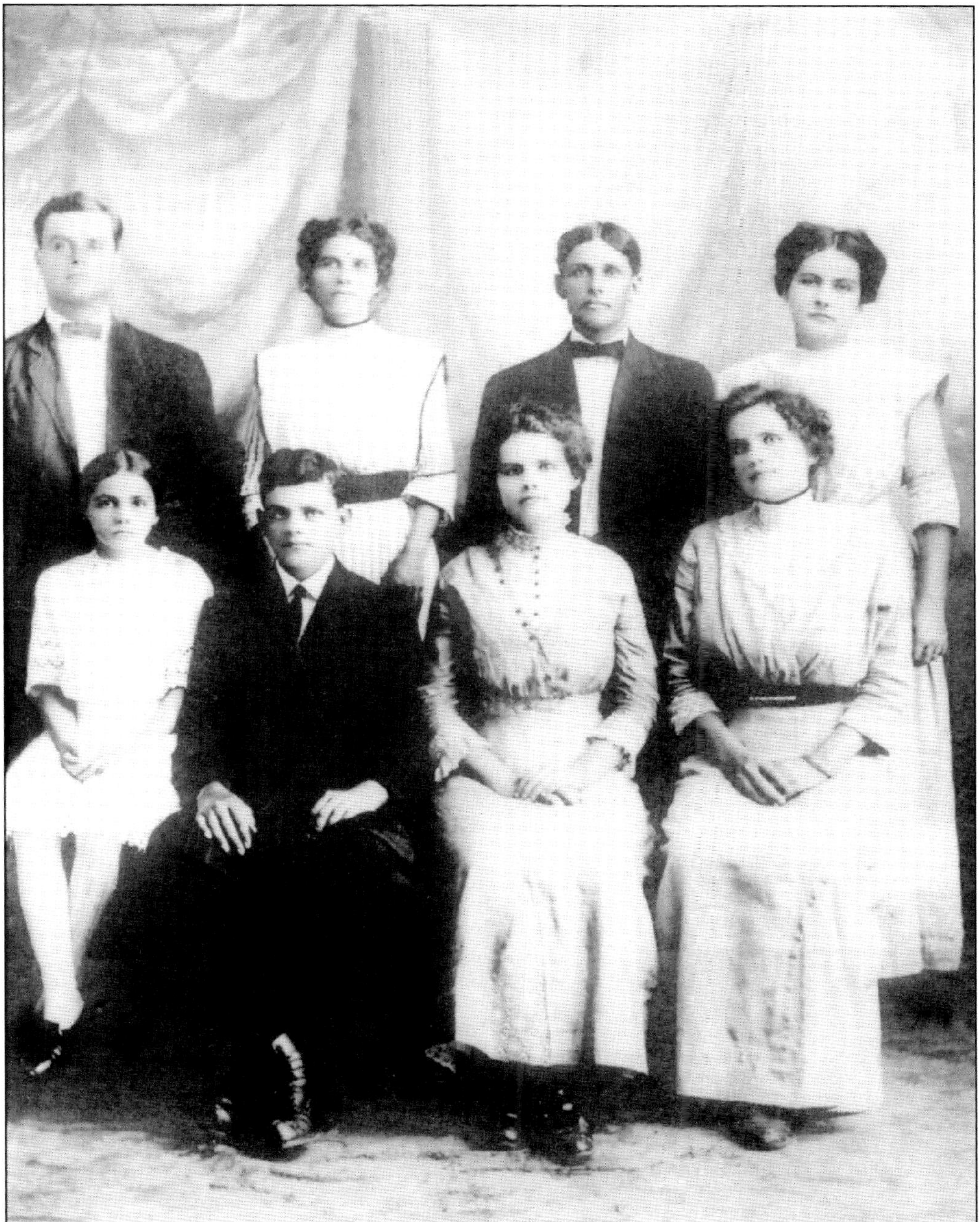

The Meeks family settled in the northeast end of Coffee County. Like many families in the early 1900s, they worked in agriculture and had a family church and cemetery located on their property. Most family churches and graves became public or died away as the population in the area grew. This family's church continues to thrive on New Forest Highway. While most of the members are family, it is open to the public. Pictured here around 1907 are eight Meeks family members. They are, from left to right, (first row) Pearl, Ernest, Idell, and Dona; (second row) Charles Jefferson, Mattie, Stafford "Amos," and Mamie. (Courtesy of Martha Meeks.)

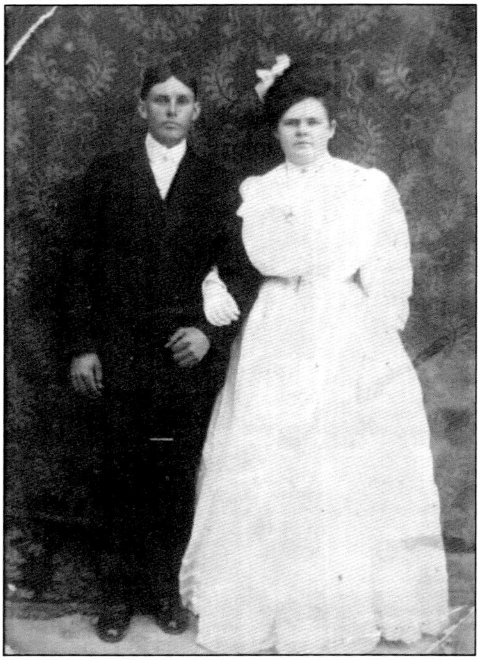

Pictured are young Stafford Amos Meeks and his bride, Amy. Their wedding took place on the front porch of her home on January 20, 1907. (Courtesy of Martha Meeks.)

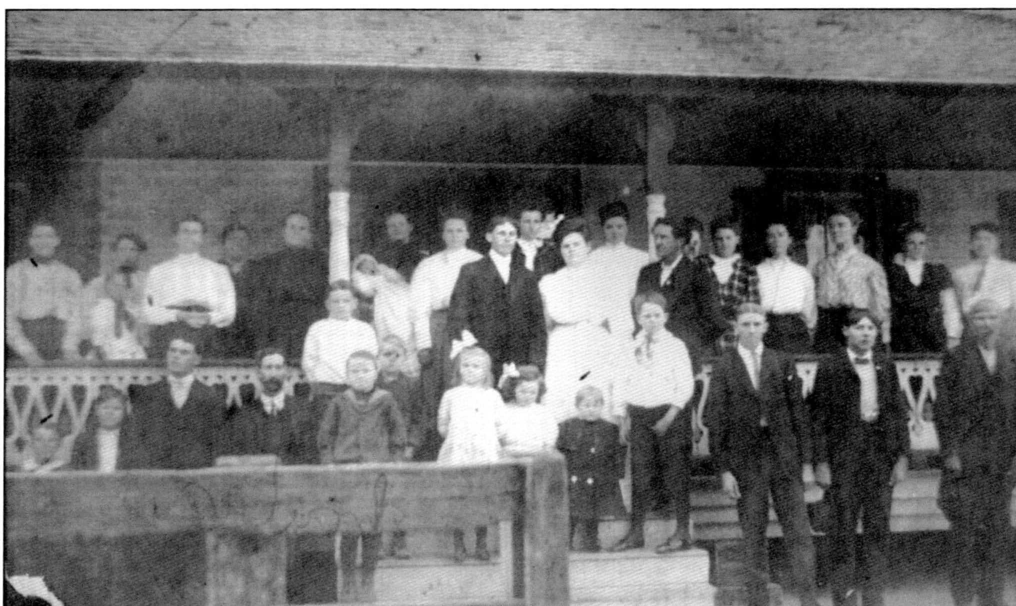

Pictured are, from left to right, (first row) unidentified, Millie Teston, Jeff Meeks, Quart Douglas, Early Meeks, Ethel Meeks, Ruby Meeks, Herbert Douglas, Malcolm Meeks, Lonnie Meeks, Lee Teston, and Ben Teston; (second row) Shafter Meeks, Amy Meeks, Amos Meeks, and Rev. Hymrick Meeks; (third row) Martha "Mattie" Meeks, Sally Ellis, Elizabeth T. Meeks, Carrie Gaskin Meeks, Linnie Doren Meeks, Mary Ann Meeks Douglas, baby Frank, Bessie Meeks, Maggie Meeks, Lula Meeks, Pearl Meeks, Tempie Meeks, Keet Douglas, Mary Jane Douglas, and Maggie Meeks Starling. (Courtesy of Martha Meeks.)

The Daniel Newbern family lost a father, mother, and four children over a span of 10 traumatic days to the spinal meningitis epidemic of February 1870. Three brothers were among the family's survivors. Standing is chief of Broxton police Lawrence Newbern; sitting are Willis (left) and Daniel Newbern. They are seen around 1912 at Lone Hill Methodist Church, near the cemetery where the family members were buried decades earlier. (Courtesy of Dr. James A. Cottingham.)

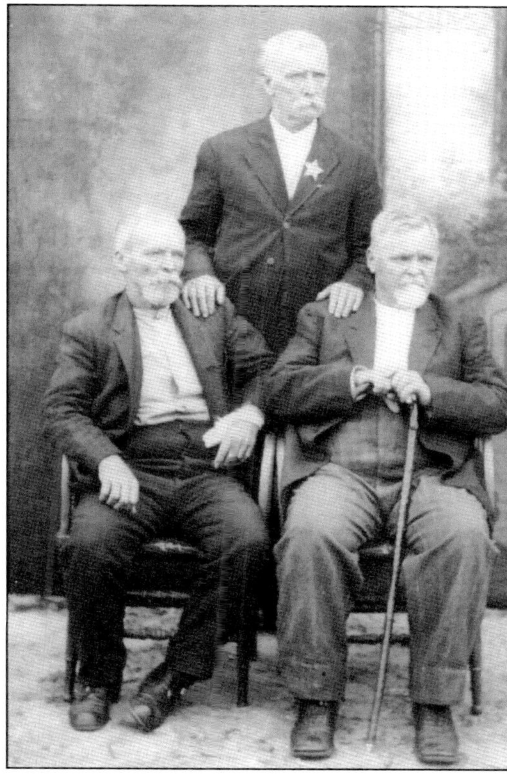

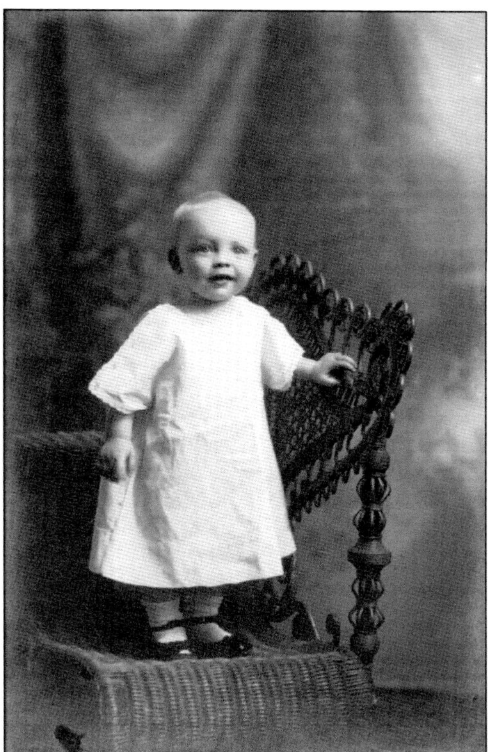

Standing still for a moment is young Tom Cottingham (1916–2012), who thrived on the opportunities his hometown of Douglas offered him. His great-grandparents were pioneers of the county. He served as president and valedictorian of the Douglas High School class of 1932. After obtaining his college education, he became teacher, registrar, and dean of students at South Georgia College. In the late 1960s, he became dean of instruction at Gaston College in North Carolina. He enjoyed his latter years in Douglas. (Courtesy of Dr. James A. Cottingham.)

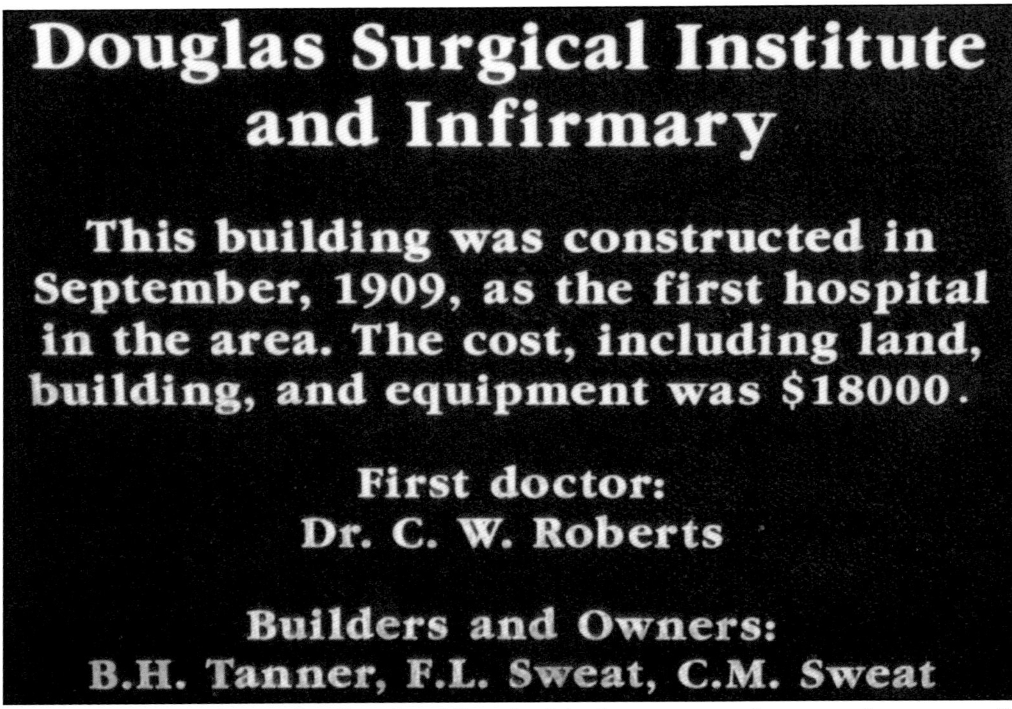

There was no public hospital in Douglas. All medical facilities were run by private doctors, usually in their homes. Downtown, one can still see the sign from the Douglas Surgical Infirmary that was established in 1909. (Courtesy of Dr. James A. Cottingham.)

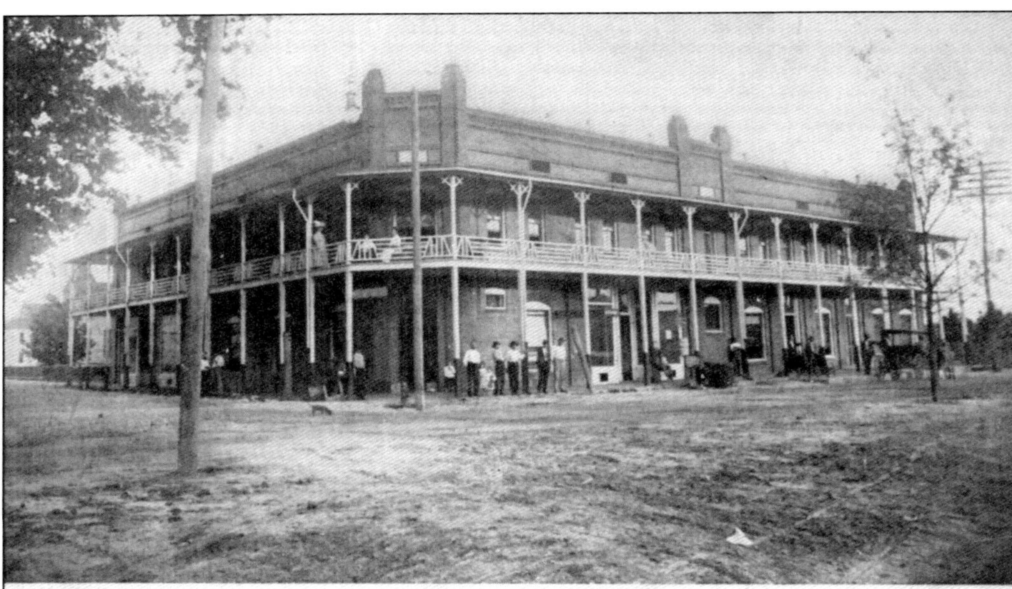

The Douglas Hotel, constructed in 1901, is the oldest building still standing in downtown Douglas. Today, it is known as the Bordeaux Suites. Built by B.H. Tanner, it was originally known as the Tanner Hotel. (Courtesy of Joanne Hanna Lott.)

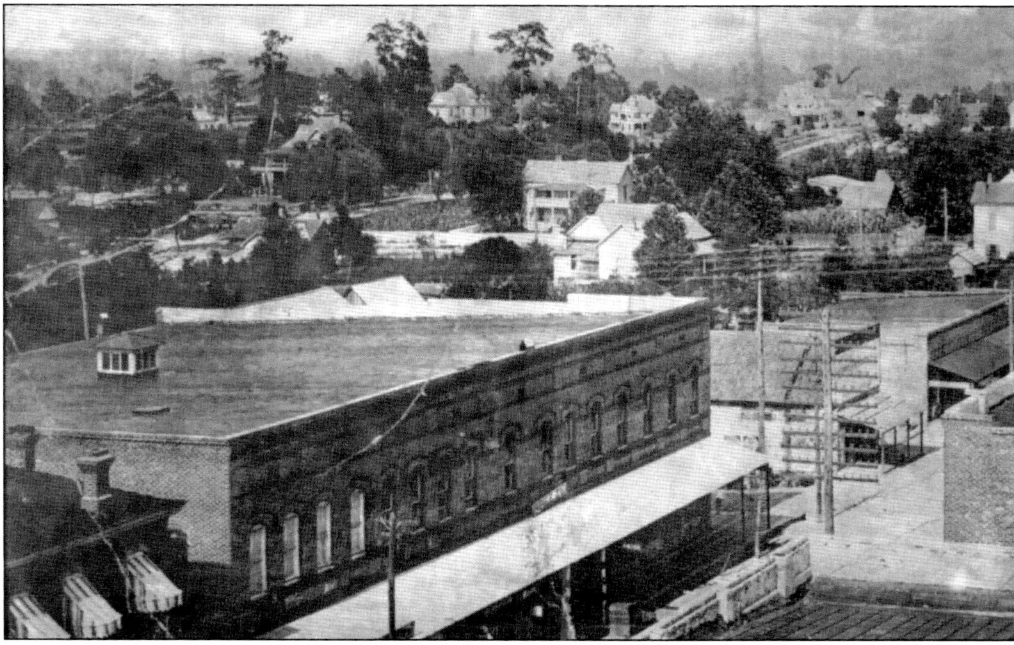

The *Douglas Enterprise* is the oldest established business in Coffee County. Founded in 1888, it was originally called the *Douglas Breeze*. One can see its offices here on the top floor of the building in the center foreground. (Courtesy of the *Douglas Enterprise*.)

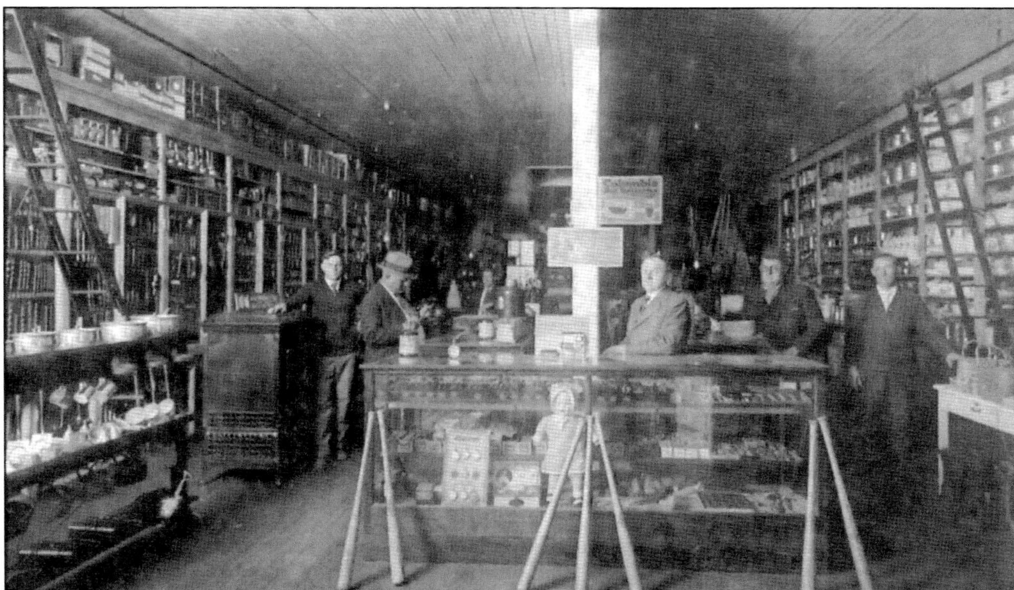

For decades, the Douglas Hardware Store was a vibrant business at 108 North Peterson Avenue, adjacent to the Union Bank. Merchandise included hardware, paint, tools, farming implements, sporting goods, china, and guns. Owner W.T. Cottingham sold an occasional Hudson automobile from there as well. He is shown here with Harry Johnson, Rexford Peterson, and two customers. (Courtesy of Dr. James. A. Cottingham.)

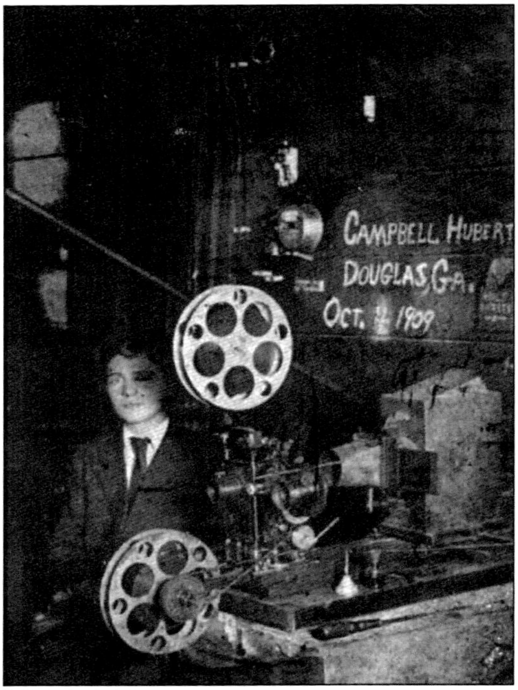

Theater houses were the center of cultural and social activity until the dawn of the television. Seen here is the Campbell Hubert Theater. (Courtesy of Joanne Hanna Lott.)

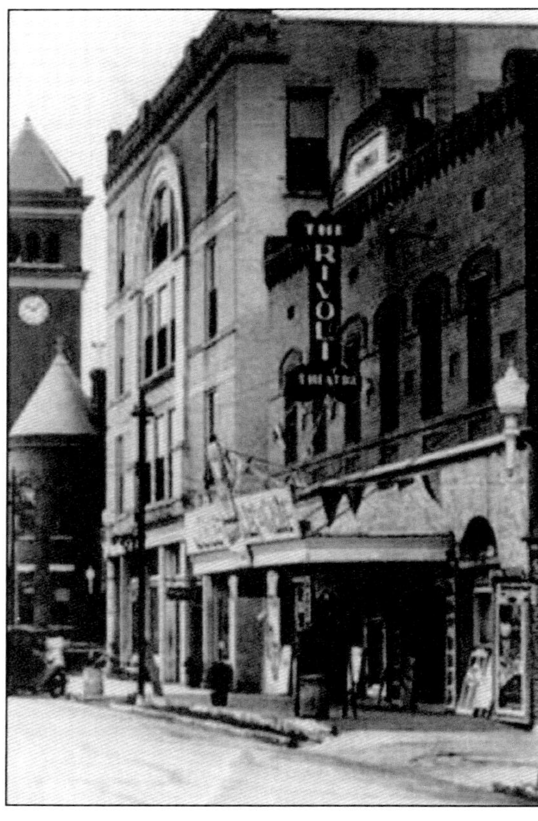

A theater house was much more than a place to see plays, concerts, and operas, it was a community center and meeting place. The Rivioli Theatre opened downtown around 1900. (Author's collection.)

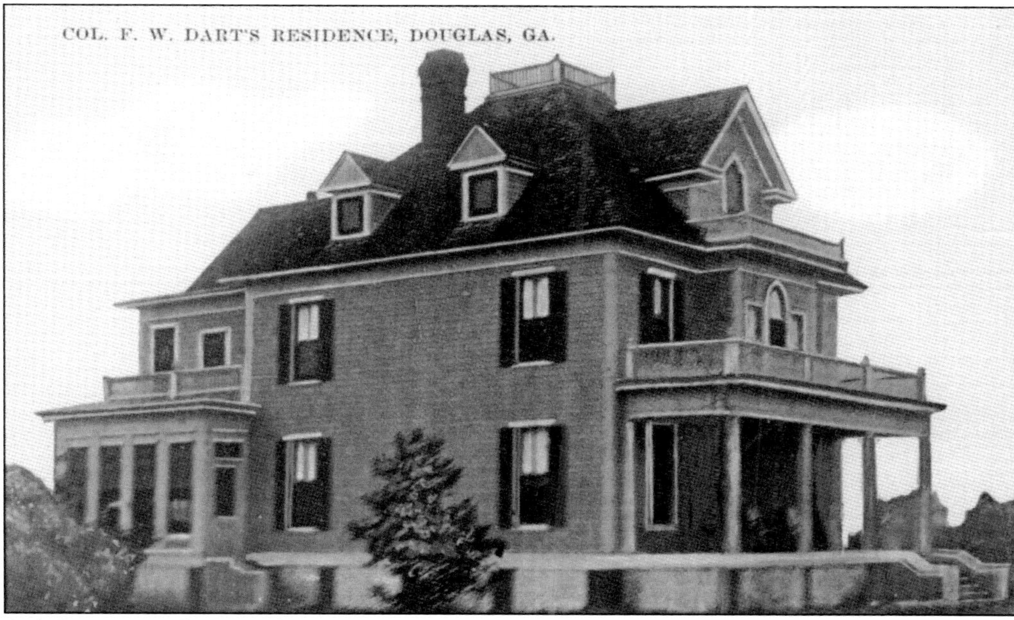

Col. Francis Willis Dart built this modified Victorian home on Gaskin Avenue in 1898. Dart was a lawyer and served as mayor of Douglas in 1907. He later moved to Florida and sold this beautiful home to his nephew (by marriage) Francis Seaborn Stubbs. Later, the first residential swimming pool in the area was added. The home then passed to Stubbs's wife. The estate was sold in 2001, and it is currently the residence of Carolyn P. Smith, an interior designer. Smith has done major renovations to the home but has kept true to the original design. (Courtesy of Joanne Hanna Lott.)

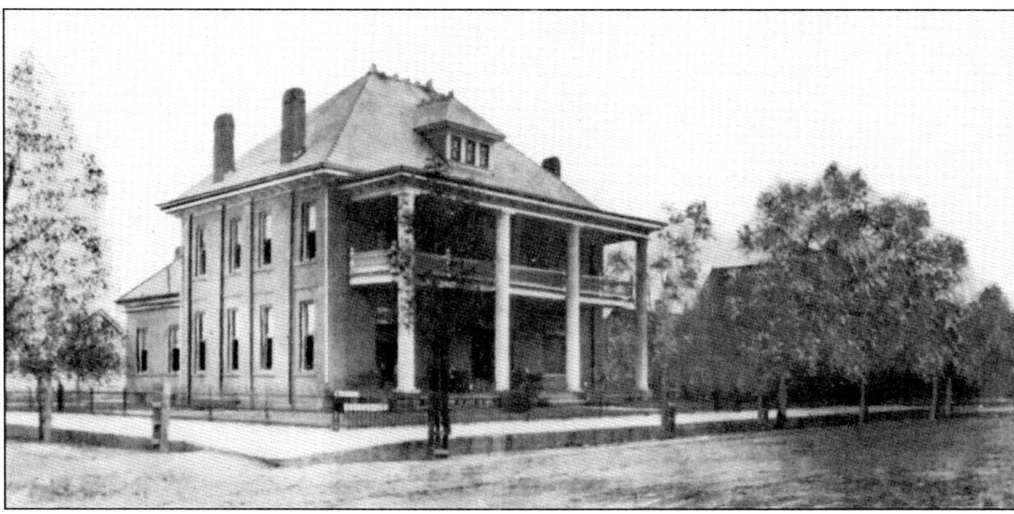

This is the Brice residence on the corner of Ward Street and Pearl Avenue. Mr. Brice was a successful banker with investments in tobacco, food distribution, and realty. The family also had a residence on Gaskin Avenue at one time. While not a native of the town, Brice married Margaret Tanner of Douglas. His father-in-law was E.L. Tanner. Tanner's efforts influenced the development of Coffee County and Toombs County. Tanner H. Brice inherited the family bank. (Courtesy of Joanne Hanna Lott.)

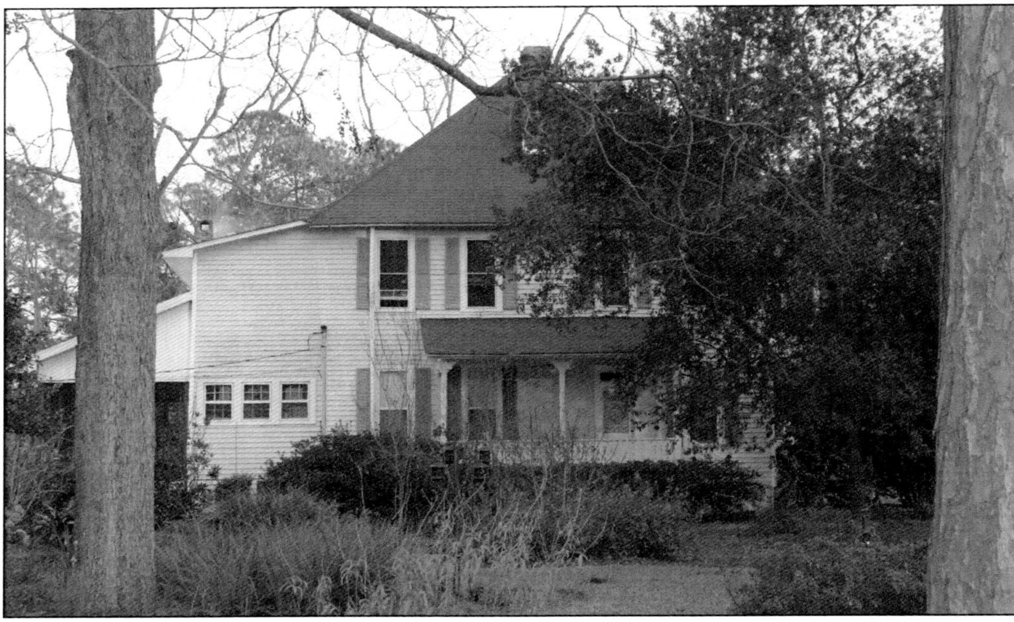

Warren Preston Ward, the founder of the *Douglas Breeze* and ordinary judge of Coffee County for 24 years, was one of the early residents of Gaskin Avenue. Reared in south Georgia by a widowed mother, he married Annie Canova, and they moved into their Gaskin Avenue home in 1899. They built the house next door for his elderly mother. In addition to being a home, the Ward residence was the site of many marriages in Coffee County. Ward presided as judge, with Annie serving as witness, for numerous weddings during his 24 years of service. Judge Ward is the author of *Ward's History of Coffee County*. (Courtesy of Charles E. Griffiths II.)

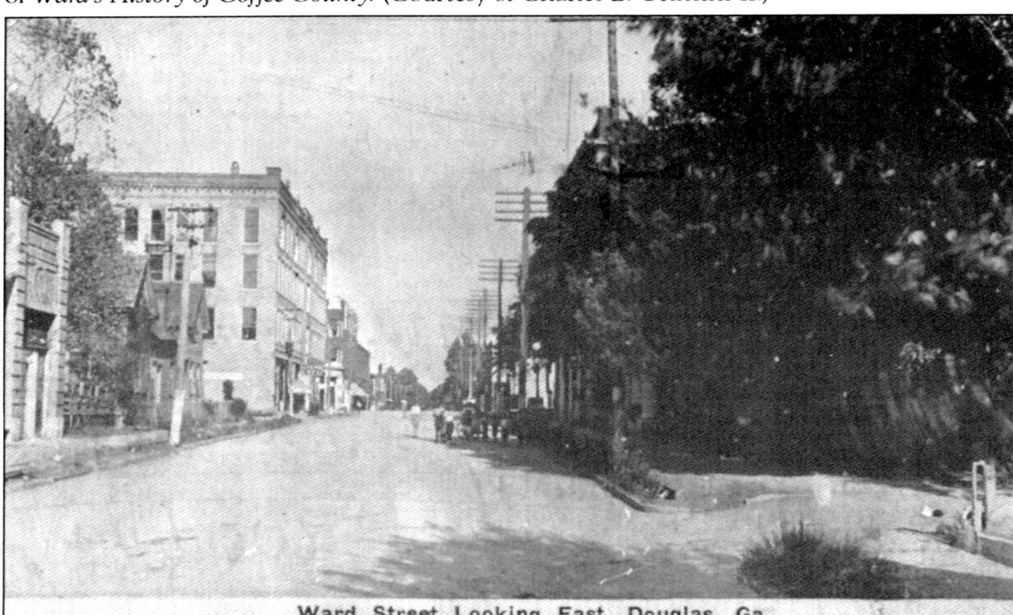

In this view of Ward Street looking east, pedestrians walk casually in the road. There is a café on the left side. (Courtesy of Joanne Hanna Lott.)

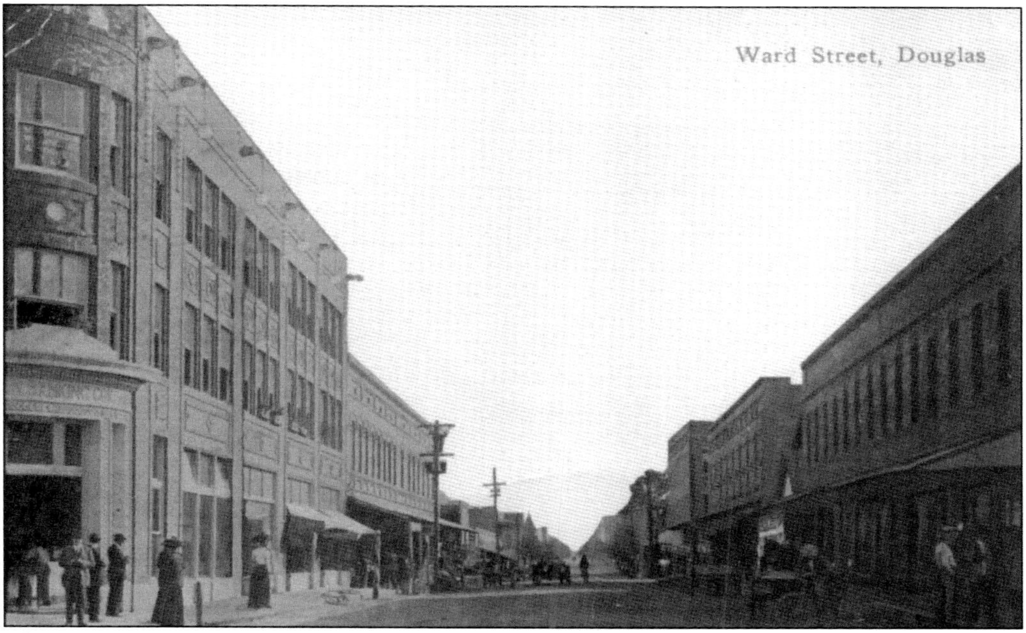

This is Ward Street by the Union Bank Building looking east. Traffic became a kaleidoscope of pedestrians, bicycles, horses, and cars. The clinic is on the far right. The building in the right foreground was damaged by fire and has been reconstructed. (Courtesy of Joanne Hanna Lott.)

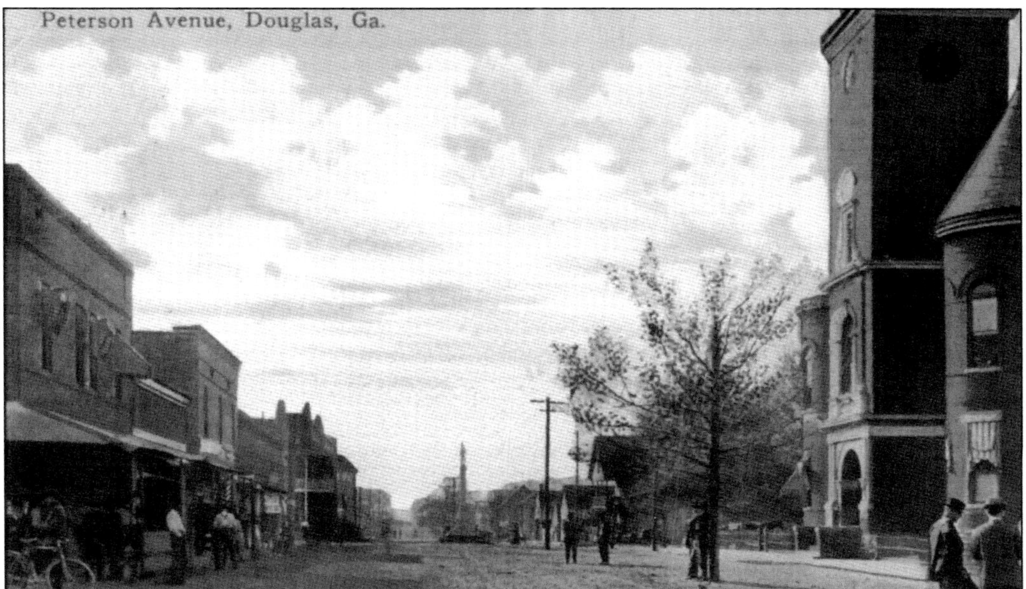

This is Peterson Avenue by the courthouse looking south. The Confederate monument is in the center of the image. Horses are corralled by the courthouse, and Kirkland's store and the barbershop are to the left. (Courtesy of Joanne Hanna Lott.)

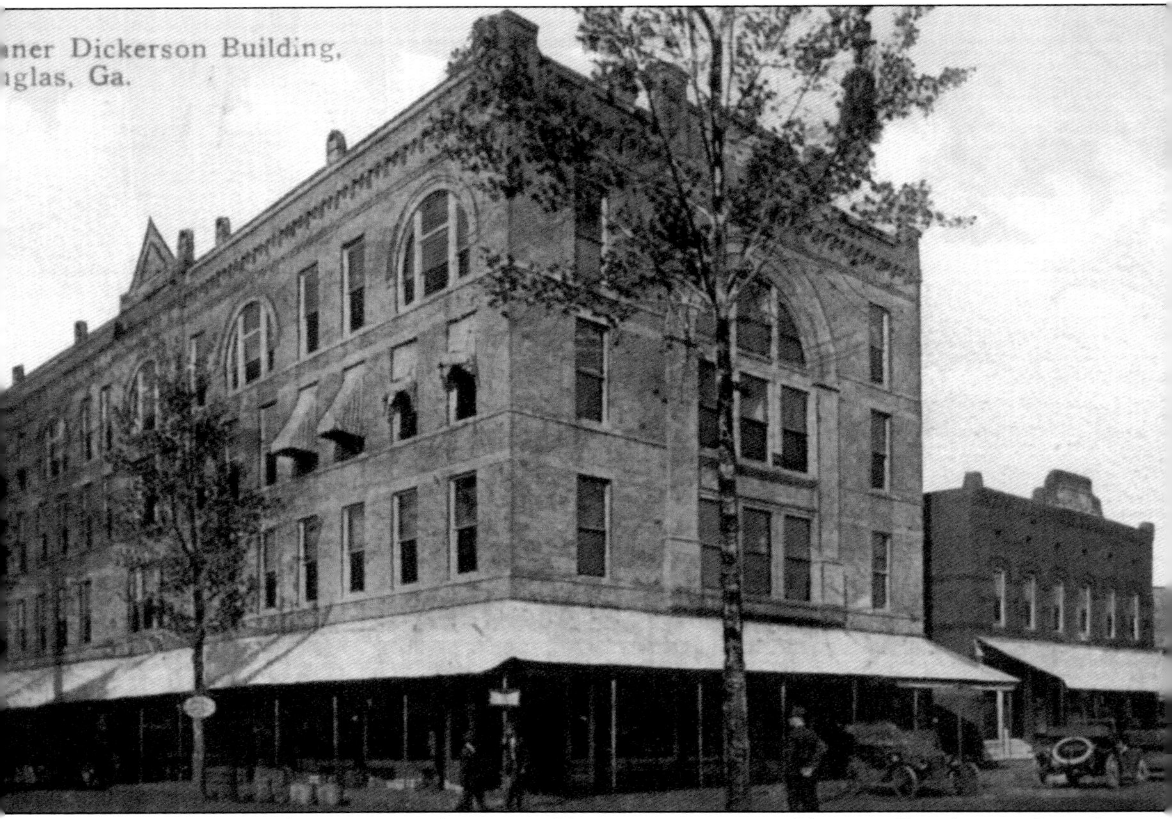

This is a scene of the Tanner-Dickerson Building just prior to World War I. Free lemonade and watermelon were passed out to encourage young men to sign up for the draft, and khaki badges were given out to show the courage of enlistees. The young ladies in town shamed their beaus if they were not wearing a badge. (Courtesy of Joanne Hanna Lott.)

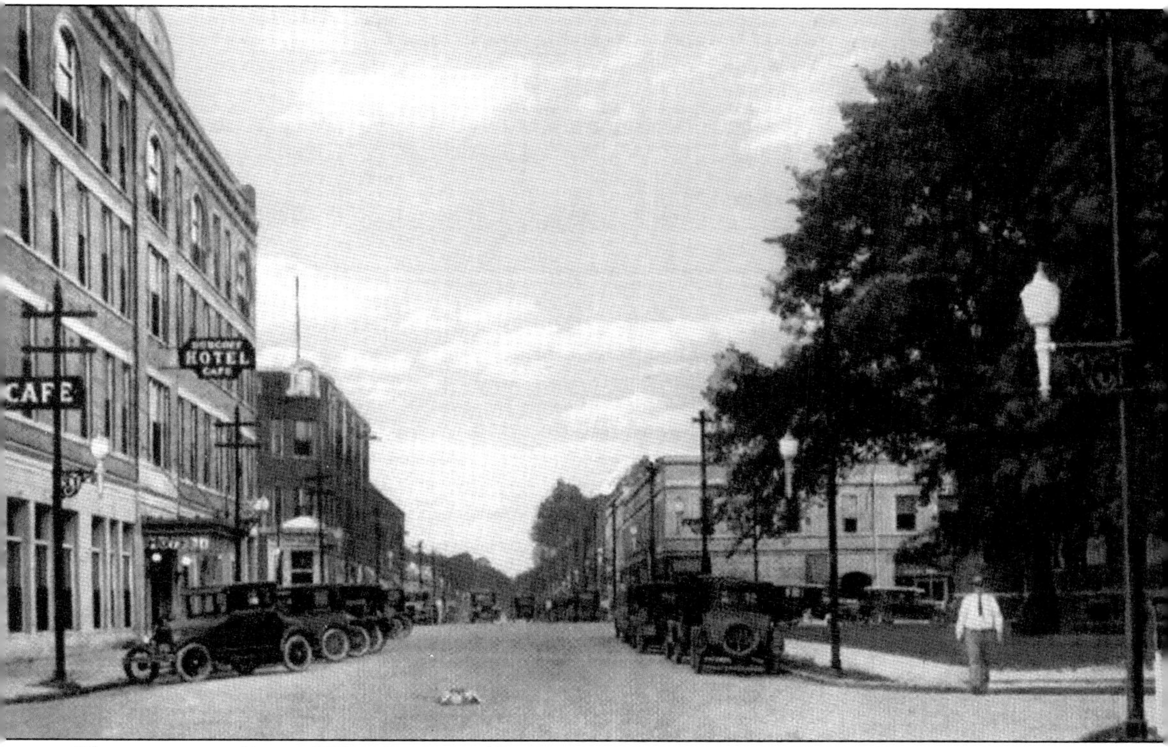

The prominent Doucoff Hotel, pictured here on Peterson Avenue, welcomed many visitors to the area. (Courtesy of Dr. James A. Cottingham.)

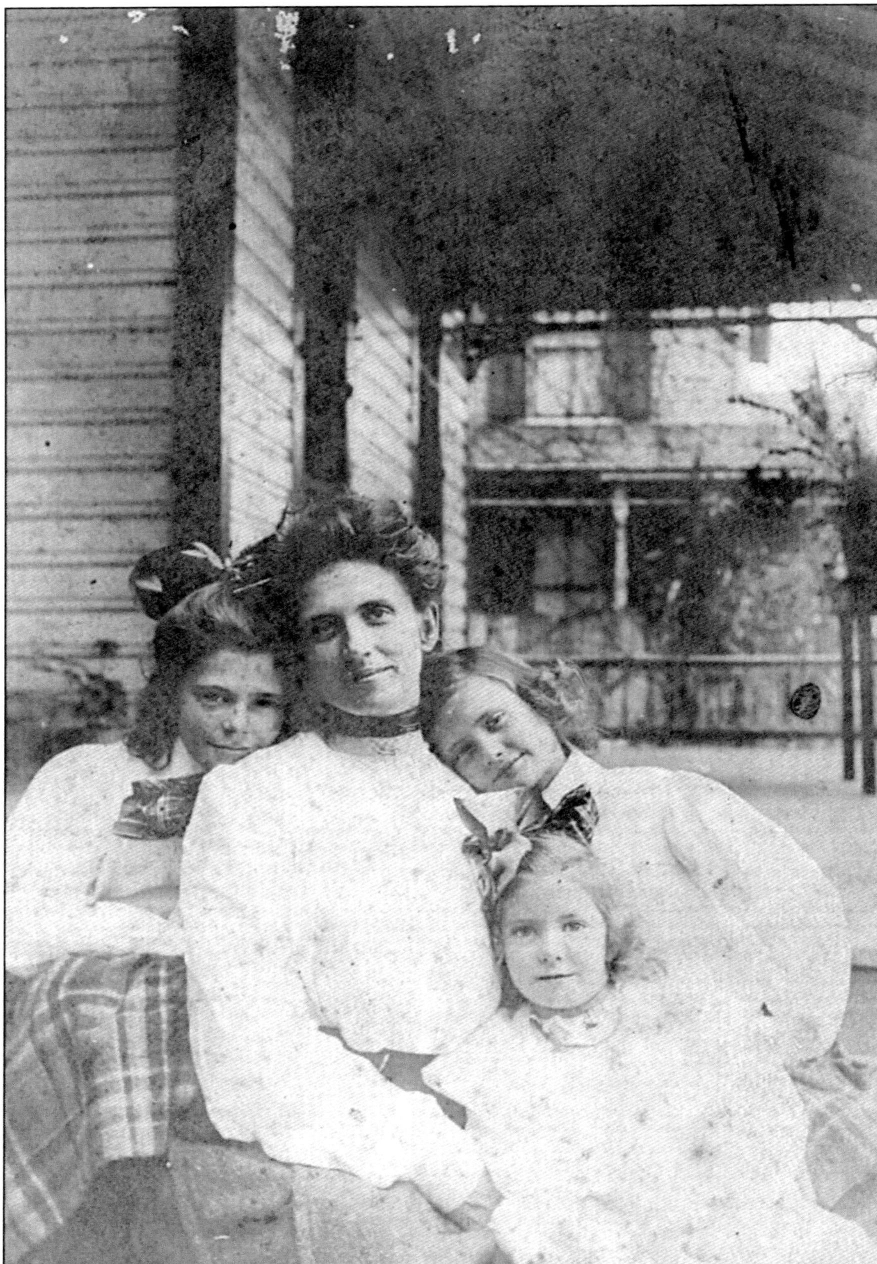

Seen here are Annie Dyer and daughters Theresa, Dorothy, and Annie Eugenia. Annie Dyer advocated for ratification of the 19th Amendment for years, petitioning, protesting in parades, and picketing for the cause. Other women on Gaskin Avenue quietly persuaded their husbands and brothers to vote for it and insisted their names be on the deeds to their homes. Annie lined up in the cold on voting day and was the first woman in Coffee County to vote. She continued her work fighting for the property rights for women. Many of the local husbands transferred the deeds to the family home to their wives during this period. (Courtesy of Mary Clyde Scott.)

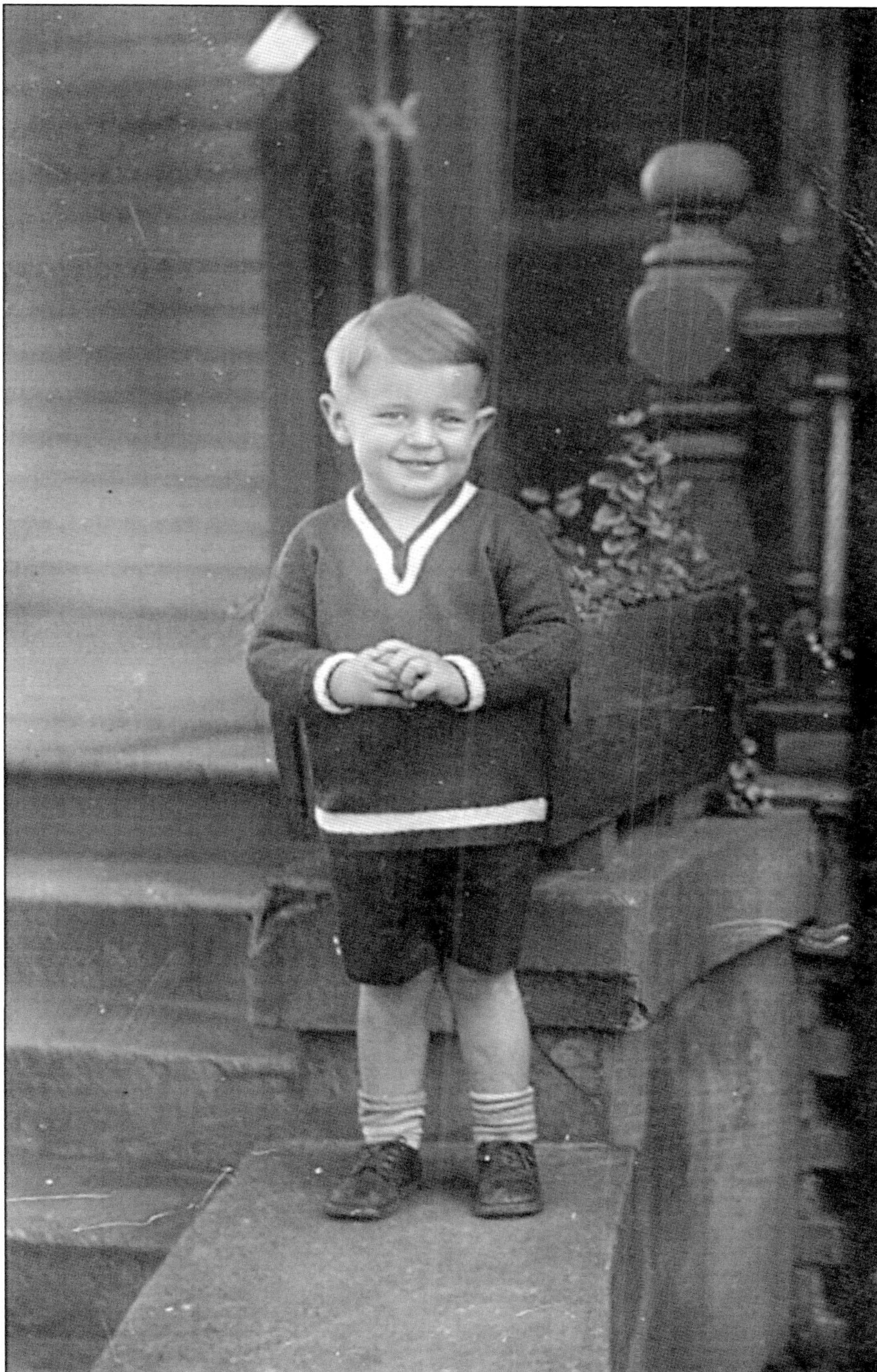

Here is Alexander Dyer Williams, son of Annie Eugenia Dyer and George Smith Williams, on the steps of his family home in 1929. He served in the US Navy in the years following World Wars I and II. After his service, he became a prominent lawyer. (Courtesy of Mary Clyde Scott.)

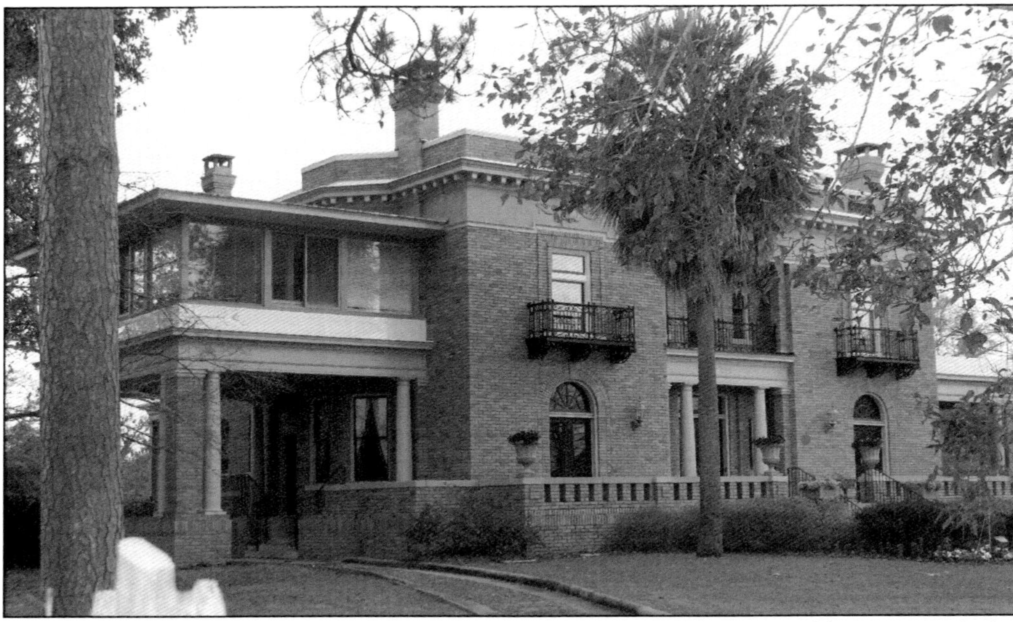

The Ashley-Slater House was built in 1912 by John Marshall Ashley as a wedding present for his wife, Ada. This mansion features hand-carved molding, beautiful woodwork, and a mural. The couple had a child who died, and John Marshall cursed God for taking his infant and then died of a stroke shortly after. Ada remarried, and her new husband, John Slater, committed suicide at the age of 38. Ada lived to age 92 and died of natural causes. It is said that the home is haunted. It has been restored by concerned citizens and is now a welcome center. Visitors can tour the home or rent rooms for special occasions. (Courtesy of Charles E. Griffiths II.)

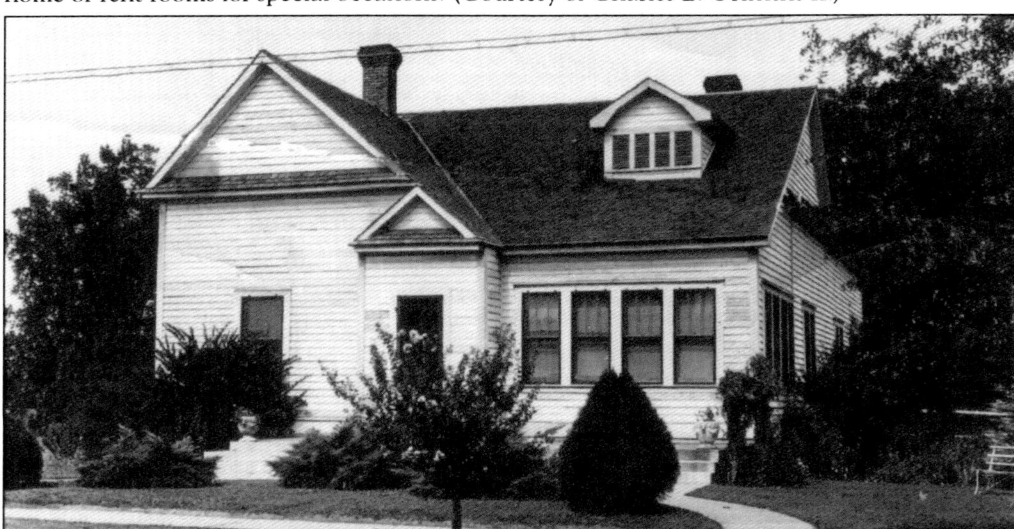

This is one of the original homes built in the Gaskin Avenue District located at 611 North Gaskin Avenue. It was erected in 1906 by Lillian Lott and Evans Parks Fillingin. The Moore family purchased the home in 1908 and lived there until they died in the 1970s. The home was demolished to make room for construction of a new house at that time. (Courtesy of Mary Clyde Scott.)

Rufus Moore practiced law at Langford & Dickerson. He handled many important cases, some of which were heard before the Georgia Supreme Court. He served as mayor of Douglas from 1923 to 1924 and also served one term as a representative in the Georgia Legislature and regional counsel to the Atlanta, Birmingham & Coast and Atlantic Coastline Railroads. (Courtesy of Mary Clyde Scott.)

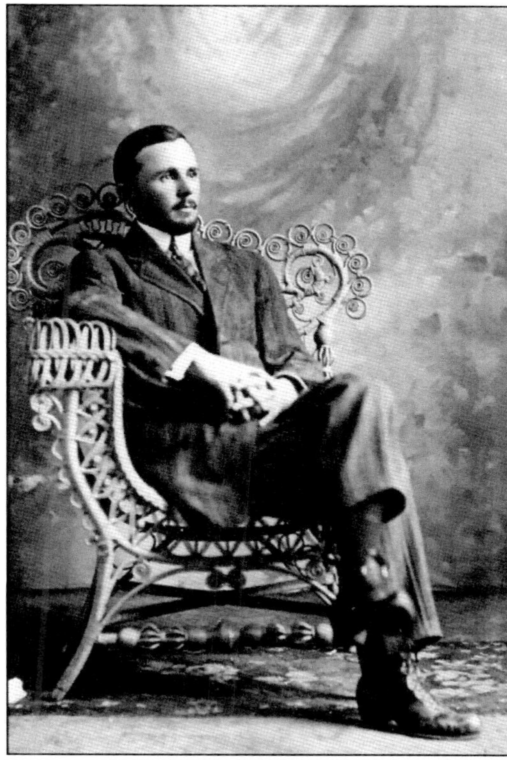

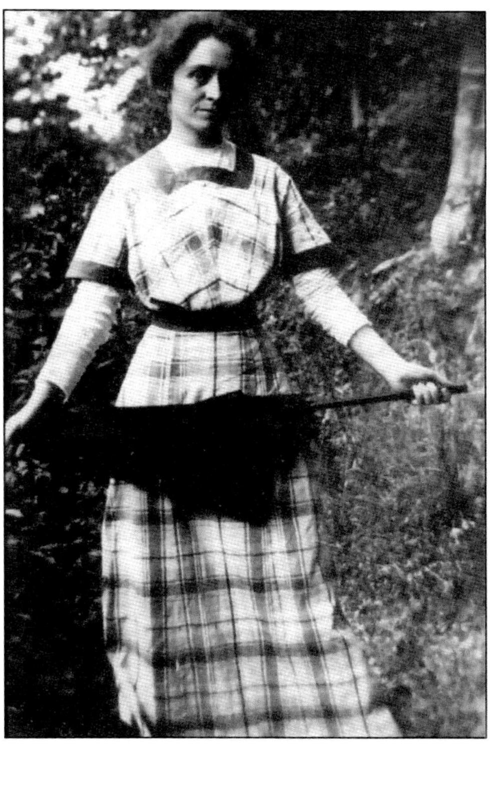

Rufus Moore met his wife, Julia Stell Harris, at the Methodist church, and they were married after a whirlwind courtship. Julia Stell-Moore was active in the Garden Club and served as president of the Women's Club from 1930 to 1932. The couple had one child, Julia Kathryn Moore, who grew up to become a local educator. This 1903 image shows Julia Stell Harris before she was married. (Courtesy of Mary Clyde Scott.)

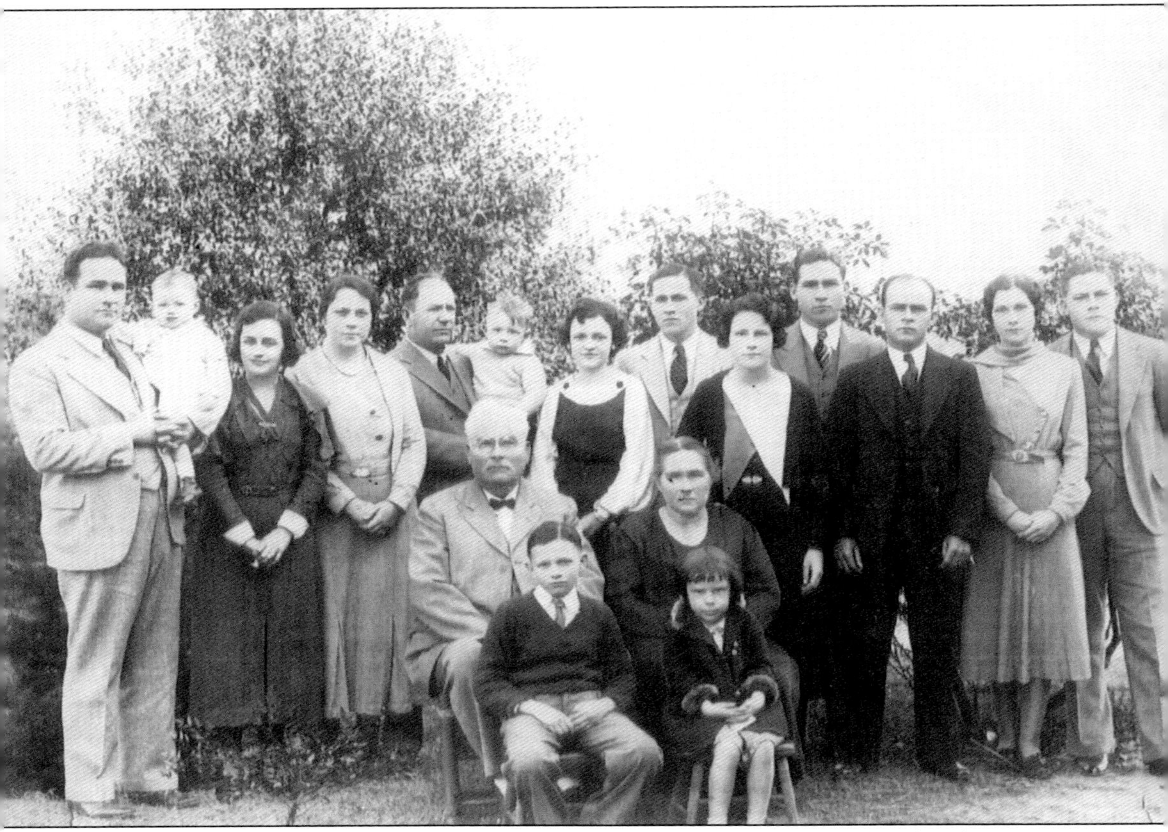

Members of the Moorman family seen here include Emory (holding Mary Claire) Roberts, Maggie Mae Moorman (Emory's wife), Cora Lee Roberts and Henry Roberts (holding Henry Clay Roberts), Frances and Warren Moorman, IvyLyn Moorman, Ross Moorman, Clara Mae Moorman, Guy Moorman, Ivy W. and Eliza V. Moorman, Oscar Moorman, and Dora Beth Roberts. (Courtesy of Mary Clyde Scott.)

Bathing beauty Clyde Griffin Tanner of Douglas, Georgia, vacationed at a summer home in St. Simons Island in 1915. At this time, there were no bridges to the island; they would be constructed in the 1920s, and the island was developed for tourism when a causeway was complete. (Courtesy of Mary Clyde Scott.)

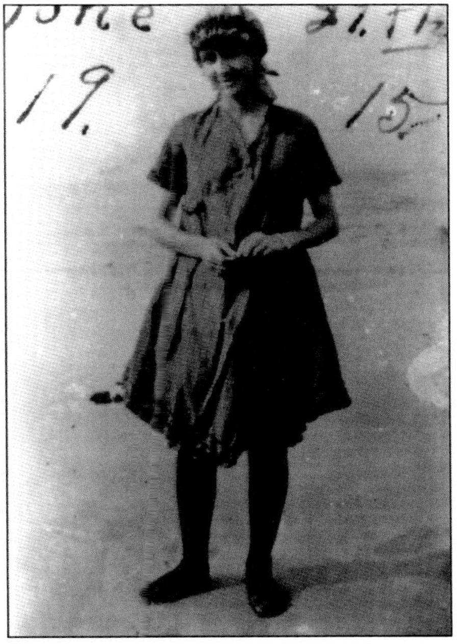

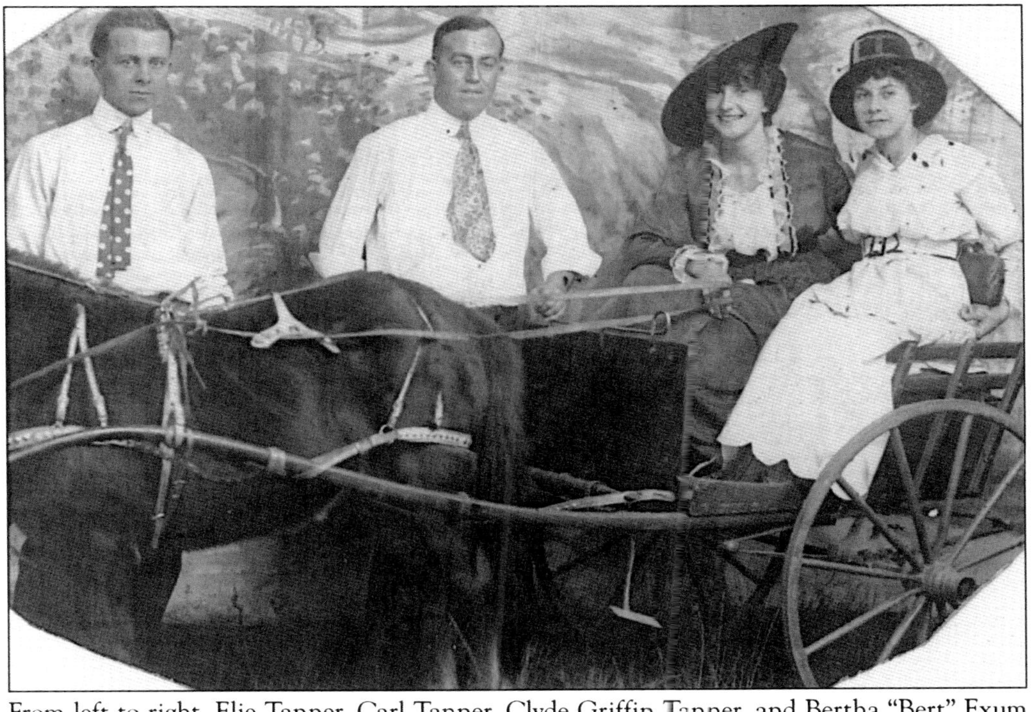

From left to right, Elie Tanner, Carl Tanner, Clyde Griffin Tanner, and Bertha "Bert" Exum Tanner go for a ride around Douglas. After they were married, the two young couples lived on the corner of Gaskin Avenue and Jackson Street. Carl and Elie Tanner took over their father's business, the Tanner Mercantile Company, when he died. After Carl's untimely death at the age of 42, Bert invested the money in insurance with business partner Jimmy Crabb to support the family. (Courtesy of Mary Clyde Scott.)

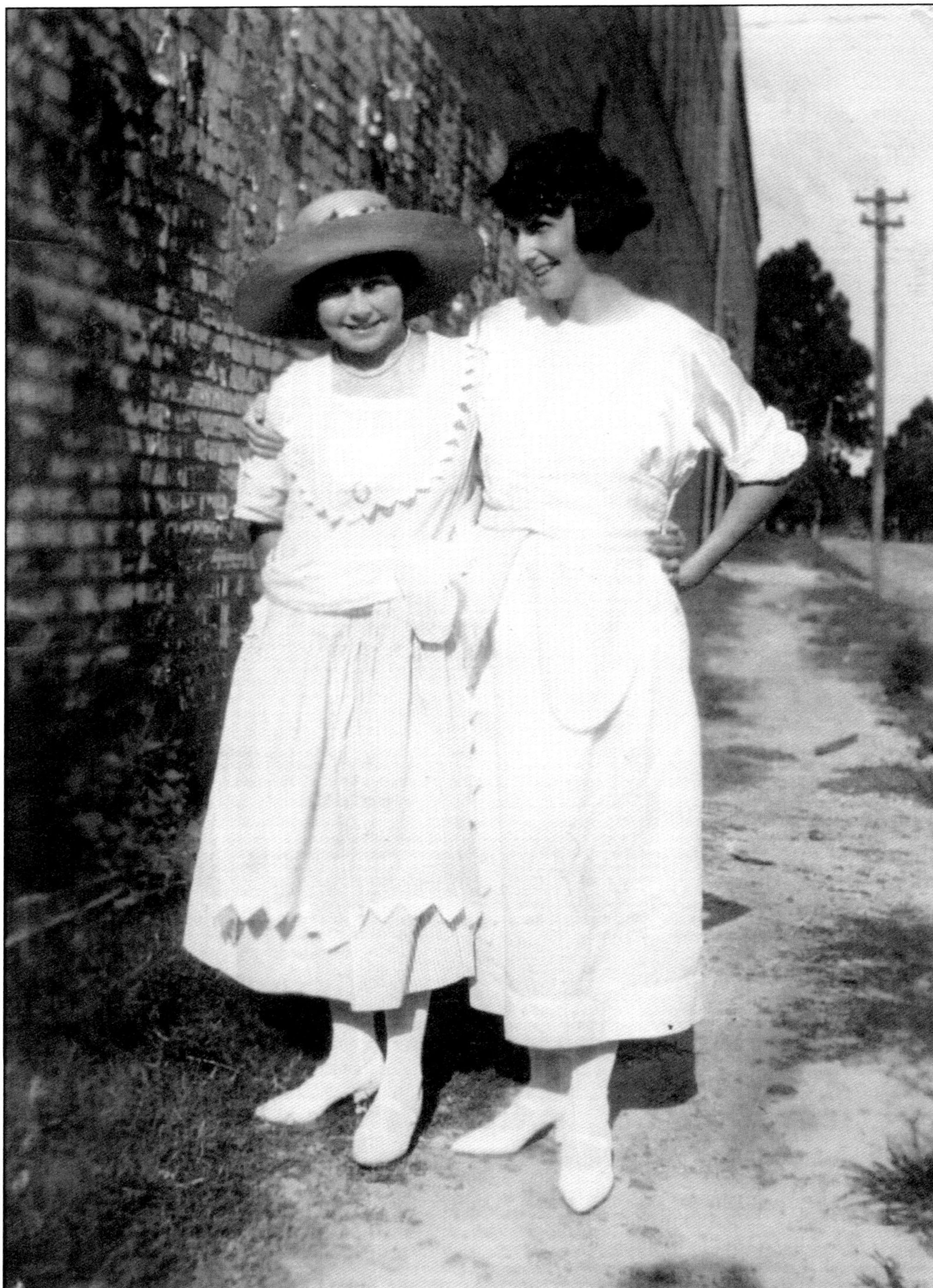

Bert Exum Tanner (left) and Clyde Griffin Tanner are seen strolling in downtown Douglas around 1915. This photograph was most likely taken near the Exum Family Store. The young ladies were being courted by Carl and Elie Tanner at the time. (Courtesy of Mary Clyde Scott.)

These four generations of women are pioneers of Telfair and Coffee Counties. The Head family settled in southern Telfair County in 1807 along the Ocmulgee River. Later, the area where their family home was built became a part of Coffee County. Mary Ella Mclean and her husband, Marion Franklin Head, moved to Douglas and settled on Gaskin Avenue; however, she remained tied to her family home and attended Oak Grove Methodist Church near Broxton, Georgia. Seated are baby Myrtie Mae Head and great-grandmother Lucretia Fussell, and standing are Mary Ella McLean Head and her mother, Mary Fussell McLean. (Courtesy of Mary Clyde Scott.)

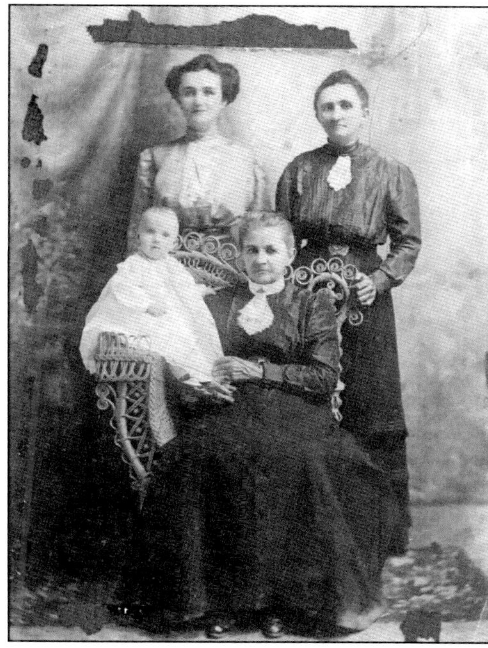

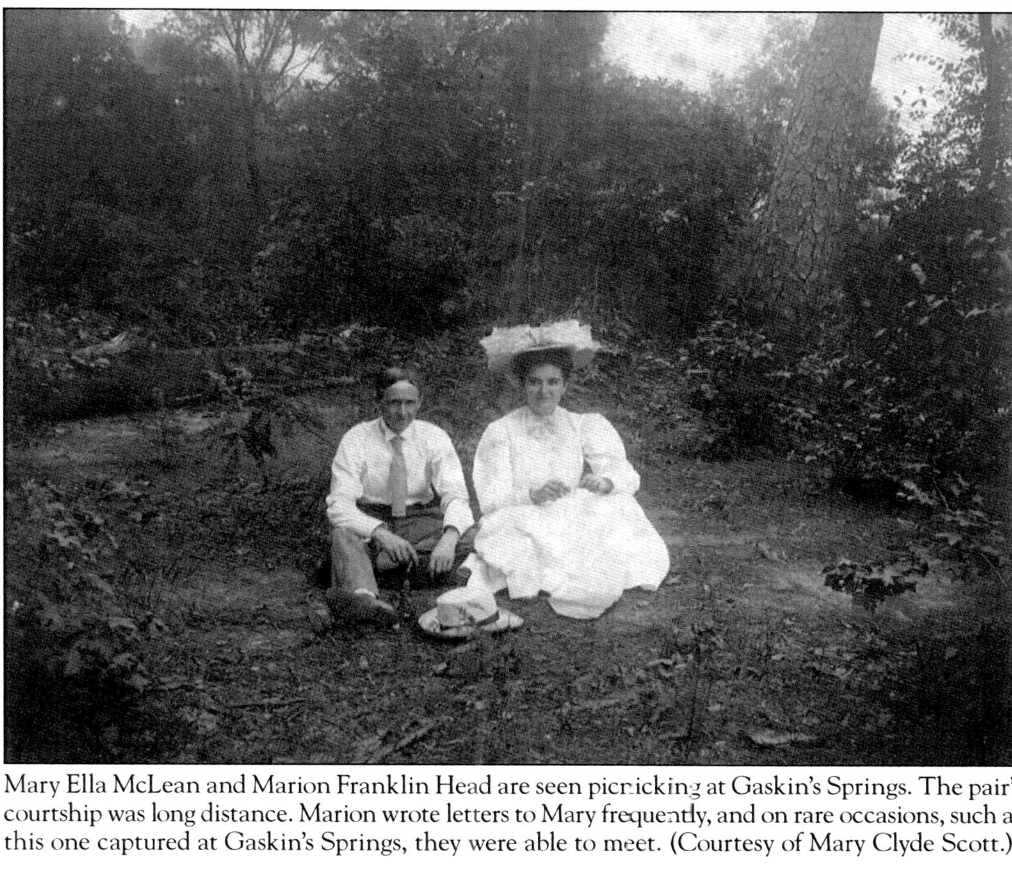

Mary Ella McLean and Marion Franklin Head are seen picnicking at Gaskin's Springs. The pair's courtship was long distance. Marion wrote letters to Mary frequently, and on rare occasions, such as this one captured at Gaskin's Springs, they were able to meet. (Courtesy of Mary Clyde Scott.)

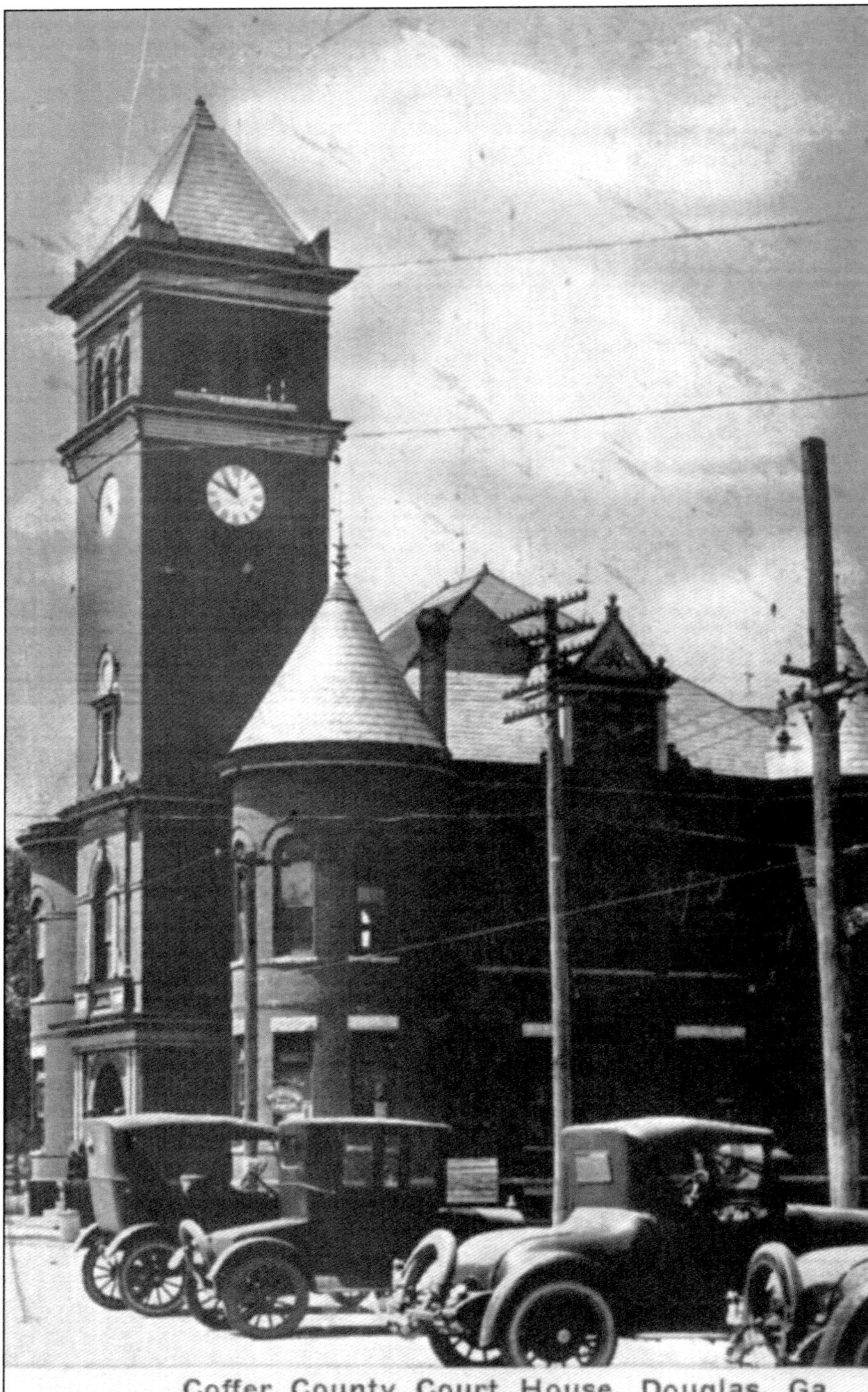

This stately building looked great and served Coffee County citizens well as a courthouse, but a few years after this photograph, in 1938, it was engulfed in fire and had to be replaced. (Courtesy of Joanne Hanna Lott.)

Three

We're Depressed

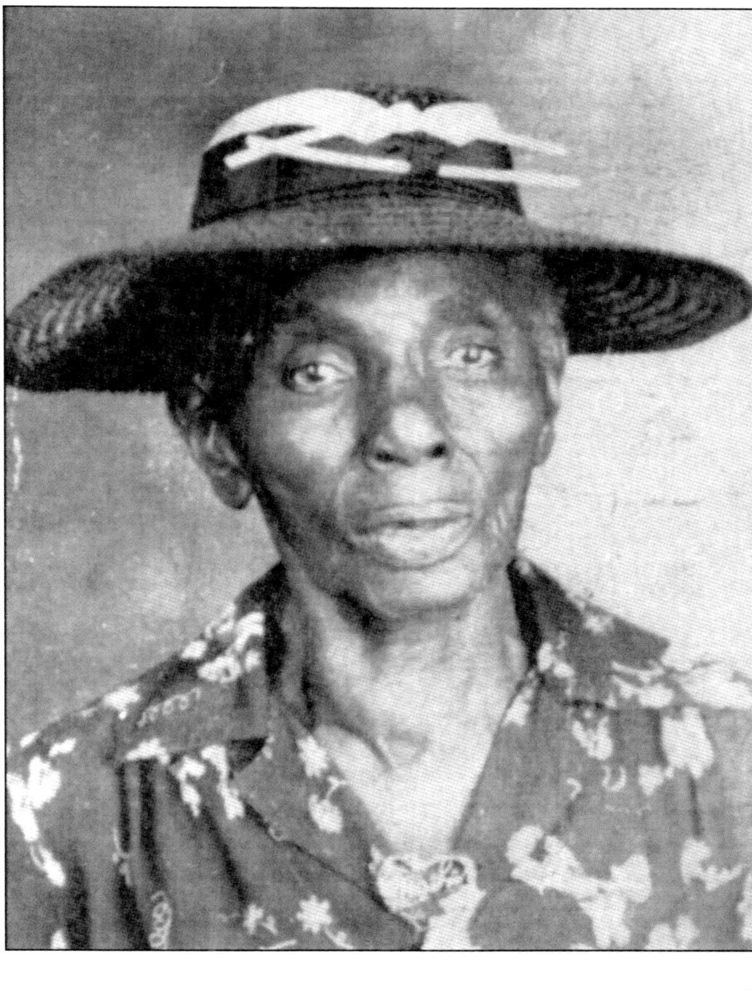

Midwife Mary Cornish Hayes began the first parent-teacher association in the African American school, began the school lunch program, provided resources for heating for the school, and donated land for the original site of the Mary Hayes School. (Courtesy of Gwendolyn Reliford.)

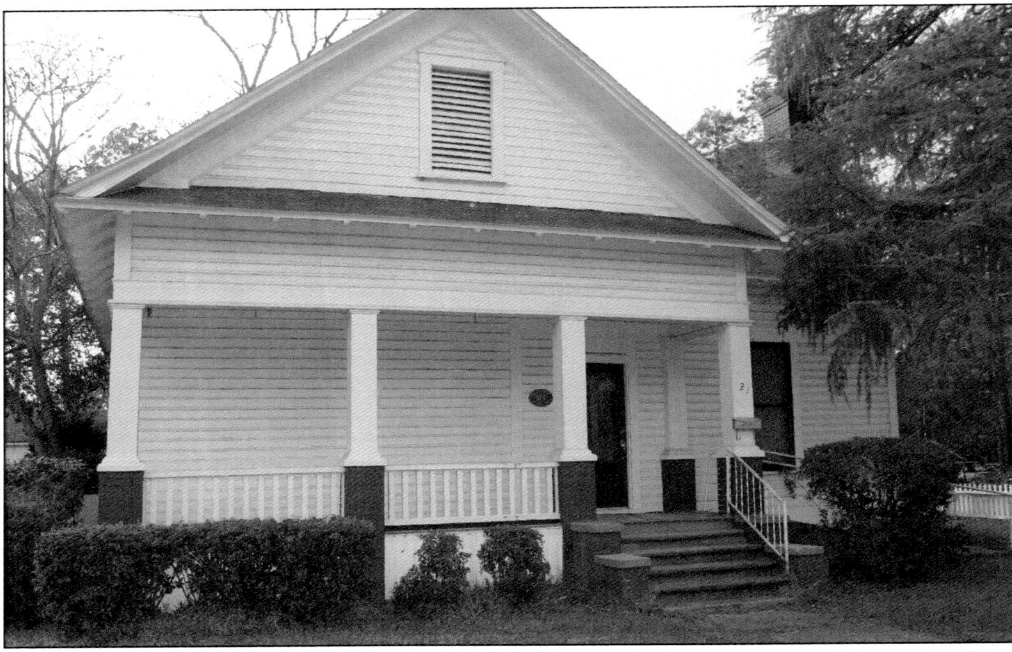

Perhaps one of the people hardest hit in Douglas during the Depression was Johnnie Wilkins. Wilkins traveled extensively with American Tobacco Company and lived on the road. When he made money in a town, he would put it in banks from that area. During the Depression, many banks closed, and he lost all of his tobacco money. His wife, Hettie Mae Wilkins, began cooking and selling food from her home to support the family during this setback. Their house on Gaskin Avenue, pictured here, became known as "Het's House." Johnnie later recovered financially and partnered with Francis Stubbs to buy the tobacco warehouse in Douglas. (Courtesy of Charles E. Griffiths II.)

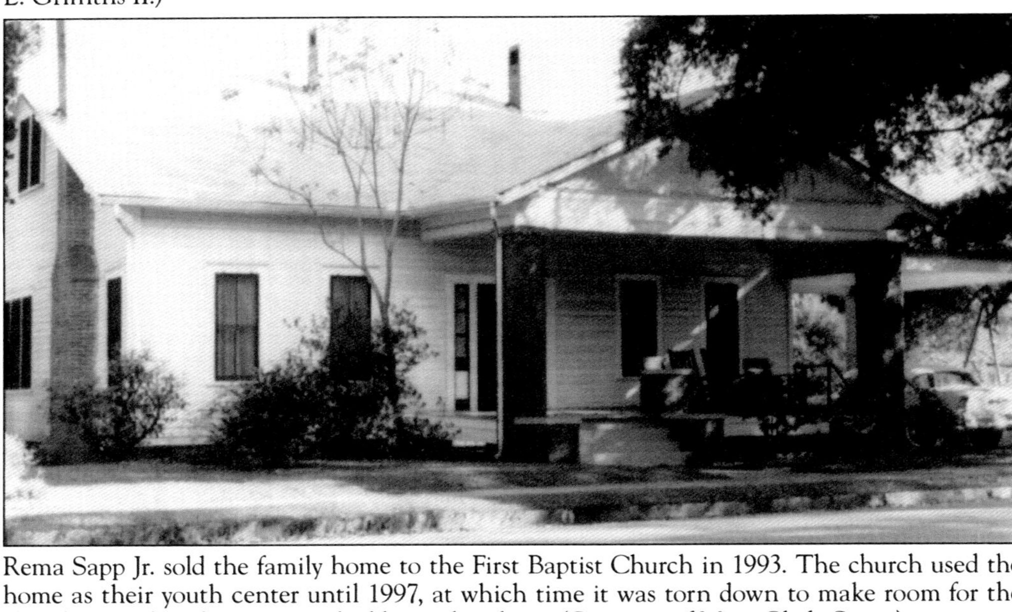

Rema Sapp Jr. sold the family home to the First Baptist Church in 1993. The church used the home as their youth center until 1997, at which time it was torn down to make room for the church's Family Life Center and additional parking. (Courtesy of Mary Clyde Scott.)

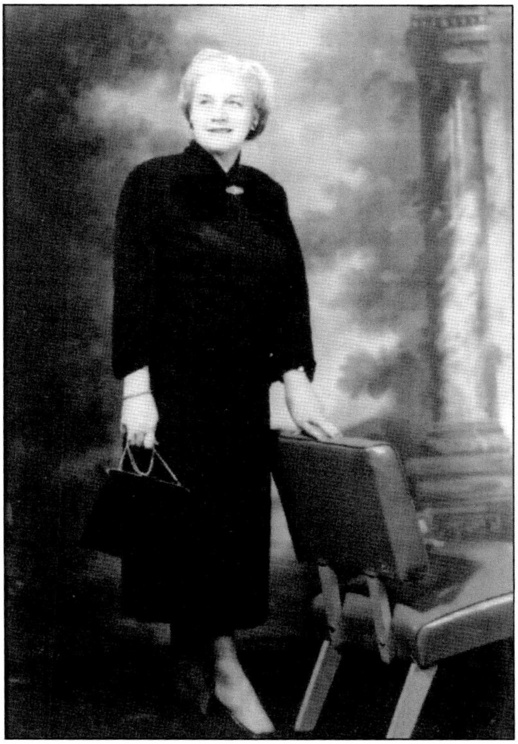

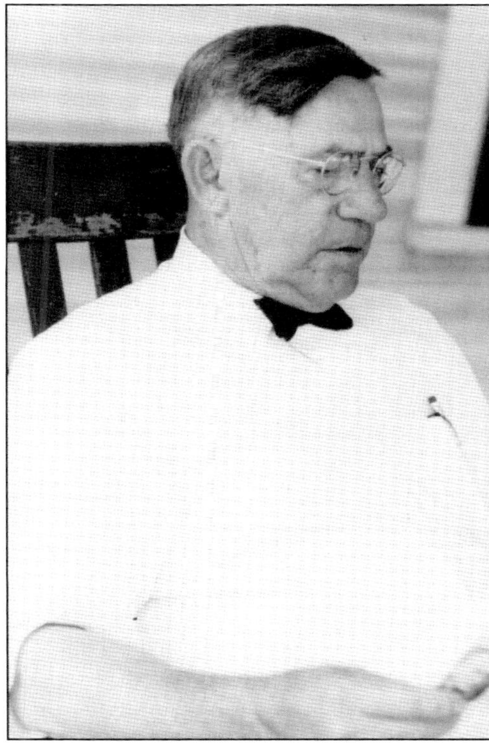

Ruby Grubbs Sapp (above, left) started the first Girl Scout troop in Coffee County. She was also Douglas's first home economics teacher and was a member of many civic organizations in addition to being an active member of the First Methodist Church and the Review Club. Rema Harris Sapp Sr. (above, right) worked as a pharmacist at Sapp's Pharmacy, originally located on Ward Street. In 1926, following the death of his father, I.C. Sapp, Rema moved Sapp's Pharmacy to the corner of Madison Avenue and Ashley Street. Rema and Ruby Sapp had two children (at right). Rema Jr., a pharmacist like his father, enjoyed photography (the photograph above of his father was most likely taken by him). Antoinette was an excellent student and talented artist. At the age of 11, she contracted acute meningitis and died a month later. (Courtesy of Mary Clyde Scott.)

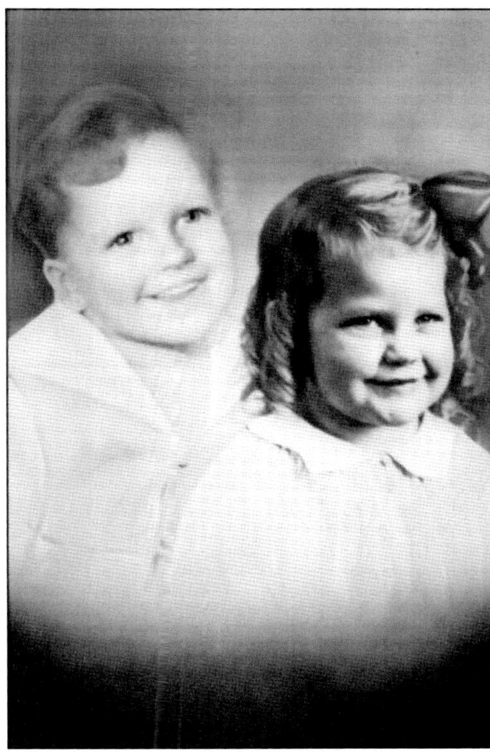

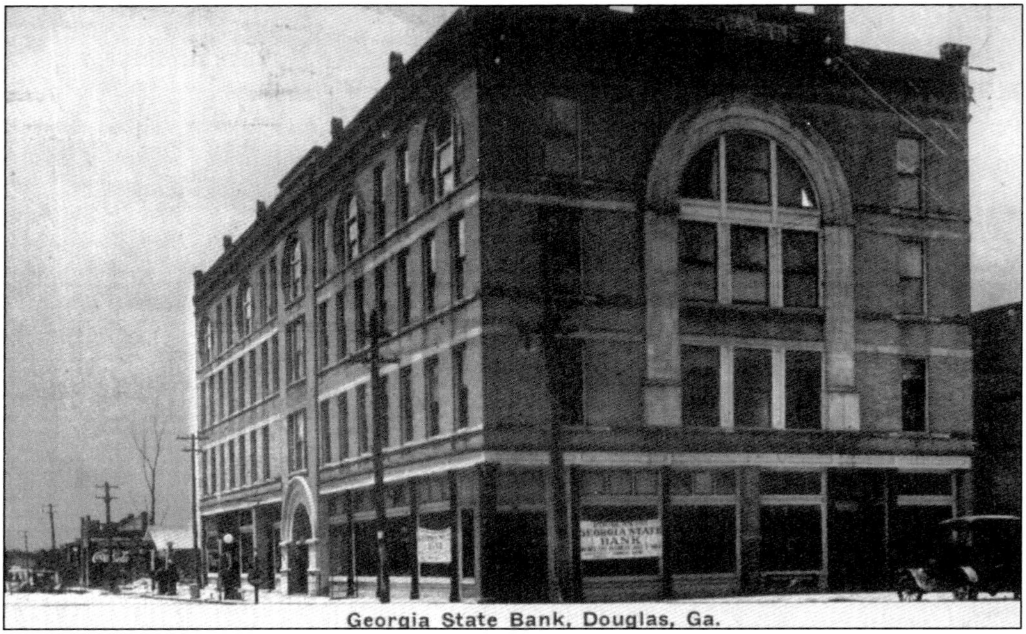

At the time of the banking crash in 1926, state and federal regulators tried to calm depositors by saying that Manleys' banks were small country banks that operated as independent units. But, before the collapse in July, the Georgia State Bank was one of the state's largest banks, with a branching network of 20 offices throughout the state. The bank failures shattered the economy in Georgia and Florida, and many depositors lost their life savings. By the time 1926 came to an end, 150 banks in Florida and Georgia were closed, and more than $30 million was lost. (Courtesy of Joanne Hanna Lott.)

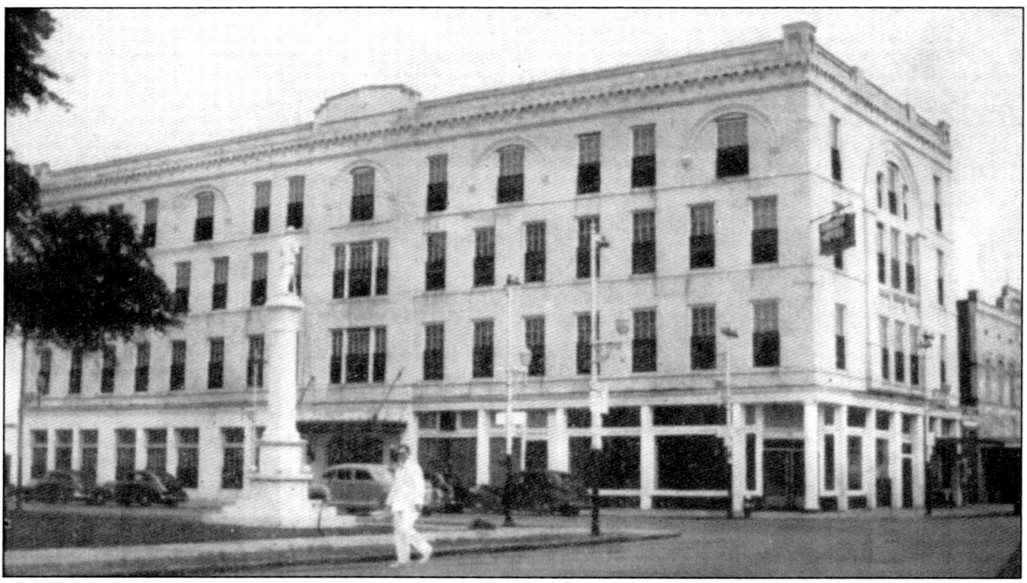

When Georgia State Bank crashed, a spacious building was left empty, so investors opened it to visitors of the area. Seen here is the new Douglas Hotel on the corner of Peterson Avenue and Ashley Street. (Courtesy of Joanne Hanna Lott.)

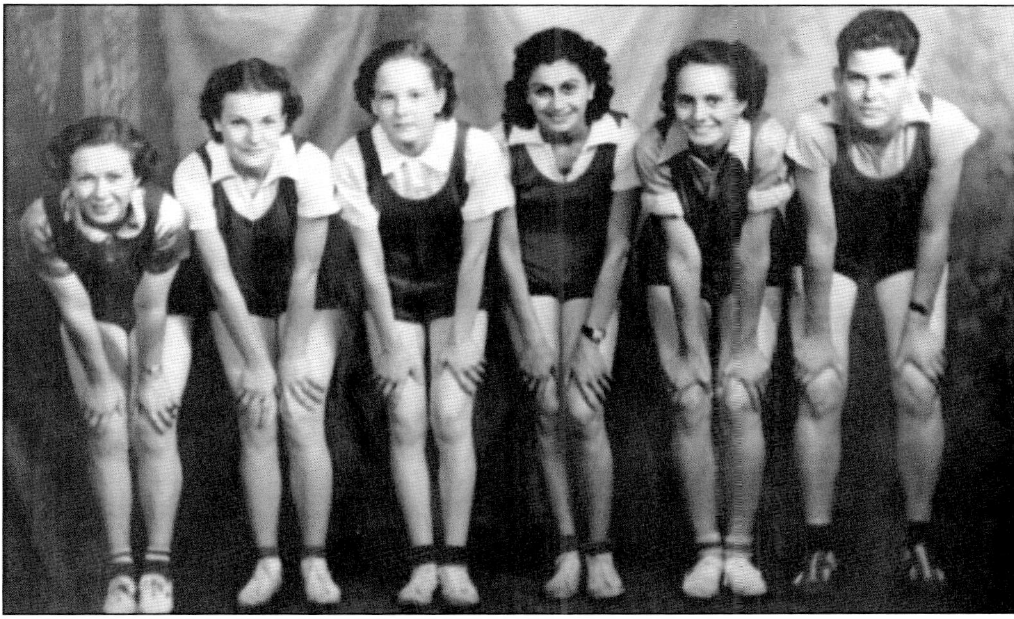

Teacher and basketball coach Willie Mae was rumored to have eyes in the back of her head. Former student Mary Clyde recalled one time passing notes in class and being afraid of getting caught. Before Willie Mae could turn around to catch her, Mary crumpled up the note and threw it out the window. The note hit the windowsill and fell to the floor, and Willie Mae assured her, "If you can't throw better than that, you won't make the team next year." The 1936 Division 3 Douglas High School varsity basketball team members posing here are, from left to right, Karlene "Chicken" Vickers, Ouida Jernigan, Runell McMilliann, Louise Hanna, Mary Clyde Tanner, and Mary Talley. Karlene earned the nickname "Chicken" because, unlike the other girls at school, she could not wring a chicken's neck. (Courtesy of Mary Clyde Scott.)

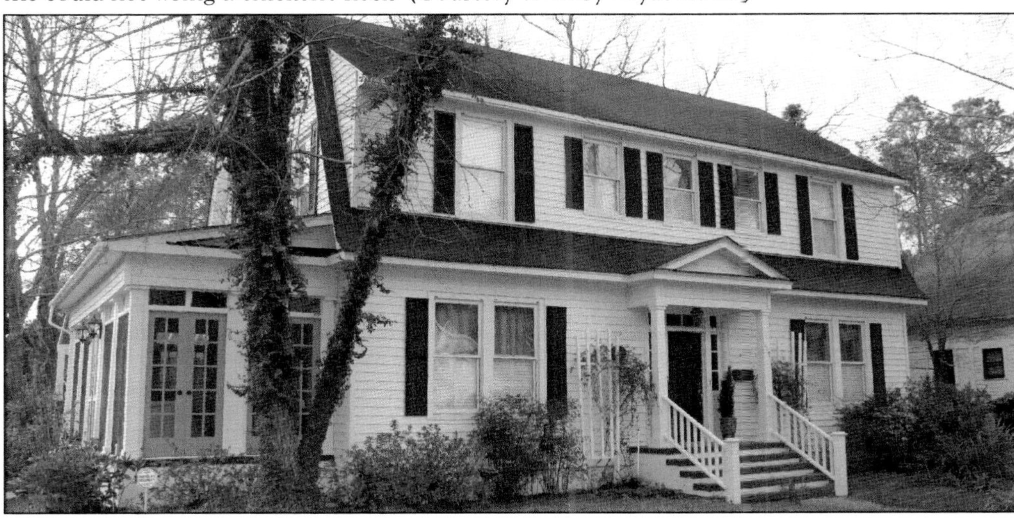

This home at 519 North Gaskin Avenue was built by Robert N. McEachren, who also constructed Union Bank. He served on the city council and on the water and light commission. For a home in southern Georgia, this Dutch Colonial building comes with an unexpected feature: a cellar. (Courtesy of Charles E. Griffiths II.)

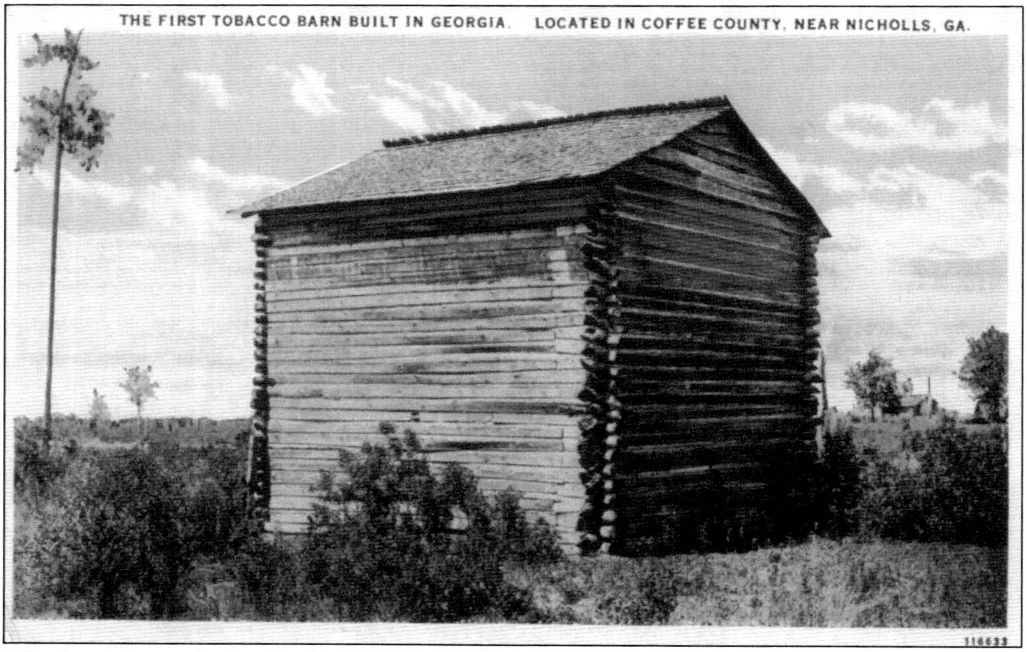

War drove down the price of cotton, and local farmers decided to try growing tobacco. Luckily, tobacco caught on just as the boll weevil infestation decimated local cotton crops. This is a picture of the first tobacco barn in Coffee County, built in Nicholls, Georgia. (Courtesy of Joanne Hanna Lott.)

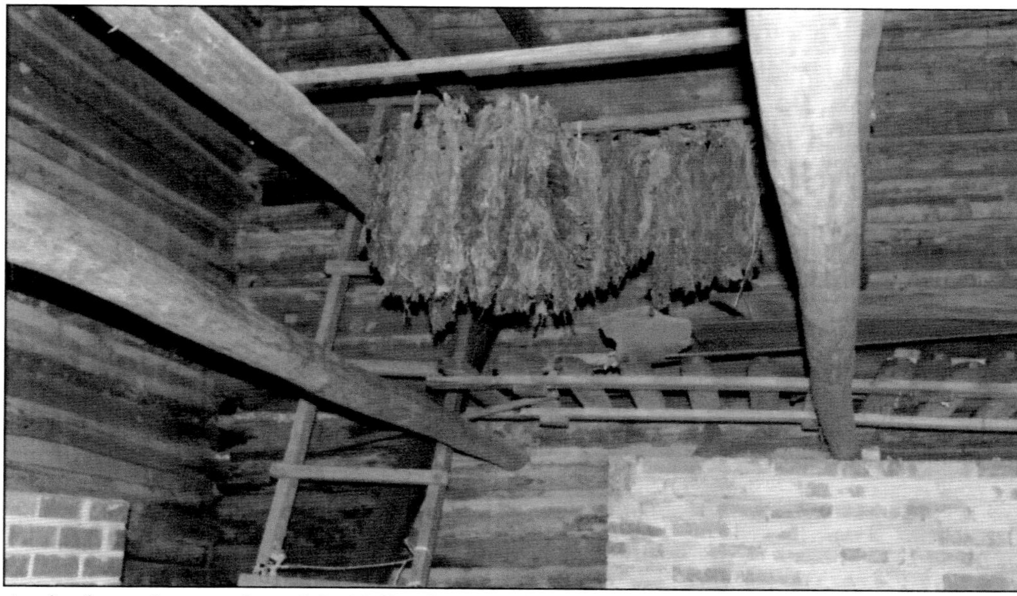

At the first tobacco sale in July 1917, tobacco sold for 20¢ a pound. The tobacco crops brought $600,000 of revenue to Douglas in 1919, and prices ranged from 17¢ to 25¢ per pound. Seen here is tobacco drying in an old barn at Heritage Farm Coffee Regional State Park. The farm is made up of buildings donated by locals and restored to preserve the agricultural heritage of the area. (Courtesy of Charles E. Griffiths II.)

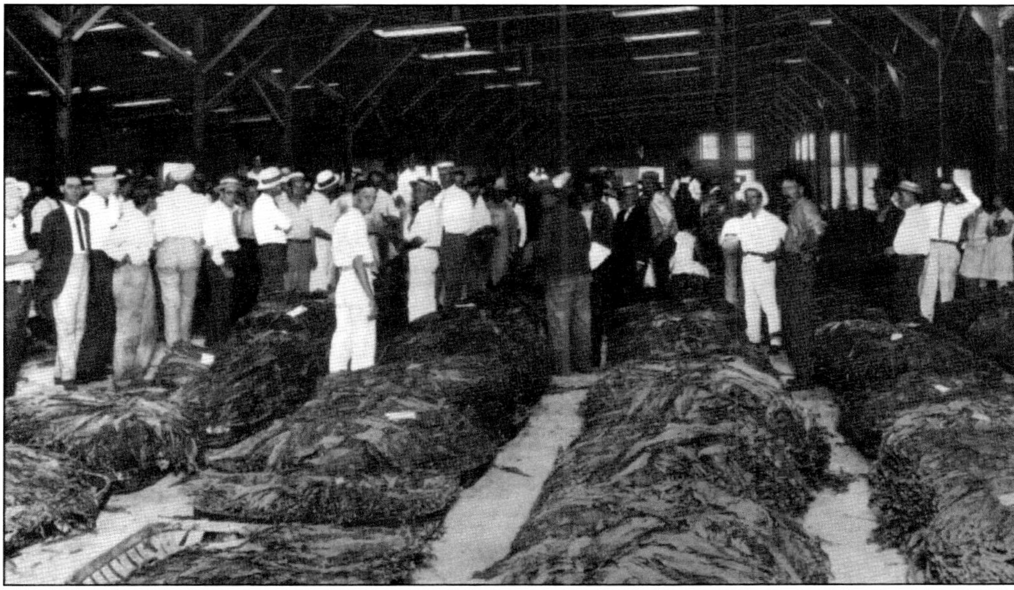

At a time when the rest of the country was suffering from the Depression, the majority of the Douglas population was rural and removed from the problems of the nation. As agriculture was the largest industry in the area, there was plenty to eat. Farmers in the area were at the forefront of the state's tobacco market. During the weeks of tobacco sales, there would be town barbecues, contests, and giveaways. The town experienced the excitement of the holidays, but instead of spending money at Christmas, many residents were earning income from tobacco and vendor sales. Prizes were given away every year to encourage farmers to sell in Douglas. Seen here are the tobacco market in 1930 (above) and the first-prize winner of best tobacco display (below). (Courtesy of Joanne Hanna Lott.)

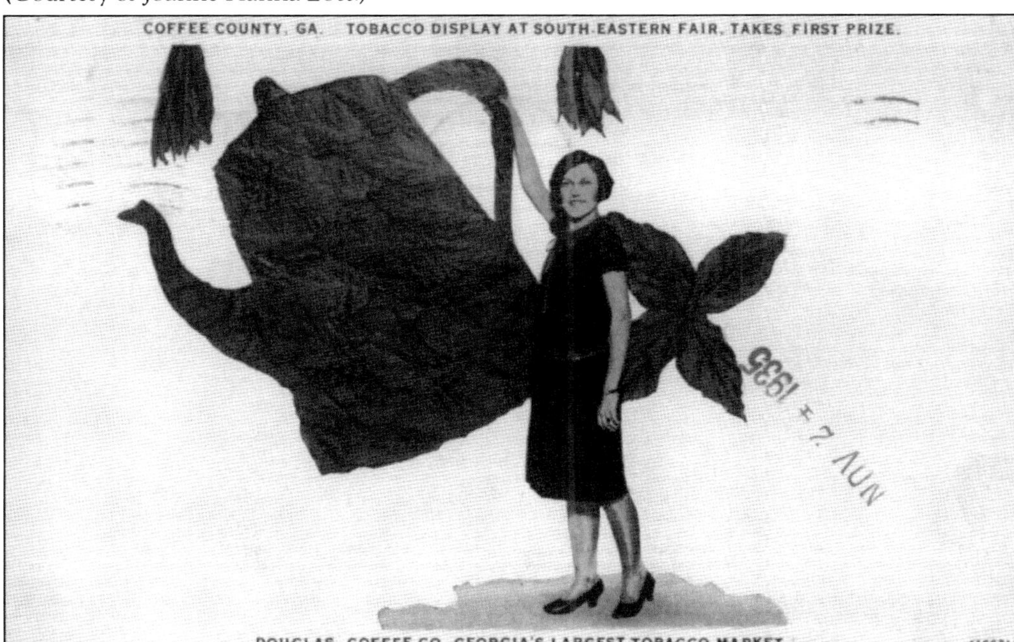

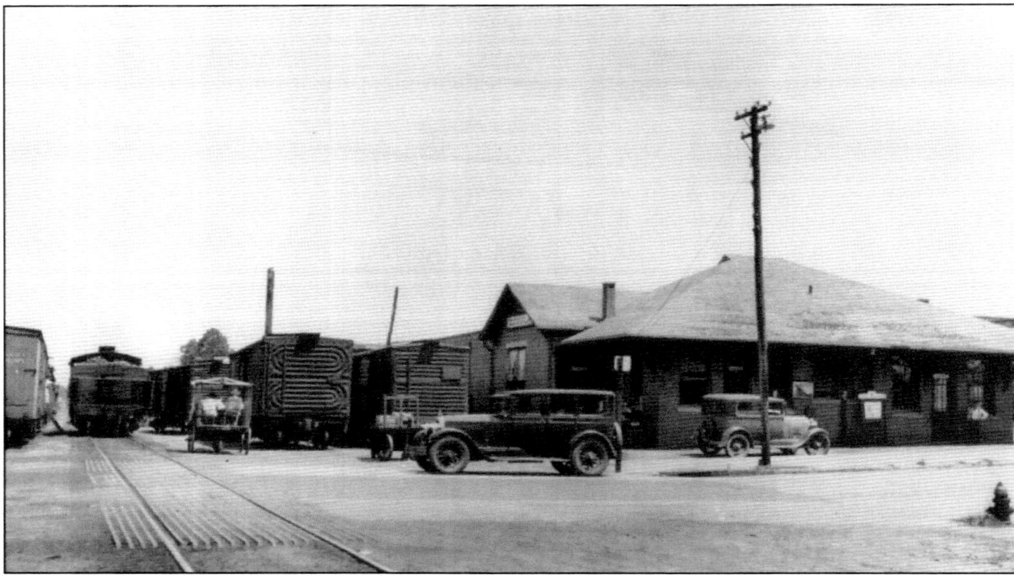

Trains were used to transport the tobacco. Shown here is the train station on market day. (Courtesy of Joanne Hanna Lott.)

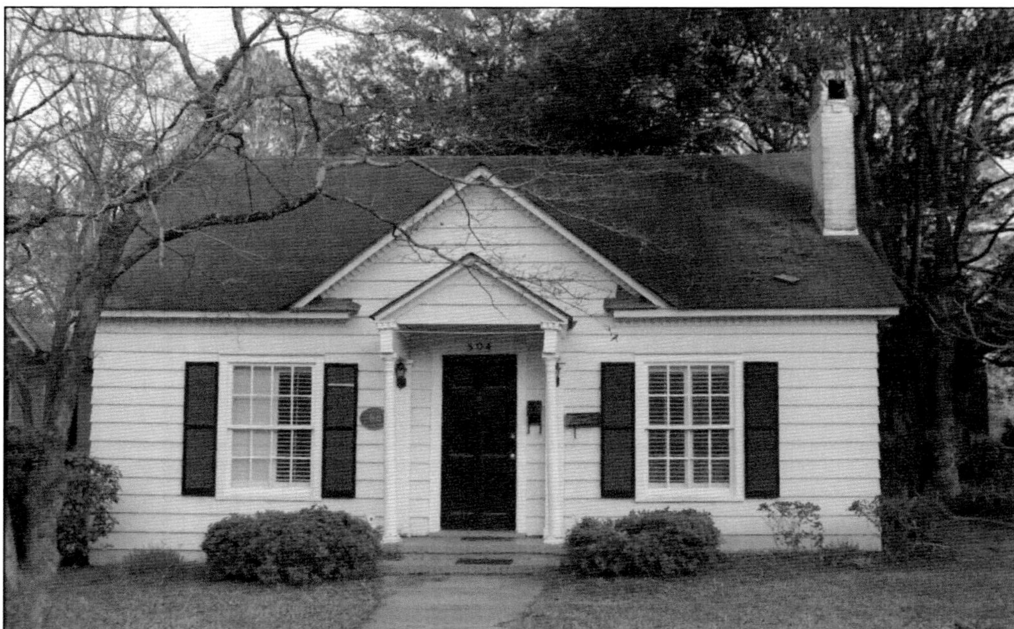

This charming cottage was built in 1931 for the principal of Douglas High School, Prof. Fussell Marion Chalker, and his wife, Lorraine Pickens. Professor Chalker was principal and counselor and was very involved with his students in activities such as the Boy Scouts, the glee club, and career development. Several of his students went on to be doctors and credit his guidance for part of their successes. He was also the author of *Pioneering Ocmulgee*. (Courtesy of Charles E. Griffiths II.)

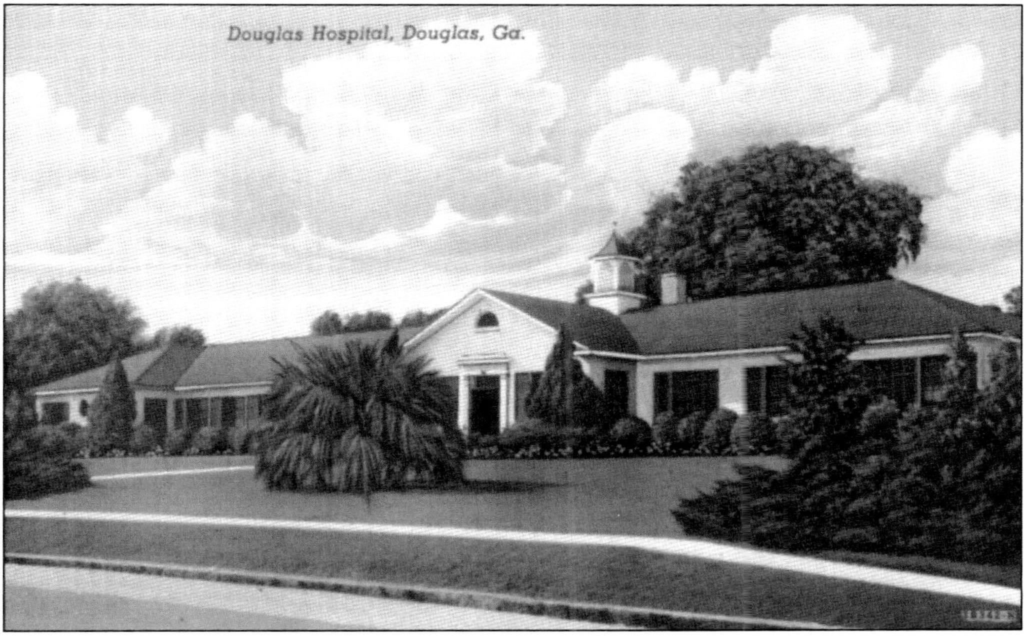

Based on the success of this clinic, the city donated land on East Ward Street for construction of Douglas Hospital. The hospital opened in 1935, but within a decade, local need had outgrown the small, $30,000 facility. This building became a public library in the early 1950s. (Courtesy of Joanne Hanna Lott.)

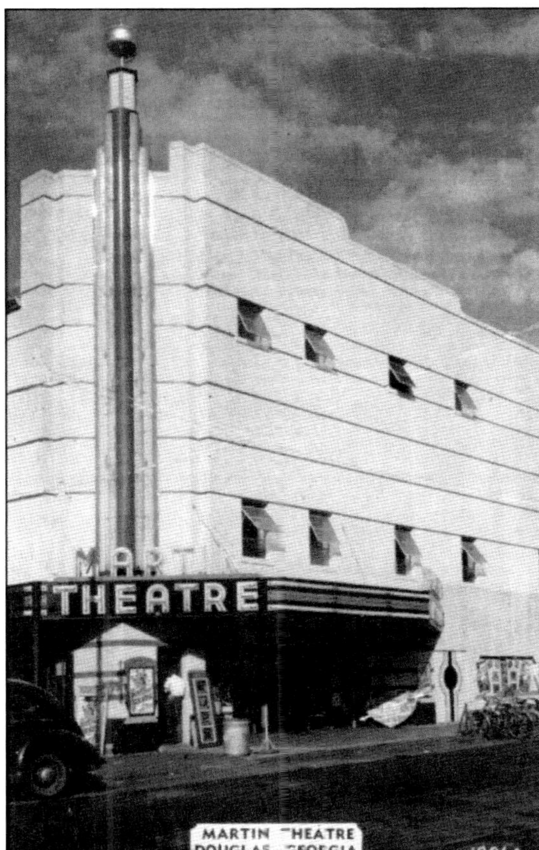

Located on Ashley Street in downtown Douglas, this historic 1940s theater has been restored to its original Art Deco splendor. The Martin Centre is still used for performing arts as well as large sales meetings, conferences, and seminars. (Courtesy of Joanne Hanna Lott.)

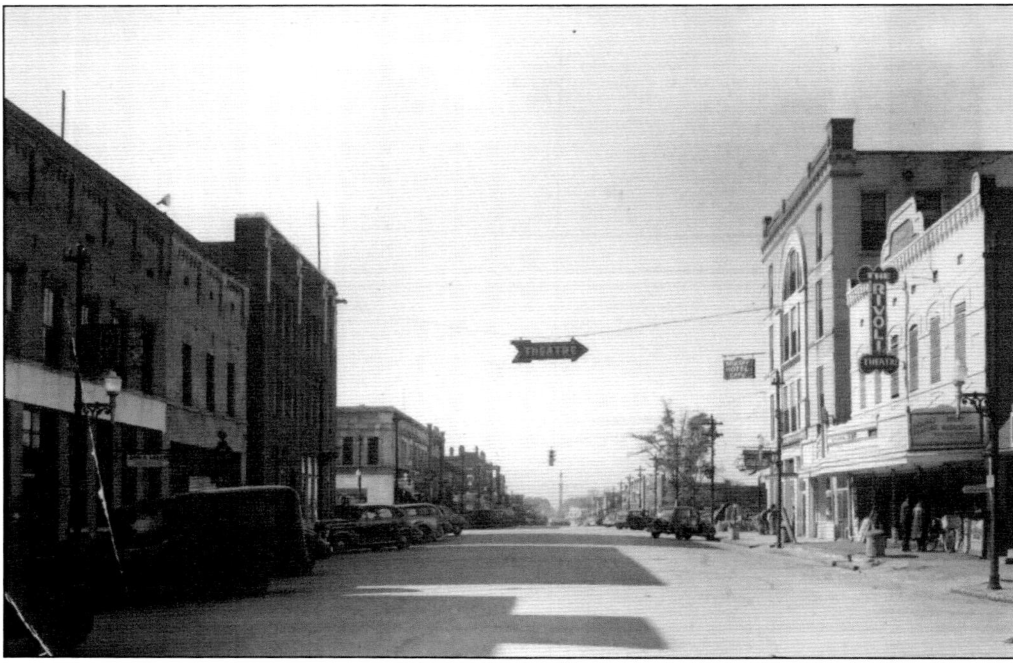

Shown is North Peterson Avenue where the Atrium, BB&T Bank, and Douglas Asphalt Company building are currently located. The Rivioli Theatre is visible on the right. Rivioli theaters were some of the best-constructed ornate theater houses established at the time. However, the war took its toll on the Rivioli theaters, as many were franchises and lacked the buying power of the competition to obtain movies. (Courtesy of Joanne Hanna Lott.)

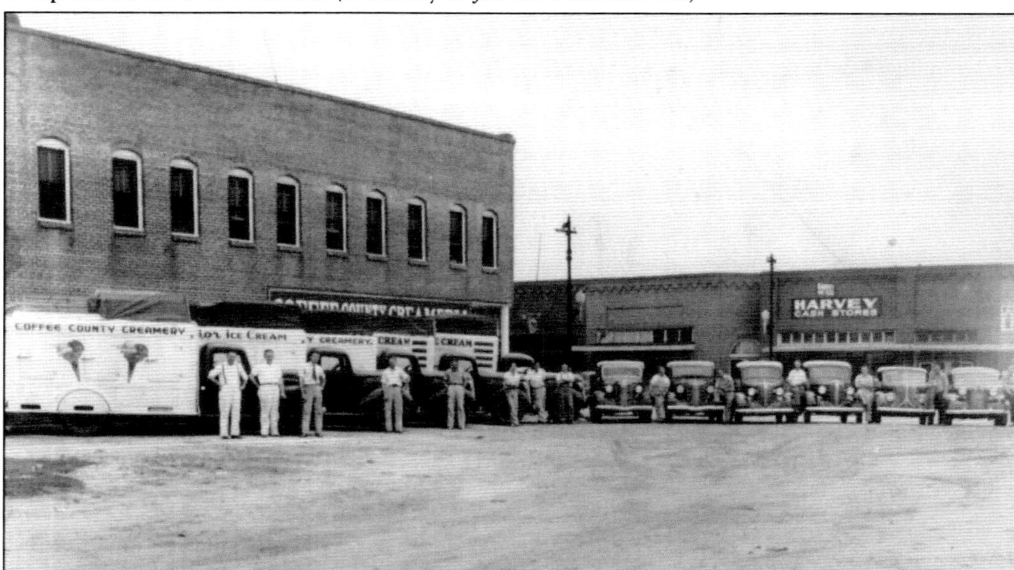

The Coffee County Creamery of Douglas is lined up and ready for the state inspection in 1937. At the time, milk was 12¢ a quart or 48¢ a gallon. This facility later became the Meadow Gold Ice Cream building. Meadow Gold still operates farms in the area, but the building is currently undergoing reconstruction. (Courtesy of Joanne Hanna Lott.)

When Georgia developed a more comprehensive public school system, the district A&M schools were no longer needed. High school principal Joseph M. Thrash rallied to convert his school into a junior college. When he did not receive the local support he needed to make this happen, he ran for the state legislature. His first act as district representative was introducing the "Thrash Bill," which incorporated his ideas of converting the school into a college and was passed by the Georgia General Assembly in 1926. Once the transition was made, the name of the school was changed to South Georgia State Junior College, and Thrash became the college's first president. He is pictured here in 1929. (Courtesy of South Georgia State College.)

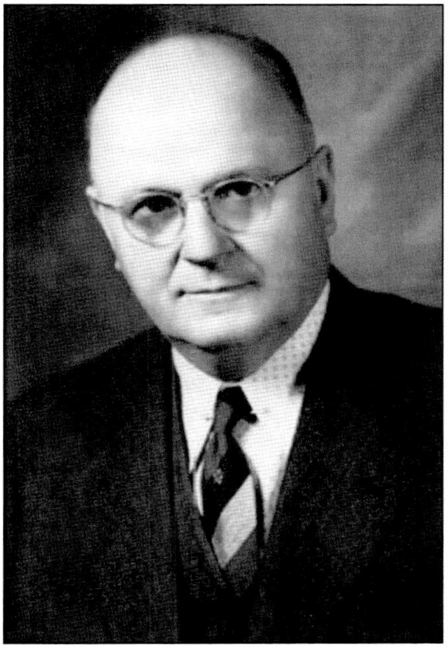

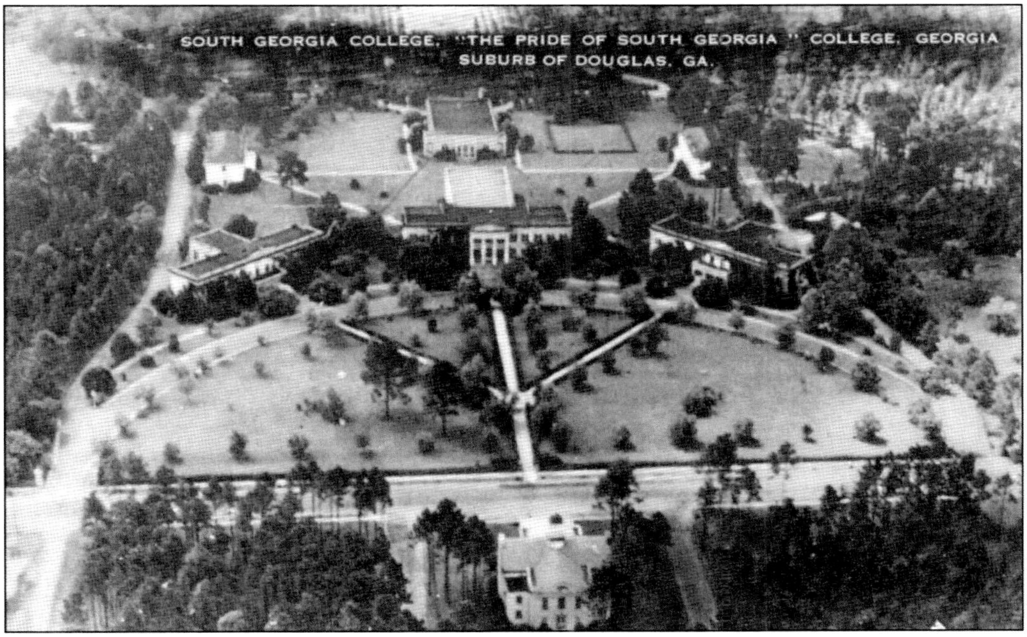

This aerial view reflects the growth of the school that was renamed South Georgia College in 1936. Additional buildings and a recreational area were added as the school expanded its program to meet wartime needs. The 63rd Army Air Forces Flying Training Detachment was originally a part of South Georgia College's pilot-training program. The library, now Thrash Hall, was built with Works Progress Administration funds in the 1930s and was located facing Davis, Peterson, and Powell Halls along Quincy Circle. Peterson Hall had an auditorium added in the back. The gymnasium, positioned south of the dining hall, was restored and now serves as the Clower Student Life Center. (Courtesy of Dr. James A. Cottingham.)

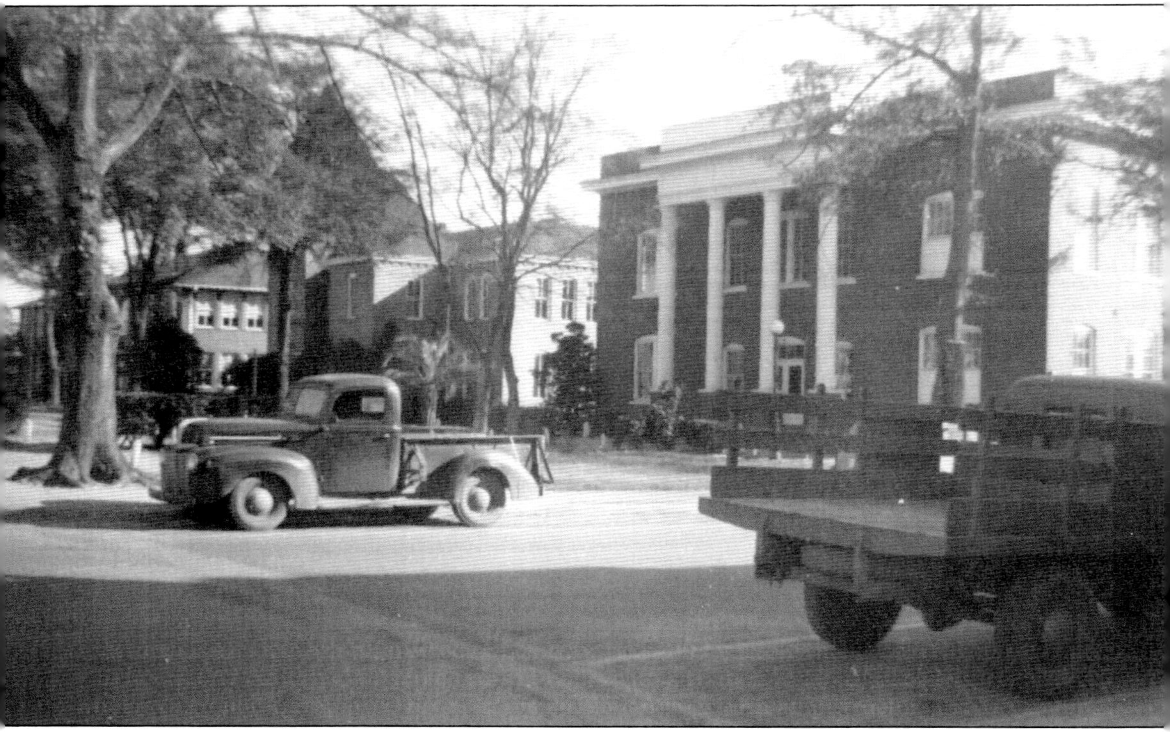

This building was formerly used for both the Georgia Normal College and Business Institute and the Douglas High School. At the time this photograph was taken, it housed the Central Elementary School complex. (Courtesy of Joanne Hanna Lott.)

Four

Winging Wartime

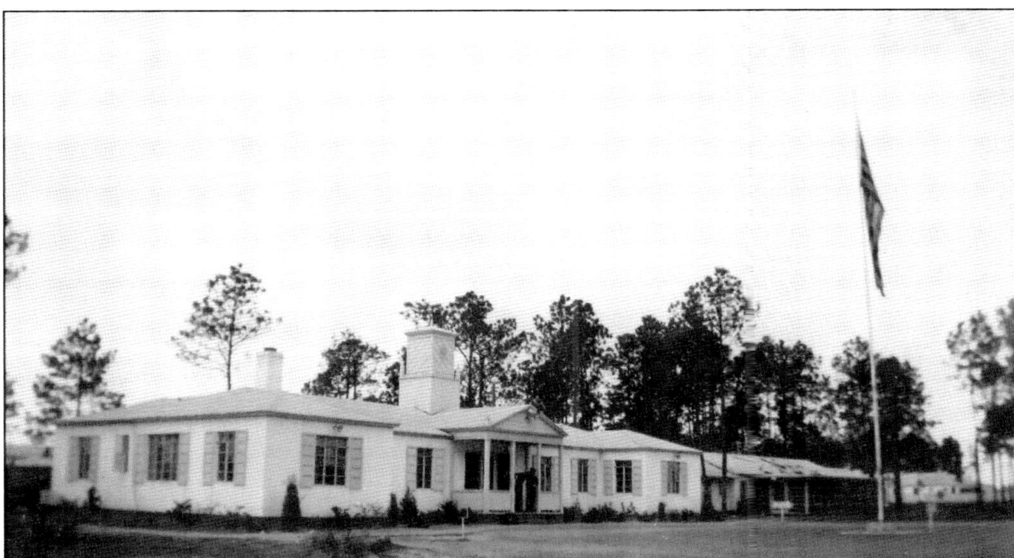

The Raymond Richard Aviation Company ran the South Georgia College pilot-training facility, but the Army Air Force oversaw the operation. Pilots were in demand for the military and were trained in this facility from 1941 to 1944. Of the 55 training centers across the United States during World Wars I and II, this facility has remained the most intact. The sign at the entrance during wartime warned that it was a restricted area. Now, the building is a museum, and admission is open to the public. (Courtesy of World War II Flight Training Museum, Don Brooks.)

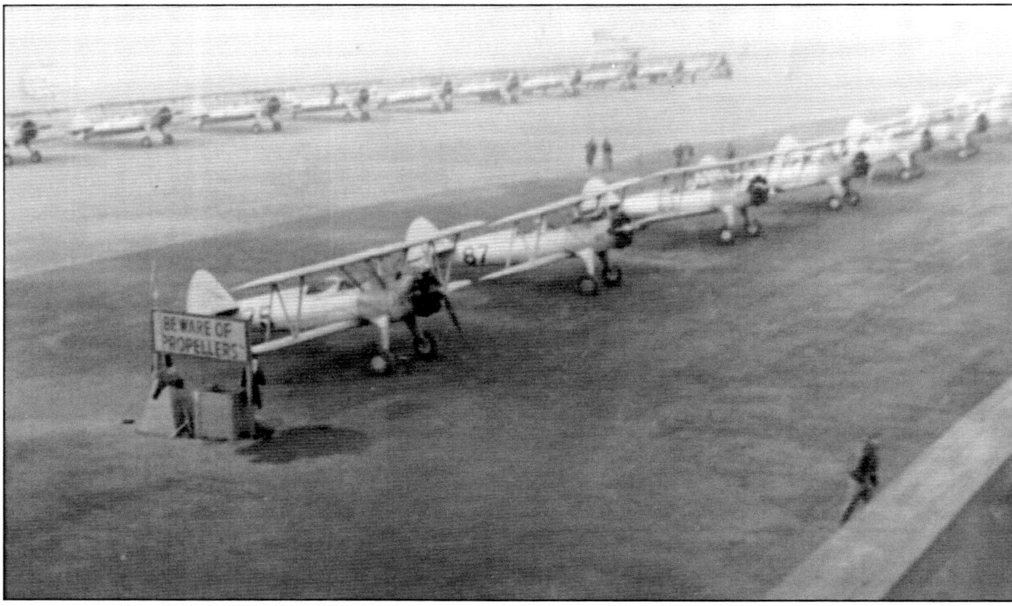

Pictured is the flight school "ready line." Note the sign warning students not to walk into propellers. Shortly after arriving, cadets were taken up for their first flight with the instructor and issued a parachute. As commercial flying was not as common then as today, many of these young men had never even seen a plane before; both riding and flying were completely new experiences. (Courtesy of World War II Flight Training Museum, Don Brooks.)

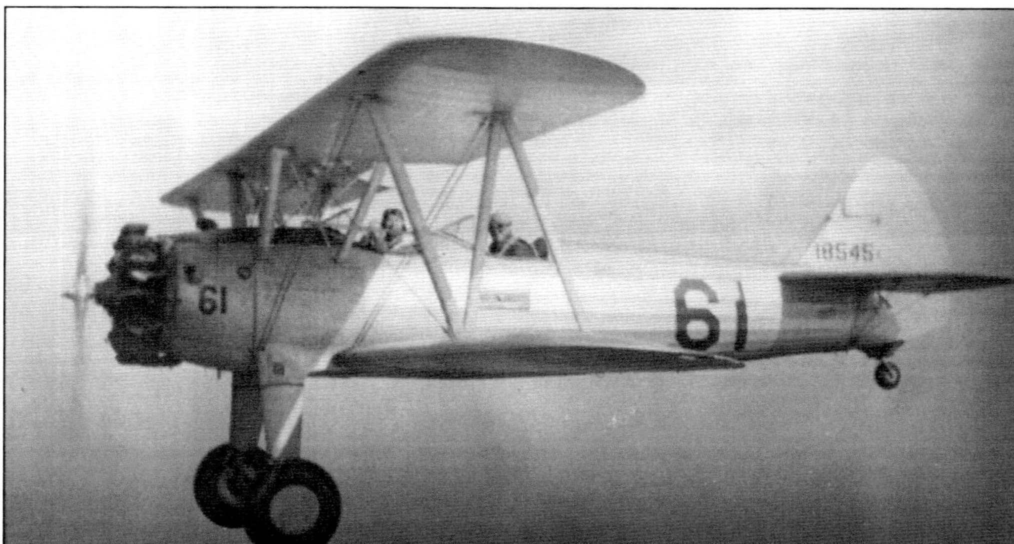

The plane used to train students in Douglas was a Stearman. The body was made of aluminum, and wings were wood and fabric, as the military had to save metal for aircraft and weapons used on the battlefront. Pictured is a cadet flying with a trainer in the back seat of a PT-17 Stearman biplane. There were officers at the school to keep the cadets incorporated in the military, but the flight instructors were civilian pilots. (Courtesy of World War II Flight Training Museum, Don Brooks.)

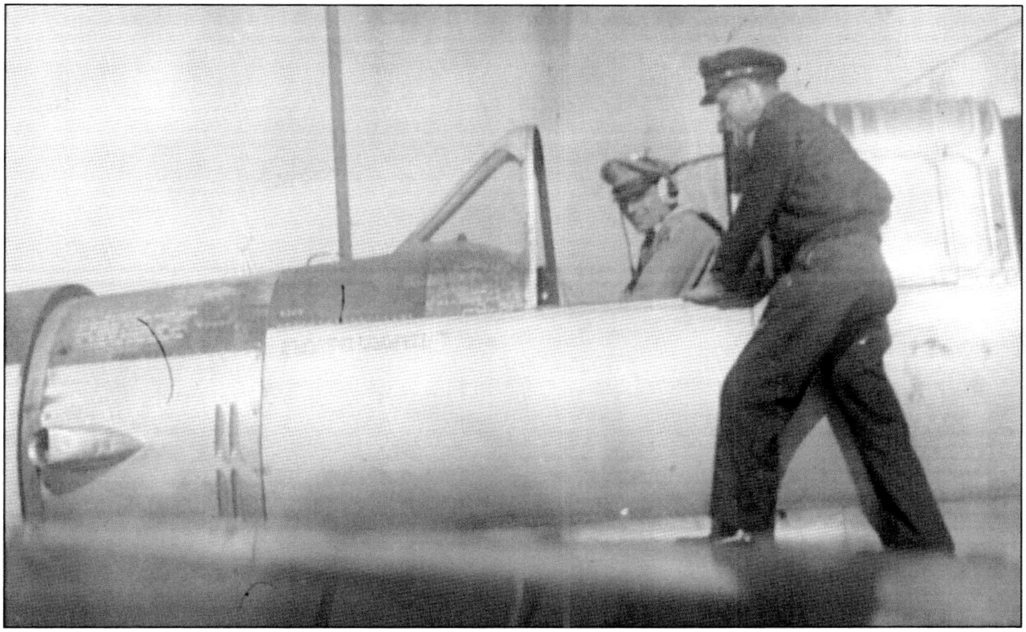

Pictured is a cadet with his instructor before he takes off for a solo flight. Solo flights were after 10 hours, and pilots had no more than 13 hours with a trainer. In Douglas, cadets received 100 hours of ground training, 60 hours in the air, 25 landings with an instructor, and 175 landings total—all in nine weeks. (Courtesy of World War II Flight Training Museum, Don Brooks.)

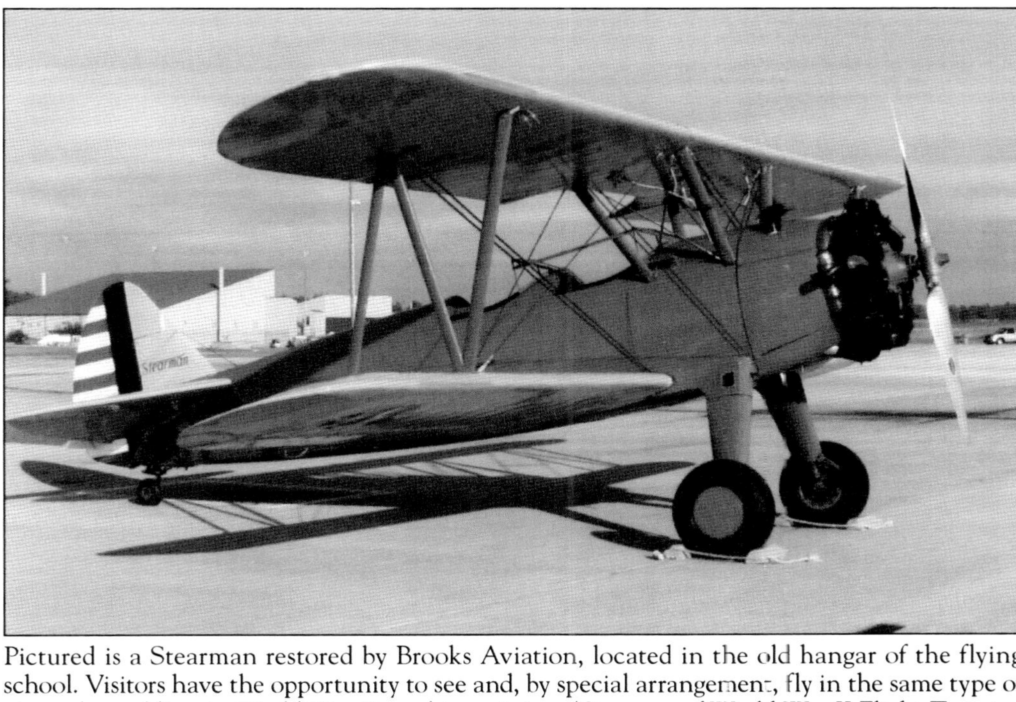

Pictured is a Stearman restored by Brooks Aviation, located in the old hangar of the flying school. Visitors have the opportunity to see and, by special arrangement, fly in the same type of plane that soldiers in World War II used in training. (Courtesy of World War II Flight Training Museum, Don Brooks.)

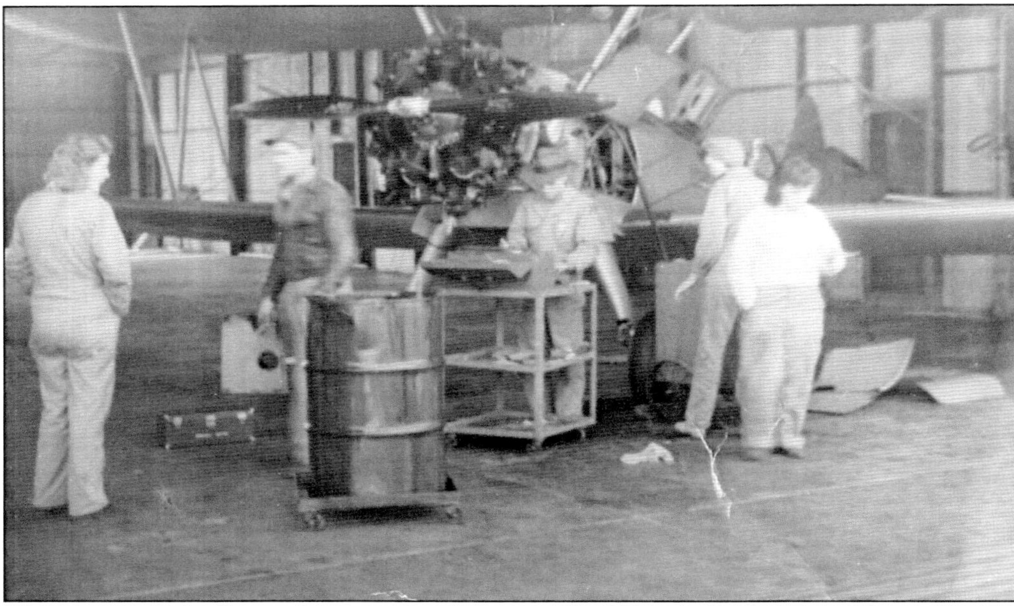

Shown are five mechanics constructing a plane. The three women received training at the school and civil air-mechanics licenses. They were hired to keep records and perform routine mechanical checks. (Courtesy of World War II Flight Training Museum, Don Brooks.)

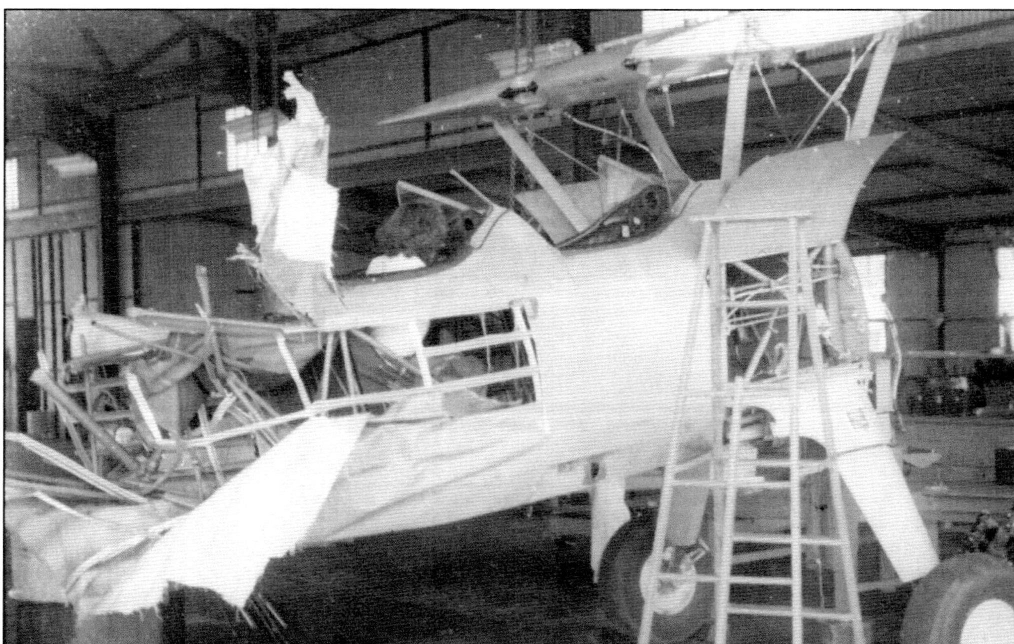

This photograph could imply that female support staff did even more than routine checks, but salvaging wrecked planes was a common occurrence. It was often difficult to get parts for the Stearman, so if repair was impossible, the parts were salvaged. (Courtesy of World War II Flight Training Museum, Don Brooks.)

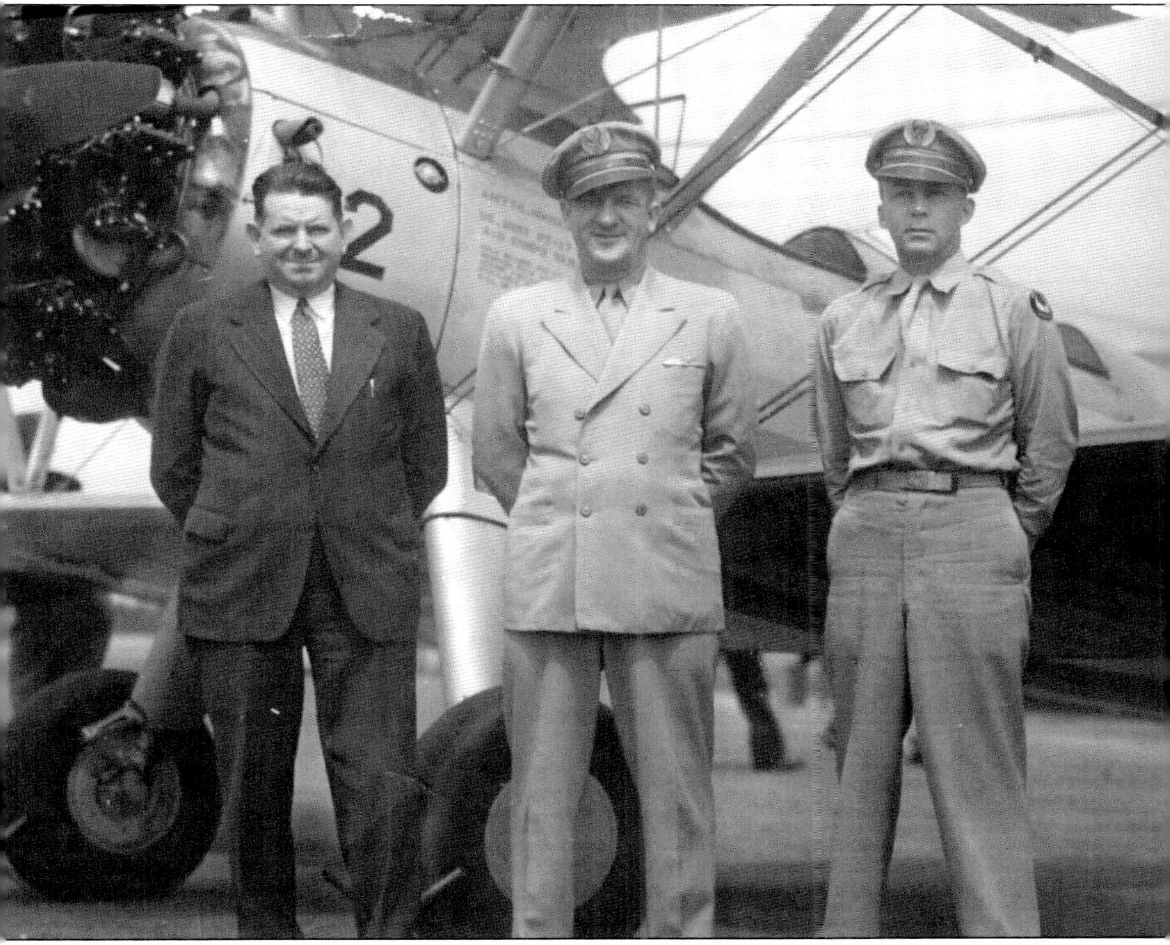

Pictured here are Wes Raymond (left), Bob Lape (center), and Bob Richardson. Raymond worked with South Georgia College and the Civil Aeronautics Authority to form a civil contract pilot school. Lape was the director of flying and a flight instructor from 1941 to 1944. Richardson was the secretary and treasurer of the Raymond Brinckerhoff Aviation Company, which later became known as the Raymond-Richmond Aviation Company. (Courtesy of World War II Flight Training Museum, Don Brooks.)

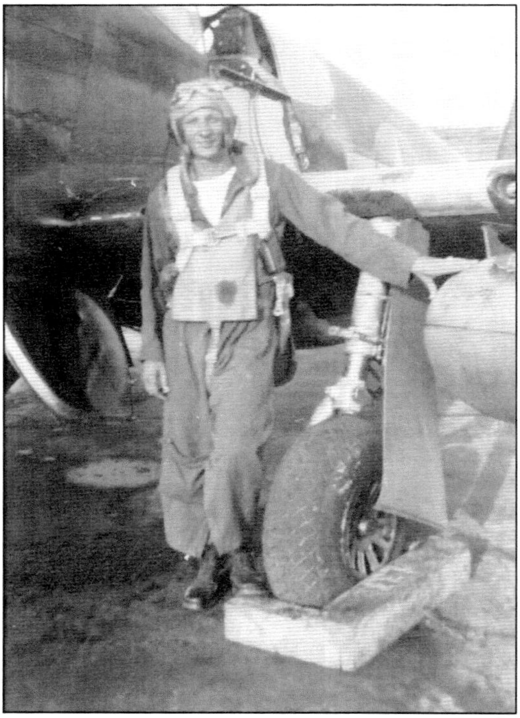

After Douglas, cadet Henry Simon (pictured) went on to fly a P-51 Mustang in Bartow, Florida, and in June 1944 in the CBI (China Burma India) Theater with the 1st Air Commando Group. (Courtesy of World War II Flight Training Museum, Don Brooks.)

Gail Updike (center) was a civilian instructor from 1943 to 1944. After the school closed, he had a career in airport management. He is seen here with students from the class of 1944-H. They are, from left to right, Calvin William Dentler, Platt K. Wiggins Jr., James N. Diacumokos, and Joseph Charles Endler Jr. (Courtesy of World War II Flight Training Museum, Don Brooks.)

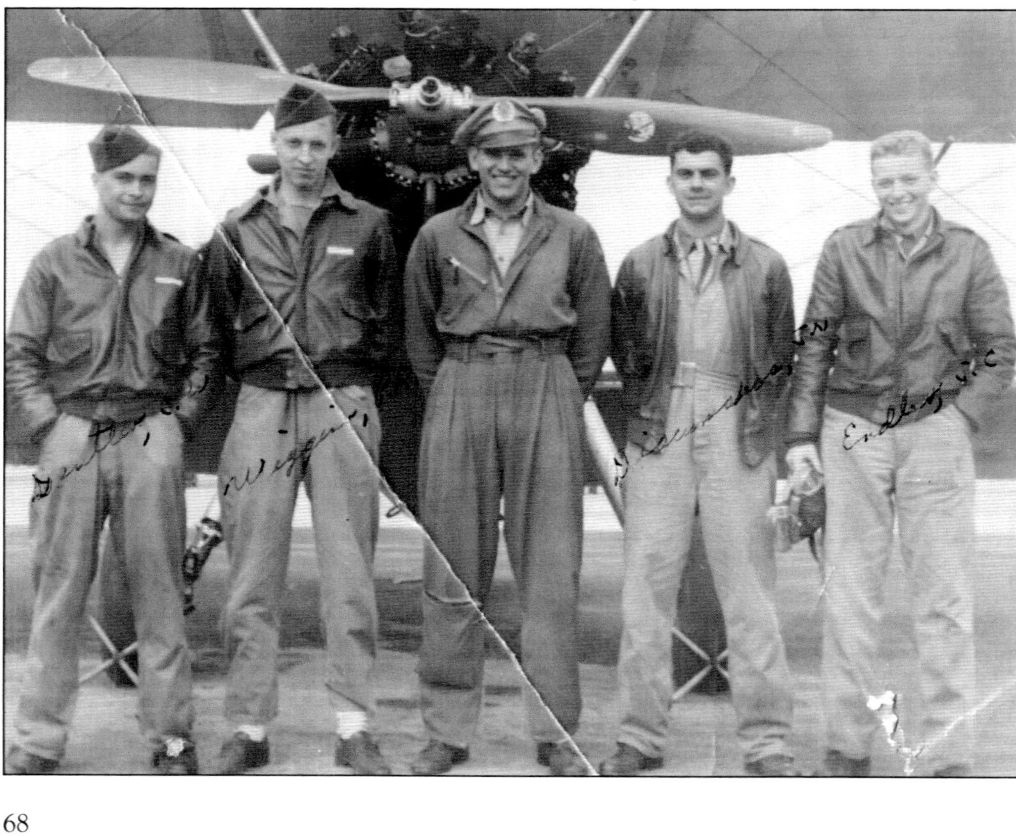

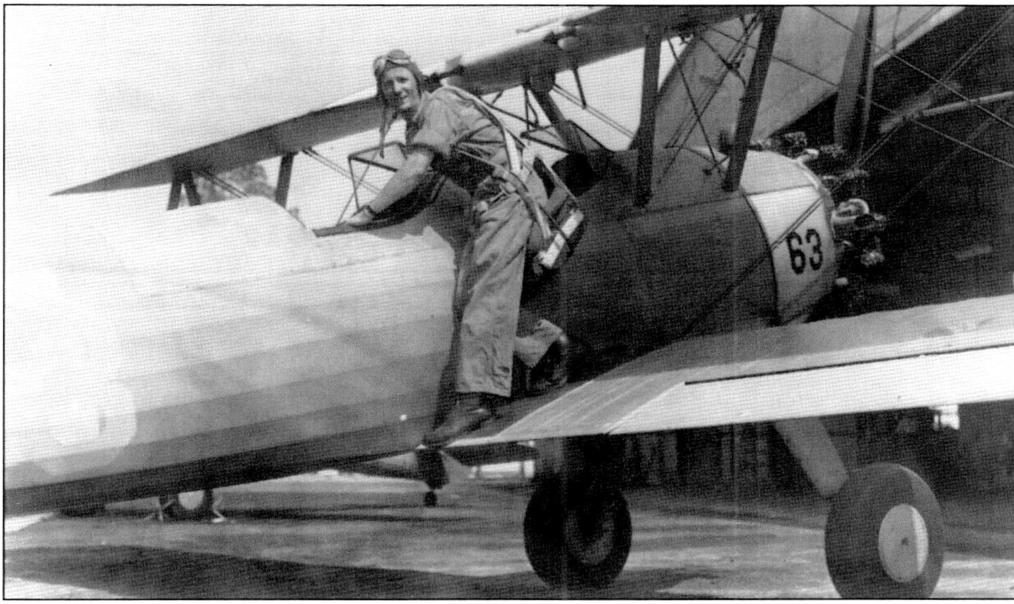

Young cadet Henry Simon is pictured in front of a Stearman plane at the flight school. This was the beginning of 34 years with the military; he would retire from the US Air Force as a major general in September 1976. (Courtesy of World War II Flight Training Museum, Don Brooks.)

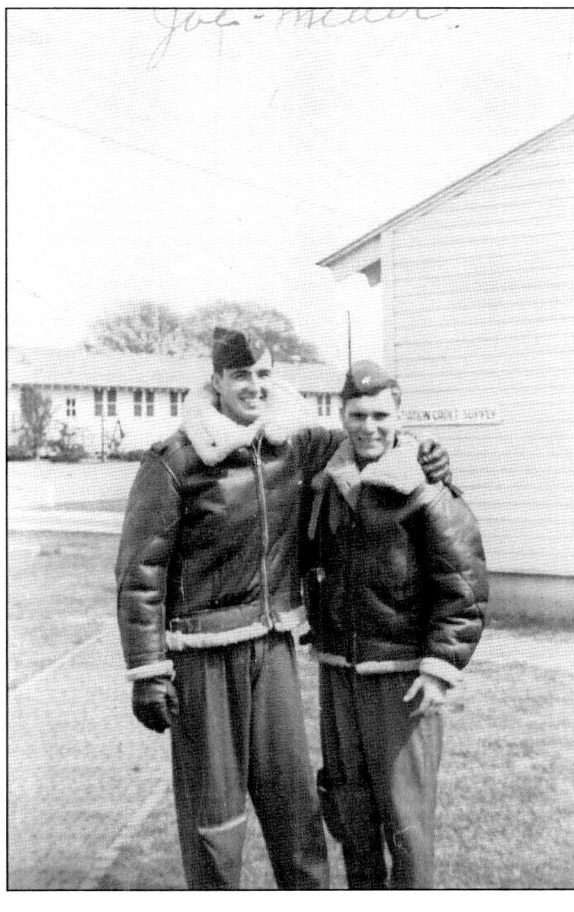

Joseph Miller from the class of 44E took this 1944 photograph of his flying buddies "Stubb" and "Milbo" next to the Cadet Ration Supply Building. They flew together in Douglas, kept in touch, and saw each other once after the war. (Courtesy of World War II Flight Training Museum, Don Brooks.)

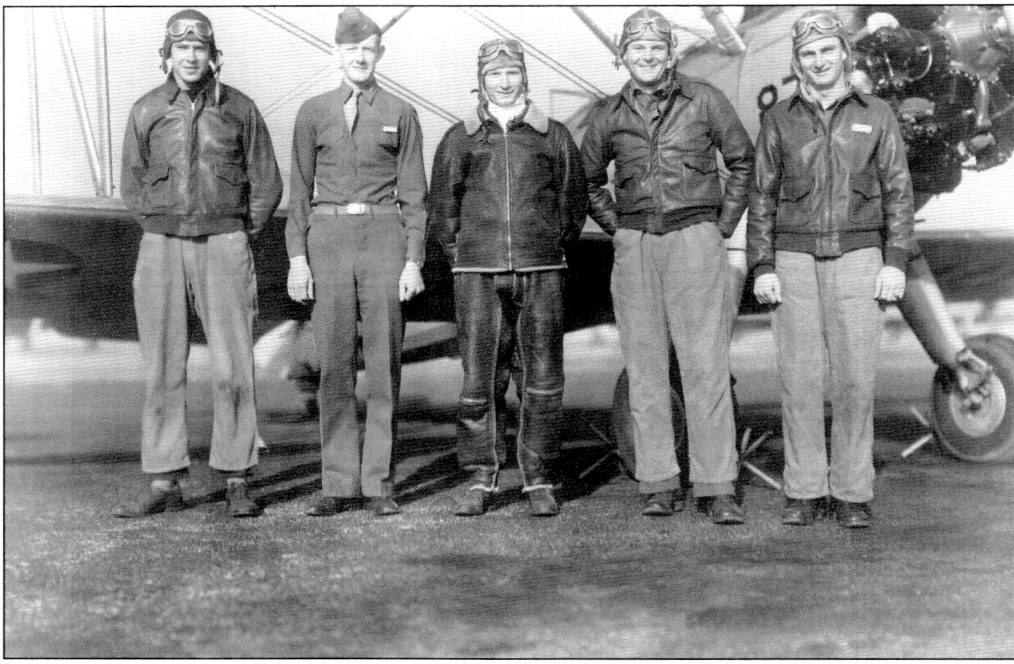

Jake Byington taught as a flight instructor from 1942 to 1944. He is seen here (second from the left) posing with four students. Students outnumbered the planes five to one, so a group of students was generally paired with an instructor and would go the course of the nine weeks together. (Courtesy of World War II Flight Training Museum, Don Brooks.)

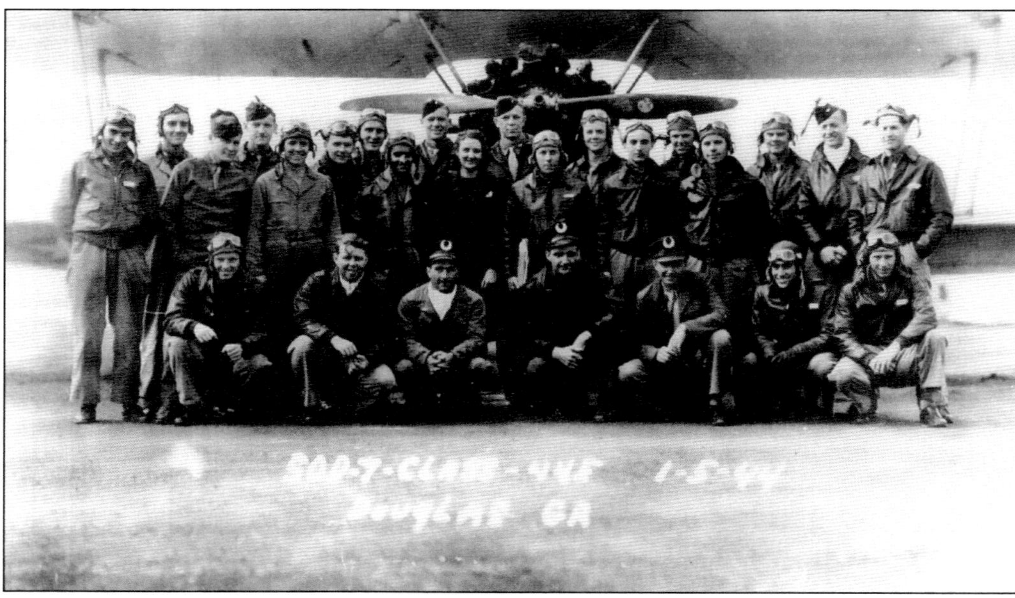

This is Squadron 7 from the class of 44E in January 1944. A total of 177 men graduated from the class. John Thurman Jr. (first row, third from the left) was a flight instructor from 1943 to 1944. When he left the school, he went on active duty until 1946. (Courtesy of World War II Flight Training Museum, Don Brooks.)

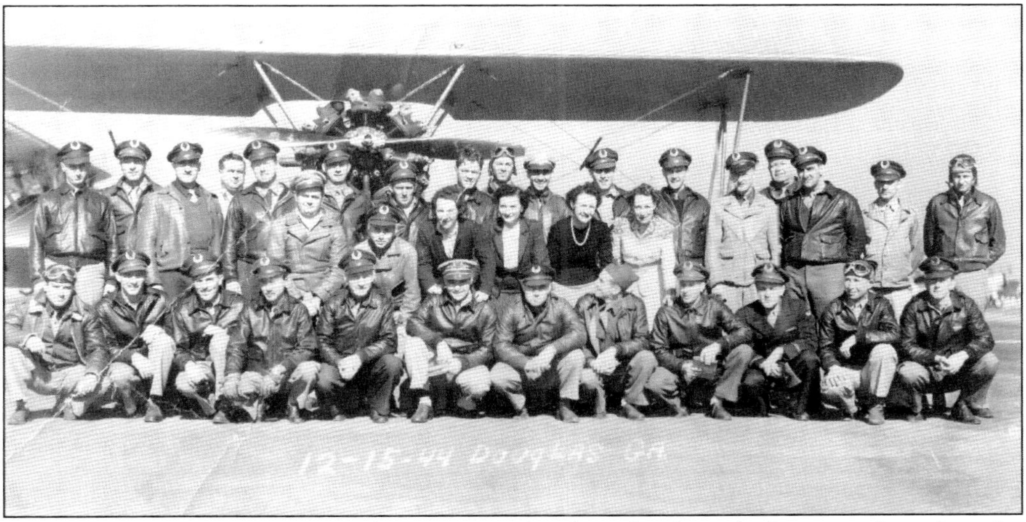

This class picture was taken December 15, 1944. The class of 44E was the last to graduate from the Douglas school. Less than a week after this photograph was taken, the flight school was abruptly decommissioned. By this time, the Army Air Forces had enough pilots, and the war was coming to an end. (Courtesy of World War II Flight Training Museum, Don Brooks.)

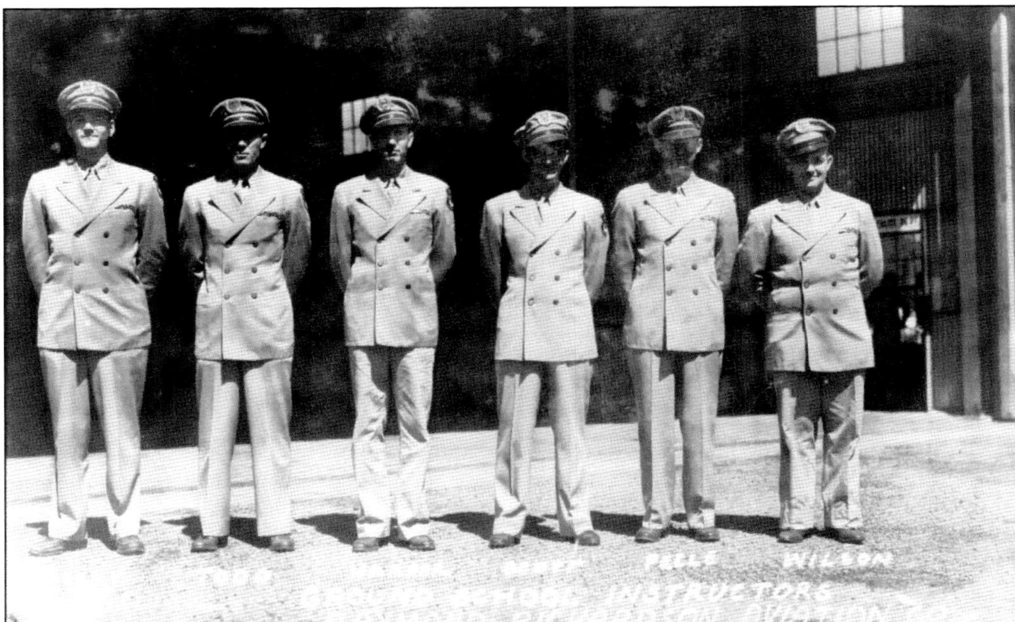

Pictured here are ground-school instructors of Raymond Richardson Aviation Company. They are, from left to right, Massey, Todd, Harper, Scott, Pelle, and Wilson. (Courtesy of World War II Flight Training Museum, Don Brooks.)

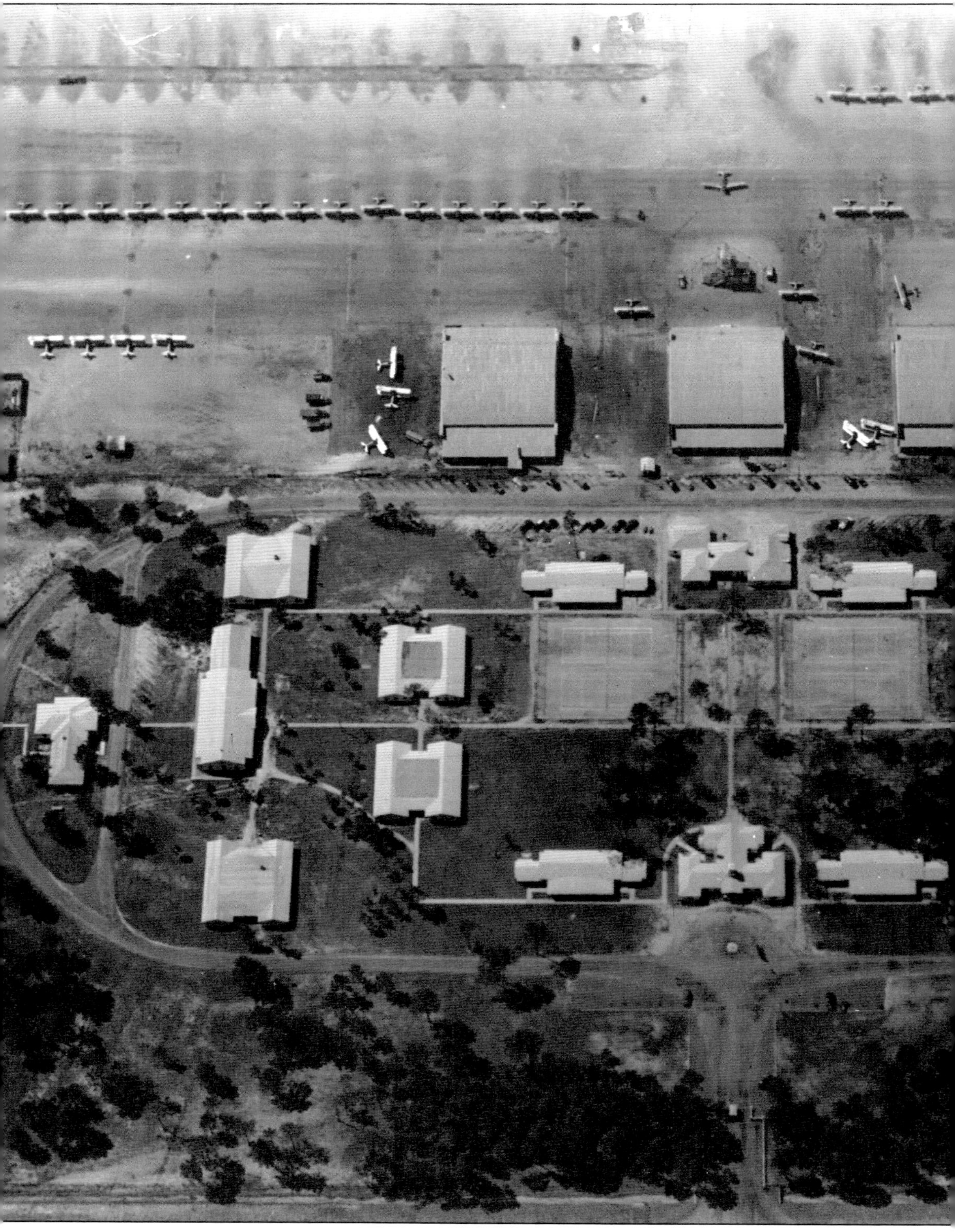

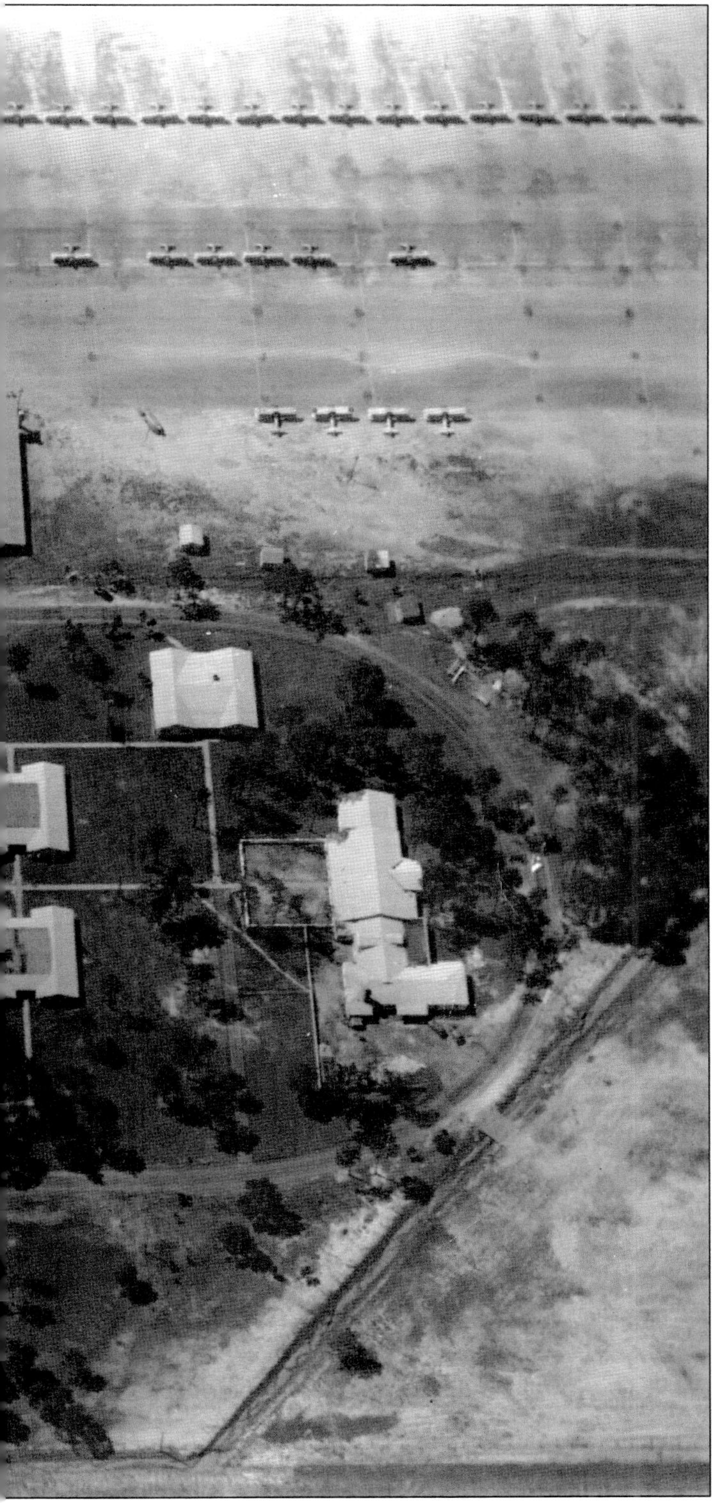

This is a 1943 aerial view of the flight school. Nine of the original buildings, the flagpole, and two hangars are still standing. The hangar to the far right and tower are now gone, and the runway has been enlarged. After the flight school closed in 1948, the buildings housed military surplus, provided a training site for the Douglas Reds, served as the home of Satilla Elementary School and the hatchery, and for a period operated as the local Georgia Bureau of Investigation facility. Today, this is the location of the Douglas Municipal Airport, the World War II Flight Training Museum, and Brooks Aviation. In addition to the functions the buildings have served over the years, the runway was extended to provide room for corporate jets to allow TRW to bring its industry to the area. (Courtesy of World War II Flight Training Museum, Don Brooks.)

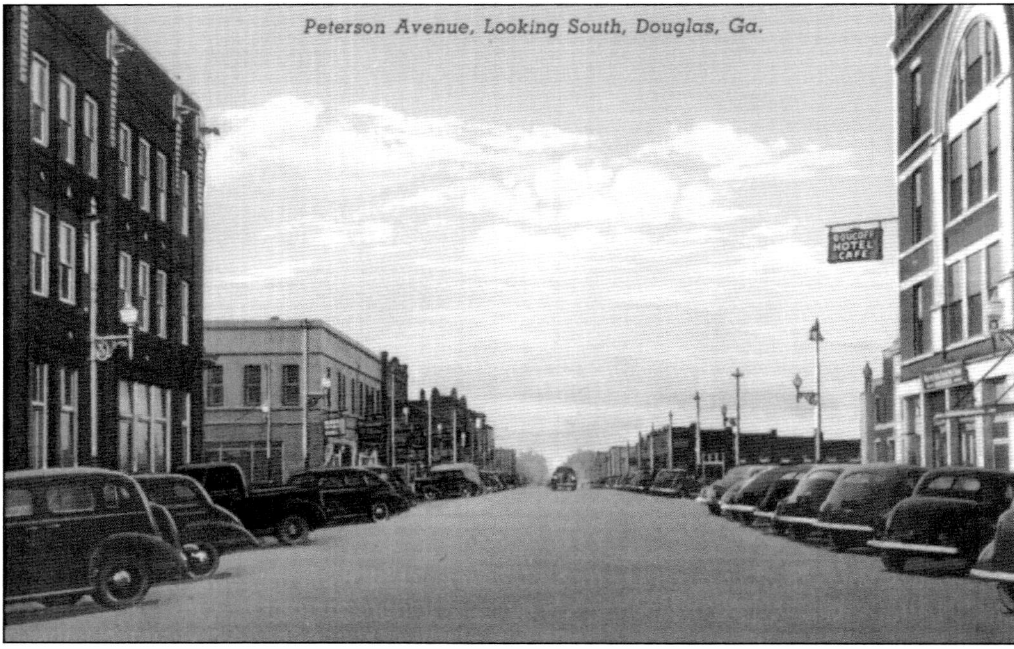

This is North Peterson Avenue looking south. To the right is the Doucoff Hotel, which burned in 1954. To the left is the Coffee County Bank, which is now Branch Banking & Trust Company (BB&T). Note the direction of the parking and the traffic; Peterson Avenue was not a one-way street at this time. (Courtesy of Joanne Hanna Lott.)

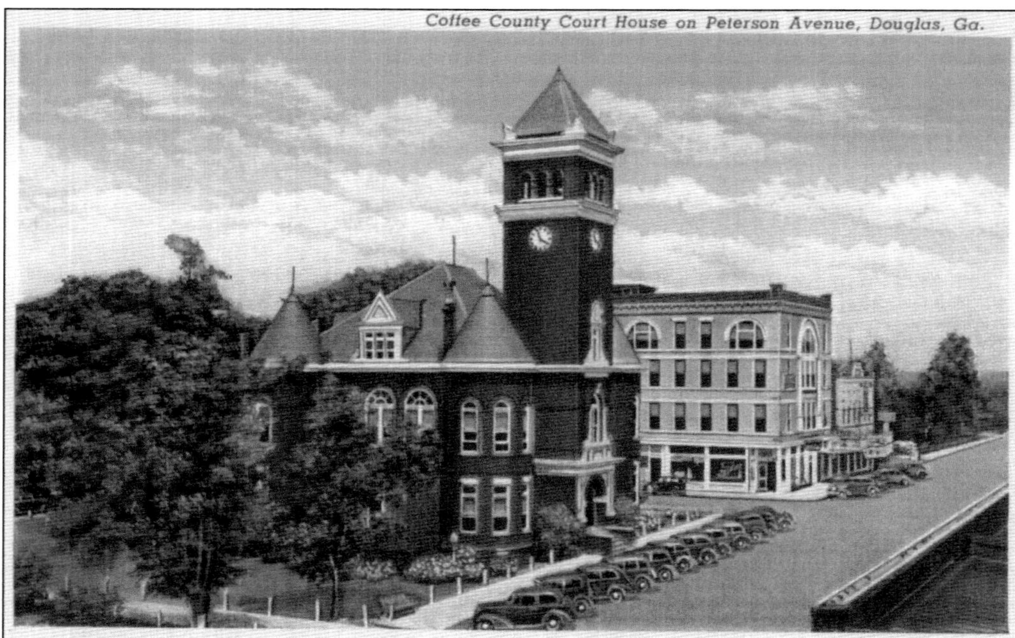

This is a bird's-eye view from the top of the Lankford Building looking north towards the old courthouse and Doucoff Hotel. (Courtesy of Joanne Hanna Lott.)

Five

THE BOYS ARE HOME

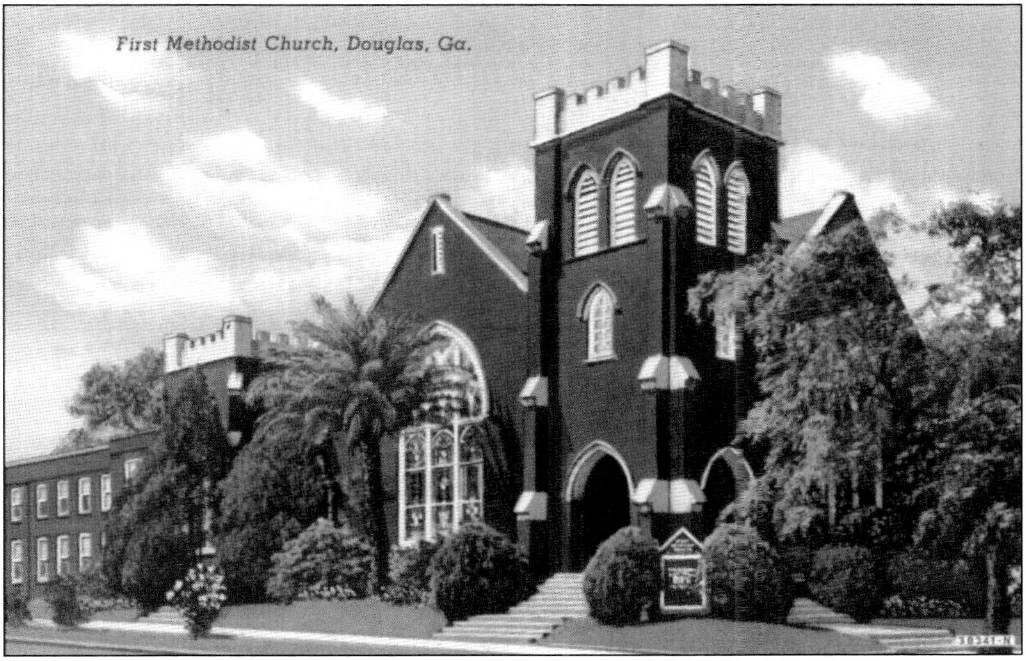

The first Boy Scout troop in Douglas was sponsored by the First United Methodist Church. The congregation's family and community activities had flourished with the new baby boomer population. As a result, the church needed a new parsonage, educational wing, church school annex, and sanctuary, as well as repair of the turret that was collapsing. To make room for these services, the church acquired the deed to the entire city block. Seen here is the building after the turret collapsed but before reconstruction was complete. (Courtesy of Joanne Hanna Lott.)

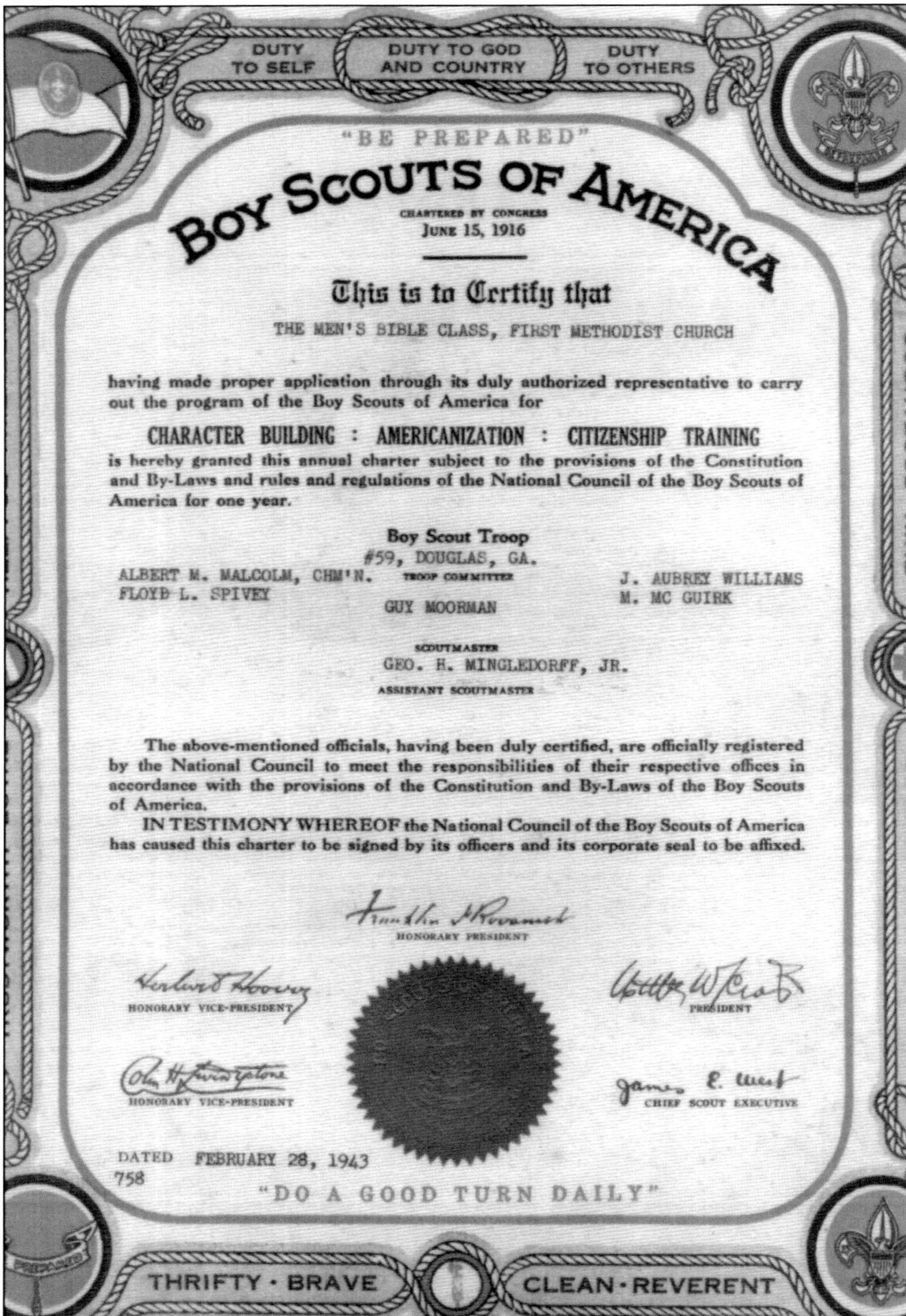
DUTY TO SELF
DUTY TO GOD AND COUNTRY
DUTY TO OTHERS

"BE PREPARED"

BOY SCOUTS OF AMERICA

CHARTERED BY CONGRESS
JUNE 15, 1916

This is to Certify that

THE MEN'S BIBLE CLASS, FIRST METHODIST CHURCH

having made proper application through its duly authorized representative to carry out the program of the Boy Scouts of America for

CHARACTER BUILDING : AMERICANIZATION : CITIZENSHIP TRAINING

is hereby granted this annual charter subject to the provisions of the Constitution and By-Laws and rules and regulations of the National Council of the Boy Scouts of America for one year.

Boy Scout Troop
#59, DOUGLAS, GA.

ALBERT M. MALCOLM, CHM'N.
FLOYD L. SPIVEY
TROOP COMMITTEE
GUY MOORMAN
J. AUBREY WILLIAMS
M. MC GUIRK

SCOUTMASTER
GEO. H. MINGLEDORFF, JR.
ASSISTANT SCOUTMASTER

The above-mentioned officials, having been duly certified, are officially registered by the National Council to meet the responsibilities of their respective offices in accordance with the provisions of the Constitution and By-Laws of the Boy Scouts of America.

IN TESTIMONY WHEREOF the National Council of the Boy Scouts of America has caused this charter to be signed by its officers and its corporate seal to be affixed.

Franklin D Roosevelt
HONORARY PRESIDENT

Herbert Hoover
HONORARY VICE-PRESIDENT

PRESIDENT

HONORARY VICE-PRESIDENT

James E. West
CHIEF SCOUT EXECUTIVE

DATED FEBRUARY 28, 1943
758

"DO A GOOD TURN DAILY"

THRIFTY · BRAVE
CLEAN · REVERENT

Originally, Boy Scout meetings were held in the schoolhouses under the supervision of Professors C. Williams and T.A. Clower. The first scoutmaster in Douglas was Fred Brewer in 1922. Shown here is the 1943 registration document for Troop No. 59i. (Courtesy of Dr. James A. Cottingham.)

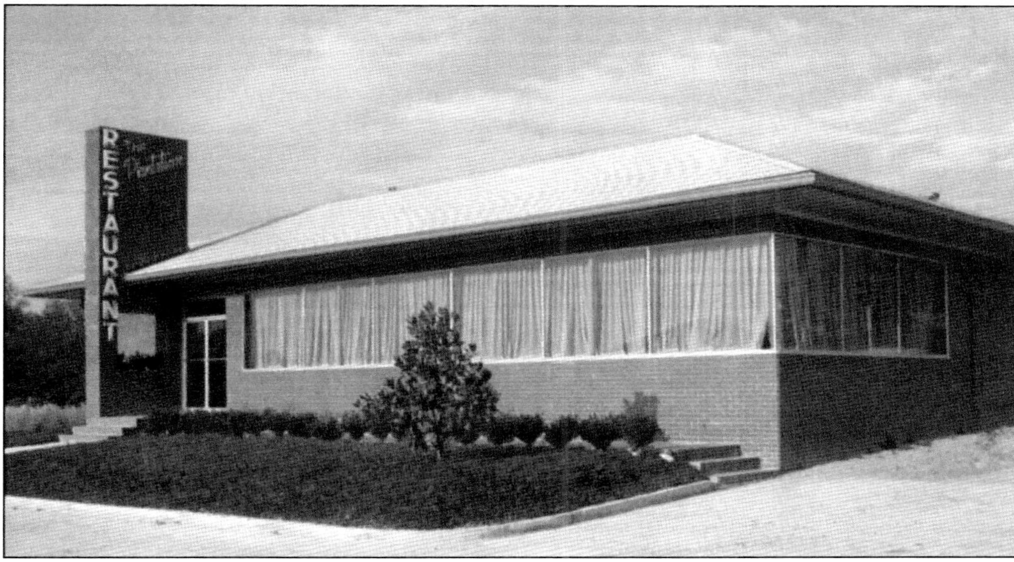

This is the diner-style Plantation Restaurant on the corner of Peterson Avenue and Walker Street. It became a Chinese restaurant in the 1980s and is now home to B&D Used Cars. (Courtesy of Joanne Hanna Lott.)

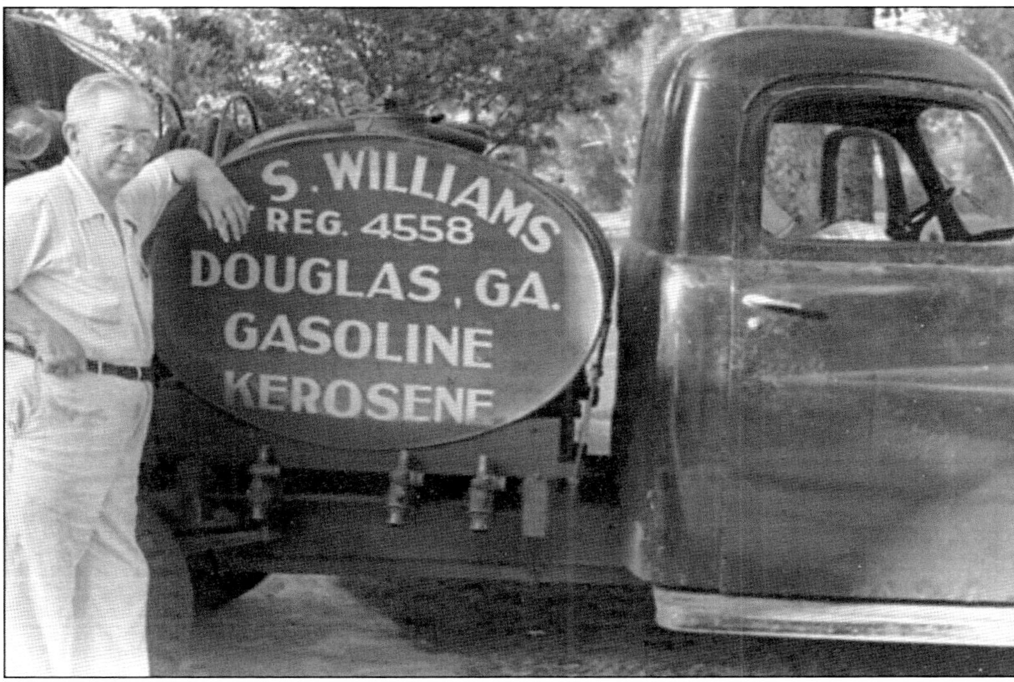

George Dyer poses in front of his family home with a Douglas Kerosene truck. Dyer was the distributor for the Standard Oil Company in Coffee and Atkinson Counties. Standard Oil dominated the oil-production market, streamlining distribution through the railroads in the area. Principle shareholder Henry Flagler was also the developer of the Florida East Coast Railway, which operated through Douglas until the mid-1980s. Standard Oil now operates under Chevron, Exxon, Mobil, and Esso names. (Courtesy of Mary Clyde Scott.)

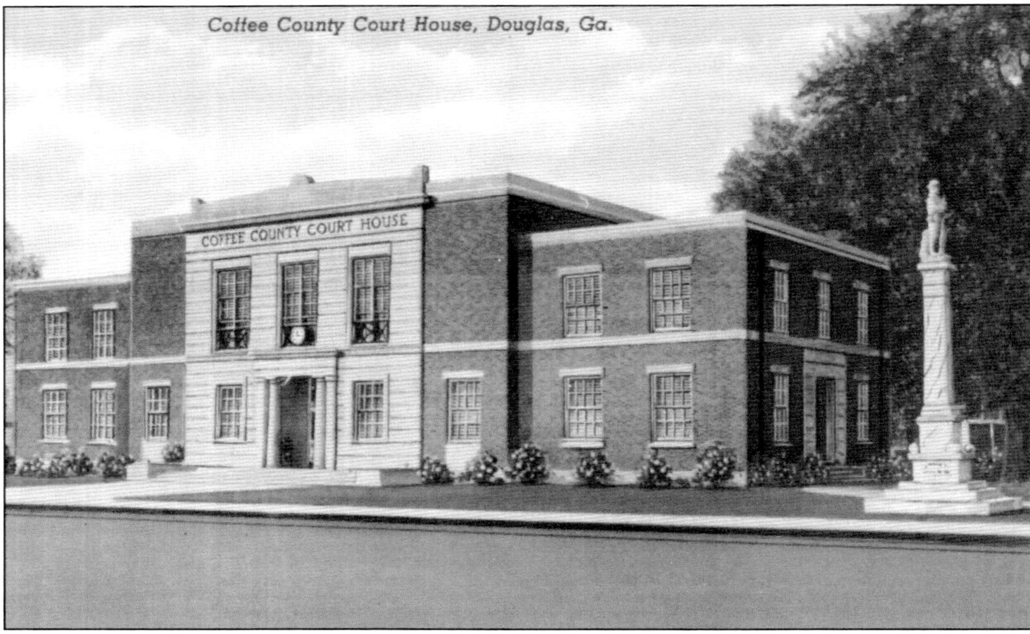

In the late 1930s, the Coffee County Courthouse was destroyed by fire. The new courthouse was built in 1940, and the Confederate monument was relocated to its present position by the courthouse on Peterson Square, facing north. (Courtesy of Joanne Hanna Lott.)

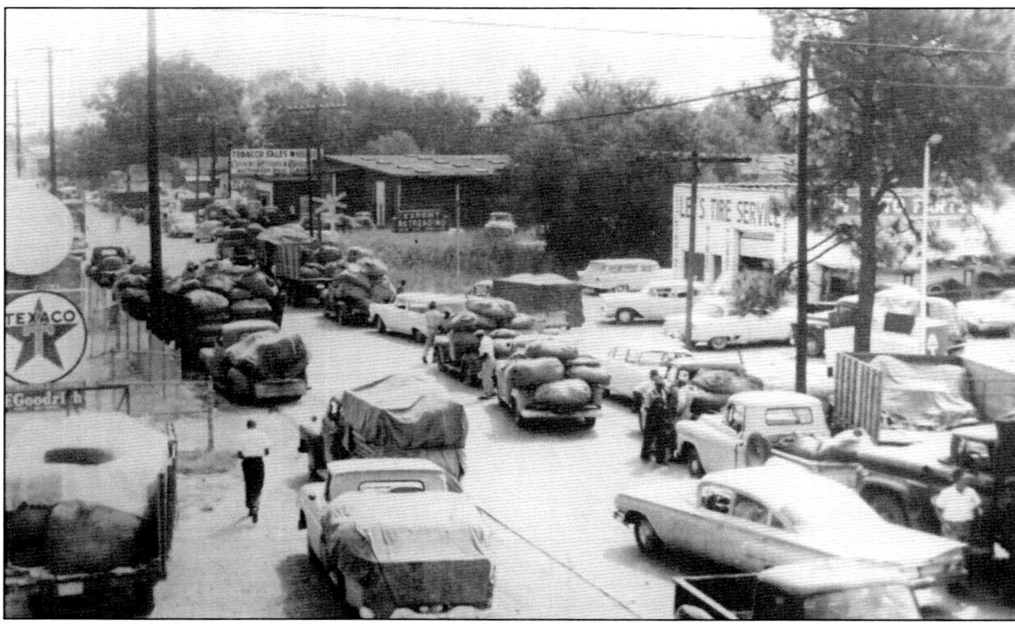

As the tobacco industry was steadily growing stronger, the town held barbeques and hosted political speakers for Market Day. In 1929, the Douglas Tobacco Company employed 400 people to process over three million pounds of tobacco. By 1950, the company employed 750 people to process over 12 million pounds of tobacco. Pictured is a street scene at the tobacco market. (Courtesy of Douglas-Coffee County Chamber of Commerce.)

Members of the Meeks family have been recognized leaders in the local agricultural community for decades. They were the first in the area to try several innovations, including deep wells, corn bins, irrigation, and raising hogs in confinement. Pictured around 1963 at the Douglas Tobacco Market are Roscoe and Martha with sons Tim (left), Tom (center), and John. (Courtesy of Martha Meeks.)

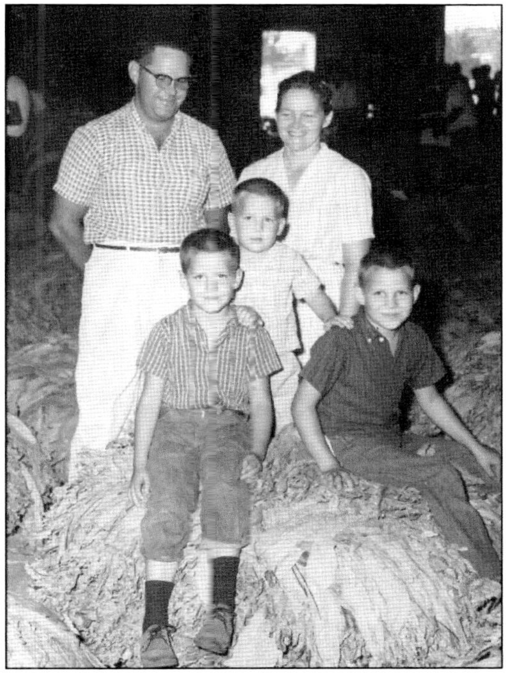

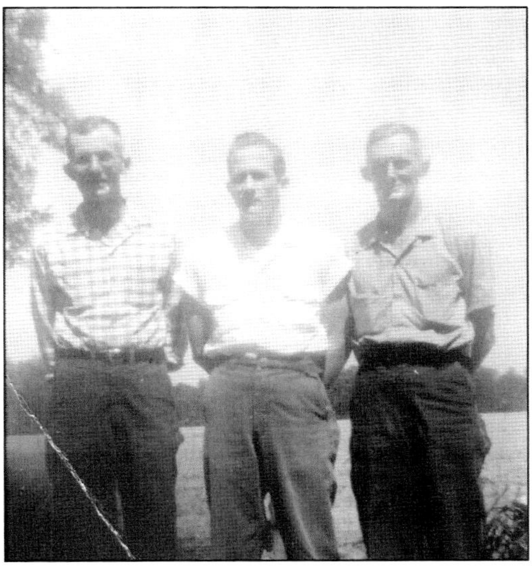

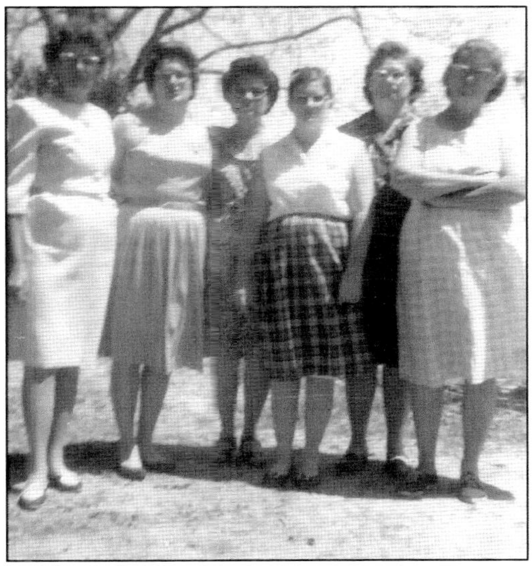

Andrew Jackson Hutchison came from South Carolina as a young man in 1870 and stayed for a short time in Irwin County. After he married and had children, he settled the family on the border of Atkinson and Coffee Counties. The Hutchison family sharecropped cotton and tobacco. Sharecropping was the agricultural labor system developed after the Civil War, which lasted in the South as late as the 1940s. Nearly a third of the state's agriculture was worked by sharecroppers. Landowners employed individuals to work the land in exchange for a share of the crops and in some cases allowed tenancy. Pictured here are the children of Andrew Hutchison's youngest son, Jacob Reason, and wife Vennie Boutwell. They are, from left to right, John "J.B.", George, Tommy, Rosa Lee, Claudine, Lucille, Florine, Mattie, and Melissa "Toad." (Courtesy of Rose Ann Martin.)

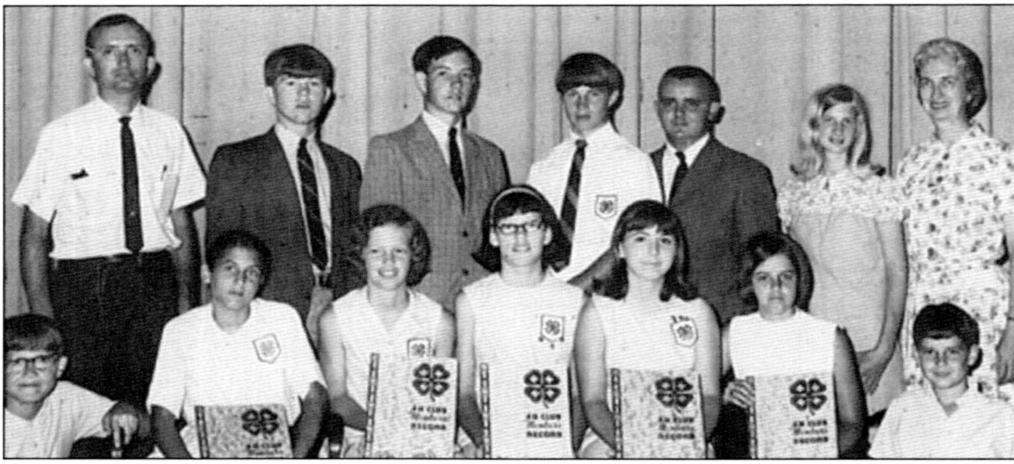

4-H began as a response to needs throughout the country rather than as the idea of one individual. The goal of the program was to extend agricultural education to rural youth by organizing boys' and girls' clubs and through "learning by doing." With the United States's entry into World War II, 4-H members across the country responded to the needs for increased agricultural production and support of the war effort. They were directly responsible for more than 77,000 head of dairy cattle, 246,000 swine, and 210,000 nondairy cattle. The organization contributed more than 40,000 tons of forage crops and 109,000 bushels of root crops. By 1942, 4-H had 1.6 million members, gaining 650,000 new members during the war. (Courtesy of JoAnne Ray Lewis.)

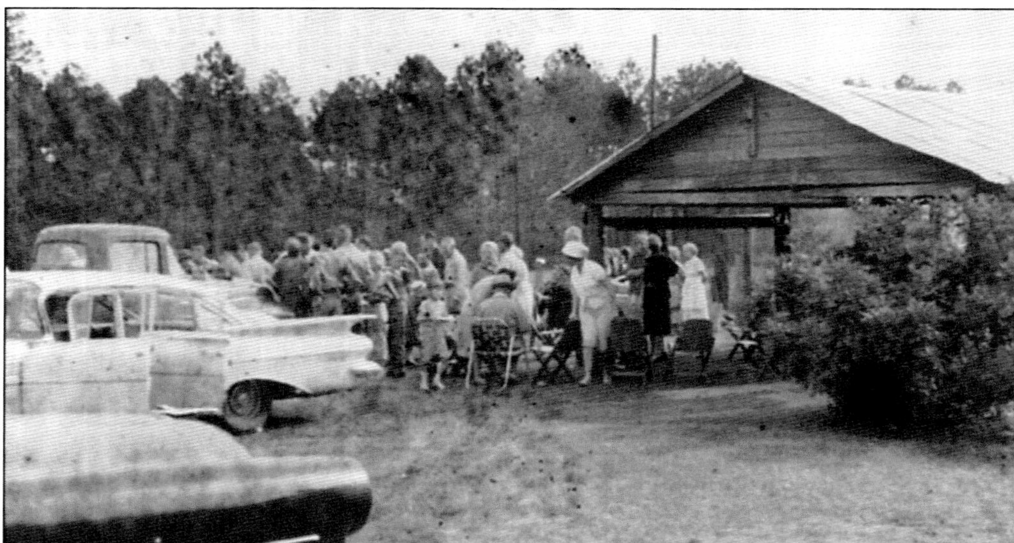

Early pioneers in the Wiregrass Region practiced variations of the Sacred Harp tradition, including singing schools and "walking time." Walking time is the activity of walking counter-clockwise to the beat of the music and is still done in Primitive Baptist churches in the area. While some still practice the Sacred Harp tradition, gospel sings and church picnics with the Methodist and Baptist churches increasingly replaced the singing schools and "dinners on the ground." Dinners on the ground were an all-day singing and fellowship event, which occurred outside with food eaten picnic style. Now, most churches have a fellowship hall and the tradition is rarely seen. Pictured is a church picnic in the West Green community. (Courtesy of JoAnne Ray Lewis.)

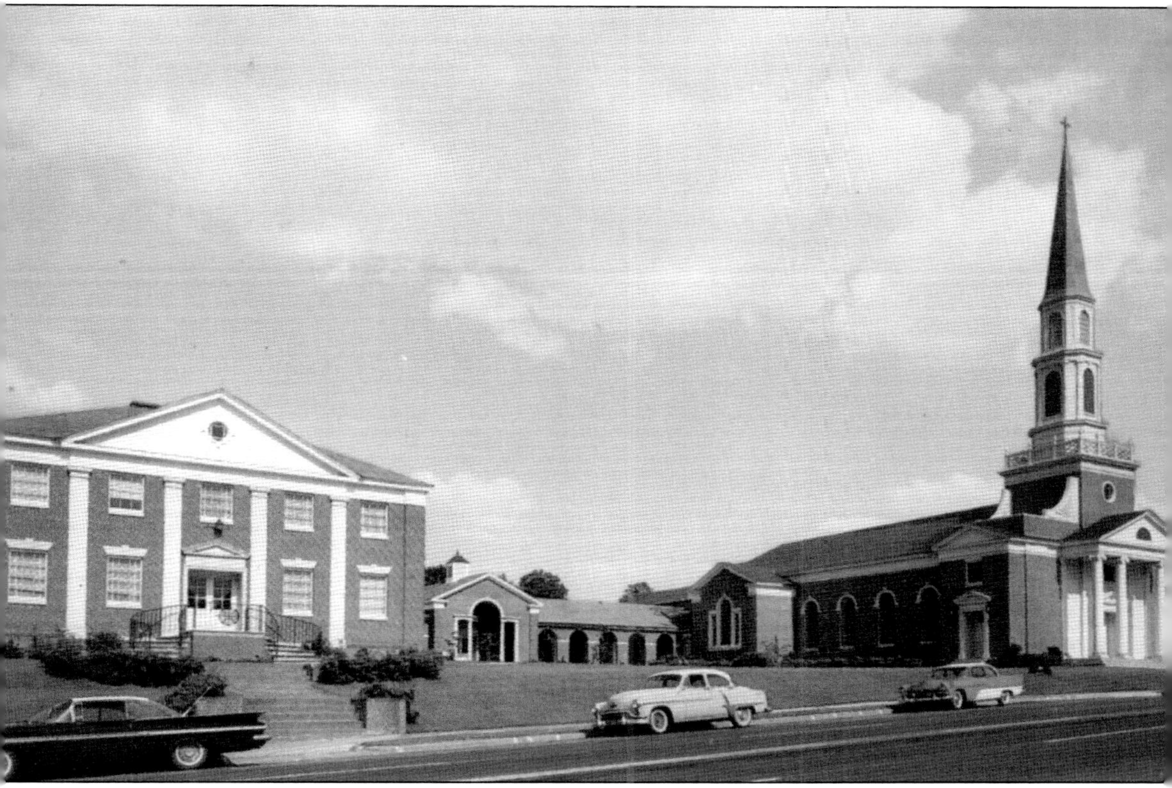

After almost two decades of reconstructing and annexing new wings, the congregation of the First United Methodist Church was able to enjoy their new building. The education wing was completed in the 1950s, and the new sanctuary was dedicated on Easter Sunday in 1960. Pictured is the expanded First United Methodist Church of Douglas on Peterson Avenue. (Courtesy of Joanne Hanna Lott.)

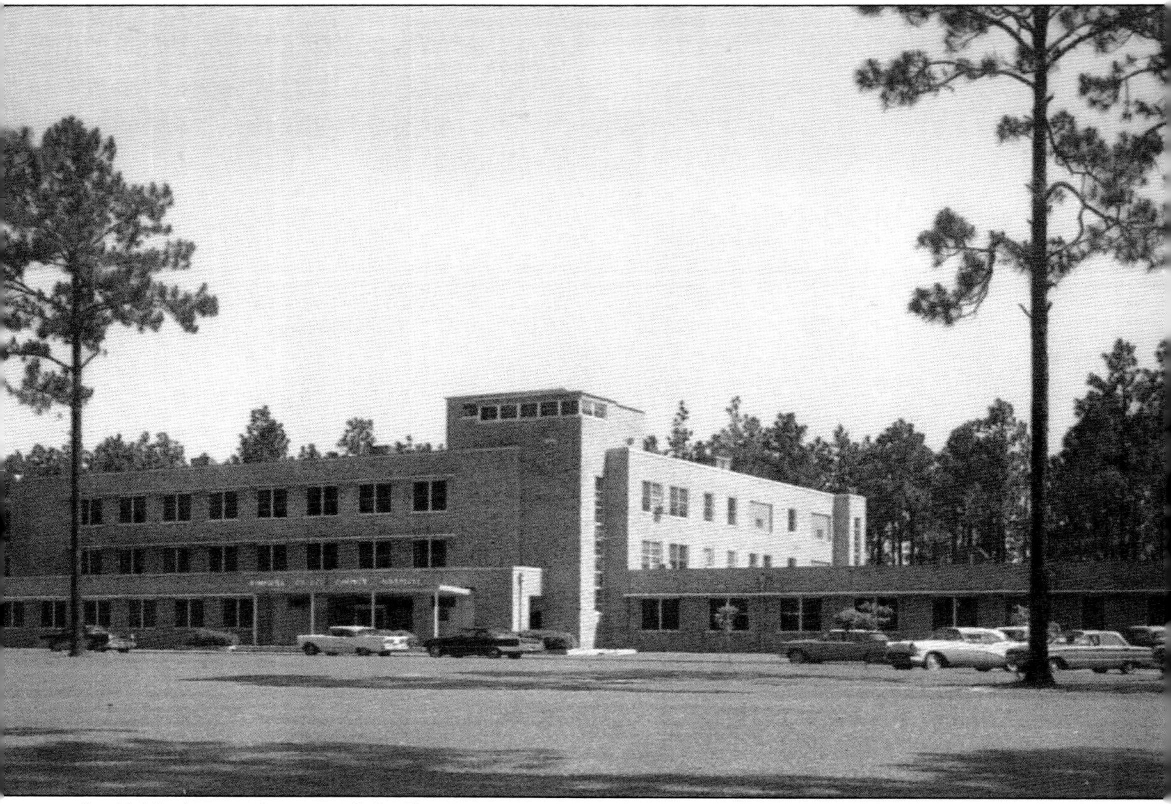

In 1946, the newly created Coffee County Hospital Authority applied for available federal funds through the recently passed Hill-Burton Act, which was designed to help states improve the nation's hospital system. Citizens voted overwhelmingly to provide necessary matching funds, and Mayor Lonnie Pope donated land for a three-story, 60-bed facility. (Courtesy of Joanne Hanna Lott.)

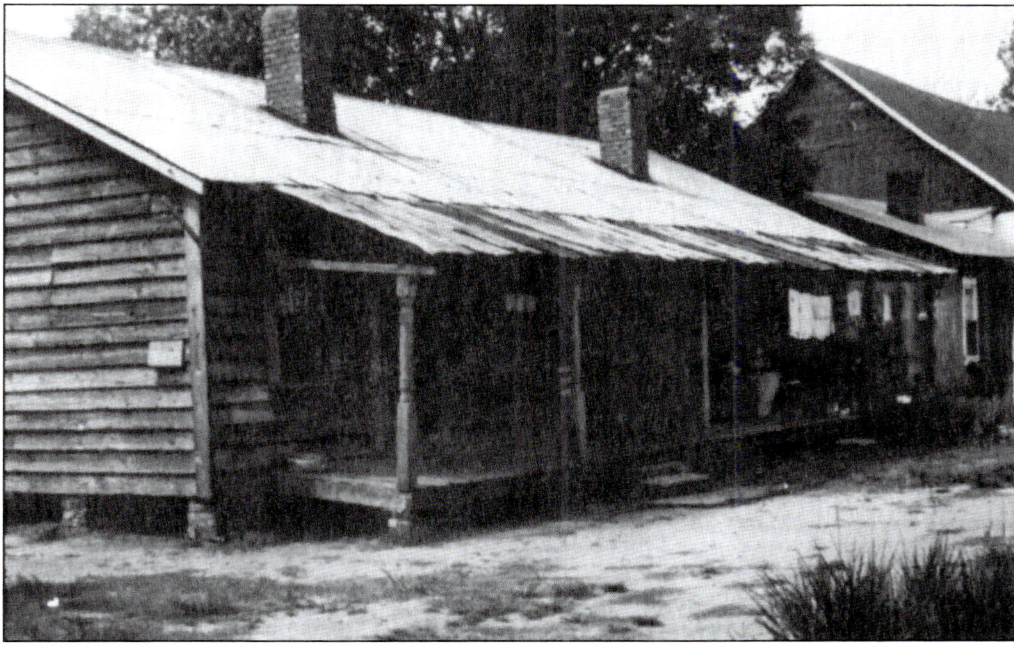

Just a few years later, in 1955, Douglas was faced with a crisis. Business was down, homes were empty, and the city was dying. Without jobs, people were forced to leave or commute out of town for work. This image shows a group of homes on "Rat Row." (Courtesy of Yvonne Brock.)

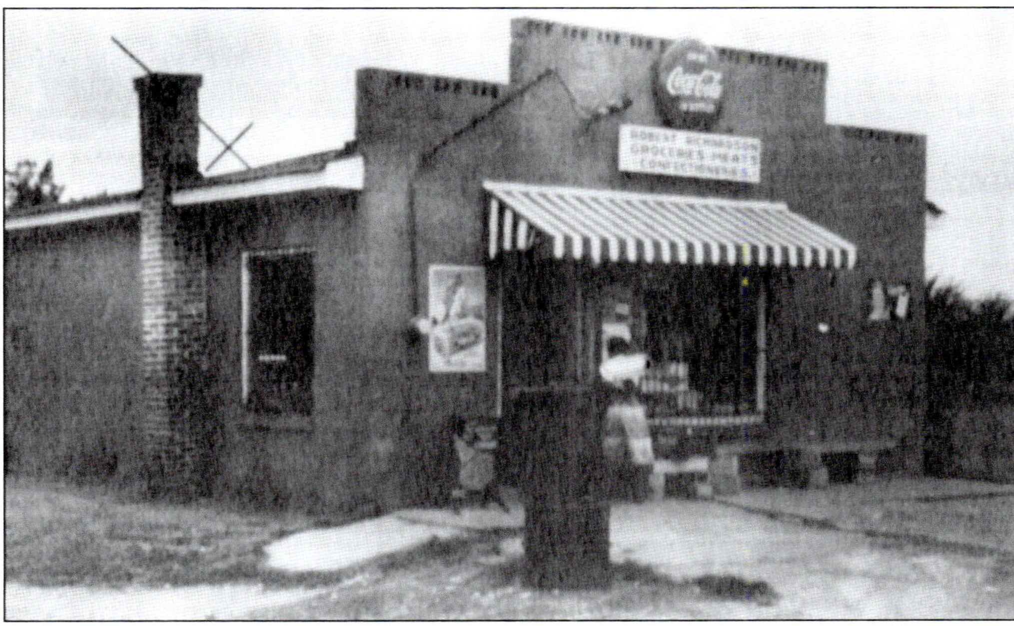

The rundown areas of town made it difficult to convince residents to stay in Douglas, and the lack of adequate housing provided little reason for anyone to move to town. There were few local jobs available, and Douglas could not attract new businesses, as it was in shambles. Big businesses wanted to locate to growing, thriving areas, but Douglas looked like a ghost town. (Courtesy of Yvonne Brock.)

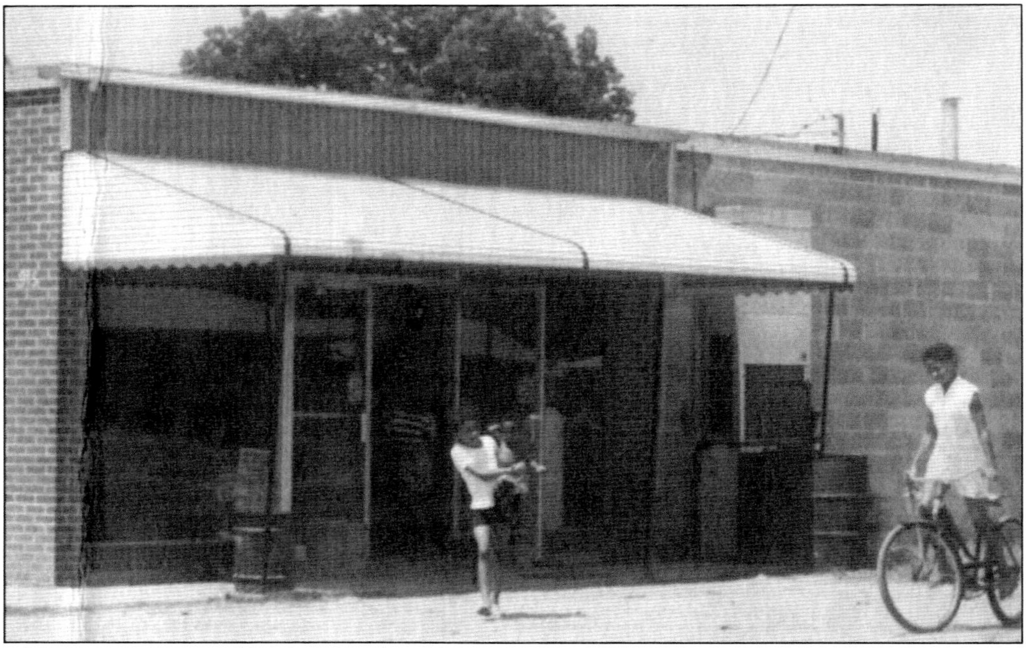

The new store pictured here replaced one located in the area locally known as Rat Row. (Courtesy of Yvonne Brock.)

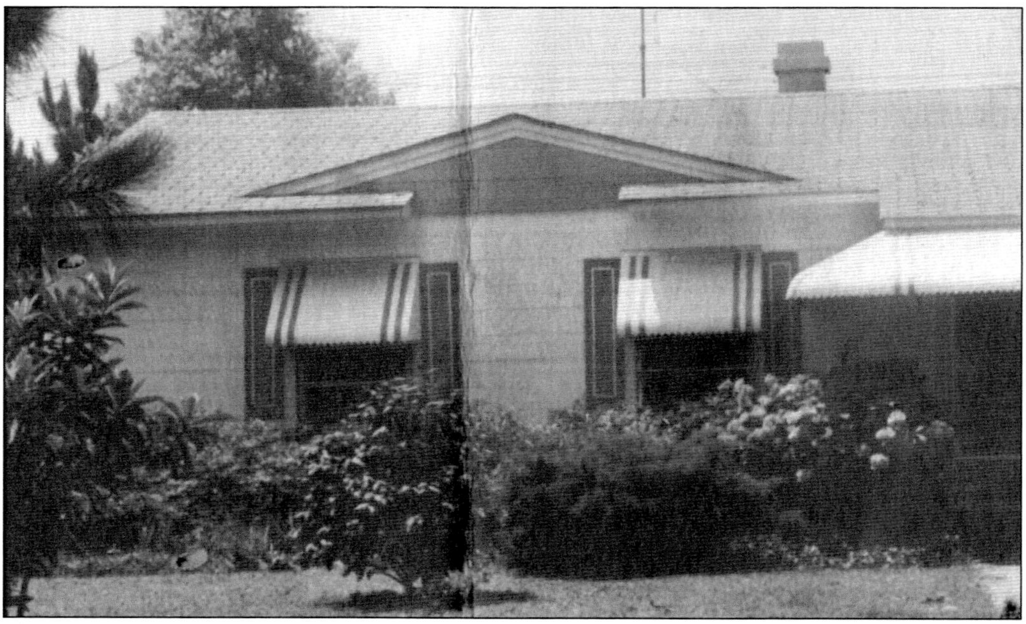

Shown is a new home for a former resident of the "Rat Row" area. Rat Row included single mothers, widows, the elderly, and the sick who could not afford owning a new home. Wendell Sears went door to door seeking funding from private citizens and banks to pay for new homes, as there was no governmental assistance available at the time. Sears's methods were novel and won him awards for urban renewal. He went on to demonstrate these practices to cities and states all over the country. (Courtesy of Yvonne Brock.)

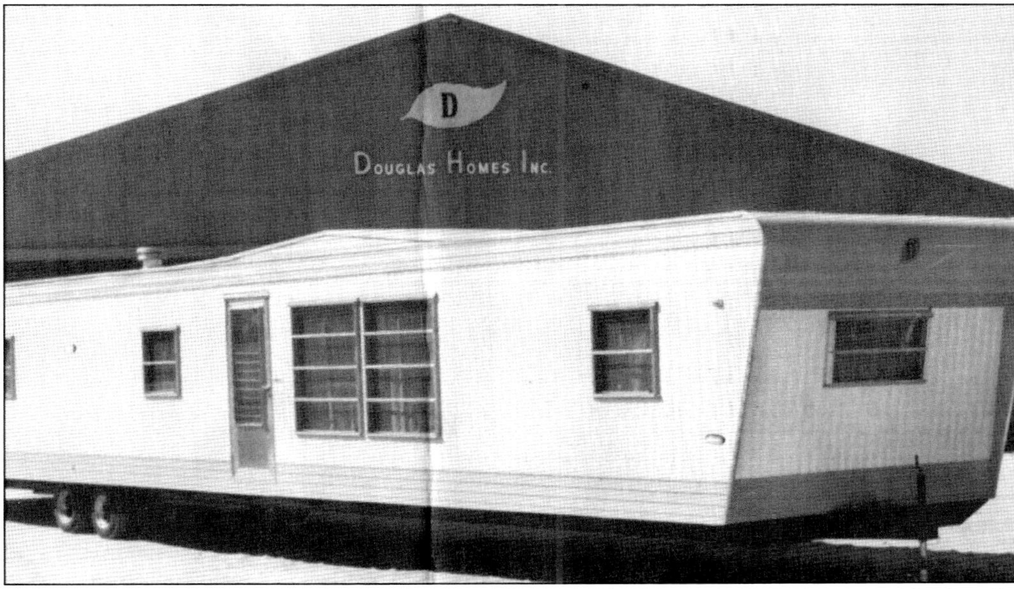

Pictured is the first mobile home for Douglas Homes, Inc. The company was actively involved in the General Neighborhood Renewal Plan that Wendell Sears created. (Courtesy of Yvonne Brock.)

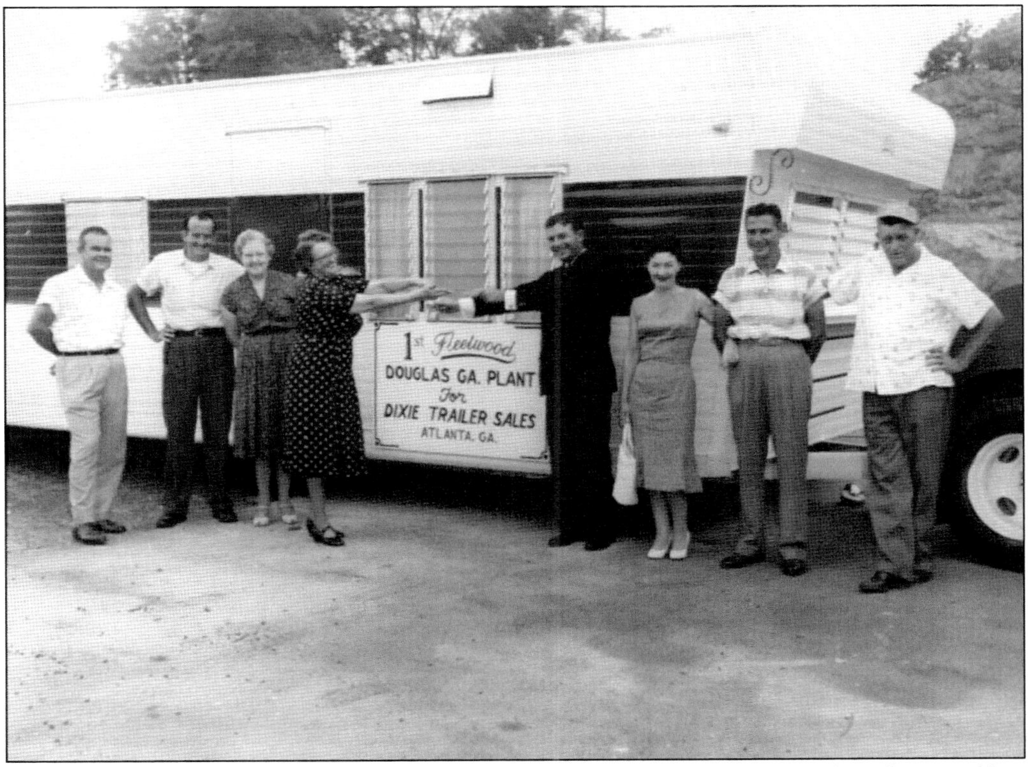

Shown is the first mobile home manufactured at the Fleetwood plant in Douglas. Fleetwood has been producing these homes since 1950. This one was made for Dixie Trailer Sales in Atlanta. (Courtesy of Douglas-Coffee County Chamber of Commerce.)

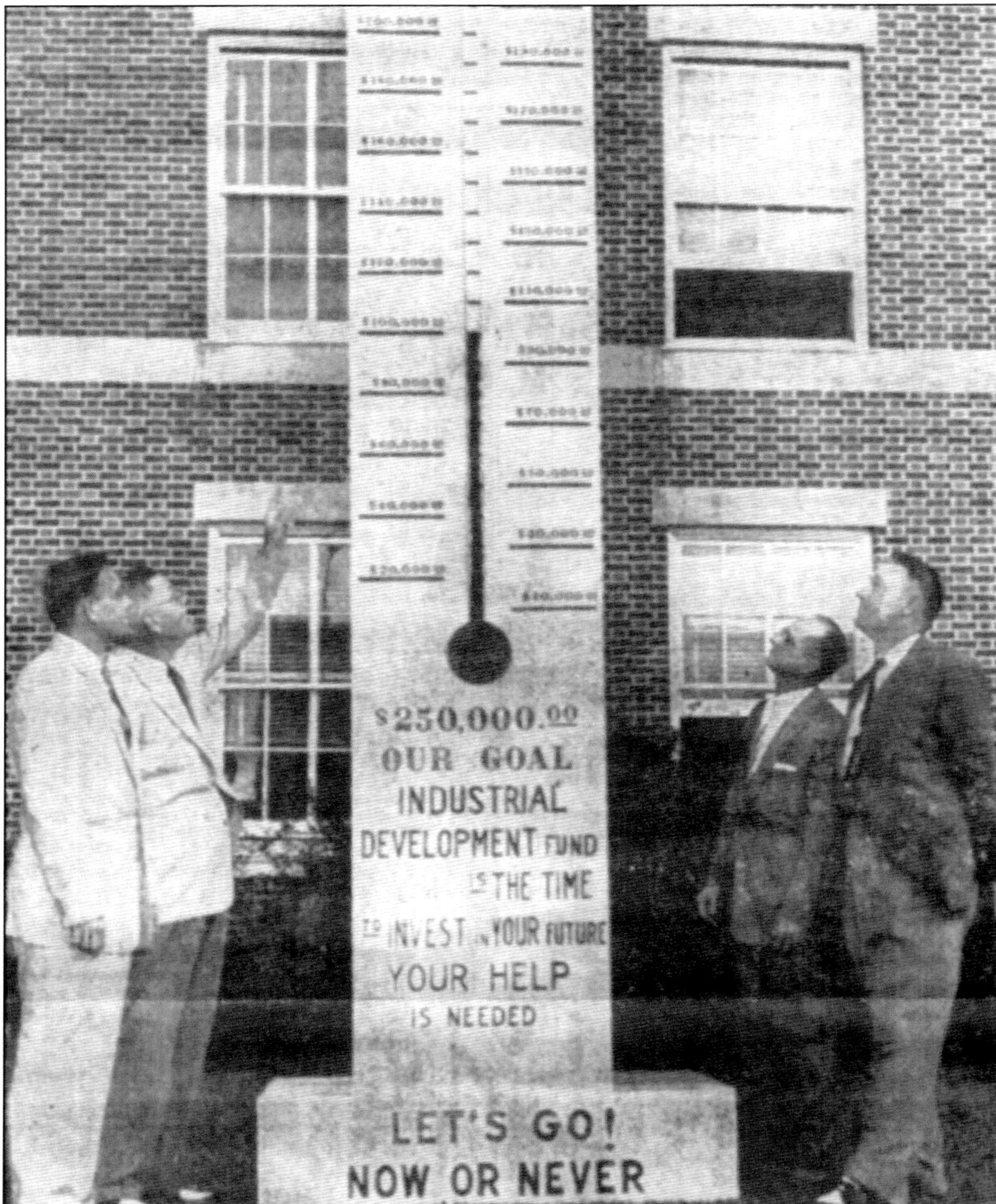

In 1957, the City of Douglas created an industrial development campaign. In two weeks, citizens raised $250,000; pennies were even collected from schoolchildren. This amount is astounding when considering that the average person made $8 a day at the time and that there were fewer than 10,000 citizen in town. The Industrial Development Authority has now established five industrial parks for the city. (Courtesy of Douglas-Coffee County Chamber of Commerce.)

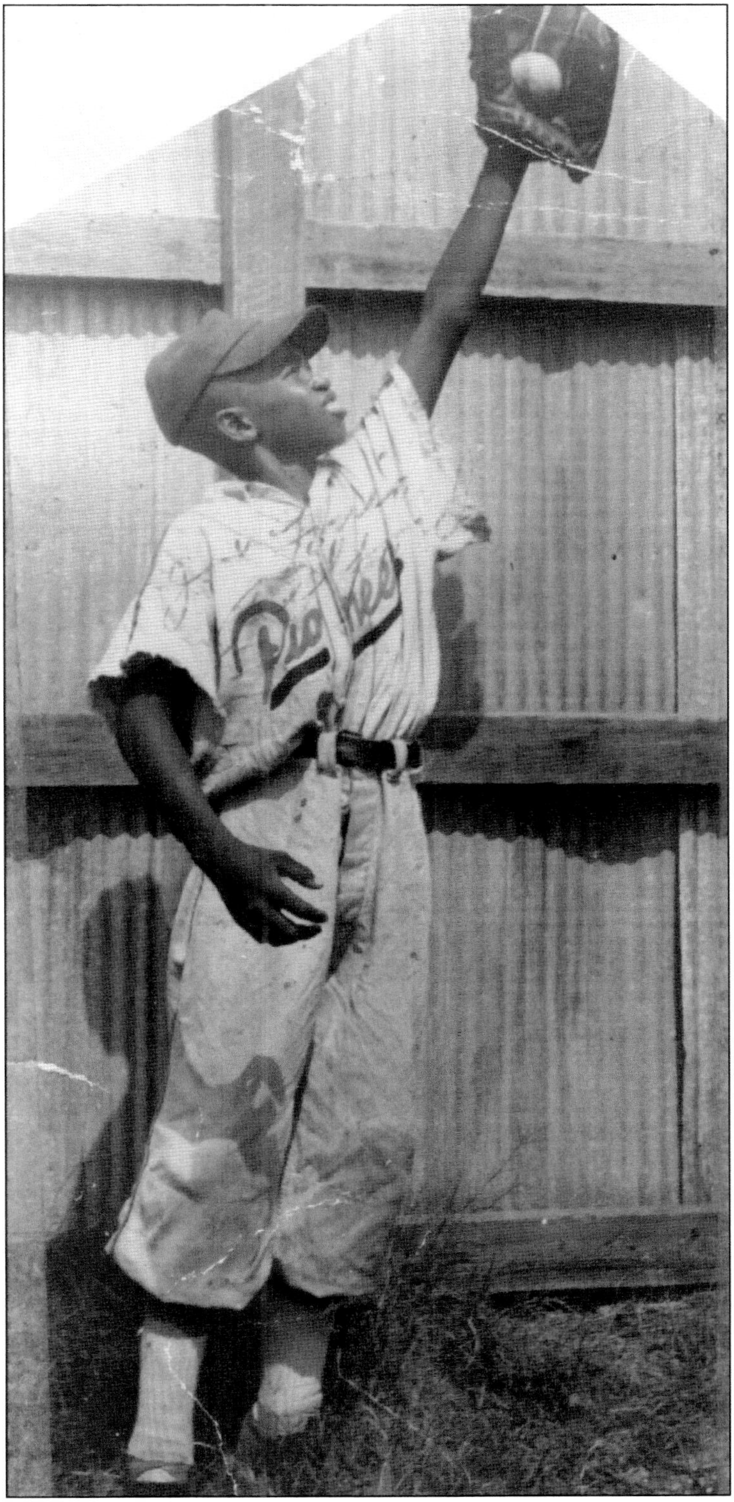

Joe Reliford was the youngest baseball player to ever play in a professional game and the first African American to play in the segregated Georgia State League. Joe's father died when he was four, and his mother was arthritic and raising 10 children alone in south Georgia. Joe just wanted to earn some money to help his mother when he asked to be a batboy for the Fitzgerald Pioneers. One day in 1952, as a joke, folks chanted to put the batboy in the game, and coach Charlie Ridgeway conceded. Reliford played well, surprising everyone. When he caught the ball that ended Harold Shuster's 21-game hitting streak, the crowd went wild. After the game, fans rushed the field. Reliford stated that he did not know what to think of this mob of white people running towards him; he closed his eyes and expected the worst. The crowd, though, came to congratulate the young player—some even stuffed his pockets with money. The Pioneers forfeited the game, and the coach was suspended, but Joe had made history. He later became a fixture in the Douglas community. (Courtesy of Joe Reliford.)

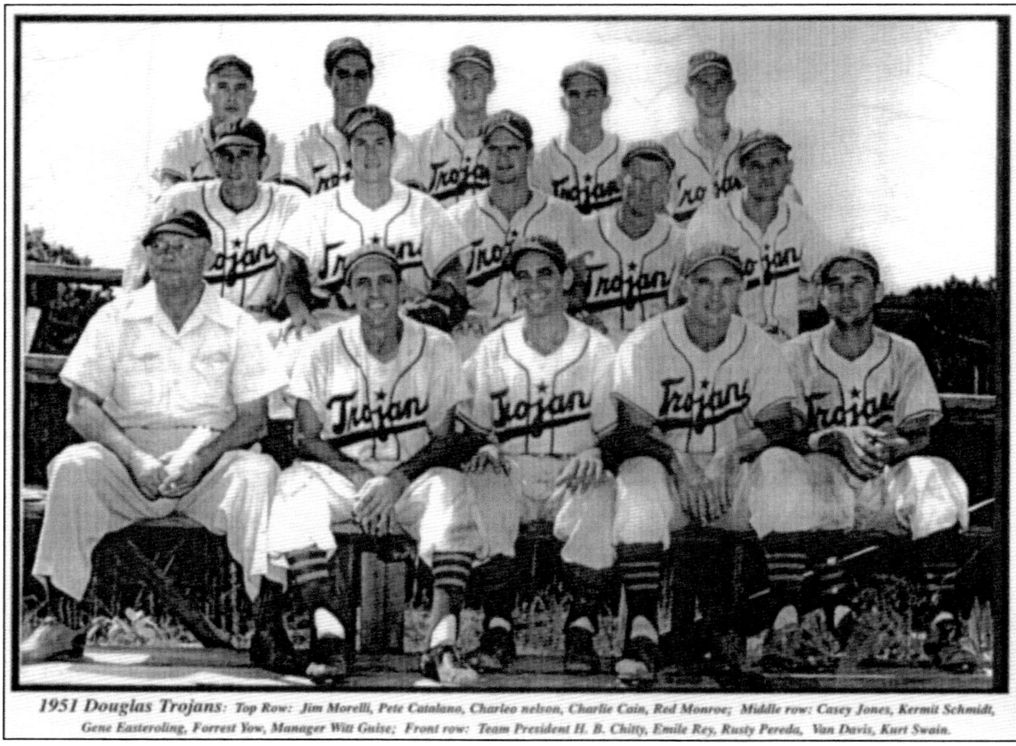

This photograph features the Douglas Trojans of 1951, who played in the Class D Georgia State League. The team was affiliated with the Cincinnati Reds. Eight players from Douglas went on to play in the major leagues, while others found various occupations. Pictured second from the right in the second row is Forest Yow, who came to town with the league, settled in the area, and became a prominent business owner. Douglas enjoyed the presence of the minor-league team from 1948 to 1956. (Courtesy of Cathy Harper.)

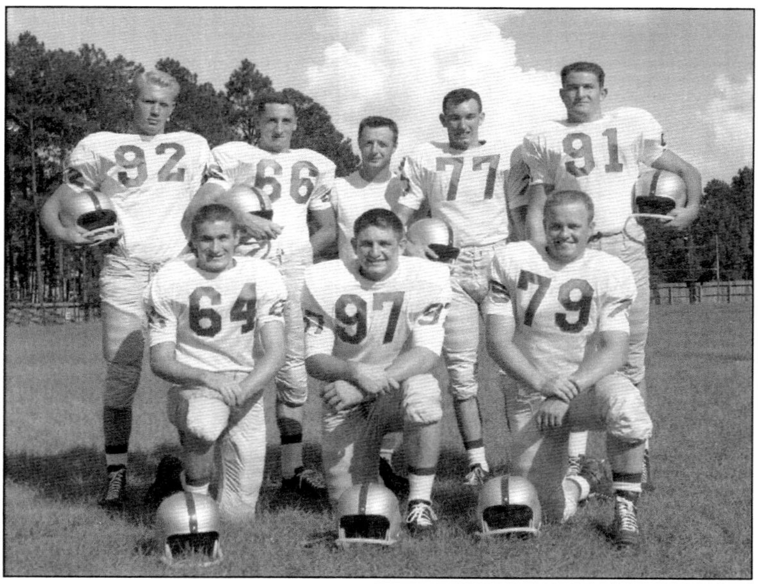

Before Bobby Bowden became the winningest coach in college football history at Florida State University, he was the head coach at South Georgia College (1955–1958). Pictured here are players from the school's 1957 team, along with coach Bowden. (Courtesy of South Georgia State College.)

Six

Cars, Pools, and Plays

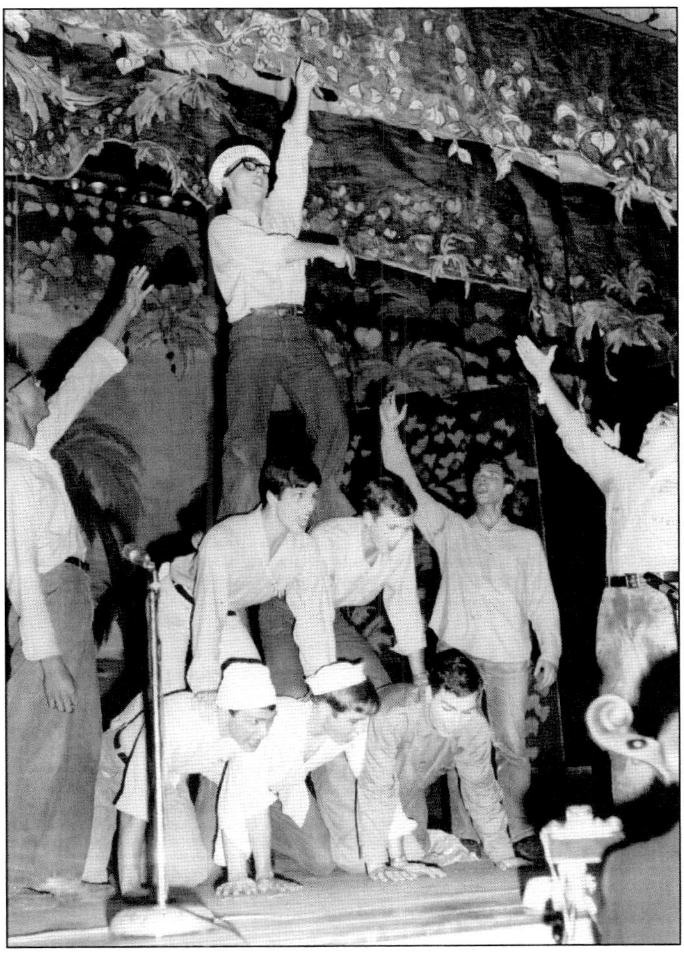

Performing arts surged after the war, and South Georgia College was the site of many plays, concerts, recitals, and other events held both by the college and the community. (Courtesy of South Georgia State College.)

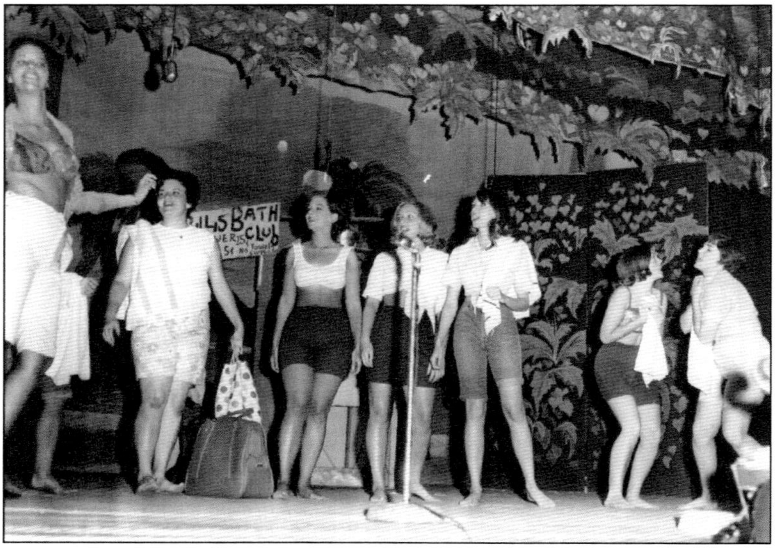

"Sock and Buskin" theater clubs wrote and performed plays held in Peterson Hall. When it was not the students' turn put on a show, they travelled and watched performances at other schools and theaters. There was a similar exchange of arts and performances by the philharmonic clubs. (Courtesy of South Georgia State College.)

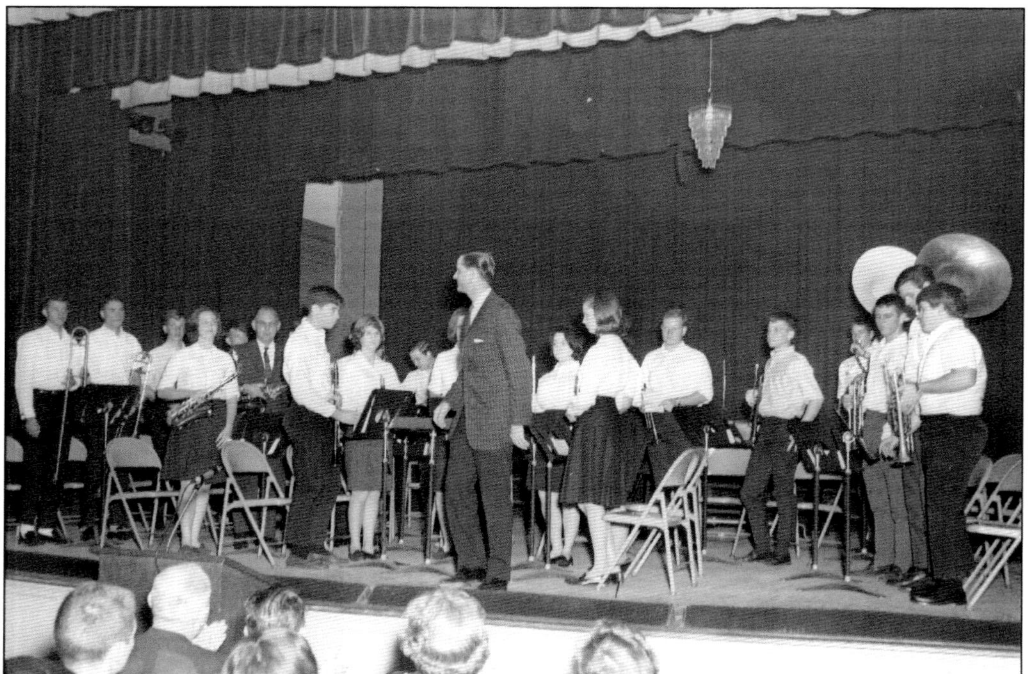

This is a photograph of a local band concert. Music was a bigger business in Georgia in the 1950s than it is today; Atlanta could have easily grown into a recording mecca like Nashville. Gospel, bluegrass, and country music were developed from the traditions of the South. Douglas had seven dance halls and four auditoriums at this time, and many music pioneers made appearances as guest singers at local performances. Douglas was the stomping ground for many greats, including James Brown, who worked here briefly after a stint in prison. (Courtesy of South Georgia State College.)

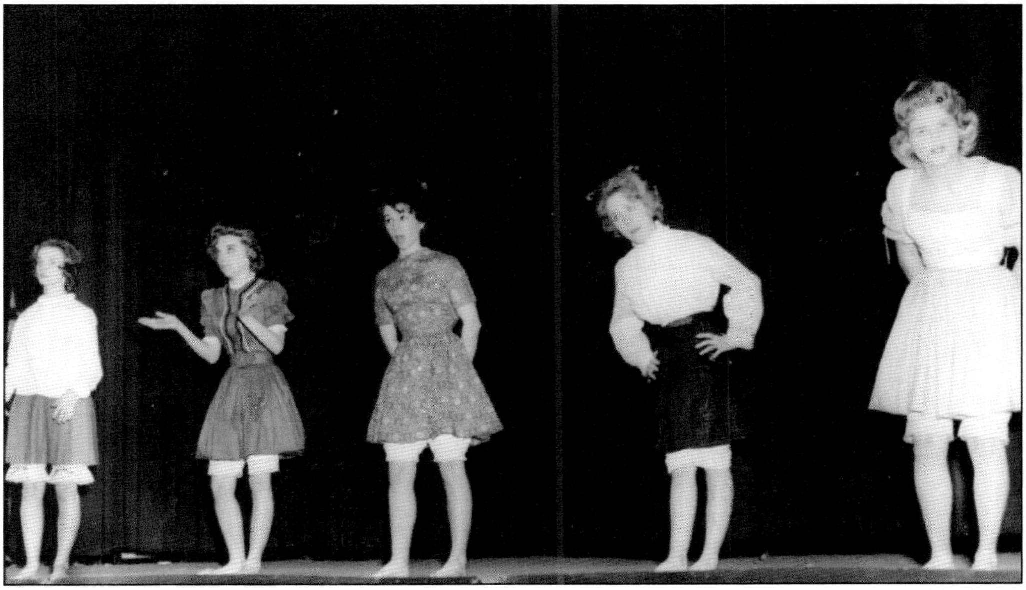

The state YMCA sponsors the Y Club in schools. Often, these clubs are referred to as Hi-Y (for boys) and Tri-Hi-Y (for girls). In 1929, Douglas High School chartered the first Tri-Hi-Y in the nation, which was a huge development for girls everywhere. By 1940, the Y was sponsoring performances by chapel choirs at colleges in Georgia. These choirs performed at schools and churches and also went caroling. (Courtesy of South Georgia State College.)

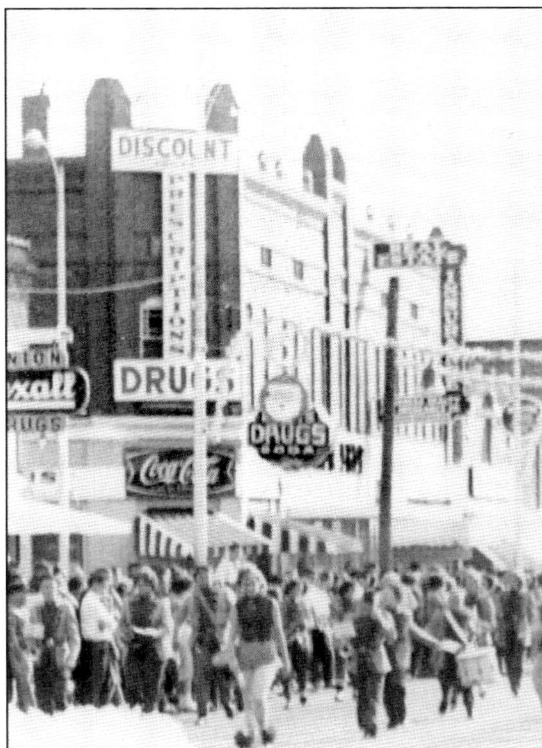

Douglas has a long tradition of parades featuring school bands, churches, local beauty pageant winners, stores, businesses, Boy Scout troops, dance studios, fire trucks, lawn mowers, horses, and people of all ages and from all walks of life. Various people from the county came to town just for work or for their monthly shopping trip, but parades brought everyone to town to celebrate Founders' Day, Homecoming, and Christmas. (Author's collection.)

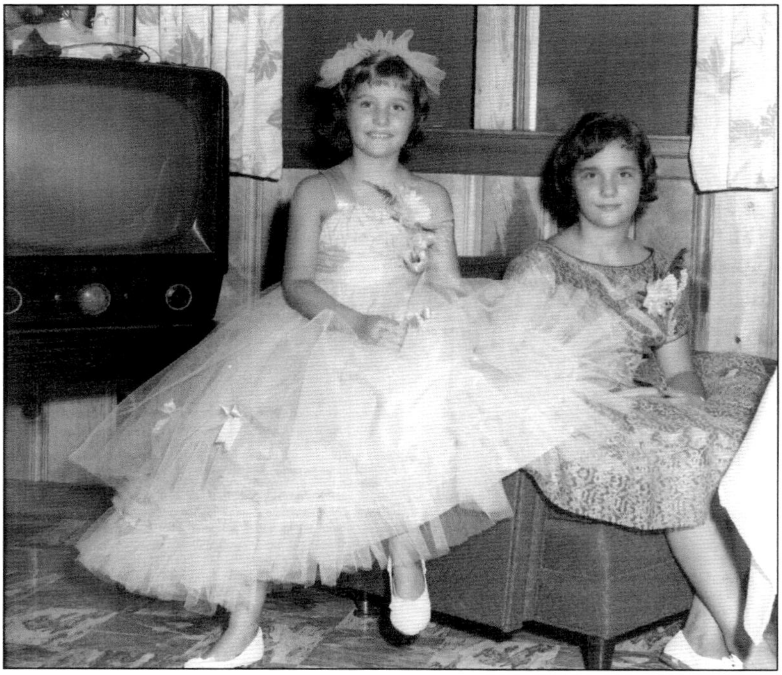

Sisters JoAnne and Carol look like little princesses, all dressed up to go to a piano recital. Today, JoAnne Lewis is president of the Douglas/Coffee County Chamber of Commerce. Carol Morgan is a retired educator. (Courtesy of JoAnne Ray Lewis.)

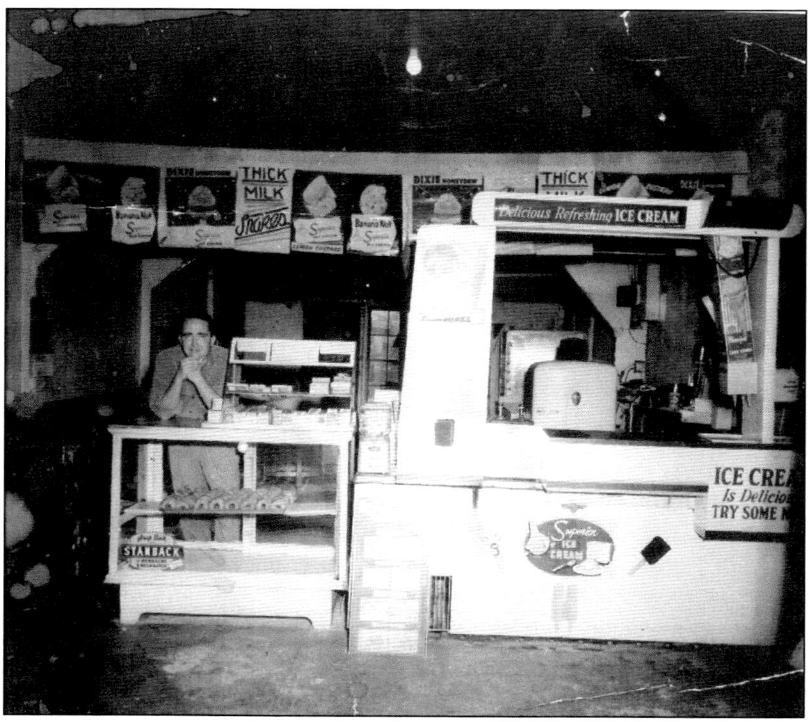

Locals would come and get donut holes here at Ed Smith's shop, The Dixie Cream. In the summer, Smith would scoop ice cream. This shop was located where the Old Town Barbershop currently stands. (Courtesy of John Martin.)

Dewey Hayes Sr. opened his law office in the Brooks Building in 1949. He practiced at that location for several years before moving to the Dickerson Building. He served as district attorney for 25 years and was also a civil advocate. He is shown here speaking at a luncheon for the support staff at public schools. Hayes worked diligently to ensure that veterans received the respect and recognition they deserved and founded the local chapter of the American Legion. (Courtesy of Dewey Hayes Jr.)

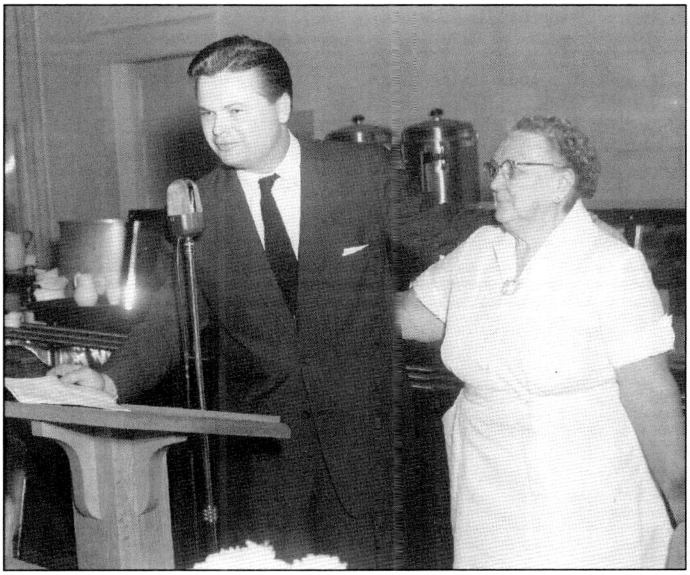

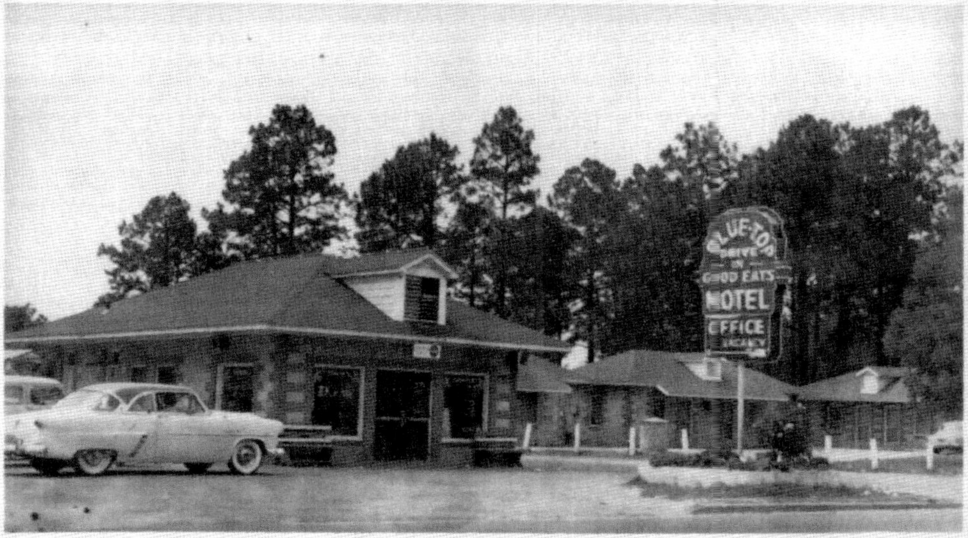

BLUE TOP – 601 N. PETERSON AVE. – DOUGLAS, GA.

In the 1930s in the United States, the lodging industry suffered greatly because of the Depression, and revenues and occupancy were at an all-time low. Just a decade later, though, many middle-class Americans were traveling, and revenues were sky high. New hotels were opened in Douglas. Shown here is the former Blue Top Hotel. (Courtesy of Joanne Hanna Lott.)

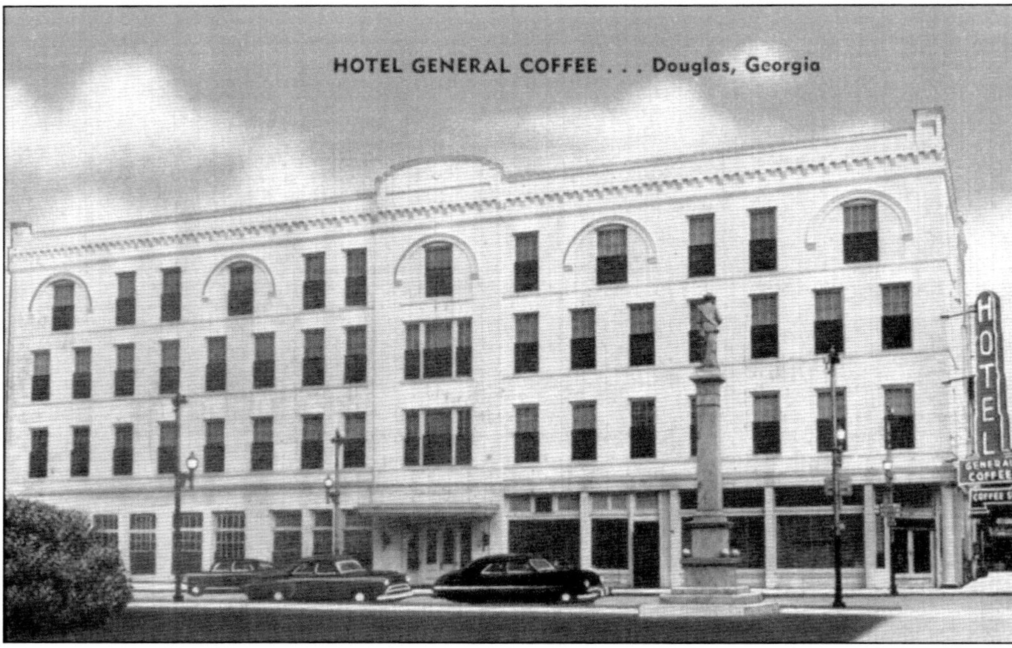

The old Doucoff Hotel changed hands in the late 1950s, and the building reopened as Hotel General Coffee. It was a very prominent hotel in town, and many of the boys training at the flight school stayed here. A coffee shop was located on the east side of the building. (Courtesy of Joanne Hanna Lott.)

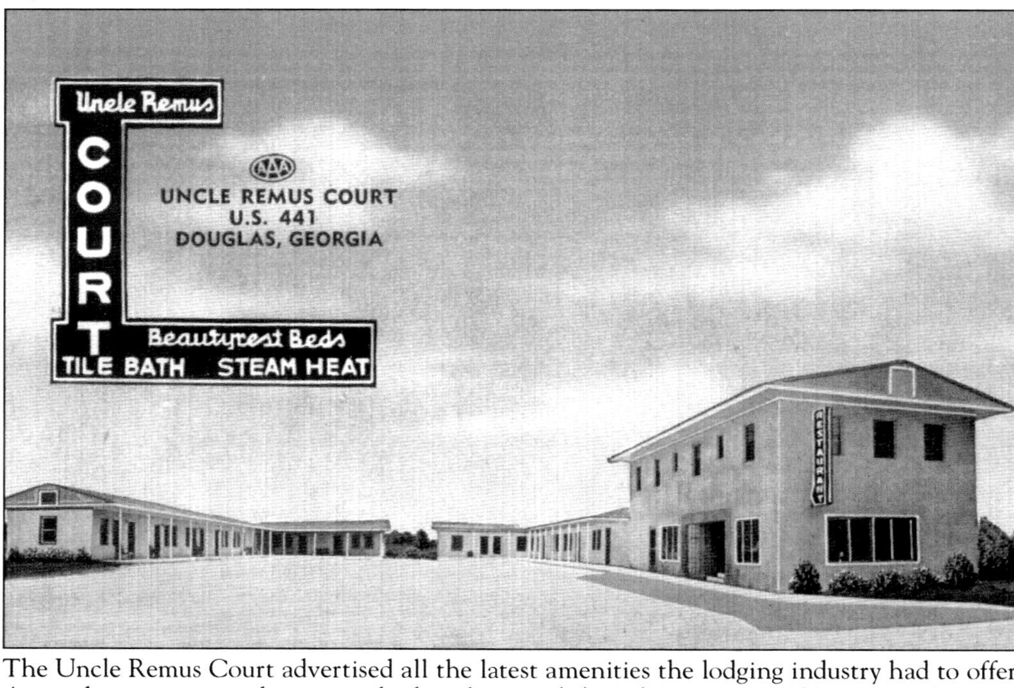

The Uncle Remus Court advertised all the latest amenities the lodging industry had to offer. A trend was recognized in steam baths, along with brand recognition. (Courtesy of Joanne Hanna Lott.)

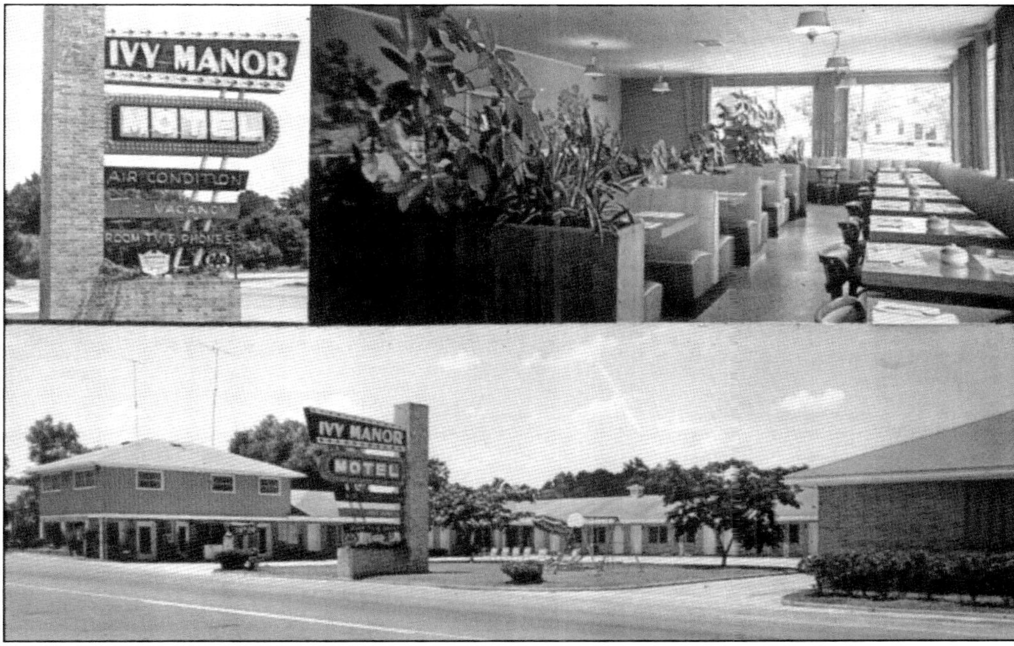

The Ivy Manor Hotel provided top-of-the-line accommodations in the 1950s, offering guests air-conditioning, phones, and televisions in each room. The air-conditioning alone made it a welcoming place to stay in balmy south Georgia at a time when only 10 percent of private homes in the south had that luxury. (Courtesy of Joanne Hanna Lott.)

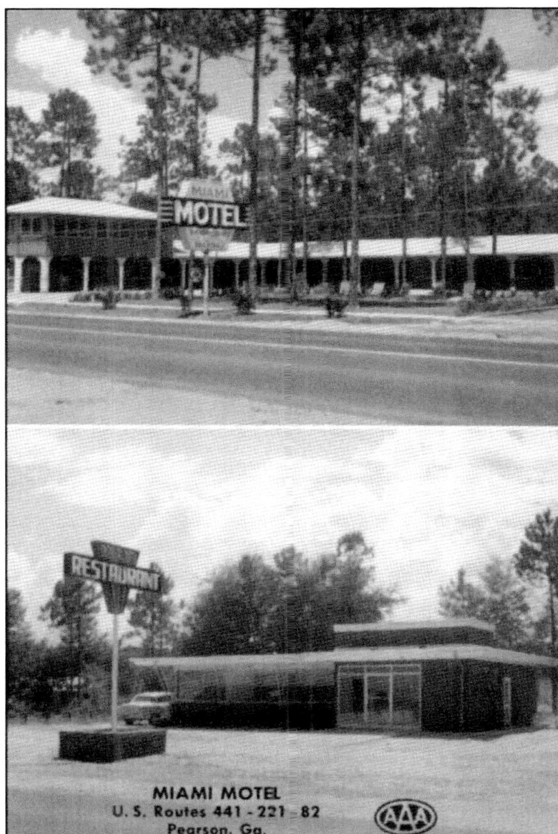

Technically, the Miami Motel is located in neighboring Atkinson County. While the hotels in Douglas were for people visiting from out of town, the Miami Motel was for the people of Douglas who just wanted to get away from it all, if only on a Friday night. (Courtesy of Joanne Hanna Lott.)

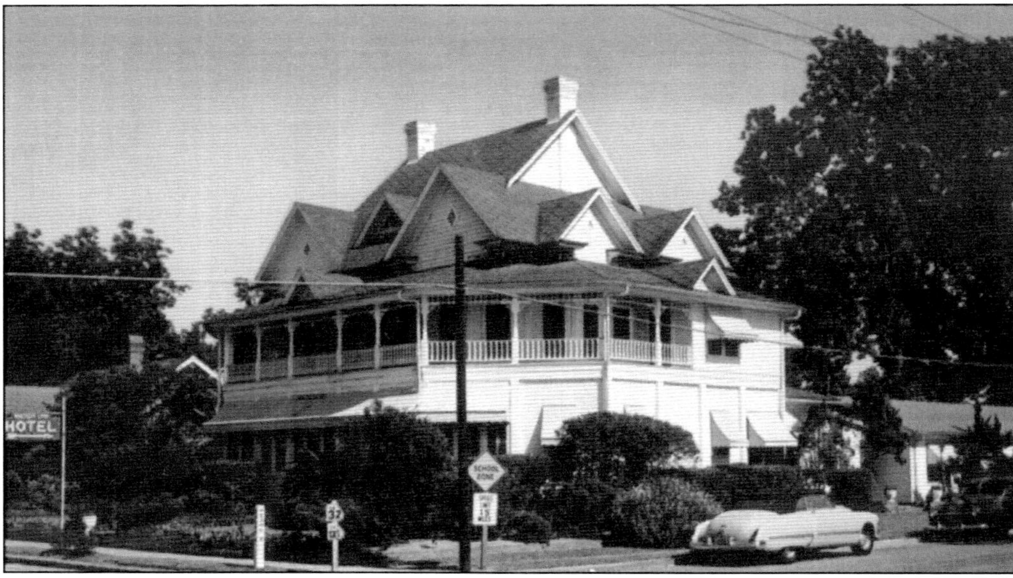

The prominent Anchor Inn Hotel on the corner of Ward Street and Pearl Avenue gave guests the opportunity to feel at home in their own private room and still enjoy a cooked meal. (Courtesy of Joanne Hanna Lott.)

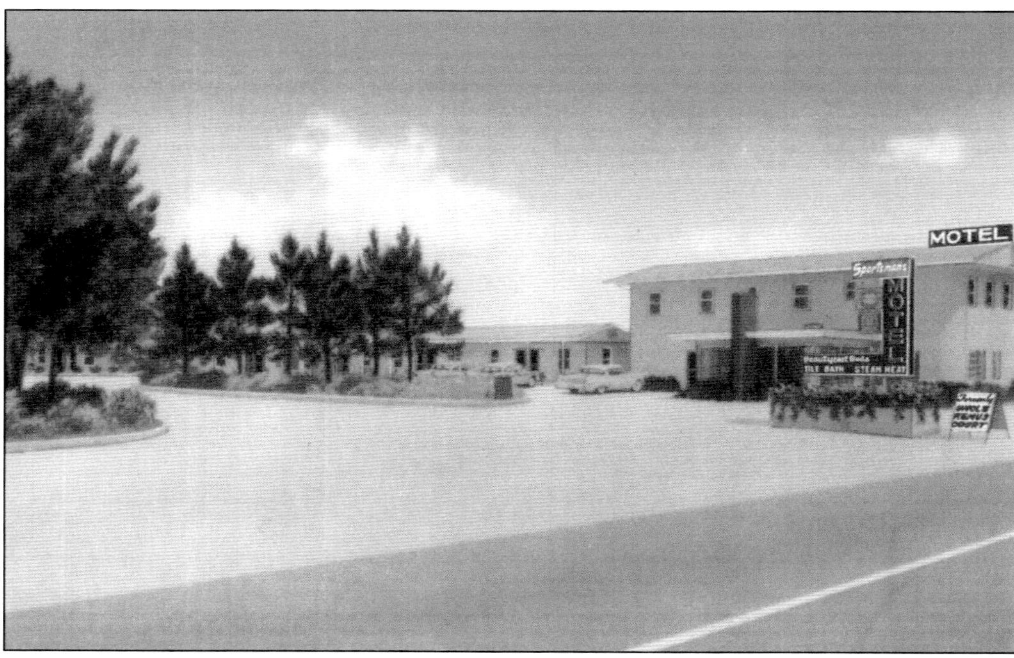

Hotels were traded on the stock exchange for the first time in 1945, and Hilton opened international locations in 1949. Even hotels with the latest amenities struggled to compete, and the Sportsman Hotel bought out the Uncle Remus. (Courtesy of Joanne Hanna Lott.)

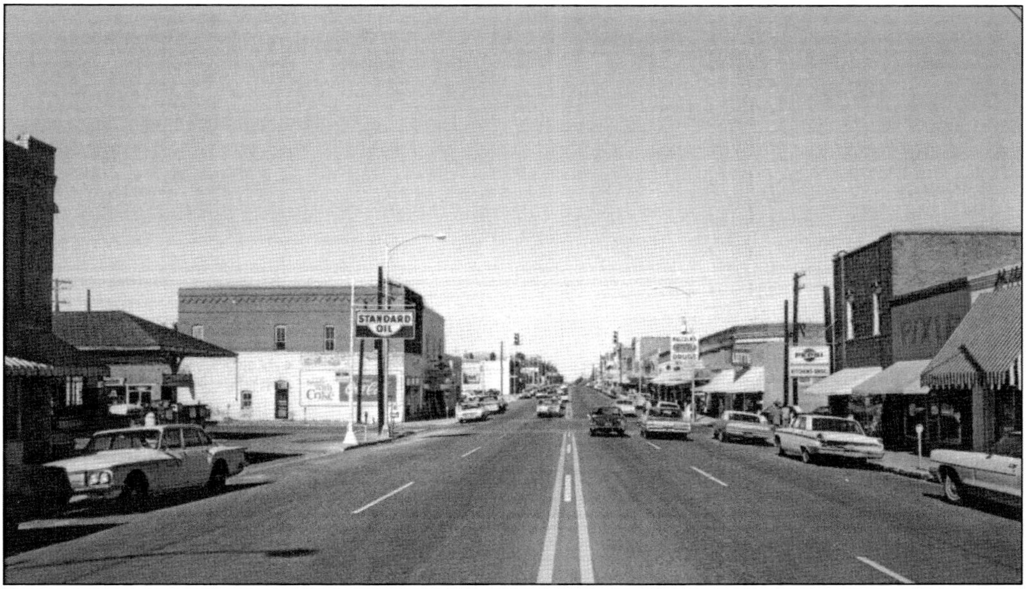

This street scene on Peterson Avenue around 1960 shows the old Kitchen's Grocery Store, Lott's Hardware, and Malcolm's on the right. The building on the left was formerly Star News Stand, with the old Standard Oil station also on the left. (Courtesy of Joanne Hanna Lott.)

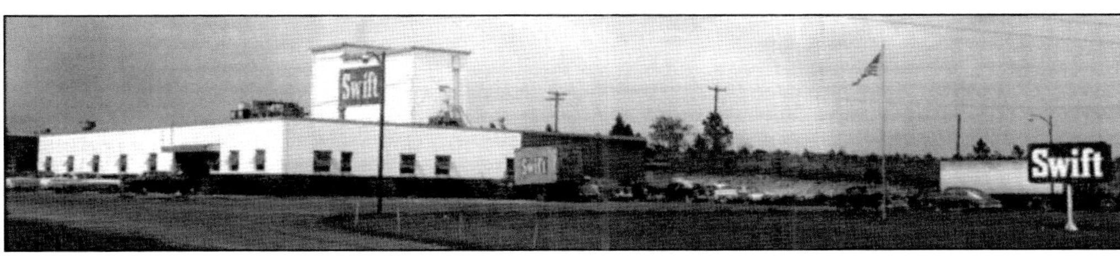

The big development push in the 1950s brought a Swift poultry-processing plant to the area. For over 60 years, poultry processing has been a key industry in Douglas. Plants have also contracted with local chicken farms and hatcheries. Recognizing that they had moved into an agricultural area, companies provided transportation to employees, as well as a company store and an on-site nurse. (Courtesy of Douglas-Coffee County Chamber of Commerce.)

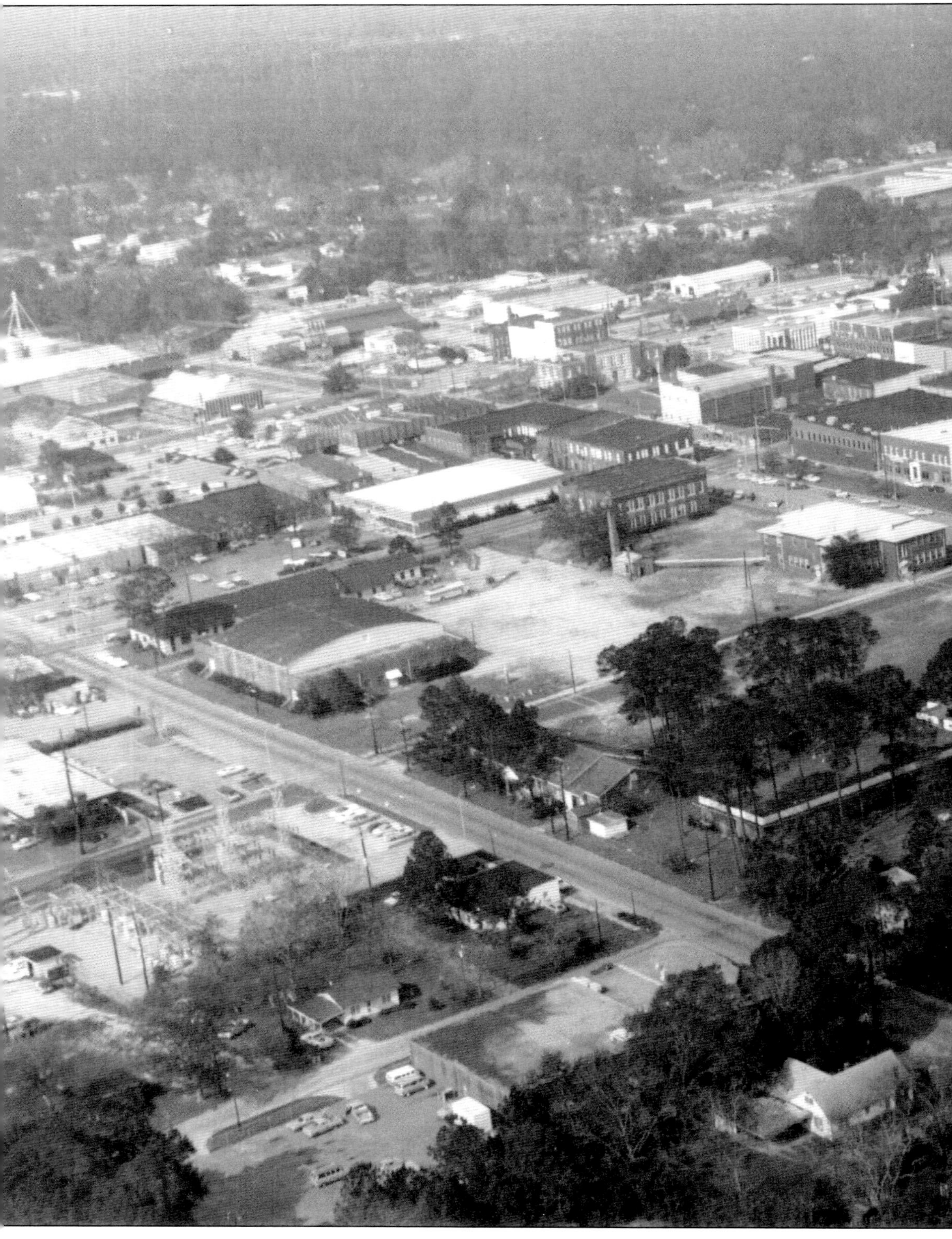

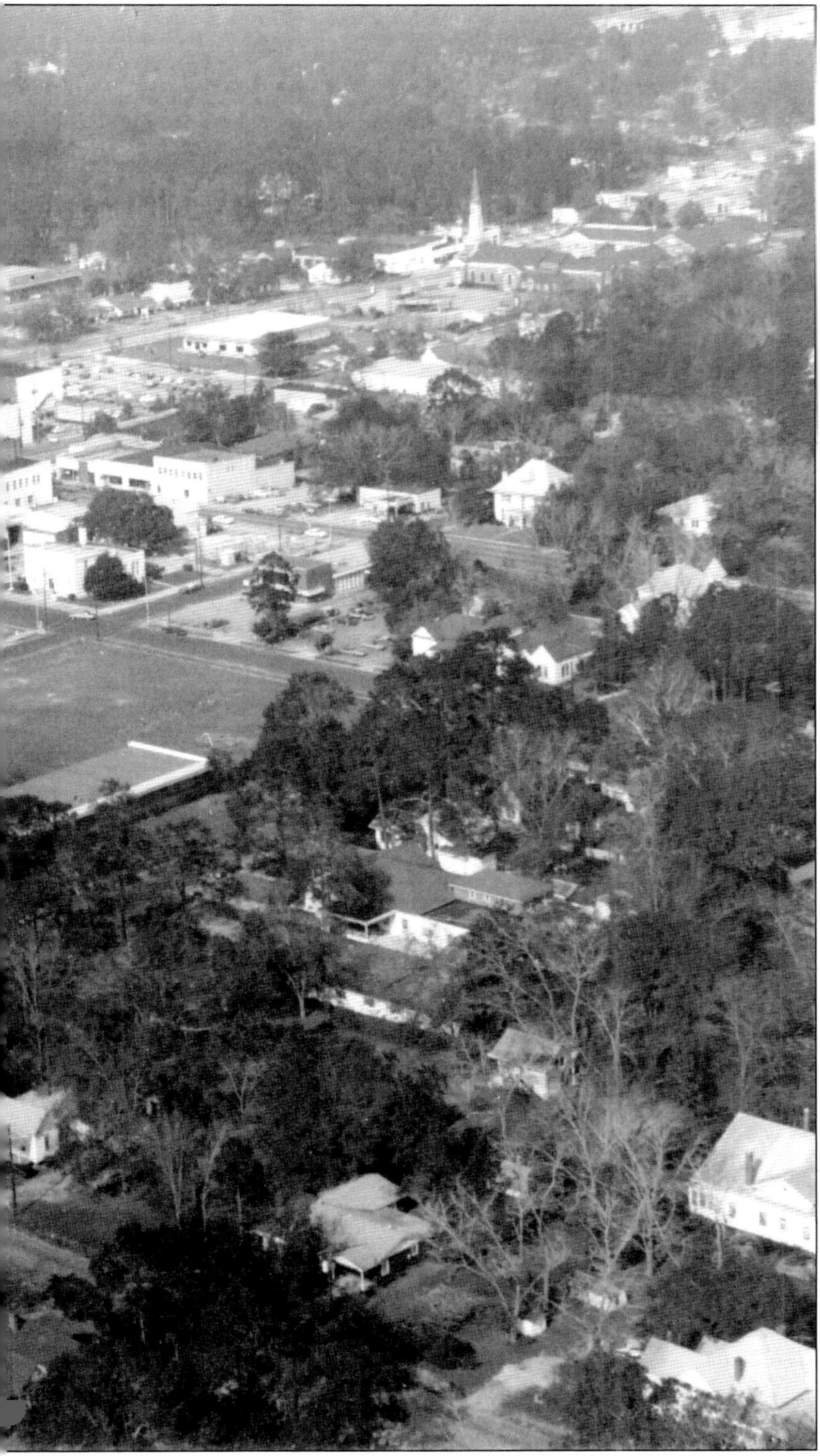

This is an aerial view of downtown Douglas from Bryan Street to a distant Jackson Street. In the upper right-hand corner lies the First United Methodist Church. The empty field in the center is now the location of Satilla Regional Library. Also recognizable in the center is the Coca-Cola Building. In the center left is the old Bryan Street Gym. The well-worn fields that surround the building hosted football and cheerleading practices for many of the children in town. Across from the Bryan Street Gym can be seen the old Western Auto location, now the Douglas Video Warehouse. (Courtesy of the City of Douglas.)

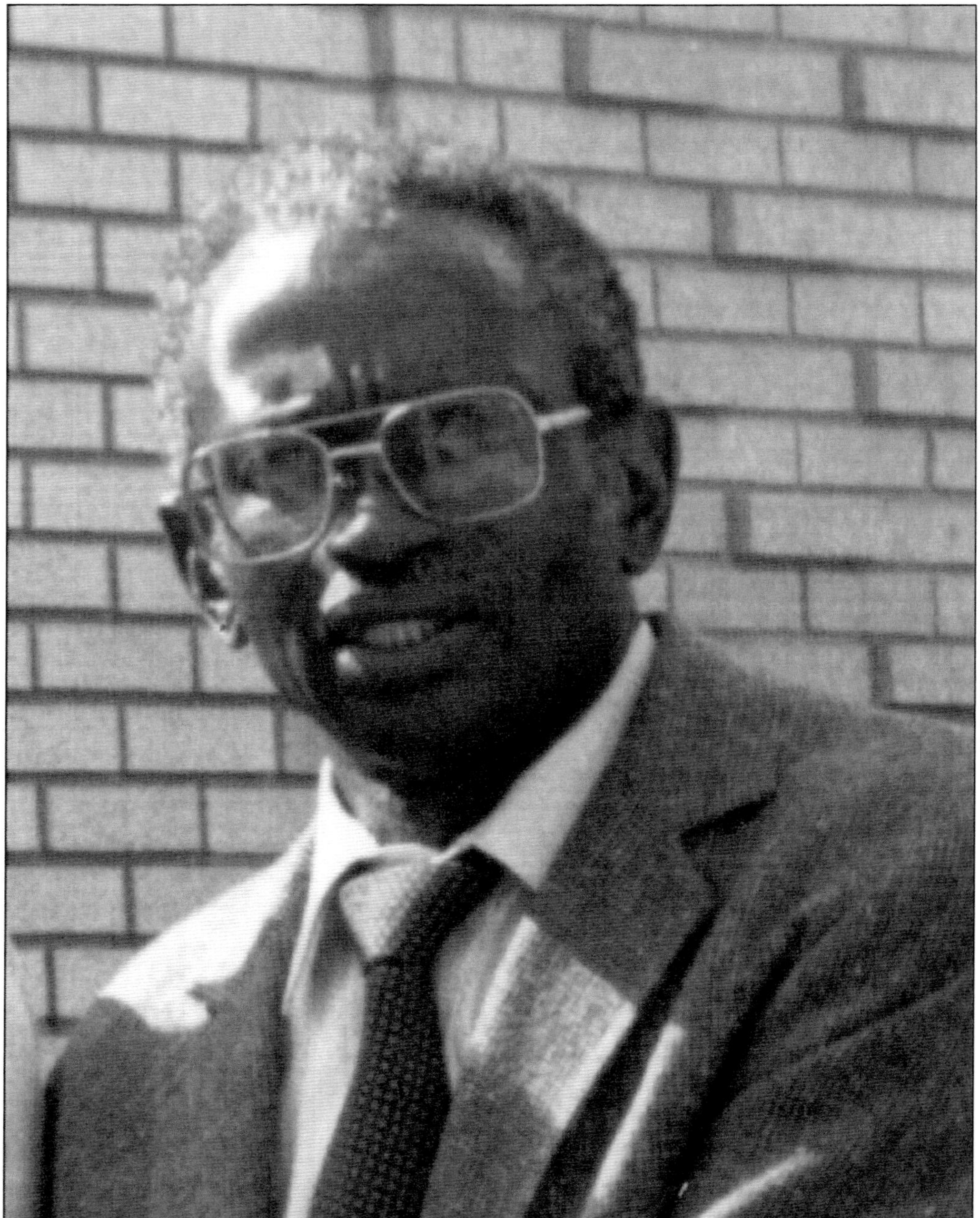

In 1967, Elisha Harrell became the first African American city commissioner of Douglas. He was part of a small class-action suit against Coffee County working actively for the reapportionment of the county's wards. He paved the way for African Americans to have positions in the municipal office. (Courtesy of Gwendolyn Reliford.)

Shown here is former child resident of Rat Row, Yvonne Brown Lott. Yvonne was born in 1942 and later married Ollie Lott of Douglas. She graduated from then-segregated Carver High School in 1962 and attended vocational and nursing school in 1969. She became one of the first African American surgical nurses at Coffee Regional Hospital in Douglas, where she worked until her retirement in 2001. (Courtesy of Yvonne Brock.)

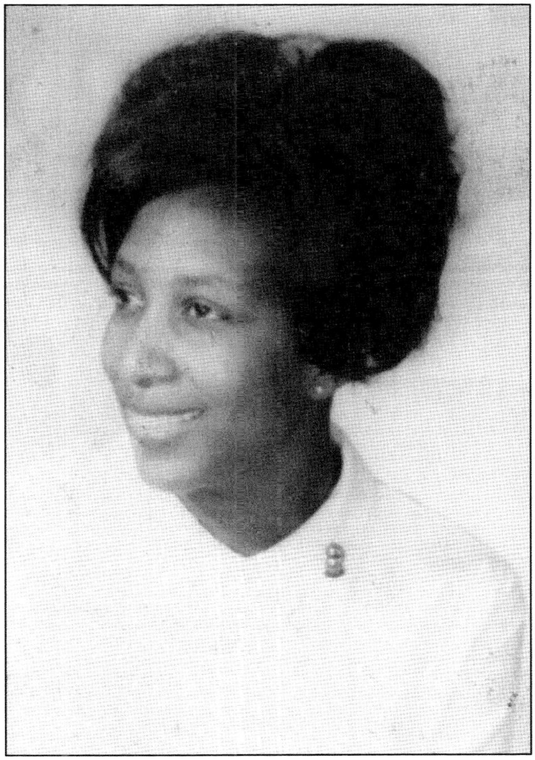

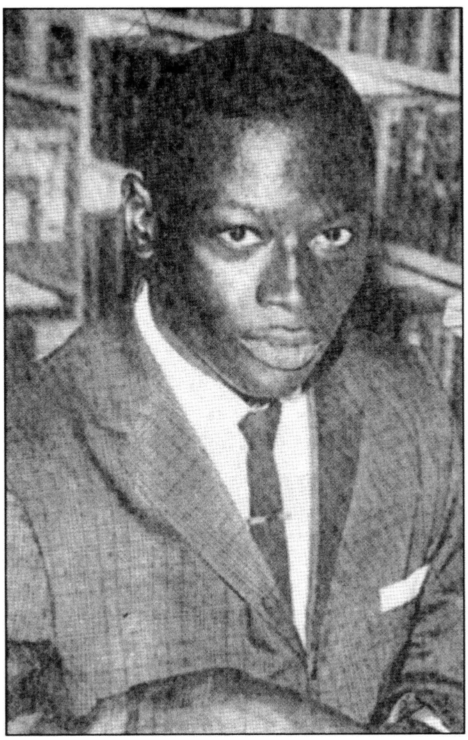

Oscar Street was the first African American to graduate from South Georgia College. He had previously graduated as salutatorian from Carver High School. Now, people may know him as the former principal of West Coffee Middle School, Sunday school teacher at Young's Chapel, member of the board at Coffee Regional Medical Center, and member of the board of directors for Ameris Bank. He has also served on the regional board for mental health and on the Coffee County Democratic Committee. (Courtesy of Gwendolyn Reliford.)

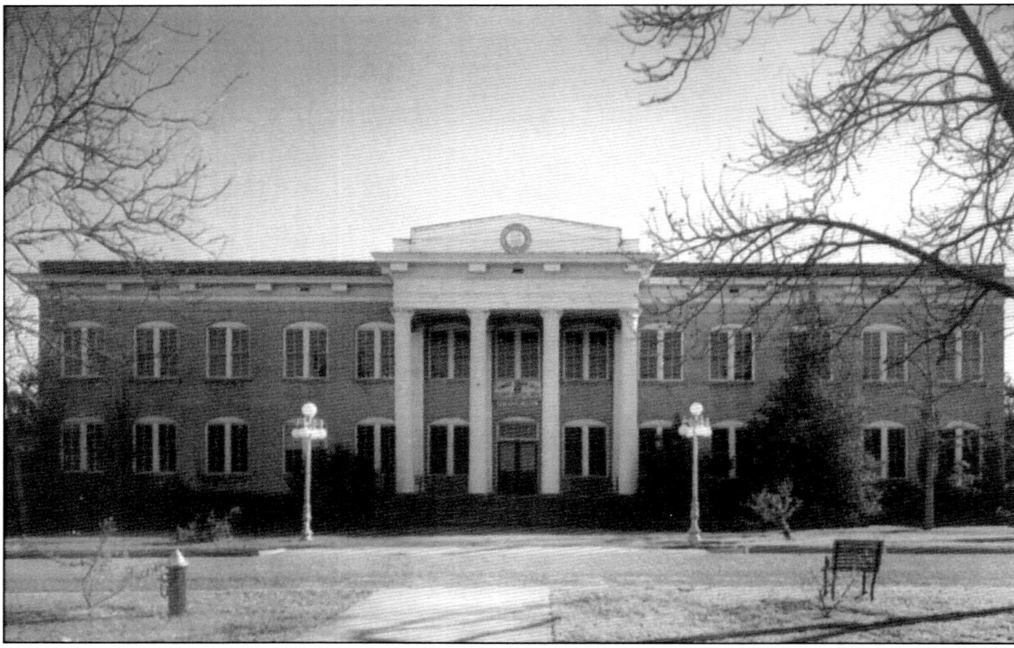

In 1995, Thrash Hall at South Georgia College went through a major renovation. It is shown here as it was originally built. (Courtesy of Joanne Hanna Lott.)

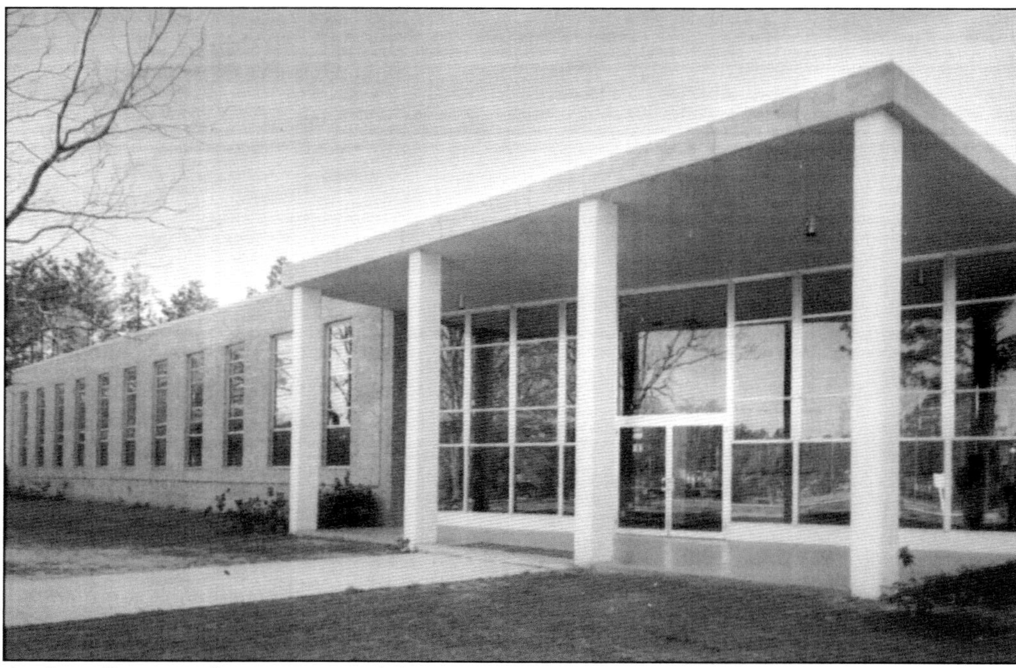

As the college enrollment grew, so did the campus. Here is the new science building, later named Stubbs Hall. (Courtesy of Joanne Hanna Lott.)

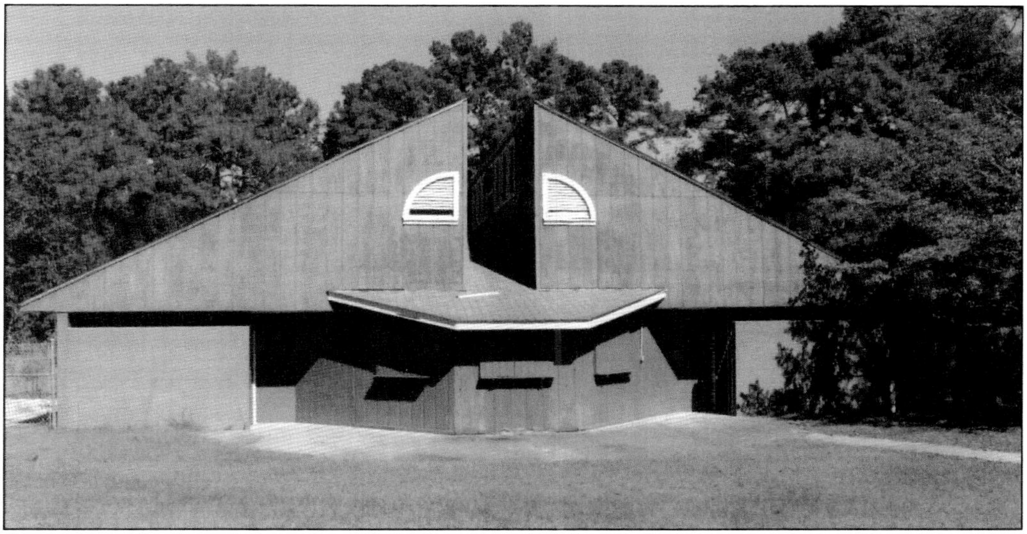

General Coffee State Park attracts more than a quarter million visitors each year. The park was donated to the state by citizens of Coffee County in the 1970s and named after Gen. John Coffee. Seen here are the concession area and showers for the pool. For the first few decades, the pool was the most popular attraction; however, because of economic reasons, 11 pools in Georgia state parks were closed in 2009. In 2013, the pool was filled in. The park now features horse trails, camping, and the 19th-century Burnham Cottage and Heritage Farm. Educational programs teach how residents of the area farmed and lived in the late 1800s and early 1900s. (Courtesy of Charles E. Griffiths II.)

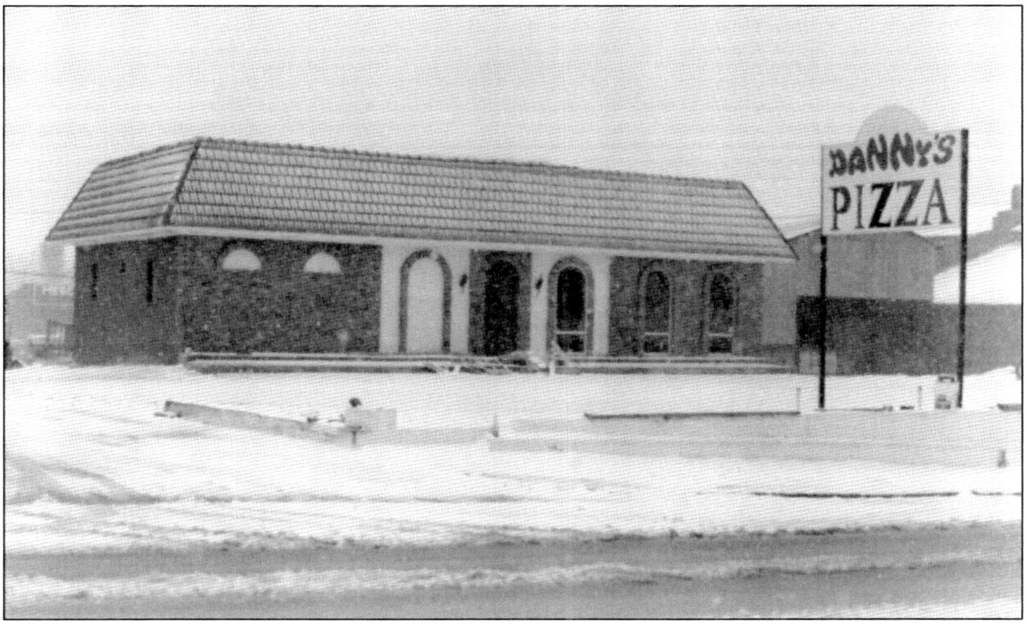

Atlanta has the Varsity, while Douglas has Danny's. For 35 years, Danny Maley's pizzeria has been a local favorite hangout after games and events. Danny has sponsored many local sporting teams and activities, and his all-star band participates in the parade every year, getting bigger and better each time. (Courtesy of Danny Maley.)

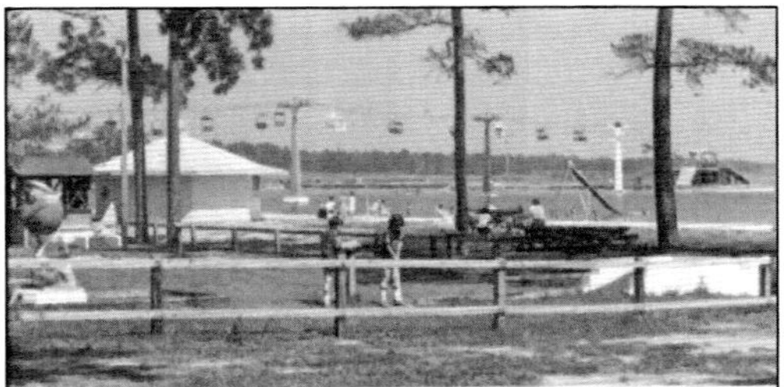

After working hard all week, folks used to go to Holiday Beach. Rest, relaxation, thrills, and excitement could all be found on these 1,350 acres of recreation space on the west side of town. (Courtesy of Joanne Hanna Lott.)

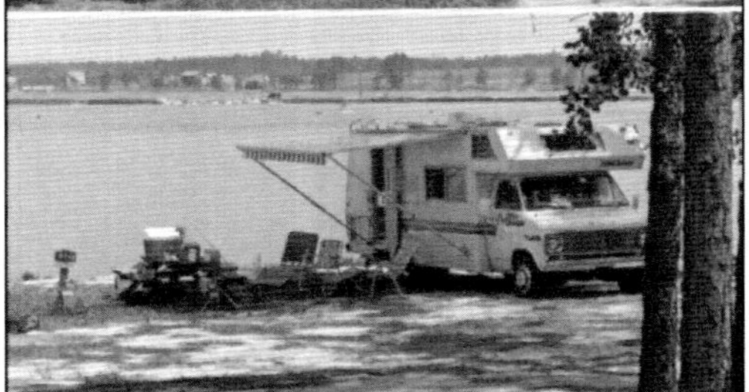

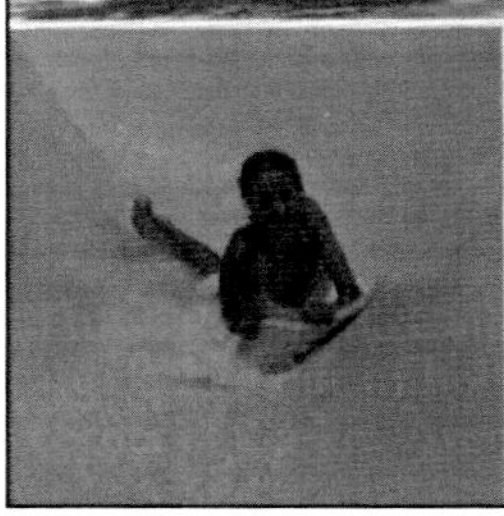

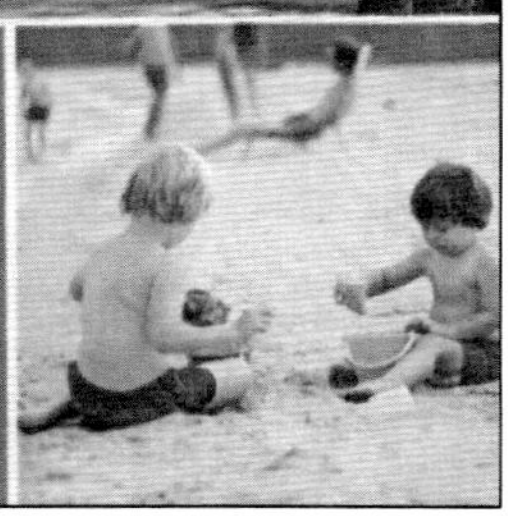

On a typical day in the 1970s and 1980s, young couples could be found lounging in the sand at the lakefront. People relaxed and tanned—nobody was particularly concerned about ultraviolet rays at the time—and Panama Jack T-shirts and suntan oil were popular with visitors. A waterslide, fun house, haunted house, restaurant, miniature golf course, airstrip, Ferris wheel, arcade, sky ride, tilt-a-whirl, helicopter, scrambler, umbrella ride, bumper-car track, and roller coaster could be found at Holiday Beach. (Courtesy of Douglas-Coffee County Chamber of Commerce.)

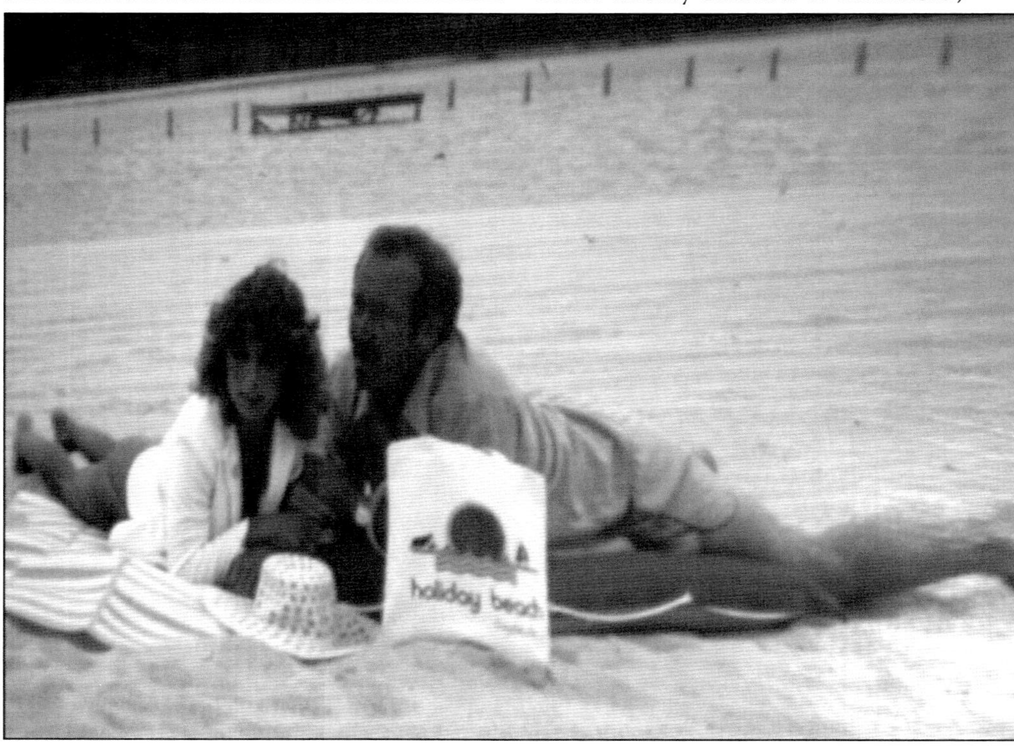

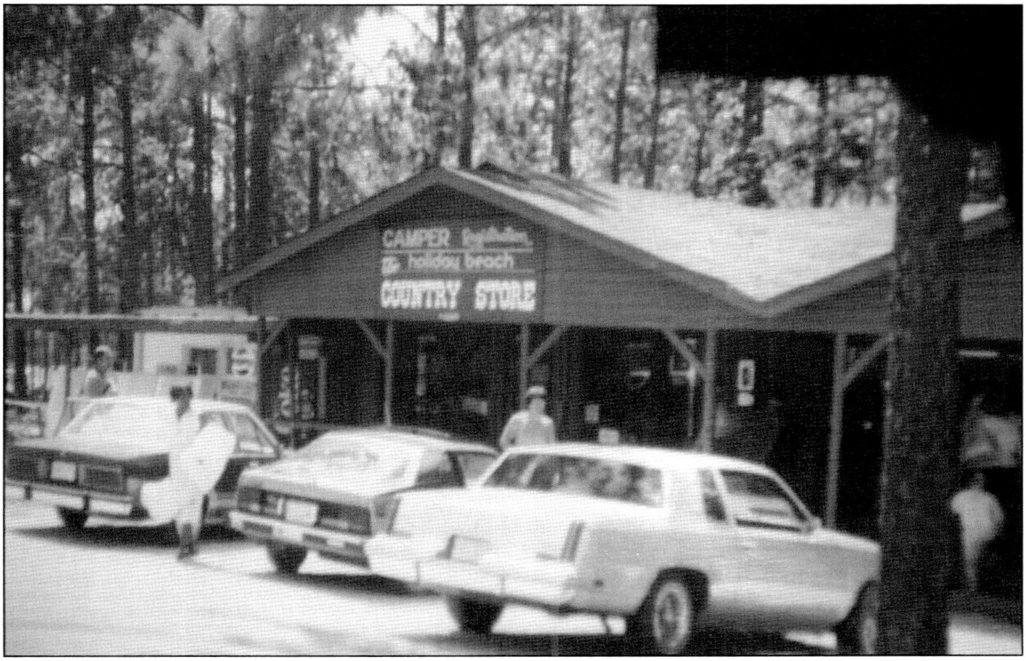

Upon entering Holiday Beach, visitors stopped here for camper registration and to pick up a few necessities at the Country Store. (Courtesy of Douglas-Coffee County Chamber of Commerce.)

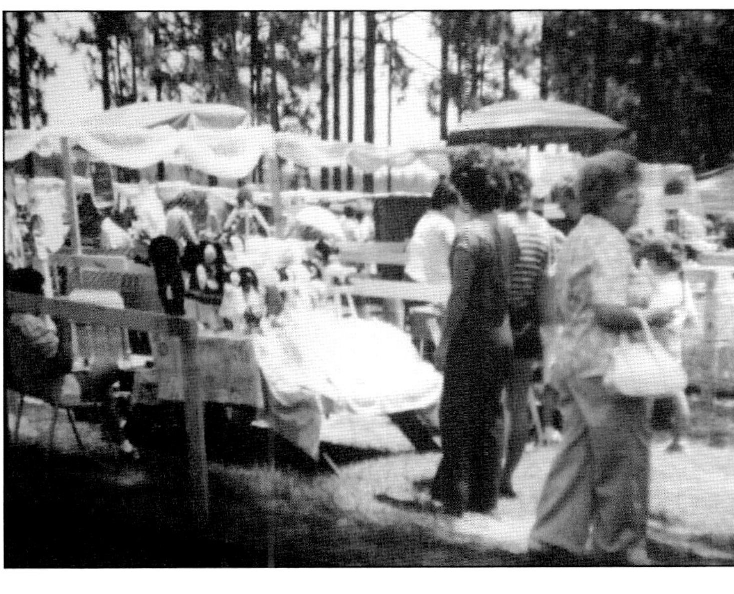

Community events, like the craft fair pictured here and concerts in the 2,500-seat Opry House, were regular occurrences. Unfortunately for the public, in October 1982, Holiday Beach was auctioned off; however, hundreds of locals can own a piece of that past, as the area became residential community called Bay Meadows. (Courtesy of Douglas-Coffee County Chamber of Commerce.)

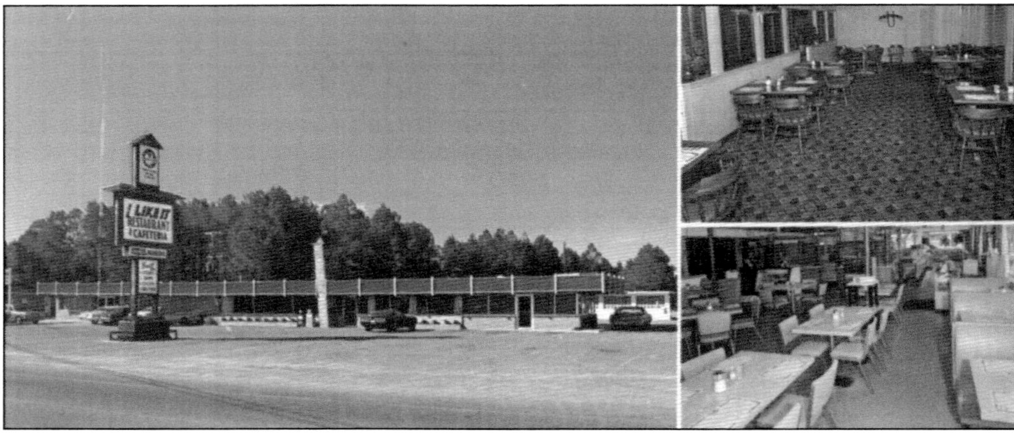

I Like It restaurant was a local favorite owned by the Mills family and located near the Douglas Airport. It unfortunately burned in the late 1980s. (Courtesy of Joanne Hanna Lott.)

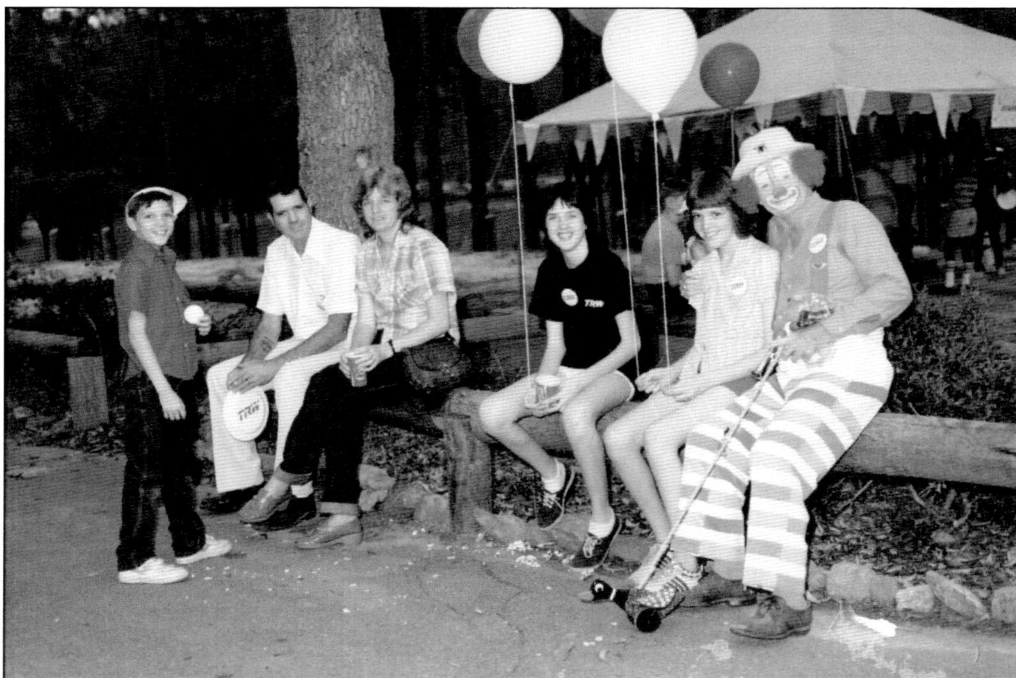

Most of the local economy was agriculturally based until the 1970s. Businesses like TRW proposed to locate to Douglas if the runway behind the old aviation school was extended to accommodate corporate jets. The community did the work on the airport, which has since been upgraded again, and TRW arrived. Seen here is the Martin family at the TRW company family picnic. (Courtesy of Richard and Rose Martin.)

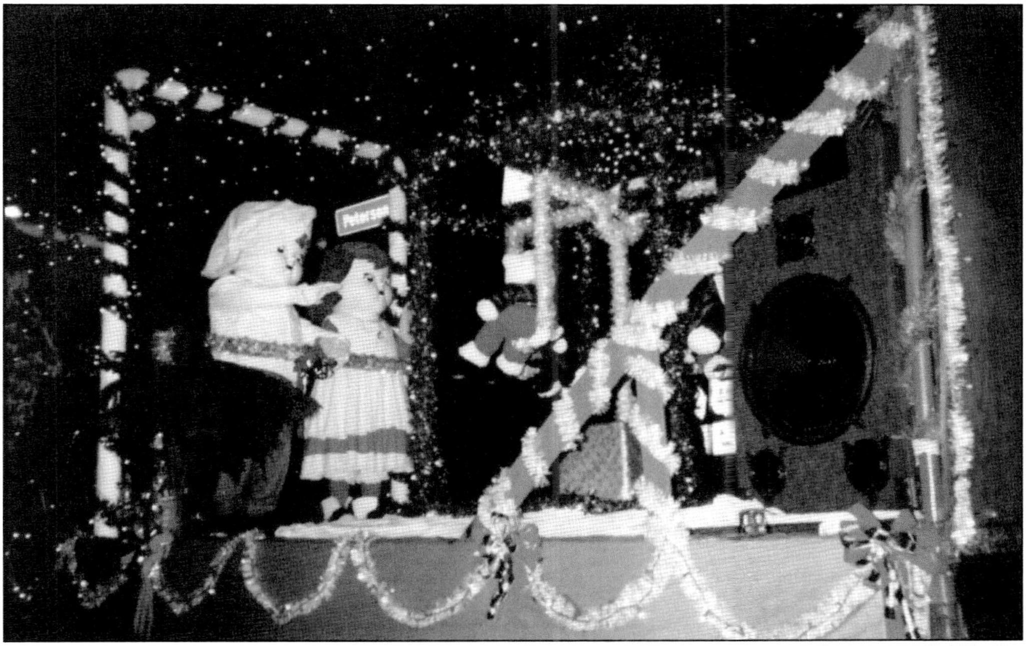

This is the Joseph Campbell's processing plant entry in the Christmas parade; the "Campbell kids" are decked out in holiday gear, tossing candy to the crowd. Joseph Campbell's operated on the corner of Gaskin Avenue and McNeil Drive until 1997. (Courtesy of Richard and Rose Martin.)

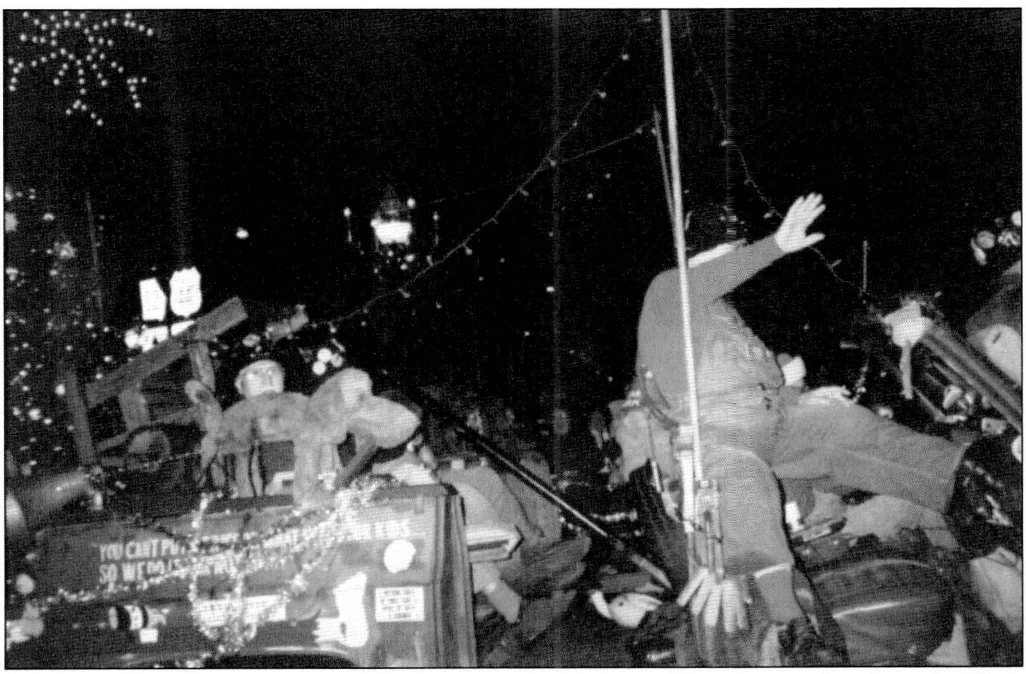

The Douglas Hobo Shriner Clowns are shown here in their paddy wagon at a local parade. Their antics were always memorable. (Courtesy of Richard and Rose Martin.)

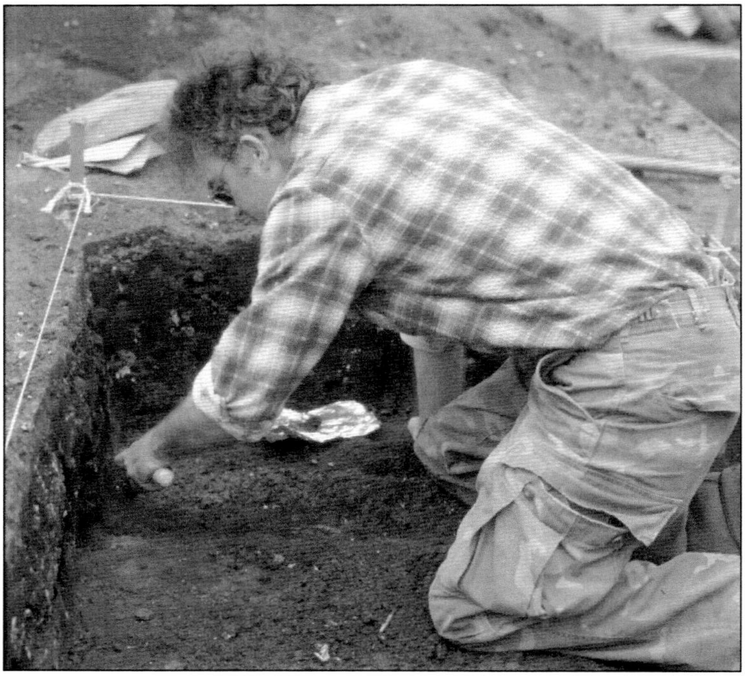

Archaeologist Frankie Snow is shown excavating a site in the northern part of the Coffee County. Snow has done extensive research on the Swift Creek people who lived in this area in prehistoric times. (Courtesy of Frankie Snow.)

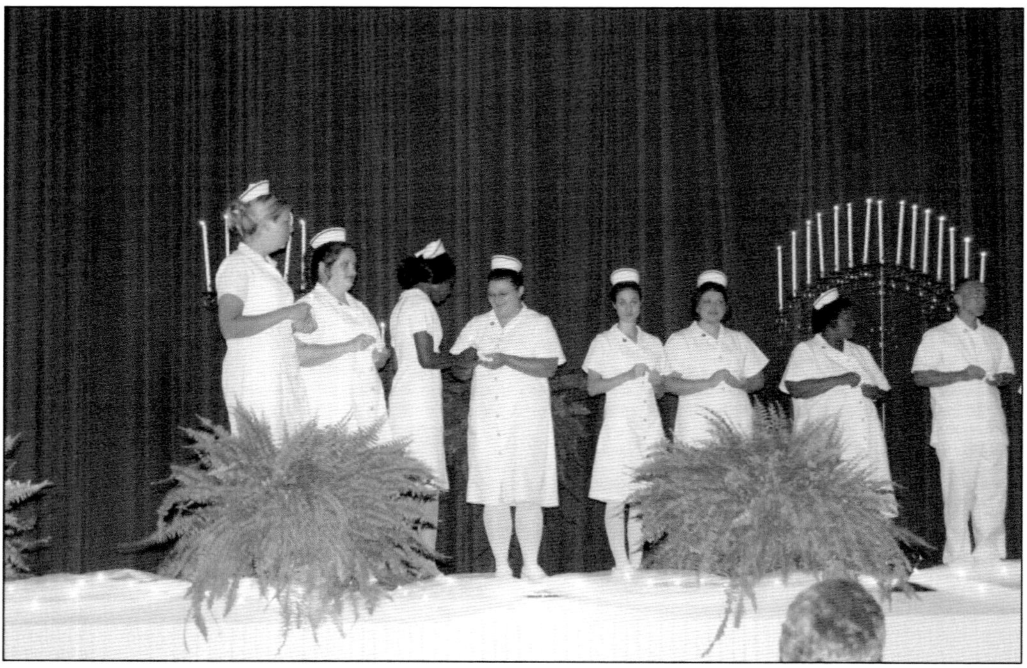

Pictured is the nurse-capping ceremony at East Central Technical College. Students train here to obtain a licensed practical nurse degree or a degree in one of dozens of other programs. East Central Technical College merged in 2009 with other technical schools and is now a campus of Wiregrass Georgia Technical College. (Courtesy of Yolanda Crosby.)

Seven

All Grown Up

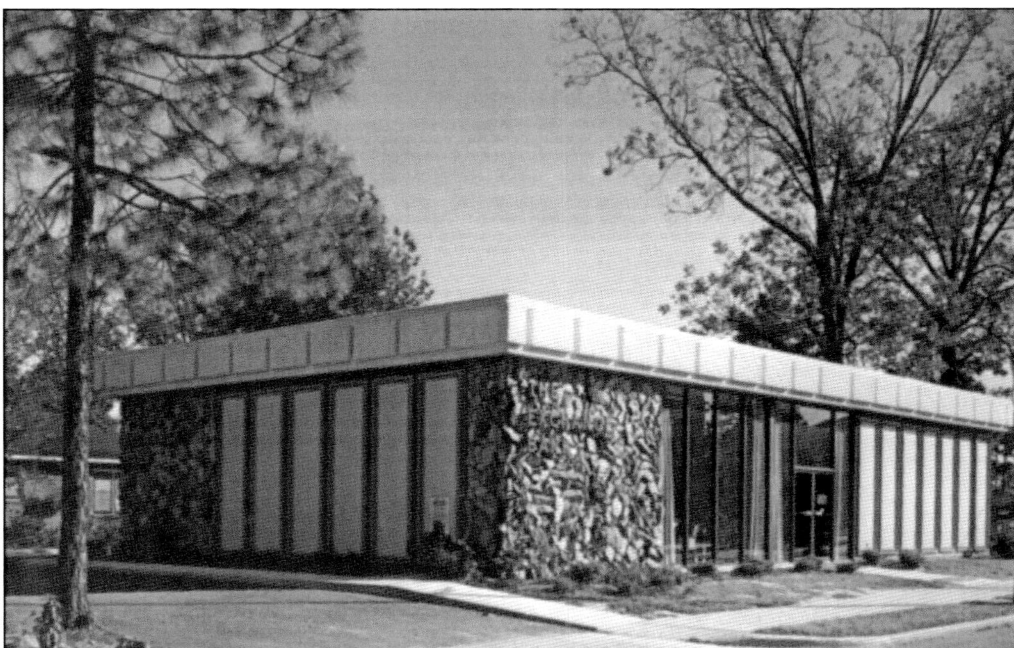

The old Exchange Bank building features Googie architecture, most notably in the flagstone rock and ground-to-ceiling glass windows. Structures during this period were influenced by noted architect Frank Lloyd Wright, and design elements similar to these were also used in the construction inside Collins Hall at South Georgia College. This building is now Ameris Bank. (Courtesy of Joanne Hanna Lott.)

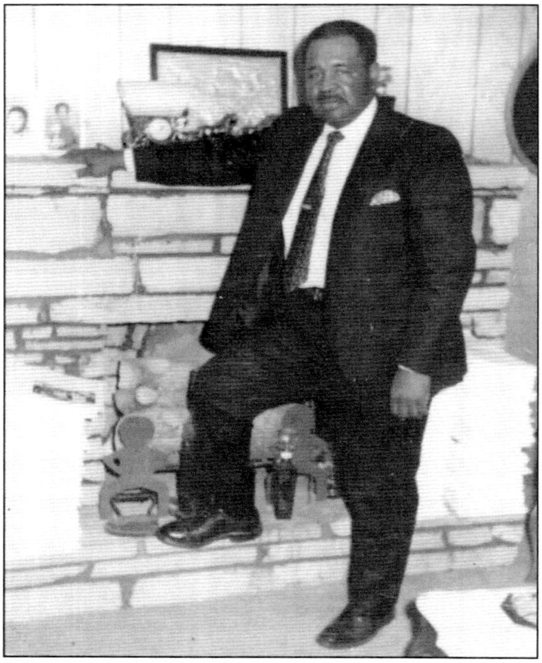

Paul Buchanan was a big man with an even bigger heart. He was married to Ophelia Baity, and together they raised 11 children. For 26 years, he delivered, produced, and frequently bought fruit to give away in his neighborhood. After his retirement in 1967, he was hired by Sheriff Lewis Sapp and became Coffee County's first African American deputy sheriff. (Courtesy of Gwendolyn Reliford.)

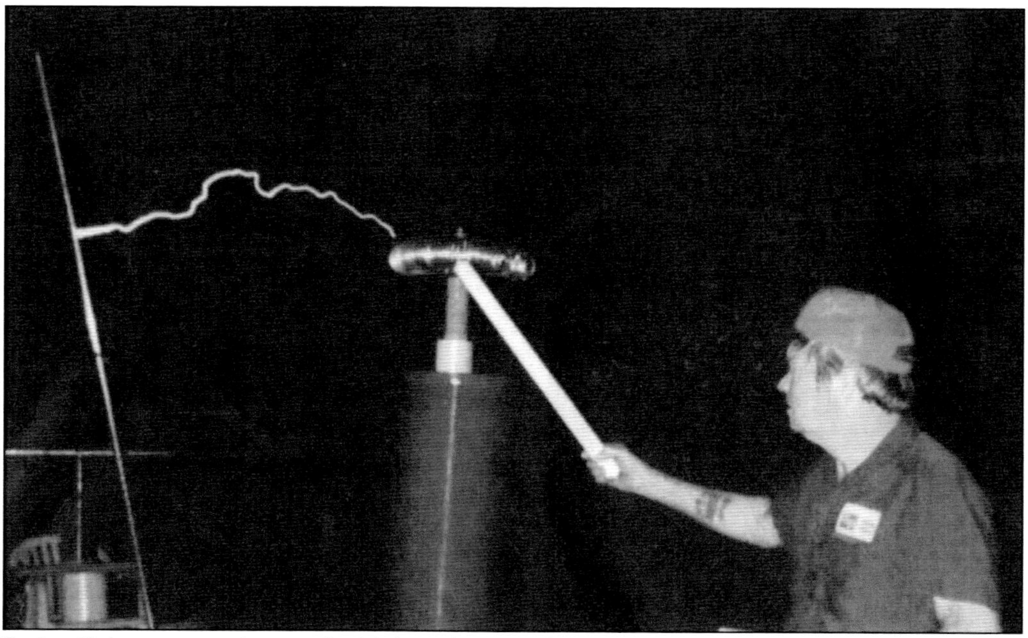

Richard Martin is seen here with a Tesla coil. Martin has constructed a number of electronic gadgets and gizmos over the years and has donated several to school science classes and to businesses for decor. Before his retirement, he was employed as an electronic troubleshooter for Gold Kist Industries. There, Martin invented a laser device to make poultry processing quicker and more efficient. He also invented a machine for Joseph Campbell's processing plant to reduce waste, effectively saving both plants millions of dollars. Though retired, he continues to troubleshoot electronics for businesses and individuals in his spare time. (Courtesy of Richard and Rose Martin.)

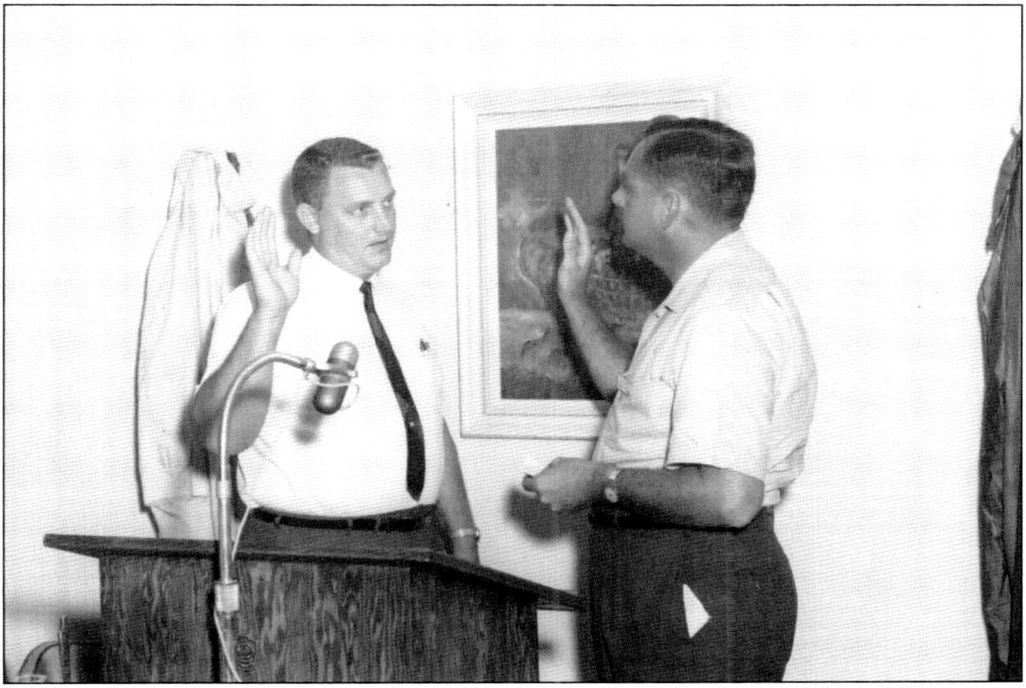

The city attorney is shown swearing in J.C. Adams. Adams served as city commissioner when Tri-Hi-Y was established and was the mayor of Douglas for 14 years. (Courtesy of the City of Douglas.)

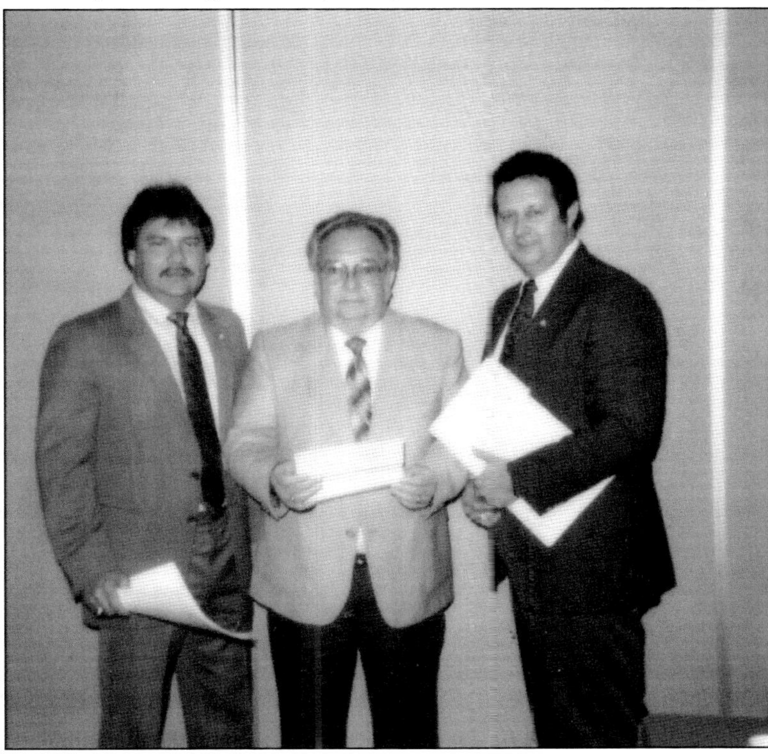

Seen here from left to right are former city mayors Derward Buchan and J.C. Adams and state representative Walter Ray. (Courtesy of the City of Douglas.)

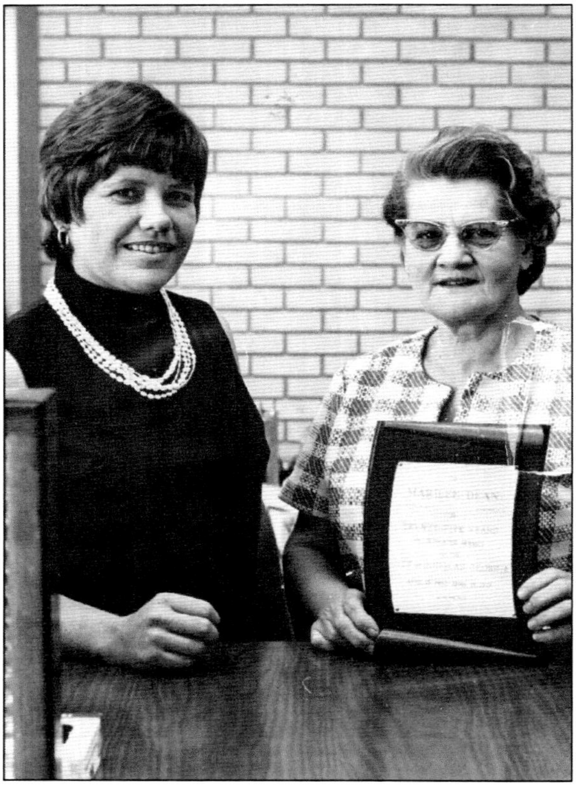

City worker Hayvene McFall (left) is shown congratulating retiree Marilee Dean, who holds the plaque she received for 25 years of service. (Courtesy of the City of Douglas.)

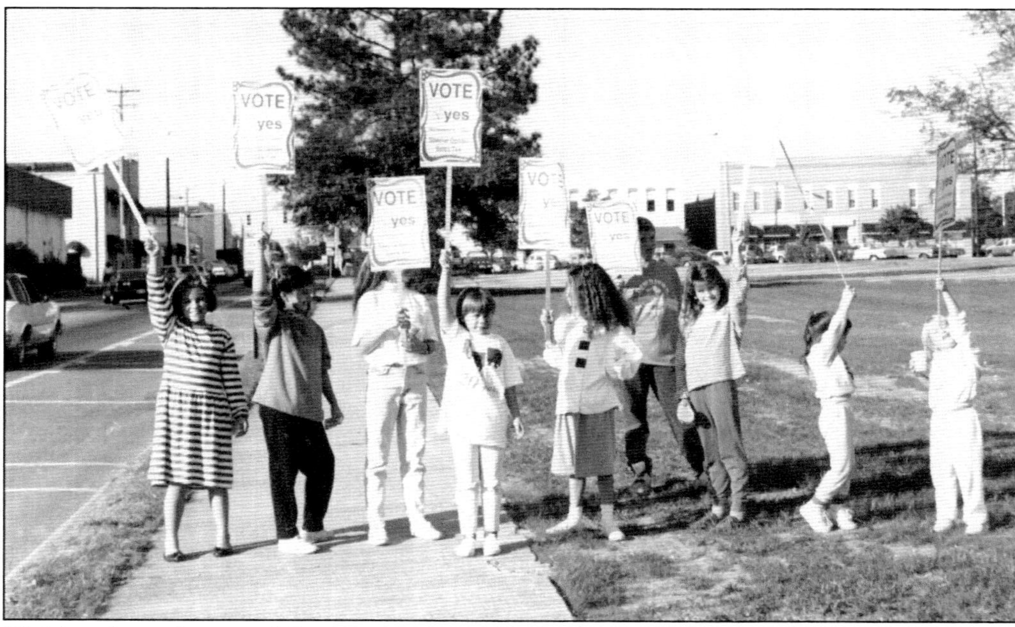

Children from the city of Douglas campaign for the first special-purpose local-option sales tax (SPLOST), which proposed an additional one-percent tax for the purpose of building parks, schools, roads, and public facilities. (Courtesy of the City of Douglas.)

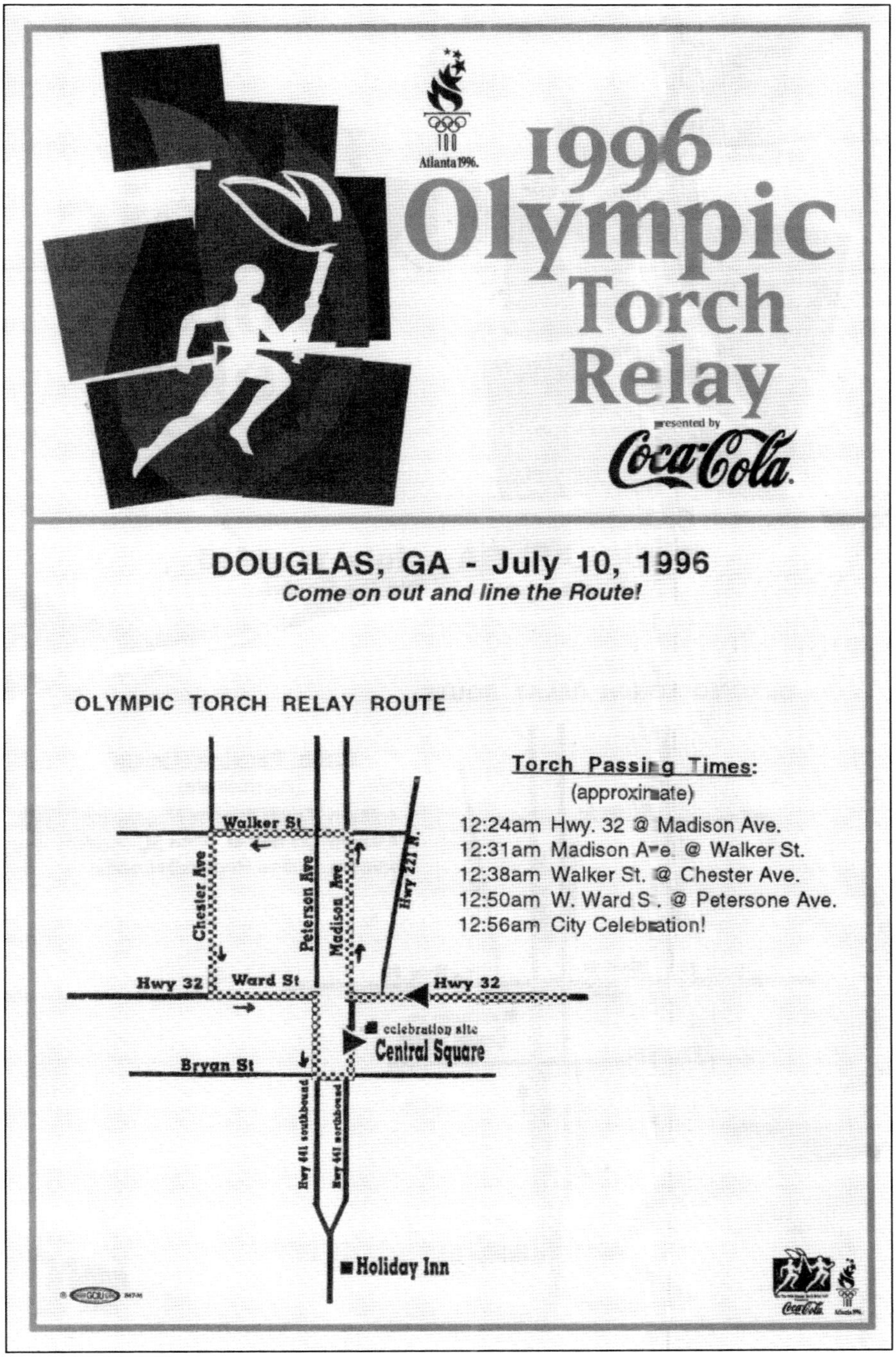

Young and old attended the events listed in this brochure for the 1996 Olympic Torch Relay. There was a feeling of national pride on this momentous occasion when Douglas took part in a time-honored tradition that has been practiced across the globe. Local celebrity torch runners included Walter Hue, Mary Francis Smith, Greg Walker, Erin Palmer, Ron Morris, and Dr. Romulo Navarro. (Author's collection.)

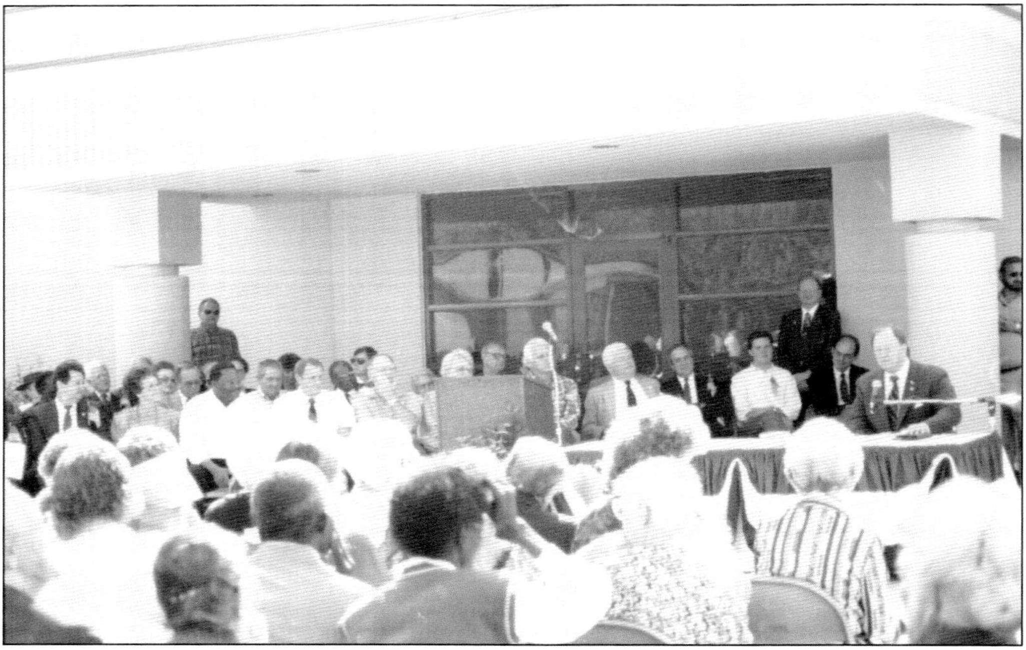

In the 1980s and 1990s, city officials and community leaders worked hard to revitalize the struggling downtown district, develop community programs, and honor veterans. Seen here is a town meeting that had to be moved outdoors to accommodate the unexpectedly large attendance. (Courtesy of the City of Douglas.)

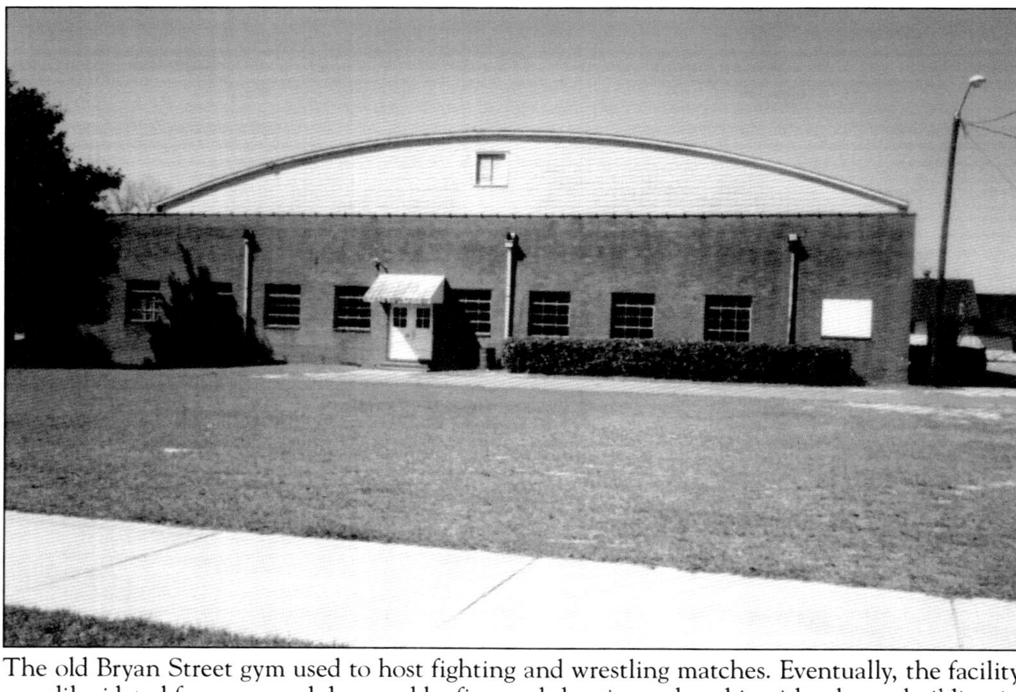

The old Bryan Street gym used to host fighting and wrestling matches. Eventually, the facility was dilapidated from age and damaged by fire, and the city replaced it with a larger building in the 1990s. (Courtesy of the City of Douglas.)

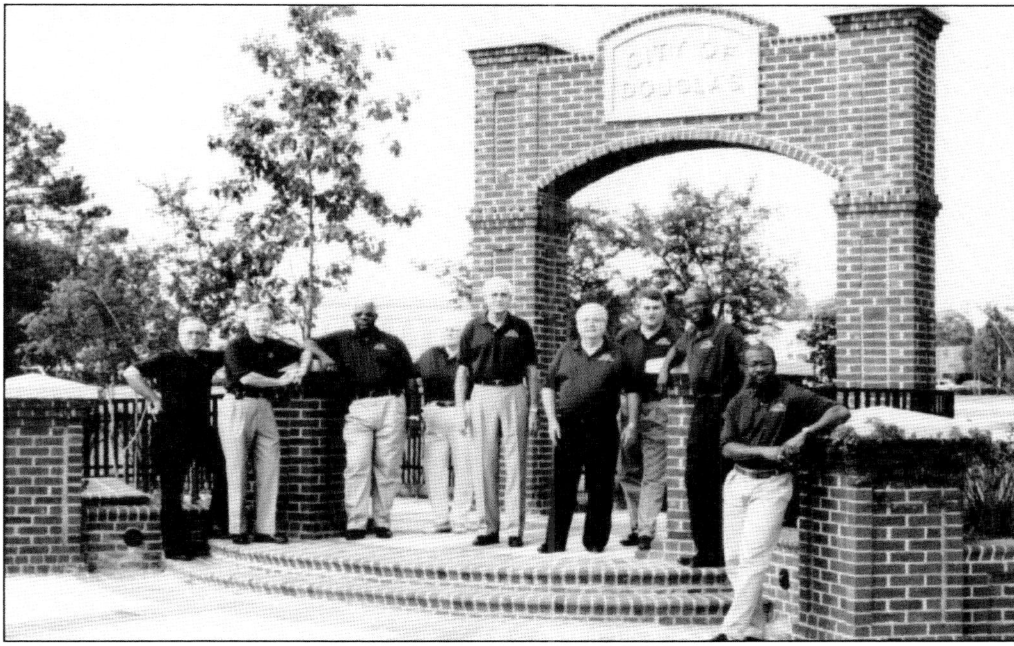

Douglas and Coffee County community leaders are seen standing before the new Douglas sign. From left to right are Bob Moore, Ronnie Anderson, Joe Reliford, Jackie Wilson, Art Davis, Derward Buchan, Danny Lewis, Elisha Harrell, and Charles Moore. (Courtesy of the City of Douglas.)

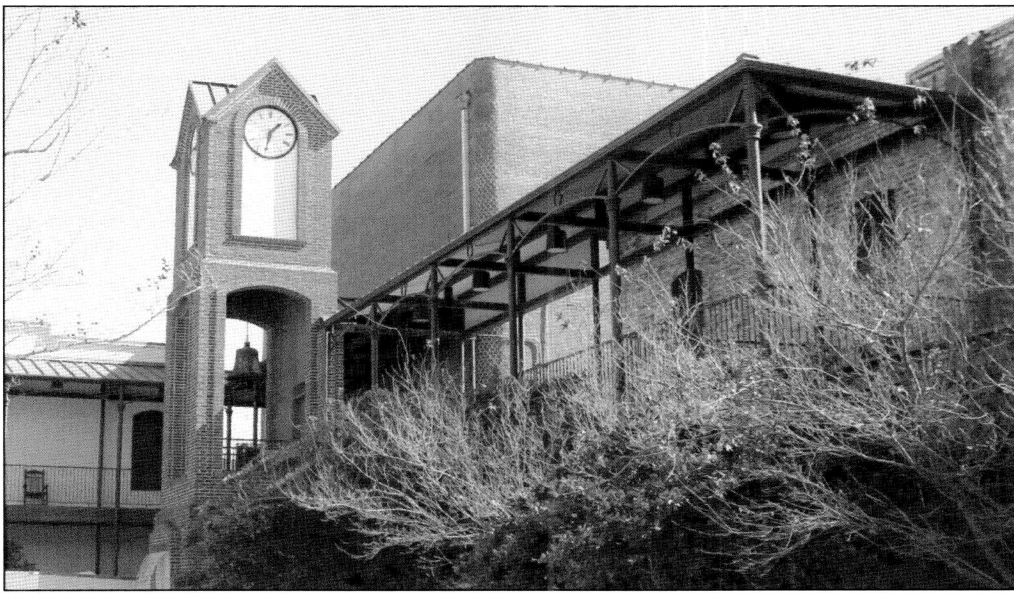

The City of Douglas Main Street Program was established in 1980 to preserve and revitalize the downtown district. The project spanned three blocks and six intersections. Business was down in the main street shops, and buildings were in need of repair. Before the restoration, this block was an eyesore; a fire had gutted the corner office and left the building open for vandals. The newly restored Hayes Building turned that corner into a relaxing area for weary shoppers, and the area is now the Atkinson Plaza. (Courtesy of Charles E. Griffiths II.)

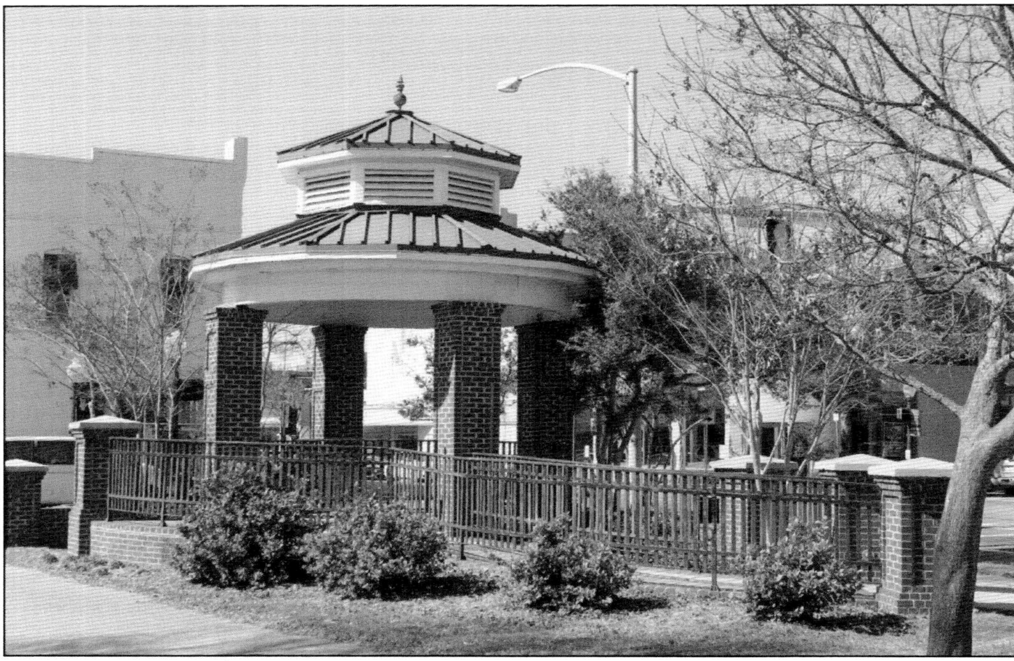

Douglas completed a $1 million downtown streetscape project rejuvenating the downtown area. The addition of brickwork, a gazebo, an arch, sitting areas, lighting, trash receptacles, and crosswalks inspired store owners to improve their buildings. (Courtesy of Charles E. Griffiths II.)

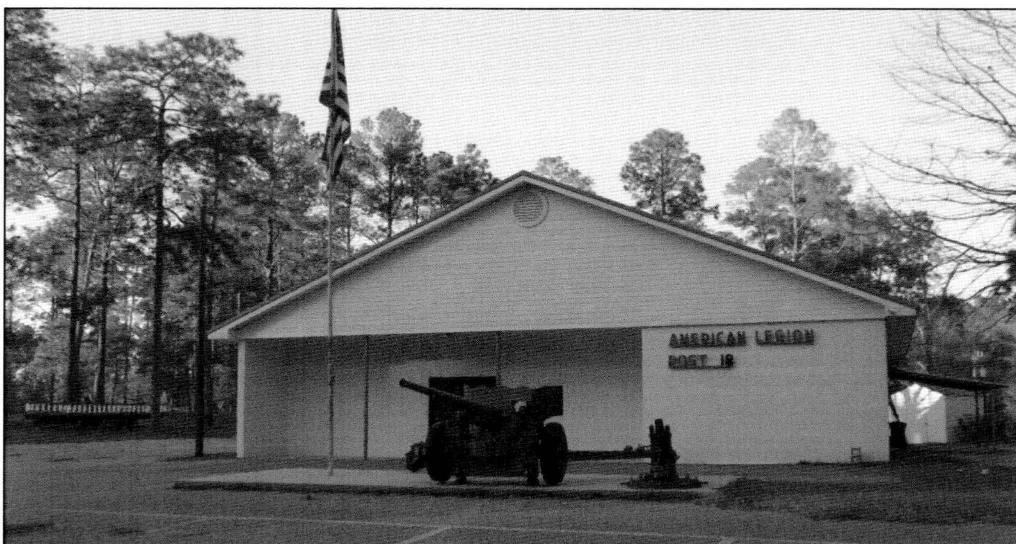

Georgia is home to almost one million veterans (one out of every five adults in the state), and the majority of the population has family members or friends who have served in the military. Many veterans have chosen to make Douglas their home because of the affordable cost of living. Local organizations to support veterans have been established, closed, and reopened as needed. The Veterans of Foreign Wars (VFW) was revitalized in 1995, and an American Legion post was established in 1999. Douglas now has two American Legion posts. (Author's collection.)

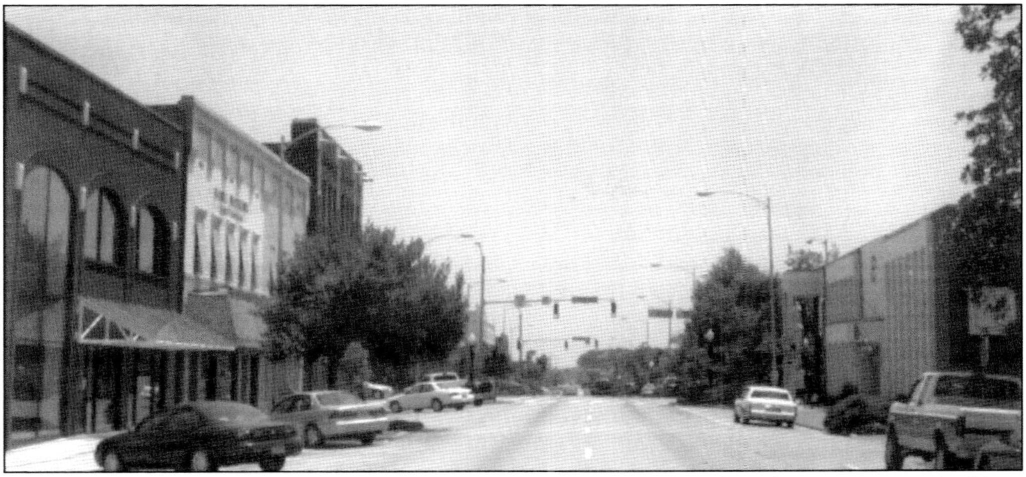

This street scene of Peterson Avenue was captured in 2004. On the left is the new Atrium Building and the former Earl Watkins, the finest men's clothing ever sold in the city of Douglas. The BB&T Bank, formerly known as the Coffee County Bank, is on the far left, and the Douglas Asphalt Company is on the right. (Courtesy of Joanne Hanna Lott.)

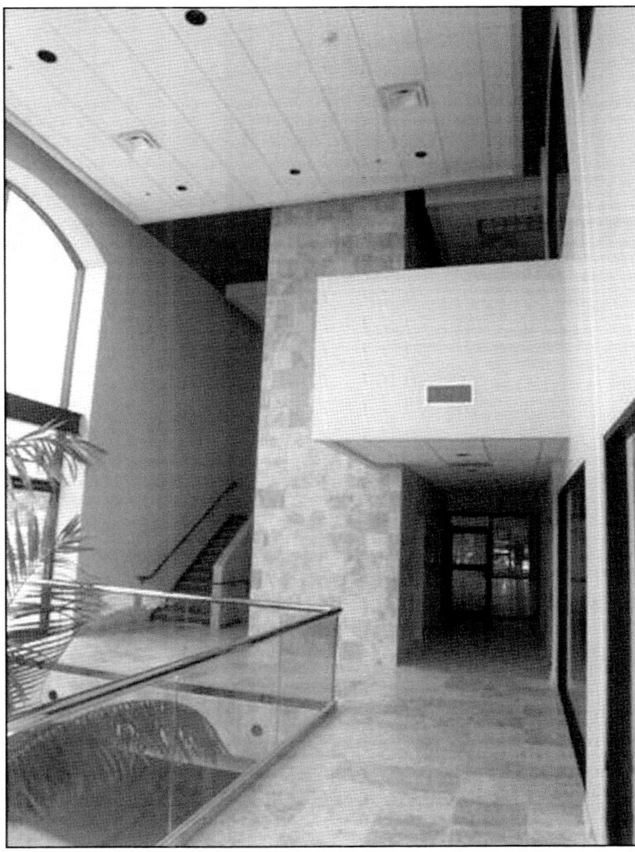

The Atrium Building is a 2005 redevelopment project headed by Francis Lott. It has since been restored and expanded to include the Atrium Event Center, a multipurpose property for retail and professional services. Events, businesses, antique shops, and restaurants can all be found here. (Courtesy of Douglas-Coffee County Chamber of Commerce.)

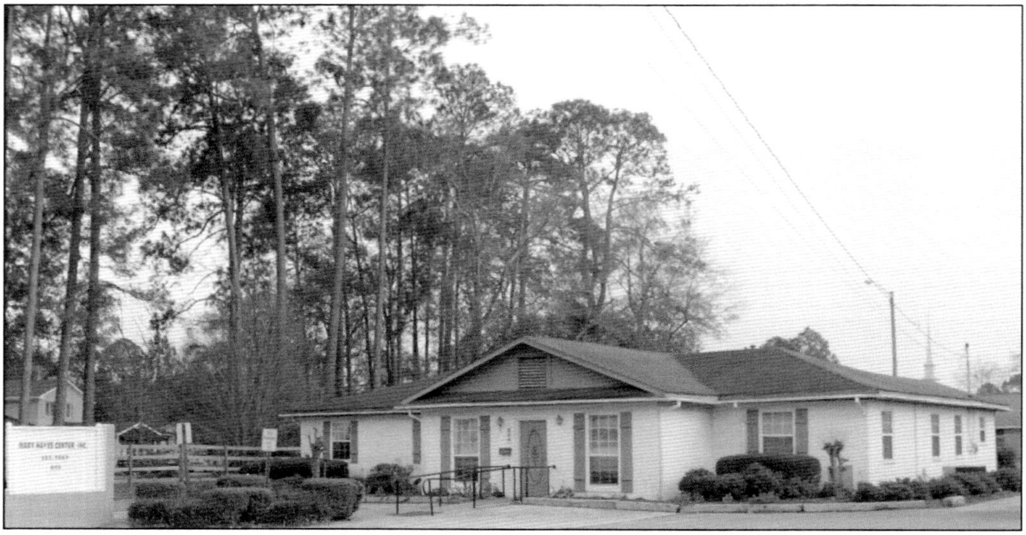

Developed in the 1990s and based on a study by the Coffee County Interagency Council, the mission of the Mary Hayes Center for Social Change is to promote the guidance of at-risk youth by providing educational and social programs. (Courtesy of Gwendolyn Reliford.)

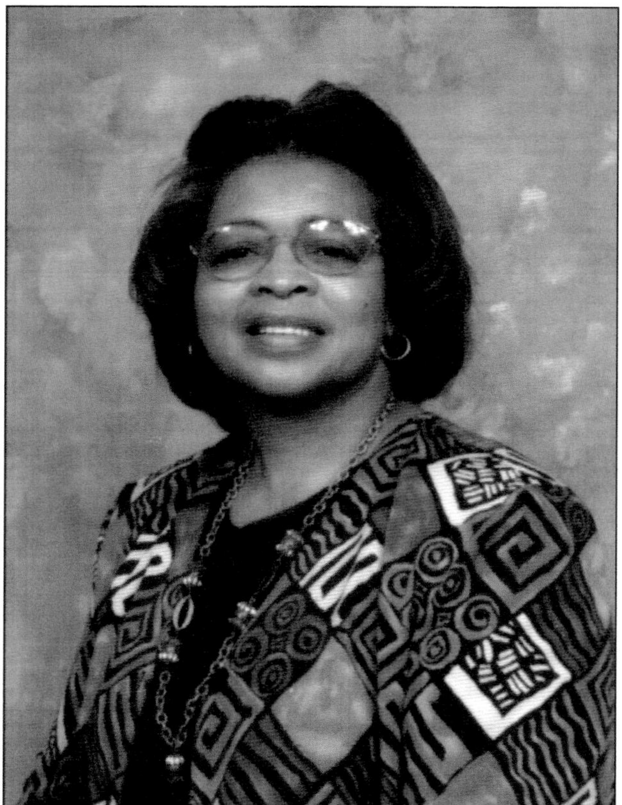

Gwendolyn Reliford was the first African American teacher of the year for Coffee County. She served as chair of social studies for 32 years. She is currently the director of the Mary Hayes Center for Social Change. (Courtesy of Gwendolyn Reliford.)

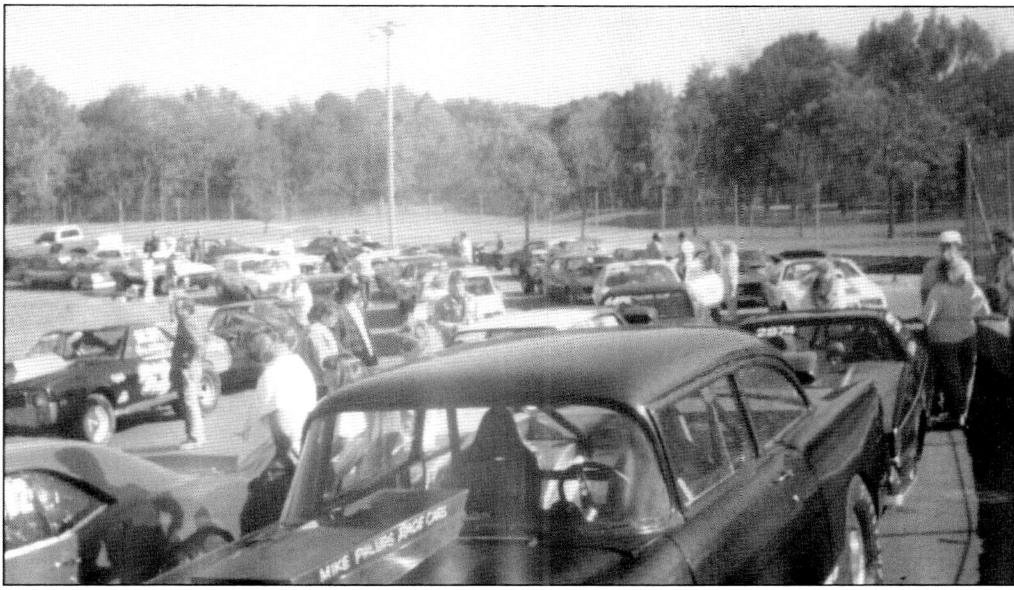

Formerly known as Southern Dragway, Douglas Motorsports Park has recently been named the International Hot Rod Association track of the year. Coffee County has been hosting racing events for over 40 years. (Courtesy of Sue McDuffie.)

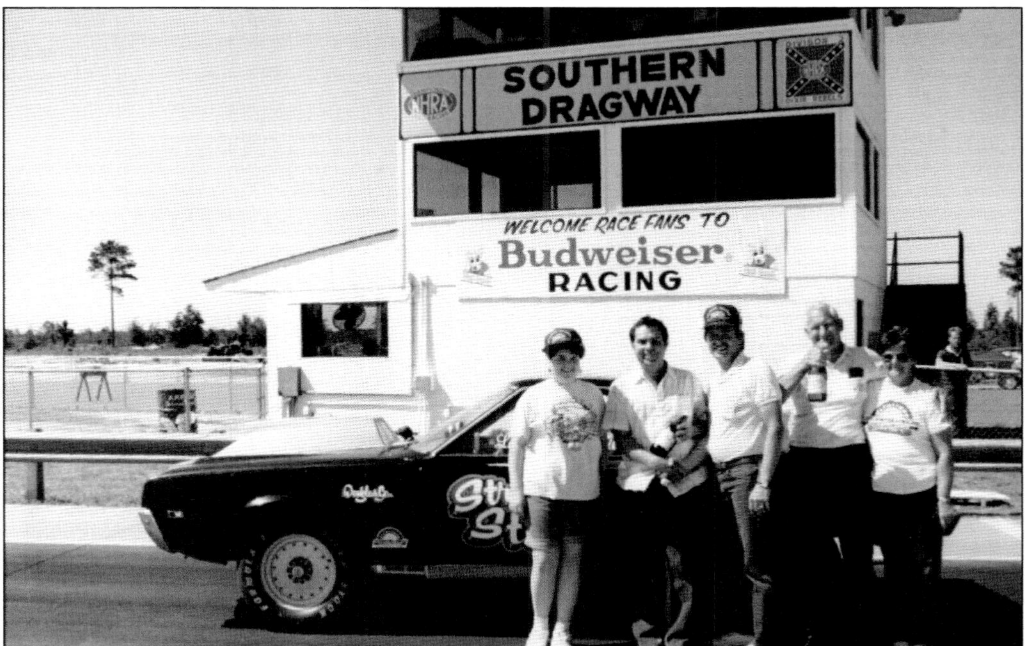

Seen here is Southeast Division E.T. racer Larry McDuffie with his AMX car *Strange Stuff*. An area resident, "Barefoot Larry" was a National Hot Rod Association Racing Summit Series two-time winner, Racer of the Year, and Southeast Division Driver of the Year. From left to right are Larry's daughter Felicia McDuffie, Larry, Timmy Miller, and Gordon and Lynette Thigpen. (Courtesy of Sue McDuffie.)

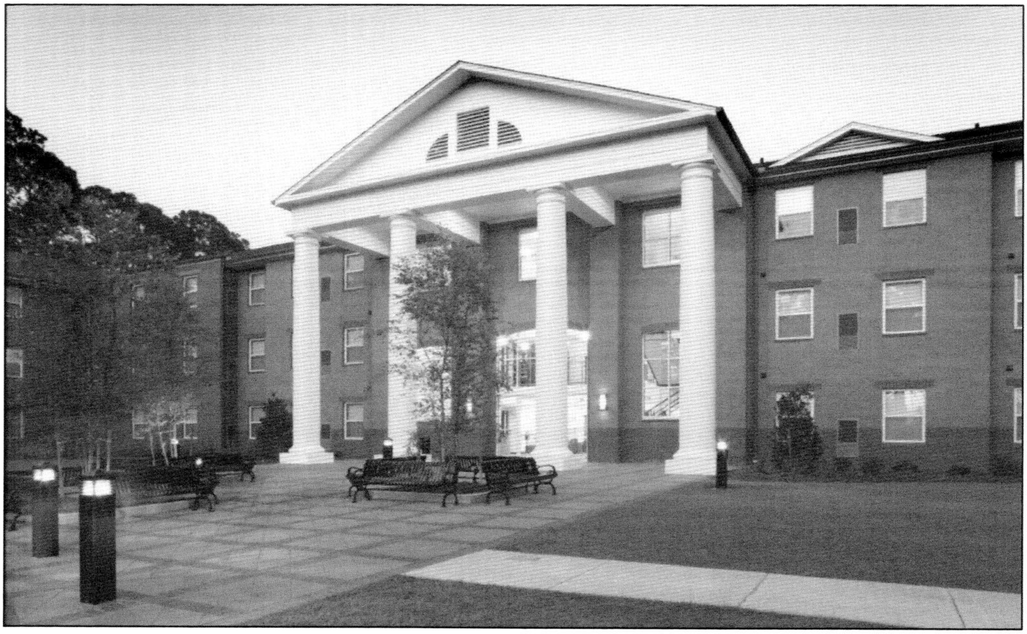

In January 2013, South Georgia College consolidated with Waycross College, and the name changed to South Georgia State College (SGSC). Seen here is Tiger II, the newest residence hall at SGSC. (Courtesy of South Georgia State College.)

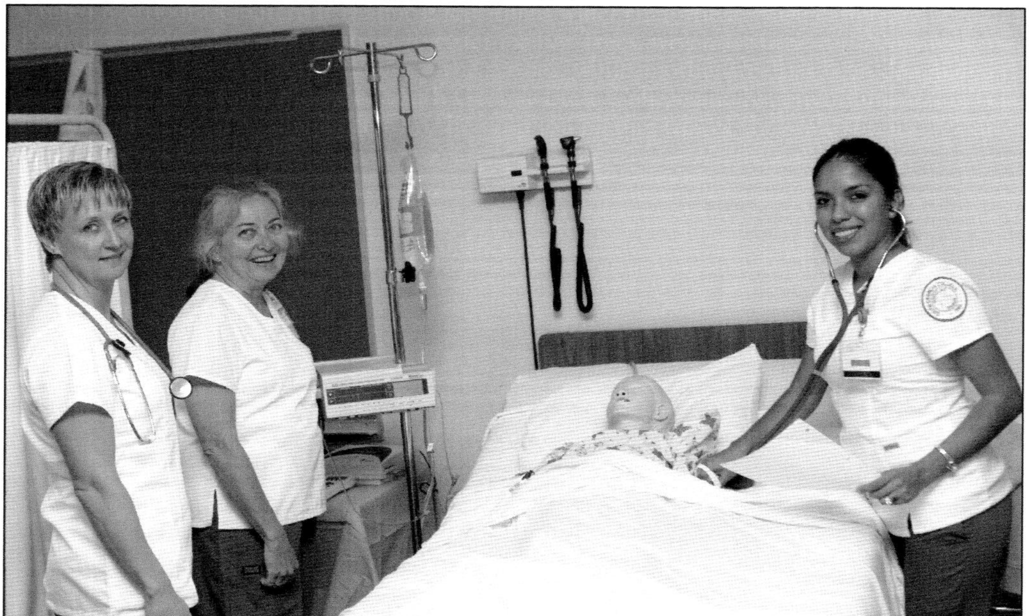

In 2011, the Georgia Board of Regents elevated the former South Georgia College to the level of "state college." This change allowed the college to offer baccalaureate degrees. Currently, the institution offers a bachelor of science in nursing degree (RN-BSN). (Courtesy of South Georgia State College.)

In 2007, Tracy McClelland opened Ycarte Health Career Center, a nursing tutorial facility designed to assist in training health-care professionals. Ycarte focuses on supplementing the education of registered nurses to help further their careers while also training certified nurse assistants to begin their professions. (Courtesy of Tracy McClelland.)

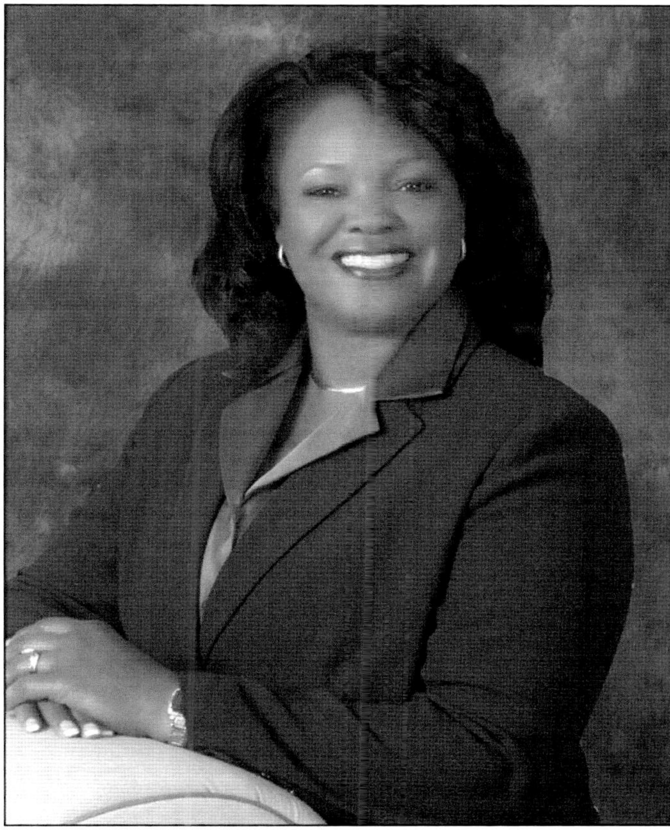

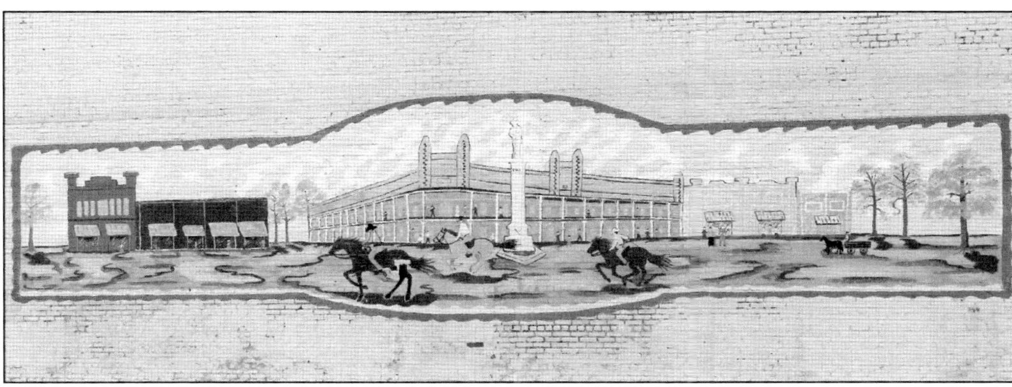

In the last few decades, the state of Georgia has experienced a large migration of Hispanic populations, with many coming to Coffee County and neighboring Atkinson County. Many have worked in agriculture and in processing plants, while some have started businesses of their own. One such business, Dos Hermanos, is housed in historic downtown Douglas. This mural expressing history and culture, painted by artist Pedro Hernandez, is found on an exterior wall. (Author's collection.)

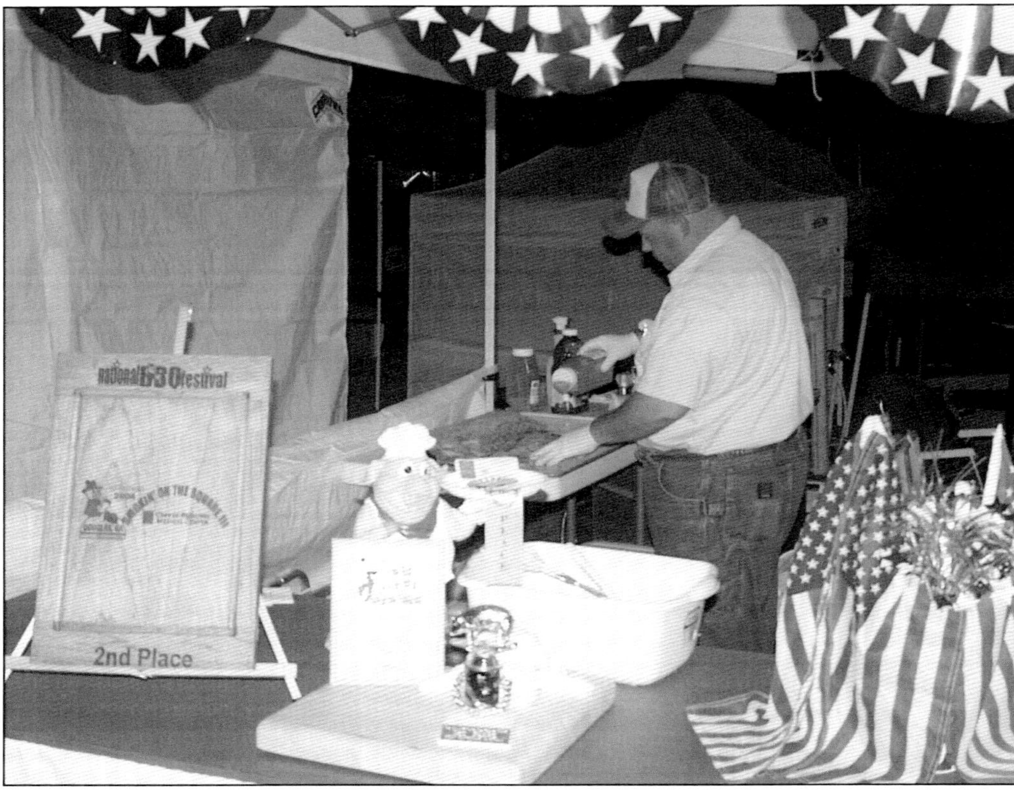

Douglas has hosted an annual event for the National Barbeque Festival from 2004 to 2011. Thousands of people come from every part of the country to compete. (Courtesy of Bill Anderson.)

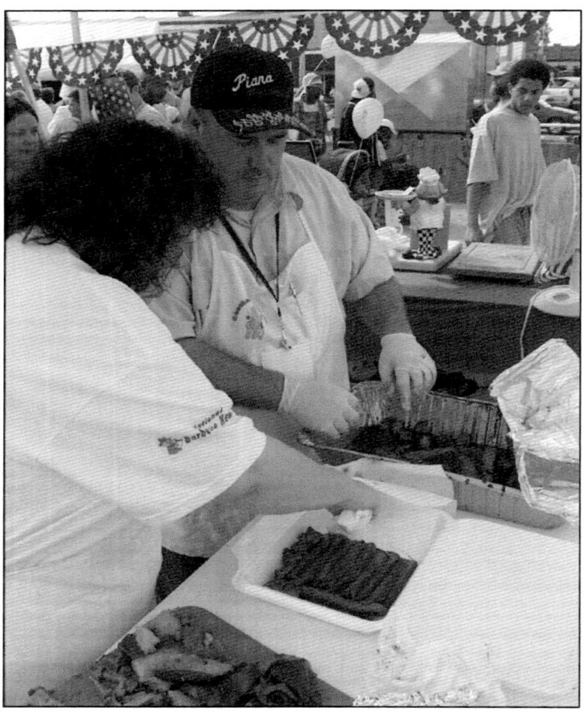

Each competitor must have won a local- or state-level barbeque contest to qualify for participation in the competition. Thousands attend the event every year to enjoy the best of the best in barbeque. (Courtesy of Bill Anderson.)

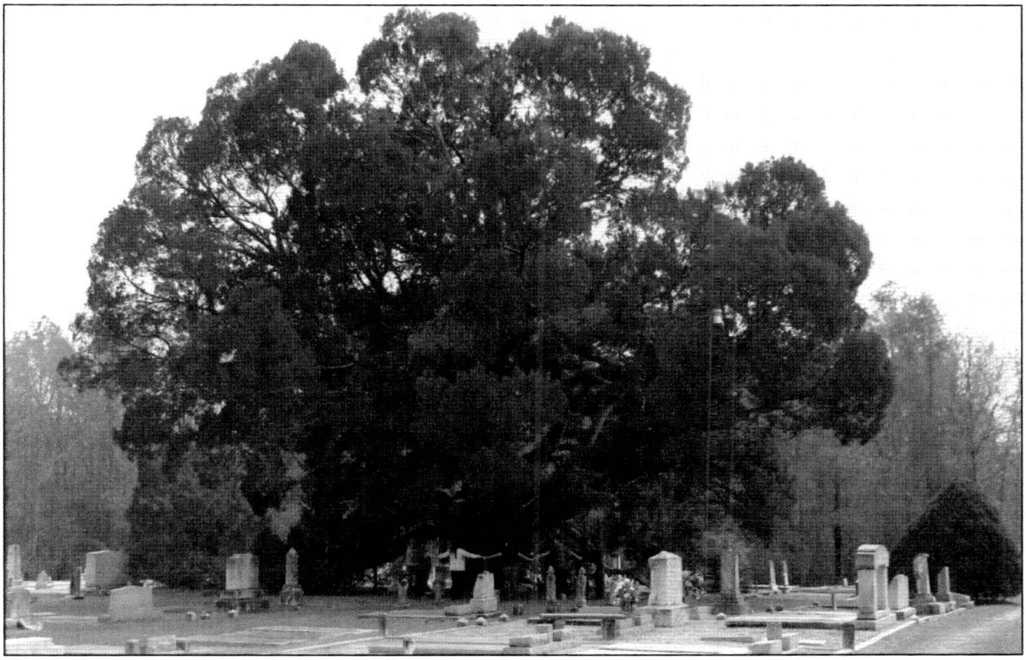

Most eastern red cedars resemble decorative bushes or Christmas trees. A mature tree can grow to 60 feet in height and spread 25 feet wide; this one dominates the cemetery of Lone Hill United Methodist Church. It is almost four times wider than the average eastern red cedar. In 1997, it was placed in the National Register for Big Trees, which lists the top 200 largest trees in the nation. The tree is the widest of the species, while another tree has been designated the tallest. Here, Prof. Kelly Moore of South Georgia State College and her environmental lab class surround the tree. The smaller tree on the right is a mature tree of the same species. (Courtesy of Charles E. Griffiths II.)

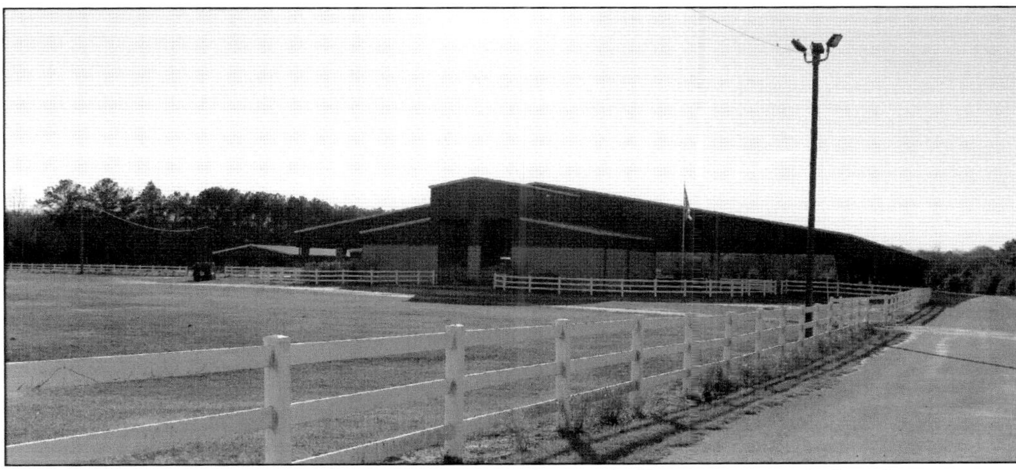

The South Georgia Wiregrass Youth Park, located in Nicholls, Georgia, includes a large covered arena. Folks from Coffee County and surrounding areas use the facility for Future Farmers of America livestock shows and 4-H activities for youth. Horse shows, livestock events, car shows, tractor pulls, concerts, flea markets, and other educational and recreational events are also held here. (Courtesy of Charles E. Griffiths II.)

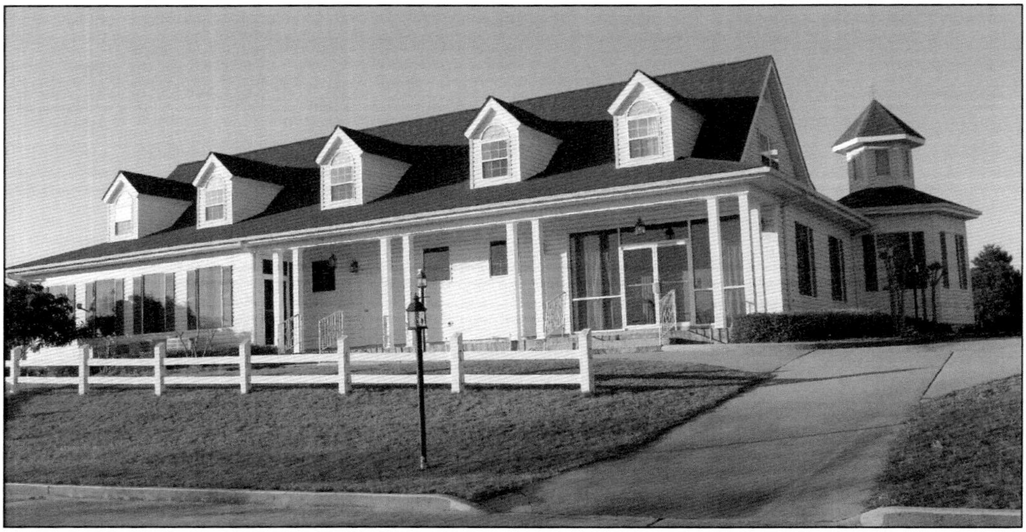

Hinson Hills, an 18-hole golf course at the Hinson Hills Golf Center facility in Douglas, was designed by general manager/golf professional Larry Hinson and opened in 1992. In 1967, Larry was the NCAA Division II men's golf champion, and he was the winner of the Greater New Orleans Open Invitational in 1969. (Courtesy of Charles E. Griffiths II.)

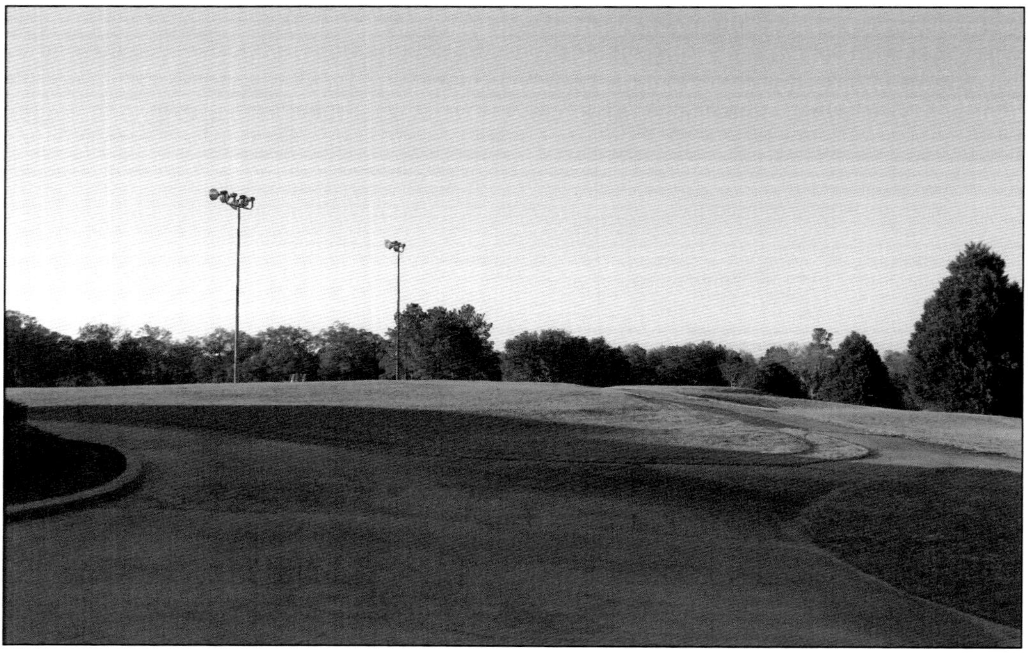

The Douglas area has four golf courses. Hinson Hills and Community Golf Course of South Georgia College are open to the public to play. The Douglas Golf & Country Club was designed in 1931 by Bobby Jones, and Beaver Creek, designed by Kirby Holton, is a semiprivate course that opened in 1988. (Courtesy of Charles E. Griffiths II.)

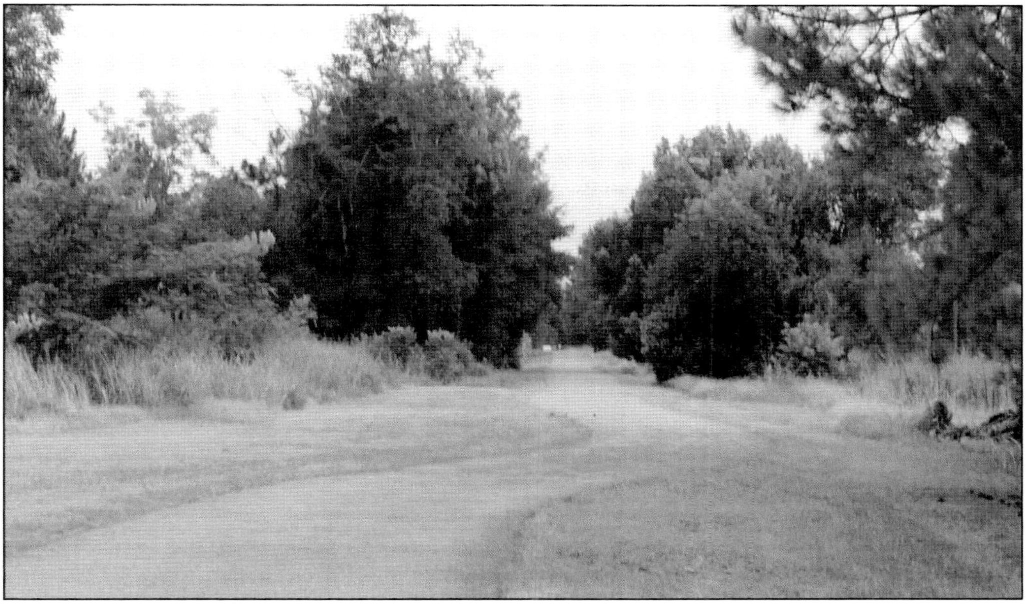

In 2012, Douglas successfully built a multiuse trail atop the bed of the old Georgia & Florida Railway, a former economic generator. From the board of education, the route meanders through the landscaped campus of South Georgia State College. It then tours through local businesses and passes several homes. Midway along the trail, on Ward Street West, it passes the old train depot, now home to the Heritage Station Museum. Continuing along a path lined with wildflowers and pines, the trail presently ends at North Chester Avenue. The City of Douglas is currently working to extend the trail on the north end. (Courtesy of Charles E. Griffiths II.)

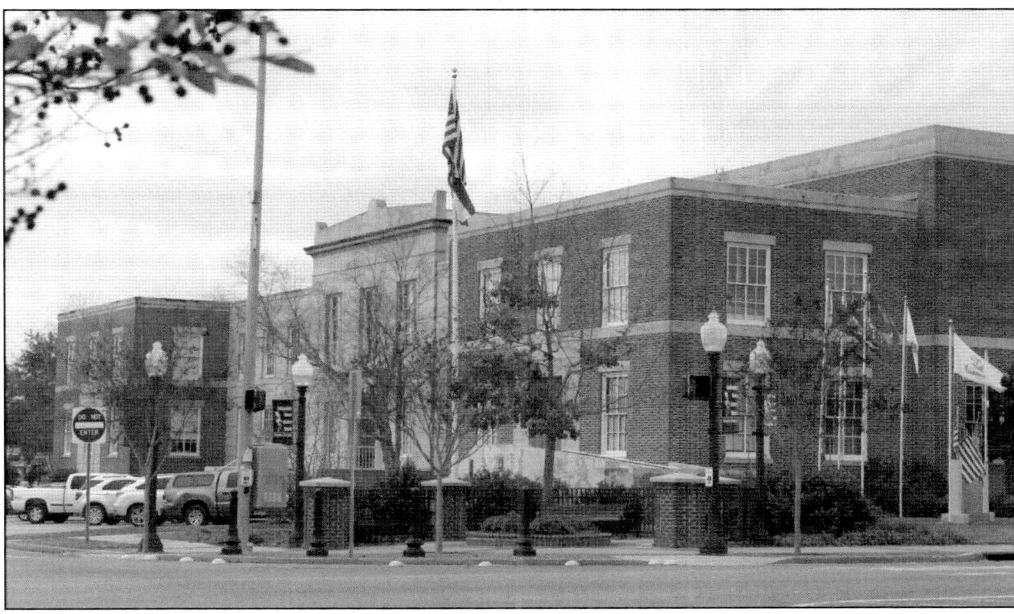

The county outgrew the original 1940 courthouse; an addition to the large two-story structure added in 1991 covers the block. Shown is the addition and courthouse building on the side by the new Veterans' Memorial. (Courtesy of Charles E. Griffiths II.)

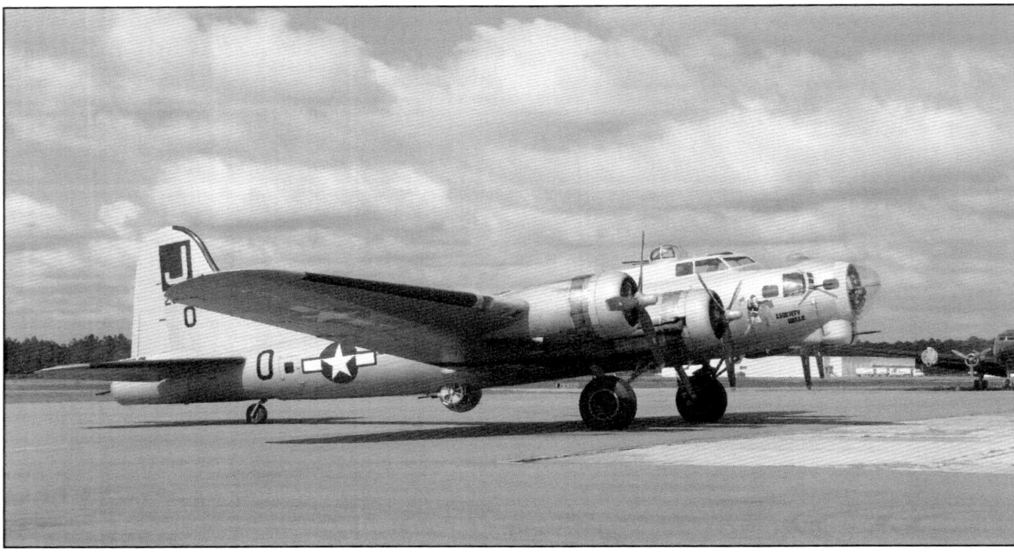

The B-17 *Liberty Belle*, after restoration, is pictured here on the Douglas airstrip. The restoration took Tom Reilly 13 years to complete. The B-17 series aircraft saw plenty of action in all theaters during World War II. (Courtesy of Brooks Aviation, Don Brooks.)

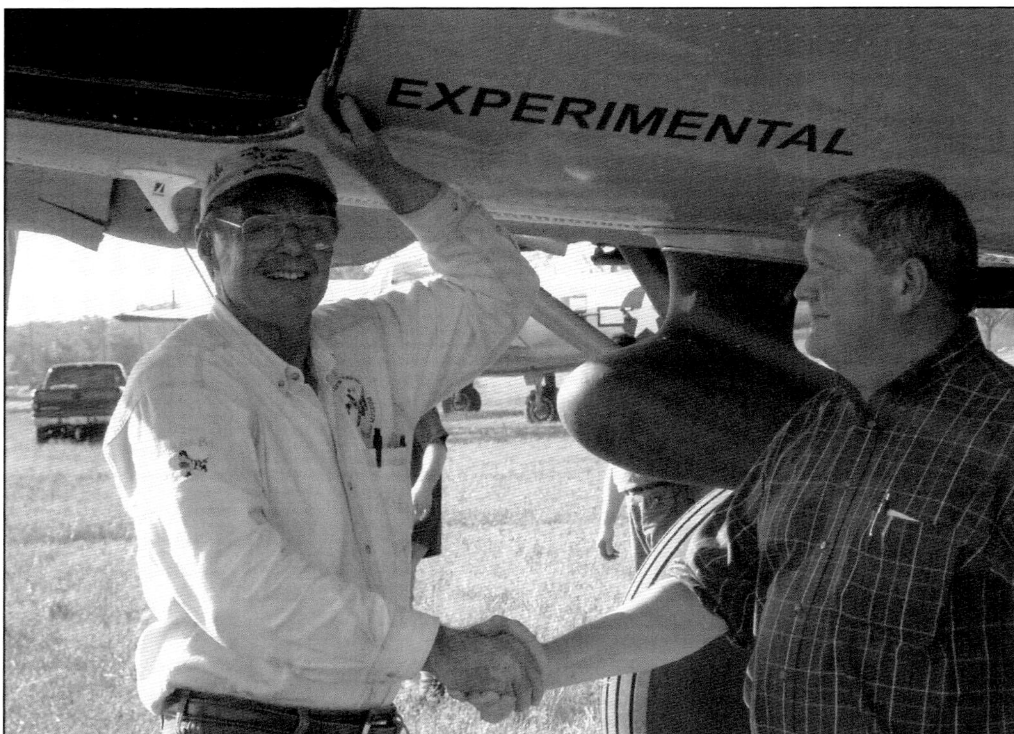

Tom Reilly (left) and Don Brooks pose in 2004 after the first flight of Don's B-17 *Liberty Belle*. With over 40 years of accident-free restorations, these men have been responsible for saving 33 significant "war birds" for future generations to experience. If not for their efforts, the majority of these aircraft would have ended up in scrap yards. (Courtesy of Brooks Aviation, Don Brooks.)

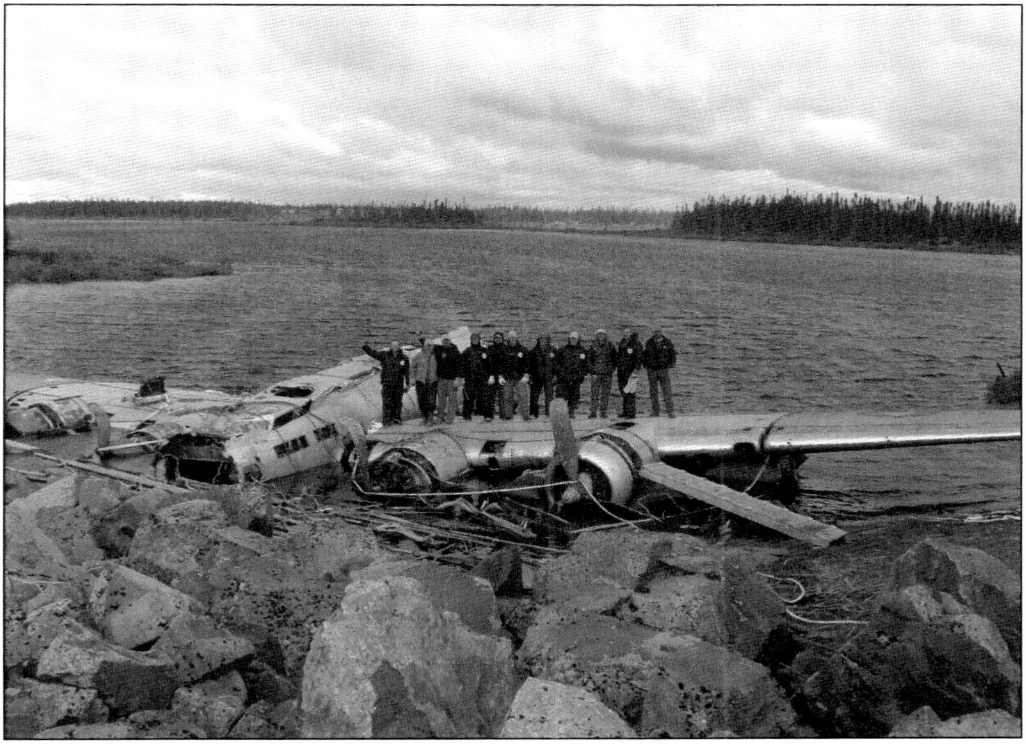

A B-17 Flying Fortress, completely damaged by a tornado in Windsor Locks, Connecticut, was recovered for restoration. Tom Reilly and his crew of highly skilled sheet-metal artisans have been taking piles of rubble and painstakingly duplicating each piece of original aircraft to re-create and save history that would otherwise have been lost to a scrapper forever. (Courtesy of Brooks Aviation, Don Brooks.)

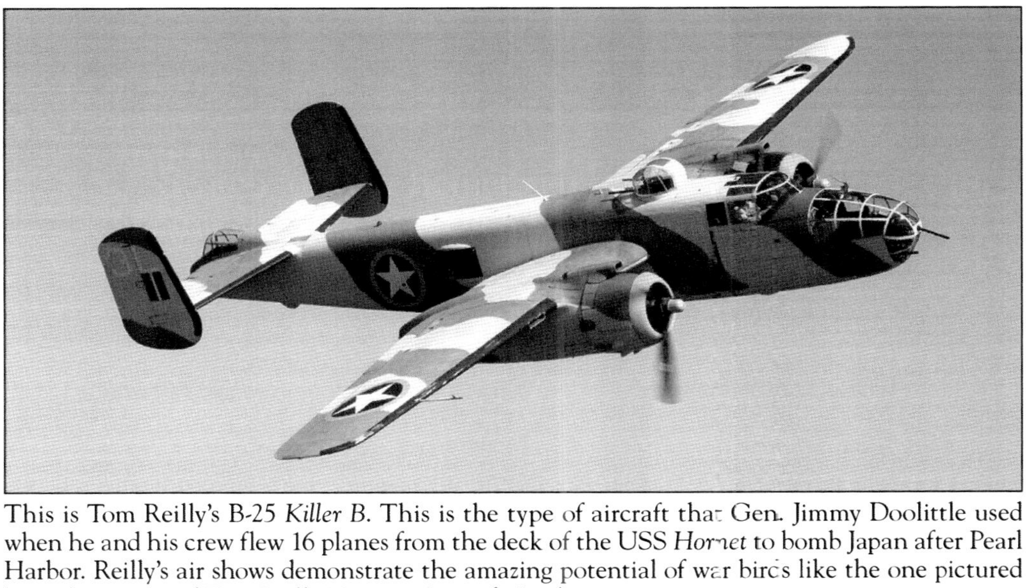

This is Tom Reilly's B-25 *Killer B*. This is the type of aircraft that Gen. Jimmy Doolittle used when he and his crew flew 16 planes from the deck of the USS *Hornet* to bomb Japan after Pearl Harbor. Reilly's air shows demonstrate the amazing potential of war birds like the one pictured here. (Courtesy of Tom Reilly Vintage Aircraft, Inc.)

IMAGES
of America

WARD POUND RIDGE RESERVATION

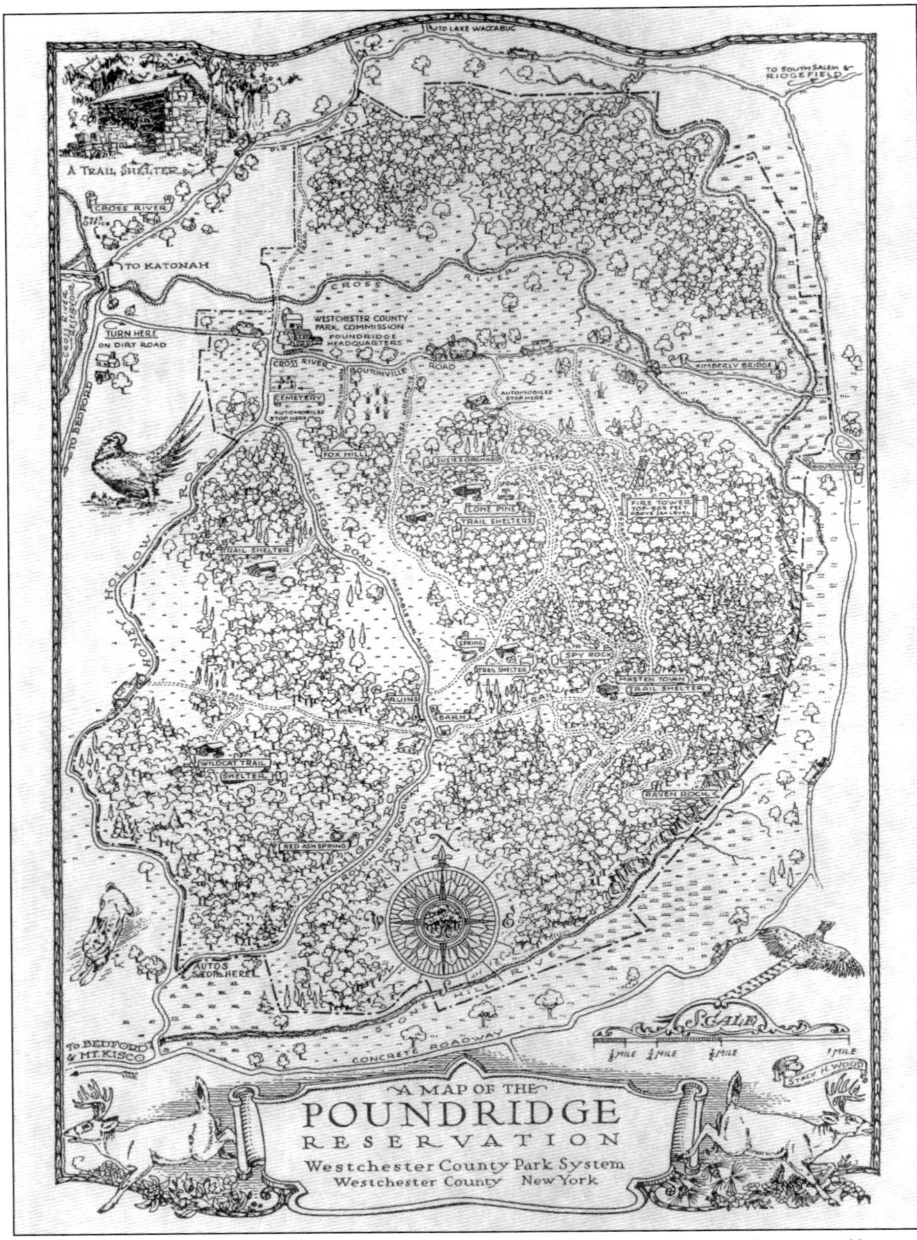

This early park map, bordered with images of wildlife and traversed by renderings of hay wagons and motorcars, highlights barns, springs, ruins, and an emerging trail system. Sweeping around the eastern arch of the reservation is the ridge of rock for which the town of Pound Ridge is named. While there were two entrances, from Routes 121 and 124, vehicles were restricted to the old Boutonville Road. (Courtesy of the Trailside Nature Museum.)

On the Cover: Sitting on a farmer's fence in 1940, a park visitor gazes across the valley. An unpaved Route 124 is in the background, and the spine of Cross River Mountain rises to the west. This photograph illustrates the story behind the Ward Pound Ridge Reservation: the connection between the people and the land. (Courtesy of the Westchester County Archives.)

IMAGES
of America

Ward Pound Ridge Reservation

Beth Herr and Maureen Koehl

ARCADIA
PUBLISHING

ISBN 978-0-7385-9905-2

Published by Arcadia Publishing
Charleston, South Carolina

Printed in the United States of America

Library of Congress Control Number: 2012951208

For all general information, please contact Arcadia Publishing:
Telephone 843-853-2070
Fax 843-853-0044
E-mail sales@arcadiapublishing.com
For customer service and orders:
Toll-Free 1-888-313-2665

Visit us on the Internet at www.arcadiapublishing.com

This book is dedicated to the people who lived, worked, and played in, and studied and interpreted the extraordinary Ward Pound Ridge Reservation.

CONTENTS

Acknowledgments

We would like to thank the following persons and organizations for their help: Jason Klein, Sharon Mammoser, Lori Morash, Bill Whitman, He Who Stands Firm, the Bedford Garden Club, and the Westchester County Archives. Unless otherwise noted, all images appear courtesy of the Trailside Nature Museum.

INTRODUCTION

Ward Pound Ridge Reservation is an extraordinary place, a gem of a park encompassing forests, meadows, wetlands, rocky ridges, and miles of walking trails. It sits like an emerald atop the map of the New York City metropolitan area, a wilderness within reach of Manhattan. Its history is rich: Native Americans left petroglyphs and place-names; the British and the New York militia skirmished here during the Revolutionary War; the legendary and secretive Leather Man camped here in a cave from 1858 to 1888; farmers changed the landscape with fields and stone walls; the Civilian Conservation Corps (CCC) called it home; and, since 1925, thousands of visitors have read this history in the land.

The creation of the park in 1925 reflected the rising tide of America's love of nature. At the turn of the century, Americans were in the midst of a nature renaissance. The popularity of the nature writers John Burroughs and John Muir, the invention of binoculars and bicycles, the declining costs of transportation, and the decreasing wilderness frontier put nature and wildlife in high demand.

The Westchester Parks Commission, formed in 1922, was aware of the need for nature. It "recognized the consistent public demand for a large reservation in the northerly part of the County, which can be reforested, if necessary, to amplify the existing forest and which would be available for camping and other forms of recreation on a large scale." The commission submitted a proposal to the county board of supervisors for the purchase of 3,000 acres at an estimated cost of $300,000. On March 30, 1925, the board voted to fund the acquisition of land for Pound Ridge Reservation.

So successful was the creation of the core of an impressive reservation that, following intense review by environmental experts, the commission recommended expanding the park to its natural topography "along ridge summits to include the slopes of the stream valley and four small secondary basins or valleys. " That brought the total appropriation to $500,000 for a total acreage of 4,171.

One man in particular led the effort to create this remarkable park. William L. Ward, Westchester's Republican leader, had the "vision and courage" to acquire the land for the people. In October 1938, four years after his death, with pomp and ceremony, the park was renamed in his honor and forever became Ward Pound Ridge Reservation.

From its inception, the reservation was managed for wildlife and for the enjoyment of people. Trees were planted (500,000 white and red pines, hemlocks, and spruces), stone camping shelters with fireplaces were built, 30 miles of "old woods roads and paths" were cleared for hiking trails, springs were cleaned and walled in, and an 85-foot fire tower was constructed on the highest point in the park.

Established as a forest preserve, the reservation initially lacked interpretive trails, brochures, or exhibits. A local conservation group, the Bedford Garden Club, took an interest in the new park. In 1931, it hired a naturalist and local bird expert, William Wheeler, to blaze a nature trail, one of the first interpretive trails in New York State. Wheeler soon became quite popular and developed a devoted following.

Two of Wheeler's biggest fans were garden club members Delia West Marble and Eloise Payne Luquer. They had the idea to create a small nature museum in the park and to install Wheeler as its naturalist. Their greatest ally in this scheme was Hermann W. Merkel, then general superintendent of the Westchester Parks Commission. He was a botanist and clearly understood the value of such a museum. Merkel, at the urging of the garden club, traveled to Washington, DC, to petition the Department of the Interior for funds to construct a nature museum. He was successful, returning with $3,600 for building materials.

The museum was built by the men of the Civilian Conservation Corps (CCC) who were stationed in the park. The design was crafted by the architects of the National Park Service, already involved in developing other CCC projects at Pound Ridge. It was one of the first nature centers to be built in America, following a similarly named museum at Bear Mountain Park. Anchored in local stone crafted by the skilled masons of the CCC, topped with a slate roof, filled with custom-made cabinets, and nestled in the stony hills, the Trailside Museum was a remarkable sight.

After the museum was completed in 1937, Wheeler wasted no time in filling the rooms with exhibits. The walls were covered from floor to ceiling with curiosities. Wheeler's annual report from 1938 lists items on exhibit: "conservation posters, colored pictures of bird and wildflowers of the current month, colored plates of fresh water fishes, a complete fern collection from the old Agassiz Association of Bedford, bird's nests, deer antlers, mounted fish, an original Audubon print, insects balls, local snakes and salamanders, turtle shells and their eggs, rock and minerals, birds and mammals."

The Bedford Garden Club continued to support the museum and its programs. It paid the curator's salary for the first three years and even kept the museum open on weekends during World War II. The club helped publish a book about the reservation's wildlife, sponsored nature lectures, and started a wildflower garden.

The ecology movement was catching on all over America, leading to the first Earth Day celebration in 1970. People were hungry for information about ecology and local natural history. It was a pivotal era for the museum and marked the arrival of Nick Shoumatoff. Now called He Who Stands Firm, Shoumatoff was a charismatic and magnetic naturalist, linguist, artist, and ethnographer. Weekday and weekend programs were expanded and drew record crowds. Shoumatoff procured federal funding for two research expeditions to collect information and plant lore from living descendants of Westchester County tribes. During his tenure, the museum was enlarged (1976), the Delaware Indian Resource Center was established, and archaeological digs were carried out at sites within the park.

Today, Ward Pound Ridge Reservation is treasured and managed for biodiversity. A biological inventory continues; rare habitats and species are monitored; vernal pools are mapped; species restoration projects and radio telemetry of endangered animals guide management toward wildlife protection. The stewardship lessons learned are shared with the public through weekend programs, school field trips, summer ecology camps, and student internships.

Given the vast expanse of the landscape, including forests, meadows, and wetlands, and given its many years of protection, the reservation is recognized as an area of rich diversity. It was designated by the Wildlife Conservation Society in 2001 as the hub of the Biotic Corridor of Northern Westchester. In 2003, the Westchester County Parks commissioner proclaimed the reservation a Biodiversity Preserve in its entirety.

One

A Park is Born

Westchester County joined the national swell of a nature appreciation culture. It followed the lead of New York State, which had just protected three natural resources to ensure their longevity: Palisades Interstate Park in 1916, then Bear Mountain and Harriman Parks in 1924. The following year, Westchester County voted to fund the acquisition of land for Pound Ridge Reservation. The decree states that "for camping and outdoor life, this reservation is comparable with the State Park areas in the Catskills and Adirondacks and can be held as a great forest preserve."

So enthusiastic was the response that the county set aside additional money for trail clearing and improvements such as "the maintenance of a few very simple public conveniences such as drinking water, comfort stations, and stone fireplaces, with some attention to existing paths and roads."

Eventually, the reservation was formed from 92 separate parcels with 55 owners. Not all acquisitions were happily transacted. Some farmers' acreage was obtained by eminent domain. Local stories and songs speak of the anger and resentment of the farmers whose lands were seized, even though they received monetary compensation.

The reservation, with its singular geology and history, is home to a wide variety of plant communities. Oak, hickory, and maple forests blanket the sloping hillsides; the wide, rich floodplains of the Cross River and tributaries slow and filter the water; steep hemlock ravines shelter bobcats and coyotes; open, wet meadows harbor rare butterflies and other insects. The area contains a remarkable suite of species available for study and enjoyment

At 4,315 acres, Ward Pound Ridge Reservation is today the county's largest park. With its varied terrain and landscapes and miles of wooded trails, the park hosts a variety of activities in all seasons. There are areas for picnicking, lean-to camping, fishing, horseback riding, and cross-country skiing. With 35 miles of hiking trails through open meadows and deep woodlands, around wetlands, and to mountaintop views, it remains a treasure for the enjoyment of all the people.

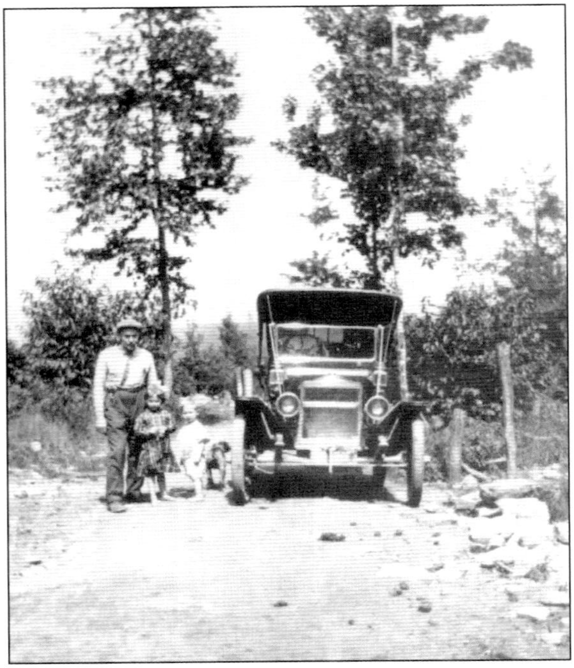

More than 3,000 acres in the new park were "immediately available for use as soon as title was acquired by the commission, because their principal charm is natural park areas of field and woodland." When the reservation first opened, visitors came in great numbers by foot, by bike, and by motorcar. The roads remained unpaved for decades, preserving the rural experience.

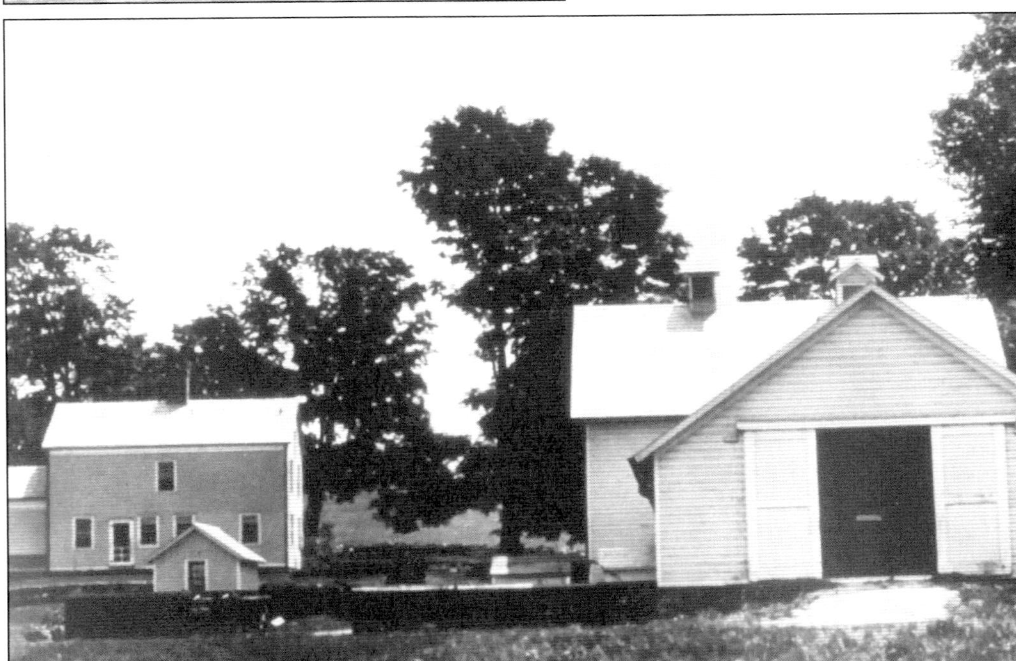

The transition from farmland to parkland took several years. Many improvements were made early on, but the cleanup of so many farm buildings took years. Most of the houses and farm sheds were destroyed, but this homestead was spared and eventually became the park headquarters. Like the farmers before them, park crews dumped debris in pits. Observant hikers can locate the remnants of early park employees' garbage and farmers' trash. The park is now a "carry in, carry out" facility, so landfills are no longer needed.

He in his bib overalls and she in her skirt, they are enjoying the breathtaking view from the Overlook after a steep climb up the mountain above the Leather Man's cave. The man points his walking stick across the Route 121 causeway and Cross River Reservoir toward the Hudson highlands and Catskill Mountains. This scene is reenacted daily. (Courtesy of the Westchester County Archives.)

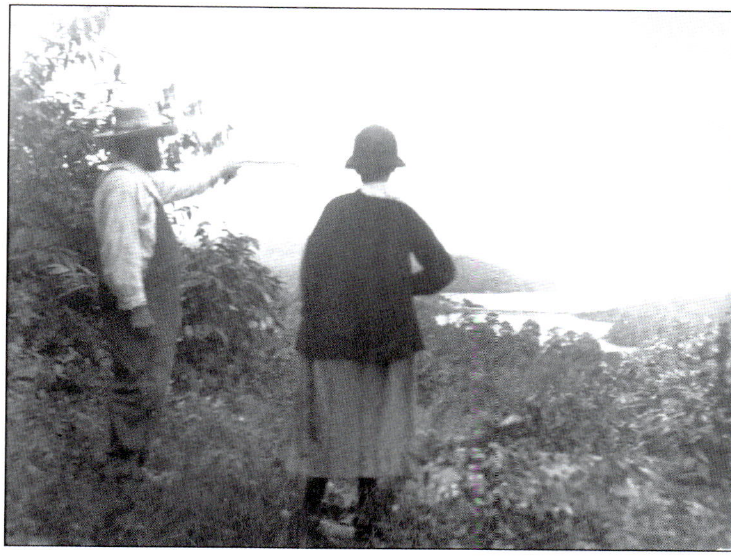

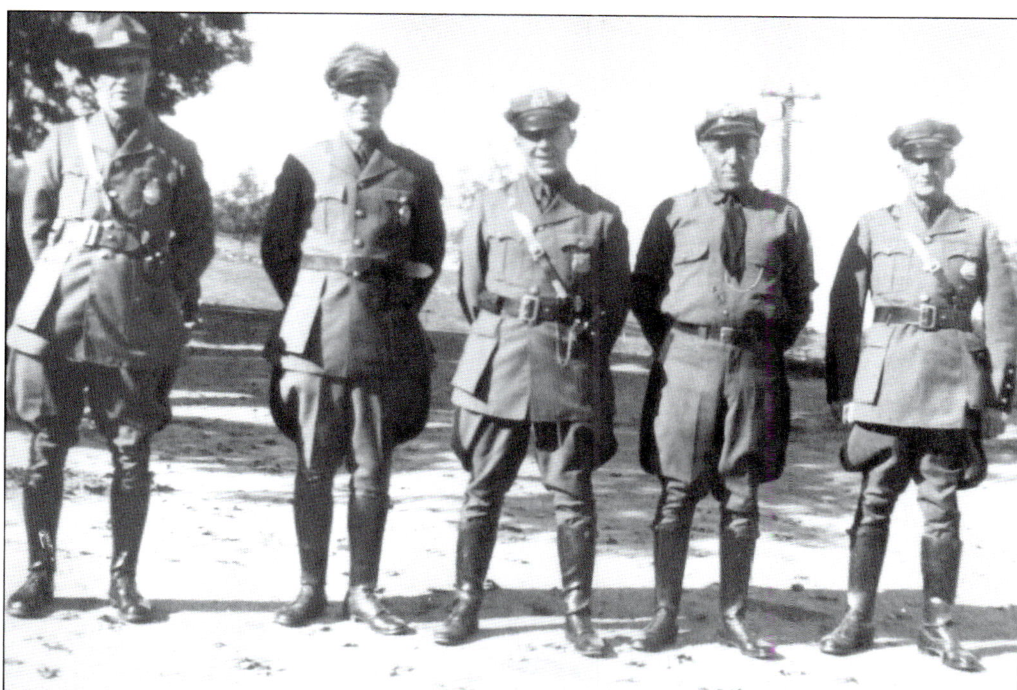

Park security was taken seriously in the early days. The reservation's impressive park patrolmen pose in full uniform in 1925. Shown here are, from left to right, William E. Whitman (also the first superintendent), ? Nash, ? Tripp, ? Nolly, and ? Green. Today, with campers spending nights in the wilderness and hikers traveling far afield, security remains essential to visitor safety.

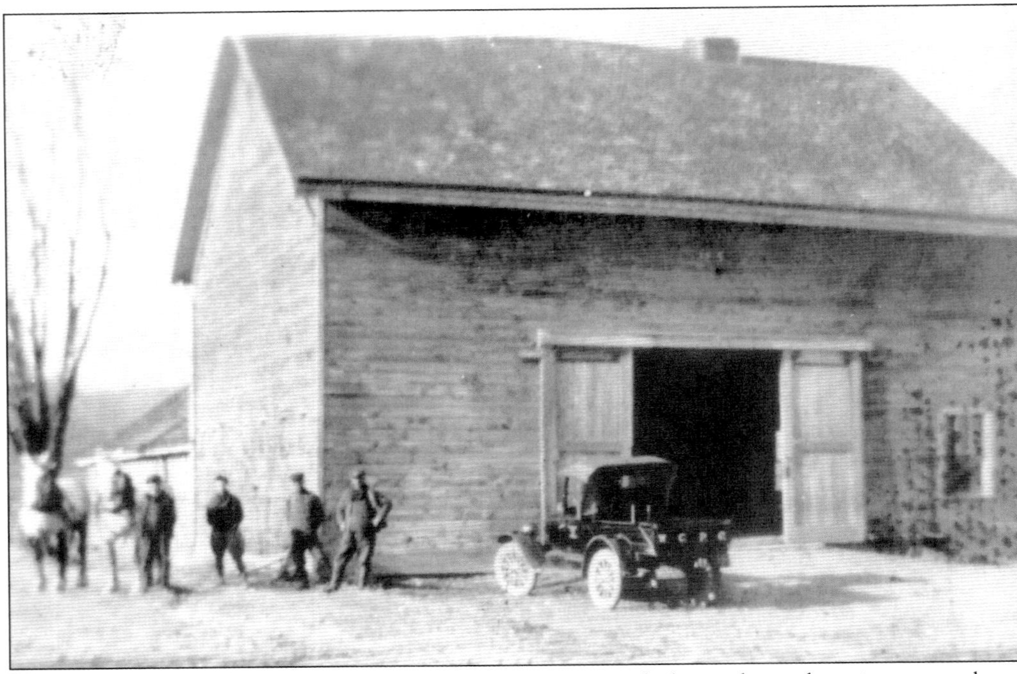

This photograph, taken the year the reservation was created, shows the park maintenance barn. Its utility had changed, from housing horses, cows, and tons of hay, to holding rakes, shovels, and park trucks. Uniformed park employees, with their horses and new park vehicle, stand proudly in front of the barn. The farmhouse nearby was converted to the park headquarters.

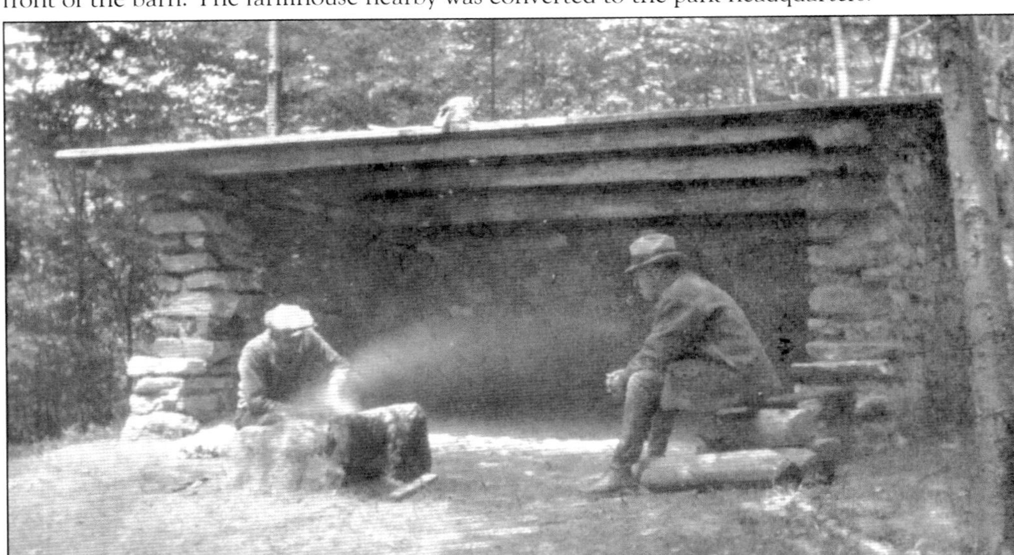

Smoke curls from a well-tended fire as two gentlemen set up camp in one of the stone lean-tos. The earliest shelter was built in 1928, its roof beams fashioned from chestnut trees felled by the blight. Many more camping shelters were added by the CCC. Most have a stone fireplace inside as well as a fire ring in front, and are used year-round.

The roads remained unpaved for decades, making travel in Model Ts a bumpy affair. This incline, just beyond Michigan Road, was the way to Boutonville. It formed a boundary between the towns of Lewisboro on the left, north side, and Pound Ridge on the right, south side. This and many of the trails in the park are lined with sugar maple trees, a testament to clever maple syrup farmers.

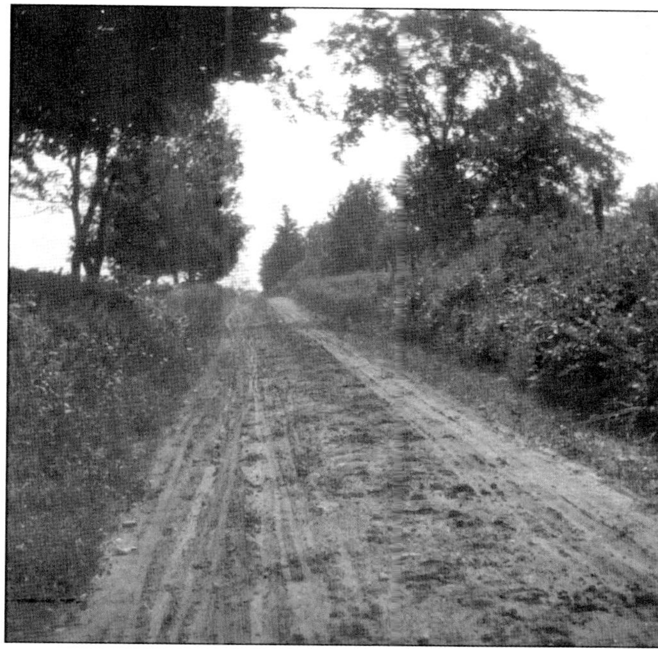

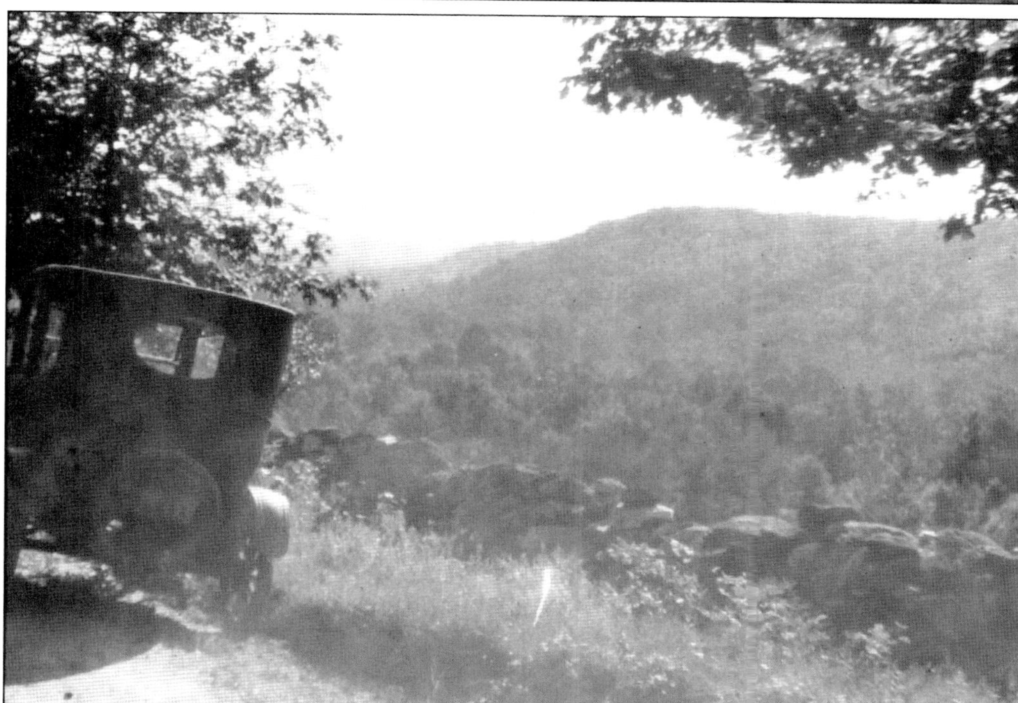

It still happens today. A casual drive through the park brings such pleasant views of bucolic landscapes that occupants are compelled to stop, turn off the motor, step outside the vehicle, and soak up the beauty. The reservation boasts some of the highest elevations in the county, and its vast acreage supports many species of plants and animals. Deer, turkey, bobcat, and coyote can be seen from the car. (Courtesy of the Westchester County Archives.)

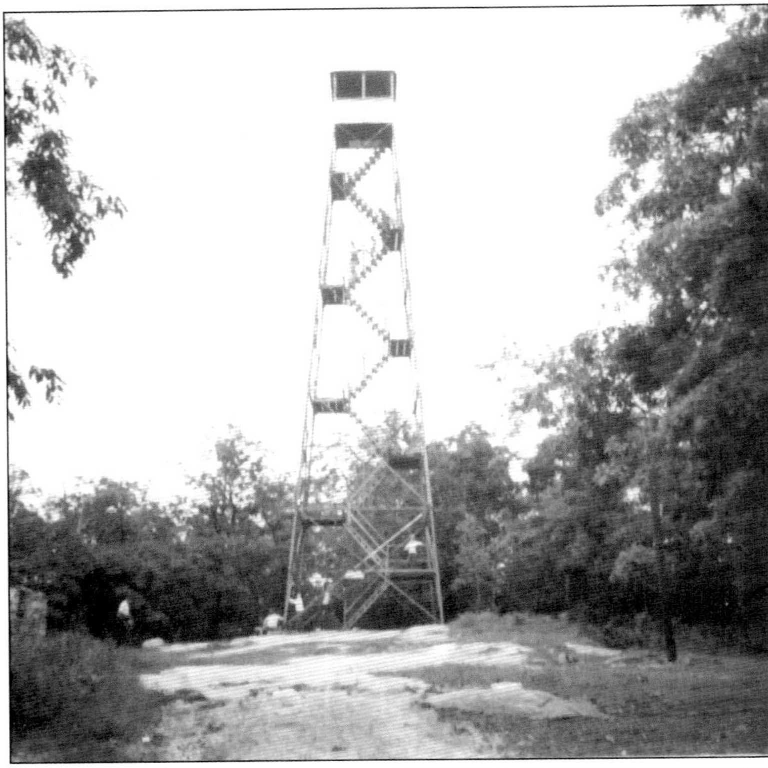

The Cross River Mountain fire tower was built in 1926 and was operated by the Westchester County Park Commission through the 1930 fire season. Control was transferred to the New York State Conservation Department in 1931 and lasted until the end of the 1970 fire season. The tower was decommissioned in 1971. The first warden was Thomas Purdy from North Salem, New York. He was paid $100 a month from April through October.

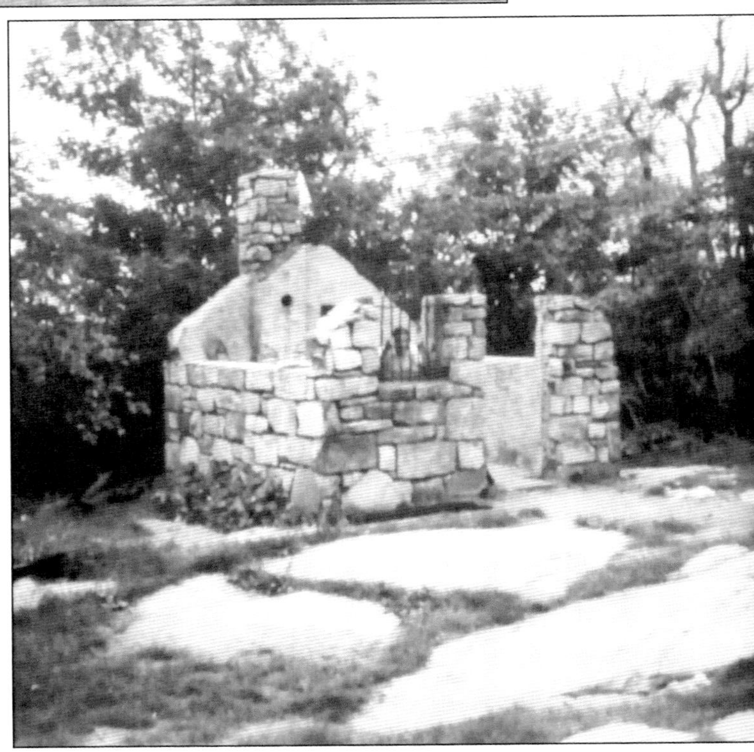

This beautiful stone building, one of two at the base of the fire tower, housed the fire warden. He spent the day in the tower watching for rising smoke and slept in the stone cabin at night. The warden relayed information by radio to the nearest tower's attendant, who relayed it to a third. By this means, the three workers helped triangulate the exact location of a fire.

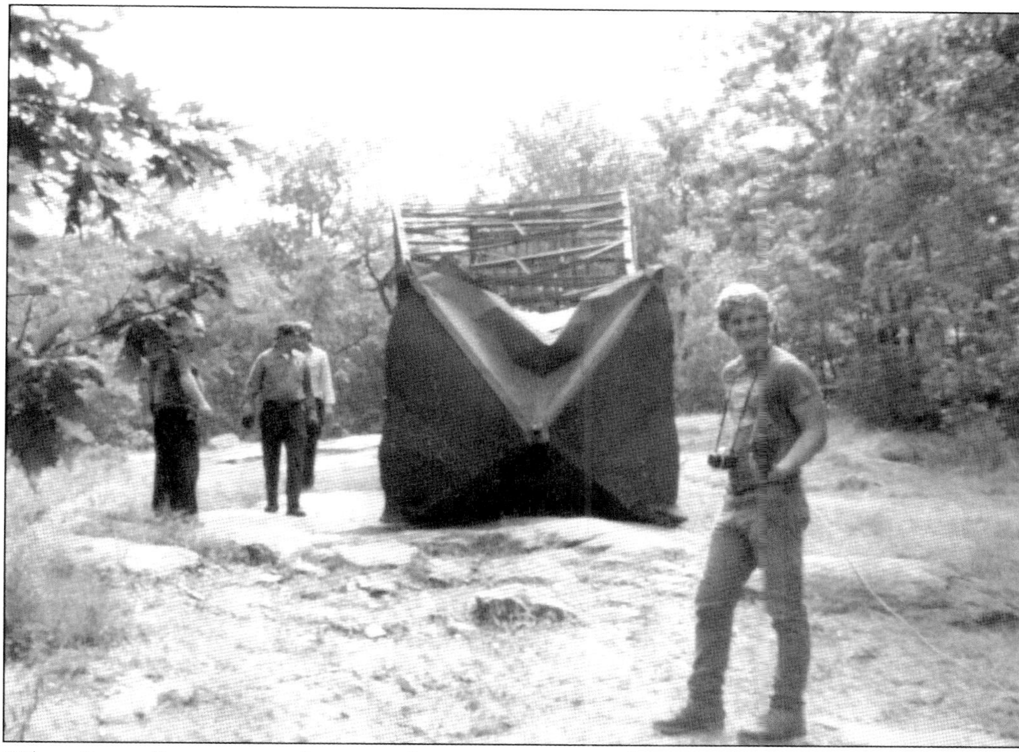

When forest fires were no longer a threat, towers were decommissioned across the state. A worker holds the cap to the reservation's fallen giant. Visitors remember that the view from the top extended to Long Island Sound and the New York City skyline. Hikers can still find their way here, climbing through several distinct plant communities. At the mountain's top sit the footprint of the tower, a US Geological Survey (USGS) marker, and a much-appreciated hand-cranked water pump.

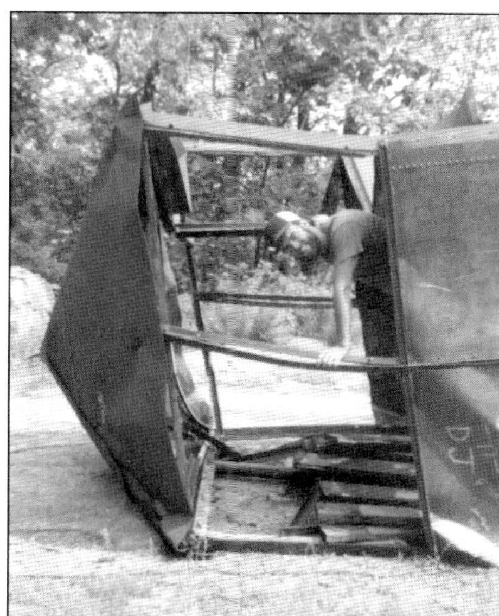

In September 1982, the fire tower was dismantled, along with 69 other towers located in New York State. Bill Whitman, a third-generation park employee, pretends to be the fire observer in the grounded steel hulk. The Friends of Trailside Nature Museum and Ward Pound Ridge Reservation hope to restore the steel structure and resurrect the views and thrills that it formerly provided.

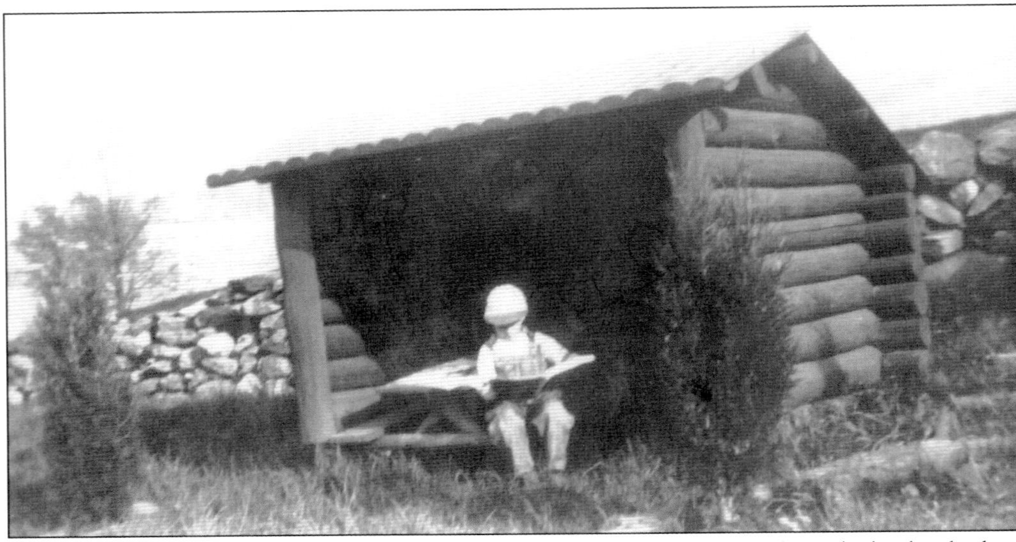

On a warm day in 1932, this young reader, dressed in coveralls and cap, brought his book along on a park outing. Most of the reservation lean-tos were made of cut local stone and are still in use today. There are no records as to how many log lean-tos were built; none of those survive.

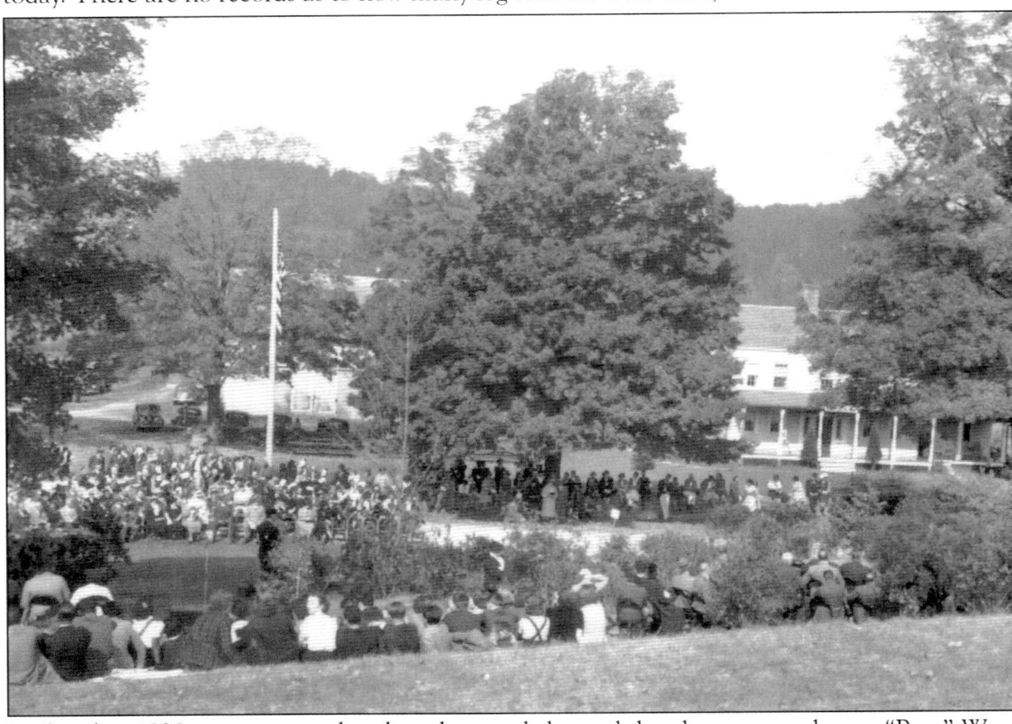

In October 1938, a great crowd gathered around the park headquarters to honor "Boss" Ward, the congressman and entrepreneur who helped create the popular reservation. Speakers included Gerard Swope, Herbert H. Lehman, and Robert Moses. A memorial plaque was unveiled, and the name of the park was changed to include Ward's name. Music was provided by local high schools, with spirituals sung by the Westchester Negro Choral Union. (Courtesy of Westchester County Archives.)

Printed on muslin, this early park sign alerts visitors to "temporary rules." Persons are warned against hunting, trapping, fishing, "except that lawful taking of upland game birds may be engaged in by citizens of this county under permit . . . hunting of foxes and other vermin may be done." Today, all plants, animals, and minerals are protected by law.

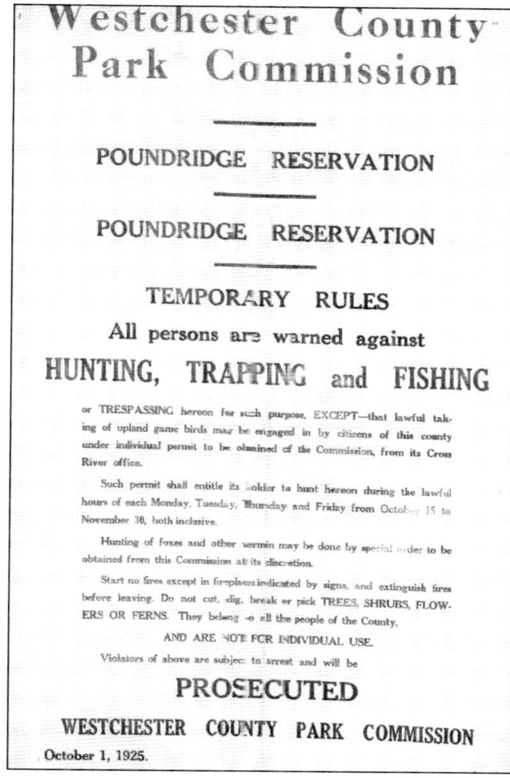

At a time when hunting was encouraged, photographs show a bounty of raccoons, foxes, skunks, minks, weasels, owls, and hawks taken from the park. The campaign against vermin became a particular focus for state conservation officials in the early 1920s. In the conservation era, the infant science of ecology had yet to influence public policy, and few people spoke out in favor of protecting entire ecosystems, predators and all.

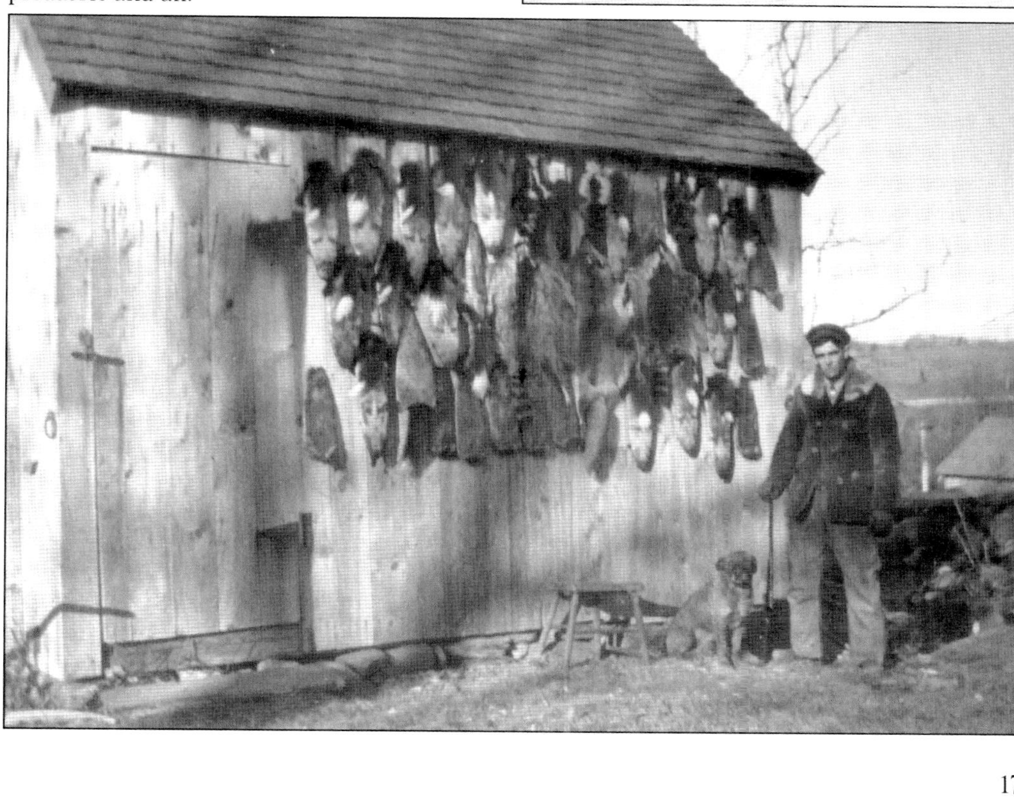

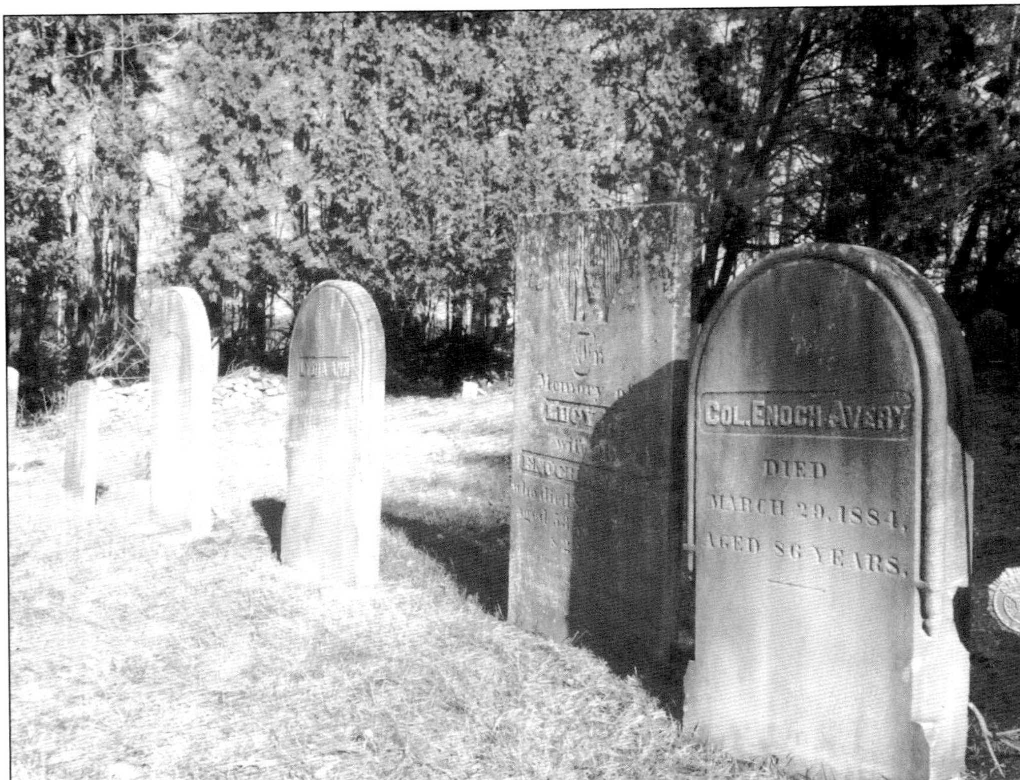

Just south of the park entrance lies the Colonel Avery Cemetery, where many town residents are buried. In addition to the tombstones of Enoch Avery and other Revolutionary War heroes, there are grave markers bearing names such as Lockwood, Webb, Mead, and Benedict. The last person buried there was Pearl Whitman, wife of William M. Whitman, whose family devoted three generations toward the caretaking of the park.

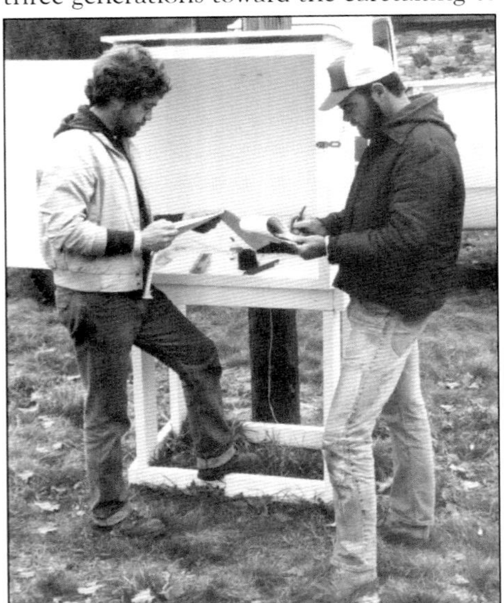

Park staff members Rick Rogers (left) and Bill Whitman record weather data from a station in the 1970s. Meteorological information, from wind speed to barometric pressure, has been collected in the reservation for decades. It is now monitored and downloaded daily by computers. Water quality in the Cross River is checked after every rain event, its purity a baseline for comparison with other county waterways.

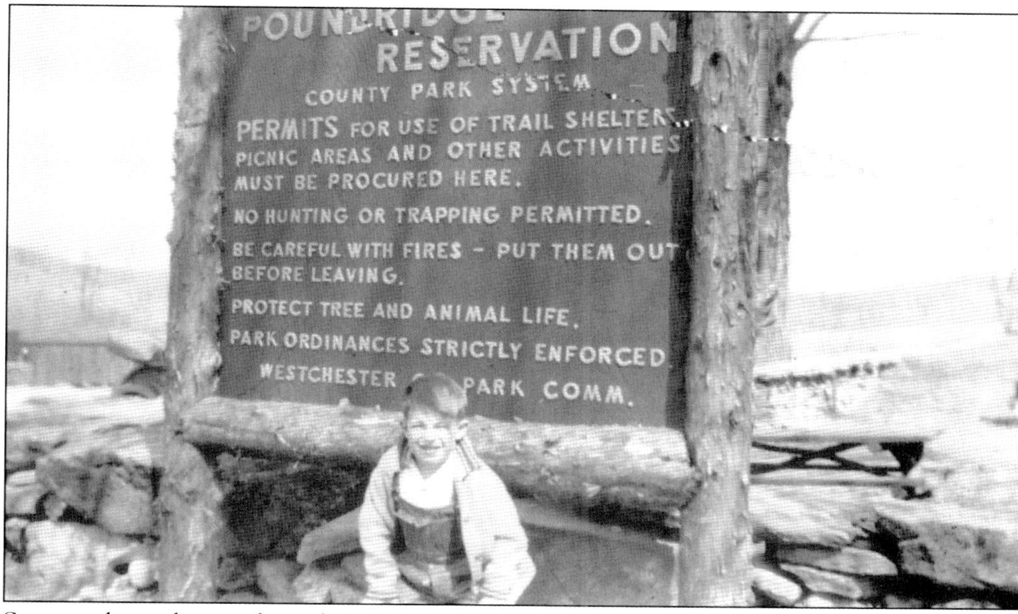

Some park regulations from the 1930s persist. Permits are required for camping, and wildlife is protected. Now, however, firewood is supplied for fear of invasive insects, and a deer management program addresses forest health. Added to the list of concerns for the integrity of the park are invasive plants, acid rain, poachers, complex multiple use, and climate change. Monitoring these impacts is essential to the integrity of this rich ecosystem.

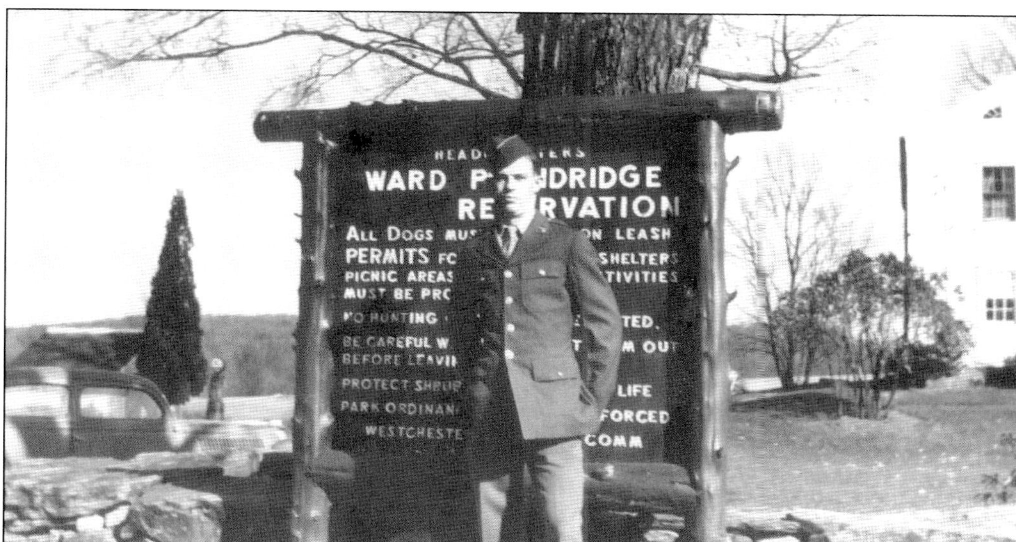

Some years later, in front of a "new" park sign with similar rules, a young soldier proudly poses for his mother or his sweetheart to remember a fond and favorite place away from home. On his left are stone carriage steps at the end of a long "walking wall" leading from the farmhouse on the right.

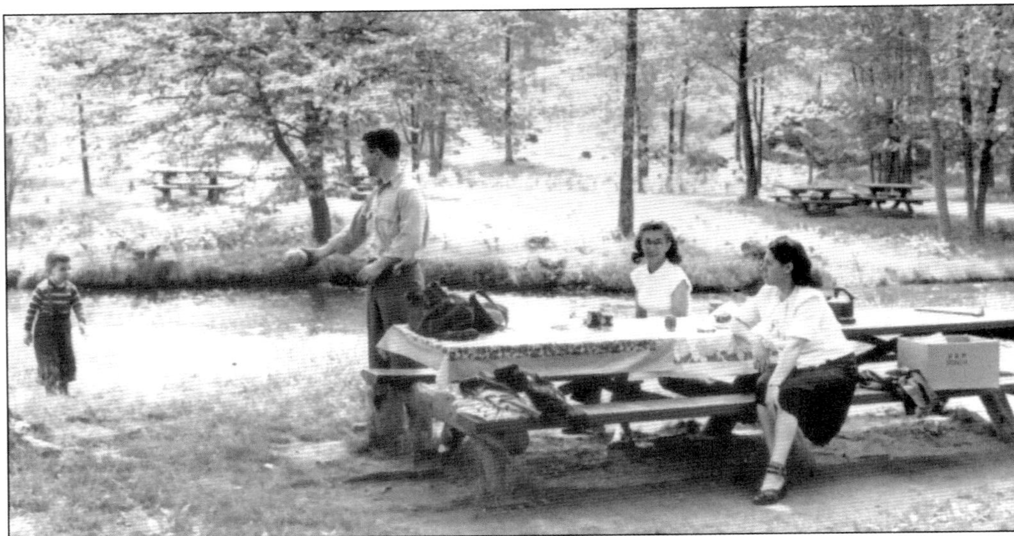

Families can enjoy a barbecue, wade in cool waters, hike miles beside the Cross River, find crayfish and minnows, or float handcrafted boats at Kimberly Bridge. The confluence with the Waccabuc River is just upstream and is labeled on an 18th-century map as "Otter Rocks." Otter tracks and scat are still seen nearby. The river empties into the Cross River Reservoir, which is part of the New York City water system.

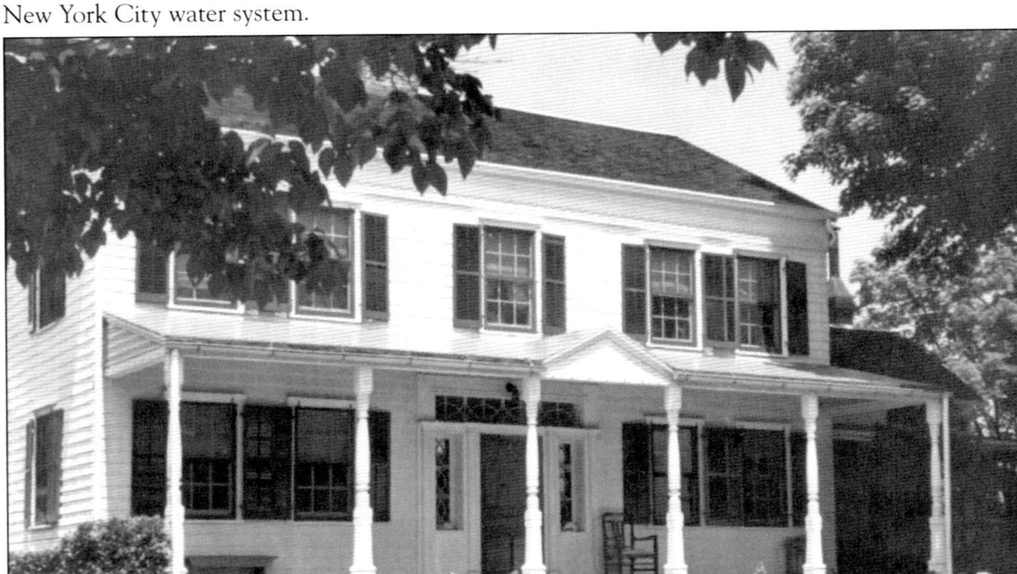

Now the park office, this building was originally the homestead of Joseph Benedict. The photograph shows the earliest part of the dwelling. On the right, with its small "eyebrow" windows, stands the first structure, built in 1726 and enlarged in 1851. The house has five fireplaces, with bake ovens surrounding a center chimney. Massive foundation stones are cut from local gneiss.

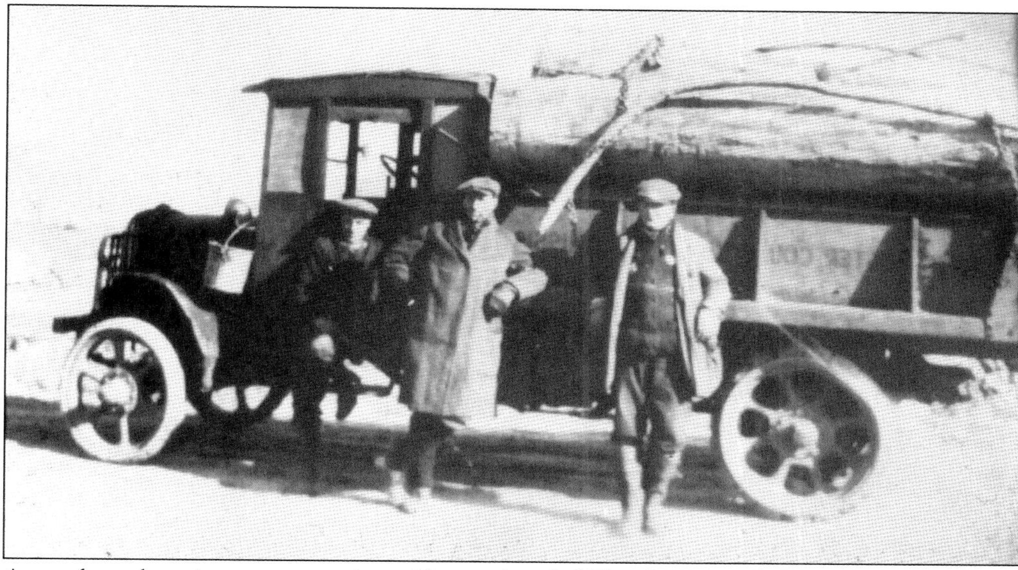

An early park maintenance truck, emblazoned with "Westchester Parks" and carrying a water bucket, stands ready for duty along with proud park employees. With miles and miles of unimproved woods roads to clear, stones to move, and trees to harvest, sturdy vehicles were a must. Today's vehicles are just as necessary, but have shocks and padded seats, something these fellows would have envied.

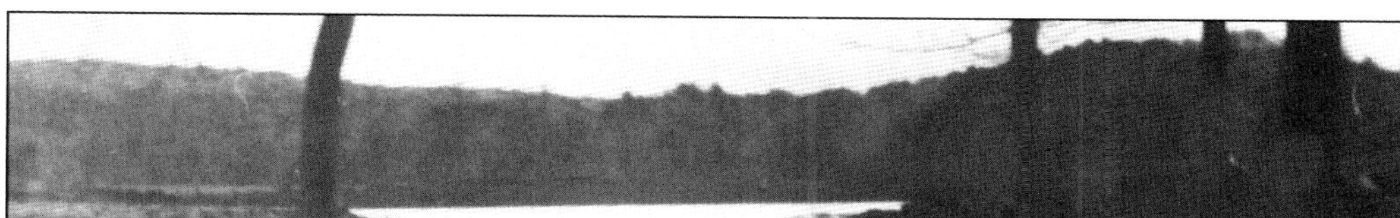

The Hurricane of 1938 inundated the Kimberly Picnic Area and destroyed the bridge, sending picnic tables miles downstream. Trails were swallowed by the deluge and many trees were downed, but the Cross River floodplain did slow the torrent, preventing property damage. With 35 miles of trails to maintain, maintenance staff dreads the inevitable cleanup after major storms.

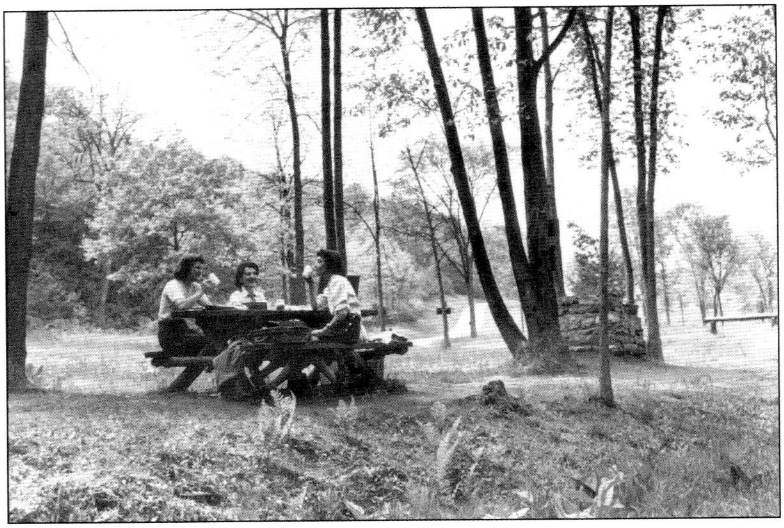

These three ladies enjoy a pleasant picnic lunch near the gurgling Cross River on the west side of the Kimberly Bridge picnic area. The stone fireplaces and grills were built by the CCC. Picnicking is still a popular activity, and groups of up to 200 can be accommodated in four different picnic groves.

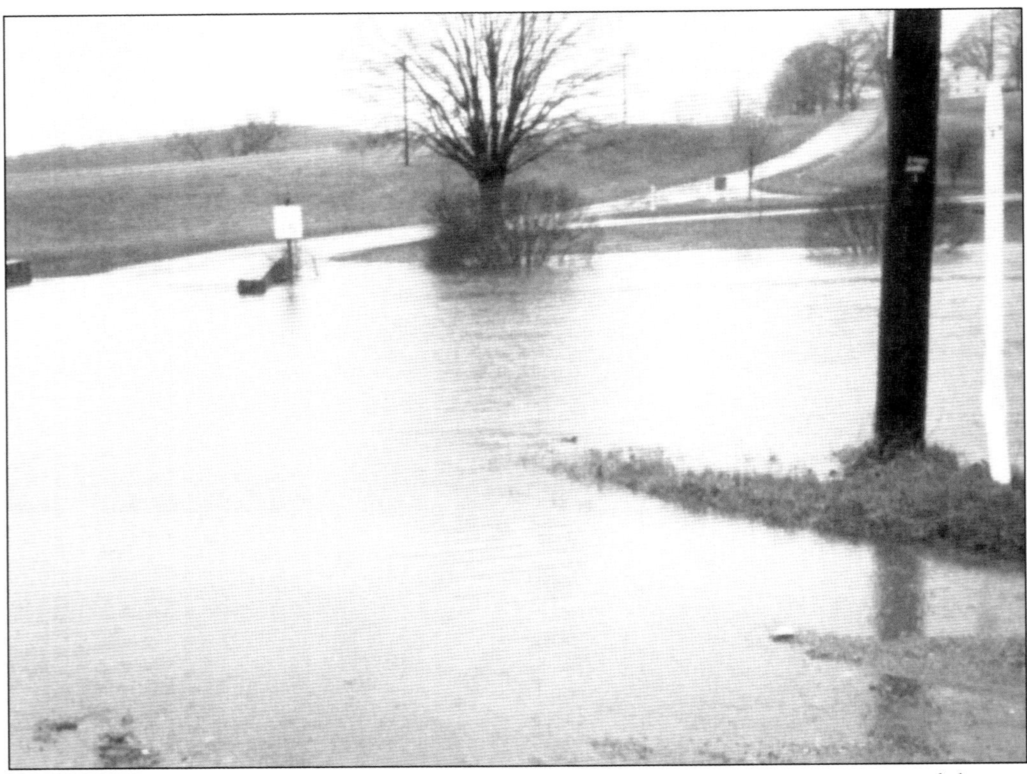

The reservation's watersheds do a fine job of protecting downstream areas by retaining and slowing down the inevitable raging waters following downpours and tropical storms. Here, Reservation Road is inundated by a swollen stream. Besides the Waccabuc and Cross Rivers, which bisect the park, the Stone Hill River ribbons around the southern boundary. The rivers' many tributaries provide quick drainage for the stony hills.

This sentinel white oak stood for centuries in the middle of the Meadow and was beloved by all park visitors. It fell in a microburst in May 2007. A local artist removed the bark from the carcass to prevent insect damage, and some of its beautiful branches still remain, to the delight of children and adults. A new oak tree was planted nearby and was dedicated in 2012. (Courtesy of Sharon Mammoser.)

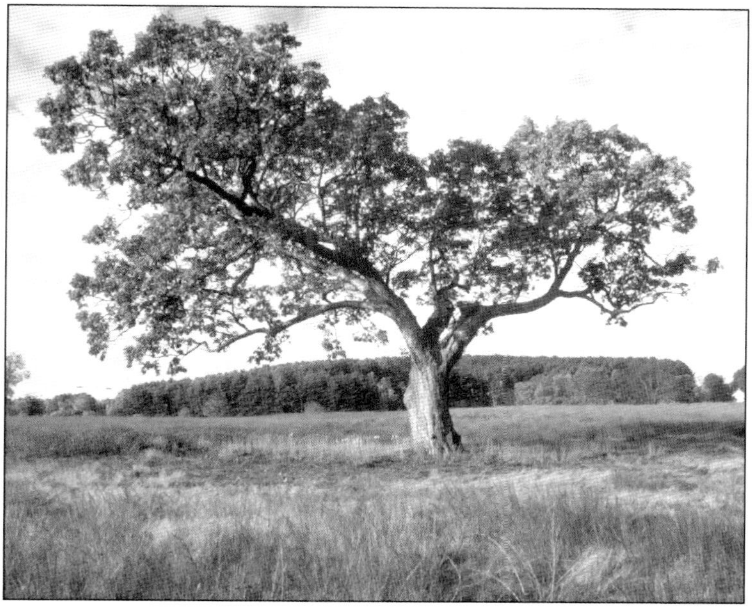

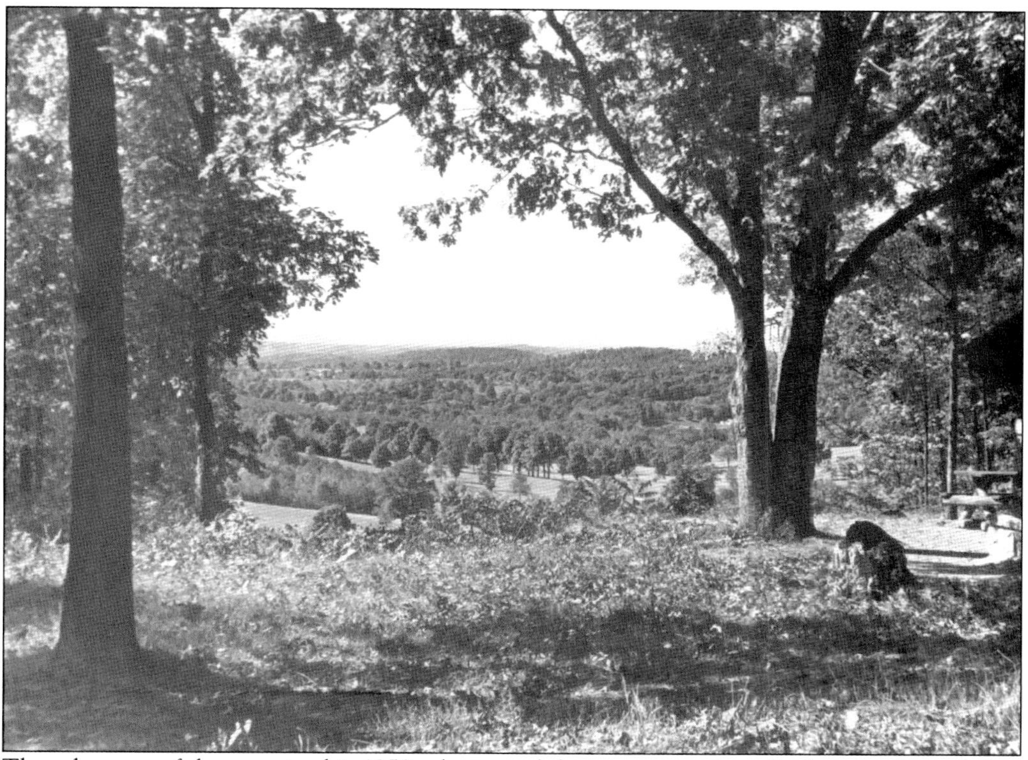

Though many of the trees in this 1950s photograph have grown quite tall, the view from shelter No. 15 on Pell Hill is still breathtaking. The Trailside Nature Museum is hidden from view, but the great Meadow lies in the center. The vista faces northwest, toward the Catskills and across the Hudson hills and highlands.

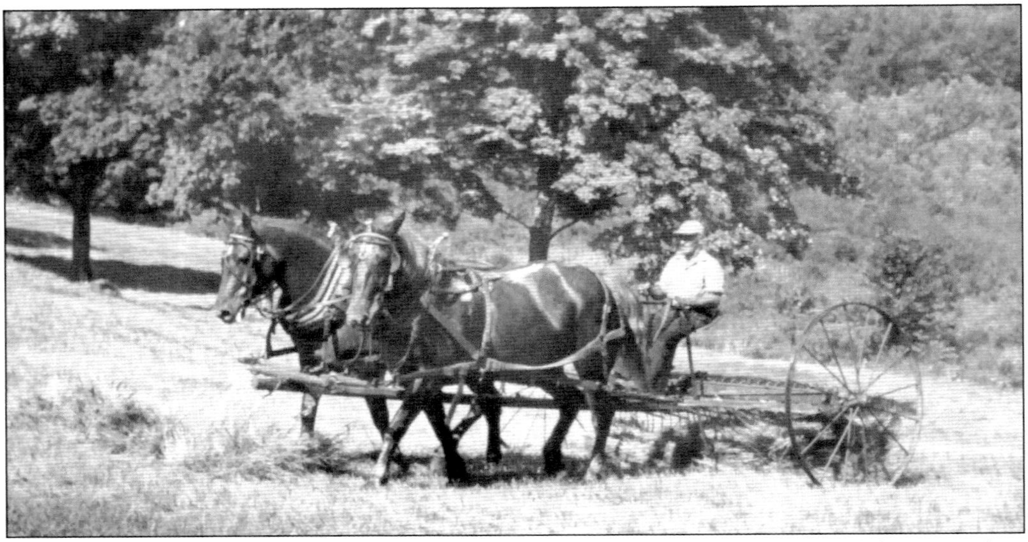

Until the 1950s, most of the park's meadows were cut by teams of horses and skilled drivers guiding mowers and hay rakes. Local farmers were allowed to use the hay, and the fields were cut regularly. Now, the meadows are managed for the benefit of wildlife and maximum biological diversity by staggered mowing regimes.

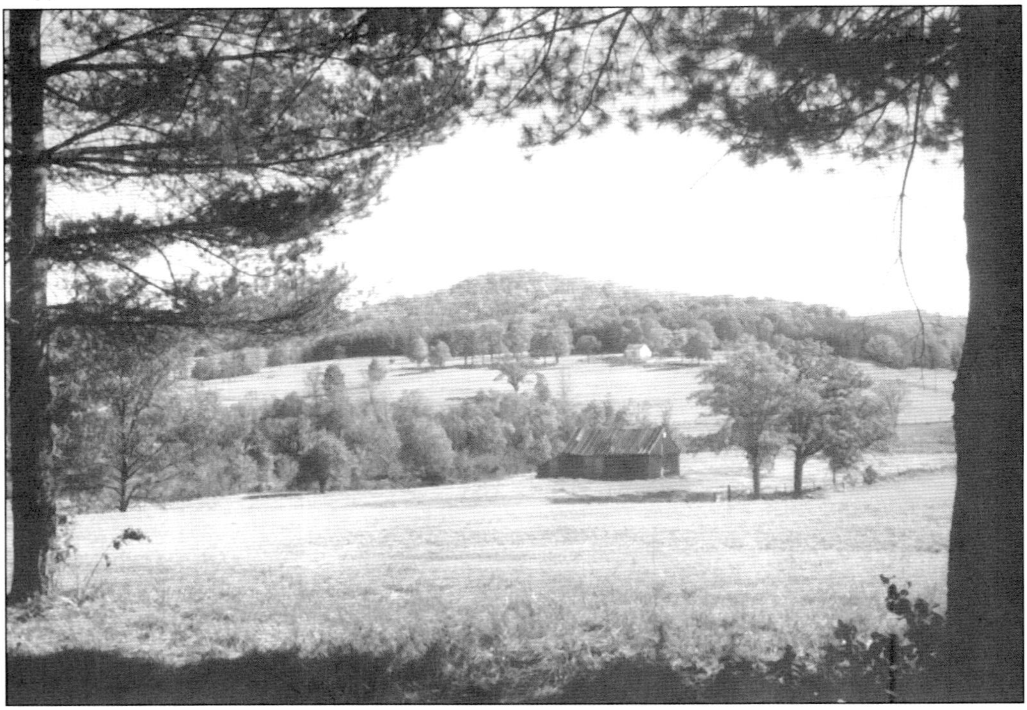

Taken from inside the conifer plantation, this photograph looks toward Fox Hill and provides a bucolic scene from the 1950s. It looks much the same today; only the barn is missing from a current view. The little white farmhouse on the hill still survives, as do the twin swamp white oaks, *Quercus bicolor.* The field today is still a tallgrass meadow, now filled with insects, birds, mammals, rare flowers, and many bluebird boxes.

Two

The Story of the Delaware Lenape

Human occupation of Ward Pound Reservation dates from the Paleolithic era, about 10,000 years ago. Little is known about the hunter-gatherers who inhabited the reservation's rock shelters during a cooler climate, when spruce forests predominated. Mastodons and giant beavers roamed the area. The Archaic period, up to 4,000 years ago, followed with a warmer climate and vegetation favorable to more species of animals. Pine and hardwood forests attracted bands of more advanced hunter-gatherers. Stone tools have been found, indicating the construction of temporary hunting camps.

By the Late Woodland period and the Contact period with Europeans, the Tankiteke and Kitchawan people of the Mohegan Nation farmed small plots, set up seasonal hunting camps, fished the streams, and built stockade "pounds" into which a team of hunters forced deer that were then killed by a barrage of weapons from a higher vantage point. These pounds, along with nearby stone ridges, gave Pound Ridge its name.

Summers were spent along the shore, but family groups migrated inland as fall and the colder months approached. Women gathered nuts and berries, while the men hunted deer and small game.

The people of the Late Archaic and Early Woodland periods had an ecological respect for their environment, taking only what they needed for food, clothing, and shelter. They treated their diseases with natural medicines and curing ceremonies. Neighboring tribes participated in a trading economy. Much changed with the coming of the Europeans. Demand for valuable furs, especially beaver, depleted abundant stocks; woodlands were cut for farming; and, most devastating, alien diseases like smallpox were introduced. Epidemics destroyed entire villages. By 1800, few native peoples remained.

Most horrendous of all was the February 1644 massacre of an entire Indian village. Capt. John Underhill and his contingent of soldiers attacked and set fire to a slumbering village assembled for a Winter Celebration. Reports list 180 warriors killed in the first onslaught; the remaining women, children, and old men who had retreated into their wigwams were burned alive when the structures were torched by the soldiers. The dead numbered between 500 and 700, the greatest massacre in the Northeast.

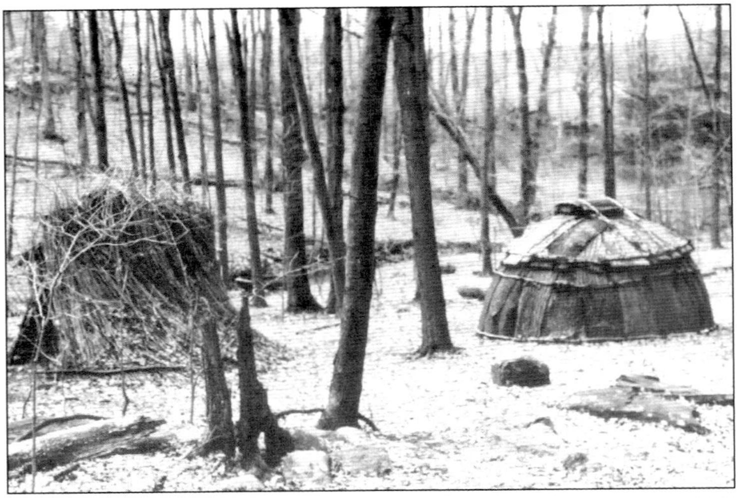

The people of the Woodland period belonged to the Mohegan Nation and spoke a dialect of the Algonquian language. A temperate climate allowed the people to spend their summers along the shore of Long Island Sound, then, as fall approached, they ventured inland to hunt game and gather berries. In late winter, temporary camps were used for maple sugaring.

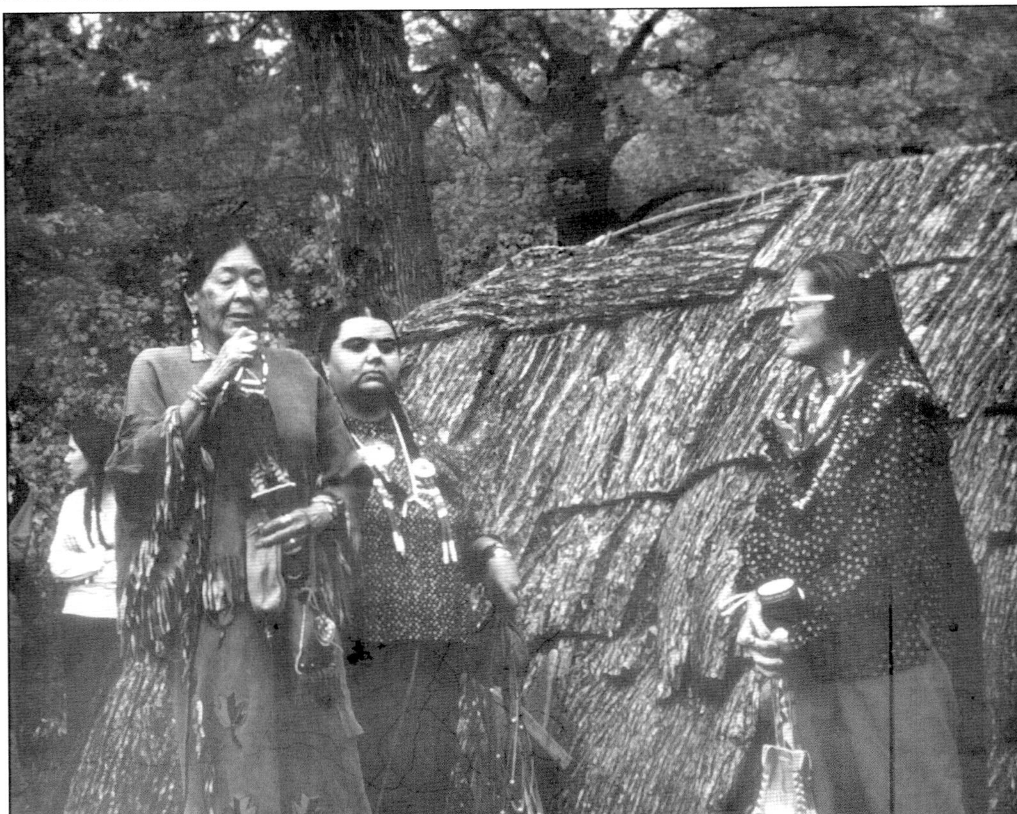

Members of the Delaware Lenape Nation visited Ward Pound Ridge Reservation to teach the museum staff and visitors the ways of the Native Americans who inhabited the area 300 years ago. Small farming plots provided for the cultivation of the Three Sisters (beans, squash, and corn) so vital to the sustenance of families. Stone fish weirs were constructed along the waterways of the reservation. Abundant vegetation supplied nutritious nuts, berries, and roots. Maple trees supplied sweet maple sap.

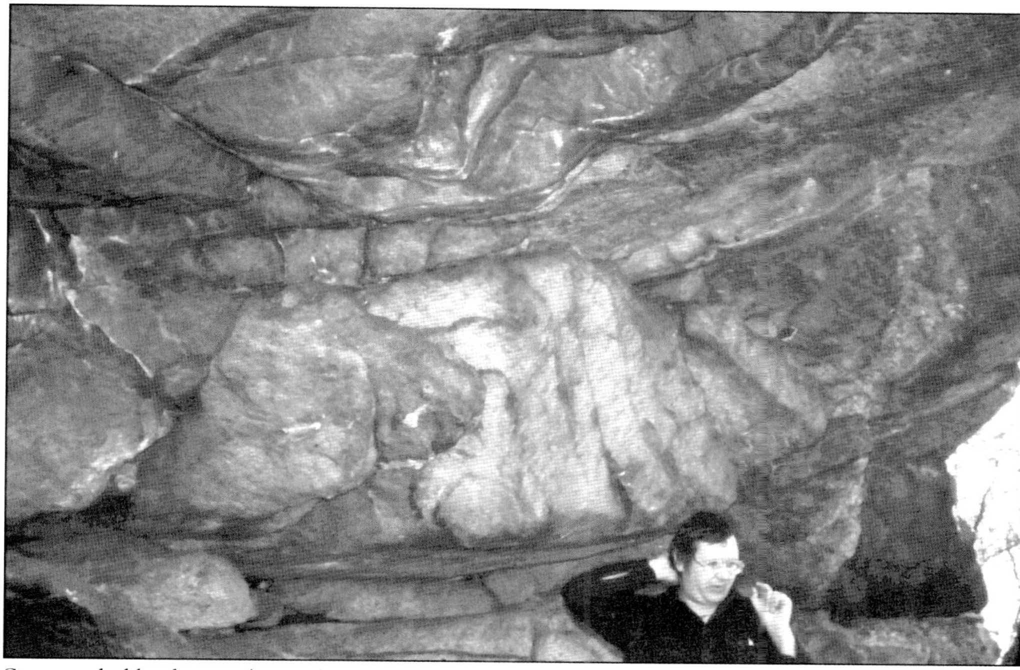

Surrounded by forest, this Indian Rock Shelter is believed to have housed hunters as far back as the Archaic period, 4,000 years ago. There is evidence that the cave-like shelter was also used by hunters of the Woodland era (around 1000 A.D.). Usage was dated by projectile points and stone tools found within the shelter. Smoke from ancient hearth fires has blackened one face of the cave. Trailside curator Nicholas Shoumatoff is pictured here.

Ancient spear points, stone tools, and more recent arrowheads have all been found along the pathways and in the stone shelters of Ward Pound Ridge Reservation, indicating a Native American presence. The type of tools and points found during an archaeological excavation in the 1970s at the Indian Rock Shelter, a park feature, indicates that the inhabitants were using the area for transient hunting camps, not permanent home sites.

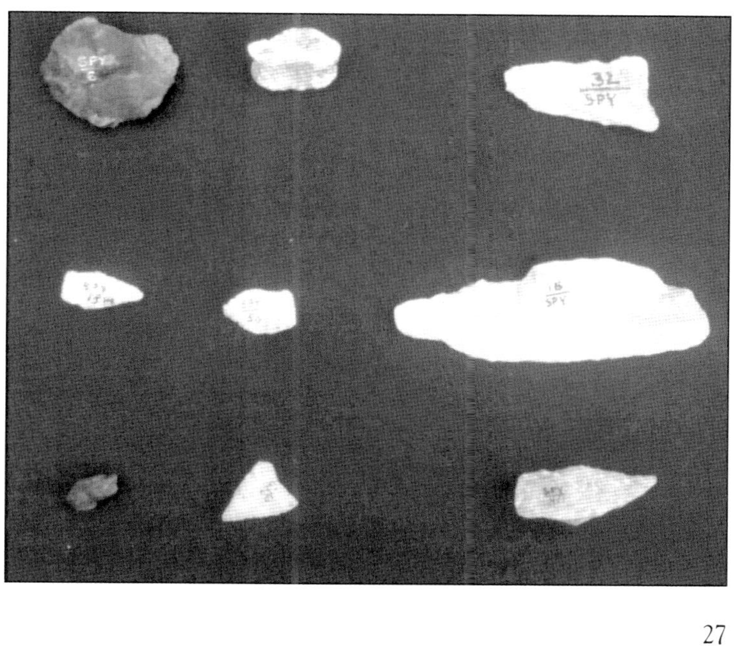

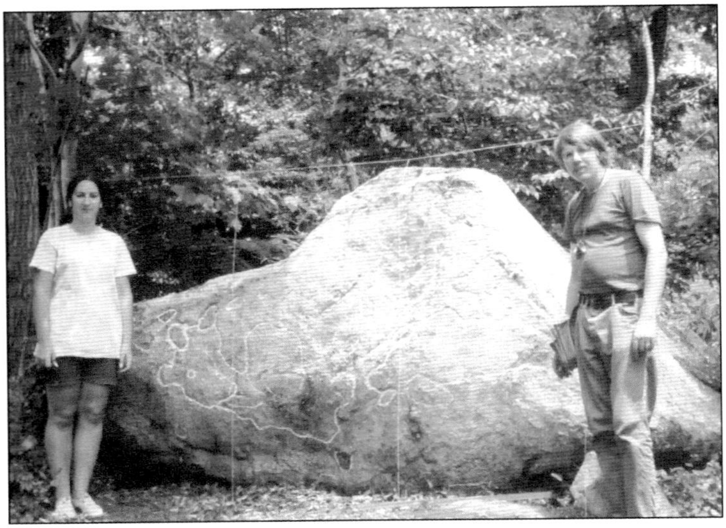

Bear Rock Petroglyph is one of the more curious features of the park. The strange markings on this large granite boulder located on the Dancing Rock Trail have invited numerous interpretations since they were discovered by curator Nick Shoumatoff and two students in 1971. The designs inscribed in the rock appear to be of a bear, a deer, and a turkey—all game sought by the indigenous people of 1,000 years ago.

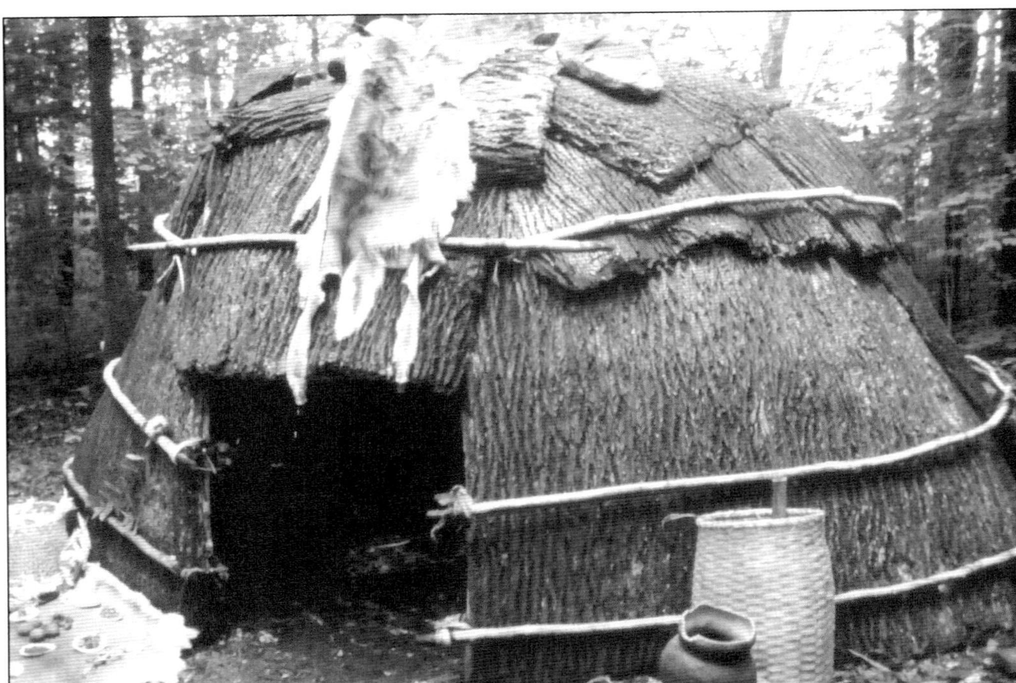

What a wonderful way to present the Native American way of life to today's schoolchildren and park visitors. This replica of a Woodland-era wigwam, located behind the Trailside Museum, is constructed in the traditional way, using young saplings bent into a semispherical base covered with slabs of bark, woven rush mats, or skins. The wigwam offers a hands-on, all-senses approach to learning.

Explaining the Native American and European Contact period to park visitors is a goal of the Trailside Museum. Celebrating with a reenactment of the first Thanksgiving was one way that curator Nick Shoumatoff chose to do this. He was well-known for his portrayals of historic figures and his knowledge of Indian lore. Here, Shoumatoff stands tall among the visitors and interpreters.

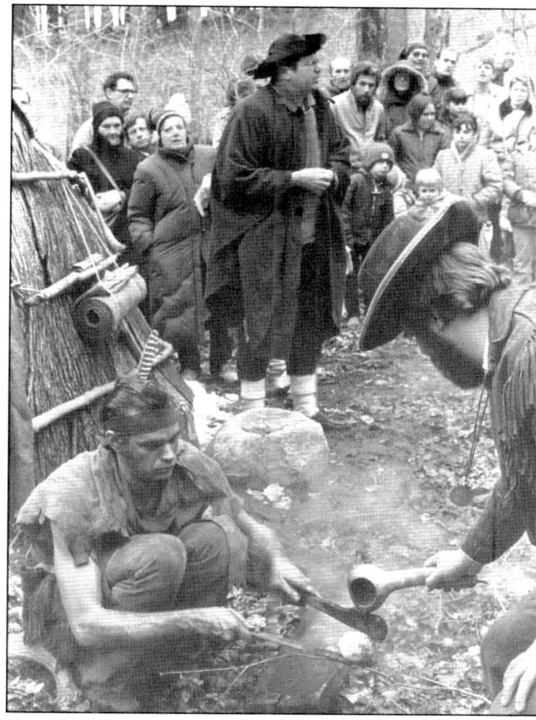

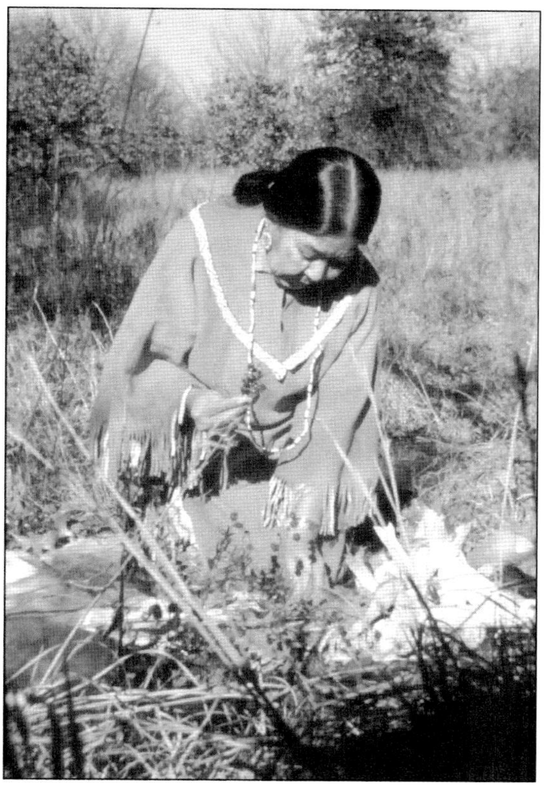

Touching Leaves (Nora Thompson Dean), a member of the Delaware Lenape Nation, was well versed in the traditional customs and medicinal ways of her people. She was an herbalist and a linguist who welcomed Trailside curator Nick Shoumatoff to her Oklahoma reservation and instructed him in the ways and language of her people. Touching Leaves visited Ward Pound Ridge in the 1970s and shared her knowledge of the time her people lived here.

Touching Leaves, possibly the last full-blooded member of the Delaware Lenape Nation, was well respected throughout the country for her knowledge of the traditional ways of her people. She worked with linguists and anthropologists to preserve the language and customs of her ancestors. Nick Shoumatoff visited her on the Bartlesville, Oklahoma, reservation, where she instructed him in the ancient customs and language. Touching Leaves died in 1984 at the age of 77.

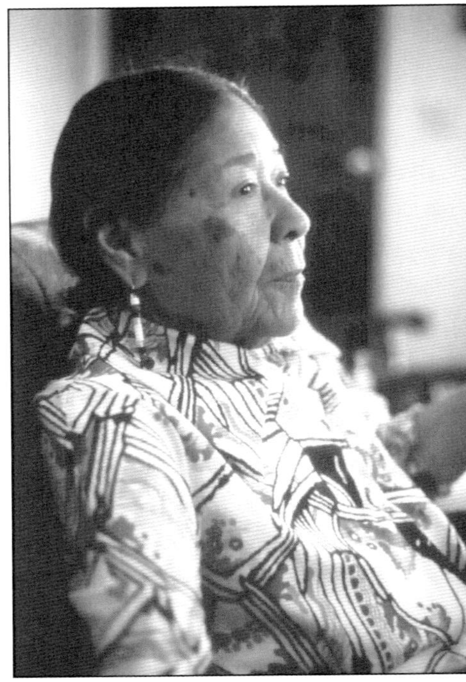

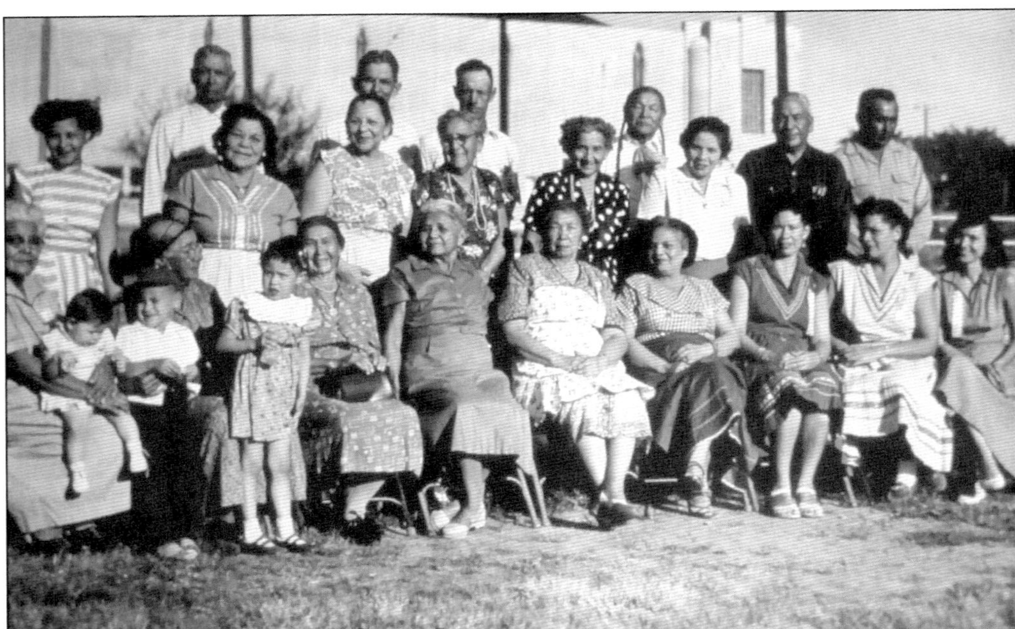

Members of the Oklahoma Delaware Reservation pose for this 1970s photograph. The Delaware Nation originally inhabited the area that is now Delaware, New Jersey, southeastern New York, and southern Connecticut, but moved west and north after the Revolutionary War. Most members of the tribe now live in Canada and Oklahoma, although there are still Delaware people living in their eastern ancestral homelands. Tribal officials ensure that traditional customs and oral traditions are kept alive for today's generation.

Three

Working the Land

It is not hard to imagine the rolling fields and lowlands of Ward Pound Ridge Reservation as farmland. The settlers of the New York Colony were farming here by the early 1700s. The villages of Cross River and Boutonville provided blacksmiths, carriage makers, shoemakers, and general stores. Boutonville boasted a hat factory and a fulling mill, and both villages had gristmills and sawmills. Cross River had a tavern, a Baptist church, and a Methodist Episcopal church. Each village had a school.

The farmland in both the Pound Ridge section and the Lewisboro section were part of the Van Cortlandt Manor lands that were divided into "great lots" of about 3,000 acres each. These lots were further divided into 300-acre farms. Lots No. 9 and No. 10 made up most of the Lewisboro section of the reservation. By the 1760s, these farms were sold off in parcels of between 150 and 300 acres. By the end of the Revolutionary War, farms in the Pound Ridge section had been sold or divided as well. For years, this land had been tilled, planted, and harvested by tenant farmers for the Van Cortlandts, or by "squatters" from the adjoining Stamford Patent. By the late 1800s, the farms averaged 50 acres because of the division of the land among heirs and in-laws.

Rocky terrain made some of the area unsuitable for farming. This land provided family woodlots of anywhere from seven to forty acres during the 18th and 19th centuries. A charcoal industry flourished during this time, as did a tanin bark operation, using the bark from oak and chestnut trees. Each year, 2,000 oxcart loads of charcoal made their way to merchants in Stamford.

Toward the end of the 19th century, farming gave way to railroad speculation. The Westchester Northern Railroad proposed tracks along the Stone Hill River on the southern border of the reservation lands, along Route 124 through Boutonville, then through Lewisboro to Danbury. Farmers were eager to buy shares in the project, but hard times fell on the country, and the railroad remained a dream. By 1924, farming in the vicinity had ended, and the fields were reverting to untamed vegetation.

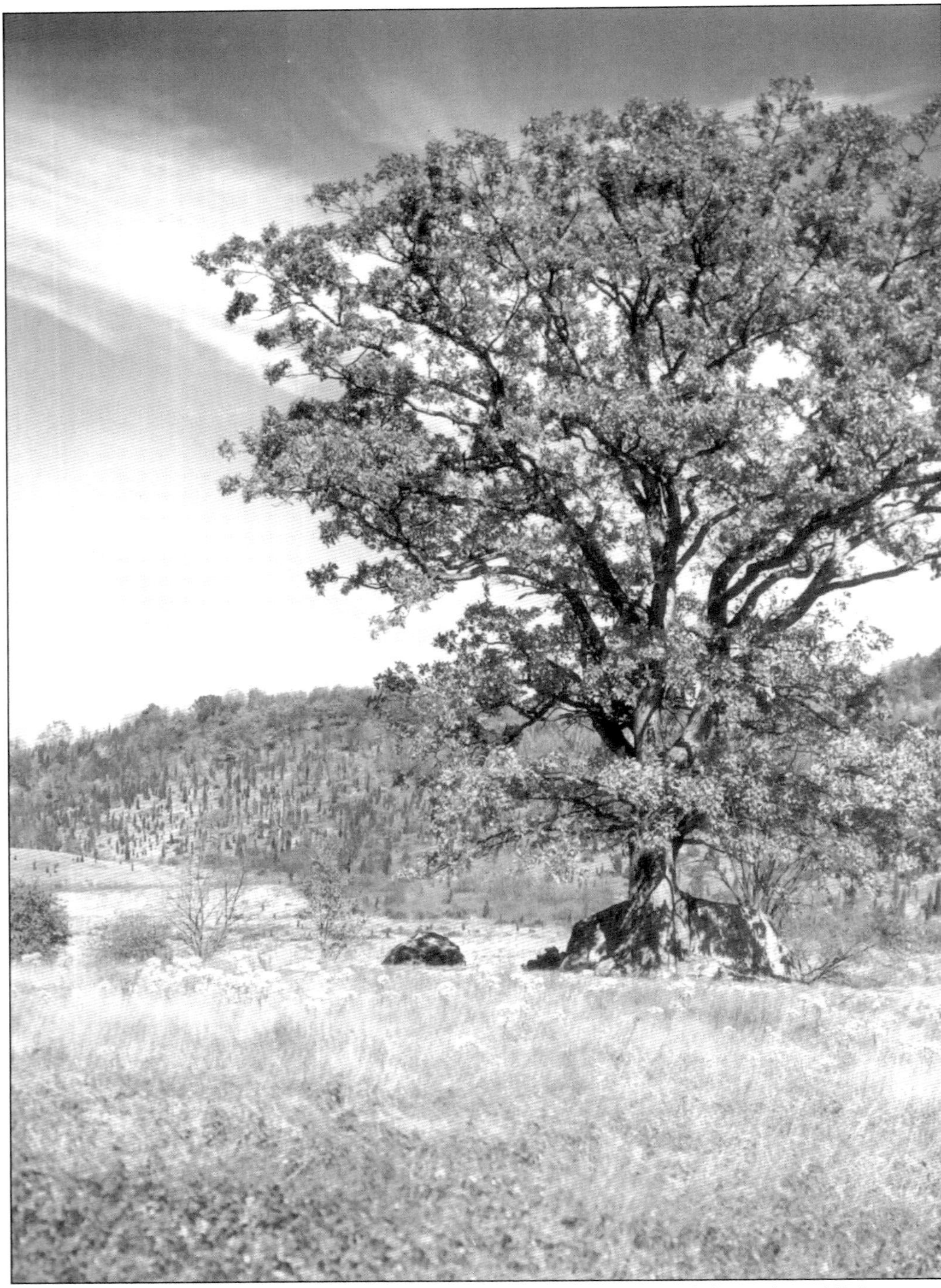

As the landscape shifted from farm plots to woodlands, so, too, changed the park's wildlife species. While there are few biological records to tell the exact story, pictures illustrate this transformation. Here is an immense wolf tree in the 1930s that thrived next to a large rock for centuries. Surrounded by open fields, the tree could reach its full shape without impingement.

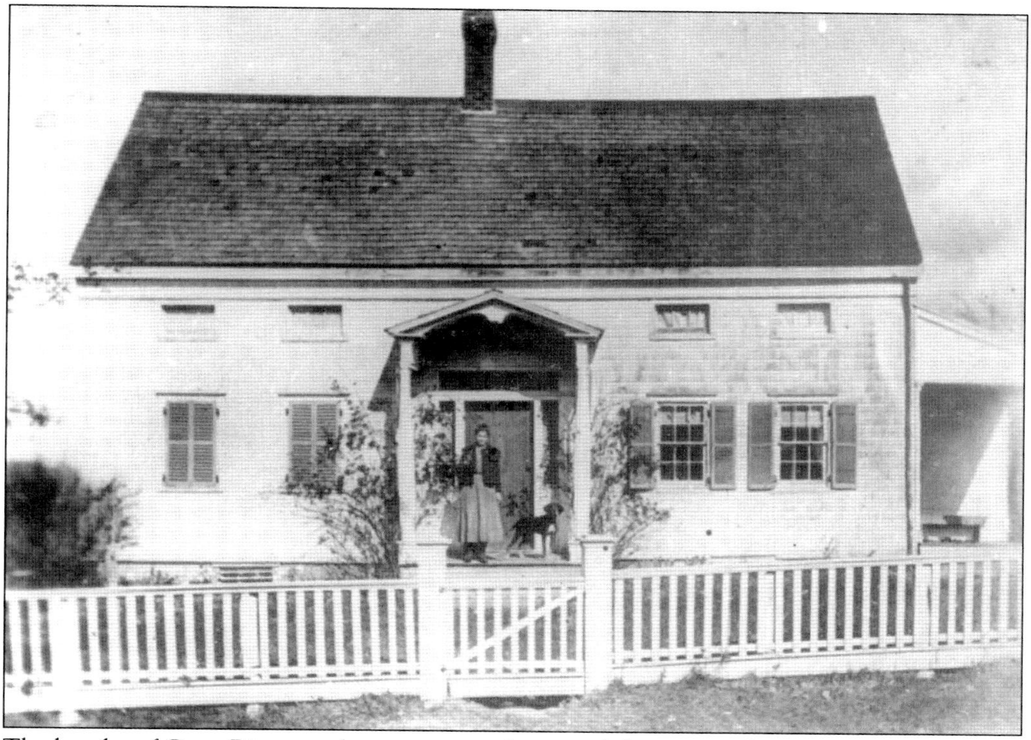

The hamlet of Cross River was home to many farms with houses similar to this one. The story-and-a-half Whitman homestead, with its eyebrow windows, dates to the early 19th century. The center chimney caps a large kitchen fireplace that supplied warmth and a cooking fire. The house, minus the picket fence, still stands on Boutonville Road. Once the main thoroughfare of the village, Boutonville is now a side road bordering the park.

The oxen team played an important part on the Whitman farm. Bull calves were castrated in their first year; by four years, the animal was considered ready for hard work. Hauling manure and plowing a straight line was springtime work; in winter, the team hauled logs from the woodlot, often wearing cleated shoes to travel over the ice. Slow and steady and stout of heart was the oxen team.

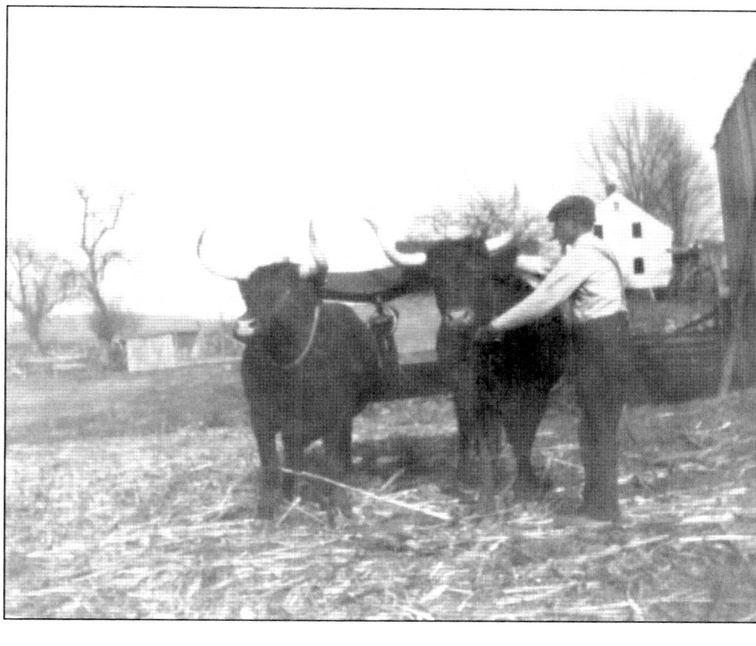

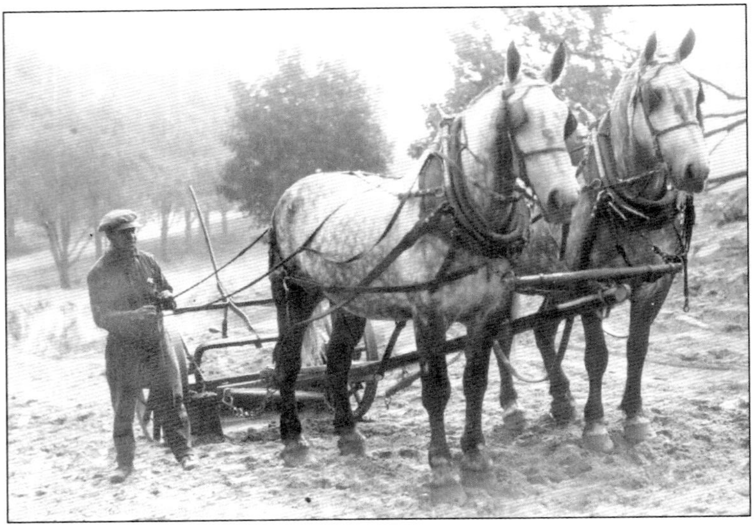

Compared to the oxen, the teams of horses did the "easy" work, including pulling the walk-behind plow and preparing the fields for planting oats, barley, wheat, flax, potatoes, pumpkins, and corn. Horses could also work faster than oxen. Farm animals were a vital part of a family's existence and were given names and treated almost as part of the family.

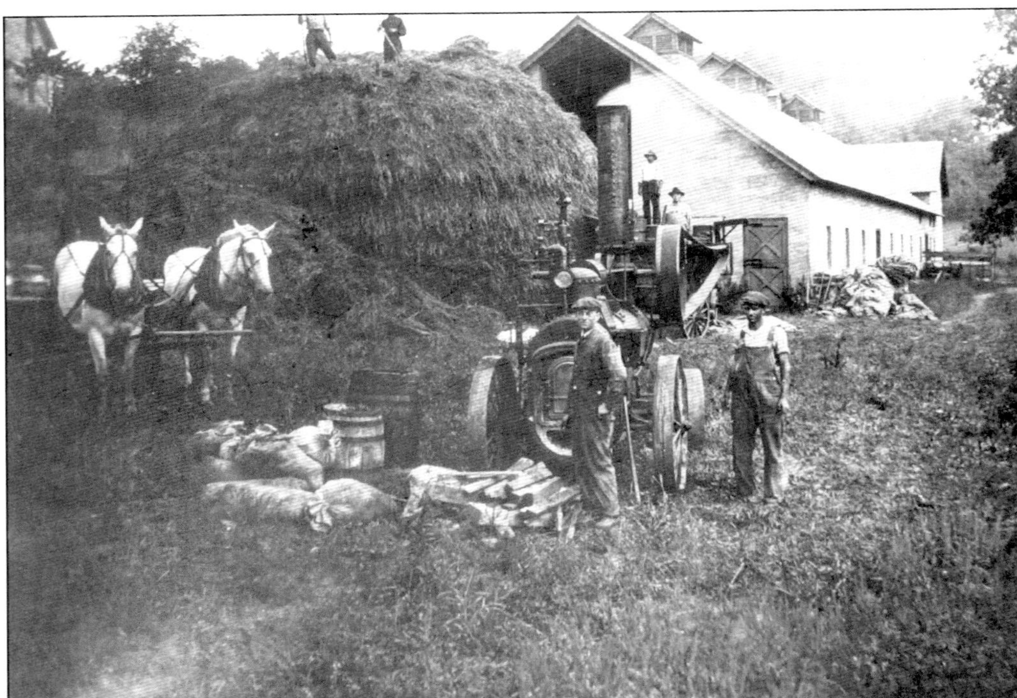

Threshing wheat and getting the hay in were important activities in the farmer's year. The farmer had to "make hay while the sun shines." Rainy weather meant wet hay, and wet hay in the haymow put winter animal feed in jeopardy. All hands helped during haying, as seen in this early-20th-century photograph of the Whitman farm. The grain was taken to nearby gristmills to be ground into flour.

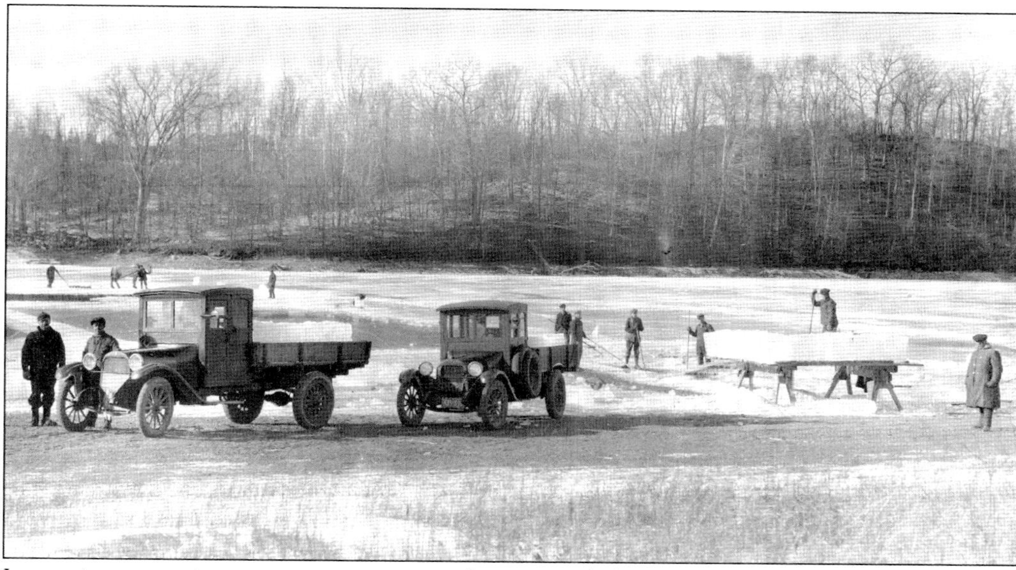

Ice cutting was an important winter activity. Ice was needed on the farms and in village households to keep food cold. By the 1930s, as pictured here on the Cross River reservoir, trucks had almost replaced the horse teams. Lots of boy- and manpower was needed to cut the ice and haul it to the icehouses. Look carefully for the horse and iceboat in this photograph.

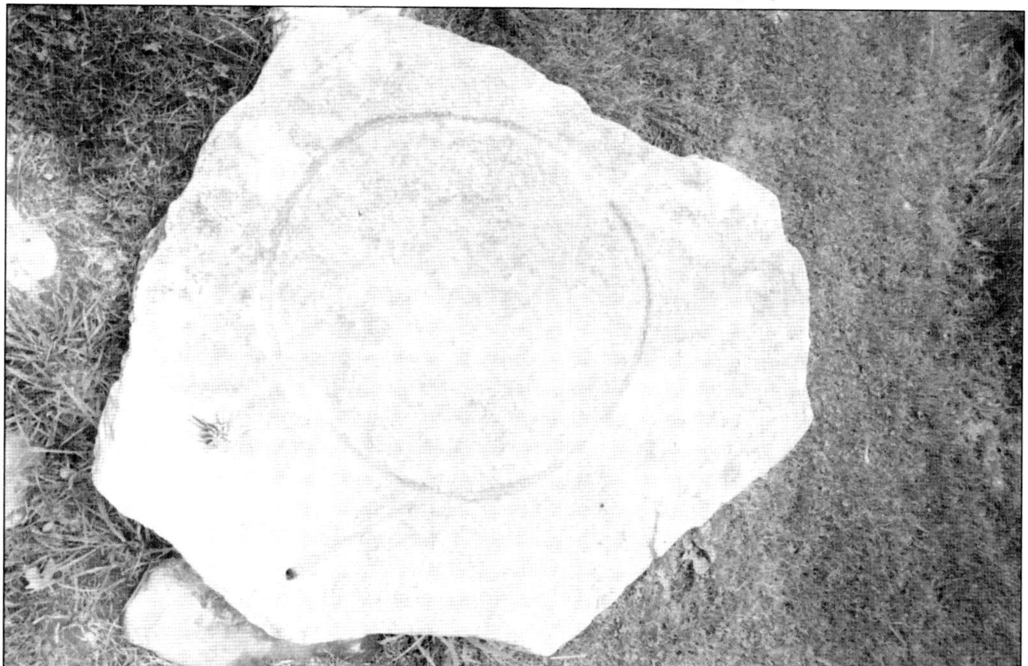

Soap making was an important task on 19th-century farms. The lye stone pictured here provided a platform for the process. A bottomless barrel filled with ashes was placed on the stone, and straw was used to cover the barrel bottom. Water was poured over the ashes, leaching out potash lye that followed a groove in the stone to a lip that funneled the liquid into a container. This solution, boiled with rendered animal fat, produced a soft soap.

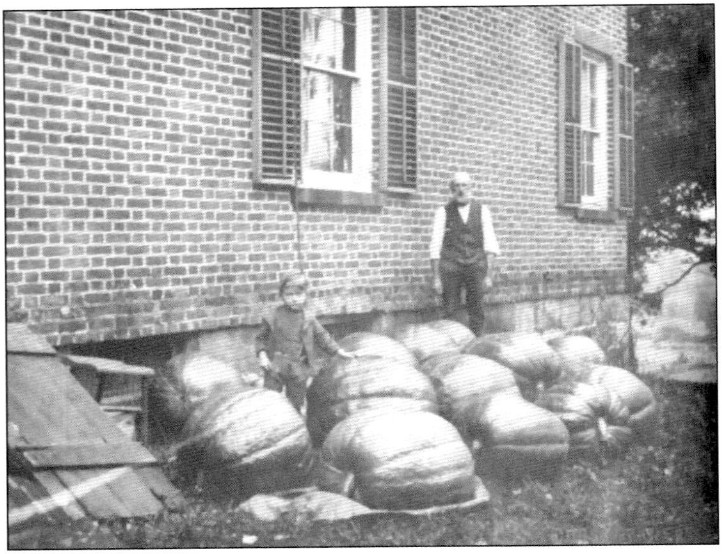

Cyrus Russell (1897–1971), pictured next to the Brick House with his father, William, and a bountiful pumpkin harvest, was a member of the Reynolds family, a Cross River founding family dating to Revolutionary times. A farm boy at heart, Russell served as Lewisboro town clerk and town supervisor during a long career of public service. He also was a construction supervisor at the CCC camp located in the park during the early 1930s.

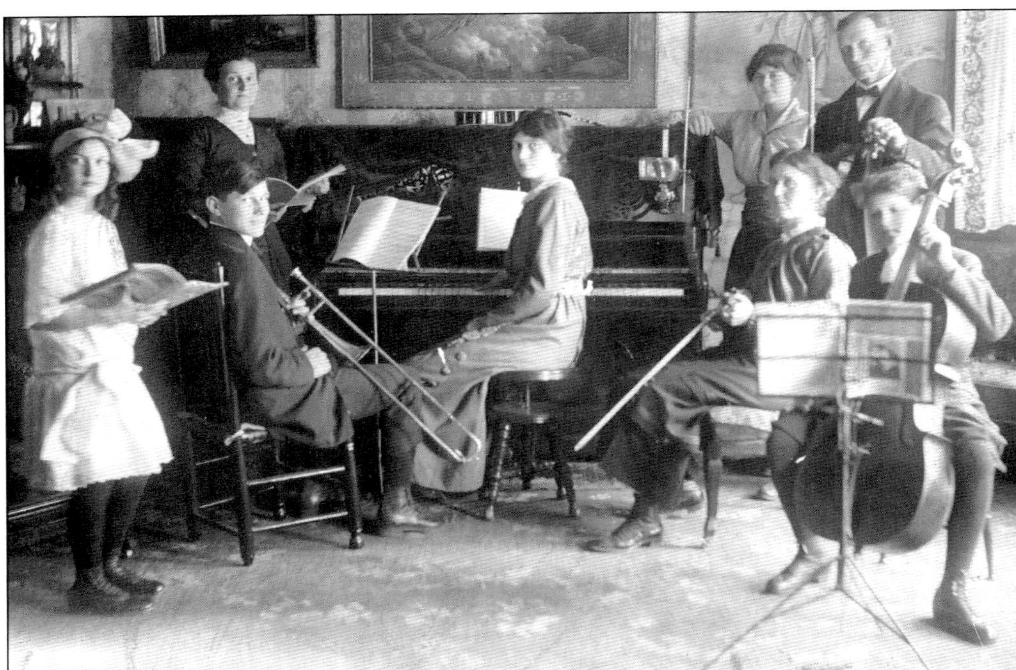

Home entertainment brightened evenings and family gatherings on the farms and in the village, as seen in this turn-of-the-century photograph of a musical ensemble at the home of the prosperous Hunt family of Cross River. Much daily activity centered on the family that owned the local gristmill and general store. Although mill remnants can still be seen, the store was razed with the coming of the reservoir.

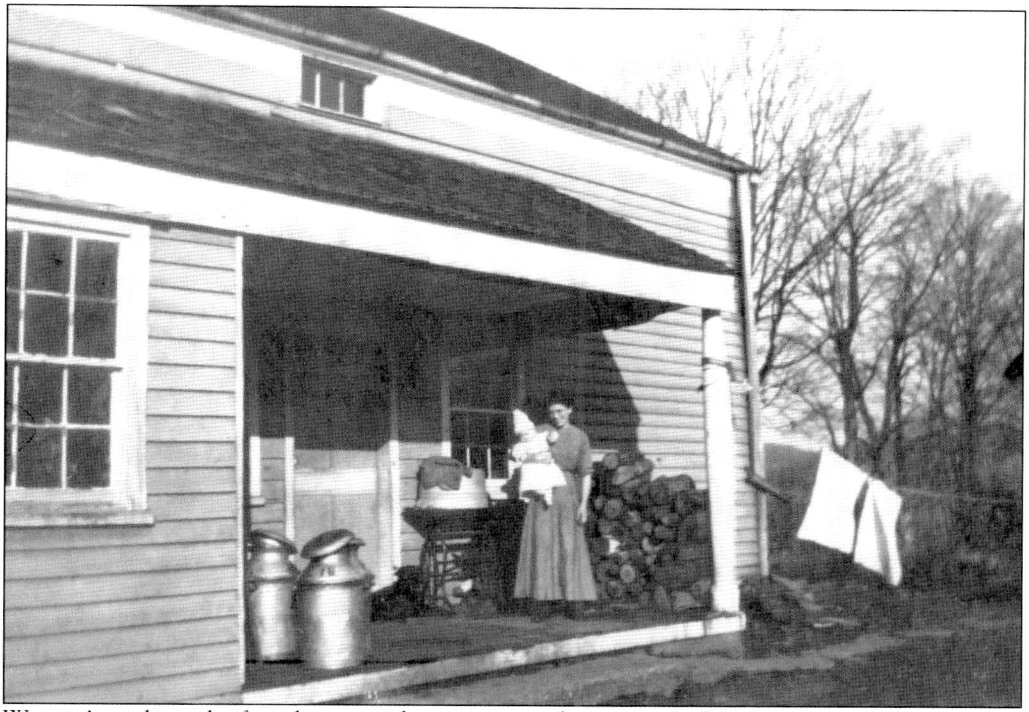

Women's work on the farm began as the sun rose and continued after the sun set. It appears that Florence Whitman is enjoying a few rays of sunshine with her young daughter, Beatrice, on the Whitman homestead back porch. The milk cans on the porch will probably be filled and the milk shipped to New York City creameries via the New York Central Railroad Harlem Division in Katonah or Goldens Bridge.

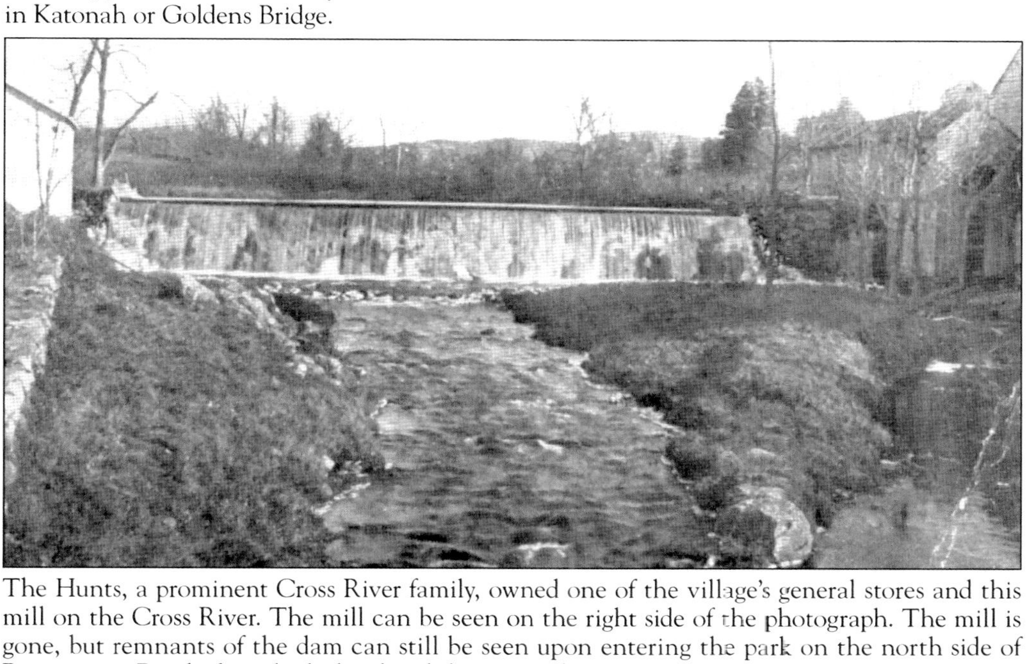

The Hunts, a prominent Cross River family, owned one of the village's general stores and this mill on the Cross River. The mill can be seen on the right side of the photograph. The mill is gone, but remnants of the dam can still be seen upon entering the park on the north side of Reservation Road, if one looks hard and the river is low.

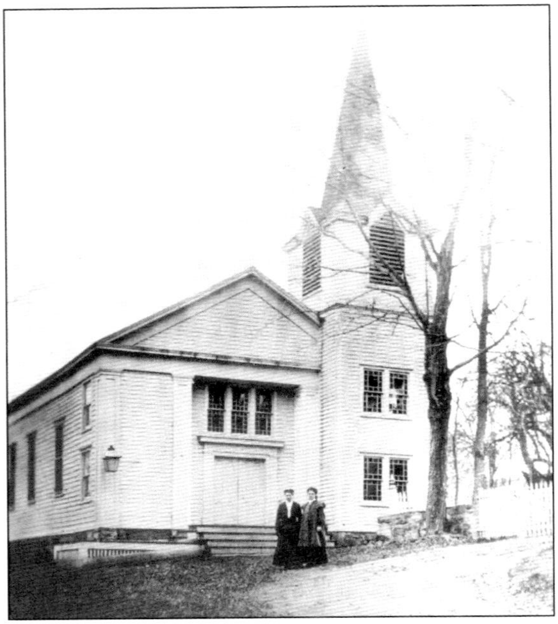

The Cross River First Baptist Church was established in 1789 by a group of families from Bedford and nearby Connecticut. It is the oldest public building in Lewisboro. Built on a low hillside at the entrance to the reservation, it did not have to be moved to make way for the new reservoir in 1906. The little church served Cross River families for more than 200 years with an active Sunday school and ministry.

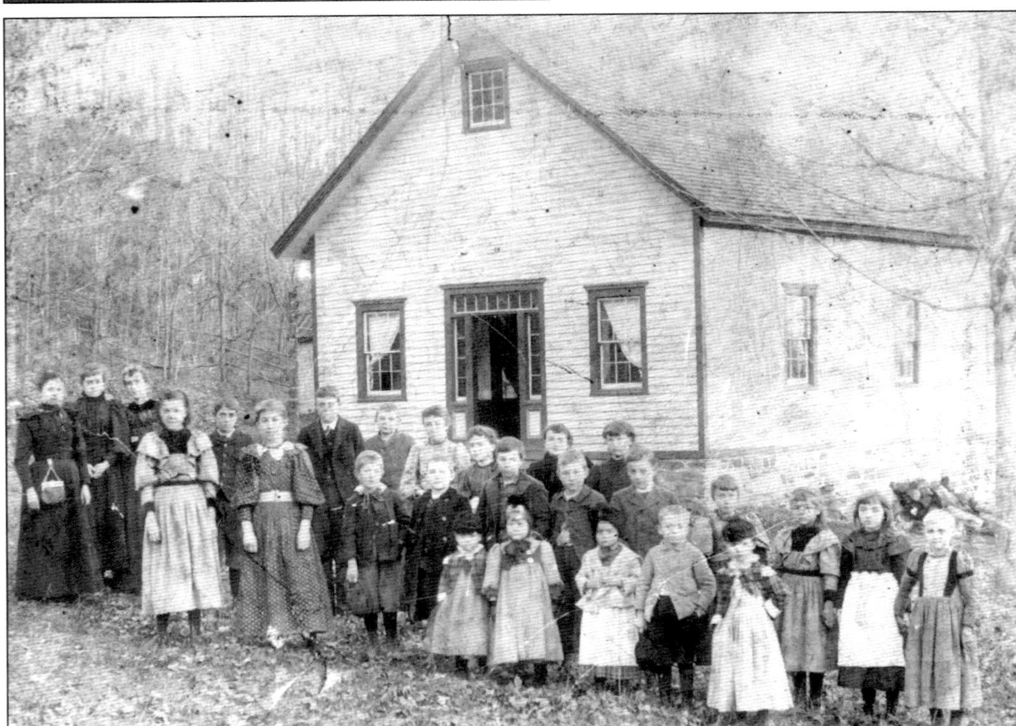

The Cross River one-room schoolhouse was built around 1866 for $1,800 to serve the needs of area farm families. Amenities included writing desks and two privies. The little school served the children of Cross River until 1941, when the town's one-room schools were consolidated into one grammar school. Electric lights were installed in 1916. One-room schools in Boutonville and on Schoolhouse Road in the park also served the farm families.

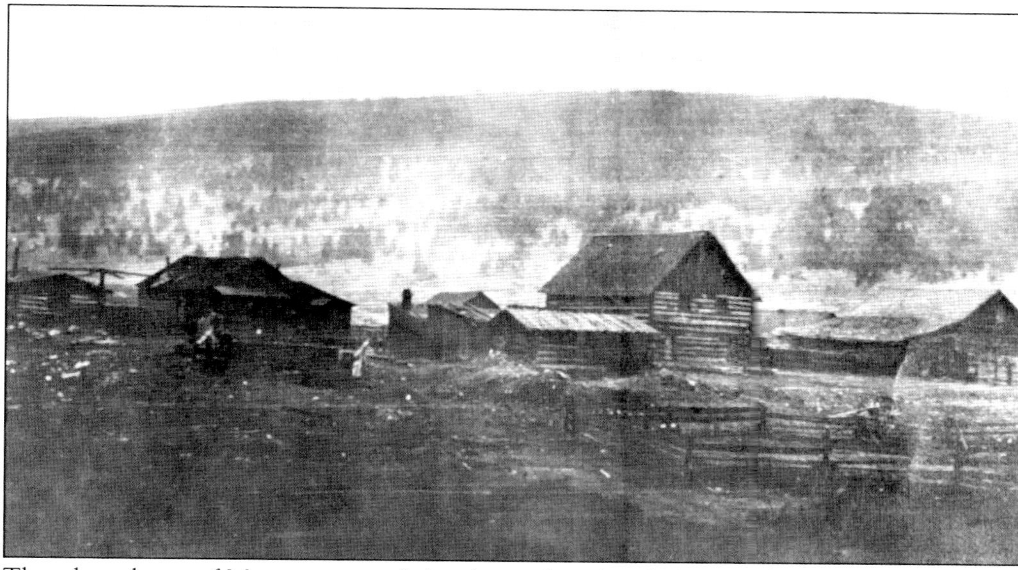

The whereabouts of Mastentown and the charcoal works of Masten Johnson, a Revolutionary War militiaman, remains one of the reservation's mysteries. Originally called Mastentown, the name was later changed to Charcoaltown. Johnson worked the pits from 1780 to 1840. Charcoal production was an important industry in the 18th and 19th centuries. Early maps locate the settlement on the west slope of Cross River Mountain, but this c. 1900 photograph is the only evidence that remains of the charcoal works.

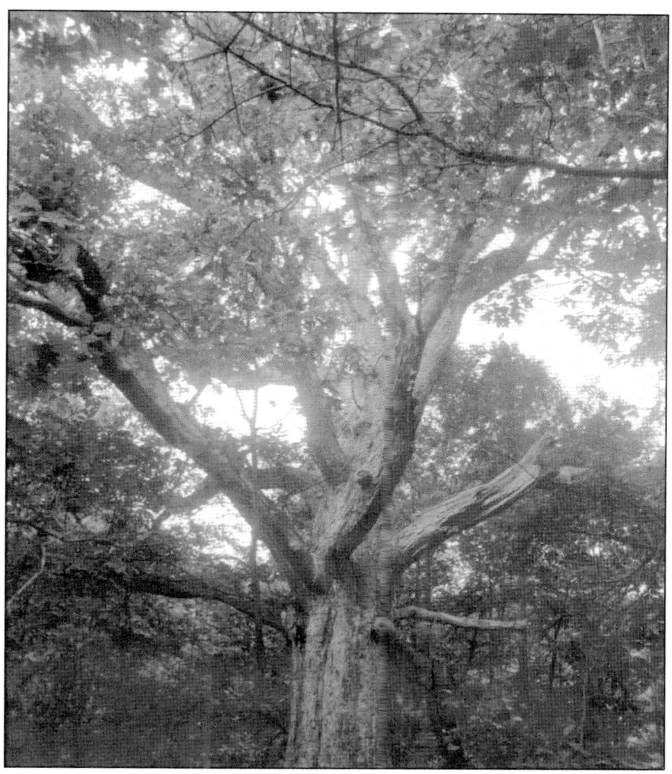

This magnificent oak on the Boutonville side of the park is said to shelter the graves of four children tragically burned to death in a house fire while their father was visiting the local tavern on a cold, windy night. Oral tradition has it that the children were buried by concerned neighbors, and that the father was tarred and feathered. It is said that, on dark nights, his lonely figure can be seen with a lantern, searching for the graves of his children.

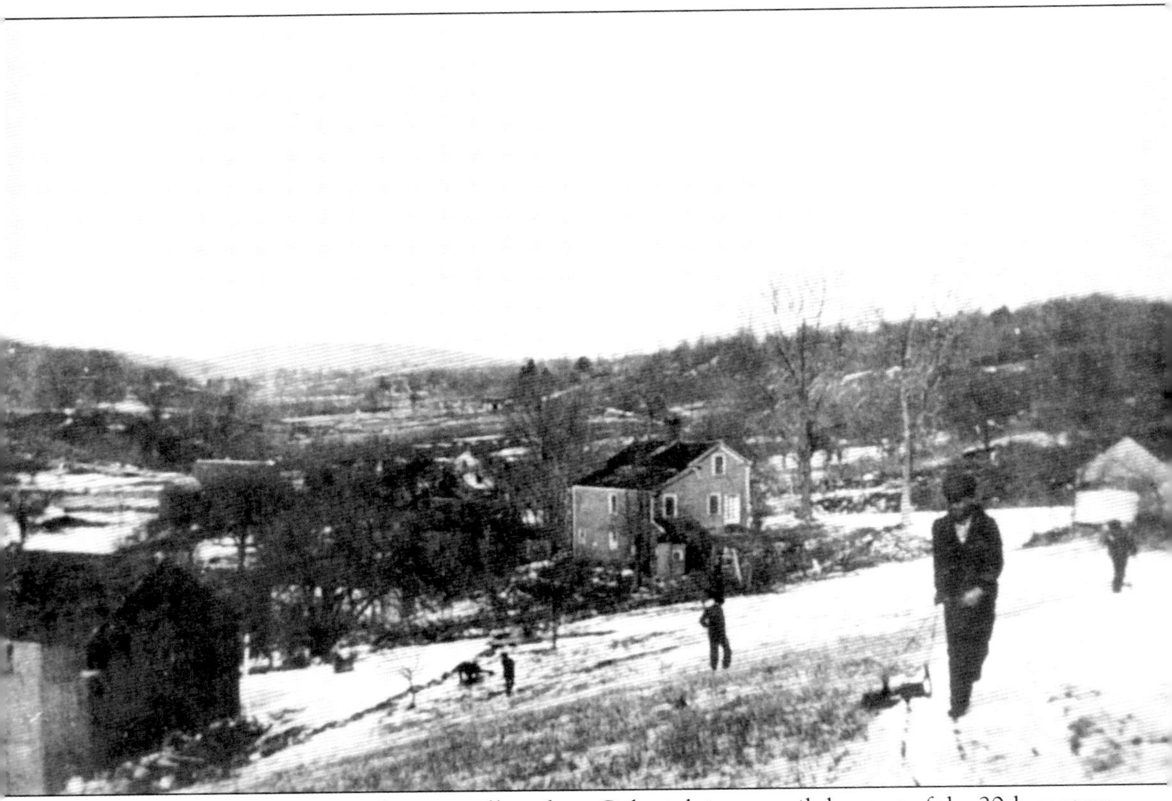

Boutonville was an active farming village from Colonial times until the start of the 20th century, with at least two mills, a school, a smithy, and a general store. Its hilly terrain was farmed; this hillside once boasted fields of cucumbers that were harvested and taken by oxcart to Stamford pickle factories. The area once known as Pickle Hill is the eastern hillside of Route 124, south of its intersection with Boutonville Road as one heads toward Pound Ridge. At the foot of Pickle Hill, a hat factory and a fulling mill and carding machine operation prepared wool from local sheep, and farmers' wives in turn made winter clothes and bedding from the material. The hill became a favorite sledding spot for Boutonville families in the early 1900s.

Four

The Boys of the Tree Army

Shortly after he became president, in March 1933, Franklin Delano Roosevelt unveiled plans to combat unemployment, contain soil erosion, and replenish the country's vanishing timber resources with a unique governmental program. His Emergency Conservation Work Act, better known by the call letters of its organization, the CCC, offered a way to put the thousands of unemployed men from the country's urban areas to work restoring the nation's resources. Known as Roosevelt's Tree Army, the program put almost three million laborers to work across the Depression-ravaged country. Teenagers and young men enlisted for six-month stints and could reenlist if they desired. Army-type camps were set up throughout the country, including Camp SP-9 (State Park No. 9) at Ward Pound Ridge Reservation. Also known as Camp No. 24 and Camp Merkel, it operated from June 1933 to 1940. The camp had five wooden barracks that housed up to 60 men each. The majority of the recruits were from the Westchester and Kingston, New York, areas.

CCC pay was $30 a month, but it was often enough to keep a corpsman's family afloat. From each paycheck, $25 had to be sent home to the family; the remaining $5 was the corpsman's to keep. The program was administered by the US Department of the Interior. Materials were supplied by the Department of Agriculture, and the camps were maintained and governed by the Army Department of War. The program offered educational programs in carpentry and forestry, as well.

At the newly dedicated 4,700-acre Ward Pound Ridge Reservation, a reforestation program was undertaken. Thousands of elm and American chestnut trees had succumbed to disease and had to be removed. Other species, such as white pine, were planted in their place. The corps cut down and burned the diseased trees. In addition to the reforestation work, local farm roads through the park were improved, and stone shelters and picnic areas were built. The CCC boys constructed latrines and bridges, erected walls, and built the Trailside Nature Museum from native stone. The legacy of the CCC is evident today throughout the park, and work is under way to mark and interpret the remains of the camp.

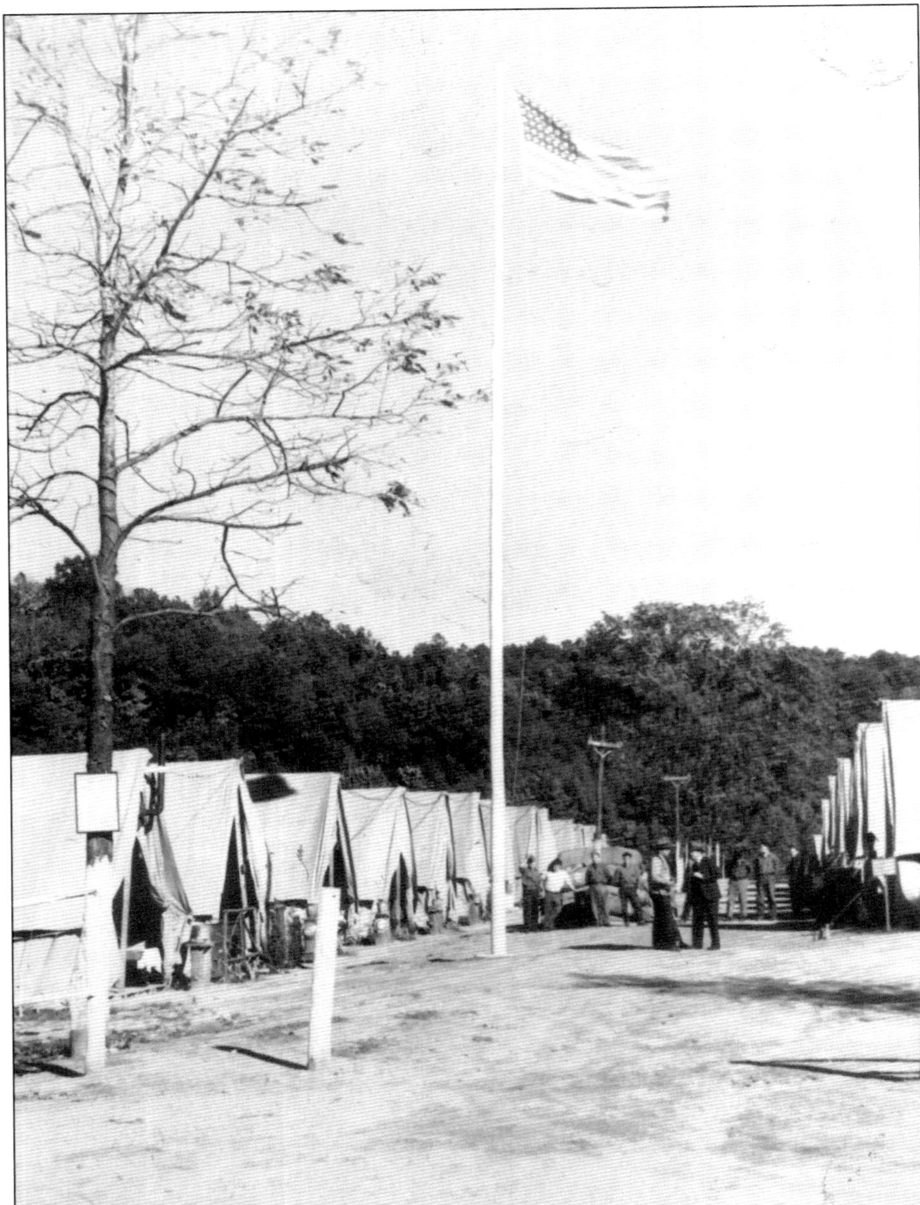

SP-9, Camp 24, 210th Company, otherwise known as Camp Merkel (named for the parks superintendent of Westchester County), was one of the earliest camps established after the CCC was founded in the late spring of 1933. It was home to about 200 enrollees during each six-month session. Males between the ages of 18 and 25 were eligible, depending on their family's needs. An enrollee had to be a US citizen, single, physically fit, and unemployed. Reenlisting was allowed in most cases. Members of the camp lived in a structured environment similar to that of the Army. Summers were spent in tent cities like the one shown here; winter housing was in wooden barracks heated by coal stoves. The enrollees were divided into work crews of up to 15 individuals. They worked hard: "60 minutes in every hour," remembered one veteran of the camp. The work was difficult, but the food was good and the friendships were lasting.

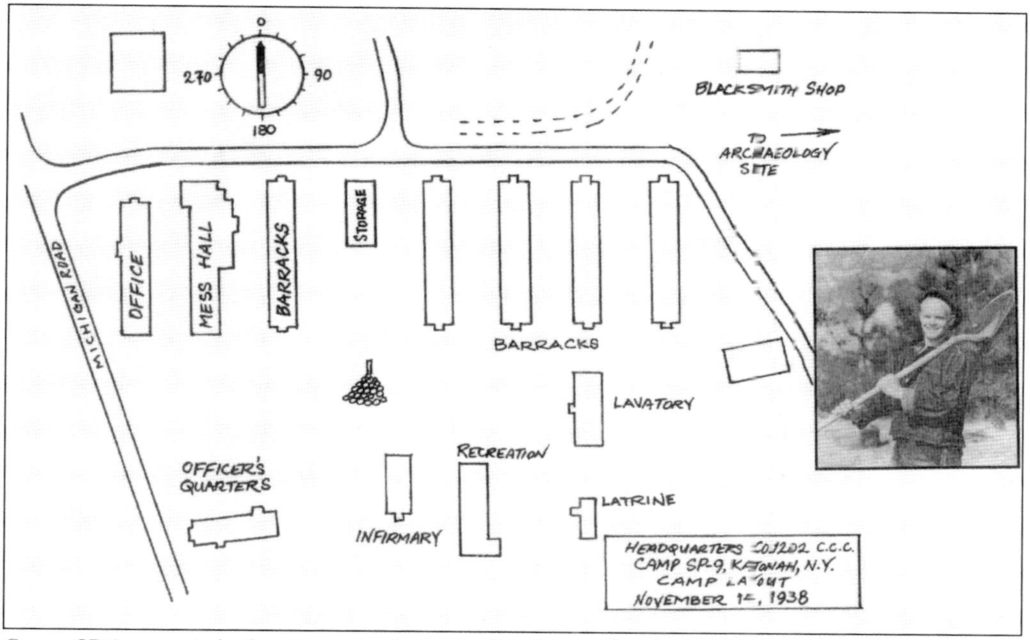

Camp SP-9 occupied a large area at the end of Michigan Road. Today, the remains of the camp's five barracks, mess hall, infirmary, recreation building, and garage are hidden by 75 years of leaf fall and forest understory. Boy Scout Eagle projects have brought new interest in the CCC's heritage in the park. Shuffling through the tangle of barberry and brush, a hiker can uncover concrete stairs and old garage metal footings.

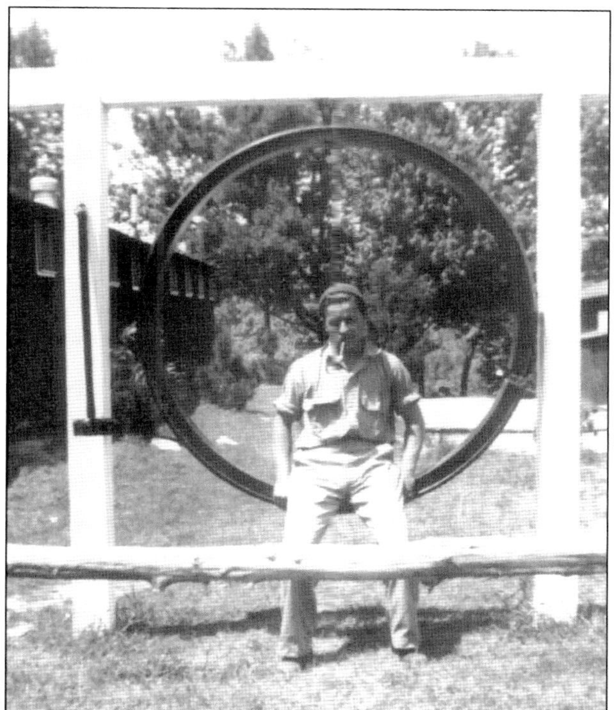

Taking time out for a smoke, a CCC corpsman rests on the fire alarm ring in the center plaza of the camp. The men worked hard, but there was leisure time, and relaxation included dances with the ladies from nearby YWCAs and church groups. The men wrote and performed in local minstrel shows, and the enrollees were invited to Halloween and Christmas festivities at the Cross River Baptist Church.

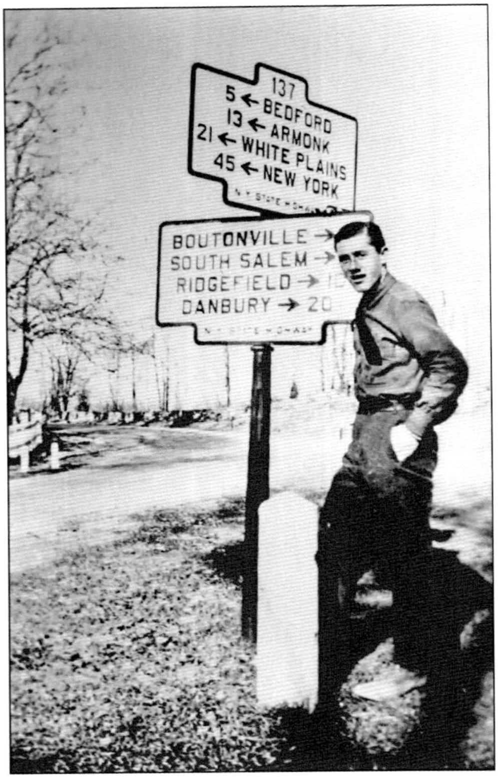

Most of the enrollees were from the local area, but some recruits were from neighboring counties and other states. This road sign could stand for the crossroads of life at which many of the recruits found themselves in the early 1930s. Recruits came by car, hitchhiked, or used shank's mare, but the destination provided a job, a salary, and a home for at least six months.

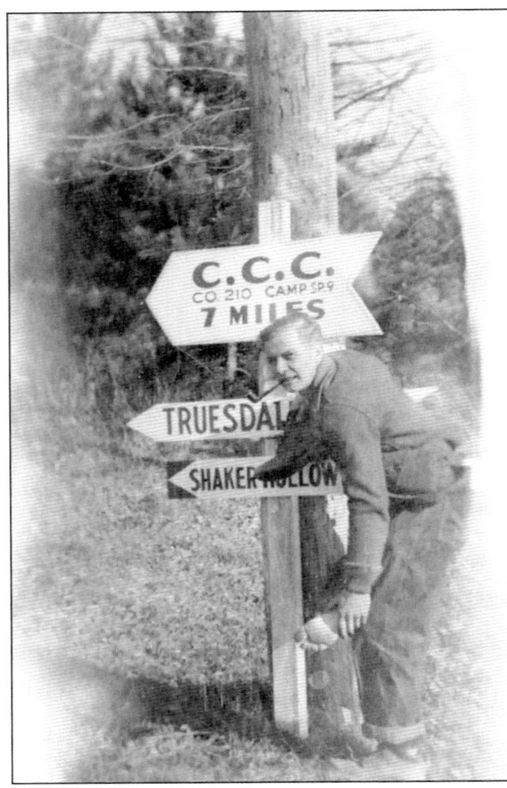

Camp SP-9 was a seven-mile walk from the train depot in Katonah. If a fellow was lucky, he might hitch a ride on a farm truck going east toward Cross River. One veteran of the camp told of walking 27 miles from his home in Peekskill, New York. No wonder this fellow has sore feet!

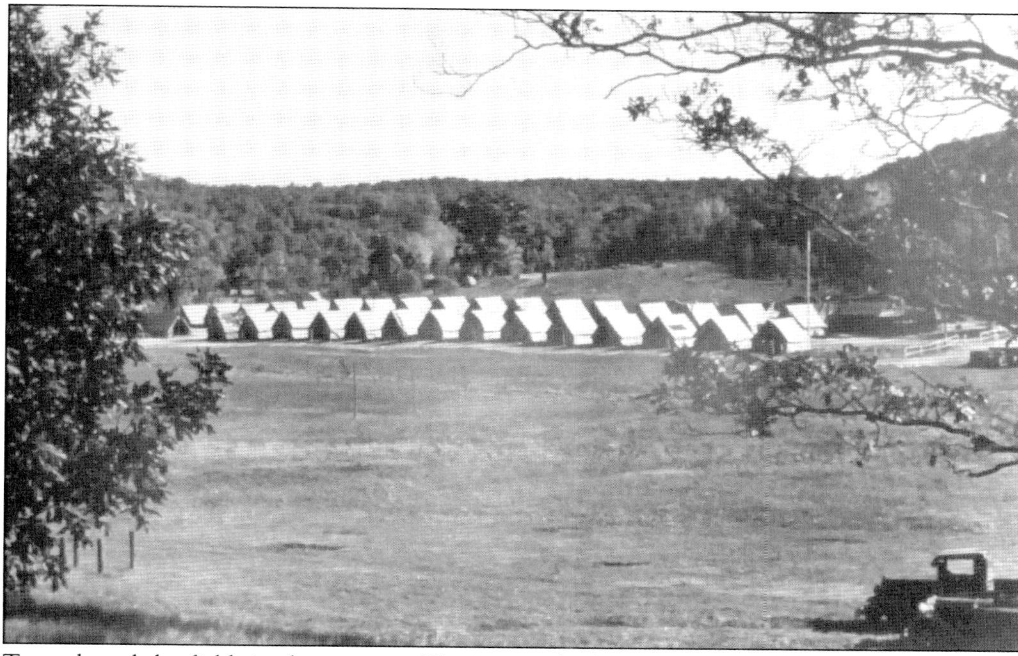

Tents dotted the fields in the summer. These were the busy months for the corps. Work details included crews engaged in tree planting, road building, and the rebuilding of park trails and the stone walls that defined the original farms and were now part of the park. Stone latrines that are still standing were built during the summer of 1935.

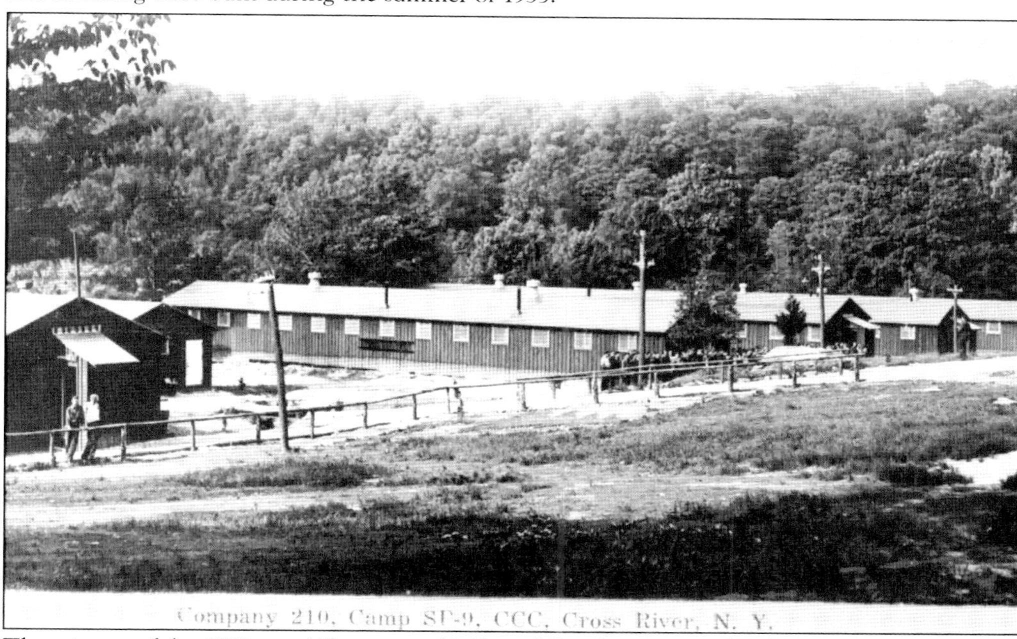

The winters of the 1930s could be very cold. Snowfalls of up to 14 inches hampered the enrollees' efforts at winter chores that included the elimination of the diseased, downed, and dead chestnut trees, eradication of tent caterpillar egg cases, and transportation of the chestnut logs from the wooded areas. The logs were used for flooring, guardrails, and other trailside structures.

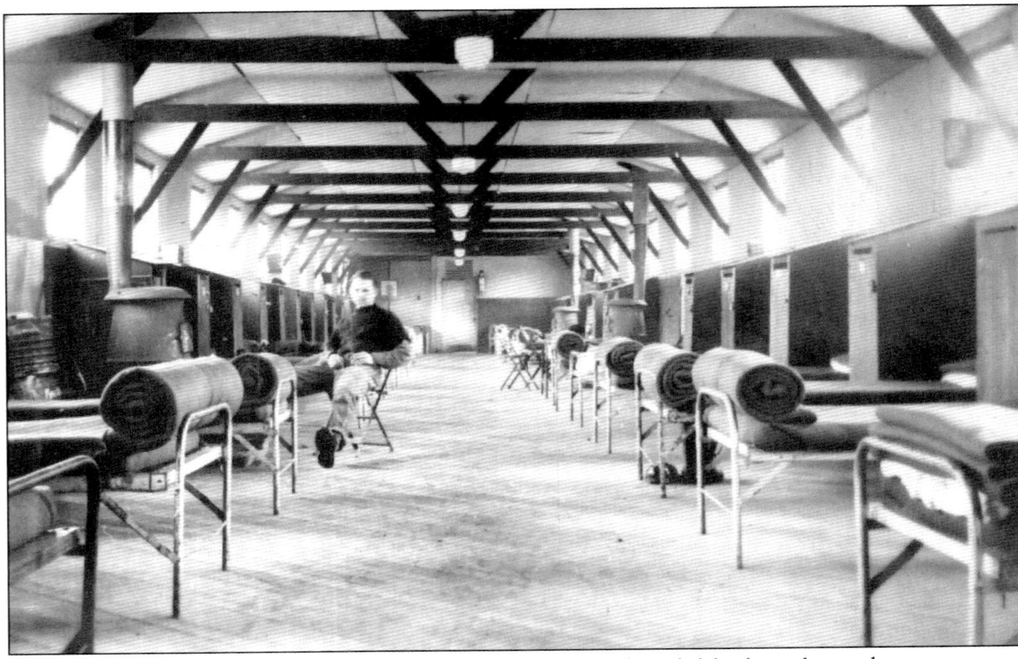

The 60-man barracks were heated by three coal stoves that did little to keep the men warm. Burlap sacks were placed under the bunks' mattresses to thwart the cold seeping through the floor. Burlap-sack rugs added a little more protection for cold feet in the morning. The men were awakened at dawn, and lights-out was 10:00 p.m. A night watchman patrolled the area to make sure rules were obeyed.

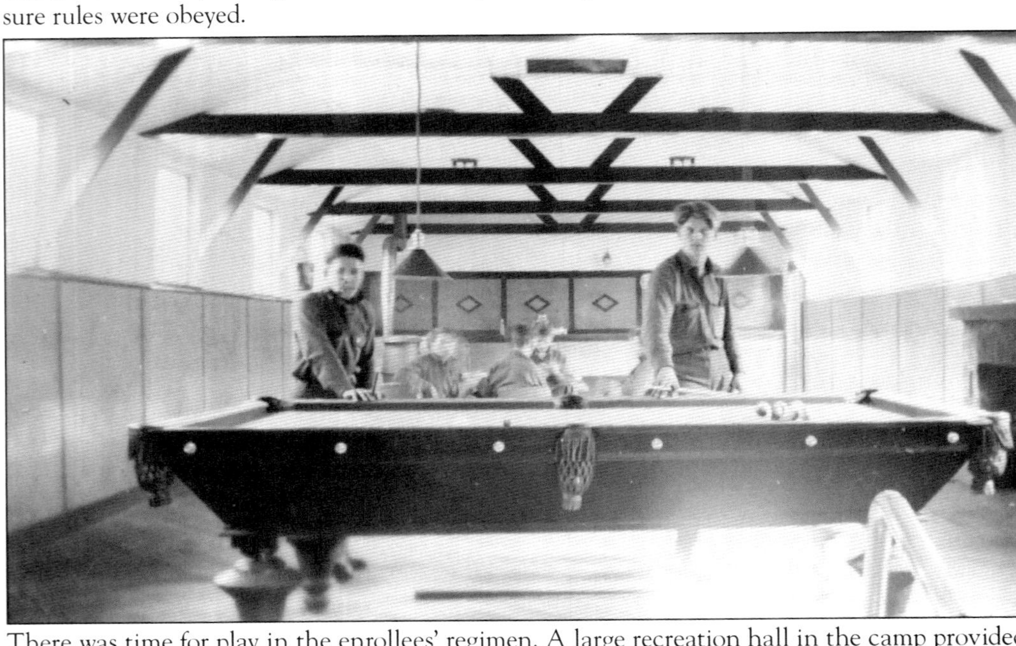

There was time for play in the enrollees' regimen. A large recreation hall in the camp provided space for games, and pool tables offered a little friendly competition. A basketball team was organized and played other teams in the area, including another CCC camp on the Katonah-Somers border near the Muscoot Reservoir.

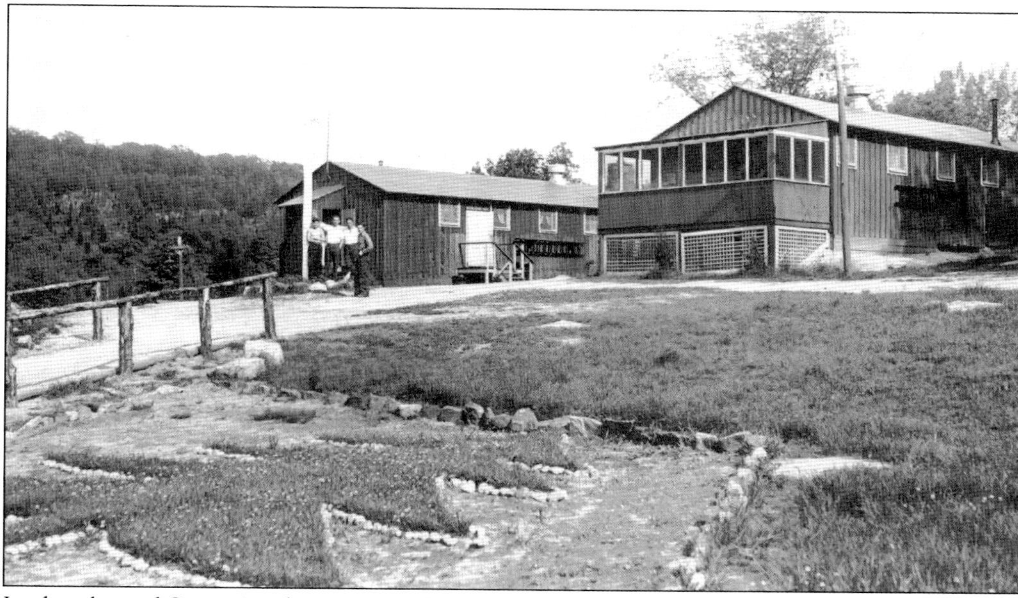

In the plaza of Camp 24, there was a Christmas tree. It was the center of attention for many of the men of that camp, and was remembered fondly. Veterans returning for CCC reunions decades later followed the trails into the woods that now hide the remains of the camp, looking for that tree, designed from carefully cut vegetation and outlined with small white rocks.

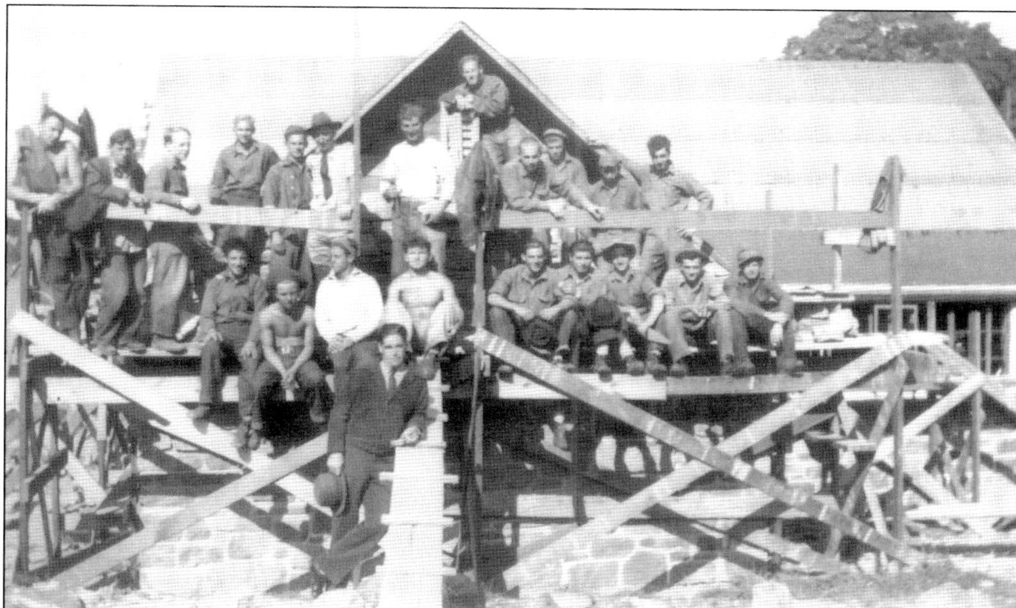

Posing in front of the partially constructed visitor center, a group of Roosevelt's Tree Army builders displays pride in their work. As much as possible, native materials, especially fieldstone, were used in the building. The structure stands opposite the gatehouse to the park, and is now called the WPA Gallery, offering frequent art shows for the public.

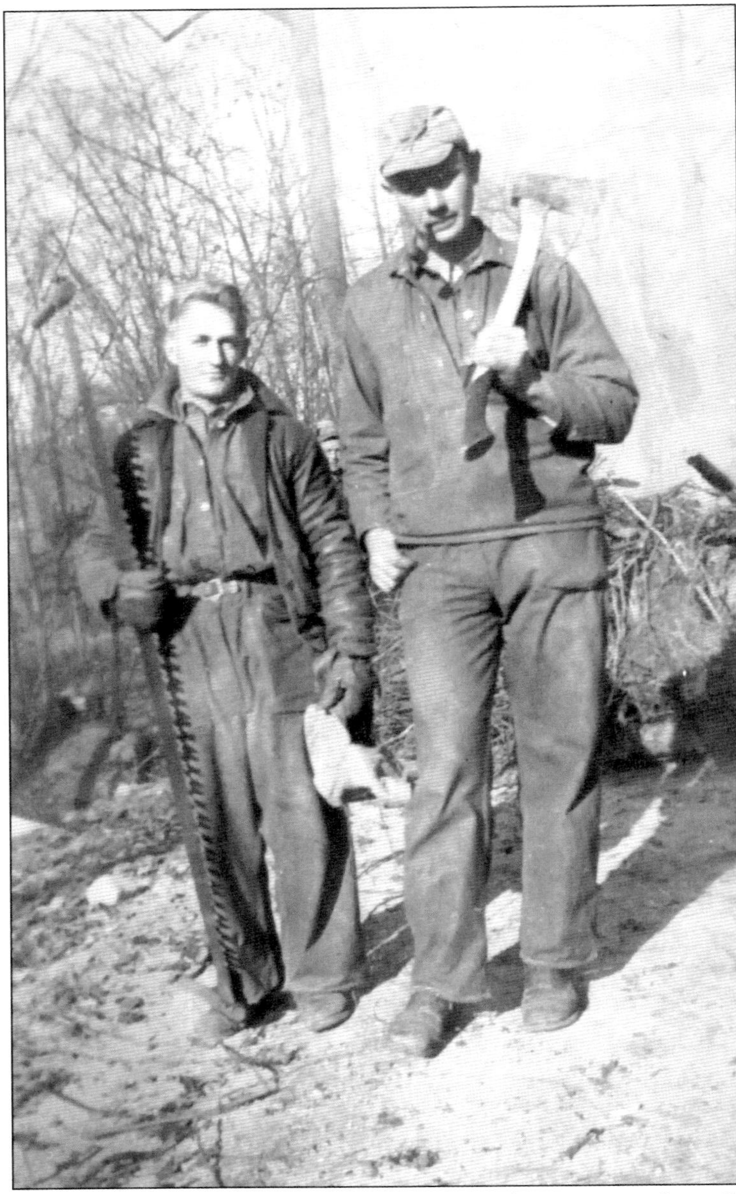

Fifteen-man CCC crews worked with Department of Agriculture personnel on efforts to control Dutch elm disease, which was rampant in the country and present in the park. The crews created a protective belt, 10 miles wide, around areas of infected trees both inside and outside the boundaries of the park. Infected trees were tagged by the Department of Agriculture, and the CCC crews cut the trees, leaving tall stumps. The stumps and logs were burned on the spot. Since the beetle causing the disease lived under the bark, the bark on the remaining stumps and twigs was pried from the trunks, and copper sulfate crystals were planted under the bark. Then, the bark was sealed to protect animals from sampling the salts. By March 1936, all 4,315 acres of the park were declared free of diseased elm trees. All dead and dying trees had been removed. The CCC workers were so adept at their job that adjoining property owners hired them to remove affected trees from their private properties.

President Roosevelt envisioned a twofold plan for his Civilian Conservation Corps: the eradication of Dutch elm disease and the reforestation of America. In addition, American chestnut trees devastated by blight had to be removed. At SP-9, Company 210 got to work planting thousands of red and white pine seedlings in the reservation and along the shores of Cross River Reservoir. The seedlings had been brought by train to Katonah and transported by truck to Cross River.

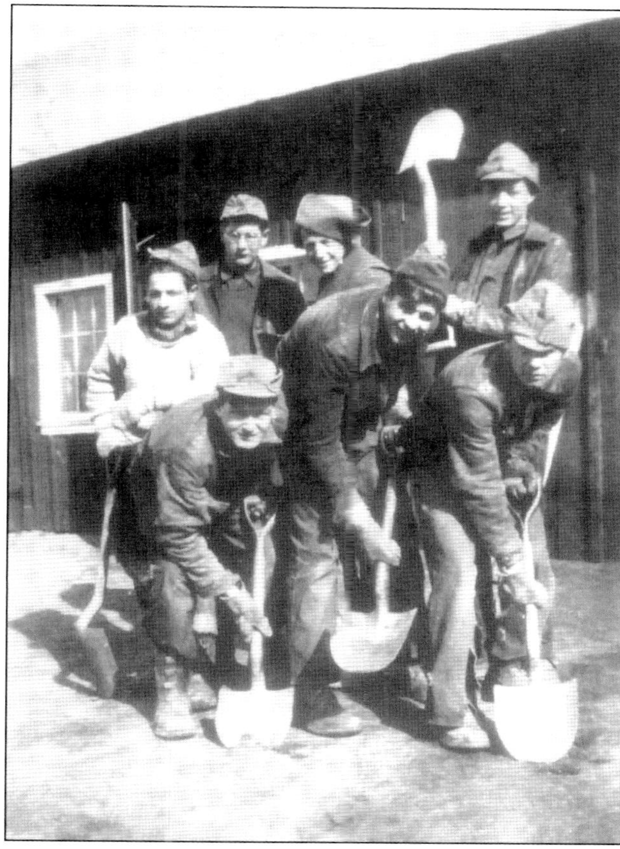

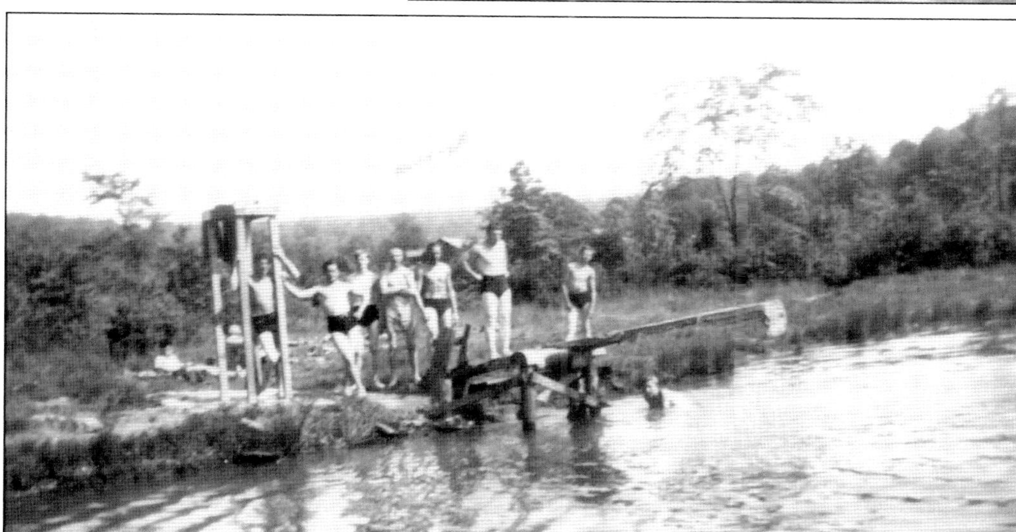

What's a camp without a summertime swimming hole? The corpsmen, being handy with tools, built themselves a diving board and dock on the shore of a small pond that had been deepened and enlarged to provide a way of cooling off after a hot day of work. The pond is still there at the end of Michigan Road.

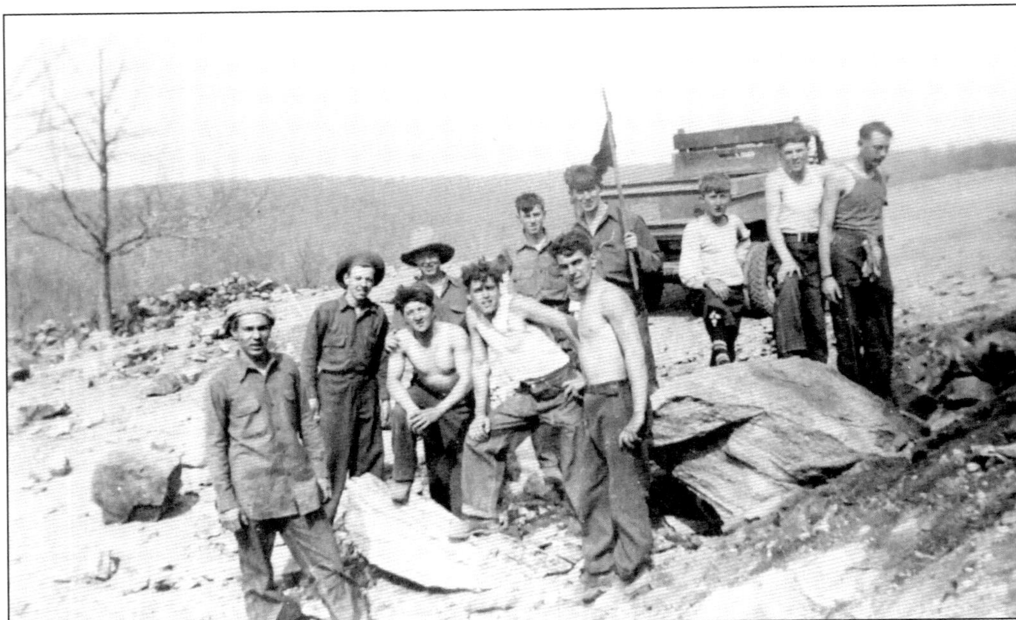

If there were not reforestation chores for the CCC work crews, there were stone wall rebuilding and road improvement details. Masons guided the stonework, and Army engineers designed the road building. Pausing to pose for the camera documenting a hot, hard day's work, this crew enjoys a respite from a battle with a large boulder along the side of the road up Pell Hill.

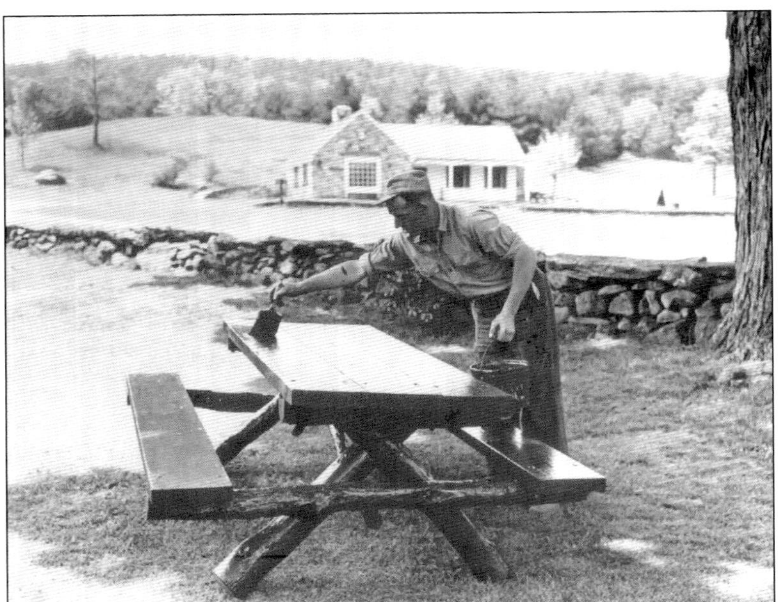

Logs from trees cut from the forested areas were made into benches, picnic tables, and guardrails by the CCC enrollees. The logs were sometimes hauled by horse and stoneboat from the swampy areas, which were too treacherous for trucks to navigate. The tables were enjoyed by the hundreds of park visitors on sunny weekend excursions to the country.

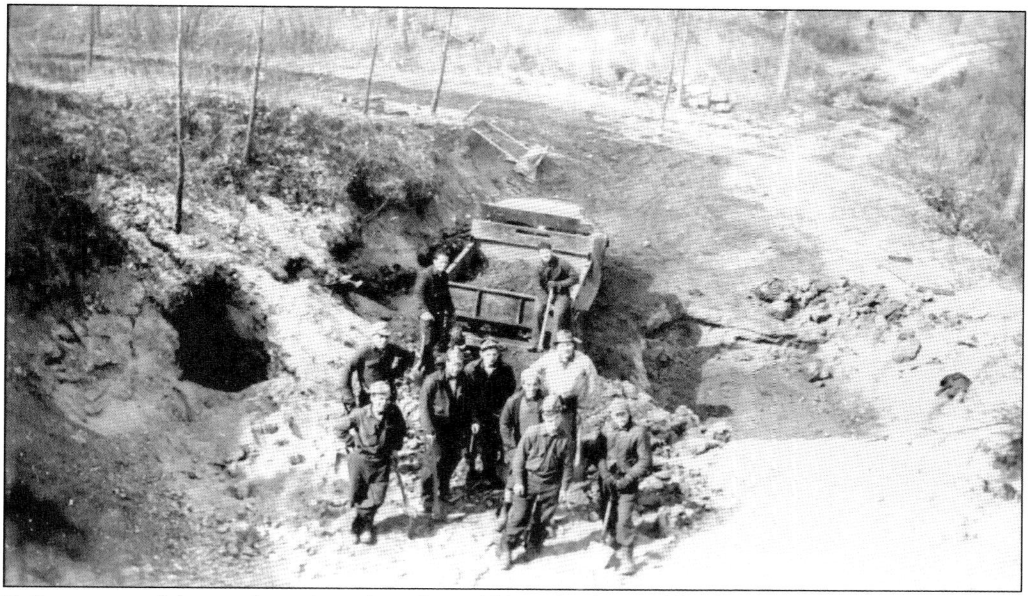

Before many of the truck trails and roads could be rebuilt, truckloads of gravel had to be brought from the park's gravel pits to provide a 10-inch base for the new road. Large rocks were removed from the old road and placed on the shoulder. A smooth sand layer was laid over the base for a well-drained and safer roadway. The Park Road and Michigan Road are examples of this road building.

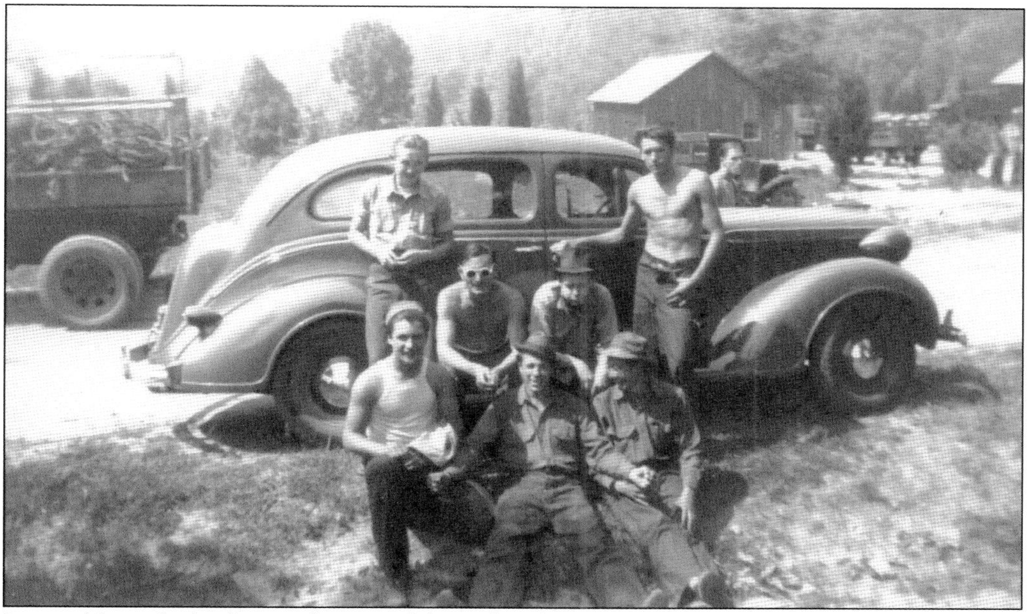

Just visible in the background is one of the eight Chevrolet trucks stationed at Camp 24. Drivers were chosen for their ability to maneuver the vehicles over rough terrain and around obstacles. Wooden planks were bolted onto the floors to prevent damage to the trucks when transporting rocks. The truck beds had removable seats and could transport 20 men easily.

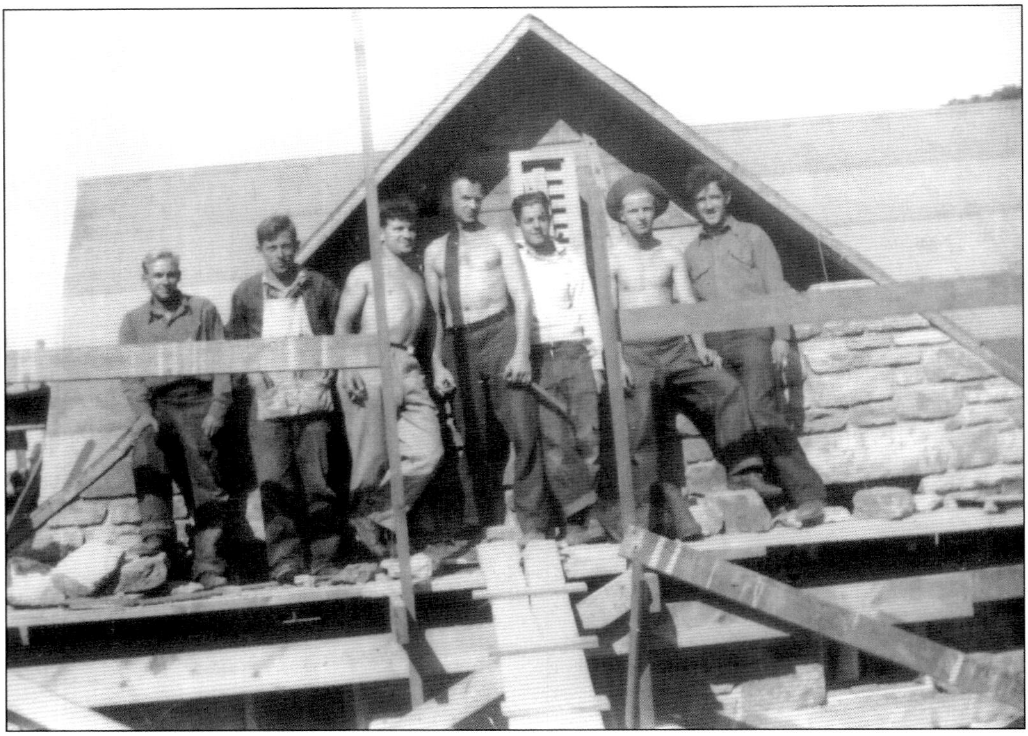

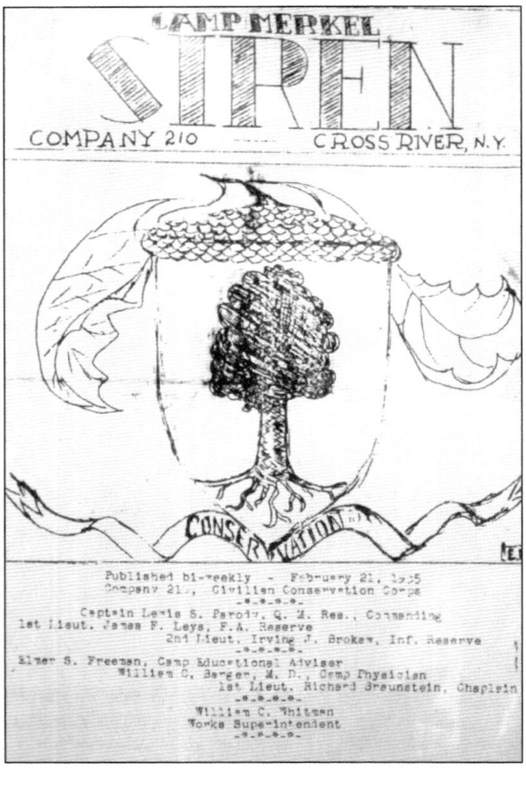

CAMP MERKEL

SIREN

COMPANY 210 CROSS RIVER, N.Y.

CONSERVATION

Published bi-weekly - February 21, 1935
Company 210, Civilian Conservation Corps
-*-*-*-*-
Captain Lewis S. Parody, Q. M. Res., Commanding
1st Lieut. James F. Leys, F.A. Reserve
2nd Lieut. Irving J. Brokaw, Inf. Reserve
-*-*-*-*-
Elmer S. Freeman, Camp Educational Adviser
William C. Berger, M. D., Camp Physician
1st Lieut. Richard Braunstein, Chaplain
-*-*-*-*-
William C. Whitman
Works Superintendent
-*-*-*-*-

CCC enrollees were organized into work crews of 15, with a supervising officer or, in the case of the stone workers, a skilled mason. Classes in forestry, crafts, drafting, and other vocations were offered as well as high school courses. Often, the skills the young men learned as CCC members gave them a life's vocation. A number of enrollees left the program and enlisted in the Army.

Company 210 of Camp 24 published a biweekly newspaper, printed from a camp mimeograph machine. Designed and written by corpsmen, it was published with the help of the camp education department. This cover illustration of an acorn and a mature oak tree symbolizes the goal of the CCC camp at Ward Pound Ridge Reservation: the reforestation of an area devastated by Dutch elm disease and the American chestnut blight.

Five

The Trailside Nature Museum

Today, nature centers come in all shapes and sizes. But in 1937, the idea of a small natural history museum surrounded by wildlife instead of city streets was a unique concept. So unusual was this little building, located not in a big city, but in the landscape it was meant to interpret, that it was featured in several magazines. Even the young ornithologist Roger Tory Peterson remarks in *Bird Lore* that "museums with marble halls require a great outlay of wealth. Not many cities can afford them—but the small outdoor museums can fill the gap. At the Pound Ridge Reservation the Bedford Garden Club has established a very fine beautiful little trailside museum."

The year the museum opened, more than 5,000 visitors signed the guest book. The following year, 1939, that number grew to 10,000, with guests from "forty of our forty-eight states, and twelve foreign countries signing the register."

A nature center is merely a building without a naturalist present to answer questions and engage the visiting public. The Trailside Museum has been guided by a series of remarkable leaders: The first naturalist, William Wheeler, stayed at the helm for almost 30 years. He was followed by Paul Friese, who upgraded the status of the naturalist, from laborer to curator. Succeeding Friese was David Junkin, who upgraded exhibits.

Nick Shoumatoff came next, in the 1970s, first as a fire tower observer, then for 15 years as curator of the museum. He greatly expanded programming, developed a huge following, enlarged the museum, added a library, and organized archaeological digs and ethnographic expeditions.

The museum has always been a "cabinet of curiosities," filled with wondrous items: animals, plants, local history artifacts, skulls, bones, and skins, and all sorts of collections. Ecological issues addressed have included the chestnut blight in the 1930s, red pine rust in the 1960s, gypsy moths in the 1980s, and Lyme ticks in the 1990s.

Nature education was the original purpose of the Trailside Nature Museum, and that tradition of quality environmental education continues today. Thousands of schoolchildren visit each year, hundreds of people are informed and entertained by weekend offerings, researchers use the libraries, and casual visitors wander in and out of its doors every day.

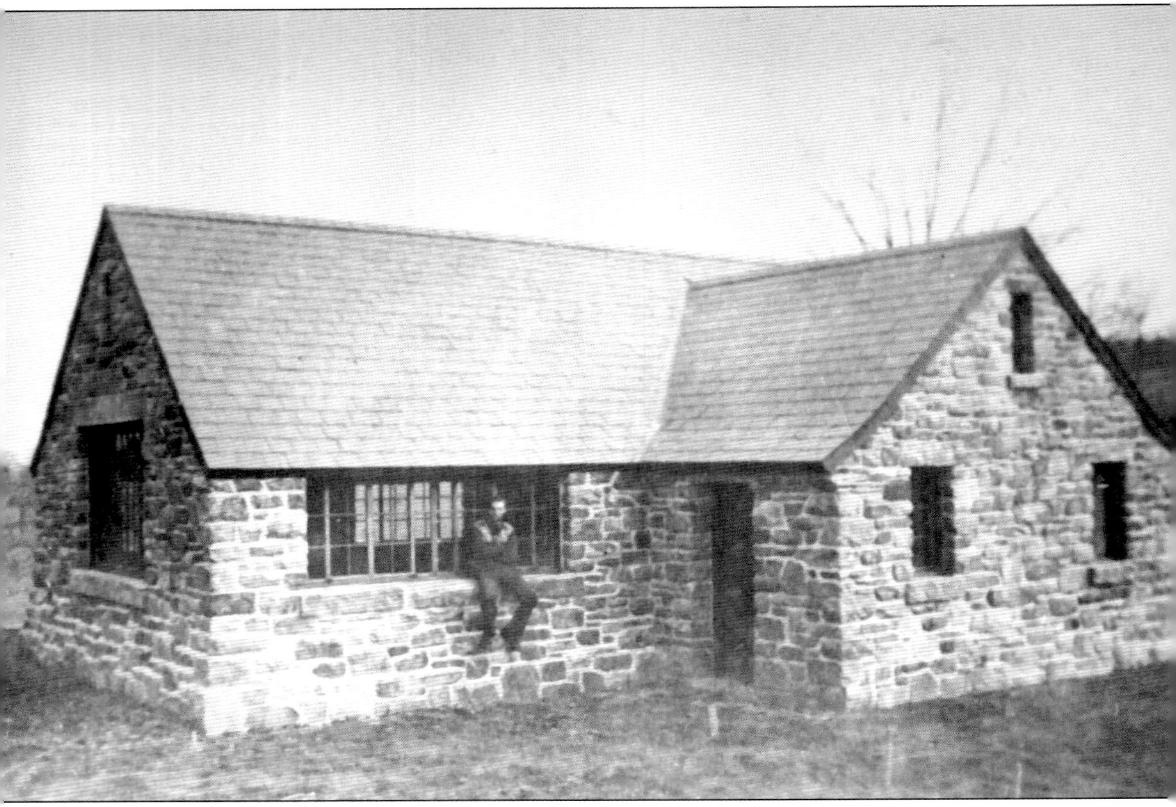

The new little nature museum, and a very proud Civilian Conservation Corps mason, welcomed the first visitors. The space inside the stone walls was soon filled with cabinets built by CCC carpenters; a topographical map created by WPA artists; artifacts donated by local naturalists; specimens fashioned by Stanley Grierson, a local taxidermist; and natural items collected by the first curator, William Wheeler.

William Wheeler (right), sought out for his birding skills, accompanied wealthy clients, like those shown here, on excursions. This reputation made him the top candidate to run the new museum. He was a protégé of the famous ornithologist Edward Howe Forbush. Their field trips, undertaken when Wheeler was just a teen, are immortalized in Forbush's classic *Birds of Massachusetts*.

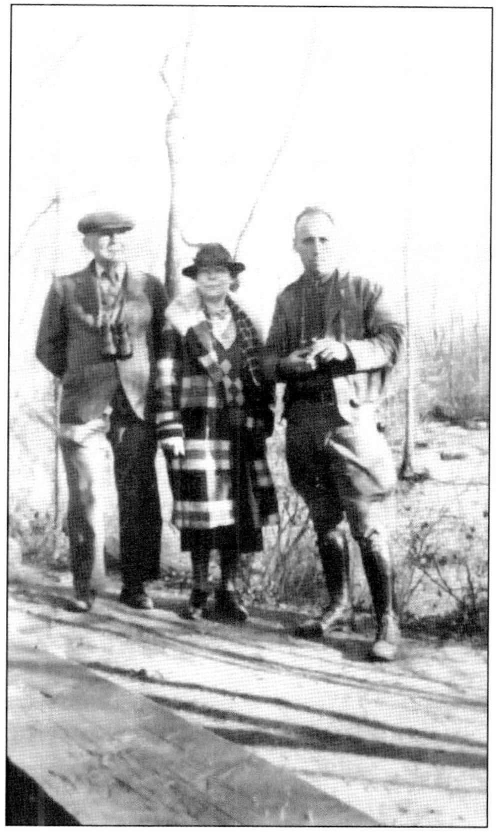

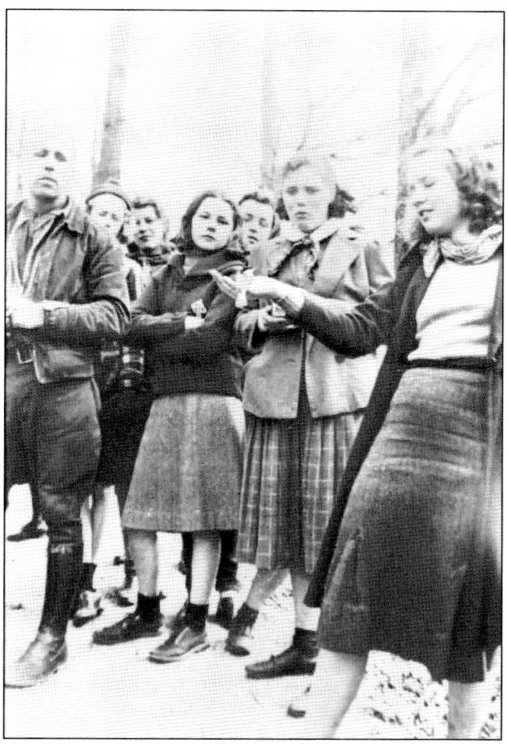

A bold black-capped chickadee, *Poecile atricapillus*, feeds atop a young visitor's hand while her friends and curator Wheeler silently watch. Wheeler was a skilled ornithologist with a reputation for mimicking birdcalls and hand-feeding birds. More than 285 species of birds have been documented in the park, and museum staff continues to offer programming during spring songbird migration season and autumn hawk migration, as well as winter bird walks and owl prowls.

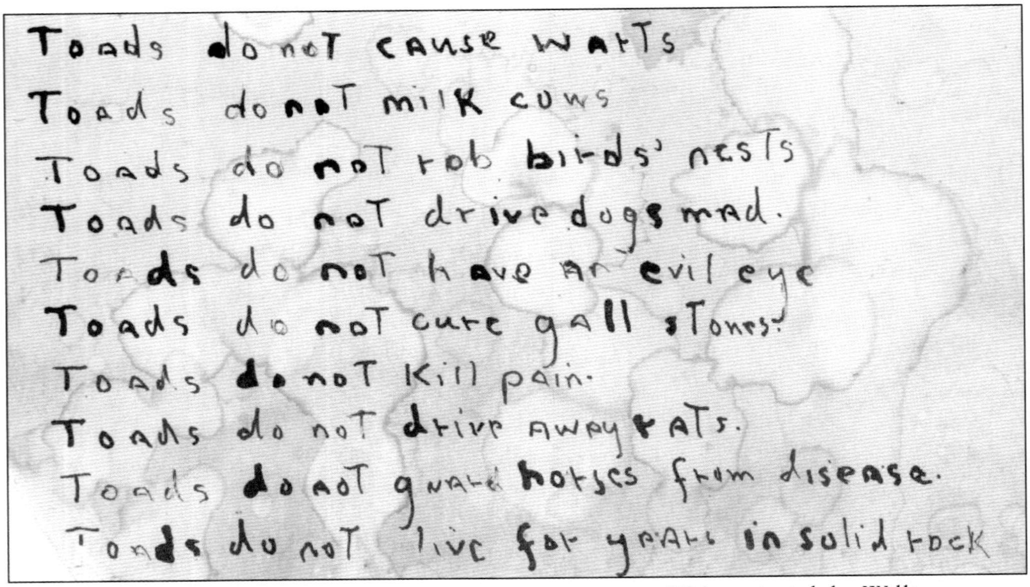
Toads do not cause warts
Toads do not milk cows
Toads do not rob birds' nests
Toads do not drive dogs mad.
Toads do not have an evil eye
Toads do not cure gall stones?
Toads do not kill pain.
Toads do not drive away rats.
Toads do not guard horses from disease.
Toads do not live for years in solid rock

Written in ink by William Wheeler, this myth-breaking exhibit helped museum visitors appreciate the unloved American toad, *Bufo americanus*. There are several species of frogs, toads, and salamanders breeding and foraging in the park. Naturalists still try to provide knowledgeable answers to questions about birds falling out of nests, "abandoned" baby deer, or black snakes found in basements.

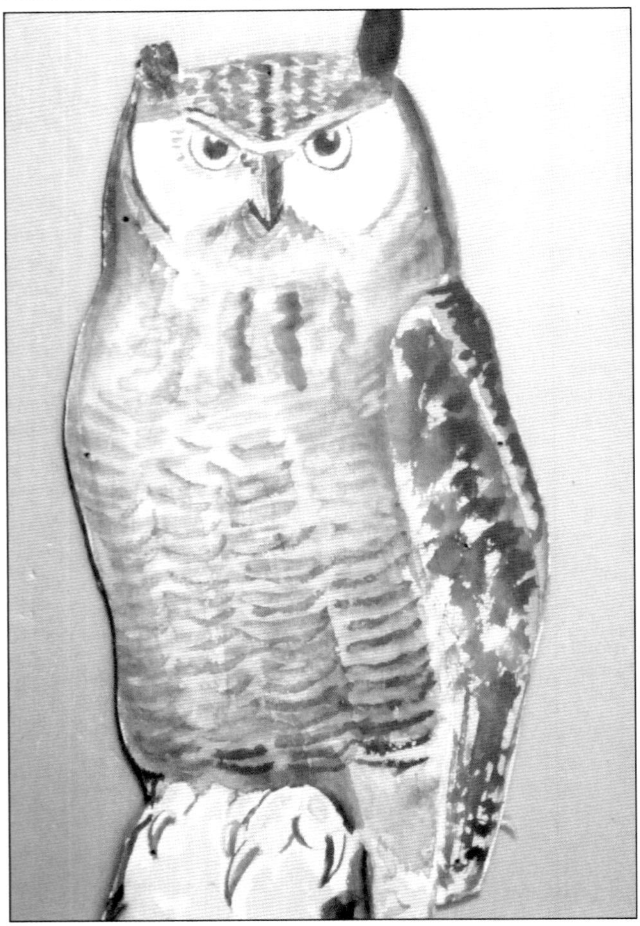

Wheeler was an amateur artist and a bird enthusiast. He needed to fill the museum with exhibits on a shoestring budget. Some of his sketches and notes survive from the 1940s, including this painting of a great horned owl, *Bubo virginianus*. Several more species of owl thrive in the reservation's forests and meadows, including the saw-whet, *Aegolius acadicus*, and long-eared, *Asio otus*.

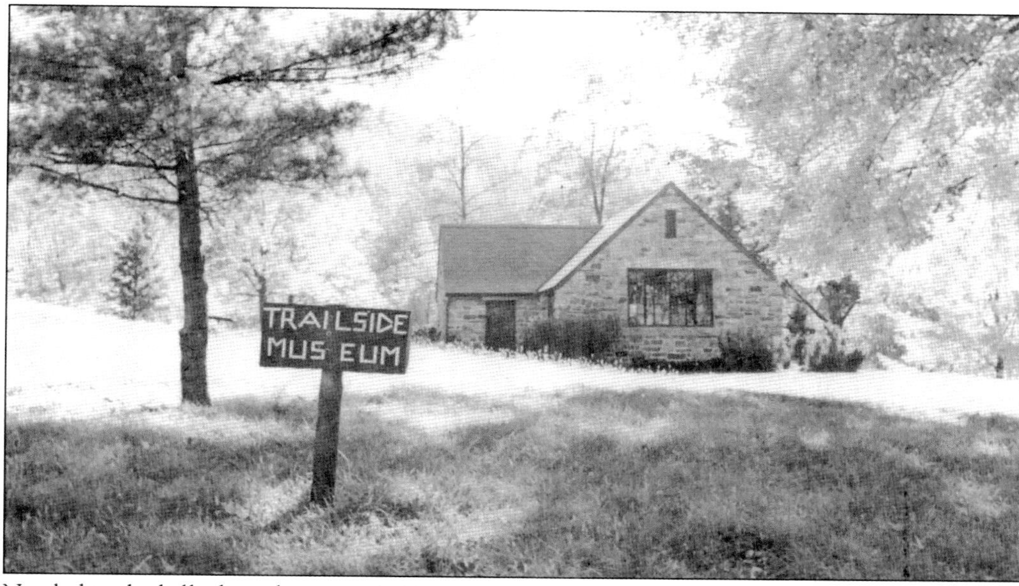

Nestled in the hillside and surrounded by stately maple trees, the little Trailside Museum was one of the first nature centers in America. The empty little building echoed at first, but soon was filled with wondrous things for visitors to see. The museum was staffed by a knowledgeable naturalist ready to answer visitors' questions; his small office was behind the door on the left.

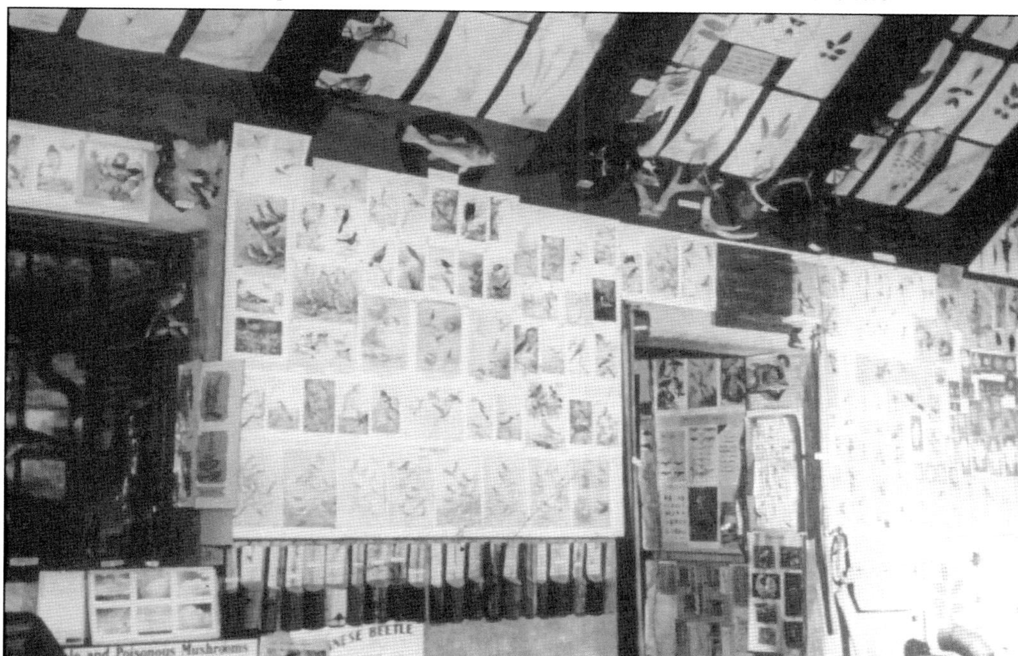

The museum has always had interesting exhibits, but the focus has matured along with the ecology movement. The collecting of specimens is now mostly replaced by observation, but nothing replaces seeing a mounted specimen up close to view adaptations, or holding a skull in hand to feel form and function. Today, most specimens are donated roadkills and are mounted by licensed taxidermists.

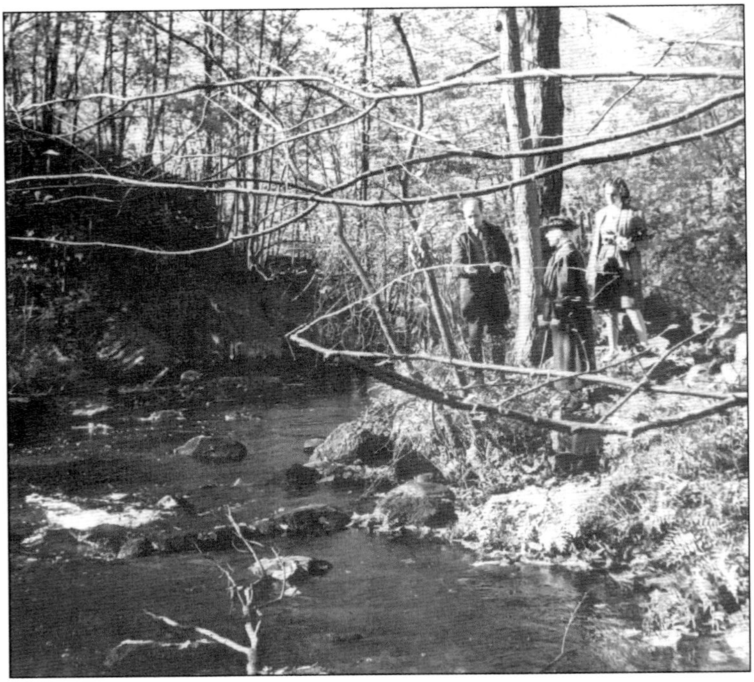

William Wheeler is seen here with Eloise Payne Luquer (center). She was the conservation committee chair of the Bedford Garden Club, an outspoken conservationist, and a devoted fan of Wheeler. It was her leadership that helped secure the building of the nature museum and Wheeler's tenure as naturalist. Here, they are likely sharing their knowledge with a newer member of the garden club in the early 1940s.

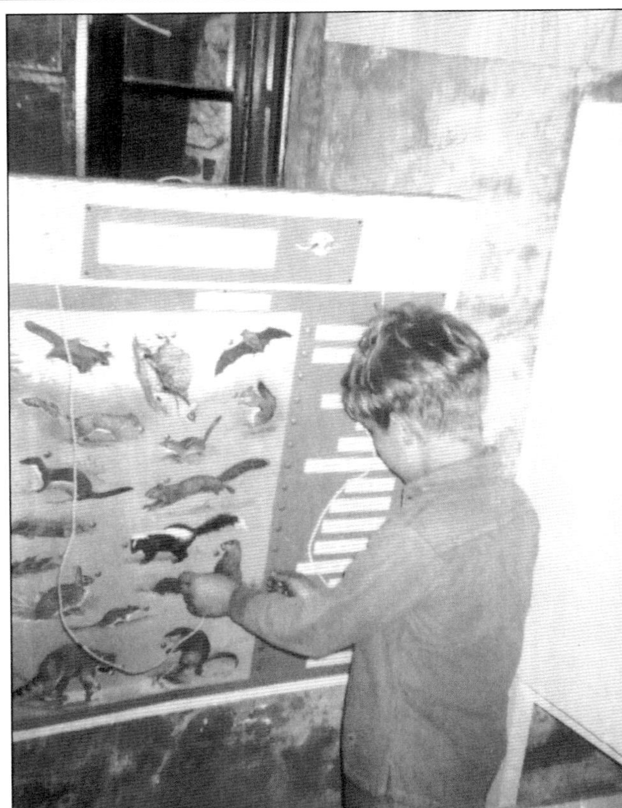

A young naturalist tries to answer questions about the reservation's mammal species on this electronic quiz board. A common exhibit in the old museum days, it provided immediate feedback on answers. The park still supports several species of mammals, from the northern flying squirrel, *Glaucomys sabrinus*, to the meadow jumping mouse, *Zapus hudsonius*. Many are secretive, like the bobcat, *Lynx rufus*, and take patience to observe.

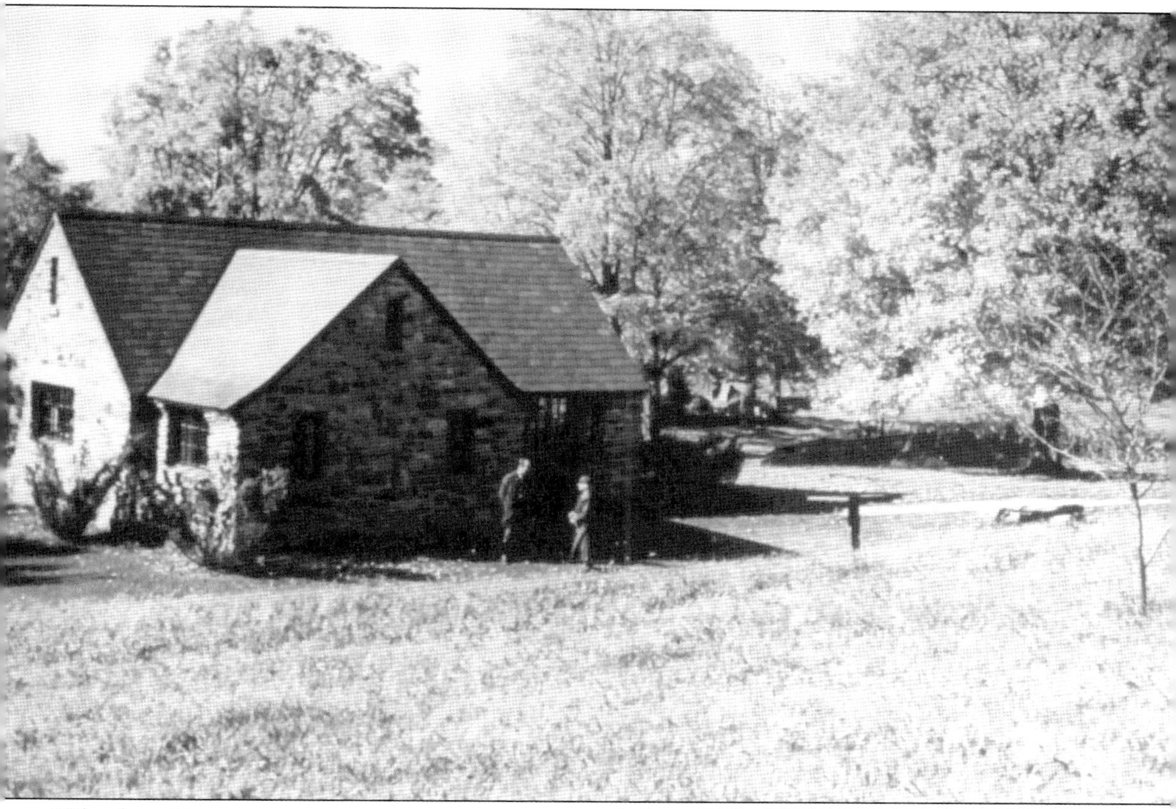

Wheeler addresses a young summertime visitor outside his office at the nature museum. The lye stone still sits near the entrance, but a demonstration planting of Christmas evergreen trees was installed in 1965, changing this view of the museum. The stately sugar maples, *Acer saccharum*, surrounding the museum stand as a testament to the farmers who made collecting maple sap as easy as they could.

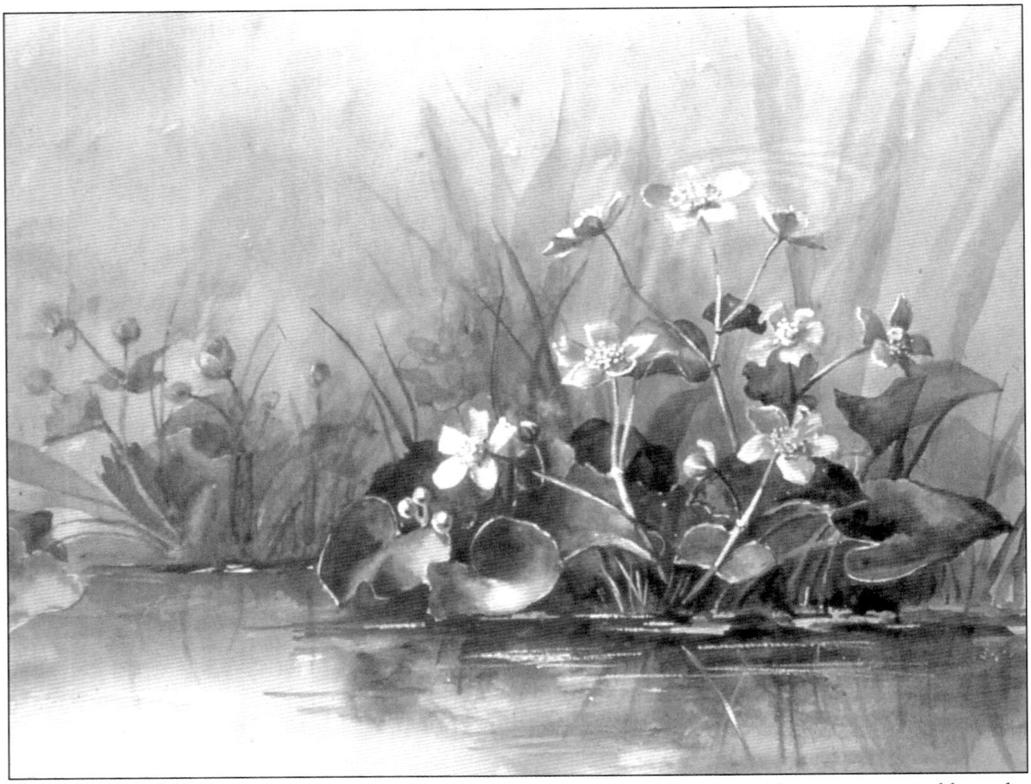

This lovely watercolor of marsh marigold, *Caltha palustris*, was painted by Luquer, a self-taught artist and botanist. She donated color slides of more than 100 paintings to the museum collection, and a large painting still hangs on the museum walls. Her paintings capture not only the beauty of the flowers, but also their habitats and their seasons. Many of her original paintings are held at the Brooklyn Botanic Garden.

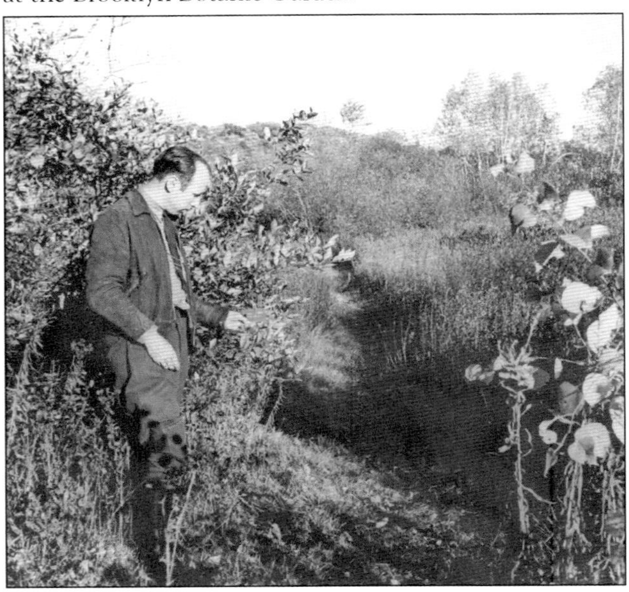

William Wheeler examines a shrub found along the nature trails he created. Behind him grows a young successional forest. He is standing in an old farm field now changing to thickets of shrubs. He wore a park ranger uniform complete with whistle and badge. Wheeler started a tradition of quality interpretive programs and trails in the reservation.

A wildflower garden was started in the 1950s with the help, again, of the Bedford Garden Club. The intention was to save threatened plants, educate visitors about native plant conservation, and create a quiet, beautiful oasis behind the museum. Over the years, other local garden clubs, young Scouts, and science interns have added to the number of species and benches. The hand-carved entrance sign was added in the 1970s.

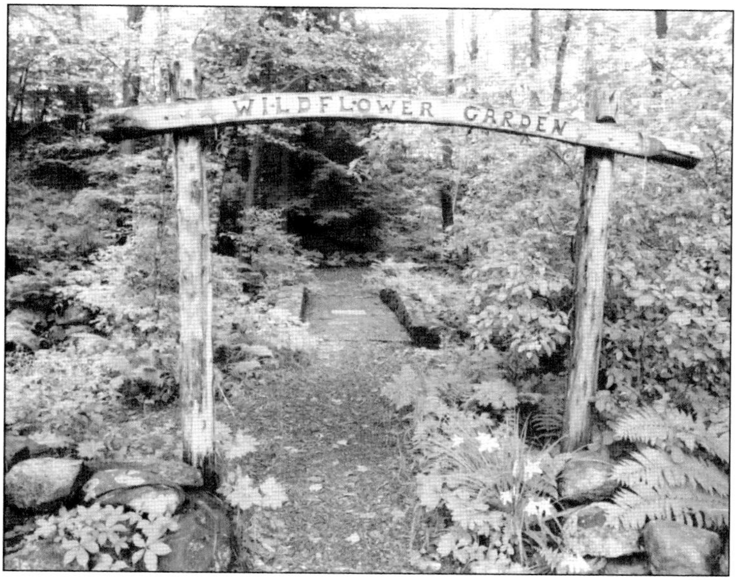

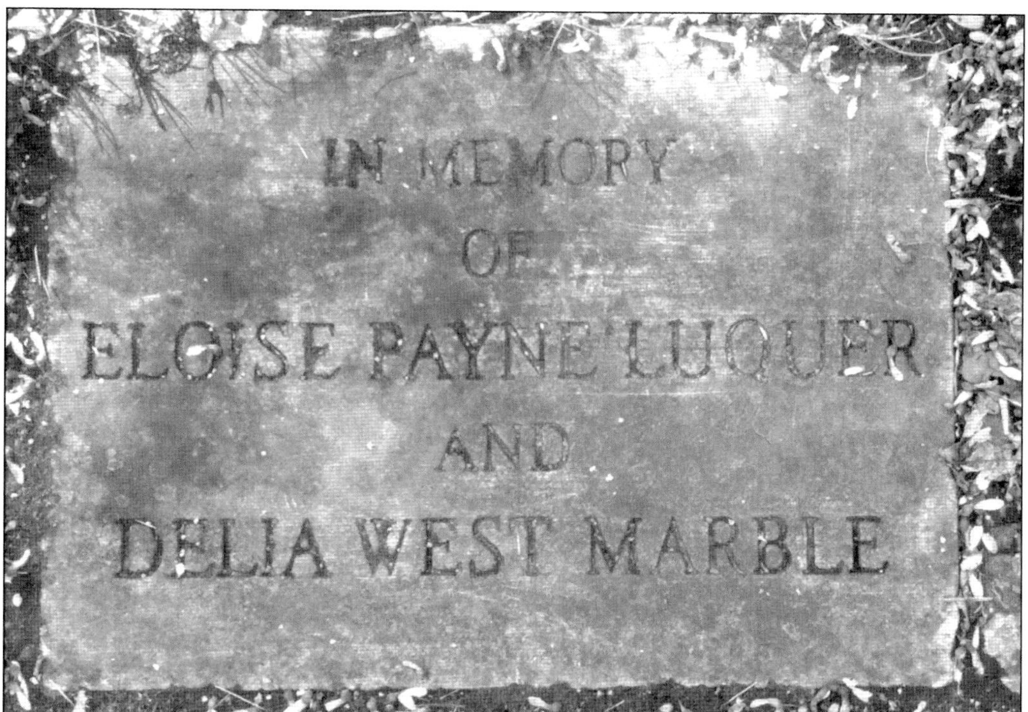

The wildflower garden straddles the Slawson Creek. Visitors are aided by wooden and stone bridges and are accompanied by the gurgle and babble of flowing water. This delightful demonstration garden was dedicated to the two women who helped with the creation of the museum—Eloise Payne Luquer and Delia West Marble. Their names are memorialized in stone on the center of the bridge.

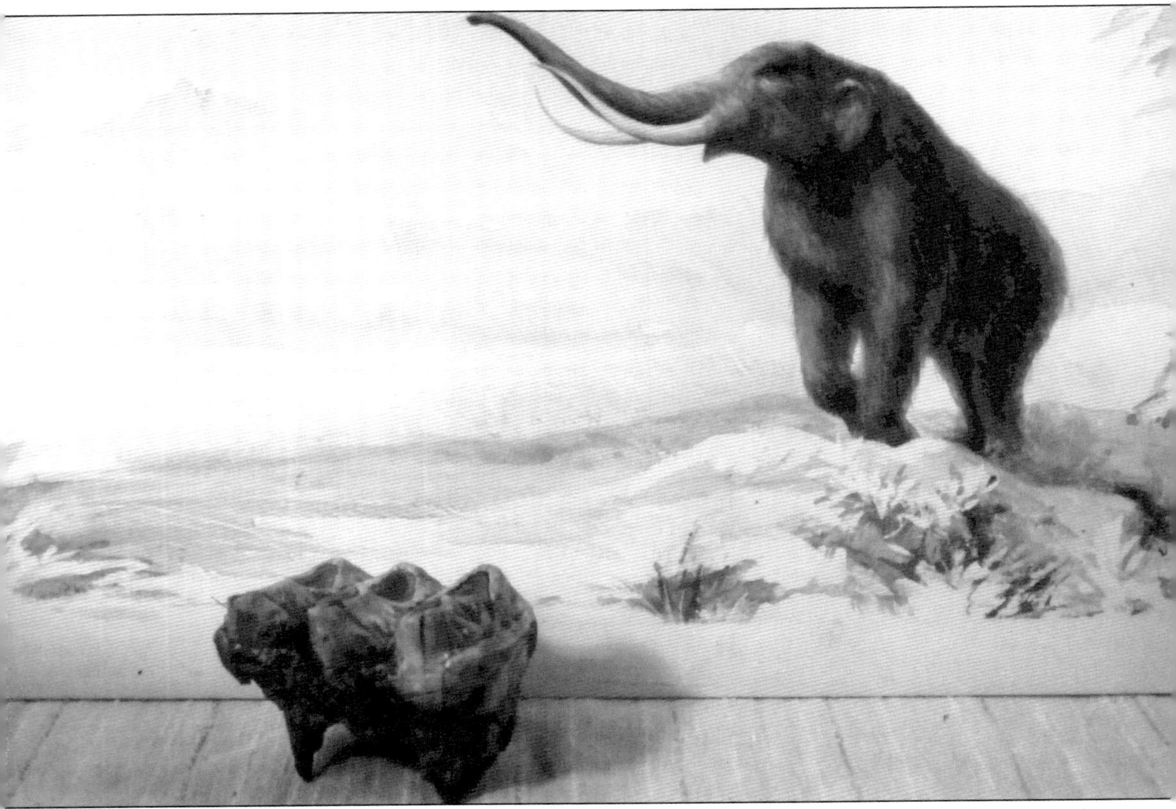

One of the most popular exhibits in the Trailside Nature Museum speaks of another age, when great mammals roamed the land. Found only two miles from the park, this mastodon tooth and many bones were unearthed in the early 1970s near Lake Kitchawan. The mammals thrived here after the retreat of the Wisconsin Glacier 13,000 years ago.

An older William Wheeler sits on a lye stone in front of the museum. He retired in 1963 after 30 years of service, leaving behind a fine nature library, a devoted following, many inspired students, and detailed notes about the park. The stone still waits by the museum, inviting questions from curious visitors.

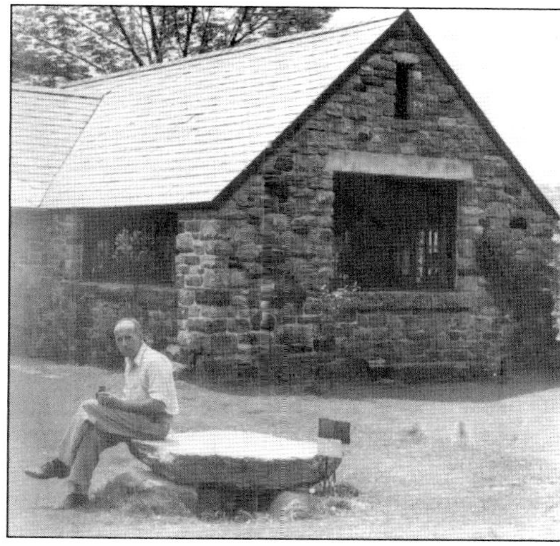

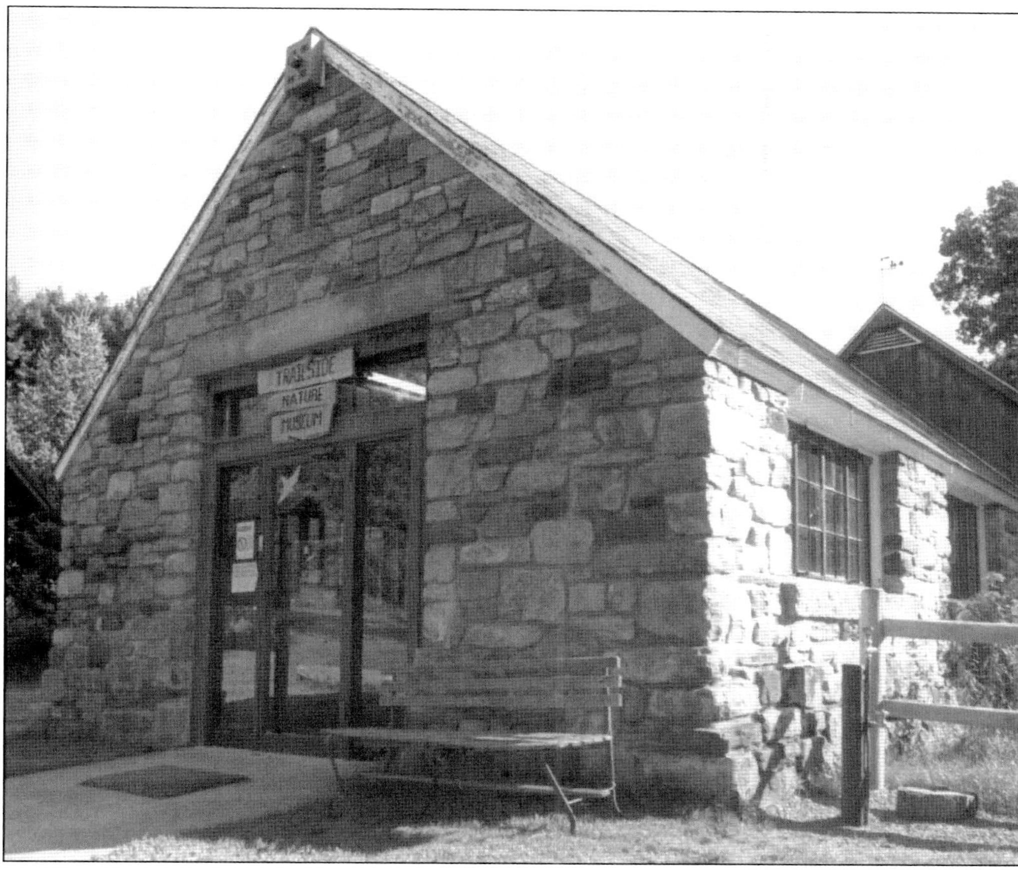

In 1976, the museum needed to expand to meet the needs of large groups. An addition provided a large meeting room, a much larger office, and a library, called the Delaware Indian Resource Center. The casement windows were replaced with glass entryways and wildlife viewing windows. That same year, a small log sugarhouse and Colonial-style log home were built behind the museum, dedicated to local history programming.

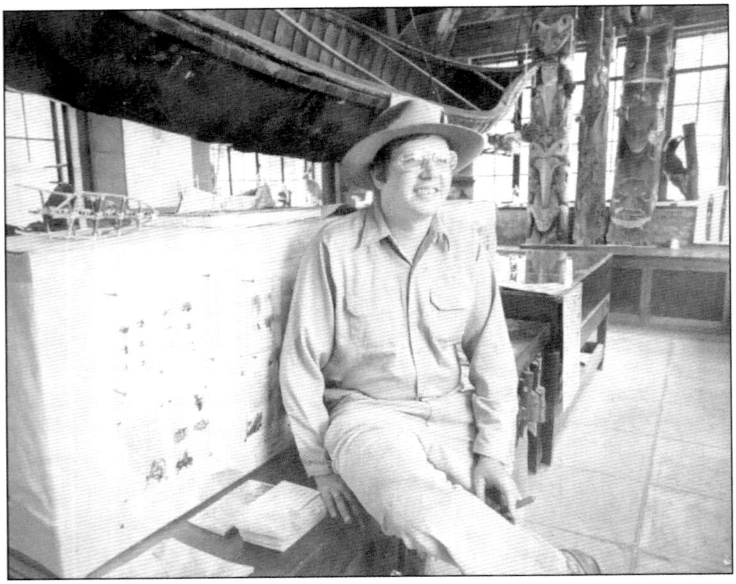

Nick Shoumatoff, in ranger badge and hat, sits under a birch bark canoe, surrounded by totem poles and Native American artifacts procured during his tenure. He lectured widely on local tribes, to the delight of museum visitors, and earned the respect of the living relatives descended from those tribes. He made many recordings of their language, place-names, plant uses, and eventually invited them to visit the museum.

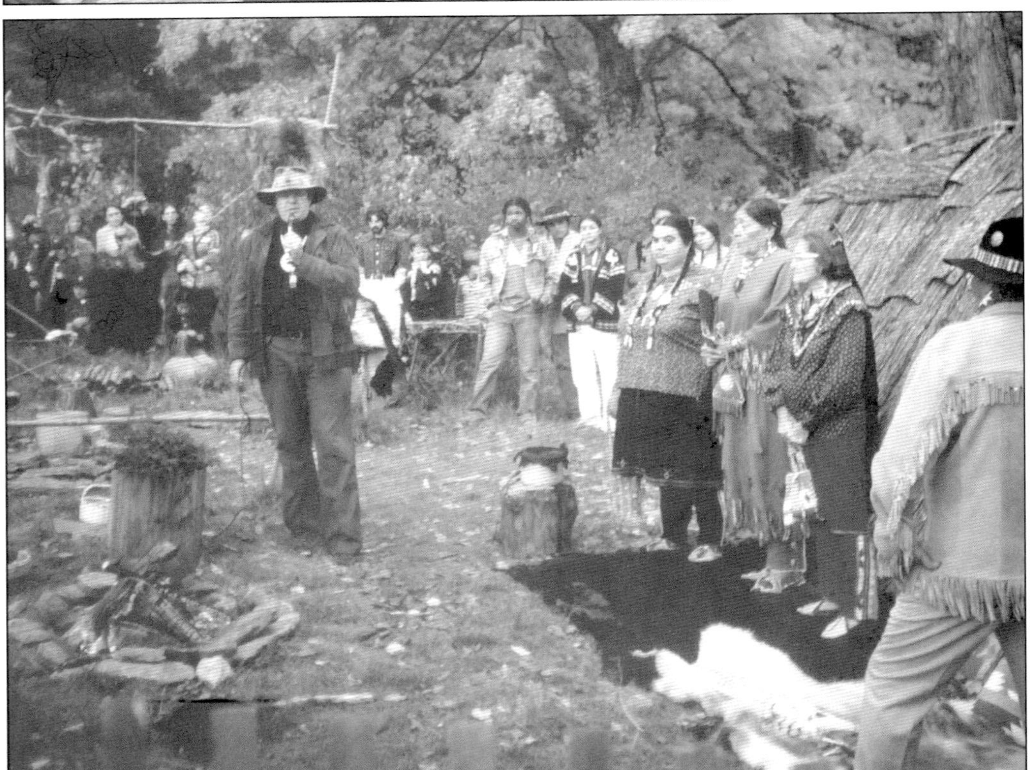

Standing at a wigwam constructed behind the museum, Nick Shoumatoff welcomes Nora Thompson Dean, an elder descended from Native Americans who lived in Westchester. Shoumatoff had procured federal funds for an expedition to her home in Oklahoma, where he was able to record and catalog place-names and genealogical information. He was honored at this ceremony and given the name He Who Stands Firm, by which he is known today.

Nick Shoumatoff, curator from 1970 to 1984, brought local history to life. He used props like this iron cauldron for maple sugaring, homesteading, and camp cooking programs. He convinced locals to donate artifacts to the museum and built an impressive library. An accomplished musician, Shoumatoff also collected songs about the region, including ones about the building of Cross River Dam in 1906 and the creation of the reservation in the 1920s.

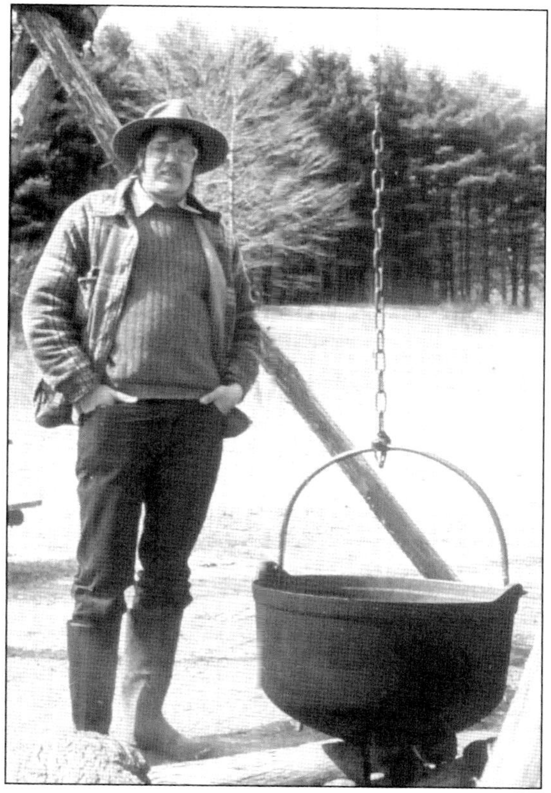

This excited group of youngsters is ready to collect maple sap with curator Shoumatoff, using yoke and buckets. The park had many healthy and huge maple trees to tap, a sugarhouse with an evaporator to boil sap, and many students to carry the buckets. A time-consuming but fun process, the tradition of making maple sugar continues at the museum.

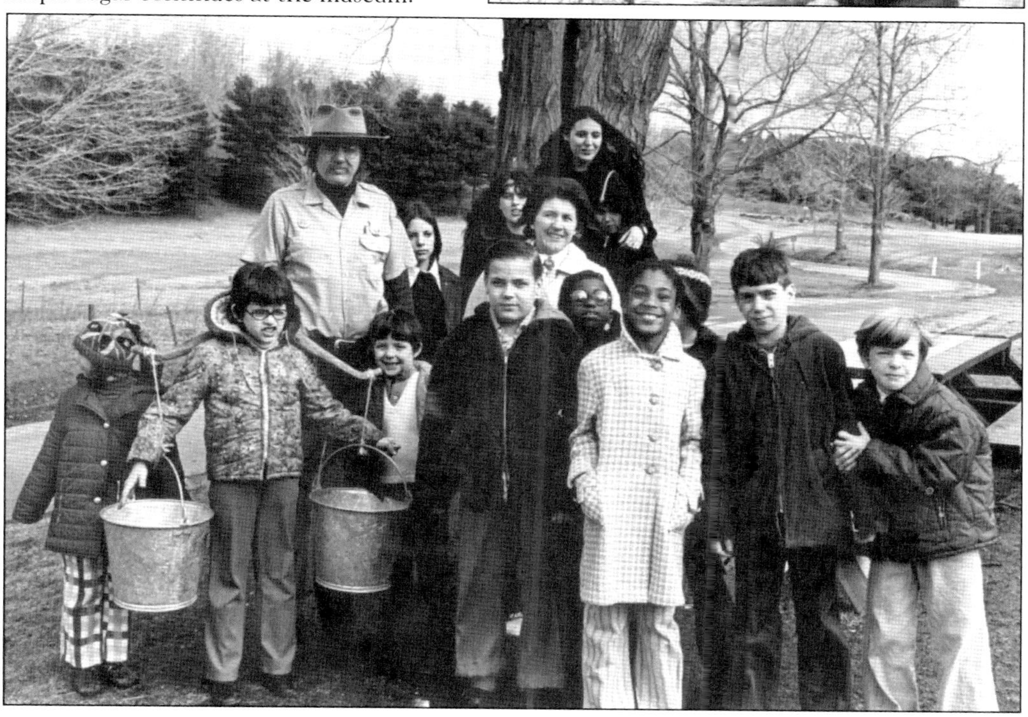

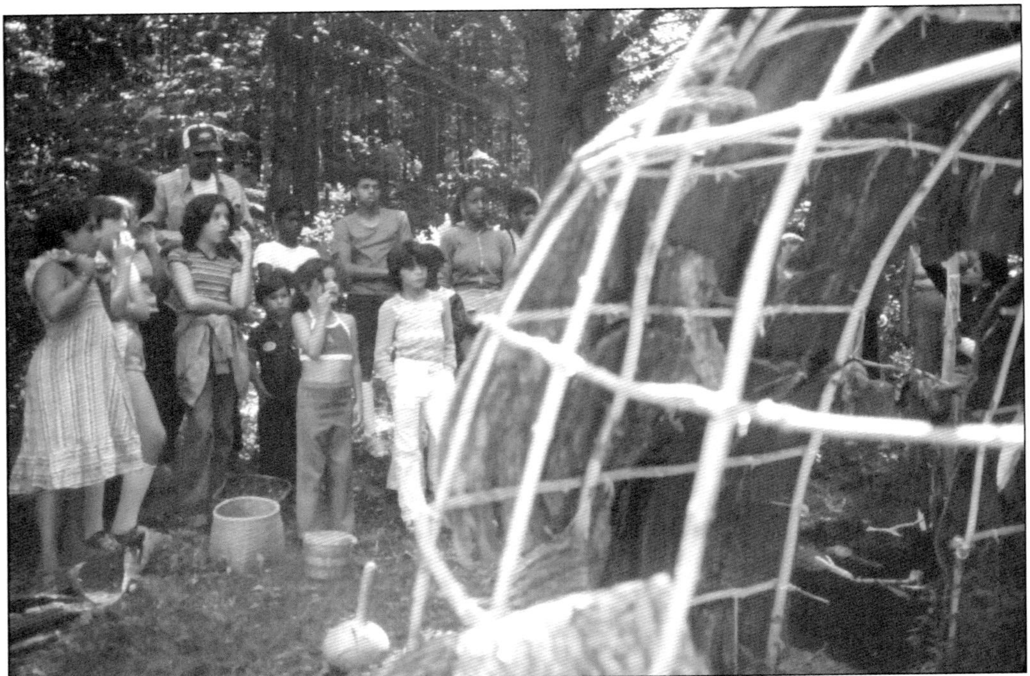

Interpreting the history of native people was, and still is, an important part of the museum's repertoire. Here, visitors watch the construction of a wigwam. Saplings were harvested and debarked, the ends sealed in fire to forestall rot. They were then lashed together with bark strips to create a frame for the dwelling. Only traditional woods and tools were used in these demonstrations. Wigwams need to be replaced every five years.

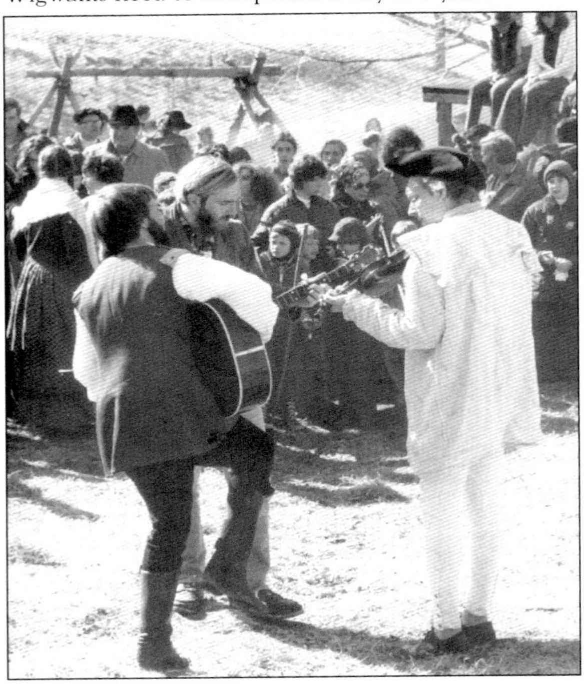

Whether it was maple sugaring, a Thanksgiving observation, or Colonial crafting, the most popular events were those that included the fiddle and the banjo. Here, a standing-room-only crowd enjoys a musical addition to a Colonial history program at the museum. Behind the group hangs a steaming cauldron supported by a log tripod with simmering goodies for the finale.

Six

Programs of the Reservation

The reservation has always hosted picnickers, campers, hikers, photographers, and artists, as well as those who simply study nature. But it was not until the museum was built in 1937 that educational and entertaining programs were offered to visitors.

Curator William Wheeler writes in his first annual report that "special groups including garden clubs, women's clubs, school children, boy scouts, girl scouts, and under-privileged children from a lower Westchester day camp" attended his lectures. He began a tradition of excellent environmental education that continues to this day. Curator Nick Shoumatoff revived programming in the 1970s, offering maple-sugaring lectures, hay mazes, First Thanksgiving reenactments, storytelling, and very popular Native American events.

In addition to the museum's natural and social history programs, large recreational events were offered, drawing big crowds. A Day in the Country, popular in the 1970s, included hot-air balloon rides, chili contests, and craft vendors. The Fiddlefest, a music venue with bluegrass bands, banjo players, and folk singers, brought thousands of fans and had a 20-year run.

In winter, then as now, when the snow falls, no formal program is necessary, as sledders from miles around know the park has the best slope for downhill thrills. The sloping meadow near the museum is wide enough to accommodate little ones on saucers, oldsters on toboggans, and daring teens on snowboards. Given just a few inches of snow, miles of trails in the reservation offer the best cross-country skiing in the region. Easy, moderate, and difficult courses are available, and beginners are content to cruise the level meadows.

There are many activities to pursue in the reservation, from bouldering to stargazing, geocaching to horseback riding. Given the richly documented history, the variety of habitats, the number of species, the quiet of the forest and meadows, the lack of light pollution, and the many acres, the possibilities for programming are endless. Ward Pound Ridge Reservation is a treasure for those seeking entertainment, recreation, knowledge, and solitude.

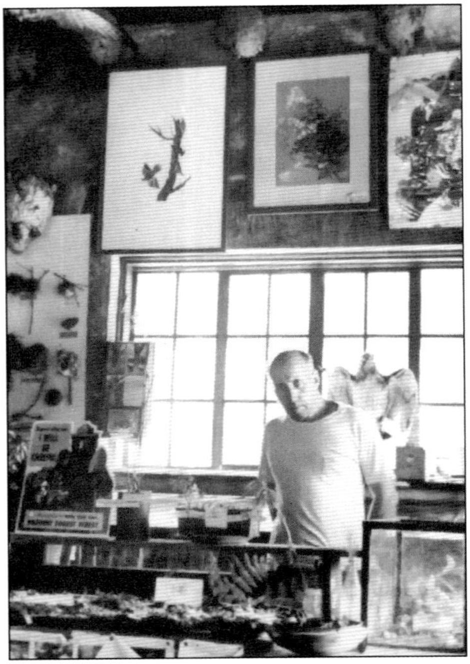

It was William Wheeler who led the first formal programs at the reservation. The science of interpretation was just developing at the time. Today, a college degree, years of field experience, and education courses are needed to be a park ranger. For the self-taught Wheeler, it was his hours in nature with experienced ornithologists and his own enthusiasm for nature's wonders that prepared him to lead so many nature hikes.

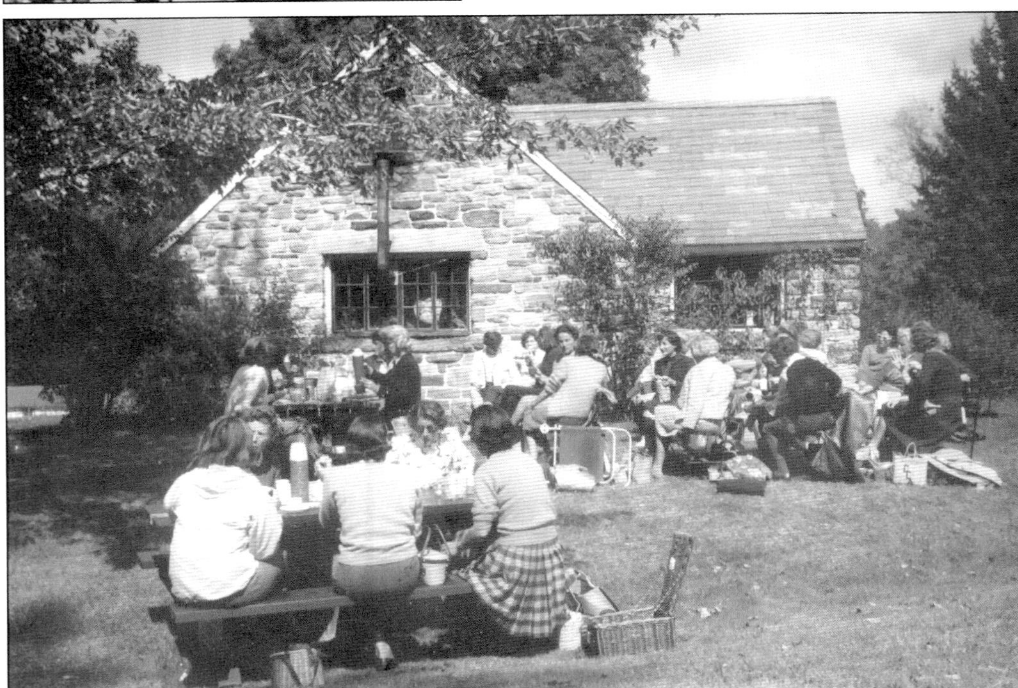

Likely members of a ladies' garden club or other organized group, these women brought thermoses, picnic baskets, and sunglasses for an al fresco lunch just outside the museum sometime in the 1950s. They may have just attended a nature outing and lecture. This is probably a local group, but, because the museum is so near the New York metropolitan area, visitors from around the globe have come to the museum.

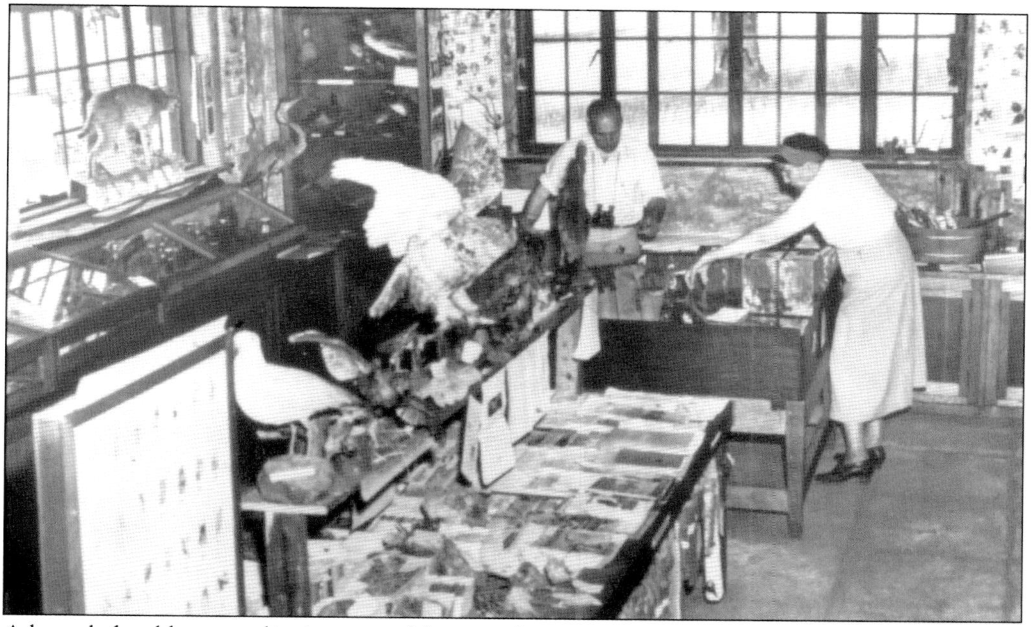

A knowledgeable naturalist is essential for a vital nature center. Impromptu programs can follow from just one question from a visitor. Here, Wheeler, binoculars at the ready, answers a patron's question. Then as now, the intention of the naturalist is to spark the curiosity that sends a visitor outside to get his or her answers in nature.

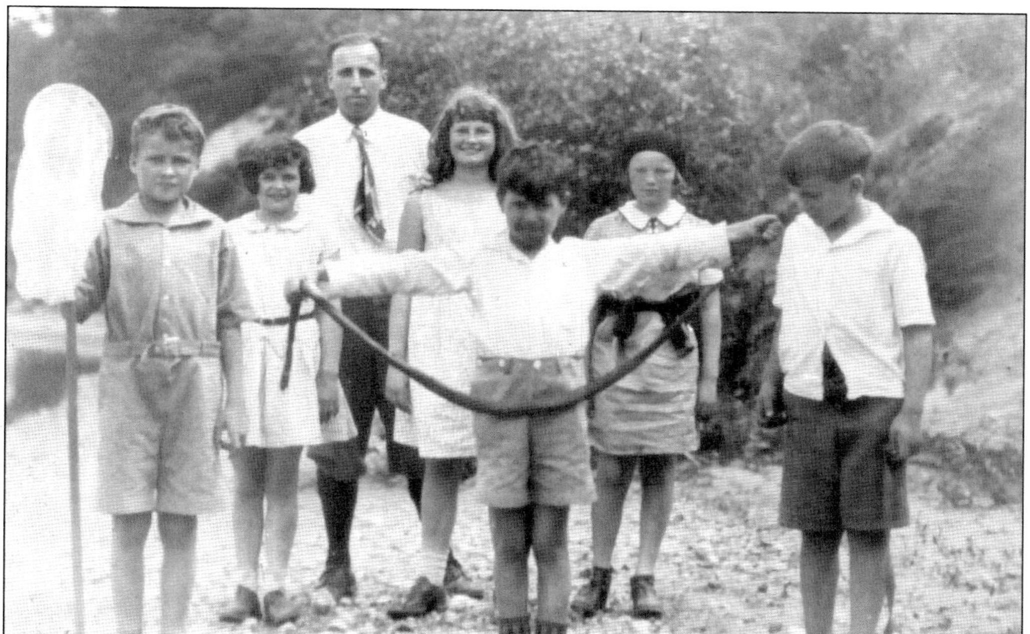

Wheeler and a group of happy, proud young naturalists show off their treasure: a very long, very dead black rat snake, *Pantherophis obsoletus*, still a common denizen of the park. One youth carries a butterfly net, suggesting that a nature discovery excursion was in progress. What a story these children could tell!

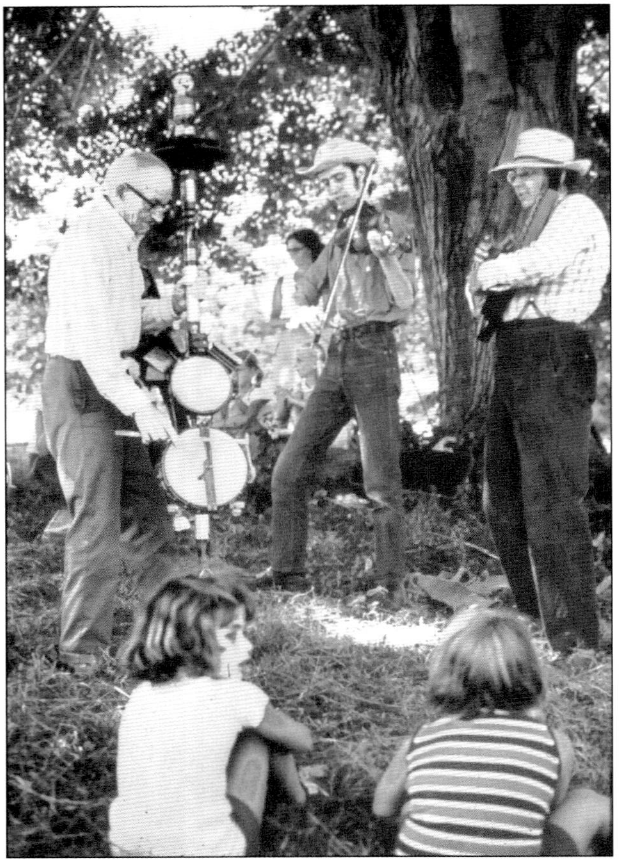

The famous Fiddlefest at the reservation, which drew thousands of bluegrass fans, got its humble start under the Grandmother Maple in front of the Trailside Museum. Nick Shoumatoff (right) plays his Autoharp, another musician plays a homemade banjo, and a third plays the fiddle. Shoumatoff recognized the hunger for old-time instruments and song.

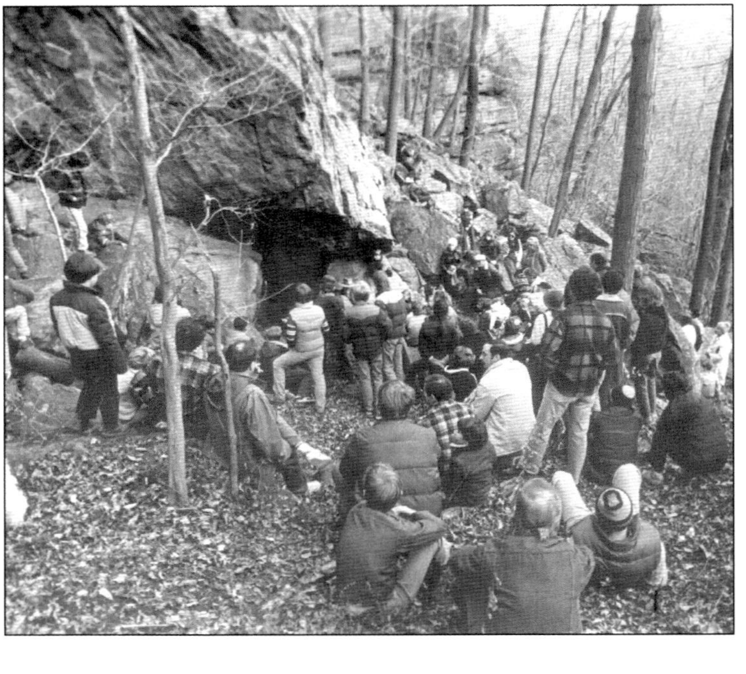

You could hear a leaf drop, so enthralled were hikers listening to stories while sitting around the dark cleft of the Leather Man's lair. Legend tells of a hermit who rarely spoke, wore a heavy suit of patched leather, and traveled a 365-day circuit once a month, begging for food, staying in huts, caves, or barns, and stopping at this rock shelter between 1858 and 1888.

Nick Shoumatoff leads a group along the trail on a late autumn day in 1975. A standard but never boring activity, a guided nature walk is the best way to introduce the public to hiking trails and to witness nature's miracles. In the fall, stone walls and foundations emerge; in spring, the wildlife returns; in summer, natural activity hums; and in winter, there are tracks to follow.

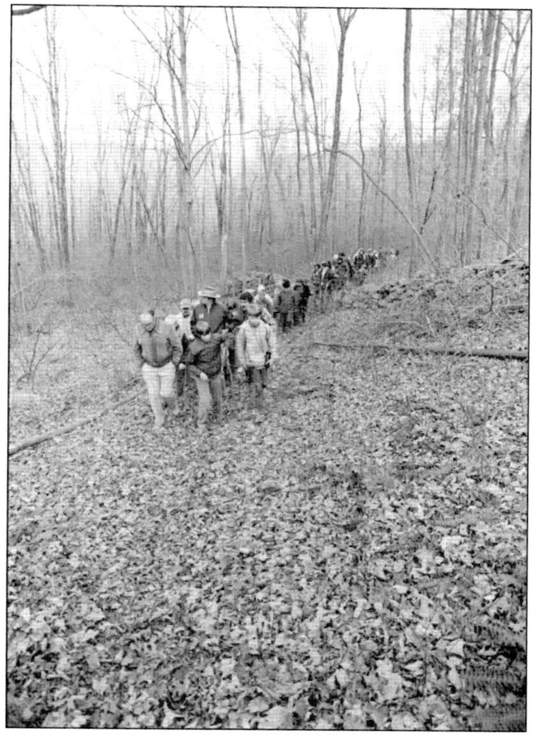

An artist at her easel finds inspiration for a sketch, while a young artist sits nearby with her feet in the cool waters of the Cross River. Artists are fond of the many viewsheds in the reservation. Art teachers bring classes for plein air instruction, and artists exhibit their work in the two galleries located in the park.

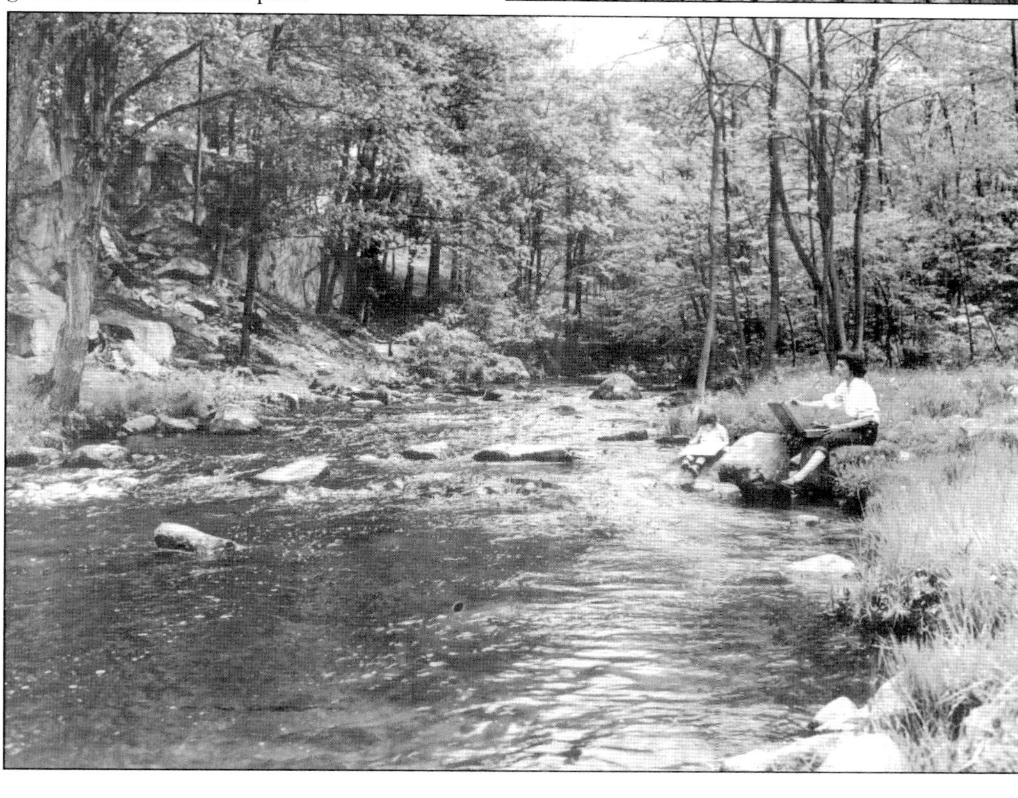

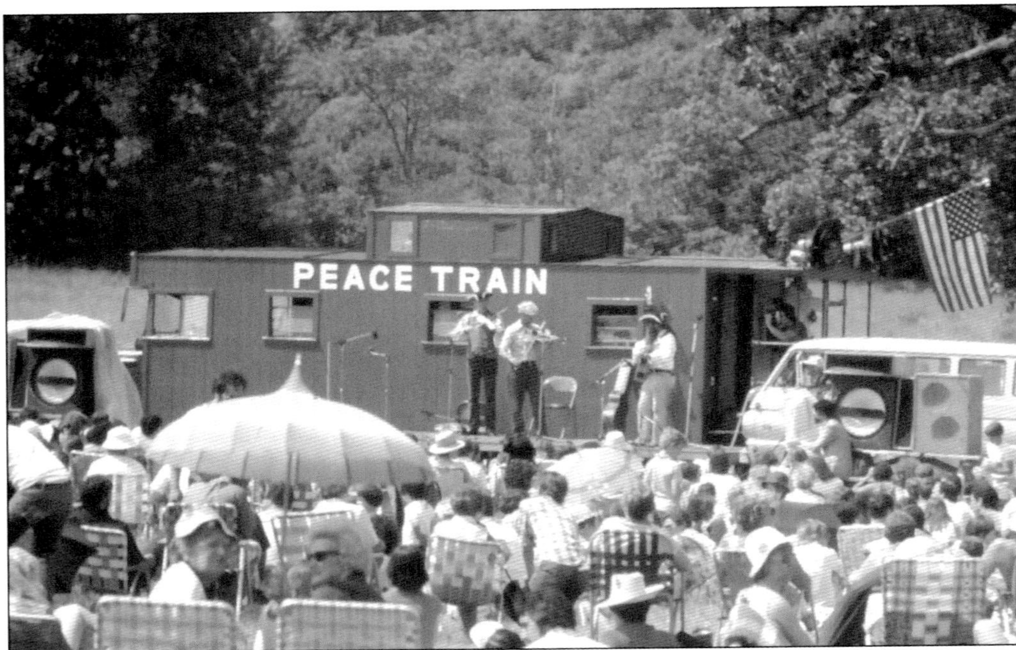

The first real Fiddlefest was held in the great Meadow with a boxcar labeled "Peace Train." This was during the 1970s, when antiwar sentiment was strong and people were hungry to reconnect with the land. Every year thereafter, the crowds grew larger, the roster of performers grew longer, and the stage and sound systems became more elaborate.

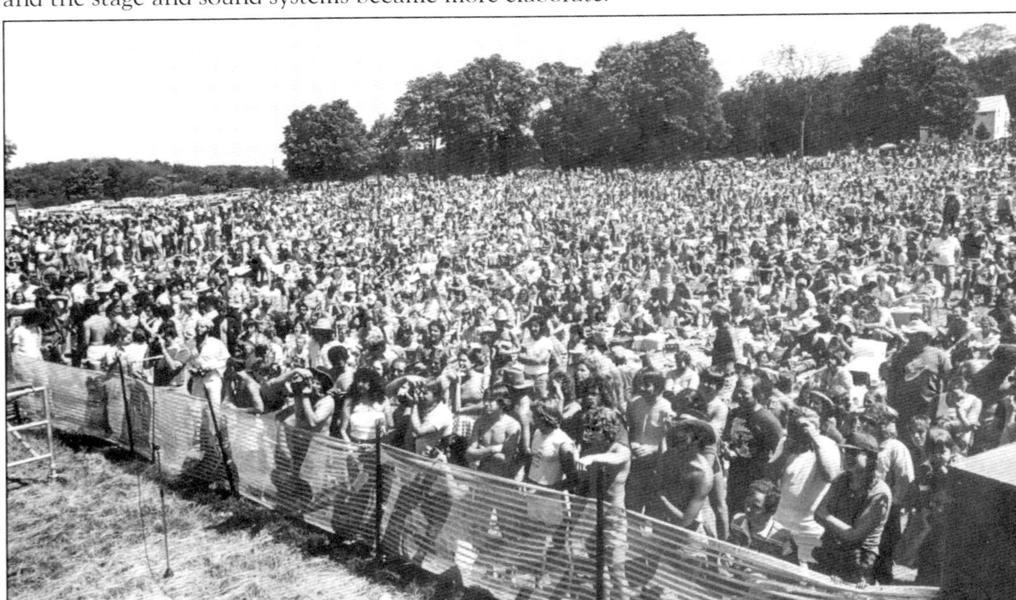

Thousands gather to hear bluegrass music, plunking banjoes, and dueling fiddles at this Fiddlefest in the 1970s. People of all ages installed themselves on the lawn of the Meadow. Children waded in the river, parents picnicked, and everyone had a good time. The festival had a 20-year run, and was legendary for its sunny weather despite gloomy forecasts.

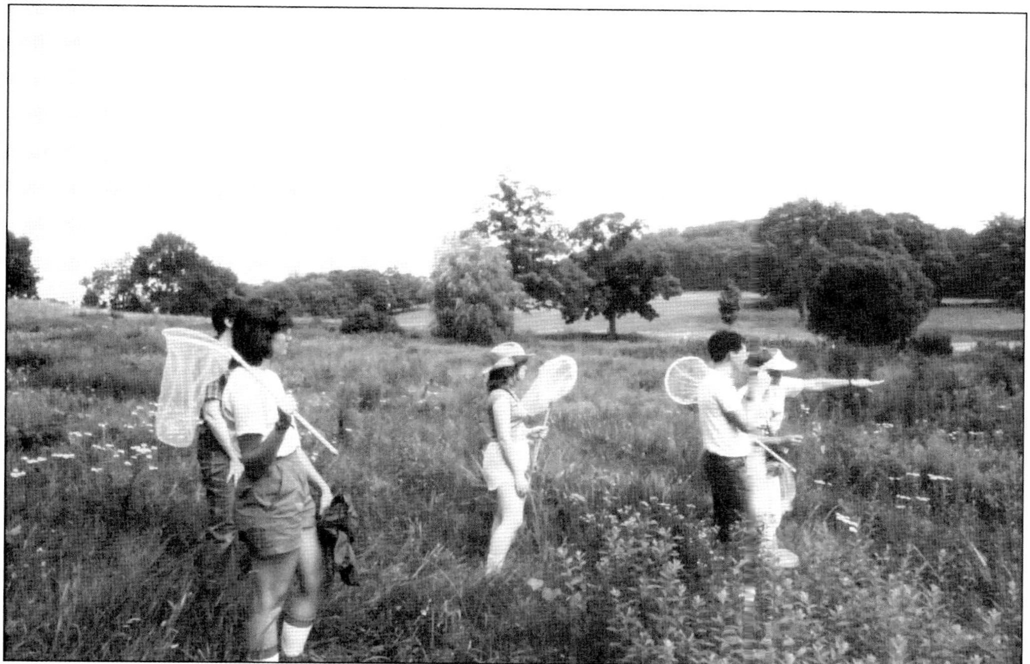

Tall grass in the park's meadows abounds with insects of all kinds, including butterflies, grasshoppers, spiders, bees, and dragonflies. There is a big difference in diversity between this meadow and a mowed lawn. Here, visitors enjoy getting a close look and learning about insect adaptations before releasing them. Collecting insects is discouraged, as observation and photographs are more effective learning tools. In this way, rare or endangered species are not diminished.

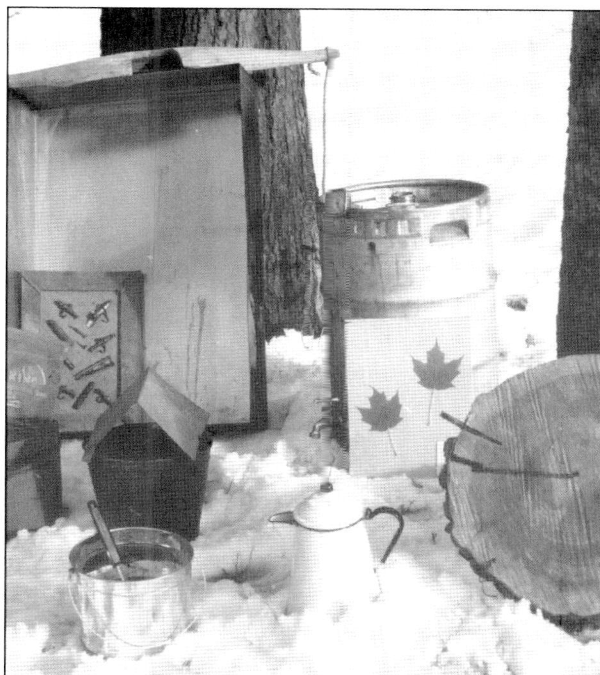

Maple sugaring, a gift from the Native Americans, was a forgotten craft in the 1960s. Trailside Museum was the first in the region to offer programs that taught the art of making sugar from maple sap. Shown here are the tools used to turn sap to sugar as practiced every spring by local farmers. Hikers in the reservation today can count the old maple trees that line the trails.

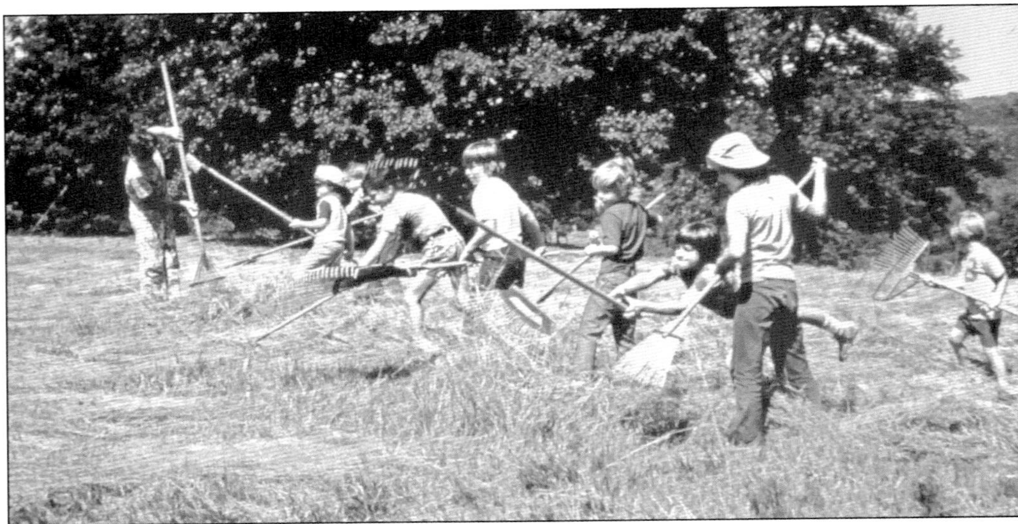

Kids love to rake leaves and straw. Here, they use old-time tools to create mazes. Traditional mead was served to sweaty hay-makers, banjo music filled the air, and everyone got a sense of the hard work that the haying season required of so many farmers in the area. In the early days of the park, local farmers were allowed to use the hay cut from the reservation's fields.

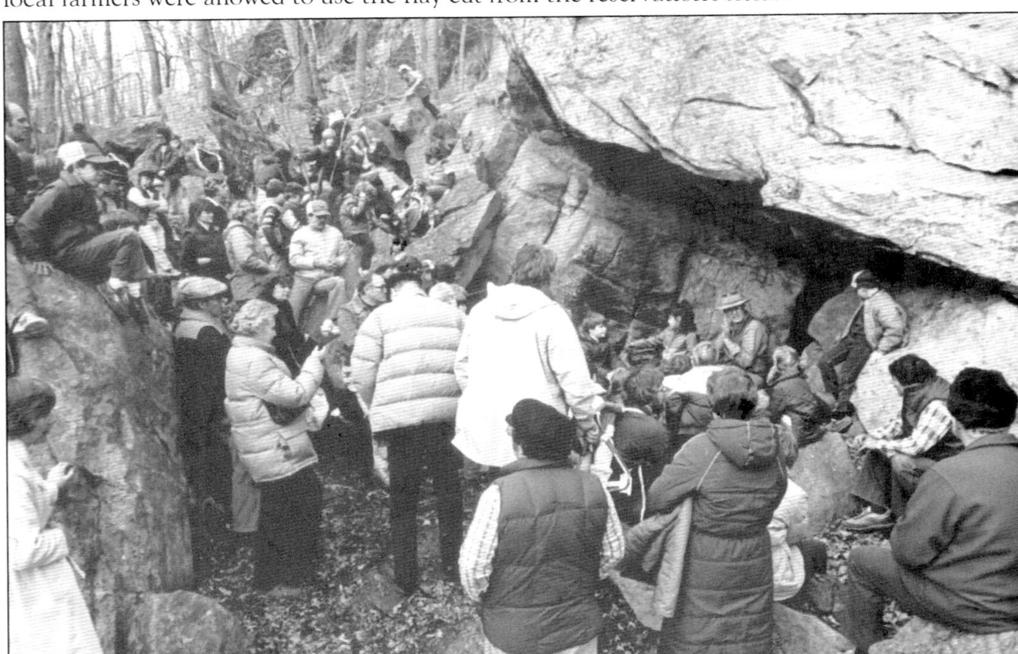

Hikers crowd around the Leather Man's cave to hear Nick Shoumatoff's stories about the local hermit. This three-mile trail, still the most popular in the park, begins at the end of Michigan Road. Though not a true cave, this south-facing rock jumble was more substantial than other rock shelters used by the hermit on his monthly route.

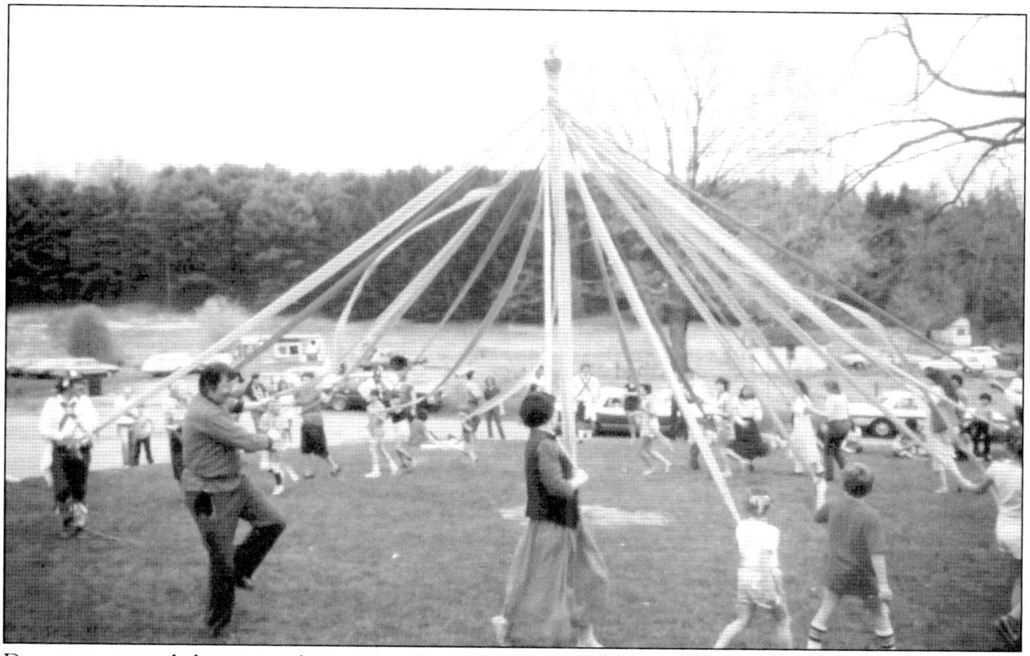

Dancing around the maypole on May Day, while still celebrated in little villages of Europe, was not that common in the United States in the 1970s. This ancient tradition celebrated the return of warmth and light, and dances ensured a good crop. Note the cars scattered along the road, as the parking lot by the museum had not yet been built.

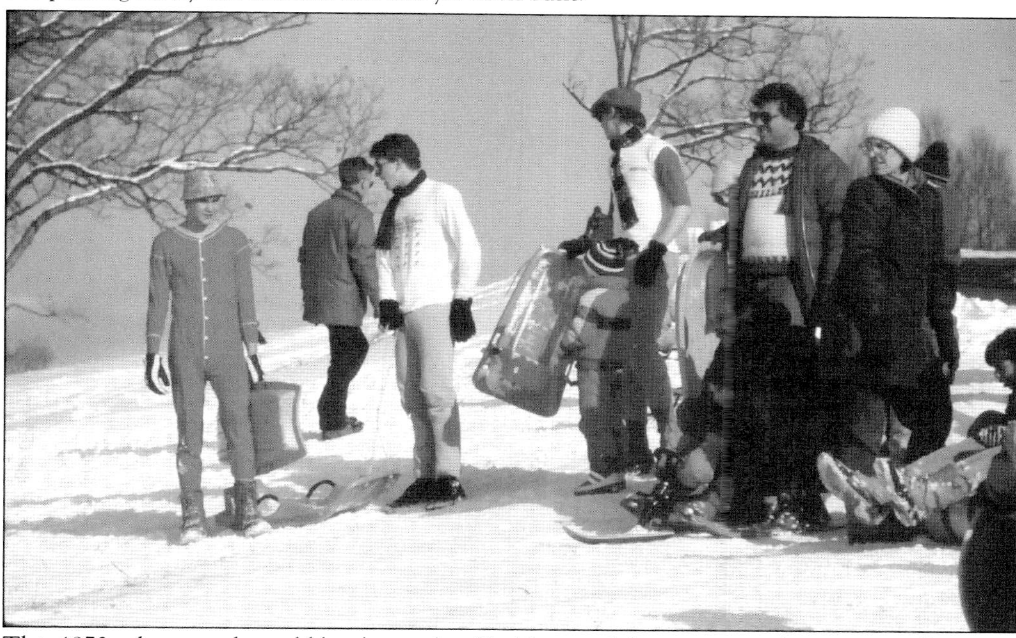

This 1970s photograph could be shot today. Sledding and skiing are timeless sports still enjoyed by visitors of all ages. All that is needed is a good blanket of snow. Sledders are welcome to sip warm cocoa in the museum while defrosting their toes. Impromptu snowball fights and snowman building keep the kids warm and happy.

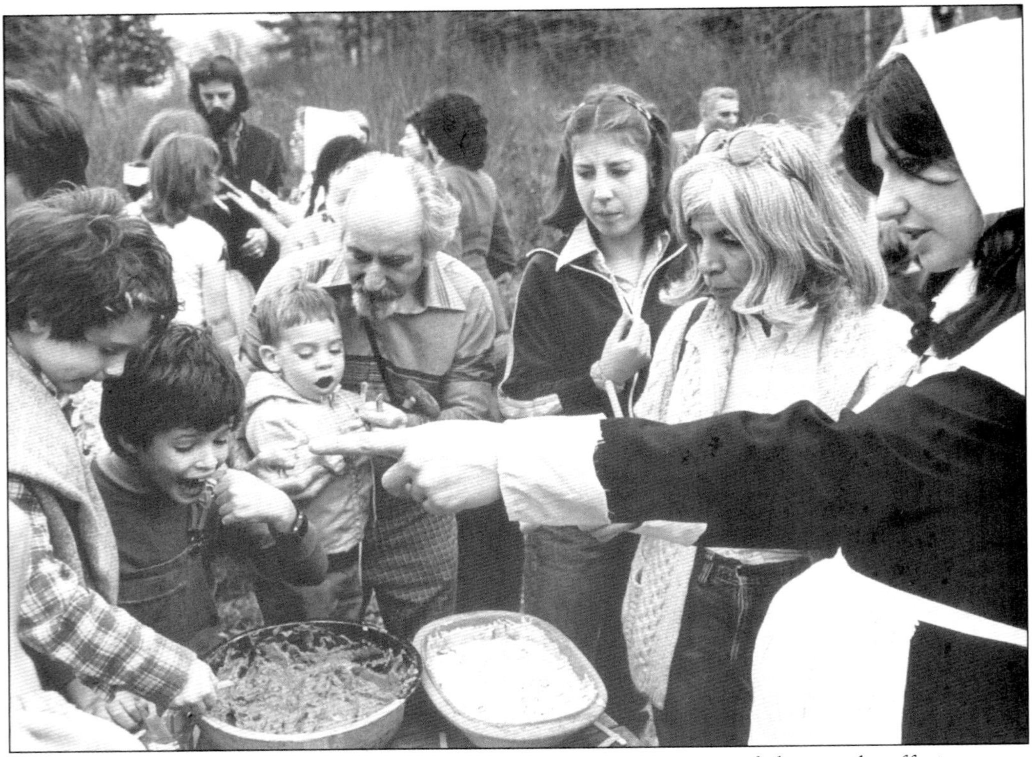

Attendees eagerly sample succotash and sweet potatoes, just part of the ample offerings at a Thanksgiving reenactment. Scores of volunteers were needed, and their participation is evidence of their devotion to the park and museum. Nothing enhances programming like replica dishes, first-person interpretations, and live music. It is no wonder that visitors still talk about these popular programs from the 1970s.

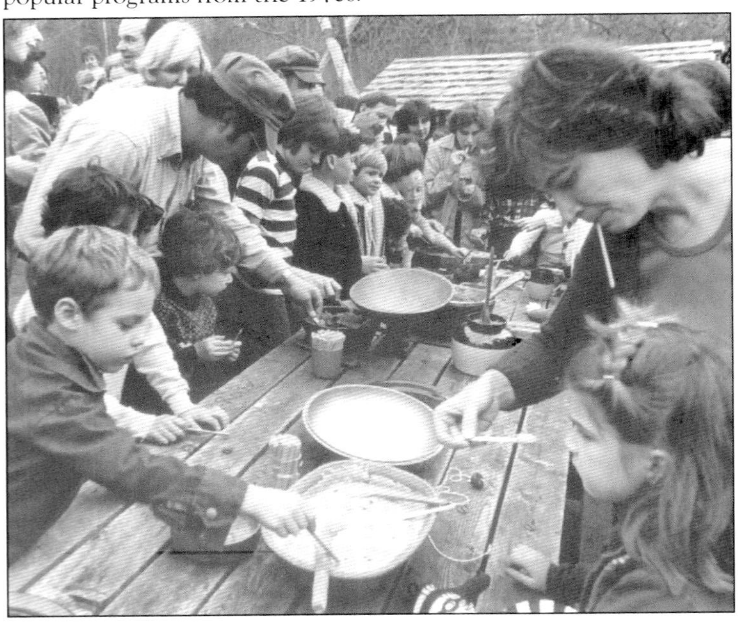

Visitors sample the gifts of the maple trees: maple sugar, maple syrup, jack wax, and maple candy. The traditional dill pickle is used to cut the sweetness so that more sugar can be eaten. The participants also witness the hard labor and long hours required for seasonal activity. Today, this activity is fun; for the early colonists of this region, it was essential, as sugar was expensive and hard to come by.

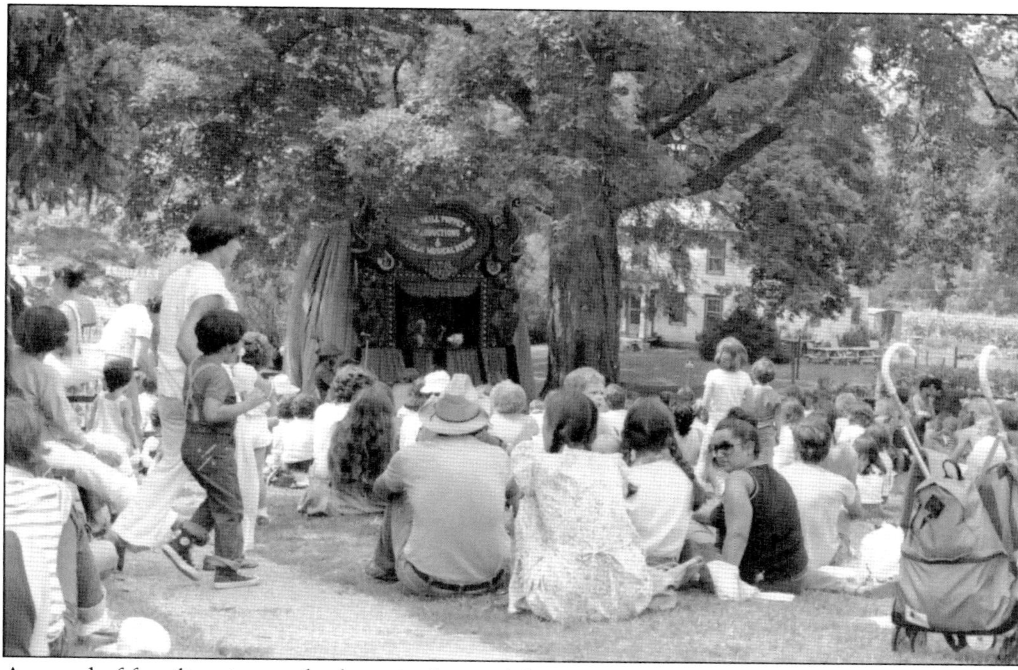

A crowd of families sits on the lawn in front of the museum to watch a puppet show. With the stage nestled under the Grandmother Maple, and the David Webb farmstead in the distance, this is a special arena for the children's theater. Another program initiated by Nick Shoumatoff, the puppet show was wildly popular.

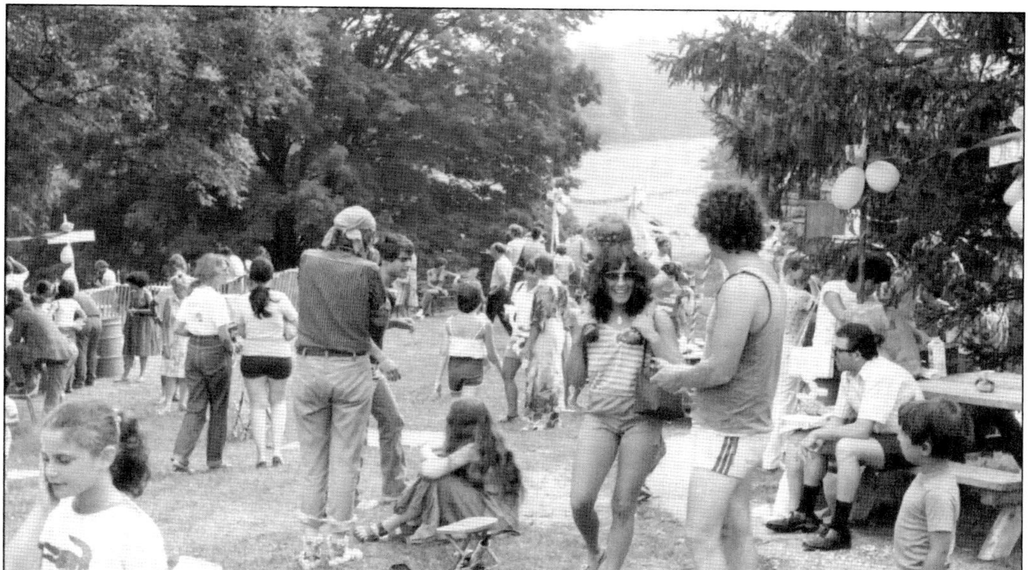

Children's Craft Day, an annual and favorite event for many years, was widely attended. Picnic tables set with crafts ranging from painting to clay creatures invited excited youngsters to create all day long without the worry of cleanup. Many crafts emphasized natural supplies or old-time skills. Often, storytellers, musicians, and bubble-makers wandered through the families. Snacks complimented a fun day.

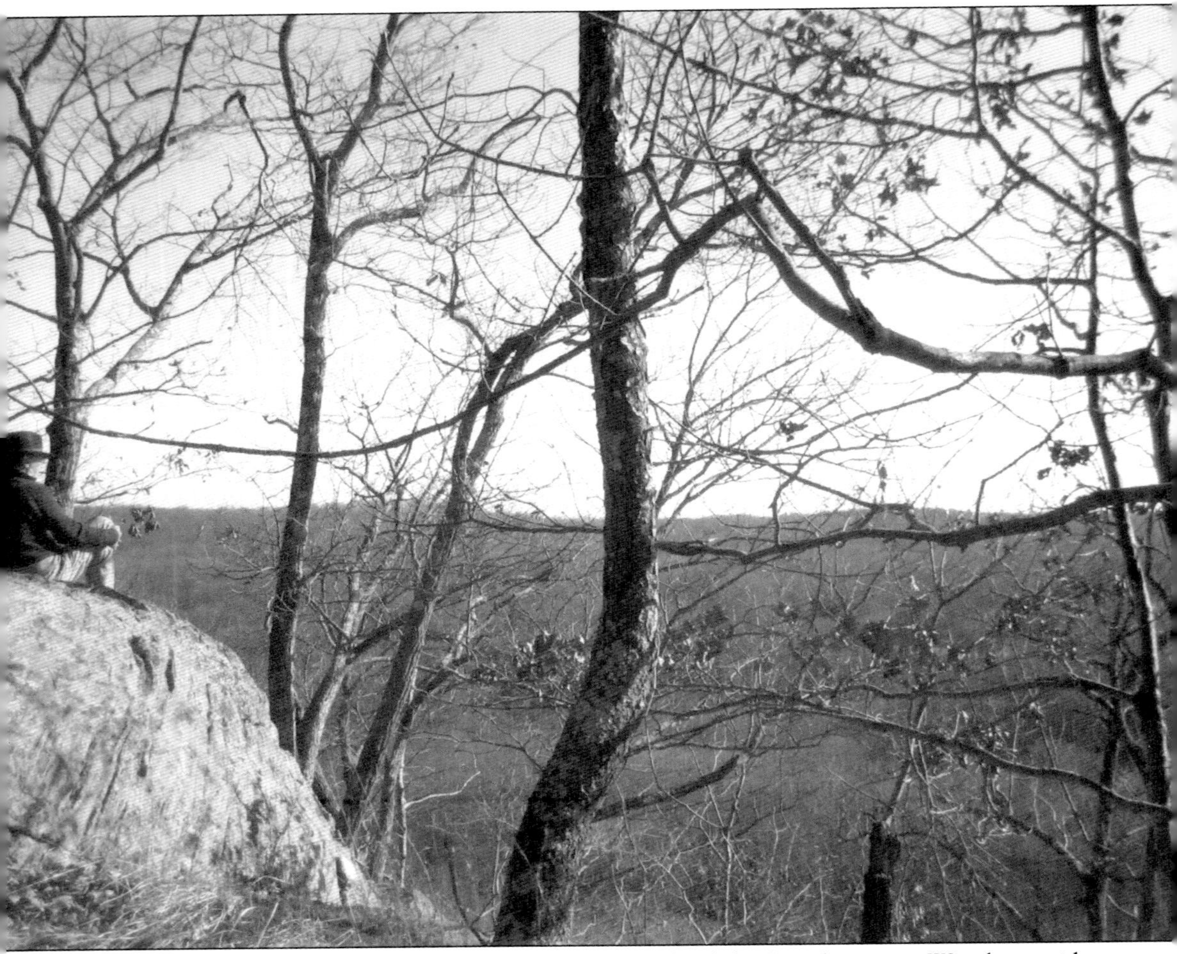

Westchester County was neutral ground during much of the Revolutionary War, but residents were subject to raids from the "cowboys" (loyalists) and "skinners" (patriots) who stole animals and food for their troops. Spy Rock is the perfect place to observe the settings of the difficult struggles and the frightening skirmishes that the colonists experienced.

Here, volunteers offer a feast to park patrons during a living history demonstration of the first Thanksgiving. The log cabin in the background was built by park staff. The cabin and a small log sugar shack for making maple syrup help to bring alive the forgotten stories of the local colonists.

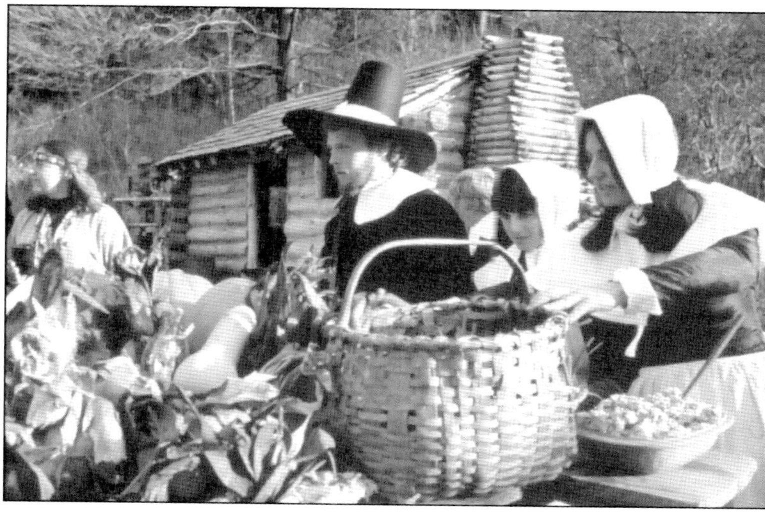

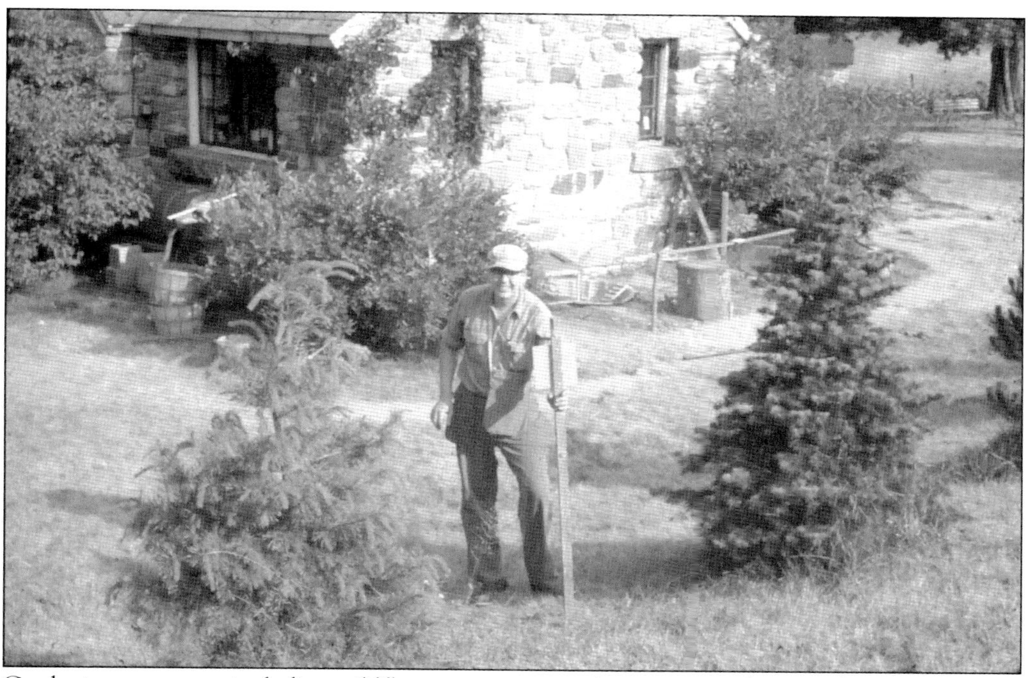

Gardening programs, including wildflower propagation, deer-resistant plantings, butterfly-friendly nectar and larval sources, and this Christmas tree farming demonstration, were offered on weekends. In 1965, several species of evergreen trees were planted near the museum to give visitors a look at the different choices for the perfect holiday tree. Included are the Douglas fir, *Pseudotsuga*, and Colorado blue spruce, *Picea pungens*, both from other regions.

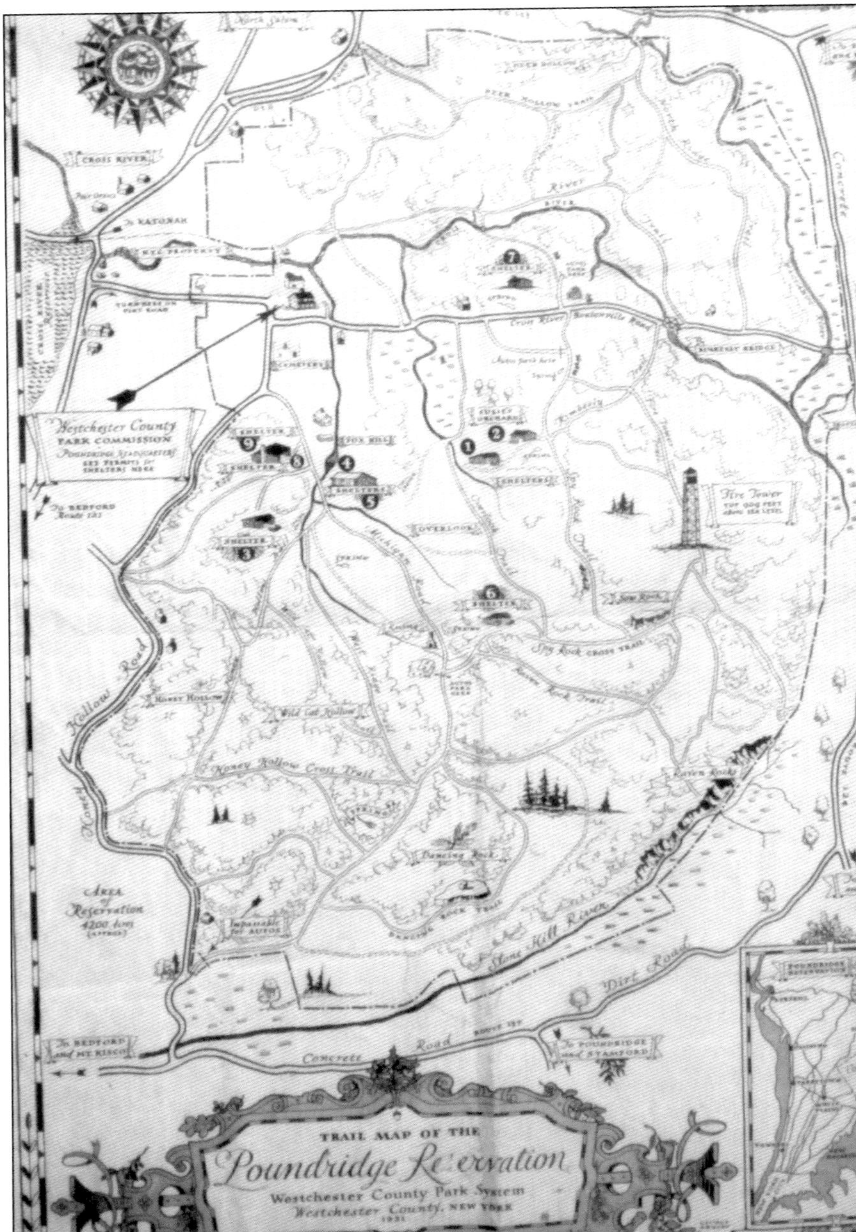

This 1931 map of the reservation highlights geological features that were and still are popular destinations. Dancing Rock, the southernmost stone outcropping, is a flat, expansive mountaintop. Farmers traditionally gathered here to celebrate the harvest with music, food, and friends. Small stone foundations are located nearby. Raven Rocks, on the southeastern border, is described thusly by Robert Bolton in his 1905 *History of the County of Westchester*: "a precipitous declivity in the mountains, nearly two hundred feet high; where, amid the stony ledges, the ravens used to build their nests of yore. The rocks here form almost a semi-circle, and bid defiance to the most daring climber, or trapper. This gloomy spot is still the favorite resort of the screech owl and crow." The map also highlights the locations of springs and concrete and dirt roads.

Seven

Rocks of the Ages

The history of Ward Pound Ridge Reservation is truly written in its stone. The story begins millennia ago, marches through vast ages of weathering and upheaval, and continues today. The long geological development provided the foundations for specific plant and animal communities.

There are three types of bedrock found within the park. Fordham gneiss, a light-and-dark-banded rock, underlies most of the acreage. This billion-year-old, pre-Cambrian metamorphic bedrock spreads all the way to the Bronx, forming the base for rocks known as the Manhattan Prong.

Sweeping through the reservation from north to south in a great crescent along the eastern side, Pound Ridge gneiss forms the backbone of the highest ridges. This later, but early, intrusion into the Fordham gneiss is dominantly a pink, medium gray. The Fordham gneiss outcrops are quite prominent in the area known as the Overlook, on the west side of the park. The Pound Ridge gneiss may be seen in the road cut just east of Kimberly Bridge near the Cross River.

Inwood marble, a metamorphic rock formed by the heating and compressing of an ancient limestone, lies hidden under the Waccabuc, Stone Hill, and upper Cross River drainage. Its parent rock was deposited at the bottom of an ocean that once covered the Pound Ridge area. Most of the marble in the park is completely buried under sediment.

The reservation was covered some 15,000 to 30,000 years ago by the Late Wisconsin Glacier, and much of the bedrock in the park shows signs of glacial action, such as polishing, striations, and large, sandy morainal deposits of glacial till. A recessional moraine topped with a split glacial deposit is seen at the end of Michigan Road.

The area's geologic action is not over, of course. It continues today, imperceptible to the hikers that wander by, ever-changing and timeless. But observant visitors will be rewarded with sculpted stone wonders in the foundations of the reservation's farmhouses, well capstones hidden on the forest floor, and in the walls of the little nature museum.

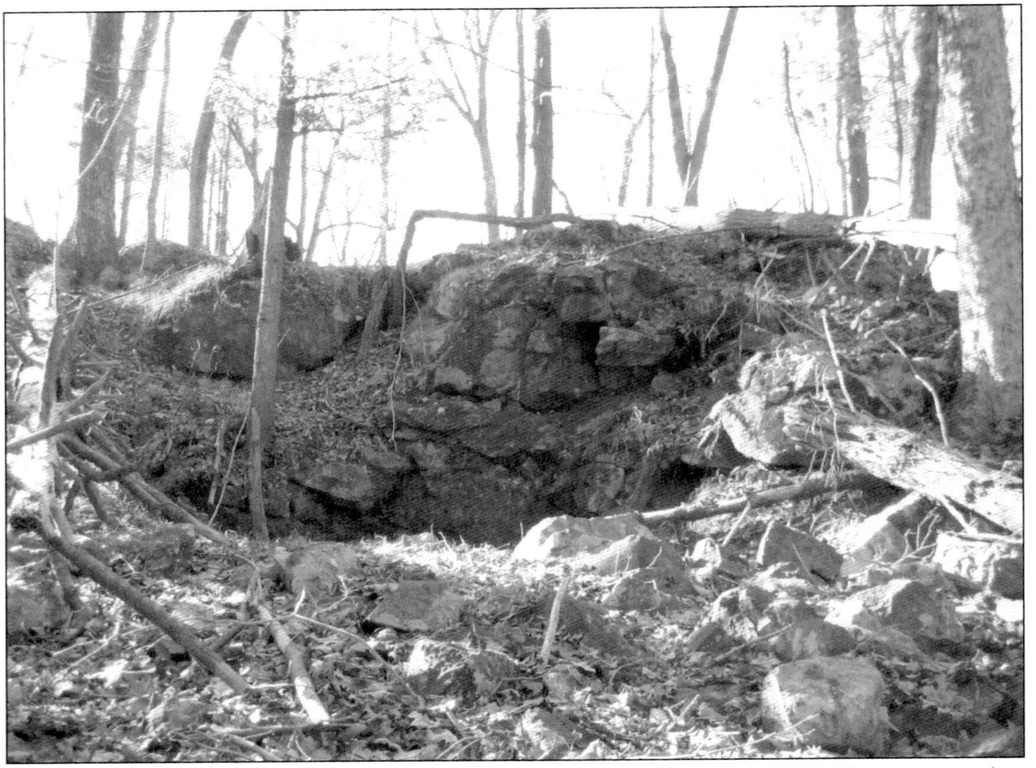

The reservation holds many geological secrets, such as this entrance to an old iron mine that may be referred to in an 1847 deed. In that document, the sellers reserve the right "to dig out on said piece." The Avery "silver" mine and a "coal pit house" are mentioned on deeds, but their exact locations remain elusive.

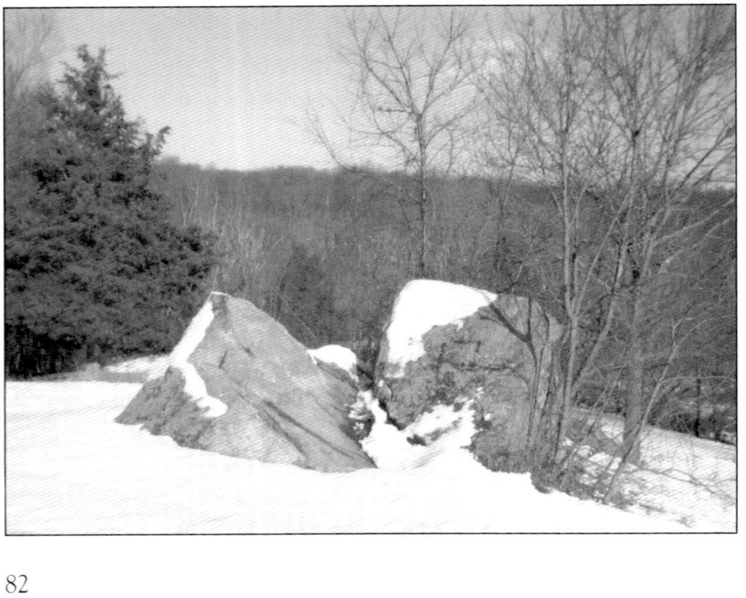

This split glacial deposit sits at the end of Michigan Road, atop the long mound of sand created by a melting glacier. Composed of local stone, it was likely sheared off of a nearby mountaintop, tumbled, was pushed by moving ice, and was left here when the glacier retreated some 13,000 years ago. Other deposits, composed of different minerals, are called erratics and can be found in the park.

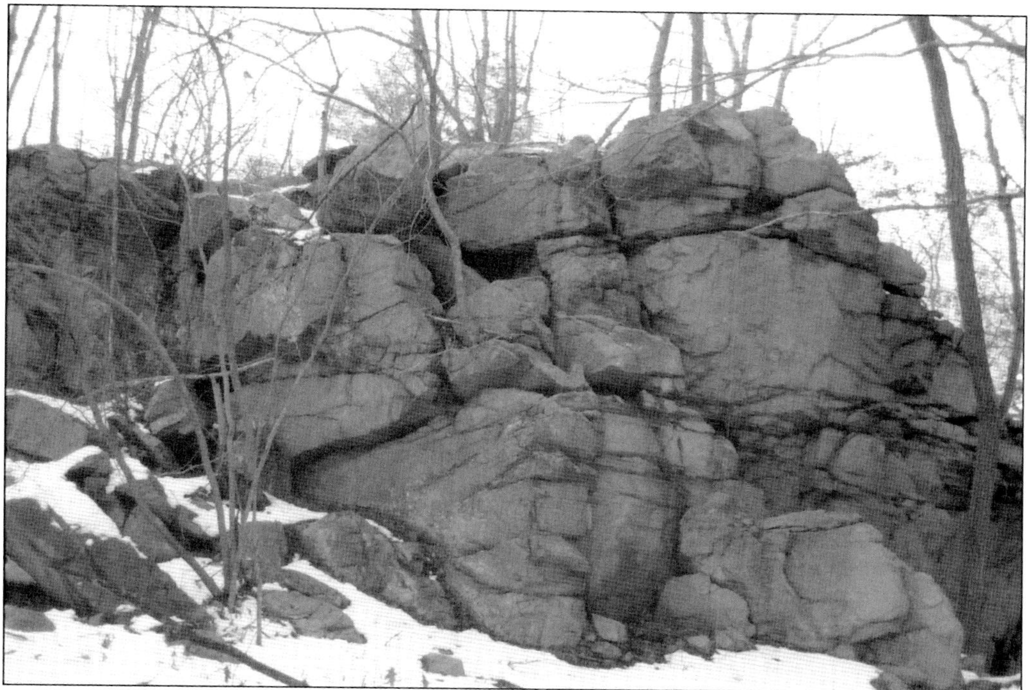

One of the best examples of glacial action in the park is the roche moutonnee (sheep back) found just south of Kimberly Bridge on the west side of the Cross River. This dramatic exposure of the pink Pound Ridge gneiss is the result of asymmetric erosion and abrasion on the "stoss" (up-ice) side of the rock and plucking on the "lee" (down-ice) side.

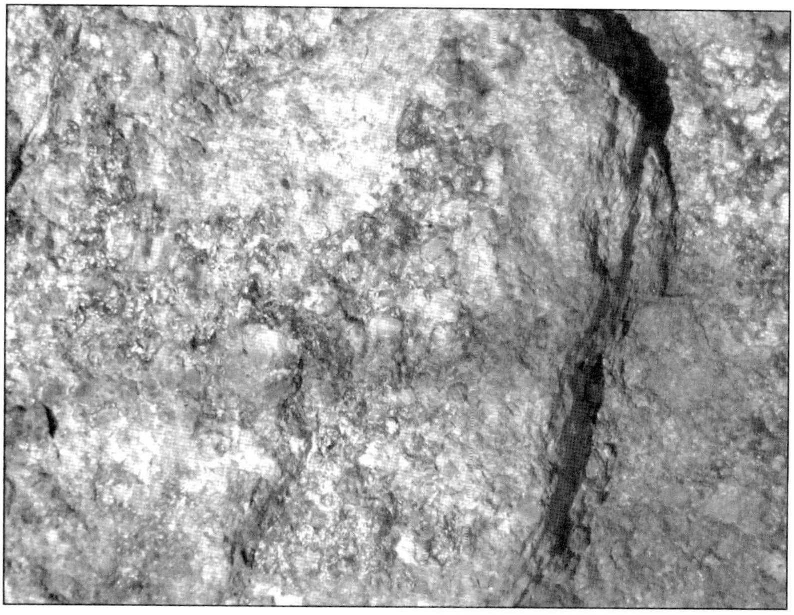

A close-up of the rock crystals found in the pinkish Pound Ridge gneiss shows quartz, potash feldspar, oligoclase, and biotite. This intrusion into the earlier Fordham gneiss bedrock also has sparkles of greywacke. The same type is found in northern Africa, evidence that the two continents were once part of a single landmass, called Pangaea.

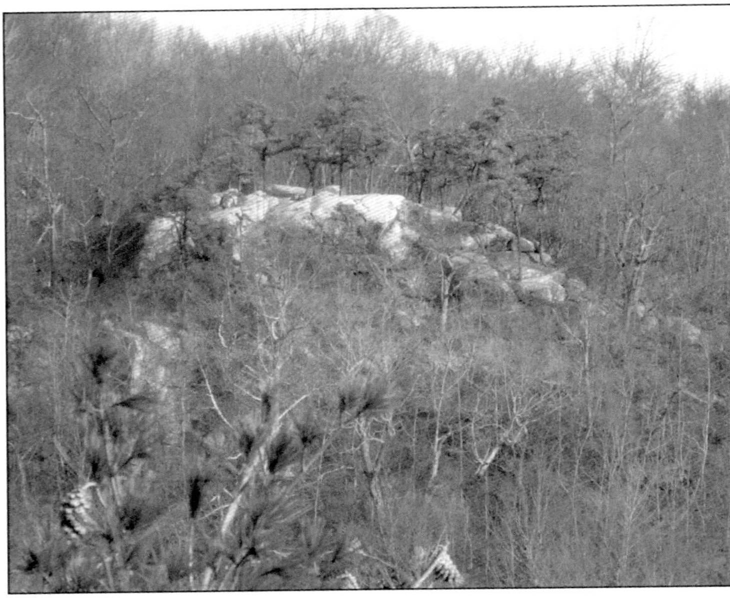

This bare knob of stone was named Sow Rock by farmers who discovered a pig with her piglets atop this isolated spot. Merely the remaining stump of a great mountain weathered over eons, it provides the stage for a plant community called an Appalachian oak-pine forest, which is not found elsewhere in the park. It can be found by hikers using a good map.

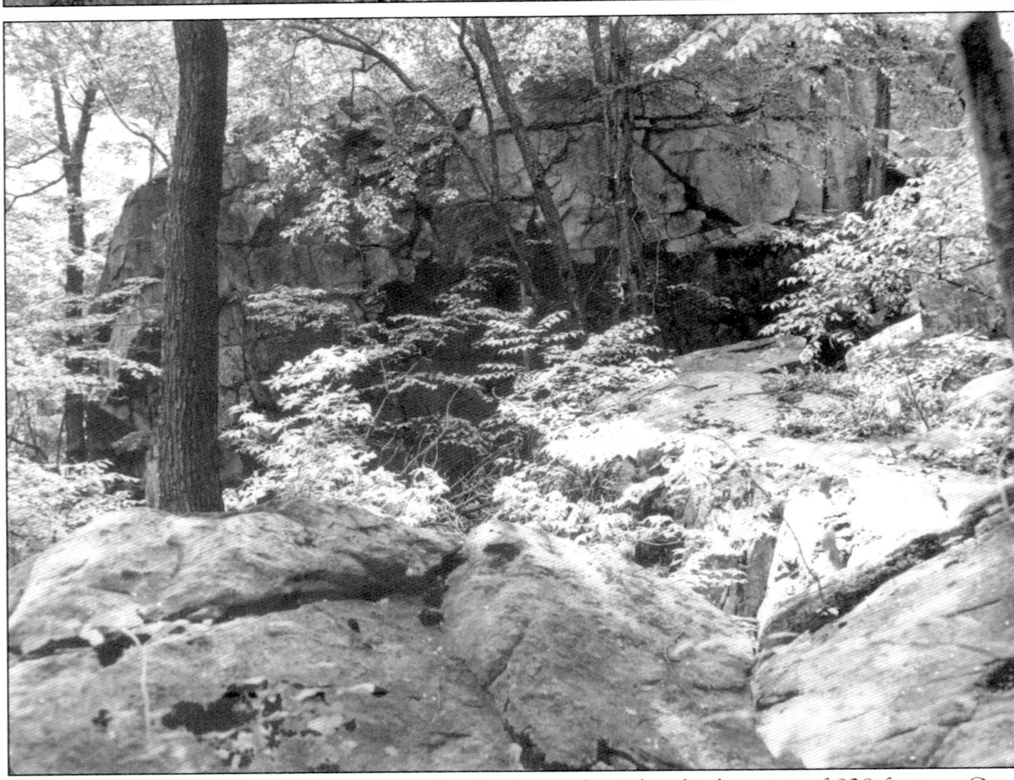

The bedrock formation of the reservation is elevated, with a high point of 938 feet on Cross River Mountain. Joe's Hill promontory to the west of the park reaches 738 feet. This makes the reservation one of the highest areas in Westchester County, creating slightly cooler temperatures and affording spectacular views from various lookout points. It also offers settings for challenging bouldering, such as here, at Castle Rock.

The dramatic rock faces found on the southern sides of the Stony Hills make for great rappelling, bouldering, and rock climbing. Similar versions of south-facing rock screes like this one, created by the passage of glacial ice over the bedrock of the park, can be found in the reservation. The most famous is the warm and sunny jumble of stones that formed the home of the Leather Man. The largest of these outward-facing scarps forms Raven Rocks, a prominent landmark.

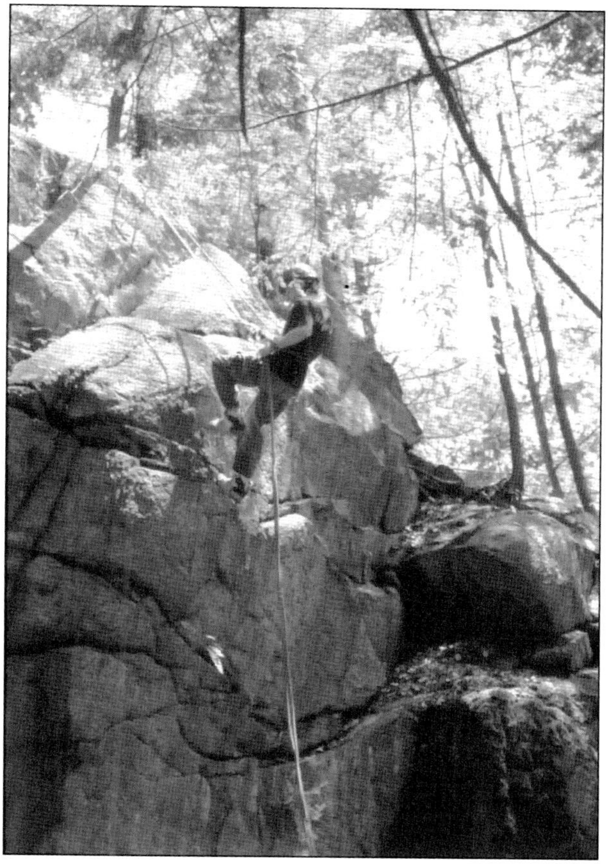

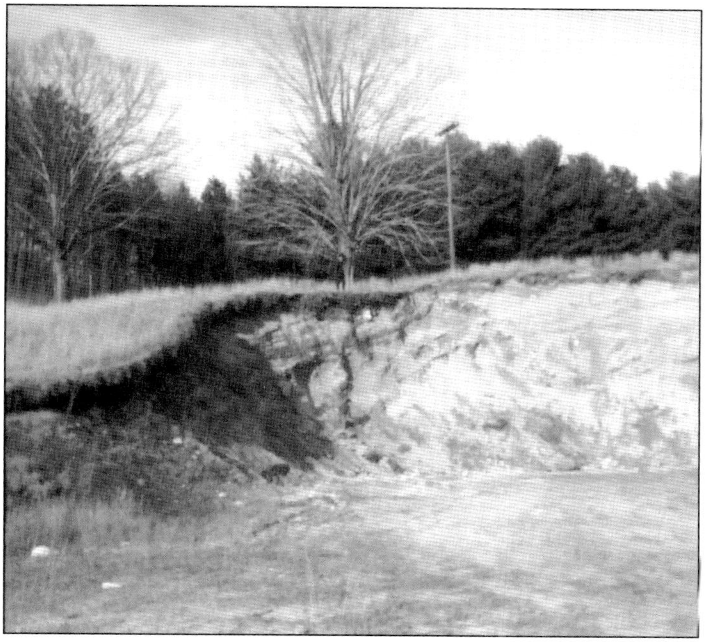

A hiker stands atop a great wall of pebbly sand deposited by melting glaciers. This moraine, found near the park office, is one of four in the park. For many years, the sand was harvested for construction projects and for use on icy park roads. Bank swallows, *Riparia riparia*, and belted kingfishers, *Megaceryle alcyon*, use the shifting sand walls for their nesting holes.

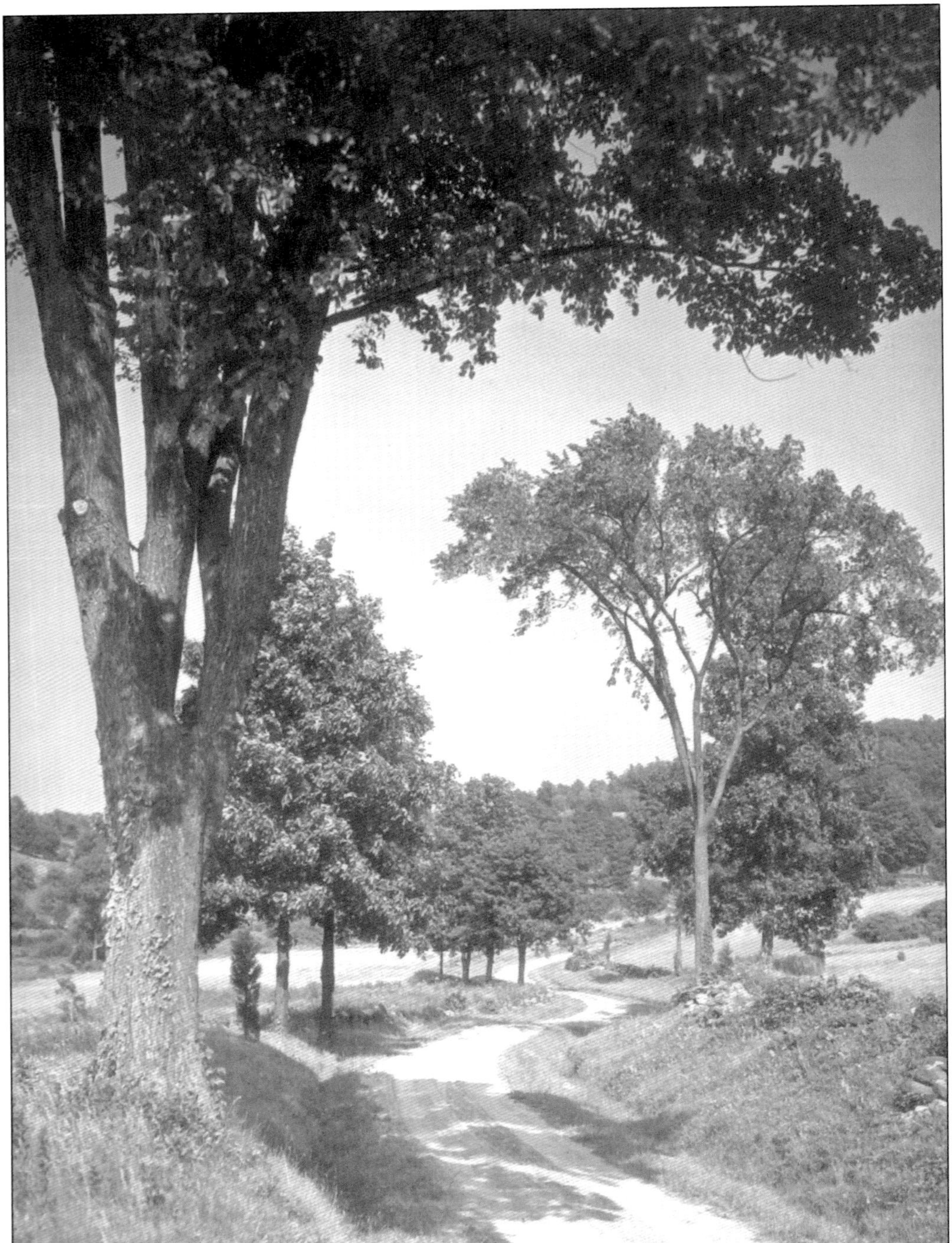

Old maple trees shade this ribbon of road as it snakes its way to the little museum. So beautiful was this vista in the 1940s that many more maples were planted over succeeding years along the other roads in the park to mimic the effect. The trees pictured here are now starting to die, but the younger trees fill the gaps, assuring lovely maple allees for the future.

Eight

Wildlife of the Reservation

Ward Pound Ridge Reservation abounds with wildlife. Like all of nature, it is not static, but ever changing. As precious as a fine tapestry with threads of silver and gold, the suite of species in the park is a finely woven complex of plants and animals worthy of study and stewardship.

In the early days of the park, trees were planted in great numbers. Hundreds of thousands of conifers were started to prevent soil erosion. Those plantations have grown tall, creating cathedral-like forests of white pines and Norway spruce. Red pines were also planted by the hundreds, but they succumbed to blight 30 years later, as did the giant chestnuts, many of which were cut down by the men of the Civilian Conservation Corps.

As throughout most of New York State, large predators that threatened the colonists were extirpated; coyotes, cougars, bears, and wolves brought lucrative bounties. Other large animals, such as deer, turkey, and beaver, were hunted for food and fur. By the 1900s, large mammals were missing from the landscape.

After the Trailside Nature Museum was built in the late 1930s, plants and animals were faithfully recorded. The lists show increases in mammals and birds, and an astounding collection of wildflowers and grasses.

In the 1980s, museum curator Ed Kanze recognized the need to catalog the park's flora and fauna. He gathered knowledgeable botanists and naturalists, and together they created a biological inventory. Observers recorded important data about abundance and location, resulting in a valuable record of species.

That inventory continues today. A recent count showed 235 flowers, 27 ferns, 85 trees and shrubs, 73 dragonflies, 83 butterflies, 18 mammals, 11 snakes, six salamanders, and six types of turtles. Bobcat, bear, coyote, turkey, otter, and even beaver have returned.

Ward Pound Ridge Reservation is a reservoir of biodiversity. It hosts pockets of protection for wildlife and corridors for those species that will likely migrate as the climate warms. The park continues to be a laboratory for study and education, a playground for nature-lovers, and a sanctuary for all.

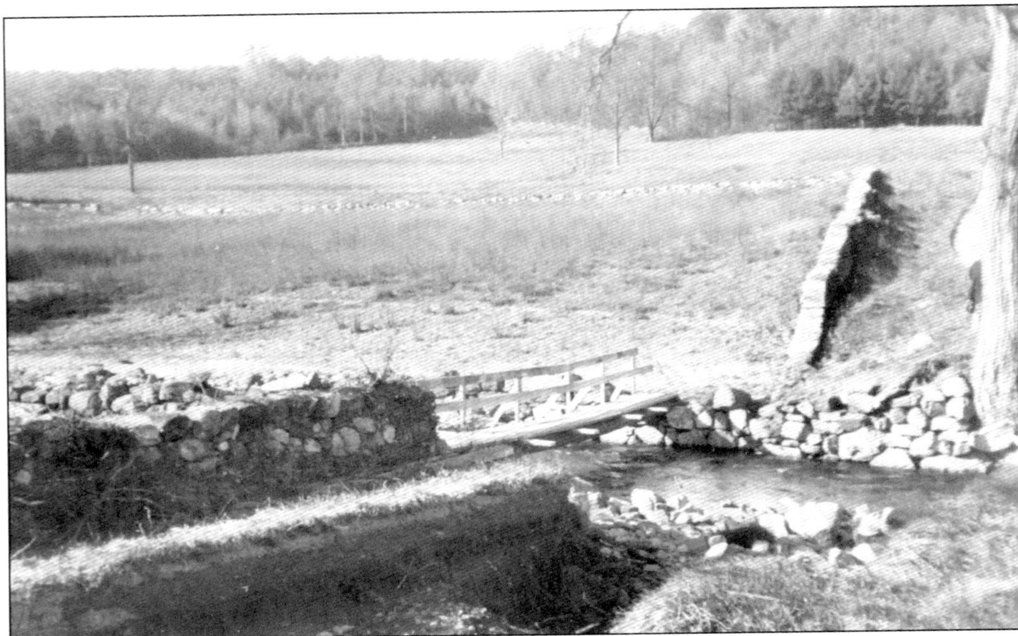

This view from the 1930s is the same today. Expansive meadows are rare in Westchester today; the park's meadows are mowed to encourage biodiversity. These wet lowlands sparkle with fireflies on summer evenings and are home to hosts of insects, mammals, and unusual flowers, making them biological hot spots. The little bridge spanning the Cross River, the only way to access the little farmhouse pictured below, was replaced.

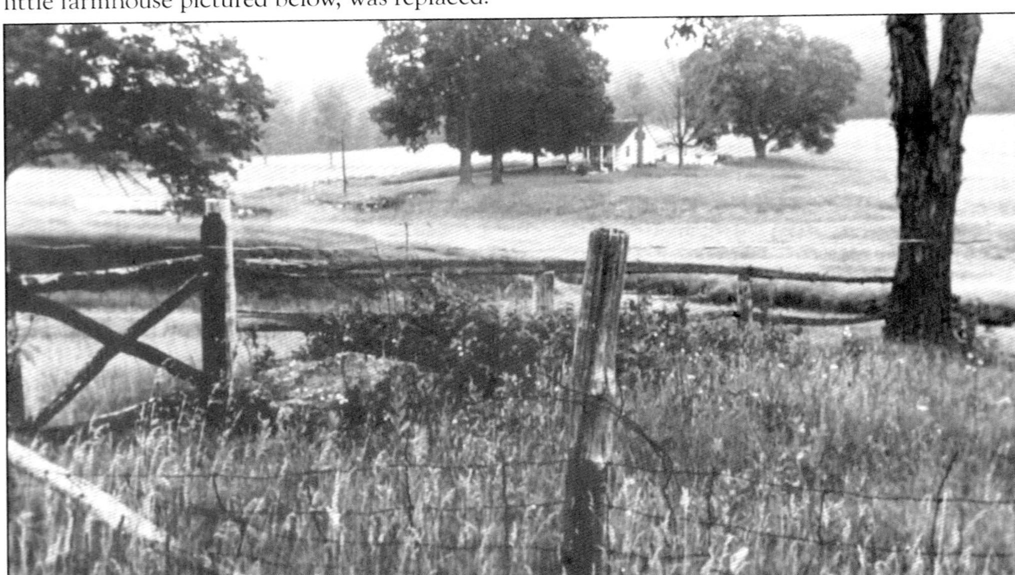

Native Americans managed this landscape, creating edge habitats teeming with game by purposely setting fires. The colonists changed the land even more, by denuding the forests for lumber and firewood while introducing weeds along with their fences. This farm plot has been reclaimed by the forest, but acres of meadows are now mowed for wildlife. The little farmhouse still stands, surrounded by the same trees now grown quite large.

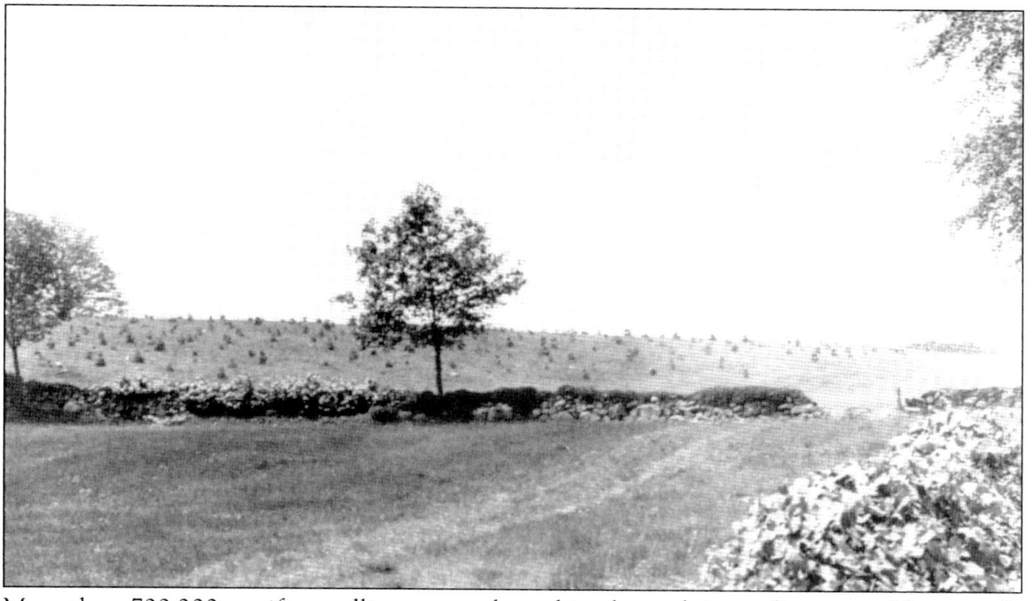

More than 700,000 conifer seedlings were planted in the park in its first years. Here, newly planted seedlings will transform an old farm field into a pine forest. Abandoned fields slowly turned to forest by natural succession. First to arrive were the pioneer species—red cedar, grey birch, and blueberry shrubs—followed by tree seedlings and more shrubs. Foxes, deer, raccoons, and songbirds likely followed.

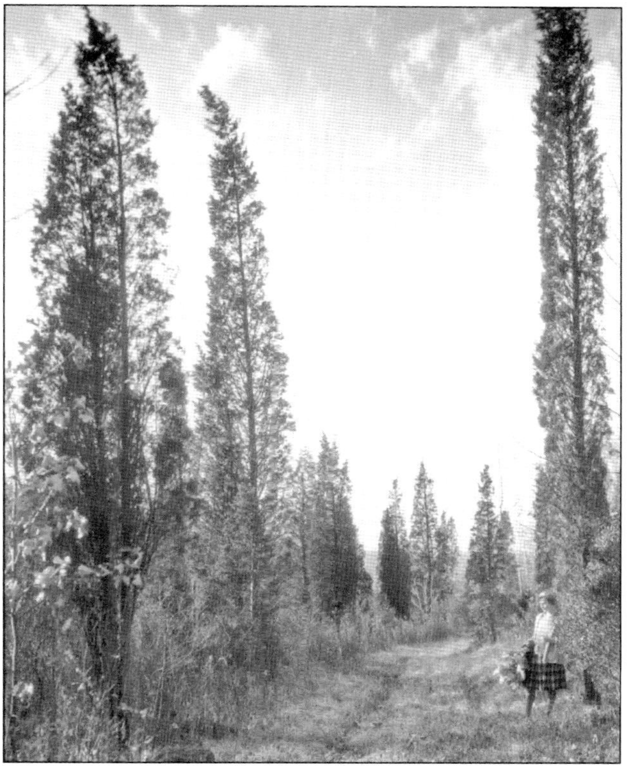

Before this photograph was taken in the 1940s, this scene was likely a cornfield. In the Northeast, nature creates forests; the first to take hold are these tall red cedars, *Juniperus virginianus*. The young woman carries a bouquet collected on her walk. While wildcrafting was not frowned upon then, picking flowers or grasses is prohibited now in order to allow everyone to enjoy their beauty. (Courtesy of Westchester County Archives.)

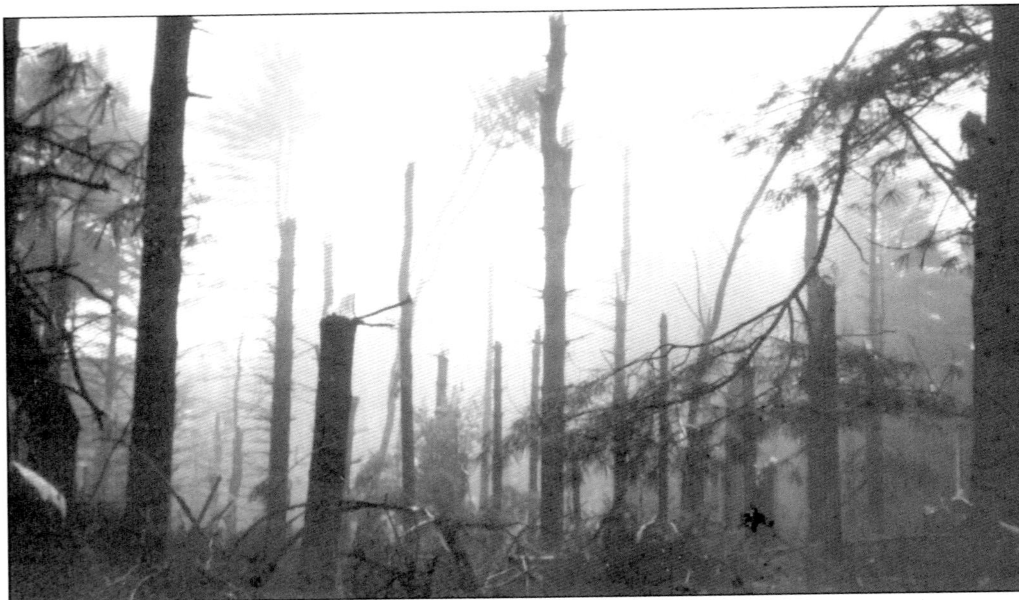

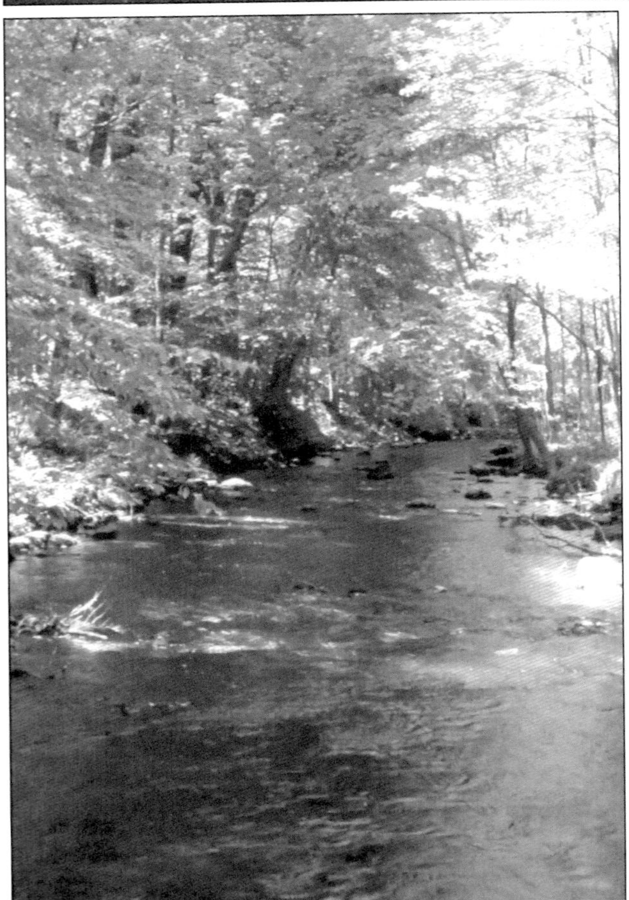

Because the conifers in the plantations have grown so tall and were never thinned, they are subject to wind damage. Nature is not static, and change like this is exciting. It can open up the forest to a whole new suite of plants and animals. After this storm damage in the 1990s, new evergreen seedlings were planted, and the area has already started to recover.

Here, the Cross River is wide and slow and draped in arching foliage. Its headwaters bubble up from swampy ground on the east side of the park, join the Waccabuc River as it wraps around from the north, and then empties into the Cross River Reservoir, eventually feeding the New York City water supply. It supports 13 species of fish, innumerable macro and micro invertebrates, and recreational fishermen.

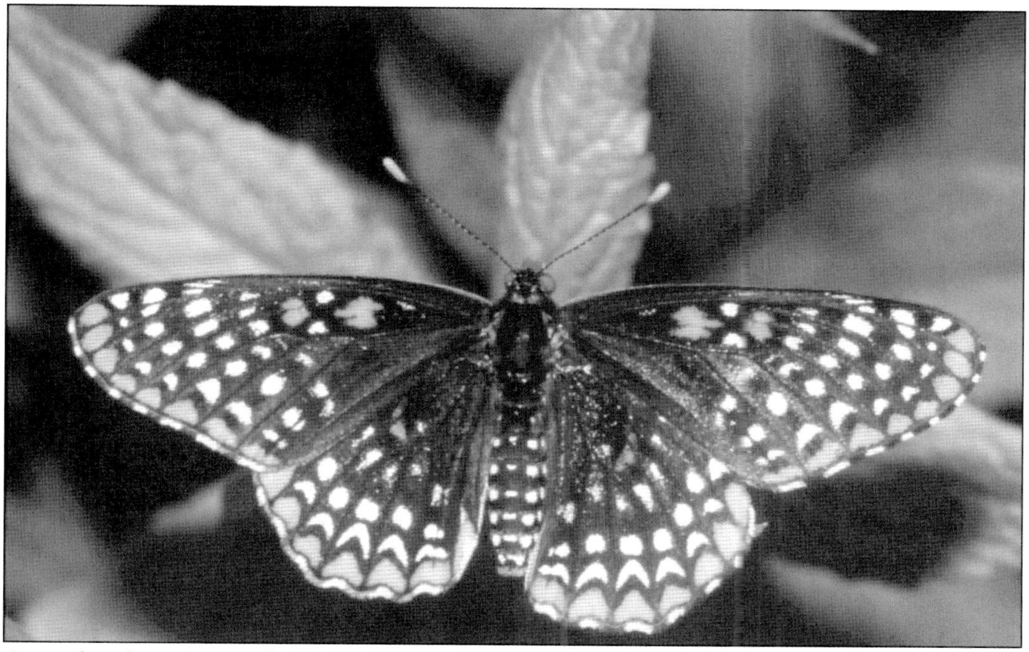

A startling beauty in its brilliant orange pageantry, this Baltimore checkerspot, *Euphydryas phaeton*, is found wherever its host plant, Turtlehead, *Chelone obliqua*, thrives. Numbers of this and other butterflies are declining in the park for complex reasons. However, the reservation continues to be one of the best places to observe butterflies in the region.

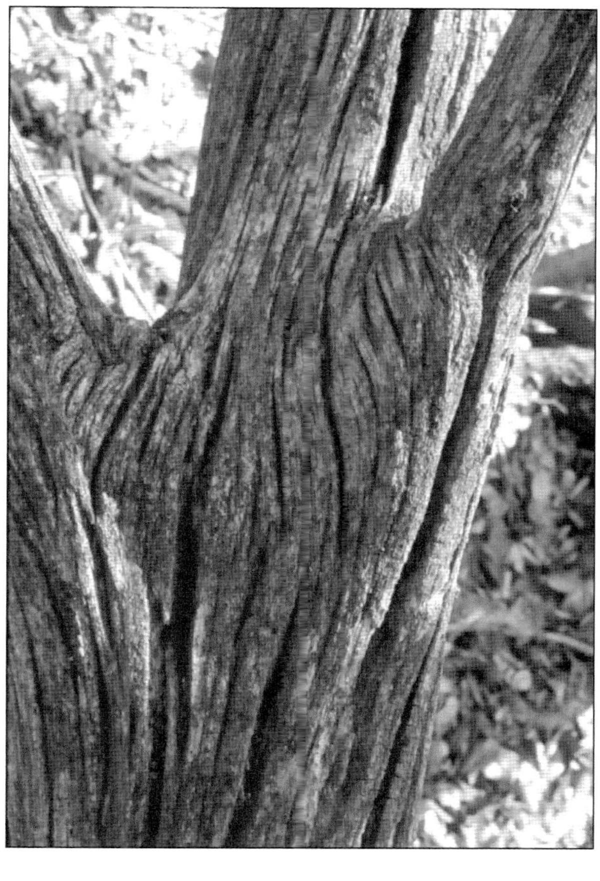

While most of the American chestnut trees, *Castanea dentate*, succumbed to blight, the wood is so dense that their trunks remain as silent sentinels of the forest. Some trees in isolated pockets of the reservation continue to flower, their pollen collected by the American Chestnut Foundation in hopes of breeding a resistant tree.

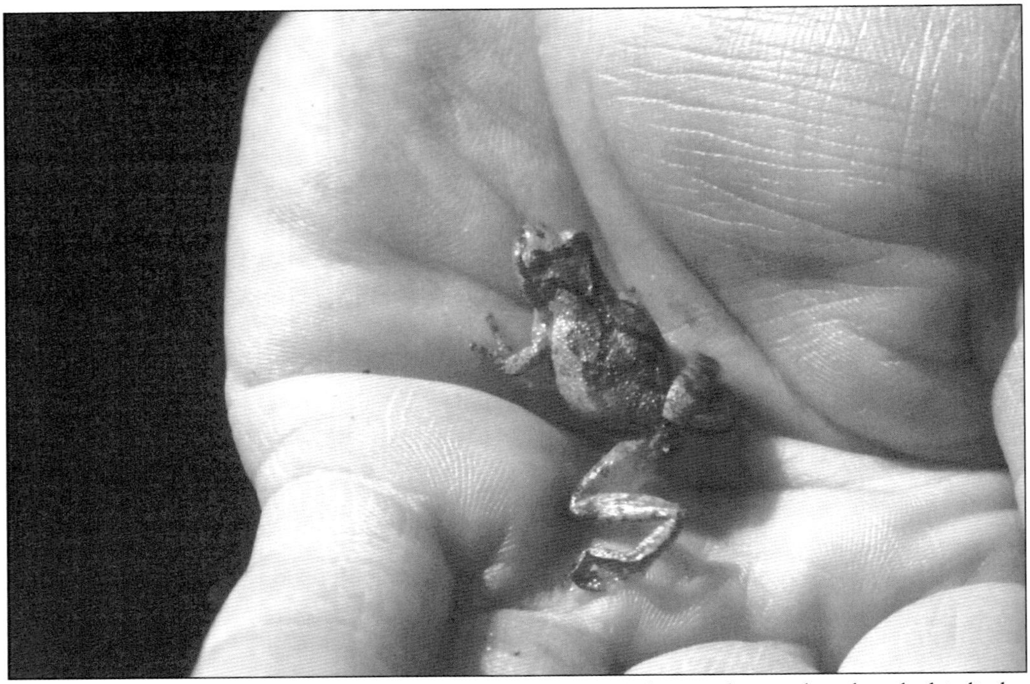

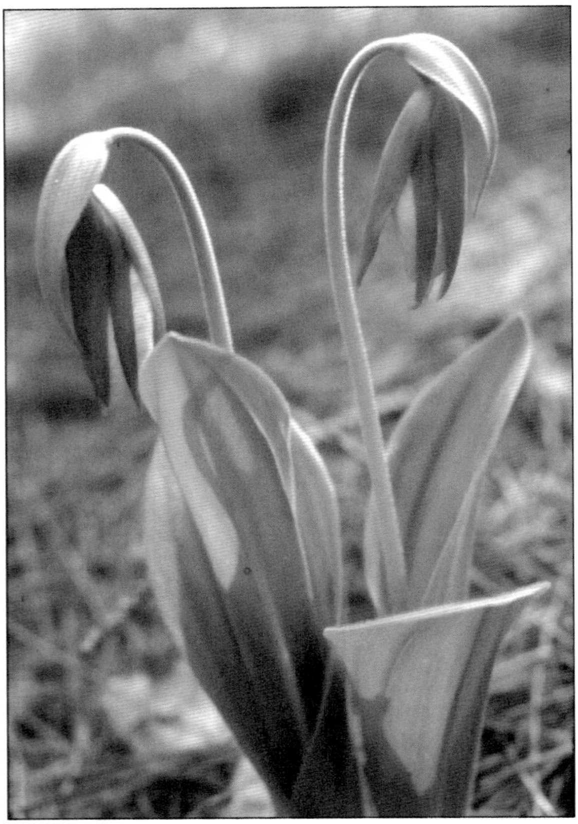

No bigger than a thumbnail, this little tree frog spends its life high in the treetops, feeding on insects. In the early spring, it migrates to breeding pools. The chorus of the spring peeper, *Pseudacris crucifer*, can be deafening in the wetlands at the end of Michigan Road, and are a sure sign that spring is just around the corner.

Several rare and unusual orchids can be found in the park, the most beloved of which, the pink lady slipper, *Cypripedium acaule*, is just unfolding in this picture. This flower, found in June on rocky, acid soils, elicits audible sounds of joy from visitors upon discovery. Because of its association with a fungus necessary for its growth, lady slippers are difficult to transplant. All plants and flowers in the reservation are protected, and picking or digging is prohibited.

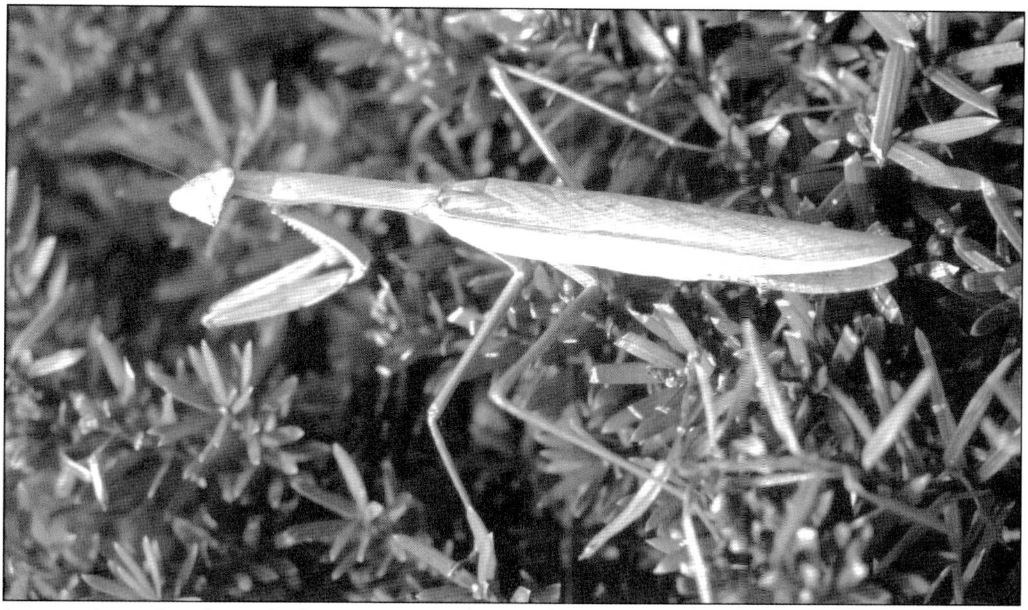

Insects abound in the park, from minute midges to this monster, the praying mantis, *Tenodera*, so named because of the prayer-like attitude of the folded forelimbs. Perfect miniatures when they hatch in the spring, they are commonly found in autumn meadows. Their foam-like egg cases can be seen all winter long.

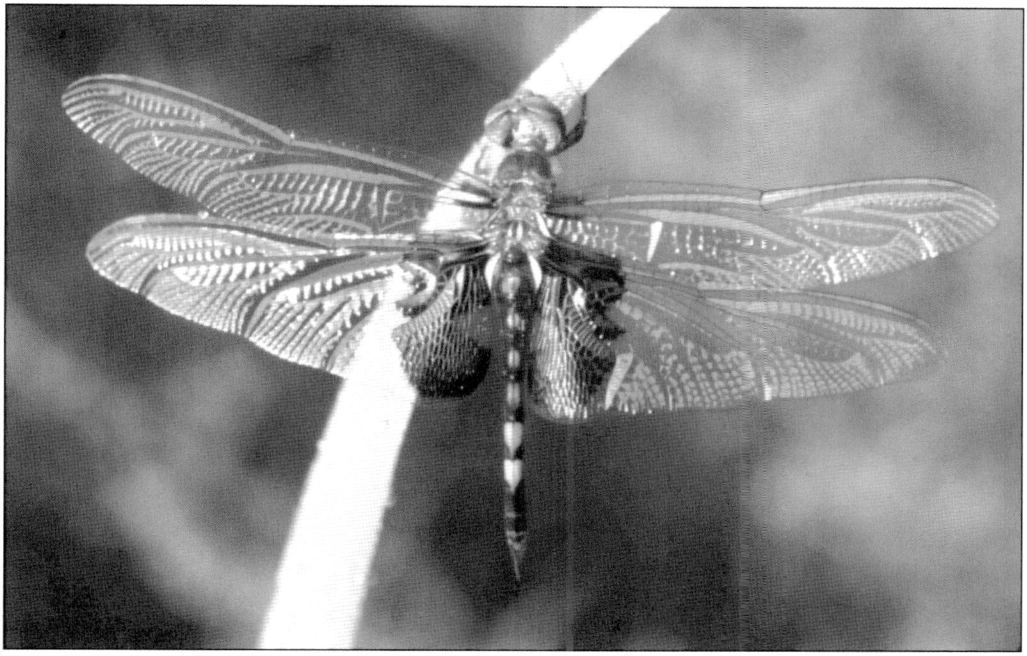

An astounding number of dragonflies and damselflies call the reservation home. This male black saddlebags, *Tramea lacerate,* is among the more than 80 species of odonates. As larva, each needs specific water bodies to survive, from cool seeps upwelling in the forest, to still ponds, to fast-moving stream riffles, to vernal pools, all of which are found in the park.

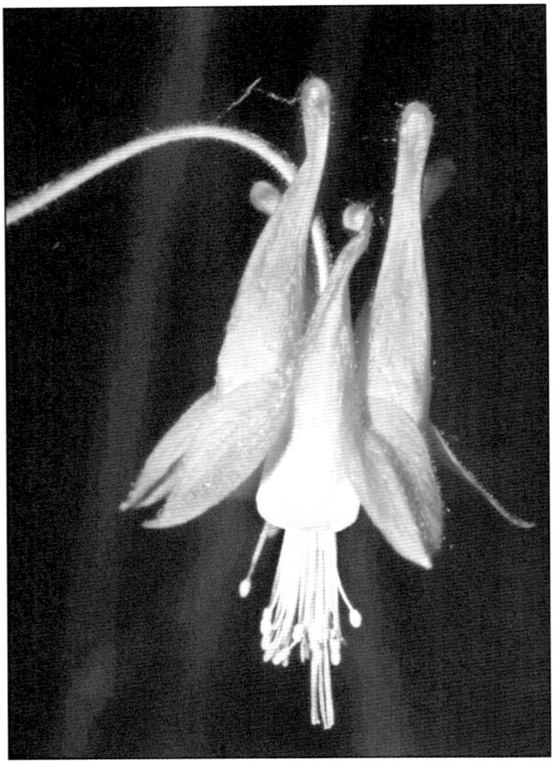

Many spring ephemerals are seen in the reservation, sometimes blanketing the forest floor before the trees leaf out. This favorite, columbine, *Aquilegia canadensis*, is especially fond of rocky areas that can protect it from being eaten or collected. The number of herbaceous species has sharply declined for complex reasons, one of which is an overabundance of white-tailed deer, *Odocoileus virginianus*.

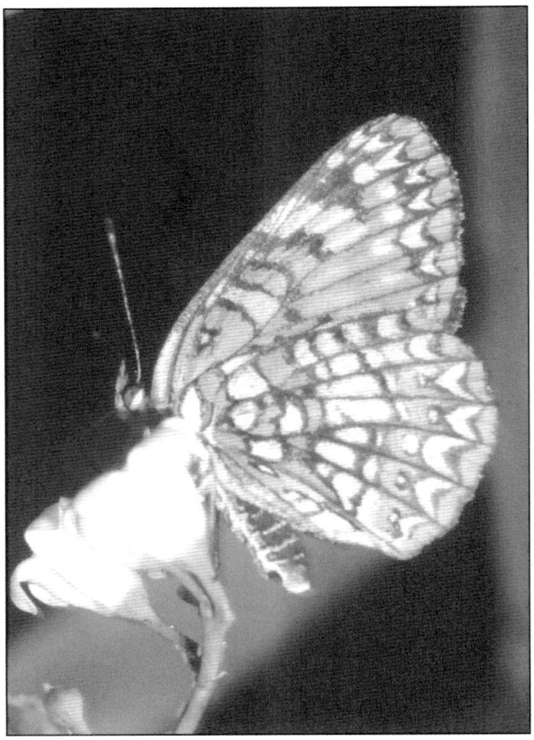

Another miniature beauty, this Harris' checkerspot, *Chlosyne harrisii*, is becoming quite rare. A colonial species, its larvae feed on one plant only, the flat-topped aster, *Doellingeria umbellate*, found in just one area in the reservation. Butterfly enthusiasts hold a count every July; their data has been invaluable in tracking butterfly abundance.

Not a cranberry at all, the highbush cranberry, *Viburnum trilobumis*, is covered with large white blossoms in May, followed by attractive red berries in fall. Several species of viburnums and dogwoods produce copious fruits in a good year. Migrating birds relish this and other fruits of the park's shrubs, making the reservation an important stopover.

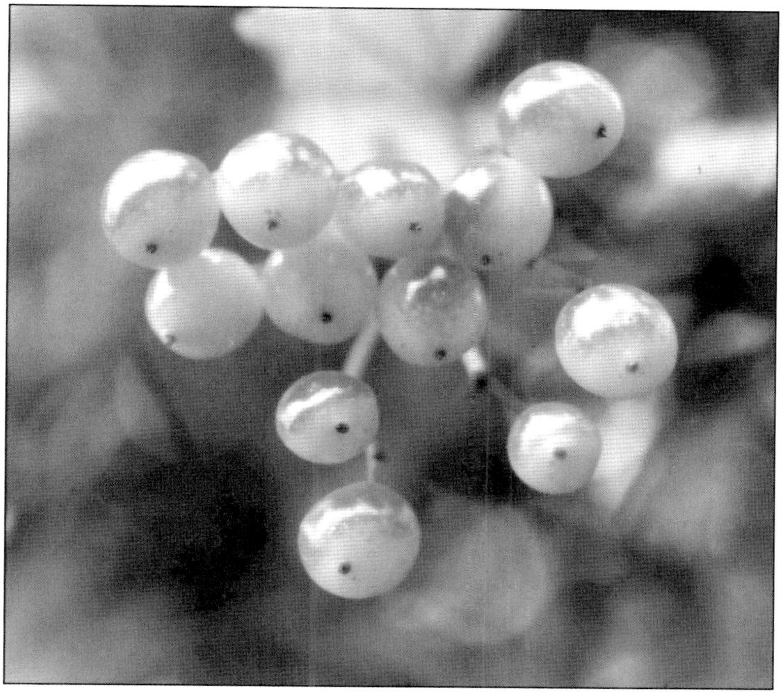

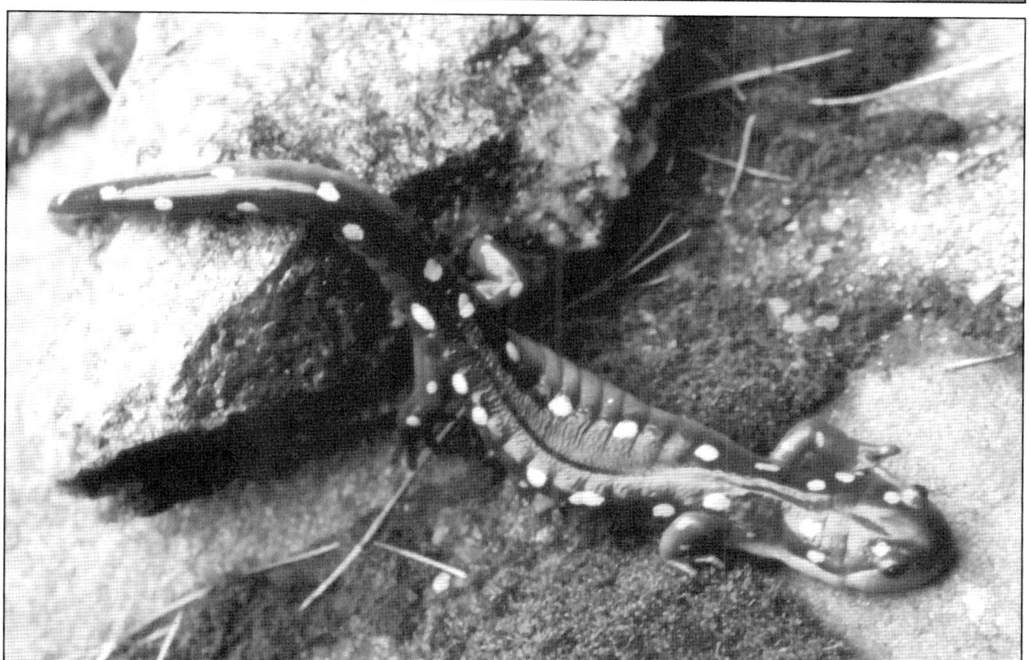

Great numbers of salamanders can be seen on rainy spring evenings as they migrate to their breeding pools. The remainder of the year, they seek moist areas under leaves and rocks and are an important part of the food chain. This spotted salamander, *Ambystoma maculatum*, is one of the largest, sometimes reaching six inches in length. The most unusual type found in the reservation is the four-toed salamander, *Hemidactylium scutatum*.

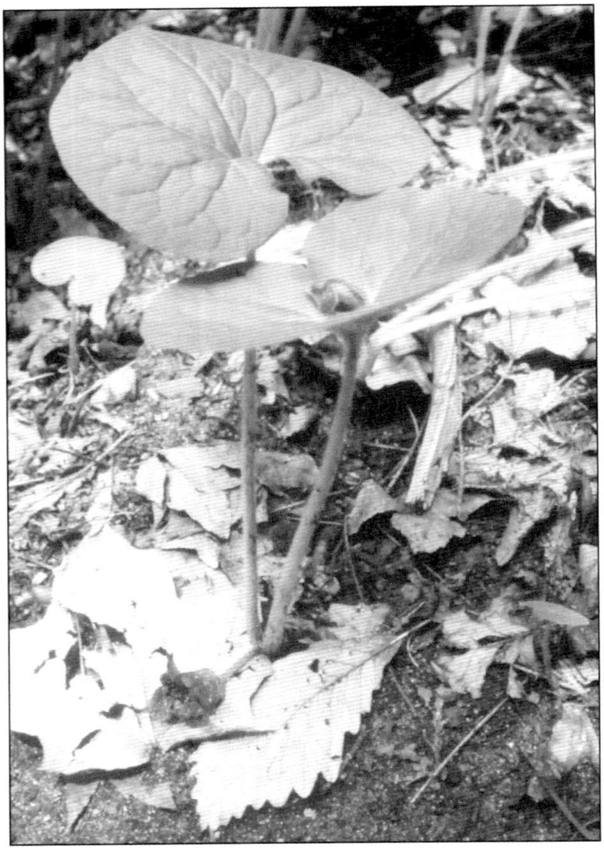

The compressed limestone hidden under the Waccabuc, Stone Hill, and upper Cross River drainage sweetens the soil, supporting some of the park's most unusual and rare wildflowers. Calcophiles like wild ginger, *Asarum*, can be found along the Laurel and River trails. Its foul-smelling red flower hugs the ground, attracting carrion flies for pollination. A few small outcrops of Inwood marble appear along the reservation's southern border.

One of the most beautiful and most rare wildflowers, the fringed gentian, *Gentianopsis crinite*, loves very wet, acidic soils. Blooming as late as mid-October, its sky-blue blossoms close if clouds cover the sun. The very fine crenulated hairs ringing the petals make it a most delicate flower. It is found in only a few places in the reservation.

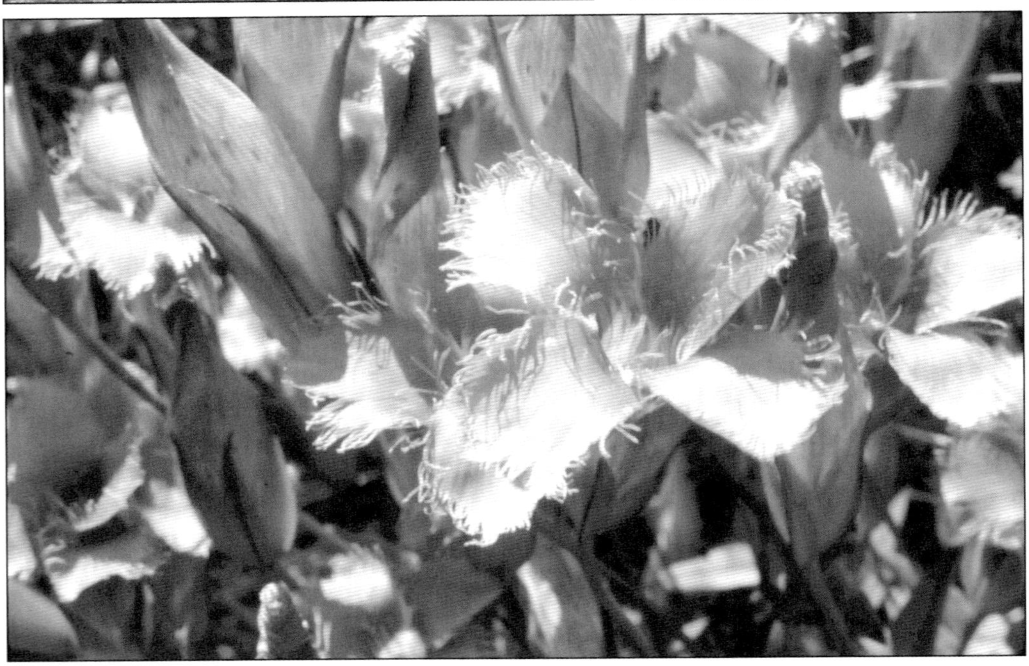

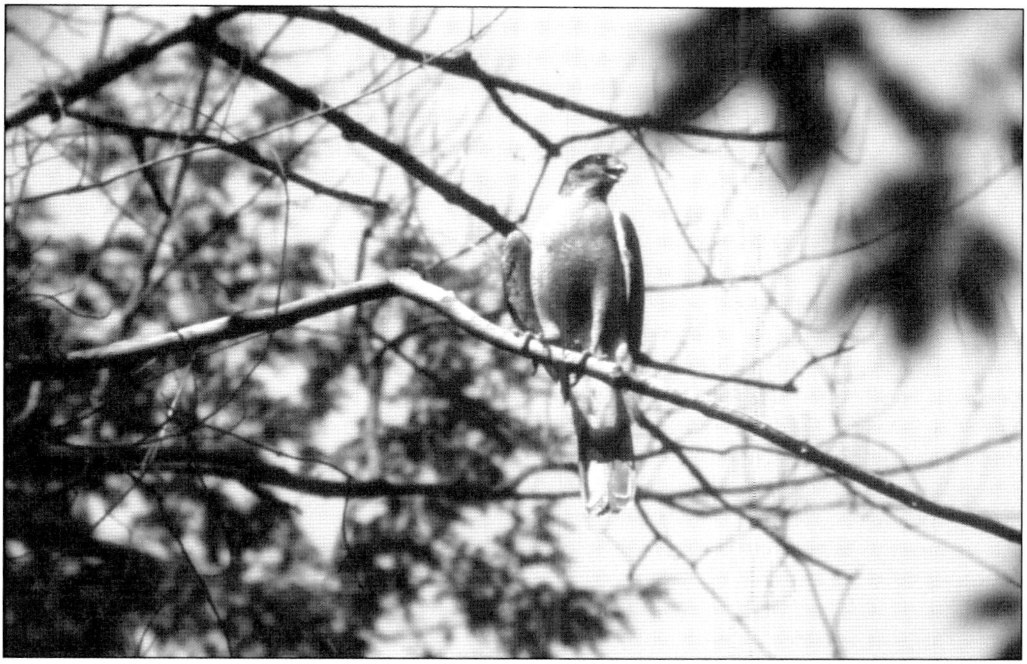

One of the largest birds of prey known to nest in the reservation is this handsome northern goshawk, *Accipiter gentili*. They prefer the tall conifers for their nest sites and can be vociferous and threatening if a hiker approaches their nests. Many hawks stop in the park during migration, especially on rainy or foggy days, when there are no thermals to carry them south.

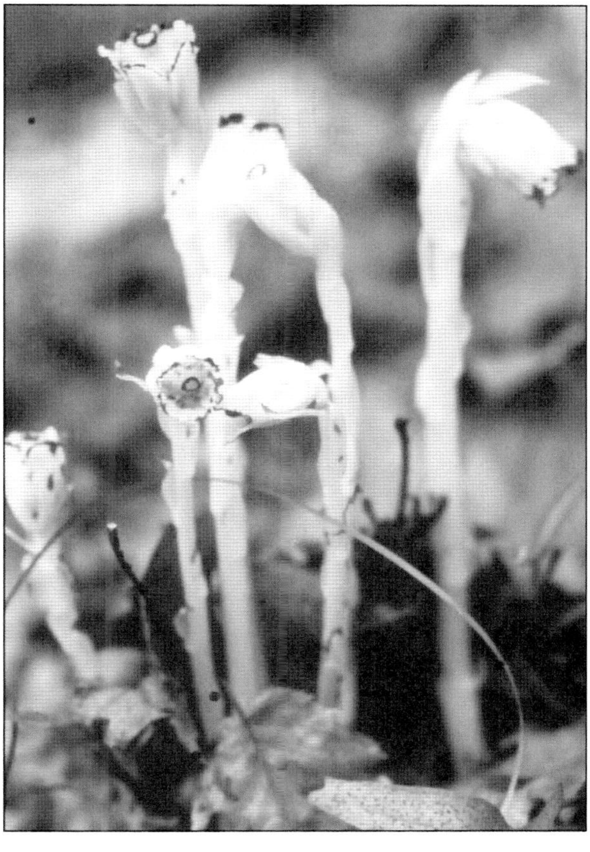

A most unusual wildflower, the Indian pipe, *Monotropa uniflora*, is found in early summer throughout the park. Also called corpse plant because it is white and contains no chlorophyll, this plant is parasitic and relies on certain fungi that are associated with trees. Because it does not need sunlight, it can be found on the dense, dark forest floor.

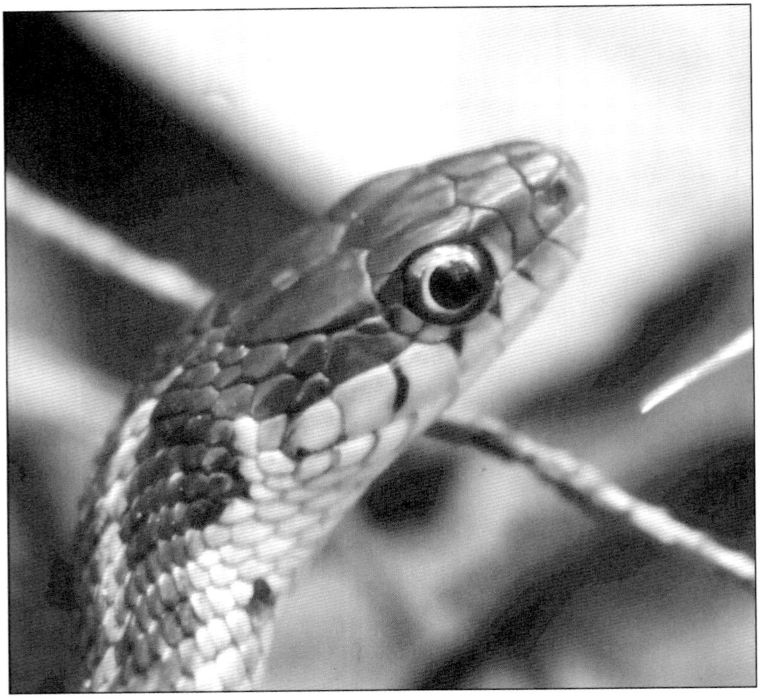

This garter snake, *Thamnophis sirtalis*, is one of 11 snake species found in the park. Some snakes are in decline in the region, including the eastern hognose, *Heterodon platirhinos*, and the copperhead, *Agkistrodon contortrix mokasen*, both of which inhabit the park. Snake boards constructed of metal and wood, which retain heat from the sun, are placed near known dens to provide safe spots for sunning and hiding.

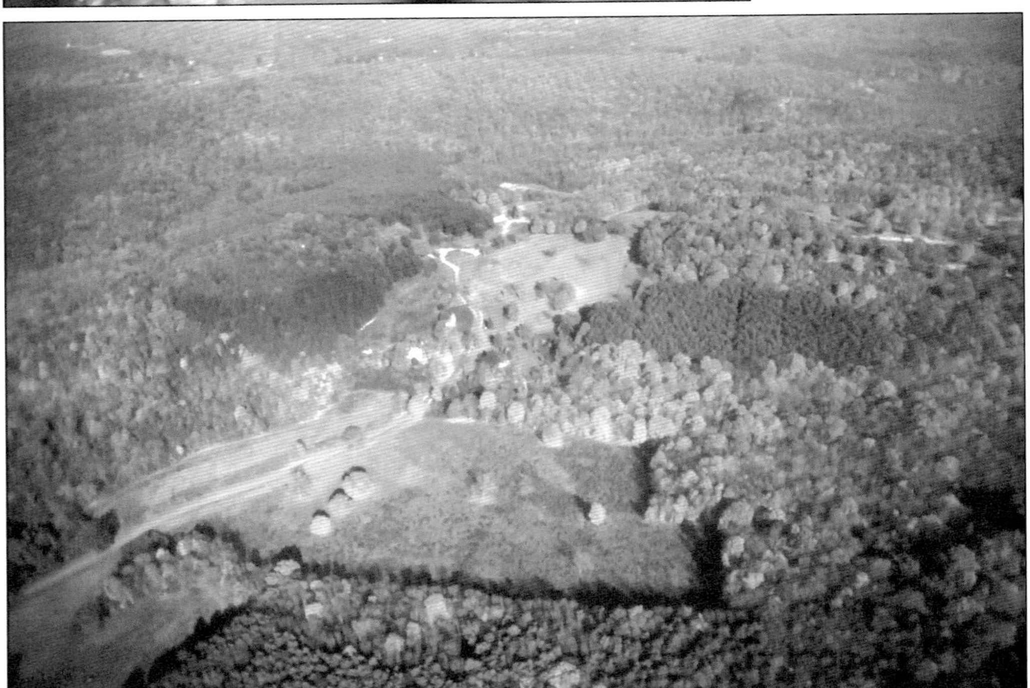

From the air, the vastness of the reservation is evident. The absence of suburban sprawl, the pine plantations, and the wildness make the park such a treasure. The roadway is shown here, extending eastward. In the center of the photograph is the sledding area on Pell Hill, near the Trailside Museum.

This broadwing hawk, *Buteo platypterus*, alights on a wire to get a good view of voles, mice, and shrews in the tall grass. Meadows in the park support great numbers of these little mammals, making the area an important feeding ground for birds of prey. Some fields are left unmowed during the winter to provide cover for the mammals and food for the birds.

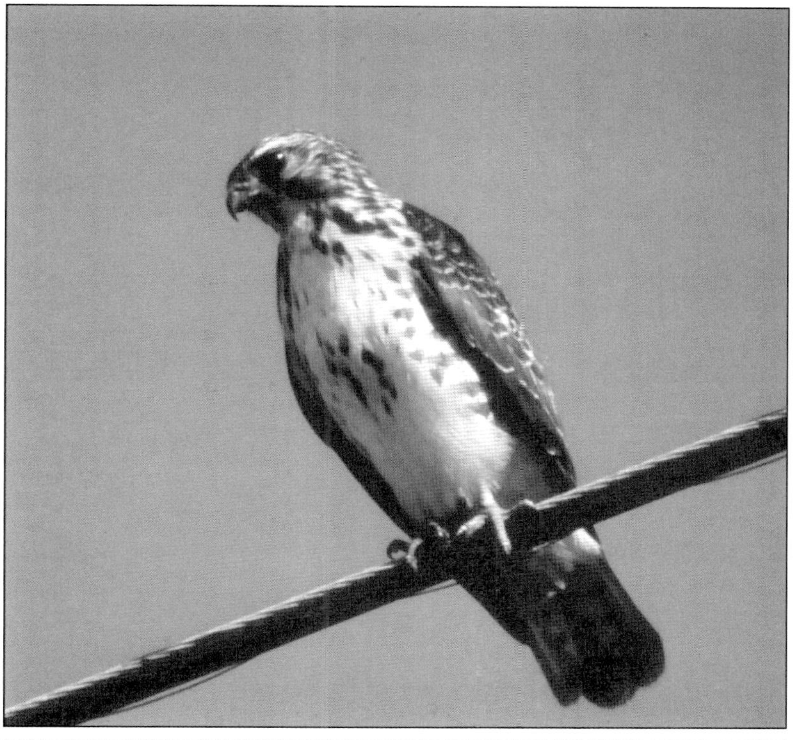

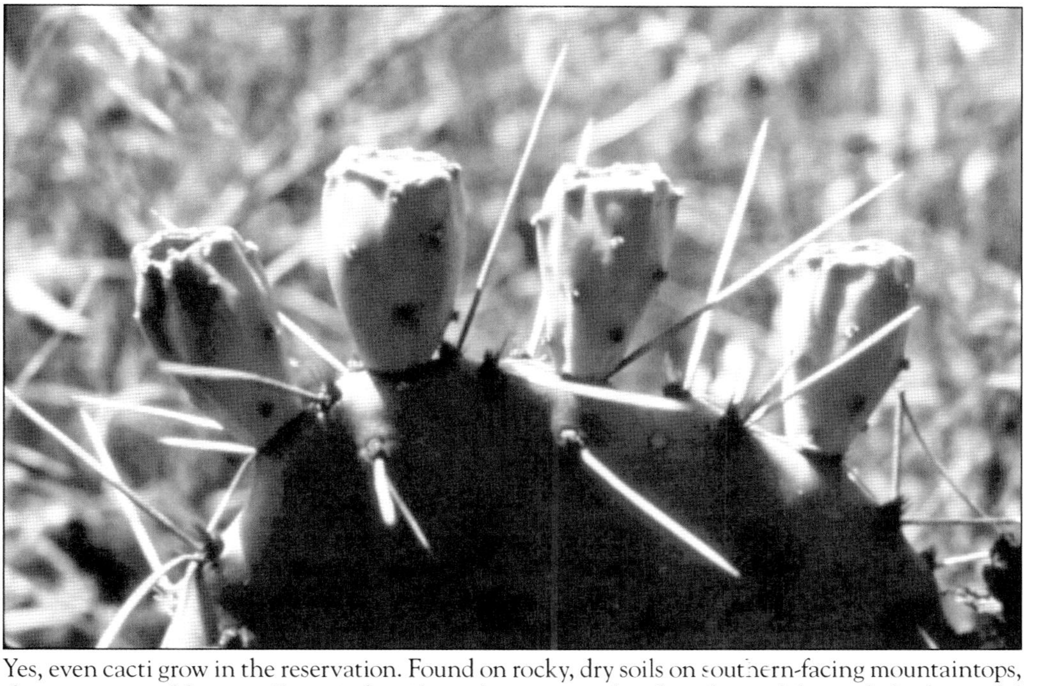

Yes, even cacti grow in the reservation. Found on rocky, dry soils on southern-facing mountaintops, the eastern prickly pear, *Opuntia humifusa*, thrives in isolated pockets of the park. Its beautiful yellow blossoms are a thrill to find, but beware—the spines are minute, almost invisible, and very painful to remove.

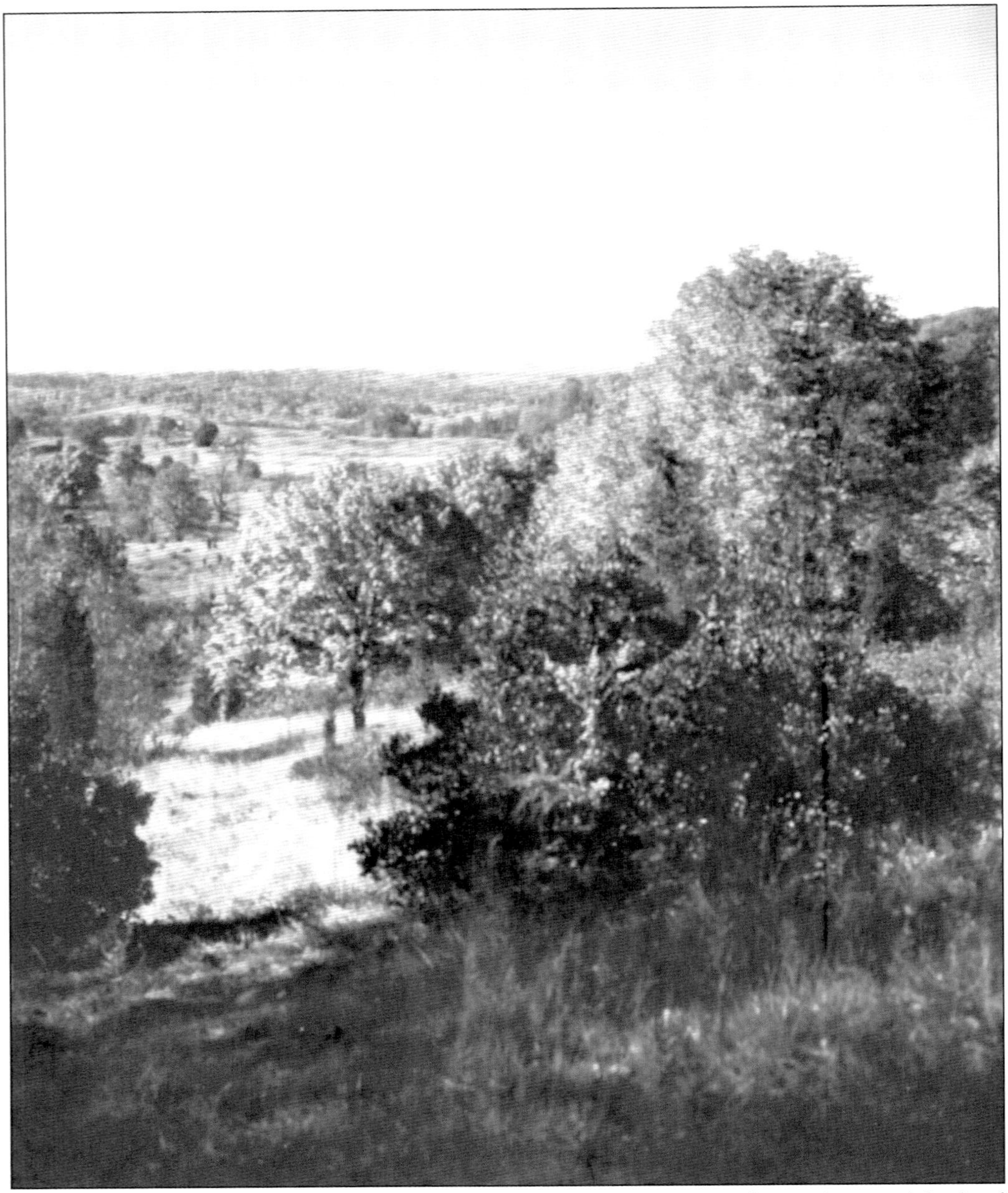

Trees provide shade and a pleasant vista, as this view toward the west shows. As use of the land for farming disappeared, and the fields were no longer plowed, the pastures began to grow up and shrubs, brush, and trees took the place of wheat and corn as nature's law of succession took over. From this viewpoint at the top of Pell Hill, near one of the camping shelters, footpaths created by campers leading to the museum can be seen. (Courtesy of the Westchester County Archives.)

Nine

People of the Reservation

Ward Pound Ridge Reservation, tucked away in northern Westchester County, is an exceptional piece of landscape that has always attracted noteworthy people. William Lukens Ward, sometimes called "Boss Ward," became the namesake of this most diverse of Westchester County's parks at its dedication in 1938. His idea for the park came as a revelation. He was watching city children and their nursemaids at play in an Atlantic City park in the early 1920s amid Keep Off the Grass signs. He told a friend, "We've got to have a place in our county where the kids can go and romp all over the fields. We want birds and animals and all the things to make a real welcome place for kiddies." Ward, commissioner of parks in 1922 and chair of the Republican Party, was well liked and respected. By 1926, his vision was fulfilled with the establishment of this park and Saxon Woods and Blue Mountain Parks.

Helping the park evolve over the decades into the inviting place it is today were many outstanding individuals who, in various ways, left a lasting mark on the reservation. Politicians, businessmen, conservationists, curators, and park employees all played an important role in the history of Ward Pound Ridge Reservation. Two remarkable women had a lasting impact on the reservation. Eloise Payne Luquer and Delia West Marble, conservationists with the Bedford Garden Club, had the idea to establish nature trails and a museum in the park. They were the catalysts for what has become an outstanding environmental education center.

Alice R. Ireys, a noted landscape architect, planned the park's wildflower garden. Important to the understanding of the natural and human world around us have been the museum curators; all of whom left a legacy that was built upon over the years by their successors. A park of more than 4,315 acres needs its caretakers, and, from the beginning, this park has been gifted with dedicated superintendents and caretakers who keep the seasonal rhythm of the year in focus. A number of these folks were members of the families whose farms became part of the reservation.

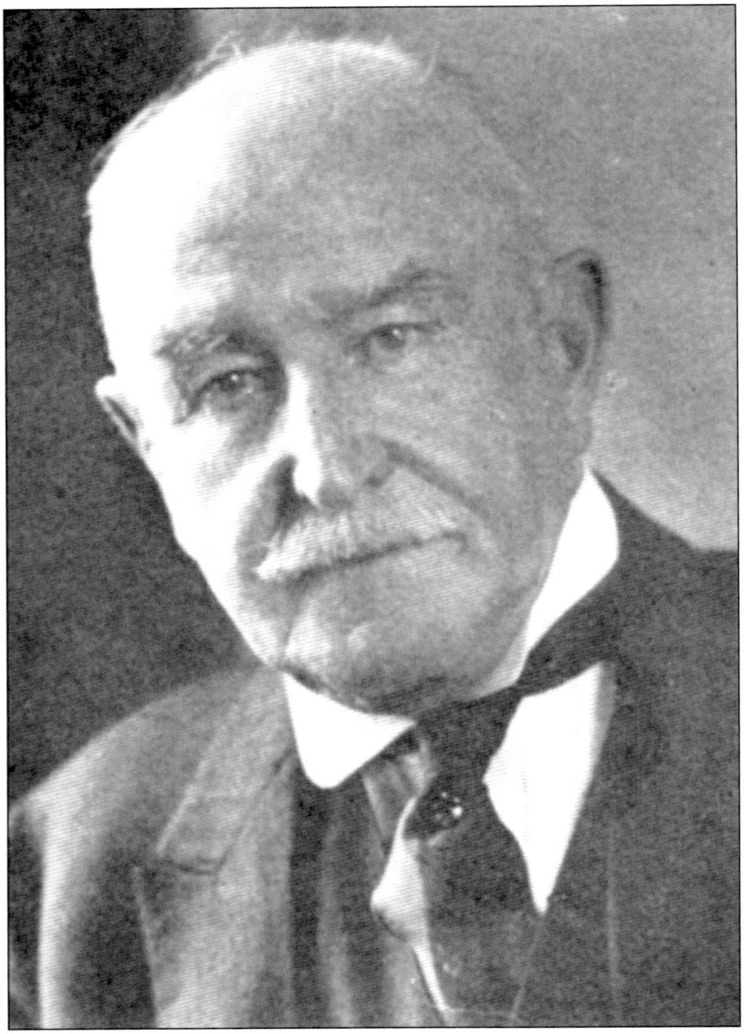

William Lukens Ward (1856–1933) was instrumental in the inception of Ward Pound Ridge Reservation and several other county parks during his reign as Westchester County commissioner of parks. As chairman of the Republican Party, he carried a lot of influence in county politics. Ward served a term as congressman (1897–1899), then returned to his home in Port Chester, where he was engaged in the manufacture of nuts, bolts, and rivets. The park was dedicated to him in a 1938 ceremony. This marker stands on a knoll near the entrance to the park.

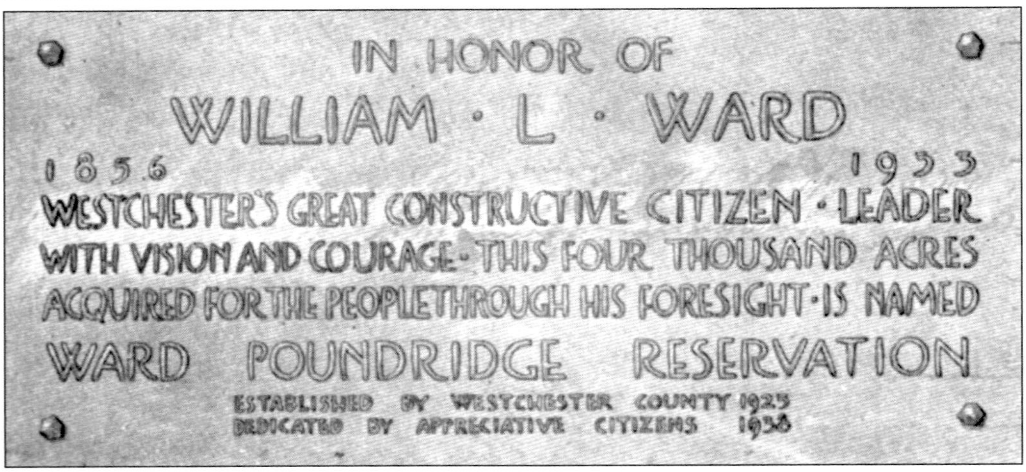

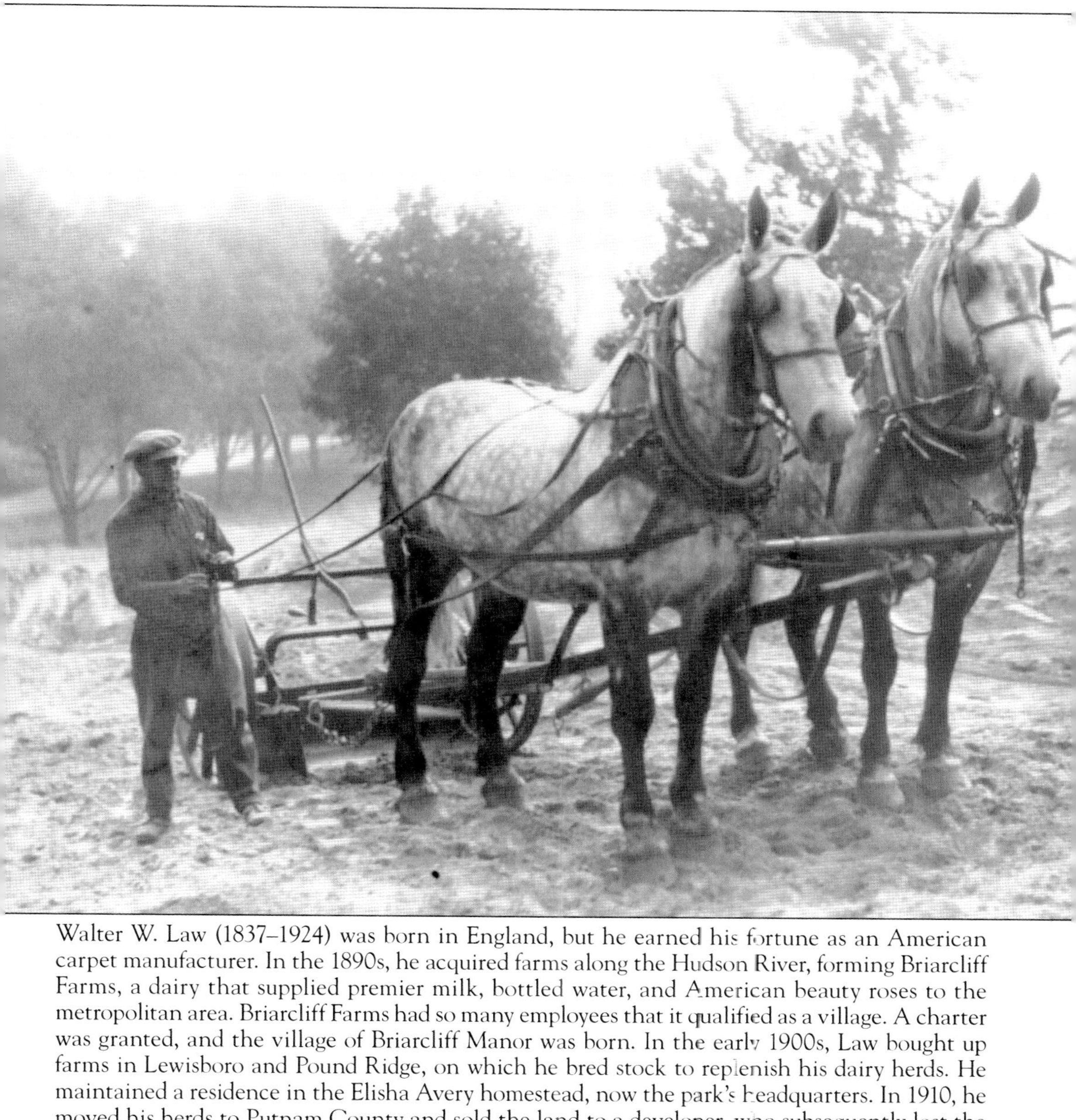

Walter W. Law (1837–1924) was born in England, but he earned his fortune as an American carpet manufacturer. In the 1890s, he acquired farms along the Hudson River, forming Briarcliff Farms, a dairy that supplied premier milk, bottled water, and American beauty roses to the metropolitan area. Briarcliff Farms had so many employees that it qualified as a village. A charter was granted, and the village of Briarcliff Manor was born. In the early 1900s, Law bought up farms in Lewisboro and Pound Ridge, on which he bred stock to replenish his dairy herds. He maintained a residence in the Elisha Avery homestead, now the park's headquarters. In 1910, he moved his herds to Putnam County and sold the land to a developer, who subsequently lost the land. Law took the property back. After his death, his firm, Briarcliff Realty, sold the 821 acres to Westchester County for $93,750. This early photograph shows a farmhand working a team near the homestead.

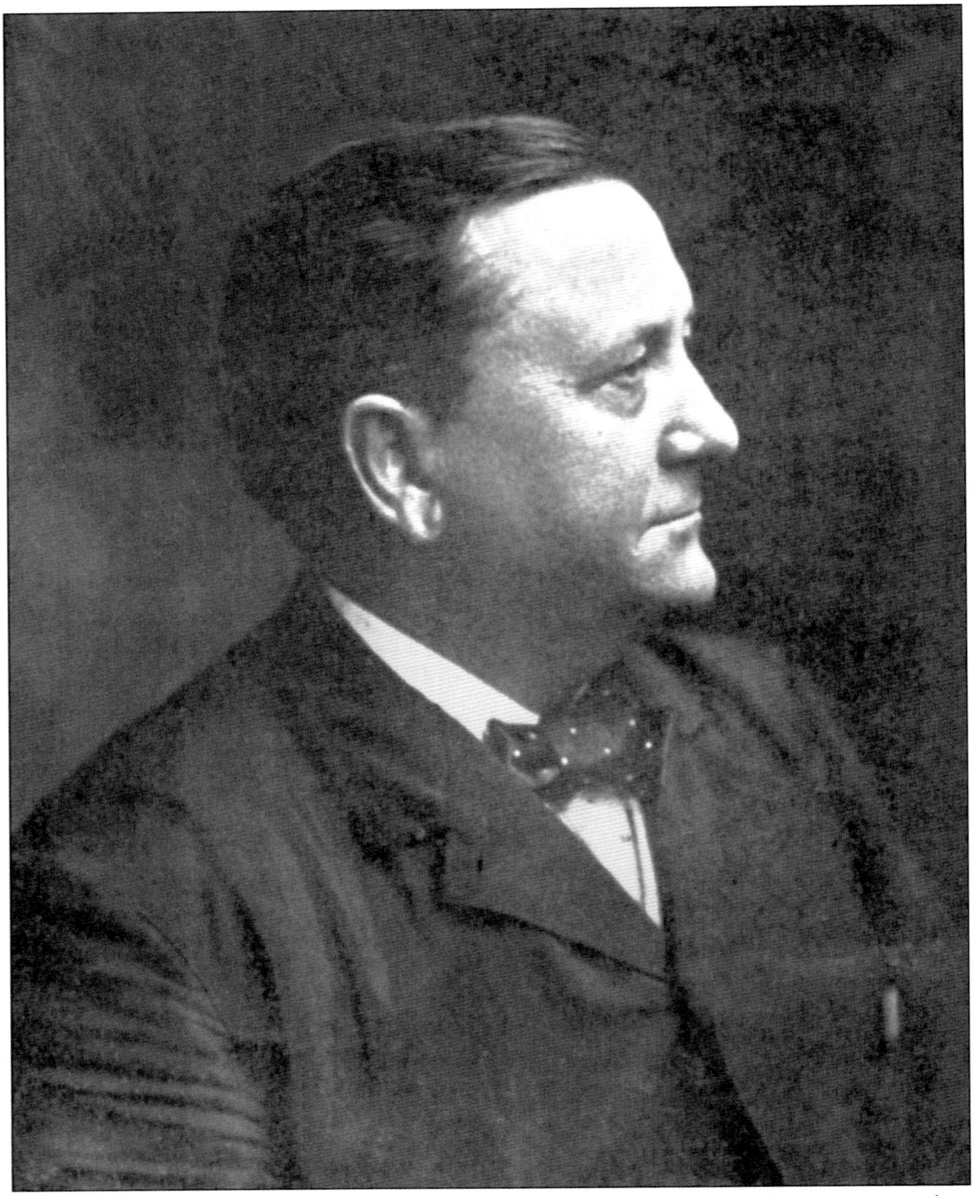

Edward F. Brush, MD, served as the first mayor of Mount Vernon, New York. He was president of the Westchester County Medical Society from 1884 to 1885, and held many other positions in the medical field. He had a legacy with the reservation as well. Dr. Brush developed a milk product called Kumyss based on a fortified milk beverage drunk by the Tartars and nomads roving the Russian steppes. His product claimed to "restore health to the weak, hope to the consumptive, and life to the sufferers from indigestion." His main Kumyss factory was in Mount Vernon, with a subsidiary in Tuckahoe. He established a dairy farm in Pound Ridge to supply "superior" milk for his Kumyss processing plants. Although it is unlikely that Dr. Brush ever resided in Pound Ridge, his farm was one of the largest in what is now the park. By 1909, he had amassed more than 600 acres. Dr. Brush owned the land from 1891 to 1924, selling the property to Westchester County when the park was formed.

William C. Wheeler was the first park naturalist and creator of one of the first interpretive nature trails in New York. He cut nature trails and created hand-painted signs from recycled tin that offered tidbits of nature lore or identified trees and shrubs. Hikers can still find his signs on the Wheeler Trail near the museum. In 1938, Wheeler became curator of the new museum, a position he held for more than 30 years.

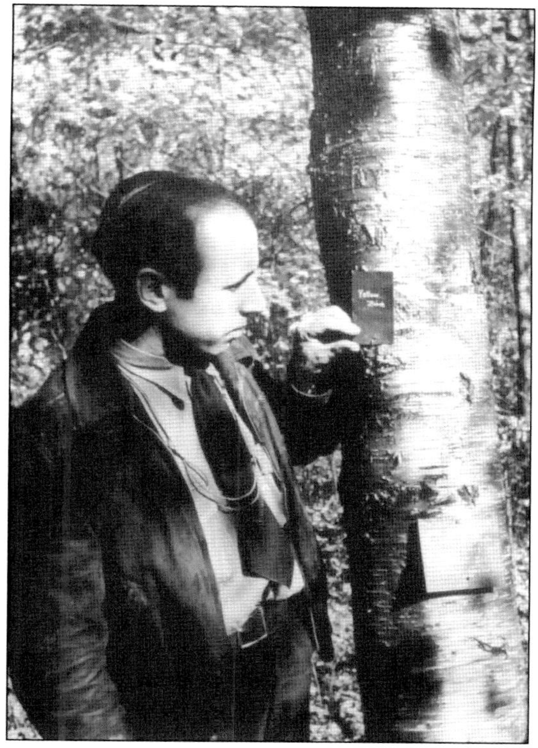

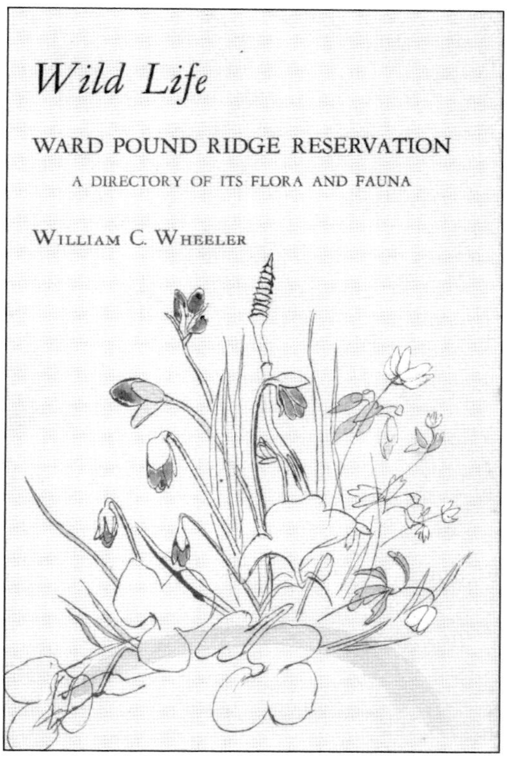

A naturalist and ornithologist, William C. Wheeler loved nature. During the early years of the park, Wheeler worked one day a week as a nature guide, his salary paid by the Bedford Garden Club. In the 1960s, while suffering from Parkinson's disease, he painstakingly wrote *Wild Life*, a privately published guidebook to the flora and fauna species of the reservation, explaining where and when to find each one.

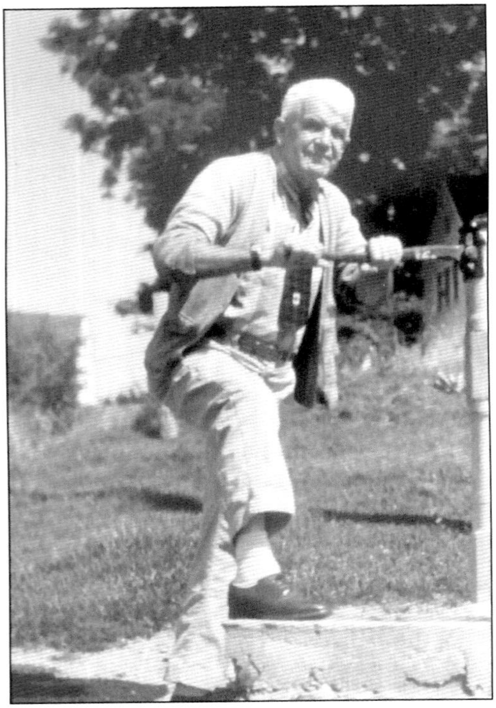

Pa Whitman took great pleasure in keeping Ward Pound Ridge Reservation running smoothly for the benefit of park visitors. Here, he is trying his hand at operating one of the water pumps in the park. This love of the park continued into the third generation of Whitmans, as, like his father, his two sons were career park employees, too.

William M. "Pa" Whitman represented the second generation of Whitmans to work in the reservation. His father, William Whitman Sr., was the park's first superintendent. Pa Whitman took over the management of the park when he returned from World War II. He spent a lifetime caring for his beloved park. He raised his family in the building that is now the park office, which is visible in the background of this photograph.

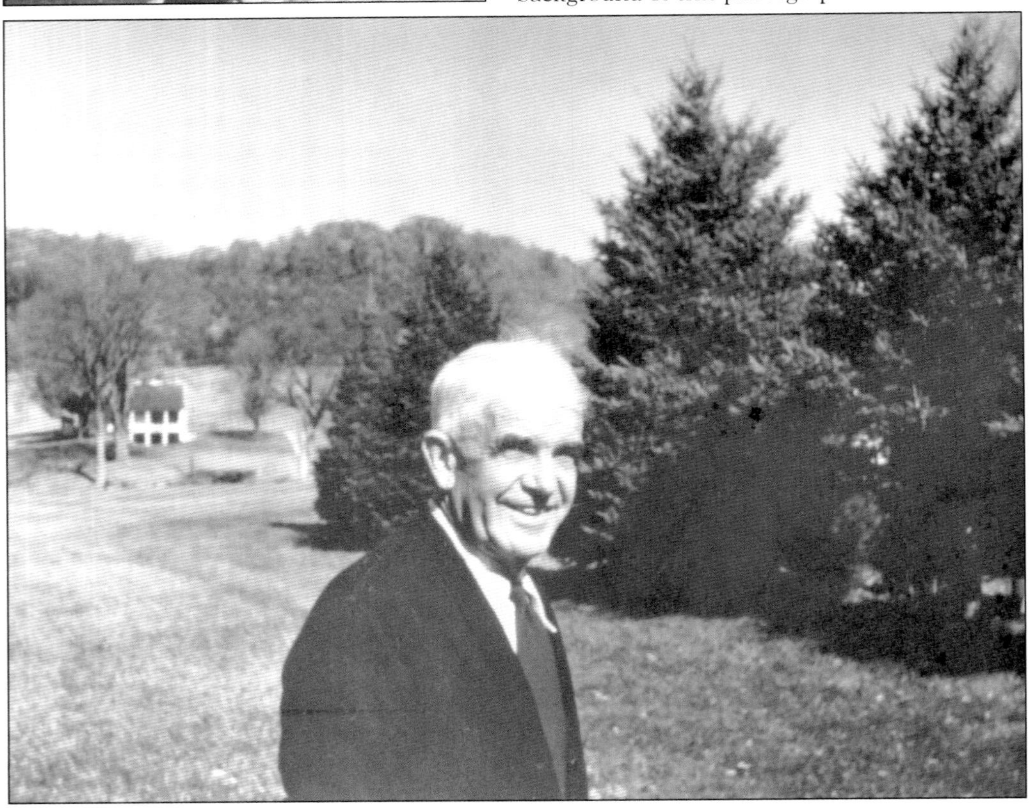

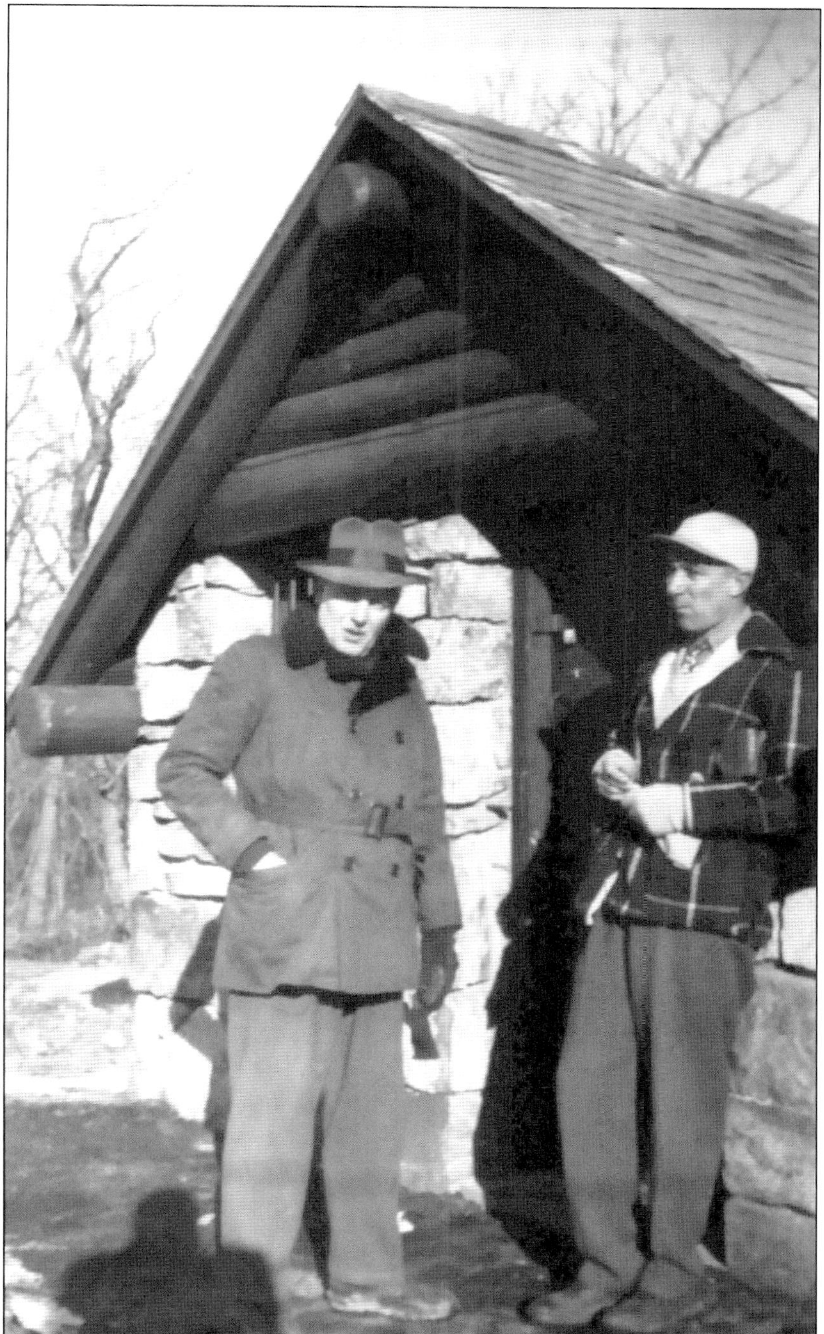

The park is a haven for people seeking to enjoy and explore nature and to share their knowledge with others. Oliver Knapp (right), seen here in the 1940s with an unidentified man, was a coworker of William Wheeler at the telephone company in Mount Kisco. He later became the village historian of Mount Kisco. Knapp had a collection of telephone memorabilia he displayed at Trailside Museum.

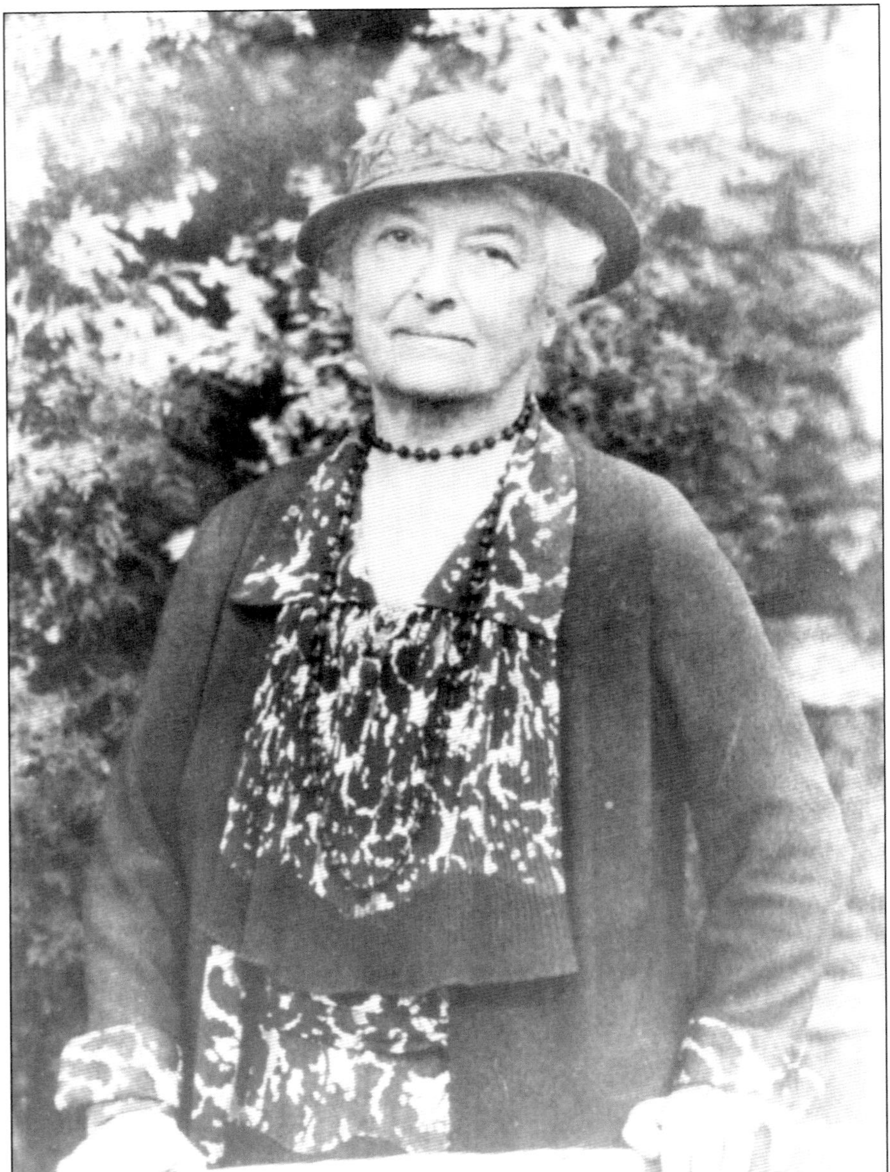

Eloise Payne Luquer (1862–1947) was born in Brooklyn, but at the age of four came to Bedford when her father became rector of St. Matthew's Church. Her intense interest in flowers led to her study of botany. This, combined with a talent for painting, produced a marvelous botanical artist. The majority of her almost 400 wildflower paintings are at the Brooklyn Botanic Garden. Luquer lectured widely on wildflower conservation and was involved in many community organizations. She was a founding member of the Bedford Garden Club. One of her goals in life was to bring people to "a greater love of nature." Luquer, with her friend Delia West Marble, initiated the idea for a nature trail and museum at the newly established Pound Ridge County Park. She and Marble marked the first nature trail and, with the help of naturalist William Wheeler, began what has become an outstanding nature program at the park.

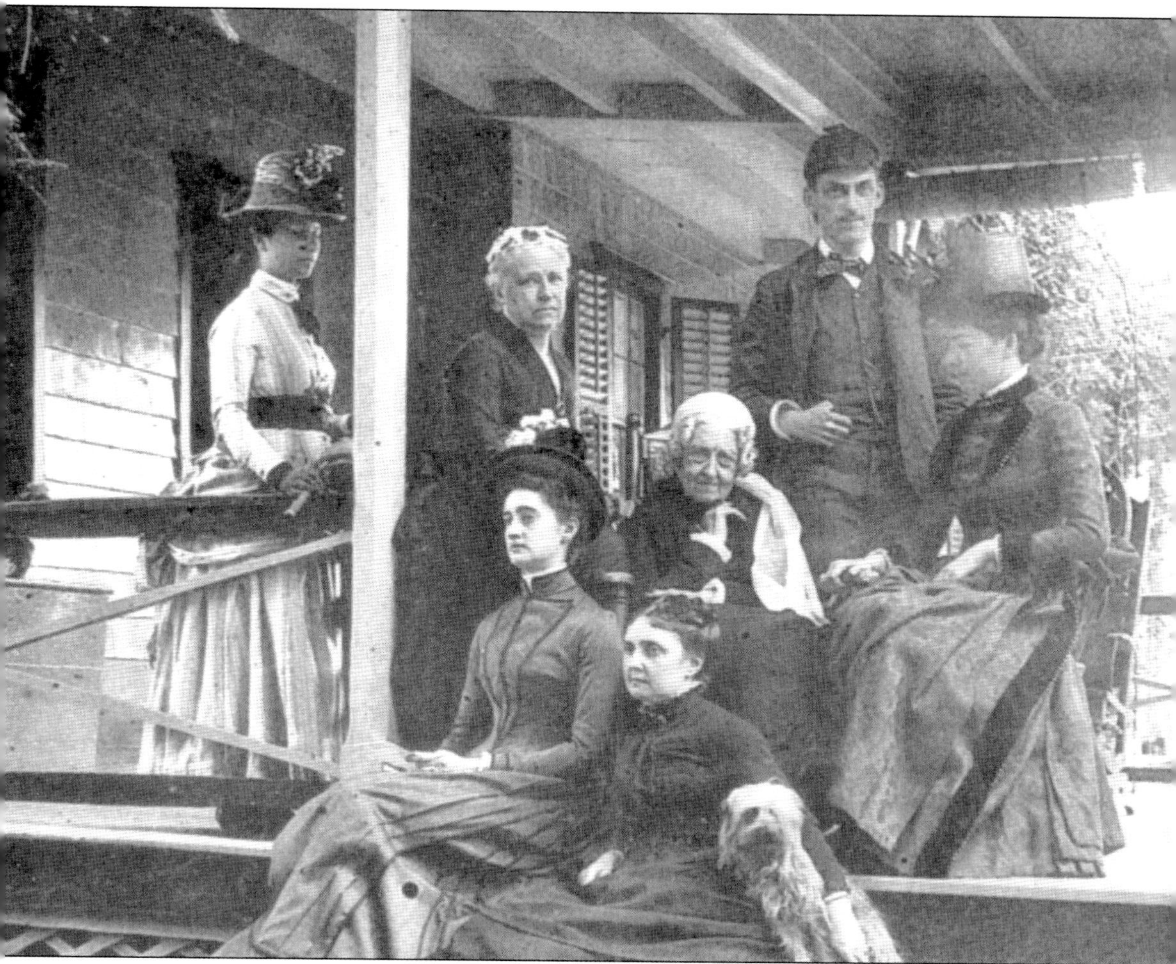

Delia West Marble (standing left) (1868–1951) was the daughter of the owner of the *New York World* newspaper. She lived in Bedford and was passionate about flowers. During World War I, she was president of the Bedford Garden Club. The club was looking for a patriotic cause, which led Marble to become involved with the Woman's Land Army of America and the Bedford Women's Agricultural Camp. She offered her farm as a training camp. Here, the farmerettes were trained to do farmwork so that they could replace the men who had gone to war. The girls were hired by local farmers. After the war, Marble and the Bedford Garden Club took an active interest in nearby Pound Ridge Reservation. She and her friend Eloise Payne Luquer worked tirelessly to develop the nature trails and new museum in the park. The wildflower garden planted in 1954 was dedicated to the two women.

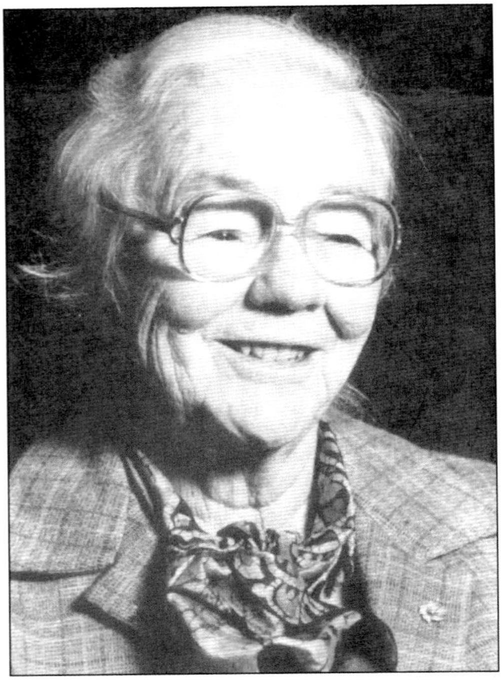

Alice Recknagel Ireys (1911–2000), a pioneer in landscape architecture, was the designer of the wildflower garden at Ward Pound Ridge Reservation. A lifelong resident of Brooklyn Heights who considered the Brooklyn Botanic Garden her second home, Ireys created public botanic spaces in many cities and suburban areas. One of her favorites was the Fragrance Garden at the Brooklyn Botanic Garden. Her garden designs provided a horticultural bridge between the 19th and 20th centuries.

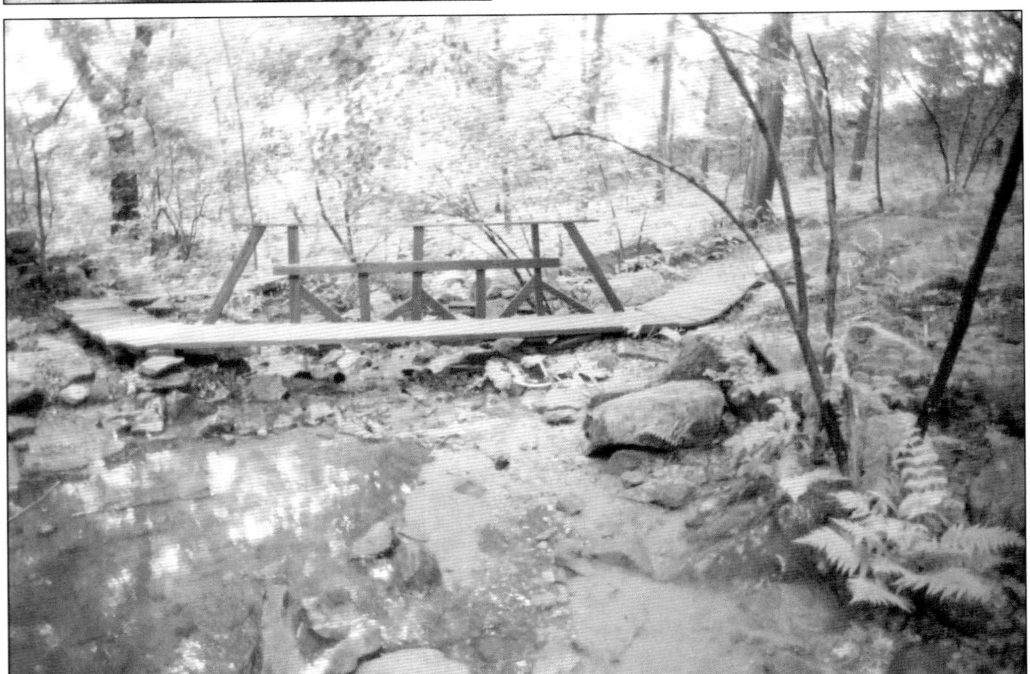

Ireys believed that simplicity encouraged an appreciation for a garden's beauty. Her wildflower garden, with its rustic bridge, was planted in 1954. The Luquer-Marble wildflower garden flourished under the guidance of the Bedford Garden Club and the volunteers who spent hours helping to maintain it. The wildflower garden highlights the many indigenous plants of the reservation. In the springtime, the garden is a beautiful spot to spend a peaceful hour.

Scott Piatt was a descendant of a venerable Cross River family. Several family members served in the Civil War. The Piatts' house stood behind the Trailside Museum in the late 1800s. Evelyn Russell of Cross River, a Piatt descendant, remembers Scott's wife by a family nickname, "Grandma Peanut." A man of many energies, Piatt raised cattle and logged cedar on his property, sending it by rail to be milled.

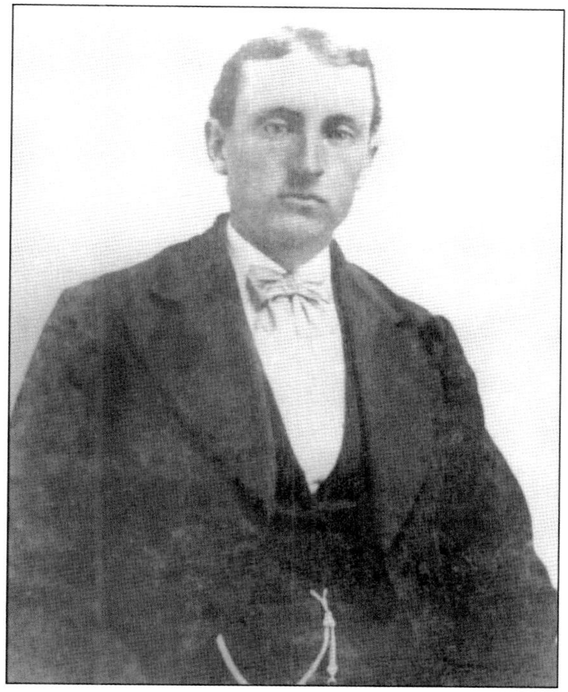

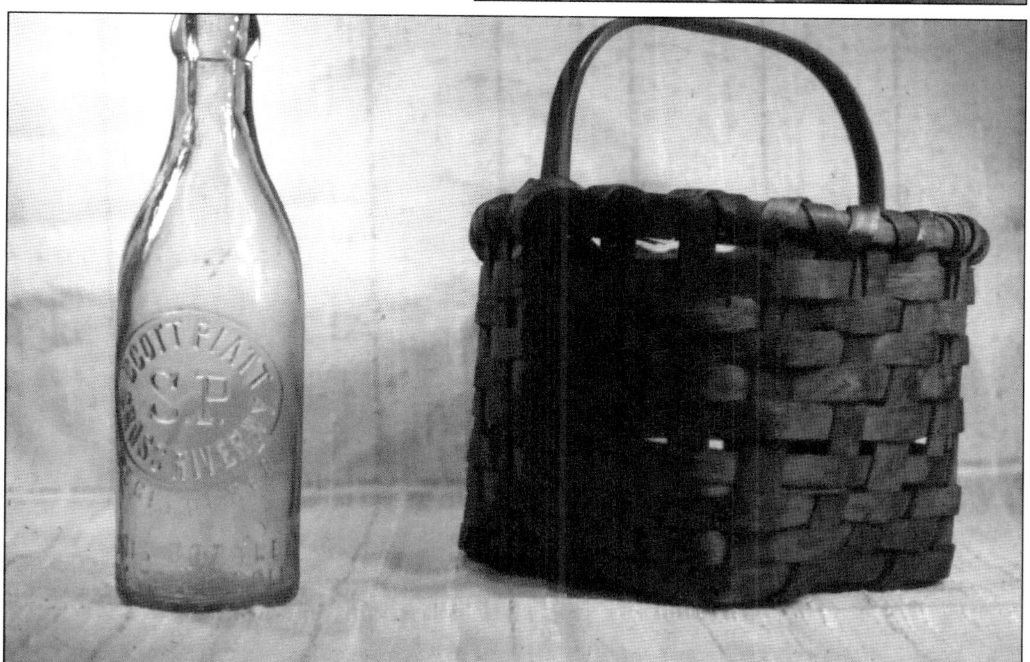

Two artifacts in the museum came from the Piatt farm: a split-ash basket and a Scott Piatt beer bottle. Scott Piatt plied several trades to provide for his family. He was a basket maker and was famous for his Scott Piatt beer, which was actually Schaefer Beer that came in kegs by rail to Katonah. He carted it to Cross River, where he bottled it in his own bottles, which are now local collectibles.

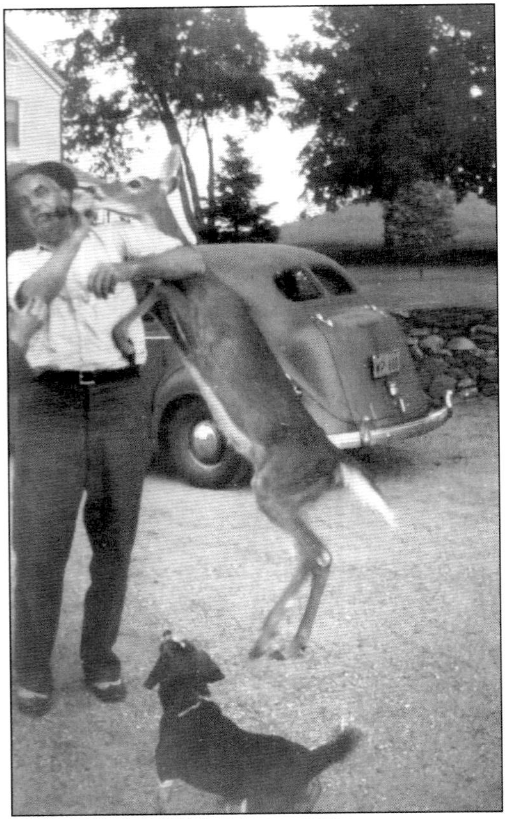

Do not worry. Pa Whitman is not being attacked by a white-tailed deer. Dottie, as she was affectionately known, was tame and readily took food from him and park visitors. She had been bottle-fed as a fawn. Deer were not as abundant as they are today, so this gentle "wild" creature was a treat for the public to enjoy. It was nature close-up.

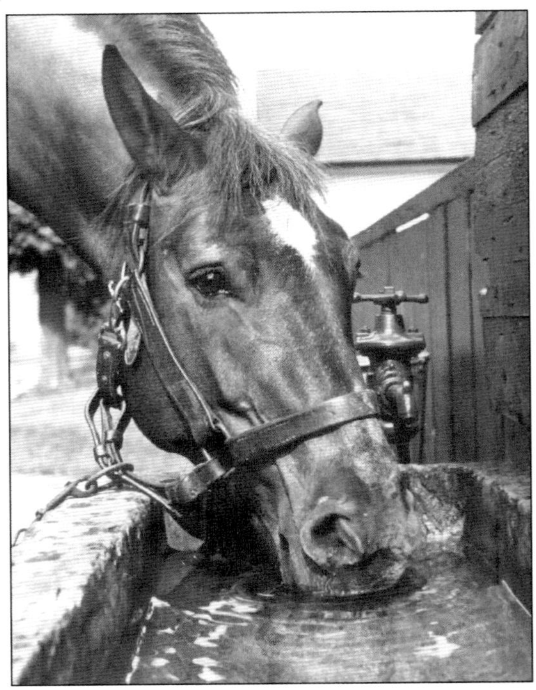

Barney, a favorite of park employees and visitors, was one of the reservation's draft horses. In the 1920s and 1930s, the heavy work of plowing, hauling, and mowing was done by horses. When Barney went to that horse heaven in the sky, he was buried in the park, and the sign for his stall still hangs in the park office.

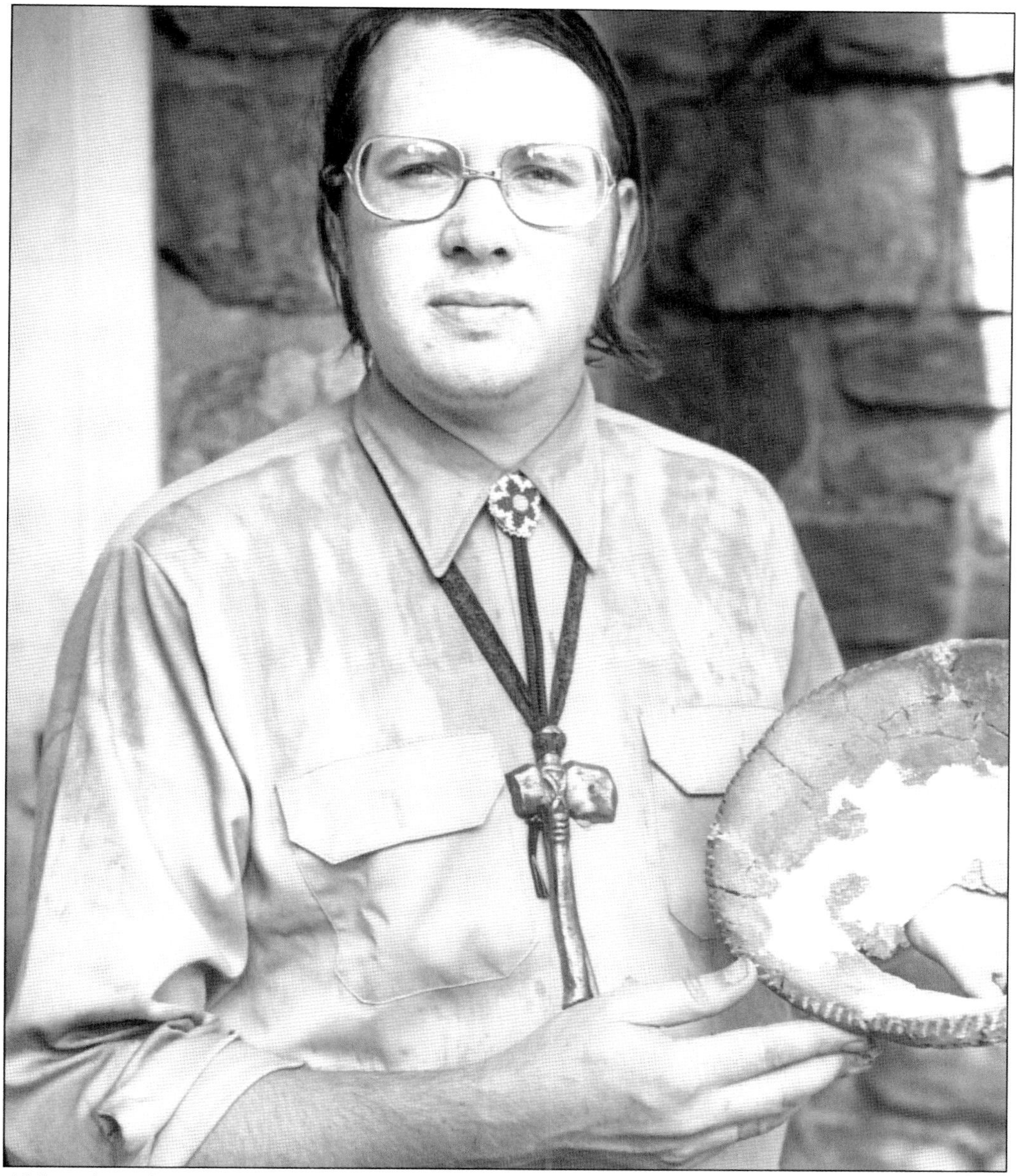

Although Nicholas Shoumatoff grew up in a family of scientific types, he had more of an artistic outlook on life. A native of Bedford, he spent the early years of his life exploring the park and Trailside Museum. He became interested in the lives of the Delaware Lenape people, early inhabitants of the area. In 1973, he met a Lenape woman named Nora Thompson Dean, called Touching Leaves in the Delaware Unami language, and immersed himself in her people's culture. In 1977, in a solemn naming ceremony at the Trailside Museum attended by important Native American leaders from Canada and the United States, Shoumatoff received the Lenape name He Who Stands Firm. At the time, he was the curator of the museum, a position he held from 1970 to 1984. As curator, He Who Stands Firm introduced many educational nature programs for schoolchildren and families, started the popular annual FiddleFest, and began the extensive Delaware Indian Resource Center, which included hours of taped conversations with Touching Leaves.

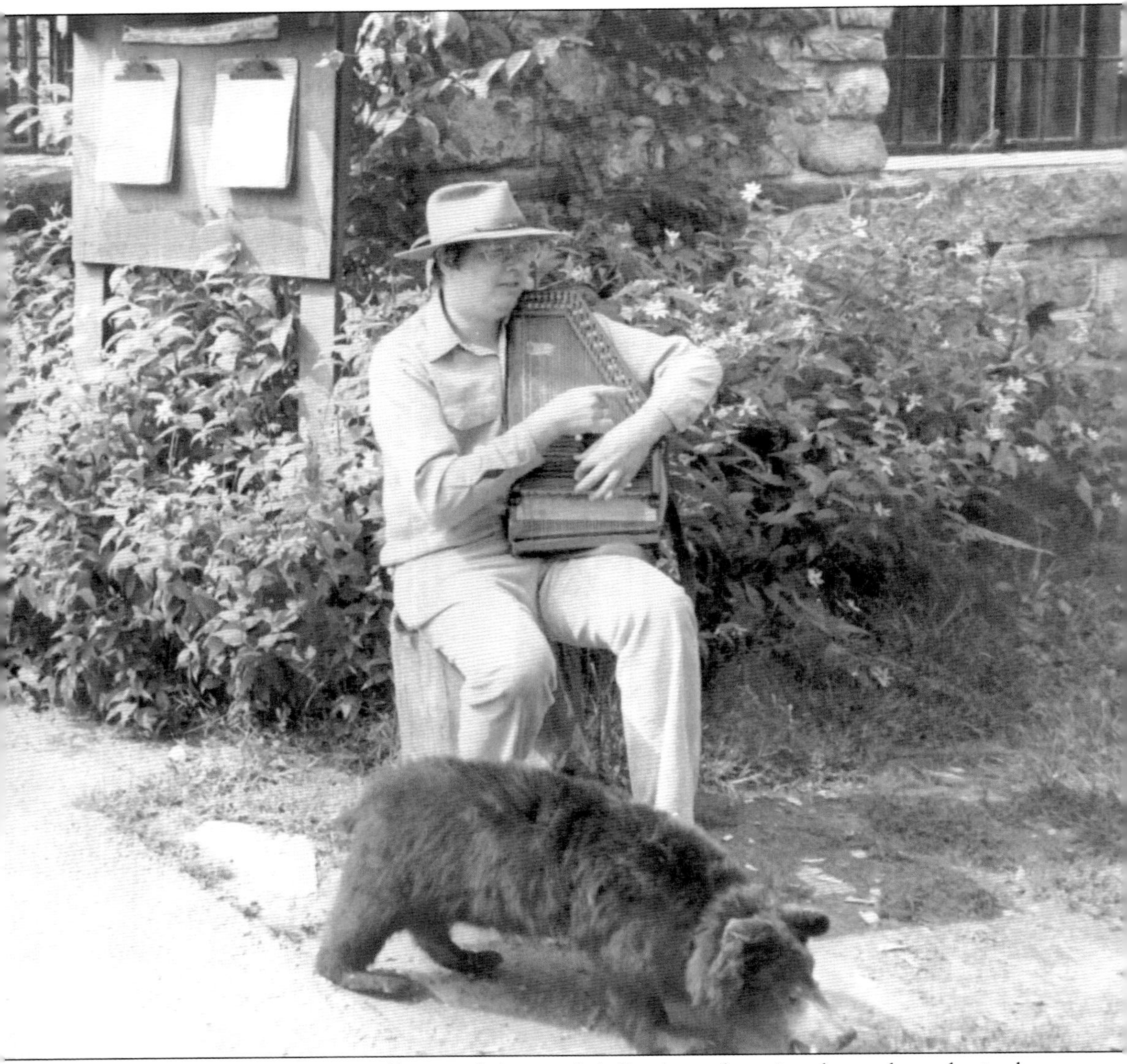

He Who Stands Firm is a collector of ideas and skills. An ardent Autoharp player, he is always ready to play and sing an original song based on historic vignettes. In this 1970s photograph, he can be seen with his instrument and, no, not a pet—it is one of the museum's mounted animals, a black bear. He Who Stands Firm began his career in the reservation as an observer in the fire tower and lived at the base of the park's tower for several seasons from 1968 to 1969. It was from his perch atop the tower on the highest point in the park that he formed what became his vision for the park. Noting how the land spread out before him, he realized that "the layers of the land represented the land and its people"—one era in a geologic sense and in a human sense built upon what came before. This idea, he believed, should be the foundation of the park's mission.

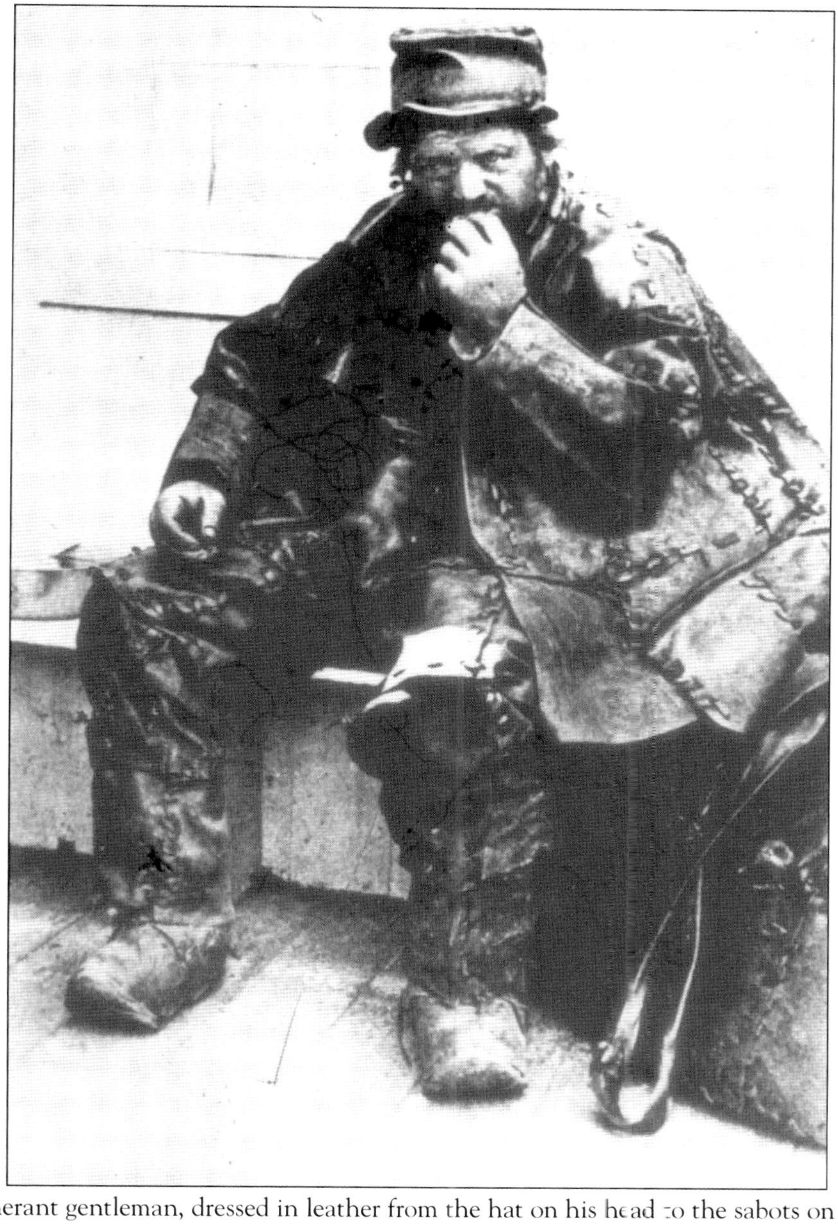

This itinerant gentleman, dressed in leather from the hat on his head to the sabots on his feet, was first seen in the area in 1858. For 31 years, until his death in 1889, the Leather Man led the lonely life of a tramp, receiving handouts from villagers and farmers along his route. He was stocky in appearance, about five feet, seven inches tall, had a swarthy complexion, shaggy brown hair that curled from under his cap, and blue-gray eyes. Legend says he was born in France but, denied in his love for the daughter of a rich leather factory owner, came to America to hide his sorrow. He seldom spoke, did not work for his handouts, never took money, and was grateful for donations of leather. He traveled a 365-day path from the Connecticut River and Long Island Sound to the Hudson River on a schedule as regular as clockwork, every 34 days. Housewives welcomed him and marked their calendars by the Leather Man's appearance at their doorsteps. The Leather Man walked 10 to 12 miles a day, no matter what the weather.

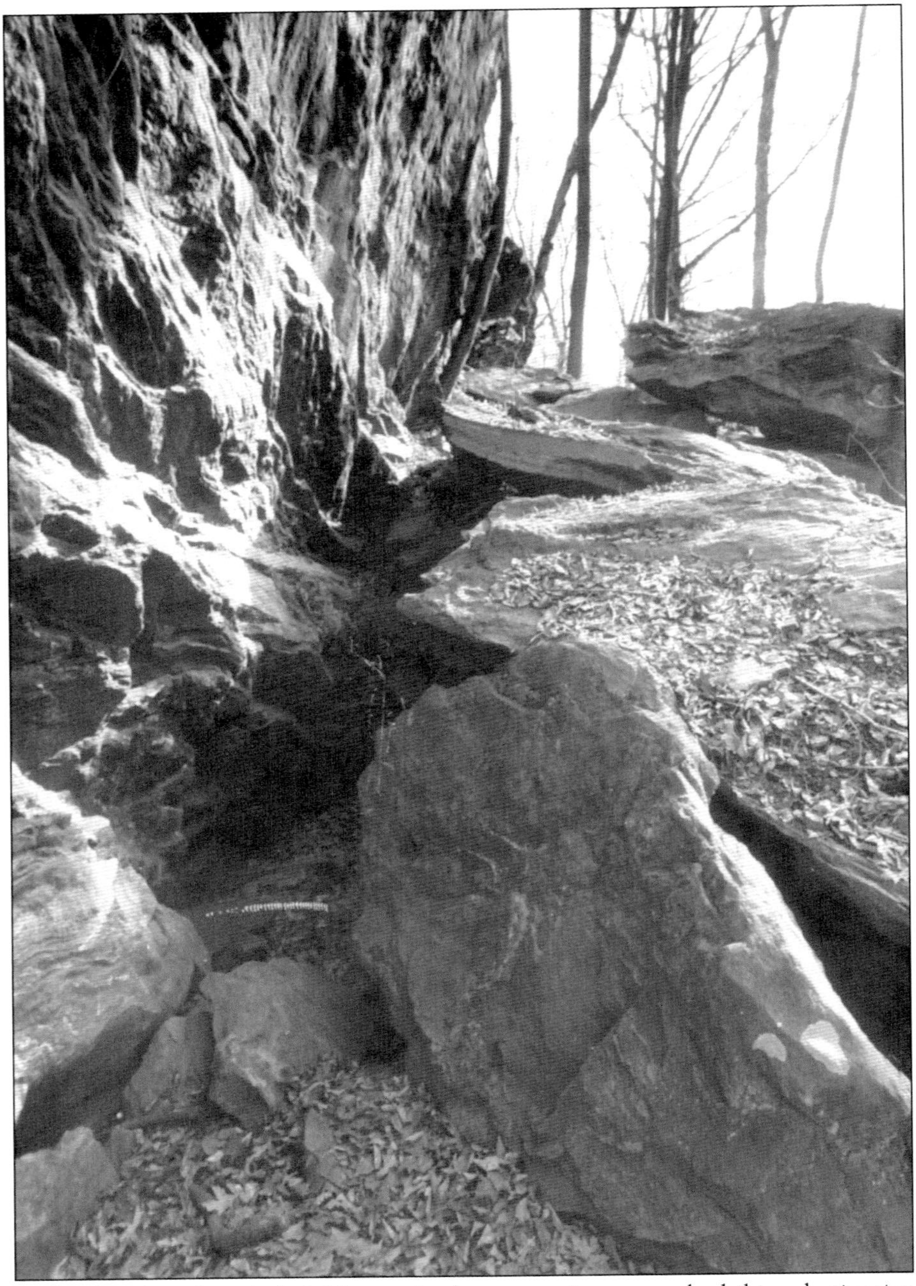

The Leather Man's path included this cave in the reservation, a popular hiking destination. The Leather Man died in March 1889 in a cave near Sing Sing, on a farm owned by George Dell. His body was discovered by a construction worker laboring on the Croton Aqueduct. His March 26, 1889, obituary claims that the inquest held in Sing Sing found that his death was caused "by blood poisoning resulting from a cancer, which had eaten away part of the lower jaw." A new theory concerning the Leather Man's roots sets his heritage as French Canadian and Native American, a much more logical origin for a traveling man who spent most of his lifetime tramping the roads of Westchester and New England.

Ten

MAPS

Are maps anachronistic these days? Are they really needed in this age of electronics and ubiquitous GPS systems? In many ways, yes. Maps show not only the lay of the land, but the changes the land has seen. George Washington's mapmaker, Robert Erskine, mapped the area during the Revolutionary War, showing strategic locations like Guard Hill in Bedford and the Croton and Cross Rivers in Lewisboro. Even today's Google Maps printouts tell a story. F.W. Beers and other itinerant mapmakers traveled throughout the country in the 19th century selling their atlases to farmers and townspeople, and making money doing it. The atlases marked not only the roads, but the owners of the properties along each highway and byway. These books are a boon to local historians trying to draw a picture of the past. A number of maps have been drawn of Ward Pound Ridge Reservation, showing how the area has changed and illustrating how mapmaking has developed, from the simple line drawings of the early cart roads to the sophisticated maps drawn with the help of aerial photography and satellite imaging. The park's catalog of maps includes all types, from easy-to-follow hiking trail layouts to more difficult orienteering maps.

Bjorn Kjellstrom, a transplanted Swede, played an important role in the development of Ward Pound Ridge Reservation as an orienteering mecca. He was a cofounder of Silva, the compass and navigational equipment company. In 1932, he helped develop the liquid-filled, protractor-based compass necessary for the sport of orienteering. These compasses could be placed flat on the maps to take bearings, making finding the way easier. Kjellstrom lived on the border of the reservation and blazed many of the trails used for the sport in the park today.

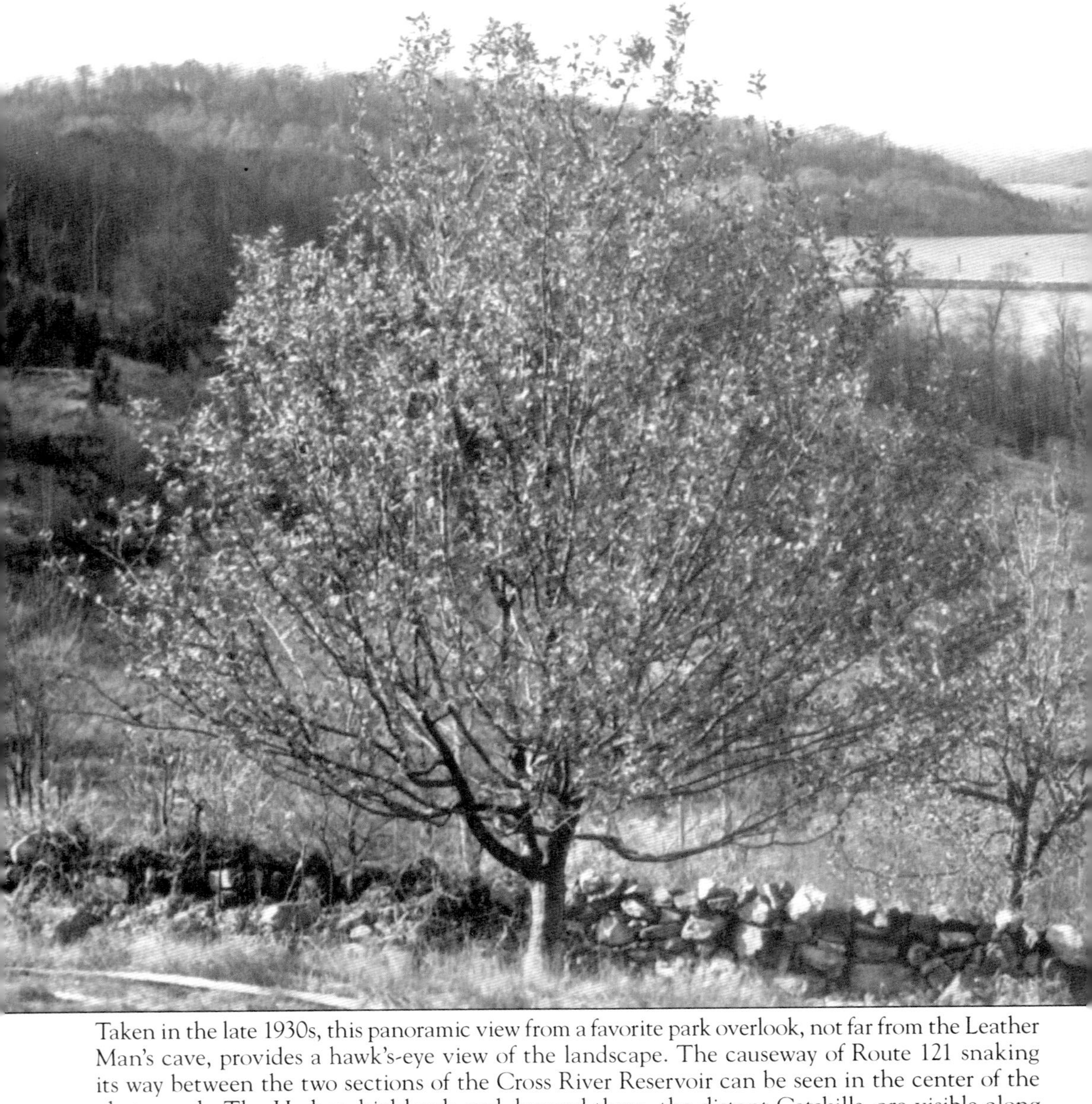

Taken in the late 1930s, this panoramic view from a favorite park overlook, not far from the Leather Man's cave, provides a hawk's-eye view of the landscape. The causeway of Route 121 snaking its way between the two sections of the Cross River Reservoir can be seen in the center of the photograph. The Hudson highlands and, beyond them, the distant Catskills, are visible along

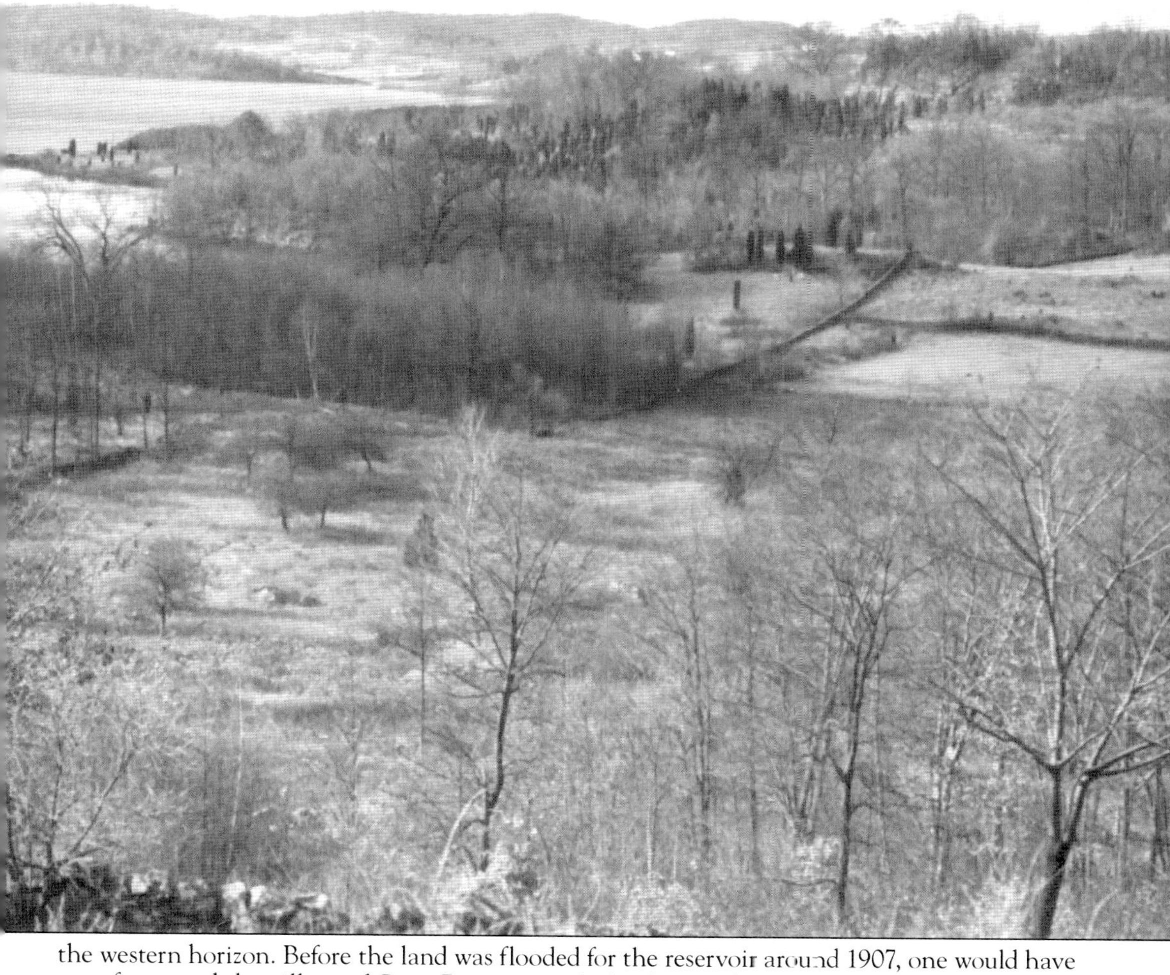

the western horizon. Before the land was flooded for the reservoir around 1907, one would have seen farms and the village of Cross River instead of a three-mile-long body of water. (Courtesy of the Westchester County Archives.)

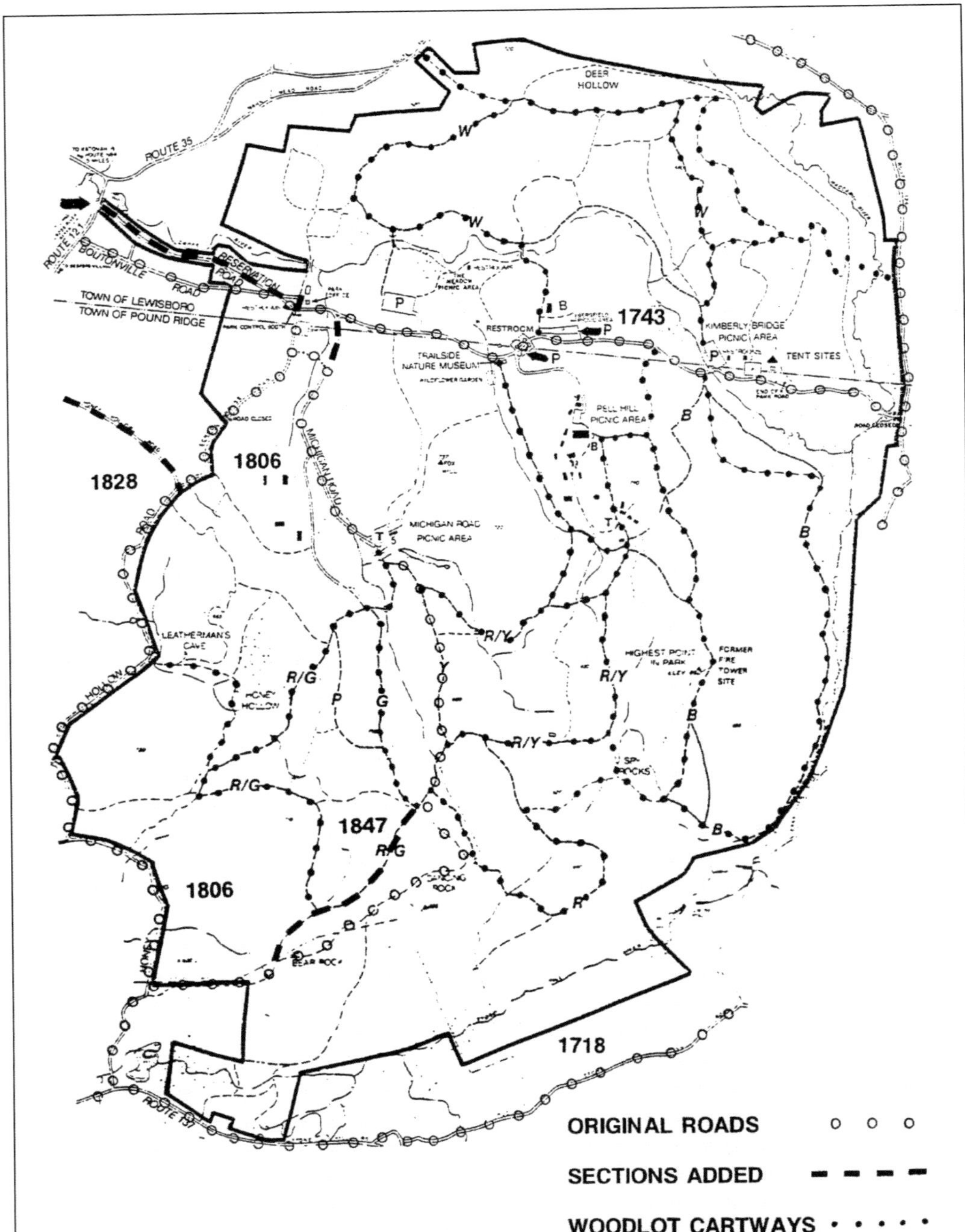

This map shows the progression of the road system in the area encompassed by the reservation. A couple of the "original roads" are now the busy state highways that traverse the towns of Pound Ridge, Bedford, and Lewisboro. Other early throughways are park roads like Michigan Road and Schoolhouse Road. The woodlot cartways have become part of the park's extensive trail system.

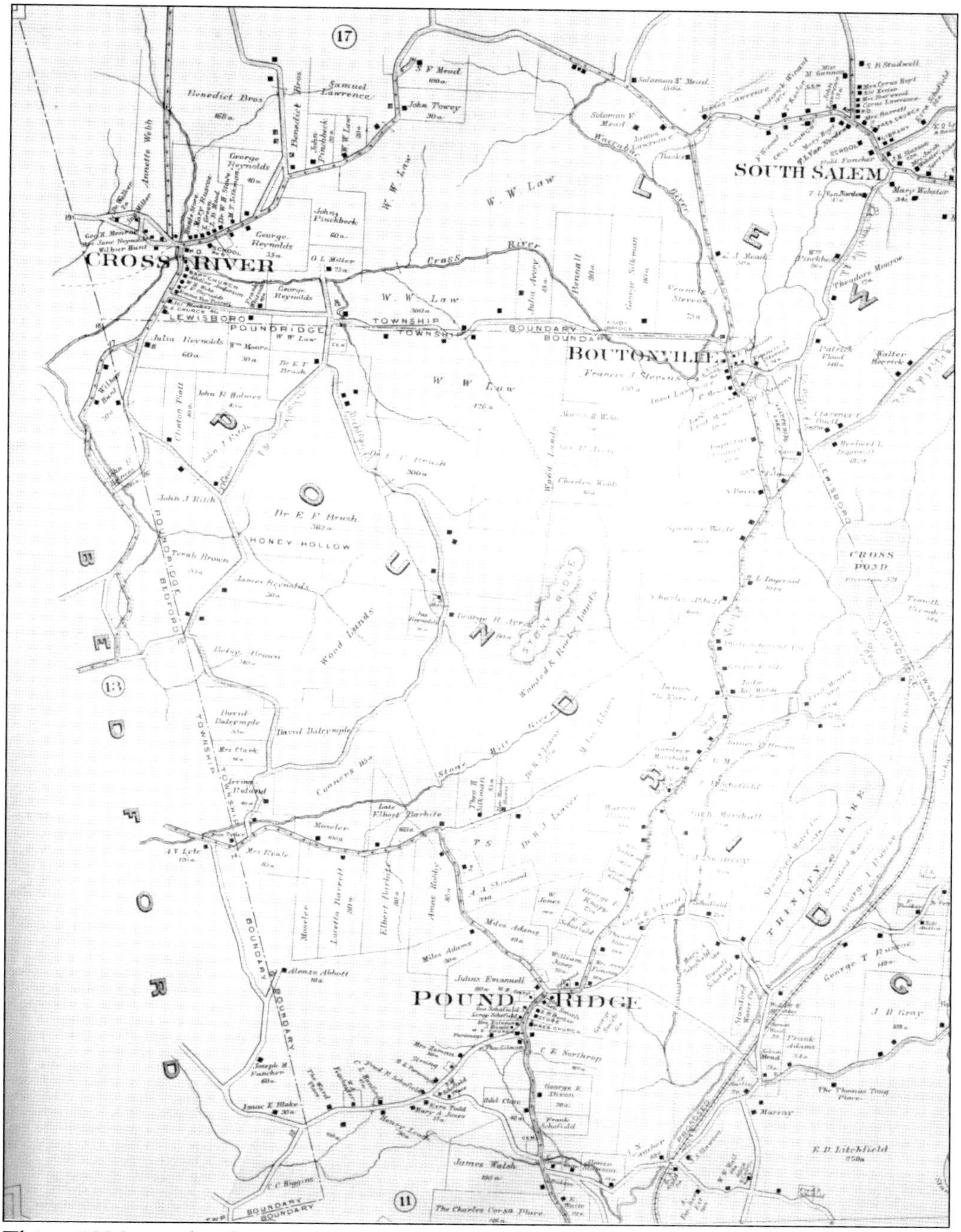

This c. 1906 map details property ownership and acreage of Lewisboro and Pound Ridge farms, many of which were destined to be sold to Westchester County to form the combined 4,315 acres of Ward Pound Ridge Reservation. Note the large holdings of Walter W. Law and Edward Brush. Many of the original small farms were being bought by landholding companies with the thought of developing the land into suburban housing. (Courtesy of the Lewisboro Town Historian's Office.)

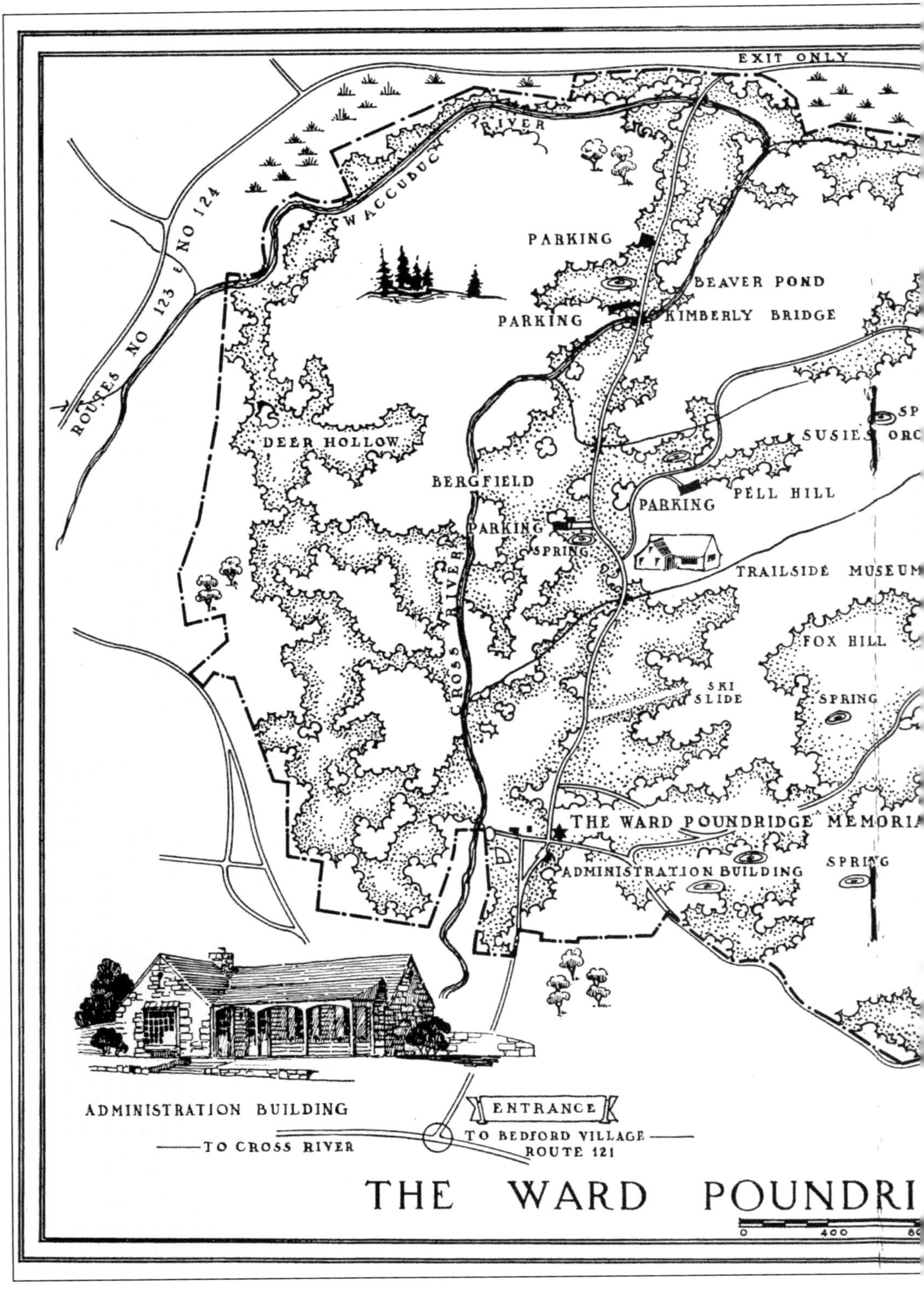

EXIT ONLY
WACCUBUC RIVER
ROUTES NO 123 & NO 124
PARKING
BEAVER POND
PARKING
KIMBERLY BRIDGE
DEER HOLLOW
SUSIES ORC
PELL HILL
BERGFIELD
PARKING
PARKING
SPRING
CROSS RIVER
TRAILSIDE MUSEUM
FOX HILL
SKI SLIDE
SPRING
THE WARD POUNDRIDGE MEMORIA
ADMINISTRATION BUILDING
SPRING
ADMINISTRATION BUILDING
ENTRANCE
TO CROSS RIVER
TO BEDFORD VILLAGE ROUTE 121
THE WARD POUNDRI
0 400

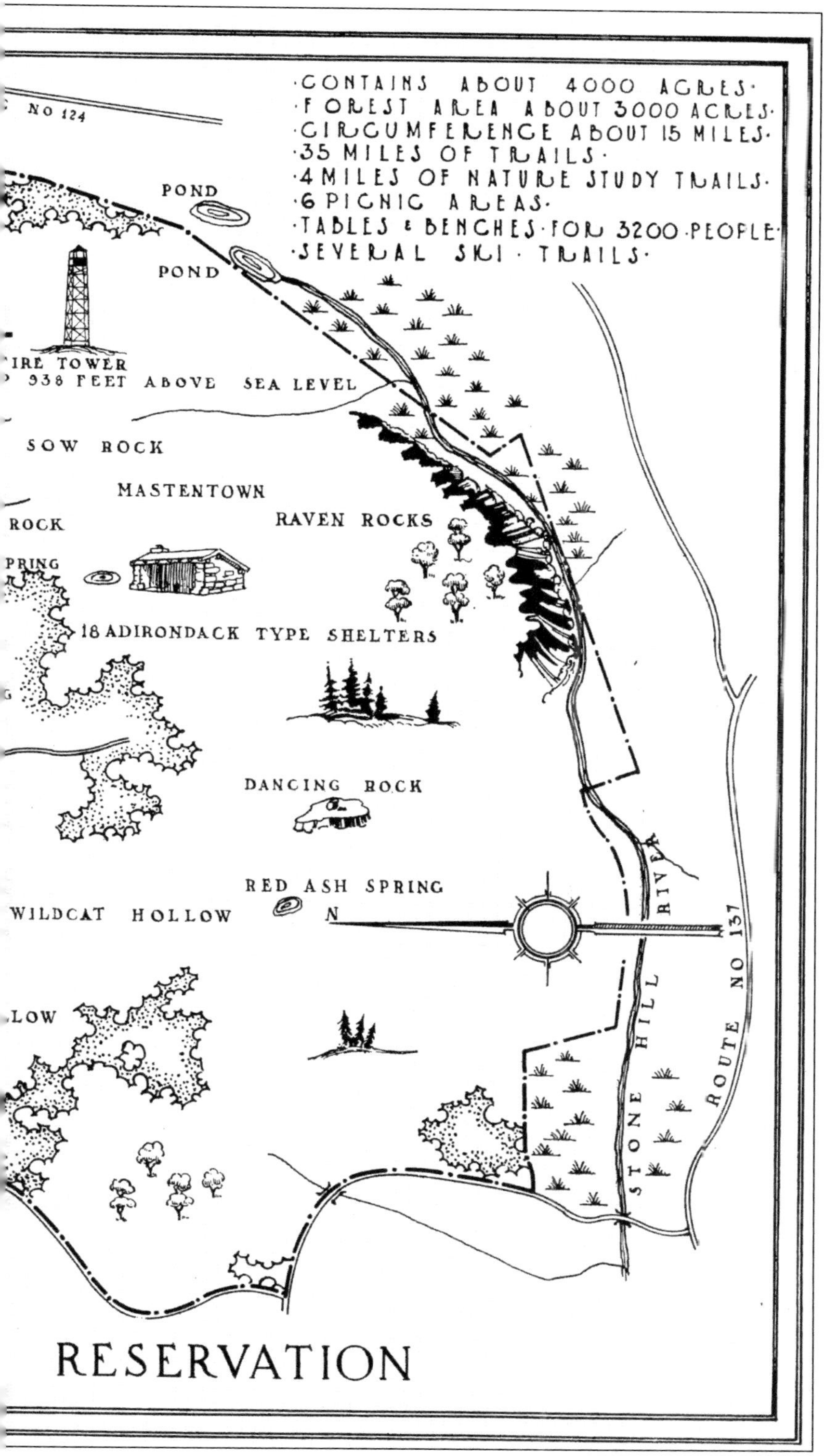

This map appears in booklet for the 1938 dedication of the Ward Pound Ridge Reservation, when the park's name was officially changed to honor William "Boss" Ward for his forward-looking philosophy in putting aside public lands for recreation. It shows the features of the park and notes that there are 35 miles of trails, 4 miles of nature trails, and tables and benches for 3,200 people.

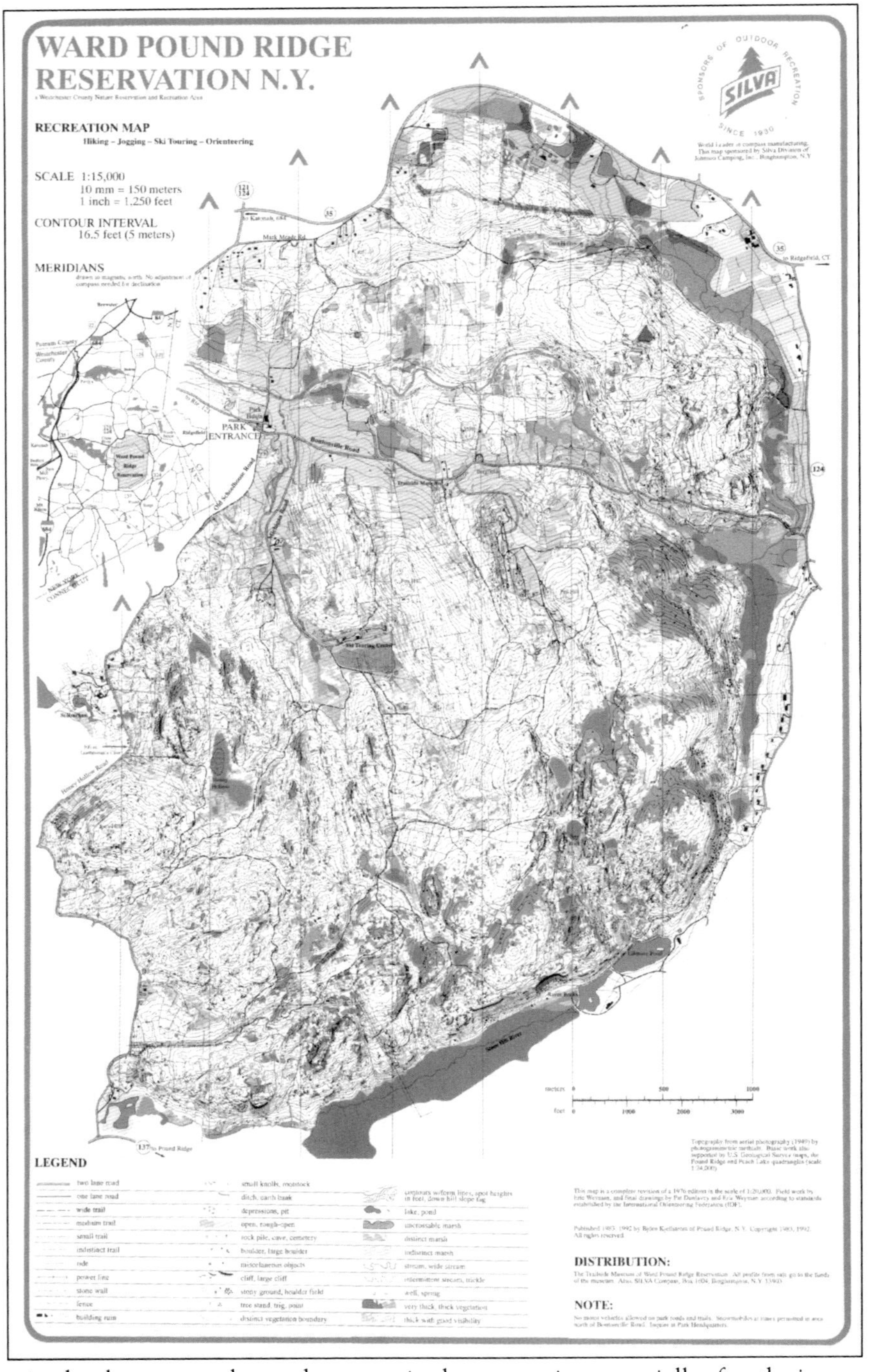

Orienteering has been a popular outdoor sport in the reservation, especially after the improvements made possible by Bjorn Kjellstrom's orienteering compass. In 1972, the park hosted the third annual US Orienteering Championships. Kjellstrom created this topographical map of the reservation with the help of Eric Weyman and Pat Dunlavey. The map can be downloaded from home computers.

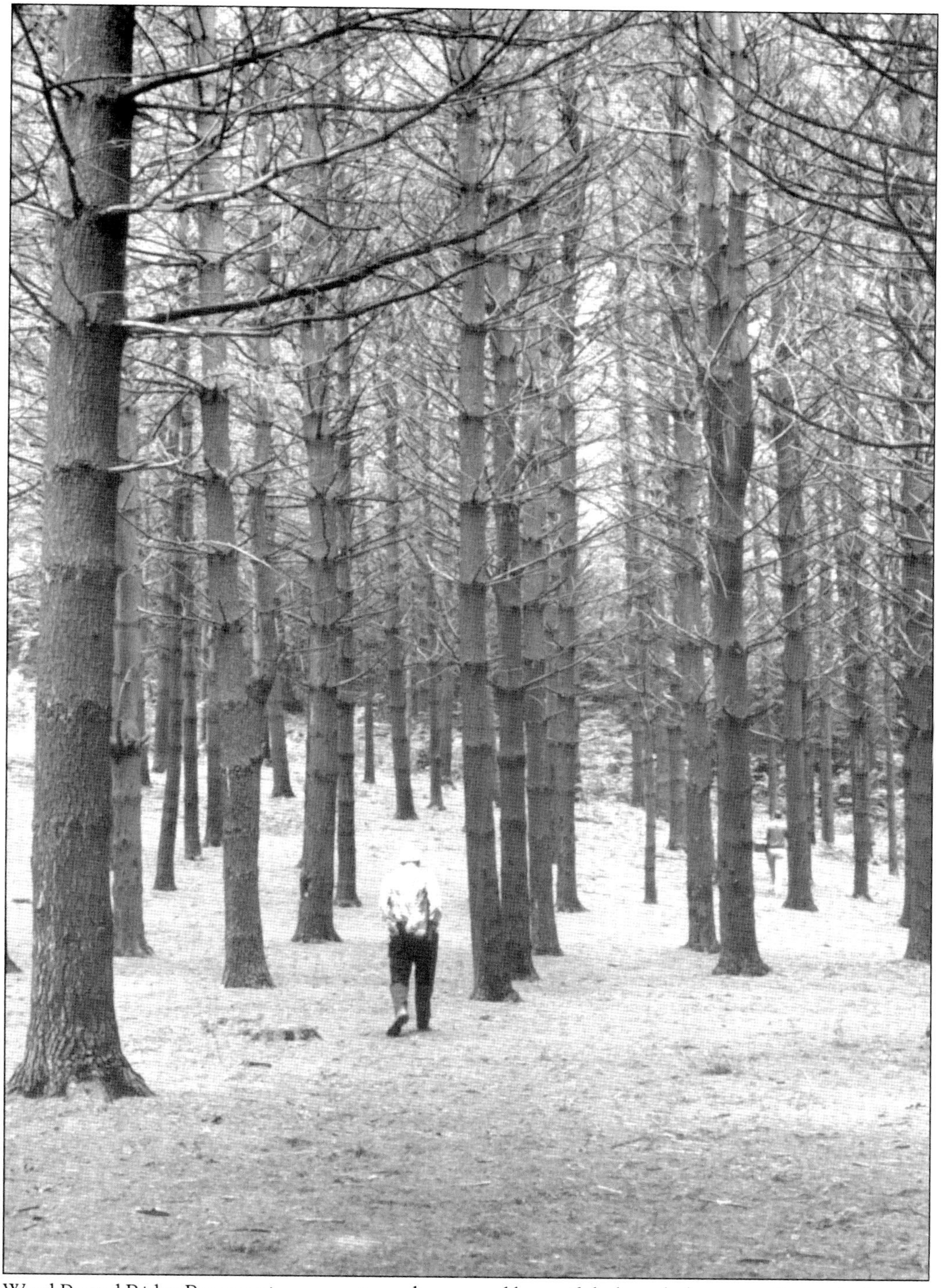

Ward Pound Ridge Reservation, an extraordinary and beautiful place, belongs to all people forever. Though the scenery may change, the park endures. Hikers, like this gentleman in his solitude, will always be able to find the serenity and restoration that nature provides.

Bibliography

Bedford Garden Club Collected Minutes, 1955–1971. Bedford (NY) Library.

Bolton, Rev. Robert. *The History of the County of Westchester.* New York: Jno. J. Cass, 1905.

Craig, Robert L. CCC Narrative Reports, 1933–1940. Cross River, NY: US Department of the Interior.

Crider, John H. *William Lukens Ward, Boss Ward: The Story of a Modern Westchester.* Privately published.

Descriptive of and Illustrating of the American Journal of Commerce, New York. Trailside Museum archives.

Jordan, Alvin R. *A History of the Town of Lewisboro.* South Salem, NY: South Salem Library Association, 1994.

Luquer, Eloise Payne. *Old Bedford Days: Recollections of Eloise Payne Luquer.* Bedford Village, NY: St. Matthew's Church, 1953.

Pessoni, Philip A. *Historical Notes on the Ward Pound Ridge Reservation, 1640–1940.* Boutonville, NY: self-published, 1995.

Reichenbecher, Martin C. *Geologic Report, Poundridge Reservation, 1938.*

Wheeler, William C. *Wild Life: Ward Pound Ridge Reservation, A Directory of Its Flora and Fauna.* Katonah, NY: privately published, 1965.

About the Organization

The Friends of Trailside Nature Museum and Ward Pound Ridge Reservation has made the publication of this book possible through its support of local history collections, archival materials, and digitization of photographs.

The Friends is dedicated to promoting a better appreciation and understanding of the natural world and the relationship between people and the land. Through its support of the Trailside Nature Museum and Ward Pound Ridge Reservation, the Friends provides financial and volunteer aid for exhibits, schools, and educational programs.